Suburban "Land Conversion in the United States:

AN ECONOMIC AND GOVERNMENTAL PROCESS

MARION CLAWSON

///

Published for
Resources for the Future, Inc.
by
The Johns Hopkins Press, Baltimore and London

RESOURCES FOR THE FUTURE, INC.
1755 Massachusetts Avenue, N.W., Washington, D.C. 20036

Resources for the Future is a nonprofit corporation for research and education in the development, conservation, and use of natural resources and the improvement of the quality of the environment. It was established in 1952 with the cooperation of the Ford Foundation. Part of the work of Resources for the Future is carried out by its resident staff; part is supported by grants to universities and other nonprofit organizations. Unless otherwise stated, interpretations and conclusions in RFF publications are those of the authors; the organization takes responsibility for the selection of significant subjects for study, the competence of the researchers, and their freedom of inquiry.

This book is one of RFF's studies in land use and management, which are directed by Marion Clawson. The manuscript was edited by Roma K. McNickle. The illustrations were drawn by Frank J. Ford and Clare Ford. The index was prepared by Penelope Stafford.

RFF editors: Henry Jarrett, Vera W. Dodds, Nora E. Roots, Tadd Fisher.

Copyright © 1971 by The Johns Hopkins Press
All rights reserved
Manufactured in the United States of America

The Johns Hopkins Press, Baltimore, Maryland 21218
The Johns Hopkins Press Ltd., London

Library of Congress Catalog Card Number 70-149239
Standard Book Number 0-8018-1313-1

FOREWORD

The United States, as a nation and as a culture, is relatively young by world standards; movement, change, and action have always characterized us. In the 19th century, we swept westward across the continent in a land colonization and settlement that was unprecedented in scale and speed. True, there had been earlier geographic spread from the original points of settlement along the Atlantic Coast, but it was in the 19th century that the flood tide was reached.

Today in the latter half of the twentieth century, we are engaged in another massive and rapid redistribution of population. Rural-urban migration is leading to a partial depopulation of more than half of the counties of the United States. Actually, the depopulation is greater and more serious than the available statistics suggest, for it is the young people who are leaving in greatest numbers. As the present aging population dies, the rural decline will be still swifter. To the extent that people are leaving rural areas for the cities, the United States is experiencing a concentration of population.

At the same time a decentralization of population is under way. Large numbers of people are moving out of the older city centers into the rapidly growing suburban areas. In this respect, as in many others relating to land use, the grain of the study, or the degree of refinement in the detail of inquiry, affects the results. At one scale or level, the dominant movement is toward cities; at a finer scale, the dominant movement is outward from the city center.

All of these population movements are highly differentiated by race, income, and age classifications. The U.S. developments have parallels elsewhere in the world, as rural people flock to cities and cities spread outward. In the United States, the automobile and the highway system have made the average citizen highly mobile, permitting residence in locations relatively remote from the place of work, and hence on the whole our suburbanization is more far-flung than elsewhere in the world.

One of the most important land use changes going on in the United States today is this suburbanization process. In the current jargon, suburbs are where the action is. Land transfers, conversion of land from one use to another, and marked changes in land prices characterize the suburban fringe, which in most cases extends beyond the actual settled areas for a few miles. Land speculators, land agents, land assemblers, developers, builders, financial institutions, insurance companies, public utility companies, and above all the buyers of residential property are engaged, under rules and programs laid down by various governmental organizations, in changing land from some open or relatively unused state to a developed and used one.

The process is imperfectly understood. There has been a great deal of writing about it. Indeed, this may be one reason why it is not better understood as a whole, since so much of the writing has been concerned with one aspect, or one area, or one viewpoint. Perhaps no one can see it whole; contemporaries often fail to understand fully what is going on all around them.

Considerations of this sort led Resources for the Future a few years ago to initiate a series of studies on the process of urban growth and development. Two of these studies have been published: *Converting Land from Rural to Urban Uses*, by A. Allan Schmid, and *The Suburban Apartment Boom*, by Max Neutze, both published by Resources for the Future in 1968. Additional studies are under way. We seek to take a broad view of the suburbanization process, although we naturally suffer from the same shortcomings of narrow viewpoint as do most groups which look at their own times.

In order to secure understanding of the actual process of suburban growth, Resources for the Future undertook the study of three metropolitan areas where suburbanization has occurred under varying circumstances and at different tempos: Washington, D.C.; Wilmington, Delaware; and Springfield, Massachusetts. Some highlights of the findings are summarized in Chapters 11 and 12 of this book.

Concurrently, and in parallel, a study of British urbanization experience was undertaken by Political and Economic Planning, an independent research organization headquartered in London. That study had generally similar aims and purposes, although of course the governmental and institutional framework is different in the two countries, and available data differ also, so that the studies necessarily had to be organized somewhat differently. We have had it in mind from the outset that, when the studies in each country were brought to the publication stage, a further volume would be prepared to contrast the suburbanization process in the two countries and the roles played by the differing governmental structures. The PEP study of the British experience is scheduled to be published toward the end of 1972 by Allen & Unwin (London) in two volumes, under the title *Megalopolis Denied: Planning and the Control of Urban Growth in England, 1945–70*.

It is to be hoped that these studies will contribute to the understanding of a process which is going on in all of the world's developed countries. Better understanding of suburbanization may lead to realization of its potentials for social good and the avoidance of its potentials for disaster.

Marion Clawson
Director, Land Use and Management Program
Resources for the Future, Inc.

30 October 1970

ACKNOWLEDGMENTS

A large number of people have contributed in one way or another to this book. In mentioning some, I run the grave risk of omitting others, whose forgiveness is hereby asked. In the first place, extensive use has been made of a very wide range of printed materials; I have drawn ideas, facts, and judgments from scores of persons, many of whom, unfortunately for me, I do not know personally. Material once printed is in the general public domain, and there is no better illustration of this than the use made herein of the writings cited. To all these many persons, my thanks.

More directly, I have been helped by a number of colleagues on this study, and by the British research team working on the companion study. Several conferences, many individual discussions, and much correspondence with Peter Hall, Ray Thomas, Roy Drewitt, and Harry L. Gracey of the British group have been most stimulating. They have forced me to explain many matters that seemed obvious to me but were less easily understood by outsiders. George A. McBride spent three years on the RFF staff, working on this project, and we consulted and discussed frequently. His studies of Fairfax County, Virginia, provided many ideas which have been developed in this book. Some very revealing studies of the Wilmington SMSA were made by Gerald L. Cole and Gerald F. Vaughn of the University of Delaware, and their ideas have found expression in many ways in this book.

Of particular help was J. B. Wyckoff of the University of Massachusetts. Working under grant from RFF and stationed in RFF offices, he not only made the study of the Springfield SMSA, from which I drew many useful ideas and facts, but also wrote the first draft of Chapter 12 of this book. His counsel and criticism has been particularly valuable throughout the latter part of this study. Joanna Seltzer Hirst served as my research assistant during the summer of 1968, and was very helpful indeed.

Others of my colleagues at RFF have also been helpful: Joseph L. Fisher, Michael F. Brewer, Harvey S. Perloff (who has since moved to the University of California at Los Angeles), Lowden Wingo, Irving Hoch, Mason Gaffney, Neal Potter, and others.

In addition to these persons, the following reviewed a first draft of this book, and their comments were especially helpful in its revision:

Maurice Ash, Totnes, Devon, England
Robin H. Best, Wye College (University of London), Near Ashford, Kent*
Robert F. Boxley, Jr., U.S. Department of Agriculture

* Organization is listed for identification only; persons were asked to comment as individuals.

John Callahan, Advisory Commission on Intergovernmental Relations
Grady Clay, *Landscape Architecture*
Melvin L. Cotner, U.S. Department of Agriculture
Maurice Criz, Bureau of the Census
Jeanne Davis, U.S. Department of Agriculture
Henry Dill, U.S. Department of Agriculture
William R. Ewald, Jr., Development consultant, Washington, D.C.
John Gerba, Department of Transportation
Karl Gertel, U.S. Department of Agriculture
Frank Goode, U.S. Department of Agriculture
Stanley D. Heckman, Barrett, Knapp, Smith & Schapiro, New York
Hugh Johnson, U.S. Department of Agriculture
Walter K. Johnson, Delaware Valley Regional Planning Commission
Burnham Kelly, Cornell University
Robert C. Klove, Bureau of the Census
Garland Marple, Bureau of Public Roads
Richard McArdle, U.S. Department of Agriculture
Frederick A. McLaughlin, Jr., Department of Housing and Urban Development
David P. McNelis, Bureau of the Census
Grace Milgram, Institute of Urban Environment, Columbia University
Walter Miller, U.S. Department of Agriculture
G. Max Neutze, Australian National University, Canberra
Robert Otte, U.S. Department of Agriculture
James H. Pickford, Advisory Commission on Intergovernmental Relations
Dwight F. Rettie, Department of Housing and Urban Development
Henry B. Schechter, Department of Housing and Urban Development[†]
A. Allan Schmid, Michigan State University
Elizabeth Schoenecker, Department of Housing and Urban Development
Ronald L. Shelton, Center for Aerial Photographic Studies, Cornell University
William L. Slayton, Urban America[‡]
Arthur K. Stellhorn, Department of Housing and Urban Development
Alan Stevens, Bureau of the Census
David M. Trubek, Yale University
Alan M. Voorhees, Alan M. Voorhees & Associates, McLean, Virginia
Shirley F. Weiss, University of North Carolina
The help of all these persons is gratefully acknowledged; responsibility for what is said herein is mine alone, of course.

[†] At the time of review; now at the Library of Congress.
[‡] At the time of review; now with American Institute of Architects.

CONTENTS

5

6

7

8

9

LIST OF TABLES

LIST OF FIGURES

SUBURBAN LAND CONVERSION IN THE UNITED STATES:
AN ECONOMIC AND GOVERNMENTAL PROCESS

SCOPE, FOCUS, AND DESIGN OF THE BOOK

As many Americans know at first hand and most of the others have been informed by the communications media, the problems of the modern city are formidable and highly complex. There are economic problems of income, output, and employment; problems of design in buildings, streets, and public areas; planning problems; transportation problems. The city's welfare problems are felt not only by the poor, many of whom belong to racial or ethnic minorities, but also by the taxpayers who must foot the bill for welfare. All citizens pay the price of social problems like crime, anomie, alienation, and violence. And it is in the cities that problems of environmental pollution are often seen in their most acute form.

Cities must be concerned with growth—in population, in area, in economic output, in housing. They must also be concerned with renewal, particularly of their older areas which were designed for a past society and economy and are now deteriorating rapidly.

At bottom, the problems of the modern city involve the whole purpose, goal, and style of modern life, for modern man is an urban man. But the problems are highly interrelated. Although there is value in examining the economic problems separately, or the political problems or any of the others by themselves, in fact the various aspects of life in the city are intertwined.

Viewed in this way, the problems of the modern city seem too large and complex to be seen whole by any one person. Anyone who writes about any aspect of the modern city must focus his analysis and exposition on those aspects of most interest and concern to him.

FOCUS OF THE BOOK

This book is about land use—what activities are carried out on the land, how the use of one area relates to the use of other areas, the processes by which land use and changes in land use are carried out, and the like. Consideration of land use necessarily also includes some consideration of buildings and their construction, of transport facilities whereby the activities on one tract of land can be interrelated with those on another tract, with public improvements which often provide a substantial part of the value to private land, with finance as it affects

1

changes in land use, with credit to the home buyer and to the home builder, with land prices, and many other topics. One cannot avoid considering the socio-economic characteristics of many of the actors on the urban scene, for these characteristics influence if not determine their actions.

The focus of the book is upon land use at the expanding outward edge of cities—the suburbs. Here are the largest areas where land use is changing. Here the city of the future is being built, and the city problems of the future are probably being built at the same time. But the need for suburban expansion, and the flow of people which fuels it, are closely related to the changes which take place in the city center. In particular, the ability (or inability) of the city to renew its older parts greatly affects both the need and the impetus for suburban growth. On the farther side of the suburbs lies a more rural belt, where land is used for nonurban purposes or lies idle as it awaits the building of the suburbs of future decades. The city casts its shadow into the suburbs and the latter cast their shadow into the more distant rural countryside.

In this book, the central focus is land use in the suburbs. There is considerable discussion on other aspects of the modern city, but this material has been included only to the degree to which it seemed relevant to this central focus. The situation is analogous to a painting, where the painter has a central figure or point of interest, with background growing increasingly indistinct with distance and with foreground which helps to put the central figure in better perspective. Just as other painters may feel that the artist has made his background too prominent, or that the foreground is too hazy, or that there is some other lack of proportion between the central focus of the painting and its surroundings, so in the present case some may feel that the writer has included too much material not closely related to the expressed focus of the book, while others may have wished to focus the analysis on partly or largely different aspects of the urban scene. To them, one can only describe and defend his choice of subject and of matter to include, and urge them to write their own books if this one fails to meet their objectives.

Complexity of Suburban Land Conversion

Suburban land conversion, as the process is conceived and analyzed in this book, is also a large and complex subject. In fact, if one tries to consider this process in a reasonably complete way, he gets involved in nearly all the manifold problems of the whole city. The magnitude and interrelationships of problems may take on different proportions in the suburb than in the older city, but few aspects of life in one area are entirely missing in the other. Thus, a study which focuses on land use changes in the suburbs is unavoidably a rather detailed and complex one, if it is to be accurate. A consideration of only some of the aspects of the suburban scene—as, for instance, the zoning problem, or the planning problem, or the school problem—may well be misleading. A considerable review of professional literature and a modest acquaintance with popular and semi-popular writing and talking about suburban problems suggests that much of what has been said is misleading simply because, by focusing on a part of the whole, it leads the reader or the hearer to believe that this part is in fact the whole.

This book seeks to take a comprehensive view of suburban land conversion. Subject to the constraints imposed by the choice of its focus, a considerable body of data and many concepts are included and thus the book is rather long and somewhat detailed. Hopefully, it avoids unnecessary details while at the same time not sacrificing essential matter. Short books, simply and directly written to a central point, have many virtues. But an effort to describe briefly and simply what is in fact complex and involved may be more misleading than helpful. There are no instant solutions to deep-seated social and economic problems; neither is there an instant description and analysis of them. The politician who will not read more than one page, no matter what the problem or the issue, is perhaps no more superficial than the scholar or intellectual who thinks that all that is worth saying on any subject can be compressed into some limited number of pages. Brevity is indeed desirable, and has been sought; but accuracy has been preferred to brevity, and relevance to either.

As later discussion will demonstrate in some detail, suburban land conversion is a field notably lacking in solid data of clear meaning. Time and again, anyone who deals with this subject must use data that are considerably less than perfect. Even scholars of considerable ability who work with care have not infrequently used some available information as if the data meant what they simply do not mean when carefully analyzed. Statements of "fact" or suggestions about policy have at times been based upon a foundation of data which will not support the superstructure. As a result, this book goes to some pains in several places to explain what the available data mean and do not mean, so that the reader will understand what is said here and will be able to avoid pitfalls in his own analyses. This, too, makes for some length and detail, which it would be desirable to omit if it were not so necessary.

General Purpose of the Study

The general purpose of this study has been to understand and to explain the present land use situation on the suburban fringe, how and why it arose, and by what processes it has changed and is changing. Three philosophic attitudes or hypotheses underlay the inquiry and have been strongly reinforced as a result of it.

1. Major improvements in the suburban land conversion process are badly needed. The results of the past and present process are needlessly bad and needlessly costly. The suburbs have failed to meet the needs of a very large segment of the population—the poorer third or half of the total population and the racial minorities. For those people who have been housed in the suburbs, the resulting life environment has been less satisfying than it could have been, and they have had to pay too high a price for housing and services.

2. Although major improvement is both necessary and feasible, there is no national crisis in suburban land conversion. The problems of the cities, complex and many-sided as they are, are still not the totality of our national problems; and the problems of the suburbs are far from the totality of all urban problems. If there should be no significant improvement in the suburban land conversion process

over the next few decades, the United States would still be an economically power-ful nation and millions of people would still be well and pleasantly housed. More-over, were suburban land development by some miracle to become perfect, many deep-seated problems of the cities would still remain.

3. Improvement in the process of suburban land conversion is both possible and feasible, given some real input of thought and effort, but perfection in the process is not possible. If one sets up a utopia or an ideal, it is likely to be impossible of attainment, especially in a complex situation. If one seeks progress toward such a goal, then substantial gains may be readily possible. The best is the enemy of the good in suburban land development as well as in many other aspects of life. This study has suggested to the author many ways in which the process of suburban land conversion might be improved, and these are outlined in the final chapter. But improvements will not come quickly nor easily, and in any case may be only part of what is desirable.

In keeping with the role of Resources for the Future and of its research staff, this book does not advocate a particular program. The final chapter outlines a number of programs which might be undertaken singly or in various combinations to improve the suburban land conversion process, and it does try to provide some basis for their evaluation. Just as there is no instant solution to complex urban problems, likewise there is no single solution.

Perhaps the most basic intellectual conviction underlying this study is that all effective economic and social programs must be based upon accurate understanding of facts, relationships, and processes. Any effective program for improving life in the suburbs must be based upon an accurate understanding of the matters discussed in this book. Understanding might, of course, be obtained from other sources than the book but hopefully the book will help.

Design of the Book

The book is made up of this introductory chapter and three parts. Part I (Chap-ters 2 to 9) explores the nature of the processes of suburban growth and develop-ment in the United States as a whole, where of course it varies from region to region. These chapters are based largely on previously published professional writing, but they offer a system of analysis which is designed to provide more order and clarity than has been available heretofore. There is a good bit of description and presentation of factual materials, but it is hoped that the analysis and synthesis of widely scattered information will be helpful to the reader. The study concen-trates on the years since World War II, but much of the discussion is likely to be relevant for a decade or two in the future. A final comment on Part I is that it tries to examine the process of suburban growth and development as a whole, giv-ing attention to the role of various public agencies and private parties.

Part II (Chapters 10 to 14) is concerned with the urbanized areas of north-eastern United States—what is known as "Megalopolis"—in the postwar period. Two chapters give the highlights of the three case studies made for Resources for the Future, and another presents brief accounts of suburbanization in several other metropolitan areas in the Northeast. The final chapter in this section considers the regional complex that is emerging along the northeastern seaboard. Although Part II is an integral section of the book, readers who are not interested in the Northeast may proceed directly from Part I to Part III.

Part III considers the future of urban and suburban growth in the United States. After a summary appraisal of the suburban land conversion process as it has worked since World War II, there is an informal projection to the year 2000 of the suburban land conversion process as it now operates. The book ends with a chapter on alternatives for the future, which suggests where effective action might be taken to modify the present suburbanization process. No program is presented, no line of change supported. The chapter seeks to identify, appraise, and evaluate alternatives.

SOME MAJOR CONCLUSIONS

In an effort to whet the reader's appetite and help him to evaluate the evidence as it unfolds in the book, the following few pages provide a brief summarization of some of the book's major conclusions. These flow from the data and the analyses of the book, although obviously the prior experiences and the thought processes of the author have affected both his modes of analysis and his choice of material for analysis. Some of these conclusions are stated explicitly in the following chapters, but others are less sharply drawn in the text. Only the major conclusions of the book are summarized, and those of course have not been fully developed here, much less documented.

1. Decision-making in the suburban land conversion process is highly diffused; there are many actors and many processes, complexly interrelated, with numerous feedbacks. For instance, land developers who benefit from rezoning do not wait patiently for plums to fall into their open mouths but vigorously shake the tree. The diffusion of the decision-making process is hardly a novel concept, but it is richly documented and illustrated in several chapters. No single person, group, or public agency is responsible for the kinds of suburbs that are built; as one result, there is no single point at which major change in the suburban land conversion process could be implemented.

2. Public programs of many kinds, including several federal programs, have greatly affected the decision-making process. Credit, mortgage insurance, transportation, taxation, and other programs, particularly in their specific administration, have directed or influenced many private actions in the suburban land conversion process.

3. The results of the suburban development process flow from the nature of that process; if the process remains relatively unchanged, the results will likewise remain relatively unchanged.

—Suburban sprawl, discontinuity in land development areas, rising land prices, and extensive speculation in suburban land arise from the nature of the market for suburban land, which is described in some detail in Chapter 7. Here, as elsewhere, the market structure affects the functioning of the market.

—Externalities and interdependencies in land use affect the use and value of each tract of land more than do actions within each tract. Yet the mechanisms to reduce or eliminate negative externalities and/or to increase positive externalities are weak or absent. As a result, the economic and operational potentialities of most suburban situations are not realized in practice.

—The provision of public services such as sewers or schools, including the methods of pricing their output or of meeting their costs, is a part of this suburban land conversion process. By and large, provision of these services has been dominated by an accommodation to other economic and political forces, rather than used as a conscious tool to guide the suburban land conversion process.

—The nature of the suburban land conversion process in any metropolitan area depends in considerable part upon its speed. Rapid population and economic growth of a metropolitan area, with a consequent rapid suburban land conversion, leads to frantic activity in the land market, to steeply rising land prices, to a much more active speculation in land, and to a more evident inadequacy of public processes involved in suburban expansion. Slow population and economic growth leads to quite different processes. To use an extreme example, bribery of public officials in connection with land zoning may occur in a rapidly developing suburban area but is much less likely in a slow-growing one.

4. The results of the suburban land conversion process as it has operated over the past two decades are both good and bad. On the one hand, a great deal of comfortable housing and many pleasant suburban communities have been built; and the increased housing supply in the suburbs has clearly released a lot of older housing nearer the city center for the use of some groups. But the suburban land conversion process has been needlessly costly. The inadequate and fragmentary data on this point are reviewed in some detail, and some rough estimates developed in the text. More seriously, the suburbs have failed to meet the housing needs of the lower-income segment of the population, perhaps as much as half the total. This general conclusion is hardly novel, but it is documented and illustrated and to some extent quantified in several chapters, perhaps more fully than is available elsewhere.

5. The city or metropolitan planning process is, explicitly or implicitly, brought under rather heavy criticism at several points in the book. The nominal planners are often not the real planners; sewer builders, transportation agencies, and other units of government often usurp the role assigned to the planning agency. There is often a serious communication gap between the planners and the general public, and between them and the other officials in government. Frequently, plans are developed by the planners and then their official and public acceptance sought; rarely are they developed cooperatively with these other groups. Perhaps most seriously of all, city planning has been too much concerned with a goal or a plan at some future specific date, and too little concerned with the processes of urban and suburban growth and change. One need only observe the fault line that is created when the rezoning of a tract is under consideration; instead of a neat shift from one classification to another in response to accepted processes and standards, frequently a major controversy develops and absorbs much time and energy.

6. Zoning, as it has operated to date, is a tool of social control over land use that

is too weak to be effective in the growing suburbs. In older developed urban areas, pressures for zoning changes are largely offset by counter-pressures to retain the status quo. The results may be good or bad, depending upon one's viewpoint, but a rather high degree of stability in zoning and in land use results and intruding nonconforming land uses are largely kept out. In the developing suburbs, the political situation is different, and zoning has proven largely ineffective. Where land is yet to be developed, land use zones, based upon a general plan or on some other grounds, have generally had little popular support when initially adopted or when changes are proposed. Such zoning may even have had negative results; it may be easier and cheaper to break the existing zoning than to conform to it. Zoning, as a legal expression of a general plan, is essential for growing suburbs but it is unlikely to be effective unless complemented by other measures of control.

7. The housing problems of the poor grow out of income disparities or income dispersion, not out of the absolute level of the incomes of the poor. Raising per capita incomes of the whole population to any level but leaving the income dispersion unchanged will not solve, and may not help, the housing problems of the poor. A more direct attack on their poverty problem is necessary.

8. The suggestion is advanced that perhaps the time has come for some of the lower-income blacks of the city center (the ghettos) to break away from their present locations and obtain housing in some of the suburbs built in the earlier postwar years. While it would be highly desirable for these people, as for everyone, to have *new* housing, this appears financially out of the question for most of them for some time, if not indefinitely. But it is not necessary that they be restricted to city centers unless they choose to be. Just as they have taken over many *older* residential areas in the city so they might take over suburban areas in the next decade or two.

9. The available data on urban land use are poor and often are misleading. Geographical units which may be entirely suitable for summarization of data on population, employment, and income are often quite misleading as units for summarization of data on land use. The geographical "grain" of an inquiry often dominates the results, unless the inquirer is particularly alert; the use of county or Standard Metropolitan Statistical Area data will often produce one picture, while data for smaller areas will produce an entirely different result. For instance, classification of counties as "urban" if they have an overall density of 1,000 persons per square mile grossly exaggerates the size of truly urban areas, as these would be defined from aerial photographs where tracts of 40 acres or less were the units of land classification. Land use data from the Bureau of the Census delineation of "urbanized areas" do not mean what they purport to mean; a substantial part of such areas are, in fact, not urbanized, and there is a sharp discrepancy (in practice, more than in stated definition) between the 1950 and 1960 urbanized areas which makes any comparison based on them seriously misleading.

10. Data about land use (and population data also) are poor for cities for another reason. The usual Census or other data on cities are based upon the geographical area within the legal city; because the boundaries have been extended from time to time, comparisons are for an expanding total area. If based on a constantly defined area, population and land use relationships for the past would

often have been quite different than they seemed, when analyzed for a changing city area; and some of the changes of the past two decades which appear novel would be found to have existed in many earlier decades.

11. Suburbs are lavish users of land if the standard of comparison is the larger older cities, although the difference is often less than is asserted because of data deficiencies. But they are thrifty users of land if the basis of comparison is the smaller cities and towns where land is used even more lavishly. If one looks only at the usual statistics on land use or on density of settlement in metropolitan areas, it would appear that the trend is toward a sharply lower density. If one uses statistics for the whole urban population and statistics which more accurately reflect actual land use, then the decline in density is much less and may even not exist at all.

12. A great deal of land is available for future growth within the larger urban complexes, including those of the northeastern United States, often called Megalopolis. The "urbanized area" (as defined by the Bureau of the Census) of this region in 1960 was but 17 percent of its total land area, yet contained 83 percent of the population. Perhaps as much as 30 percent of its "urbanized area" was, in fact, not urban in its land use; perhaps as much as two decades of normal population growth could be accommodated within the 1960 urbanized area, were measures taken to confine growth to it and to use its land fully; in fact, of course, suburban land conversion is spreading beyond the 1960 "urbanized area." While choice land in choice locations is scarce and costly (and always has been and always will be, for this is inherent in the very word "choice"), yet there is no serious overall land scarcity within the most heavily urbanized region of the United States.

13. Since the focus of this study is on suburban land conversion, relatively little attention is directed to "new towns." While there are many attractive features of the new town concept, there are obvious difficulties too. It is a gross error to assume that new towns will not experience the problems and suffer the shortcomings of the older towns. At the greatest development of new towns that seems within the range of possibility, the bulk of the urban population growth must occur within the present urban complexes, including their expanding suburbs.

14. The final chapter offers a number of alternative means of changing (and, hopefully, improving) the suburban land conversion process. These might be undertaken singly, but would be much more effective in combination. Their major outlines are as follows:

Various measures can be used to improve the present processes of suburban land conversion. Among them are: better planning; zoning more carefully based upon plans; better coordination of public improvements among themselves and with general plans; and pricing of public services to provide an incentive to private business and to individuals to undertake activities in conformity with the general plans and with social objectives. While all of these are important, and in most areas urgently needed, yet they alone cannot effect a substantial modification of the suburban development process.

Other measures can be used to improve the functioning of the suburban land market and to "deprofitize" some aspects of the present process. Of particular importance would be various tax reforms. If some of the intense economic pressures to break established plans and zoning ordinances could be siphoned off, the more conventional planning and zoning approach would have greater possibilities of success.

Reorganization of local government, to increase its capacity to deal with the difficult problems of suburban land conversion, is desirable; but there are serious difficulties in the way of its achievement.

The potential and the economics of large-scale public purchase of suburban land, for later development by private builders, is explored in modest detail. The judgment is offered that no really fundamental change in suburban land conversion—including provision of new homes for lower-income people in the suburbs—is possible in the absence of relatively large-scale purchase of land by some public body. The interrelationship of such land purchase to other suggestions is also considered rather carefully.

Although programs to alleviate poverty are outside the primary focus of this study, yet the potential for housing and for land use of some direct attack on poverty, such as a guaranteed annual income, cannot be overlooked, and is considered briefly. Likewise, urban renewal in the older areas of cities has a bearing upon suburban land conversion. The potential for stimulating urban renewal is considered briefly, and some specific suggestions are made for aiding private renewal efforts.

The intellectually stimulating but practically very difficult idea of internalizing some part of the externalities affecting land value and land use is considered, and a few modest suggestions offered.

The chapter concludes with a consideration of the gains possible from combining these separate alternatives for improvement of suburban land conversion into more comprehensive approaches. The interactions among separable parts may be very great. Improved local government would greatly aid public acquisition of land, which could be used to strengthen land zoning and land taxation. Some means of public capture of profits from the suburban land conversion process would tame the rampant speculative pressures which have so often made a mockery of land planning and zoning. Many other interrelations exist or can exist. If the process of suburbanization is to be changed for the better, some or all of these measures would contribute to such a change.

part I
FORCES, PROCESSES, ACTORS

SOME 2 MEASURES OF URBANIZATION

hroughout the world today, cities are growing faster than their rural hinterlands in population and in economic activity. Migration to the cities has
long characterized many countries. But in recent decades it has been so
rapid as not merely to absorb the natural increase of rural people but actually to
reduce the population in many rural areas. This urbanization of the world is a
complex demographic, economic, social, technological, and political process that
has many ramifications and interactions.

Millions of poor people live in urban centers, in what those who do not live there
call slums. There are many reasons why this type of urban growth is undesirable
and should be discouraged by governments: people live in poverty; antisocial conditions flourish; political instability is encouraged; health hazards are created. Yet the
inmigrants who live there have moved to these places voluntarily and would
strongly resist returning to farms and small towns.

While the slum is a ubiquitous feature of modern urbanism, living at a high
level of personal consumption is also a feature of the modern city. The vast
majority of the productive enterprises of modern economies are in cities.

Today's urbanization is but the continuation and acceleration of a process long
under way, and there is good reason to believe that it will accelerate and intensify
during the coming decades. There is no need to review here the history of the city's
development, but a few quantitative measures may be interesting and helpful.
Hoyt has estimated that in 1800 only slightly more than 1 percent of the world's
population lived in cities of 100,000 or more population; by 1930, the comparable
figure was 11 percent; and by 1960, 20 percent.[1] The proportion of the population
living in cities of over 100,000 in 1960 was quite uneven in different parts of the
world. Forty-two percent of Americans were located in such cities. In Europe, excluding the U.S.S.R., the proportion was 33 percent; in the U.S.S.R., 24 percent.
Asia as a whole was only 12 percent urbanized, and Africa as a whole only
8 percent.

All demographic projections of population for the world as a whole, for each
continent, and for each country envisage further striking increases in total numbers of people, even if population planning results in a marked future decline in
the rate of increase. Much of this expected national increase in numbers will be
located in the cities of the future. The scale of urbanization and the tempo of
change are likely to accelerate; the problems, as well as the opportunities, arising
out of such urbanization will likewise grow.

[1] Homer Hoyt, "The Growth of Cities from 1800 to 1960 and Forecasts to Year 2000,"
Land Economics (May 1963).

URBANIZATION IN THE UNITED STATES

In the United States it has long been customary, in population statistics and in general discussion, to define as "urban" any settlement of 2,500 or more people. Data are available for larger cities and also for villages of less than 2,500, as well as for farms and nonfarm open country. These distinctions arose and had their clearest application in a day when each city was rather easily identifiable on the ground, with a fairly clear edge between city and countryside. Today city and country tend to blend physically, economically, socially; it is both harder to distinguish the city as a separate entity and less meaningful to do so. The Bureau of the Census has wrestled with the ensuing problems and developed new concepts such as "urbanized area"; and the Bureau of the Budget has defined the "Standard Metropolitan Statistical Area" (SMSA). At numerous points throughout this book, the problems of defining meaningful areas for data analysis will be discussed. For the present, however, the usual published population data will serve to demonstrate the growth of urbanization in the United States.

In 1790, when the new nation instituted its system of regular and relatively comprehensive censuses—a concept now imitated throughout virtually the entire world —there were 3.9 million people and about 5 percent of them lived in "cities" of 2,500 or more people (Figure 1 and Appendix Table 1). As the total population of the country increased, the proportion in cities also rose. Farm population rose steadily until 1910 and remained on a somewhat uneven plateau until 1940, but by the mid-1960s it had declined to less than half its peak. "Other rural" population has continued to rise, its apparent increase approximately offsetting the decline in farm population to leave the total population outside of "cities" more or less constant. However, the "other rural" category is an extremely diverse group: relatively independent small towns of less than 2,500; unincorporated suburbs of various sizes or suburbs of less than 2,500 population if incorporated; and genuinely open-country settlement, often strung along roads. Moreover, the situation differs greatly among regions of the United States. Generally speaking, small towns and rural places which are within 30 miles of cities of 10,000 or more people or lie within regions of general population growth, have increased in population. In other parts of the country, small towns and rural places have generally lost.[2] Within each of these categories, the larger small towns have grown more and the smaller ones have grown less or even lost population. Much of the "other rural" is simply a more widely dispersed suburbia. Parts of it, however, are trade and service centers for agriculture, fishing, forestry, mining, and tourist activities.

Cities grow not merely in terms of total population but also in total employment

[2] For information on small towns and villages, see several publications by Glenn V. Fugitt: *Growing and Declining Villages in Wisconsin, 1950–1960*, No. 8, Population Series (University of Wisconsin Department of Rural Sociology, 1964) ; "The Small Town in Rural America," *Journal of Cooperative Extension* (Spring 1965) ; and "Some Characteristics of Villages in Rural America" in *Rural Poverty in the United States*, Report of the President's National Advisory Commission on Rural Poverty (U.S. Government Printing Office, 1968). See also J. F. Hart and N. E. Salisbury, "Population Change in Middlewestern Villages: A Statistical Approach," *Annals of the Association of American Geographers* (March 1965) ; and Howard W. Ottoson et al., *Land and People in the Northern Plains Transition Area* (University of Nebraska Press, 1966).

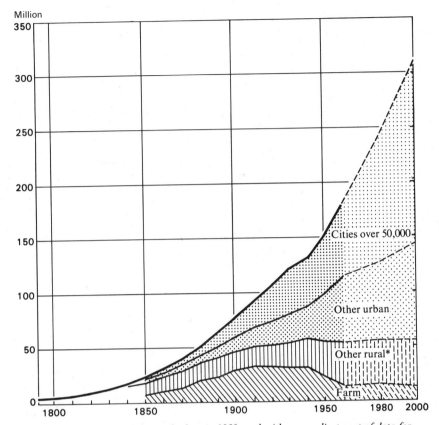

Million

*Using new Census definition of urban in 1950, and with some adjustment of data for
1940 and 1930 to put these years on same definition.

FIGURE 1. Population of the United States by urban and rural groupings, 1790–1960 and projections to 2000.

and in total income. Total employment has increased in cities more or less in proportion to growth in total population. Some cities or urban groupings of population
have higher ratios of employment to population than do rural areas, in large part
because the age distribution has often included a higher proportion of people of
working ages in the cities; but some cities have had extensive colonies of retired
persons not in the labor force. Also, in general, economic output or total personal
income has grown in cities as their total populations have increased. There are
divergences in trend in these various aspects of urban life, which in themselves
have merited and have received specialized research attention.

CLASSIFICATION OF PEOPLE BY LOCATION

At the beginning of this book, it may be helpful to consider some concepts or
general relationships which are basic to any study of urbanization as a process in
the United States. The full significance of some of these ideas may become apparent only in later chapters.

A first and perhaps basic consideration is how to classify people according to geographic location. National census, local planning, and other data on population and land use typically show population according to some geographic area: a legally defined area such as a city or only part of it, an economically defined area, or an area of origin or destination such as in a traffic survey. Without ever explicitly stating it, such processes in effect classify people according to where they "live." Popular usage does the same, as when one says that he lives in Chicago, Washington, or some other city.

Actually, nearly all such classifications are based upon where people customarily sleep at night. For the average family, this is where its home or apartment is located. In the modern United States, an increasing number and proportion of all families have a second (or third) home for vacation purposes, and an increasing proportion of all persons is found, on any given night, sleeping in commercial motels and hotels. Far more important in numerical terms are the adults who work in another location from where they sleep, often many miles away, perhaps in a wholly different governmental or economic area. While full-time workers generally spend about two-thirds as many hours on the job each week as they spend in sleep, and part-time workers spend proportionately less, yet work time and work activity is extremely important. Moreover, almost all Americans except the very young and the very old spend significant amounts of time each week in shopping, in recreation, and in education at locations which may be some distance from where they customarily sleep.

It could be argued that people "live" at each of these numerous locations, as much as they live where they sleep. Certainly many aspects of modern living take place away from the home. Whether one regards this as undesirable or as acceptable, it is a fact.

As a result of these relationships, standard data on population classified according to customary sleeping location must be supplemented by data on place of employment, on location of commercial and industrial activities, on places of recreation and of education. Transportation routes and methods and customary travel patterns are the means whereby the various scattered locations are linked together into a total living pattern for the individual and for the community. Although this study will deal primarily with population residence data based upon where people customarily sleep, it must always be borne in mind that this is but one aspect of modern urban living.

In a study of urban land use, there is perhaps more justification for concentrating on customary places of sleeping than would be the case in studies of other aspects of urban living. Residential use of urban land, in the sense of the land actually occupied by homeowners' lots, often amounts to roughly 40 percent of the total urban-use area; and the streets within residential areas may add nearly as much more land. Industrial, commercial, recreation, and other activity on land within the general urban area, while extremely important in terms of function and of focus, often occupy much smaller proportions of the land.

In the future, it will be even more difficult than it is today to classify people according to where they "live." The usual place of residence is likely to become an increasingly inaccurate description of population location; more and more families will owe more or less equal allegiance to two or more locations. The present divergence of interest of the businessman whose home is in a suburb, who works in the central city, who plays golf in rural territory, and whose children go to college in a different location may be but the forerunner of a much more fragmented interest in specific geographic locations in the future. Statistical data can be modified to meet this changing situation, but a more difficult problem may arise in having the ordinary person or even the professional student understand the complex relationships inherent in such diverse geographical interests for the same individuals.

GRAIN OF STUDY

The grain of any study of land use greatly influences, perhaps dominates, the kind of findings that result. If county data are used, one set of relationships emerges; if city (or SMSA or urbanized area) data are used for the same broad geographic area, another and perhaps sharply different set of relationships comes out; and if the grain becomes finer, by using data for census tracts—and still more if data are available by small land parcels—the results may be wholly different. The matter of the grain to use is not merely a matter of what data are available or what can be most easily calculated or mapped. It goes to the very heart of the analysis by its major, if not dominating, effect upon the conclusions.

In practice, any analysis of urban land use in the United States is severely limited by the availability of data. The analyst is forced to use relatively gross data in many instances—county data, or census tract data, or city or SMSA data—when he would much prefer to use more finely grained data. Total area and total population for a given statistical unit produces an average reliable for that whole area; but this general relationship cannot be assumed to apply to each part of the area. To anticipate some of the analysis in Part II, for instance, the average density of population for the whole Northeastern Urban Complex in 1960 was slightly less than 1,100 persons per square mile (1.7 persons per acre); in the urbanized one-sixth of this region, the average density was well over 5,000 persons per square mile (8.4 persons per acre); and in the remaining or nonurbanized part it was not much over 200 persons per square mile (0.34 persons per acre). Moreover, even these major refinements in the gross data leave enormous differences in intensity of land use within each of these categories.

One may be forced, therefore, for practical reasons of data availability to work at one scale or one grain of inquiry when he would prefer another. But he must strenuously avoid confusing himself and his readers into thinking that the results are not greatly affected thereby. They might, in exceptional cases, be the same as a finer-grained study would reveal. Typically, however, the results of a study of urban land use do depend in large part upon the grain of the study.

This book has different grains of inquiry. In Part II, for example, county data are used for some purposes; city, urbanized area, and SMSA data for others; and for still others, data for suburbs and for tracts and parcels of land. If the latter were universally available on a fully comparable basis, one could start with the finest grain and gradually build up to coarser grain that would be inclusive of broader areas. But one must be limited by what exists.

GOVERNMENTAL BOUNDARIES AND LAND USE DATA

Meaningful economic analysis of urban land use is further complicated by the fact that cities and other units of local government in the United States have boundaries which were largely determined by historical or political accident. In the settlement period in each region, county and town boundaries were often drawn on highly arbitrary lines, quite expansively in some instances and more narrowly in others. State, county, and city lines were sometimes originally established along physical boundaries, such as rivers, which may have represented logical boundaries under the travel technology and economic forces of that day. But today these physical features are as likely to serve as centers of economic activity, bringing the city and its surrounding area together rather than separating them.

For many purposes, data are needed on numbers of persons, amount of employment, volume of retail sales, and other aspects of economic or social life for units of government, and, thus it is appropriate that census reports should present data for cities, counties, states, and other units of government. However, in a great many instances these governmental units are not meaningful economic or social units. Sometimes it is possible to combine two or more governmental units in order to establish a rational economic unit. However, combination is much less satisfactory for land use data than it is for data on population, employment, income, output, and the like.

The Bureau of the Census uses Standard Metropolitan Statistical Areas to report a considerable amount of data. In general (outside New England) the boundaries of SMSAs follow county lines. This permits compilation of a reasonably meaningful total for population, labor force, and employment for a metropolitan area such as Baltimore or Philadelphia, which may include several counties and perhaps parts of two states. But the use of county lines means that relatively very large areas of completely rural land are included within these SMSAs.[3] The SMSA may include all the land used for urban purposes in a given metropolitan complex, but it typically includes several times as much land used for purely rural purposes.

The problem is different, but not much easier of solution, when city data are used for studies of urban land use. Many cities include much "undeveloped" land within their boundaries, some of which may actually be used for agriculture or other typically rural uses. In a great many cases some part of the suburban development which everyone thinks of as part of a city actually lies outside its legal boundaries. The legal city may be either larger or smaller than the economic or land use city. County data are on the whole even less useful for studies of urban land use than data on city lines. In this study, especially in Part II, data on land use by counties, SMSAs, urbanized areas, and cities, are used because there is no choice. However, it will be necessary repeatedly to speculate on what more appropriate data might show the situation to be.

---

[3] For a discussion of the limitations of the SMSA as a unit for studying urban land use, see Marion Clawson, R. Burnell Held, and Charles H. Stoddard, *Land for the Future* (Johns Hopkins Press for Resources for the Future, 1960), pp. 82–95. See also Brian J. L. Berry, *Metropolitan Area Definition: A Re-evaluation of Concept and Statistical Practice*, Working Paper No. 28 (U.S. Bureau of the Census, 1969).

The basic difficulty is that totals and averages for any one governmental unit may conceal far more differences in land use situations within the units of data analysis than between or among such governmental units. This probability may be illustrated by Figure 2, which is a schematic diagram of generalized land use for a hypothetical urban area. A large city or metropolis lies on the western bank of the river in one state, with a smaller city on the eastern bank in a different state. More or less fully "used" land takes up much—but not all—of the area within each city or metropolis but overlaps the boundaries of each. City and county boundaries are obviously arbitrary in relation to the present land use situation. Scattered outliers of residentially used land extend some miles beyond each city.

Part of the area is shown in Figure 3. The results are similar in one sense: part of each area is "used" for urban purposes, part is unoccupied, and neither follows

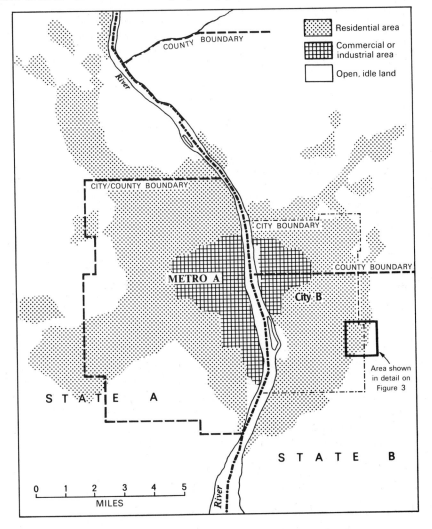

FIGURE 2.   Generalized land use picture for a hypothetical urban complex.

if he used data on urbanized areas. In addition, he would get one set of answers if data were available on dominant land use over large areas, but a very different set of answers if data were available, land parcel by land parcel.

It is no simple matter to determine the best areal units of data collection and analysis, especially for comparisons extending over considerable periods of time. Boundaries of areas for statistical purposes may be established at one time and maintained unchanged in the future. This has the advantage of showing rather clearly what is happening over time within a defined geographical area, but it is likely to miss the major economic and other changes inherent in changing land use because the major changes are likely to involve changes in areal extent itself. Another approach is to redefine continuously the areas of statistical analysis, as the city or urban area grows. This procedure measures better what is happening to the urban complex as a whole, but it may obscure changes in land use within any defined area. The best solution is to have data on both bases, that is, to know what is happening to the old defined urban areas, to know also how these are being extended over time, and what is happening within the extensions.

The Bureau of the Budget, the Bureau of the Census, and other federal statistical agencies have been well aware of these complexities. They have sought to deal with the problems particularly by use of two concepts: the Standard Metropolitan Statistical Area and the urbanized area. The SMSA concept, established to permit all federal agencies to use the same metropolitan areas, has been employed in censuses beginning in 1950. The Census Bureau thus defines the SMSA:

> The definition of an individual SMSA involves two considerations: First, a city or cities of specified population to constitute the central city and to identify the county in which it is located as the central county; and, second, economic and social relationships with contiguous counties which are metropolitan in character, so that the periphery of the specific metropolitan area may be determined. SMSAs may cross state lines.

> *Population criteria.*—The criteria for population relate to a city or cities of specified size according to the 1960 Census of Population.
>   1. Each standard metropolitan statistical area must include at least:
>   a. One city with 50,000 inhabitants or more, or
>   b. Two cities having contiguous boundaries and constituting, for general economic and social purposes, a single community with a combined population of at least 50,000, the smaller of which must have a population of at least 15,000.
>   2. If each of two or more adjacent counties has a city of 50,000 inhabitants or more (or twin cities under 1b) and the cities are within 20 miles of each other (city limits to city limits), they are to be included in the same area unless there is definite evidence that the two cities are not economically and socially integrated.

> *Criteria of metropolitan character.*—The criteria of metropolitan character relate primarily to the attributes of the contiguous county as a place of work or as a home for a concentration of nonagricultural workers.

3. At least 75 percent of the labor force of the county must be in the non-agricultural labor force.

4. In addition to criterion 3, the county must meet at least one of the following conditions:

a. It must have 50 percent or more of its population living in contiguous minor civil divisions with a density of at least 150 persons per square mile, in an unbroken chain of minor civil divisions with such density radiating from a central city in the area.

b. The number of nonagricultural workers employed in the county must equal at least 10 percent of the number of nonagricultural workers employed in the county containing the largest city in the area, or the county must be the place of employment of 10,000 nonagricultural workers.

c. The nonagricultural labor force living in the county must equal at least 10 percent of the number in the nonagricultural labor force living in the county containing the largest city in the area, or the county must be the place of residence of a nonagricultural labor force of 10,000.

5. In New England, the city and town are administratively more important than the county, and data are compiled locally for such minor civil divisions. Here, towns and cities are the units used in defining standard metropolitan statistical areas. In New England, because smaller units are used and more restricted areas result, a population density criterion of at least 100 persons per square mile is used as the measure of metropolitan character.

Criteria of integration.—The criteria of integration relate primarily to the extent of economic and social communication between the outlying counties and the central county.

6. A county is regarded as integrated with the county or counties containing the central cities of the area if either of the following criteria is met:

a. Fifteen percent of the workers living in the county work in the county or counties containing central cities of the area, or

b. Twenty-five percent of those working in the county live in the county or counties containing central cities of the area.[4]

For analysis of urban land use, SMSAs are relatively rather inclusive units; that is, they include most or all the population and the labor force that can properly be associated with a particular urban center. In so doing, they include a great deal of land which is not urban in use by any reasonable standard of "use." Their adherence to county lines (town lines in New England) would alone ensure inclusion of much nonurban land. Moreover, densities of 100 and 150 persons per square mile may result from a highly dispersed pattern of settlement or—more likely—from averaging relatively small areas of much denser settlement pattern with a great deal of open, unsettled territory. Because a great deal of other information is available on an SMSA basis, this unit of analysis will be used here, but at numerous points it will be necessary to point out its limitations as a measure of land use.

[4] U.S. Bureau of the Census, *County and City Data Book* (U.S. Government Printing Office, 1962), p. XI.

Partly in recognition of the problems of using SMSAs, the Bureau of the Census has developed a concept of "urbanized areas." It has described and defined this concept as follows:

Urbanized areas.—Although the major objective of the Bureau of the Census in delineating urbanized areas was to provide a better separation of urban and rural population in the vicinity of the larger cities, individual urbanized areas have proved to be useful statistical areas. They correspond to areas called "conurbations" in some other countries. An urbanized area contains at least one city of 50,000 inhabitants or more in 1960, as well as the surrounding closely settled incorporated places and unincorporated areas that meet the criteria listed below. An urbanized area may be thought of as divided into the central city or cities, and the remainder of the area, known as the urban fringe. All persons residing in an urbanized area are included in the urban population.

For the 1960 Census, urbanized areas were delineated in terms of the census results rather than on the basis of information available prior to the census, as was done in 1950. A peripheral zone was drawn around each 1950 urbanized area and around cities that were presumably approaching a population of 50,000. Within the unincorporated parts of this zone small enumeration districts were established, usually including no more than 1 square mile of land area and no more than 75 housing units. (An enumeration district [ED] is a small area assigned to an enumerator which must be canvassed and reported separately. In most cases, an ED contained approximately 250 housing units.)

Arrangements were made to include within the urbanized area those enumeration districts meeting specified criteria of population density as well as adjacent incorporated places. Since the urbanized area outside incorporated places was defined in terms of enumeration districts, the boundaries for the most part followed such features as roads, streets, railroads, streams, and other clearly defined lines which may be easily identified by census enumerators in the field and often do not conform to the boundaries of political units.

In addition to its central city or cities, an urbanized area also contains the following types of contiguous areas, which together constitute its urban fringe:

1. Incorporated places with 2,500 inhabitants or more.

2. Incorporated places with less than 2,500 inhabitants, provided each has a closely settled area of 100 housing units or more.

3. Towns, in the New England states, townships in New Jersey and Pennsylvania, and counties elsewhere which are classified as urban.

4. Enumeration districts in unincorporated territory with a population density of 1,000 inhabitants or more per square mile. (The areas of large nonresidential tracts devoted to such urban land uses as railroad yards, factories, and cemeteries were excluded in computing the population density of an enumeration district.)

5. Other enumeration districts in unincorporated territory with lower population density provided they served one of the following purposes:

a. To eliminate enclaves.

b. To close indentations in the urbanized areas of 1 mile or less across the open end, and

c. To link outlying enumeration districts of qualifying density that were no more than 1½ miles from the main body of the urbanized area.

Contiguous urbanized areas with central cities in the same standard metropolitan statistical area are combined. Urbanized areas with central cities in different standard metropolitan statistical areas are not combined, except that a single urbanized area was established in the New York-Northeastern New Jersey Standard Consolidated Area, and in the Chicago-Northwestern Indiana Standard Consolidated Area.

The boundaries of the urbanized areas for 1960 do not conform to those for 1950, partly because of actual changes in land use and density of settlement, and partly because of relatively minor changes in the rules used to define the boundaries. In general, however, the urbanized areas of 1950 and 1960 are based on essentially the same concept, and the figures for a given urbanized area may be used to measure the population growth of that area.[5]

Data on urbanized areas are not available for censuses prior to 1950. The statement by the Bureau of the Census as to comparability of urbanized areas in 1950 and 1960 may be true for population, employment, and other similar data. But the two definitions, as actually applied in the two years, are not comparable as far as land use is concerned. The 1960 definition not only takes in more land, which would be reasonable in view of urban spread during the preceding decade, but includes more land than can be accounted for by increased suburban population. Comparisons of land area used for urban purposes, or of density of population per unit of area, which are based on reported urbanized area in 1950 and 1960, are therefore inaccurate and may be misleading.

A considerable similarity of definition between SMSA and urbanized area is apparent; the latter is largely the built-up part of the former. However, in one SMSA in the Northeastern Complex (New London-Groton-Norwich) no urbanized area was delineated.

Although the concept of an urbanized area represents a notable attempt to define an area which is predominantly urban in land usage, more idle or rural land can be, and in fact is, included than may be apparent from a simple reading of the definition. Incorporated places, especially in the range of 2,500 to 25,000 may well contain substantial acreages of land not used for urban purposes and frequently not used at all. Towns, townships, and counties classified as urban may be so as a whole, yet may also contain much land not used for urban purposes. An enumeration district with no more than 1,000 persons per square mile may contain considerable idle or other nonurban land. The various classes of land listed under part 5, of the definition of urbanized area above—enclaved, indented, and intervening areas between settled areas and outliers—will each be predominantly nonurban in land use. For all of these reasons, urbanized areas may contain considerable acreages of land not actually used for urban purposes of any kind. The total urban-

[5] Ibid., pp. XIII, XIV.

ized acreage therefore overstates the land area in use for urban purposes. Or, to put it differently, within the area classified as urbanized there is opportunity for considerable additional settlement without disturbing any presently established land uses. The significance of this fact for various policy decisions should be apparent.

DEFINITIONS OF MAN-LAND RELATIONSHIPS

In addition to the problem of defining the most appropriate geographical unit for measuring changes in urban land use, there is a related problem of defining the best way to measure man-land relationships within any geographic unit. For both problems, the answer may be dictated as much by the availability of data as it is by the specifications of an ideal definition. Several ways have been, or might be, used to express the relation between man and land in urban areas (See Table 1). Among the major variants are these:

TABLE 1

ALTERNATIVE MEASURES OF DENSITY OF LAND USE

Measure[1]	Numerator of equation	Denominator of equation	Approximate index of area per unit of population[2]
1. Total-population/ total-area	Total population of areal unit	Total acreage of areal unit	110 to 200 plus
2. Total-population/ developed-area ("overall residential density")	Total population of areal unit	Developed or urban used acreage of areal unit[3]	100
3. Gross residential density ("gross residential density")	Residential population of areal unit	Residentially used acreage of areal unit[4]	65 to 75
4. Net residential density ("net residential density")	Residential population of areal unit	Land used only for residential purposes[5]	35 to 45
5. Residential density of private land ("site density")	Residential population of areal unit	Acreage within privately owned lots[6]	30 to 40
6. Floor area density	Residential population of areal unit	Acreage (or square footage) of floors at all levels	10 to 40

Note: See text for fuller description and definition.

[1] Words in quotation marks are the British term for the most nearly comparable measure.

[2] These are rough estimates based on examination of various city or metropolitan plans. The figures are land area per unit of population; density figures would be the inverse of these.

[3] Varying acreage of idle land within generally developed area might be included.

[4] Varying but generally small acreages of idle land or land in uses other than residential within a basically residential area might be included.

[5] In United States excluding every other use (including streets as a use) and excluding all idle land; in Britain, includes streets, hence terms are not fully comparable.

[6] Excluding all streets and all uses other than residential.

1. The simplest measure would be to divide the total population of any city, county, SMSA, urbanized area, minor civil division, enumeration district, or any other geographical unit by the total acreage of the same unit. The resulting measure might be called total-population/total-area density. (The term is cumbersome, but there appears to be no simpler one that has not been applied to other concepts.) The results of calculating total-population/total-area density would depend greatly upon the kind of area in question—more particularly, how much open, idle, undeveloped, or other essentially nonurban land is included in it. In American cities, there is often a considerable area of such land, but this varies greatly from one city to another. Bartholomew has shown, for a sample of cities, that the proportion "developed" ranges from nearly all of the total area downward to much less than half for some cities.[6] In urban counties there would usually be a larger proportion of idle land. As indicated in the first item of Table 1, the index of the amount of land required per unit of population would vary from somewhat more than 100 to a figure of twice that size or more, and the index of density from less than 50 to 90. Total-population/total-area density is not a very meaningful measure of the relation between population and land area, but it does have the great virtue of being calculable for any geographically defined area for which population data are available.

2. A much more meaningful measure of man-land relationships could be obtained if the more obviously nonurban land were excluded from the land area, as shown in the second item in Table 1. In particular, agricultural land and the larger tracts of idle land might be excluded. But land used for industrial, commercial, park, transportation, and other urban purposes, as well as for residential purposes, should be included in this measure. The result would be to include what Bartholomew calls the "developed" area of a city. This measure can best be called total-population/developed-area density; it is closely similar to what the British Ministry of Housing and Local Government calls "overall residential density."[7] In Table 1, this measure (item 2) is used as the base for the index of land area required per unit of population and for density. In the United States, at least, the use of this measure would raise some important questions including these: How small should the areas of undeveloped and/or idle land be to be excluded? How could one be sure that all of the economically and socially functional area belonging to a particular city could be included? Vacant areas within or adjacent to urban settled areas have been classified as: vacant lots, often rather small parcels, often surrounded by developed areas; leapfrogged or bypassed larger tracts, ranging upward to several hundred acres in some cases; and/or idled or "withdrawn" land on the fringes, taken out of agriculture, hopefully "ripening" for more intensive urban use.[8] The vacant lots might still be included as urban, if not too extensive, while most of the leapfrogged or withdrawn land should be excluded. In practice this might or might not be difficult.

    [6] Harland Bartholomew, *Land Uses in American Cities* (Harvard University Press, 1955), summarized in Clawson, Held, and Stoddard, *Land for the Future,* pp. 77–82.
    [7] Great Britain, Ministry of Housing and Local Government, *Residential Areas—Higher Densities* (Her Majesty's Stationery Office, 1962).
    [8] See Clawson, Held, and Stoddard, *Land for the Future,* pp. 66–77.

3. The immediately foregoing definition might be applied to a basically residential area, thus excluding the larger industrial areas, larger shopping districts, larger parks, major transportation uses of land such as major throughways and airports, and perhaps others. This measure, shown as item 3 of Table 1, may best be called gross residential density. The *Community Builders Handbook* states that "gross density is computed on the basis of gross land area devoted to streets and other non-residential uses plus one-half of bounding streets and one-quarter of bounding street intersections" but the context suggests that primarily residential areas are under consideration.[9] This is the same term used by the British Ministry of Housing and Local Government for the same measure. In this measure, how fussy should one get about local shops, schools, and small parks? Their acreage is often not large and the numerical results would not be much affected by their inclusion or omission. The index of land area per unit of population is cut by a fourth to a third, compared with the second measure, and density is increased proportionately. But this measure would result in rather different mixtures of land use in the older as compared with the newer parts of American cities and as between many American and British cities.

4. The process might be carried further, by applying the calculations to a particular housing or residential area, from which all schools, all parks, all commercial development, all street area, and every other use than residential has been excluded. This type of land definition and this man-land ratio is one which concerns the land subdivider or developer, at least in the United States. Although the term is widely misused, we call this net residential density. The *Community Builders Handbook* states that "net density represents the number of dwelling units per net acre of land devoted to residential buildings and accessory uses on the same lot within the site but excluding land for streets, public parking, playgrounds, and nonresidential uses."[10]

5. For some purposes, it would be helpful to know how much land was actually in the homeowners' lots or in apartment house lots; this measure would be similar to item 4 but might differ somewhat. Measure 5 is here termed residential density of private land; in Britain this would generally be called site density. It might measure the degree of clustering of residential units and the provision of semi-public space among them.

6. Actual floor area of buildings in residential and in other areas might also be used as a measure of land use, listed in Table 1 as floor area density or floor area ratio. The relation between number of people and floor area would reflect the degree of crowding within buildings. The relation between total floor area and gross land area would reflect, at least to some extent, the proportion of open space between buildings and the tendency of buildings to rise more than one story. The index of land area required per unit of population might vary from 10 (or less, for very high rise apartments) to perhaps 40 for detached dwellings, and density from 2½ to 10 times that of Measure No. 2.

For some purposes, especially for urban hydrology such as flood control and groundwater recharge, it would be helpful to know what proportion of the total

[9] *Community Builders Handbook* (Washington: Urban Land Institute, 1970), p. 108.
[10] Ibid.

land surface was covered by impervious surfaces such as streets, rooftops, driveways, and the like.

These general ideas may be illustrated by the map for a hypothetical small city in Figure 4. This hypothetical city has a population of 100,000 and a gross area within its boundaries of 25,000 acres; on the total-population/total-area ratio (Number 1 in Table 1), therefore, there are 4.0 persons per acre (2,560 per square mile).

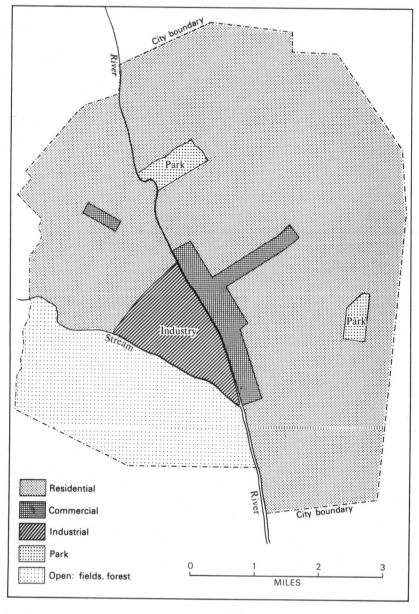

FIGURE 4. Hypothetical small city, to illustrate various measures of intensity of land use.

In the southwestern corner of the city is an undeveloped and uninhabited wooded tract, which lacks good transportation access, as well as sewer and other services. If its 3,800 acres are deducted from the city total, the remaining 21,200 acres have a developed area or "overall residential density" (Number 2 in Table 1) of 4.7 persons per acre (3,000 per square mile). Along the major river is an industrial district containing 600 acres; in two locations are major commercial areas also containing 600 acres; and two moderately large parks have 300 acres. If these 1,500 acres are deducted, the remaining 19,700 acres of more or less fully used residential area has a gross residential density (Number 3 in Table 1) of 5.1 persons per acre (3,250 per square mile). If the small area of idle land and uses other than residential and the area in local service streets is deducted, the net residential density (Number 4 in Table 1) would rise to about 10.0 persons per acre (6,400 per square mile). Floor density (Number 6 in Table 1) would be still higher. Thus, for this illustrative city, one may calculate densities of land use ranging from 4.0 to 10.0 or more persons per acre (2,560 to 6,400 or more per square smile). Each is equally accurate. Each measures a differently defined relationship, but each is equally valid if properly understood. In practice, of course, the land use situation for any city would be more complex than this simple diagram, but the general relationships would persist.

U.S. Data on Land Use

There are numerous sources of data about land use in the United States, but the various sources employ different definitions of uses or of areas for which data are available or both, so that it is extremely difficult to assemble data which are comparable from one area to another or from one date to another.[11] The Bureau of the Census obtains data on land use in farms, which are reasonably comparable from one county to another and from one Census date to another. But the data are published only on a county basis. Moreover, for our purpose these data are somewhat peripheral, for they do not directly deal with urban land uses. Although the Census Bureau obtains much information about population, employment, housing, income, and other aspects of urban life, it obtains very little information on urban land uses as such.

The most numerous sources of information about urban land uses are the special land use surveys and studies of city or metropolitan planning agencies or of transportation planning groups. These have typically been carried out city by city, with only the crudest comparability between cities, often with no means of updating the one-shot surveys, and with little historical comparability between one survey and another even for the same city. A major effort has been undertaken by some of the federal agencies most concerned to produce more usable, more comparable, and

[11] For a survey of land use information and the possibilities of its improvement, see Marion Clawson and Charles L. Stewart, *Land Use Information—A Critical Survey of U. S. Statistics, Including Possibilities for Greater Uniformity* (Resources for the Future, 1966). See particularly the appendices prepared by the federal agencies, including the *Land Use Coding Manual* prepared jointly by the U.S. Bureau of Public Roads and the Urban Renewal Administration.

easily updated land use data. Two ideas are basic to the efforts to improve data on urban land use:

1. Data as collected by observation, by interview, or from aerial photos should record actual land use in a highly detailed manner, leaving classification of such use into fewer categories for a later statistical operation.

2. Data should be obtained for the smallest recognizable parcels of land, since these can be aggregated into any desired larger areas while disaggregation is not usually possible.

Methods for employing these principles and for use of modern electronic data-analyzing machinery have been developed.

Alternative Ways of Attaining Intensities of Land Use

The average density of residential land use for some unit of area may vary from zero to well over 100 persons per acre. The average density is affected by many factors, particularly by the size of the area. The proportion of idle land and of land in uses other than residential (highways and streets, for instance) is likely to be greater for large than for small areas. But the average density of residential land use is also affected by the degree of building coverage of the land and by average building height.

Three major measures of residential building in relation to land may be distinguished:

1. Subdivision contiguity or the lack thereof, especially in suburbs. Some tracts of land of subdivision size are developed; others may not be. While subdivisions vary in size, they are usually 20 acres or more for modern residential builders and may run up to several hundred acres.

2. Building lot size, for detached single-family dwellings, within the subdivision. Within residential areas largely dominated by detached single-family houses, lots may range from 8,000 square feet (one-fifth of an acre), or even less, up to 2 acres. In estate or semi-estate subdivisions, lots may run to 5 acres or more.

3. Floor area ratio, especially for row houses and apartments, which in turn is made up of two major components: the proportion of the lot or area actually covered by the building; and the height of the building.

Although residential density of land use is a continuum over this very wide range, it is still possible to establish some broad classes of average residential density and to consider various ways in which these average densities may be obtained (Table 2). The average densities can be measured either on a relatively fine scale, corresponding more or less to density Measures 4 and 5 in Table 1, or on a coarser scale, corresponding more to Measures 2 and 3 there. In Table 2, *zero* residential density exists where land is idle, or where it is used for other purposes. The idle land may some day be developed for residential use, but the land used for other purposes is unlikely to be shifted to residential use. *Very sparse* residential land use arises where there are estates on tracts of 3 to 5 acres or more, or where lots may be much smaller but a great deal of vacant or idle land is intermixed with the residentially developed land. This density is important because the Bureau of the

Census classes any county as "urban" if it averages 1,000 persons per square mile. A *low* residential density of land use may be achieved by single-family homes on lots of 1 acre each, if the area is fully developed; or the same average density can be achieved by much smaller lots but with varying amounts of idle land between subdivisions. A considerable proportion of the newer suburbs have *average* residential densities in the general range of 3,000 persons per square mile. The average density of residential land use in the Northeastern Urban Complex, as discussed in Chapter 10, is about 4,800 per square mile. A residential area with single-family homes on half-acre lots, all developed, would produce about this average density. In the Northeastern Urban Complex, there are many apartment buildings of vary-

TABLE 2

ALTERNATIVE WAYS OF ATTAINING VARIOUS DENSITIES OF RESIDENTIAL LAND USE

General residential density characterization	On a fine scale[1]		On a coarse scale[2]	
	Persons per acre[3]	Examples	Persons per square mile[4]	Examples
Zero	0.0	Vacant land, from single lots to subdivision in size	0	Land used for other purposes, as manufacturing plants, shopping districts, highways and streets.
Very sparse	1.5	Estate country, lots 3 to 5 acres, single-family homes	1,000	Scattered subdivisions used at low or average density, but a great deal of open land interspersed.
Low	5.0	Single-family homes on lots of 1 acre each, all lots used	3,000	Subdivisions with lots of varying size, from 1 acre downward, and varying amounts of vacant land, ranging upward to half or more.
Average[5]	7.5	Single-family homes on lots of ½ acre each, all lots used	4,800	1) subdivisions of ½-acre lots, all land used; 2) diverse higher density residential areas, including row houses and low apartments, but with some intermingled open land.
High	23.0	Fully developed to row houses or walk-up apartments	15,000	Moderately high-rise apartments, up to 10 stories, with a few lower structures and limited open areas.
Extremely high	80.0	Moderate to very high-rise apartments, occupying most of site	50,000	Very high-rise apartments with extremely limited use of land for other purposes.

[1] Within a typical subdivision or by individual lots or tracts of land.

[2] Residential communities or mixed land use in urban areas.

[3] These are approximate only, with no intention of sharply marking off mutually exclusive zones; for single lots, this corresponds to Measure No. 5 (Table 1) density per individually controlled residential area; for subdivisions, it corresponds to Measure No. 4, net residential density.

[4] Also approximate; depending on size of total area under comparison, this corresponds to Measure No. 2 in Table 1 (overall residential density) where there are substantial other land uses and considerable idle land, or to Measure No. 3 (gross residential density) where the larger uses other than residential and larger vacant areas are excluded.

[5] The median density per net residential acre in the Northeastern Urban Complex, discussed in Chapter 11, is 7.5 persons per acre.

ing heights, many row houses, and many single-family homes on lots of widely varying size. Probably there is also some vacant land within the residential use category. Thus, an average density of 4,800 is achieved by a mixture of land use densities.

A relatively *high* density of residential land use can be achieved by row houses or walk-up apartments, if an area is fully developed with such structures. Moderately high-rise apartments, if surrounded by some open area and intermingled by some lower structures, may also produce the same average density of residential land use. As density rises, the alternative ways of achieving it become fewer. *Extremely high* density is achievable only by moderately high to very high apartments, with little or none of the site used for other purposes or remaining open.

The examples in Table 2 illustrate the range of residential land use densities and illustrate some of the ways of calculating them. They do not cover all the possibilities, since there are obviously other combinations between the classes shown.

POSTWAR URBANIZATION IN THE UNITED STATES

The urban proportion of the total U.S. population has risen steadily since the first Census in 1790. On a national plane, movement toward cities is a form of population aggregation, a centripetal movement of people. But, from very early days until the present, cities have grown in population by expanding outward. Hence, at the scale of the city or metropolis, the population shift is one of disaggregation, a centrifugal movement. These twin movements—population concentration on a national scale and population decentralization on a metropolitan scale—have been under way for many decades and seem likely to continue indefinitely.

A MASSIVE POPULATION REDISTRIBUTION

Young people have migrated from farms to cities ever since our nation began. In earlier decades, this was the primary way that cities grew, for many had birthrates too low to have produced much growth on their own. For a long time, only part of the rural surplus of young people migrated, and rural populations also grew. But after World War I, approximately the full surplus of young rural people migrated to cities. Since World War II, the pace of rural-urban migration has so stepped up that more than half of all counties in the United States lost population during the decade of the 1950s. In many other counties, rural areas also lost, but the gain in the major settlements offset the rural loss. Some of the counties that lost population in the 1950s had also lost it in the 1940s and earlier decades; many of these same counties were losing population in the 1960s. A vast emptying-out of the more rural parts of the United States is in process. On the whole, the rate of migration to the cities seems to have slowed down in the later 1960s. In any case, its contribution to urban population growth has declined in relative importance, largely because the size of the rural population is now too small to contribute a continuing massive migration to the cities.

In some areas, especially near large cities, the rural nonfarm population is on the increase, but these new rural residents are really urban in their employment, their life styles, and their outlook. They simply live a little farther out than the suburbanite.

At the same time, the cities and the suburbs have acquired a demographic momentum of their own, which will lead to further increases in total urban population. Population movement will take place in the future among cities and suburbs, but cities and suburbs as a total will grow primarily by their own natural increase.

The movement of population from the center to the periphery of cities has also been going on for a long time. Many writers seem to think that population loss by the older city is a new, postwar phenomenon. The usual Census data on population conceal the changes that actually have been under way for a considerable period. In many cities, in earlier decades, the city boundaries were so far beyond the line of active residential land use that large-scale building could take place on the fringes of the developed area and yet be within the city's legal (and statistical) boundaries. At the same time, a great many cities extended their boundaries at irregular intervals over the years to include additional areas, some of them quite large. But the census population data for a city were based on boundaries existing at a particular time. Such data were often used, perhaps unconsciously, as if they related to the same city over a period of time. Detailed data have existed to make corrections of the boundaries to the city, but this has rarely been done.

The importance of this point is illustrated in Figure 5 for Cleveland, Boston, and St. Louis. Cleveland, as the city was defined in 1830, reached its peak population in 1870 and by 1930 its population was below what it had been in 1830. The city as defined in 1840 continued to rise in population until 1900 but has since fallen considerably. The same was true of the legal Cleveland up to the city of 1930. The other cities in this figure do not show quite such dramatic and regular changes, but the same general situation prevails. The analysis on which Figure 5 is based ended in 1930. Since updating would be a somewhat tedious job, it has not been under-

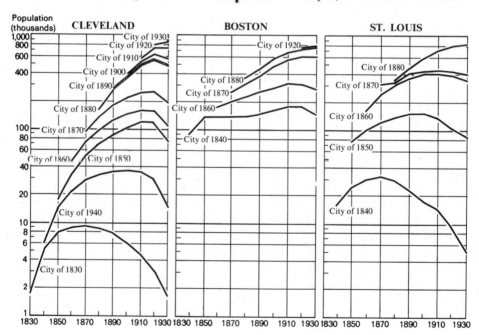

FIGURE 5. Population of three major U.S. cities at different dates, according to different city boundaries.

taken for this study. However, we know from census data that the total population of these three cities rose only slightly from 1930 to 1950 and that in each of them it declined from 1950 to 1960, in each case to a lower level than in 1930. It seems highly probable that the population of cities as they existed in earlier times has continued to decline since 1930. Many major cities have old cores in which population has declined for some decades.[1] Many of these cities began as small towns clustered around some central point. As their total population increased, the original parts were often converted to trade, commerce, manufacturing, or transportation land uses, and residences moved outward. The population decline in their older parts was thus part of a land use change.

In 1950 there were 18 cities with 500,000 or more total population (Table 3). As these cities have grown in population over the past several decades, their area has expanded. Population rose slightly more than threefold from 1890 to 1960, while total area increased by nearly 2½ times; total-population/total-area density rose from 1890 to a peak in 1950 but has since declined somewhat to a level only a third above that in 1890. The most rapid increase in their total was in the two decades preceding 1900 and again at the time of the first World War.

In 1950 there were also 73 cities with populations between 100,000 and 500,000. Their increase in total area from 1900 to 1960 was nearly threefold; their increase in total population in the same decades was only 3¼ times. Thus total-population/total-area density rose only slightly from the beginning to the end of the entire period, although it had been much higher in 1940 and 1950.

Areal expansion for each group of cities was irregular and for individual cities was extremely so. Such expansion depends in part upon the legal requirements or procedures of annexing territory and in part upon the growth in the city's economy and public services. With the passage of time, expanding cities have increasingly bumped into adjacent cities; the annexation of independent cities is extremely difficult or impossible in most states. Until 1950, it appeared that a clear slowing down in rate of territorial expansion of larger cities had occurred. But since 1950, the largest cities have grown faster in territory than in the two preceding decades, and the cities in the 100,000–500,000 group have expanded their area faster than in any previous decade.

It is thus clear that much of the reported growth of cities in earlier periods was a statistical phenomenon—that is, it was due to the fact that the city was defined differently at each successive census. But this phenomenon did not terminate in 1950. The central cities of all SMASs in the country increased in population by 10.8 percent between 1950 and 1960; but, if territorial annexations are excluded, their increase was only 1.5 percent.[2] Likewise, from 1960 to 1965, the central cities in all places of 10,000 or more population increased in population by 5.1 percent if the total area is included but only 3.5 percent if the effect of territorial annexation is eliminated. Incorporated suburbs of 10,000 or more increased in population by 16.5 percent when all their territory is included but only 13.9 percent on the basis of no annexations.

[1] Personal communication from Robert C. Klove, U.S. Bureau of the Census, 1969.
[2] Advisory Commission on Intergovernmental Relations, *Urban and Rural America: Policies For Future Growth* (U.S. Government Printing Office, 1968), pp. 3–4.

TABLE 3

Population and Area, Two Groups of Larger Cities in the United States, by Census Periods, 1890–1960

Census year	18 cities with 500,000 or more population in 1950					73 cities with 100,000 to 500,000 population in 1950				
	Total population		Total area		Density, Measure No. 1[1]	Total population		Total area		Density, Measure No. 1[1]
	1,000	Percent increase in preceding decade	Square miles	Percent increase in preceding decade		1,000	Percent increase in preceding decade	Square miles	Percent increase in preceding decade	
1890	8,424	–	1,025	25	8,220	4,191	–	–	–	–
1900	11,287	34	1,343	31	8,410	5,514	32	1,258	–	4,380
1910	14,926	32	1,458	8	10,250	8,206	49	1,610	28	5,100
1920	18,573	24	1,880	29	9,880	10,707	30	1,825	13	5,870
1930	22,980	24	2,109	12	10,900	12,955	21	2,196	20	5,900
1940	24,195	5	2,117	*	11,430	13,624	5	2,206	*	6,180
1950	26,591	10	2,241	6	11,850	15,841	16	2,541	15	6,240
1960	26,590	0	2,453	9	10,840	17,864	13	3,631	43	4,920

Sources: R. D. McKenzie, The Metropolitan Community (McGraw-Hill, 1933), App. Table IX, pp. 336–39, as updated and summarized in Marion Clawson, R. Burnell Held, and Charles H. Stoddard, Land for the Future (Johns Hopkins Press for Resources for the Future, 1960), pp. 96–103, 527–30. Updated for this book from U.S. Bureau of the Census, County and City Data Book (U.S. Government Printing Office, 1962).
* Less than 0.5.
[1] Total-population/total-area density; slide rule division, rounded.

Although migration from countryside to city and from city center to city periphery are very old phenomena in the United States, it would be a mistake to assert that the post-World War II period was no different from earlier periods. These migration processes have been speeded up in recent years, partly as the result of new forces, and they now are of a new order of magnitude.

Since World War II, the most striking and important aspect of the population redistribution, both the centripetal and centrifugal movement, has not been its numbers but its socioeconomic character. Both movements have been dominated by racial characteristics. In 1940, slightly more than half of all blacks were classified as rural; less than half were urban, many of them living in relatively small cities. By 1966, about two-thirds were urban, and the greater part lived in large cities. Moreover, the greatest concentrations of blacks were in the older city centers of the larger metropolitan areas. In one generation, the American black has gone from mostly rural to mostly urban. At the same time, the suburbs of these same metropolitan areas have frequently been "lily white."

The racial characteristic of these population movements was matched by an income differentiation. The older city centers were dominated by low-income families—most, but by no means all, of them black. Also at the centers were some higher-income, perhaps very high-income, whites, a disproportionate percentage of whom were either young adults or quite elderly. The suburbs were upper middle class and dominated by married couples with children. Sharp differences in life styles arose or were accentuated, and some part of the tensions and violence of the postwar period is due to this sorting out of people by race, income, and age.

SOCIOECONOMIC CHANGES SINCE WORLD WAR II

In order to understand suburban growth in population and in land use since World War II, it is necessary to review briefly some of the broader economic and social changes in the United States over the past generation. Some of the relevant data are found in Figure 6.

The demand for housing at any period is partly a function of income level, since people will spend some part of an increased income for more and/or better housing, and partly a function of the number of new households formed. The latter in turn is related to population increases, to numbers of new marriages, and to incomes that may force doubling up at one extreme, or at the other, may permit many individuals to have their own households. At any given date, there is a large stock of old housing; annual additions to stock rarely reach 3 percent. Many people are living in houses or apartments where they have lived for years because they have an attachment to the old place, or they cannot afford to move, or sheer inertia keeps them from doing so.

However, the number of new dwelling units (including apartments) built each year is related to the number of new households. Builders and developers in their analyses of the housing market, explicitly or implicitly, take into account the probable number of new households. To some extent, the number of new households may be influenced by the number of new housing units or by the state of

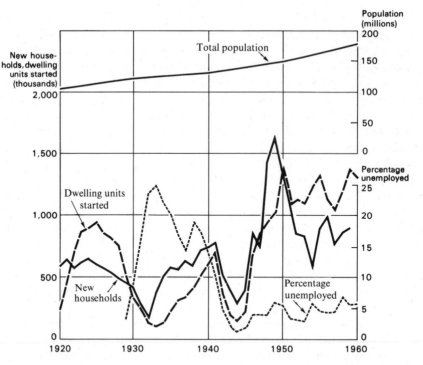

FIGURE 6.   Total population at census dates, net new households formed, dwelling units started, and percentage of labor unemployed, by years, 1920–60.

the housing market in general. When incomes permit and housing is readily avail-able—and hence probably reasonable in price by standards of the day—many indi-viduals or families seek their own households when under other circumstances, they would have lived in the households of parents or others.

In the 1920s, while the rate of new household formation was moderately high, the rate of construction of new housing units was very high by standards of that time, and unemployment was moderate. (Since employment data are not good for this period, unemployment is not shown on Figure 6.) In the economic depression of the 1930s, the most severe and massive that the United States had ever known, unemployment rose to a fourth of the labor force. New household formation fell sharply, as marriages were postponed, young married couples doubled up with parents or with other married couples, and single individuals sharply curtailed the formation of their own households. Construction of new housing units almost ceased, dropping to a figure of less than 100,000 for the entire nation in 1933. Hence, little additional land was required for residential uses in suburb, city, or countryside. Dwelling construction did pick up toward the end of the 1930s, stimu-lated in part by various federal programs.

With the coming of the second World War in the early 1940s, the situation changed dramatically. Household formation plummeted; many young men were off to war, either unmarried or with their families doubled up in parents' house-holds. But a major factor inhibiting household formation in those years was lack of available living quarters. Under wartime material controls, housing construction for civilian uses fell almost as low as it had been in the depression, and vacancies in existing apartments and houses vanished. Unemployment almost vanished also, and many people had money they would willingly have spent for housing, had it been available. Until the end of the war, the need for additional land for housing and related uses was very small on a national basis, although in localities where defense establishments expanded, additional areas were converted to such uses.

The end of the war saw another set of dramatic changes. Although unemployment rose somewhat from the abnormally low wartime levels, prosperity mounted to new highs. People had money to spend, and the demand for housing, as for many other consumption goods, was very high. New household formation and new housing moved up sharply and together, each being dependent on the other. With virtually no vacant housing units at the end of the war, households could be formed only as fast as new housing units were available; and the high potential rate of household formation helped to fuel the housing demand. Most of this immediate postwar flush of housing construction took place in the suburbs and brought a demand for large acreages of new land for urban purposes. If reliable annual data on land conversions from various rural to various urban uses were available, an increase in such land conversions more or less parallel to the increase in housing construction would almost surely be evident.

After about 1950, formation of new households, unemployment, and construction of new housing units more or less leveled off, with sharp year-to-year fluctuations around a more or less steady level. Both the accumulated housing shortage of the war period and the pent-up demand for formation of new households were worked off. A substantial upgrading in housing is now under way, as residents of older cities seek to flee from social changes going on there or as young married couples with children seek a suburban home of their own. These lead to new housing units, largely in the suburbs, and this in turn requires land conversions. Since 1968, high interest rates have restricted house buying and hence house building.

FACTORS PRODUCING POSTWAR SUBURBANIZATION

The conjunction of several factors has produced the massive postwar suburbanization in the United States. In the decade beginning with 1948, more than 10 million new households were formed, partly because of a high marriage rate, partly because of the accumulated backlog of unfilled or potential demand for separate households that had built up through depression and war. In many older cities there was relatively little vacant land on which new residential structures could be built—or the land available was not suitable for residential building. Urban renewal, whether public or private, would have been too slow in assembling and clearing sites and in building new apartments. Destruction of old housing, however poor as long as it was at all livable, would have created still more serious housing difficulties. The obvious direction to go, in providing the new housing, was toward the suburbs. The additional households simply had to be located somewhere, and neither farms nor old city centers were in good positions to absorb them.

At the same time, industrial, commercial, and other trends were all in the direction of concentration in cities. These urbanization forces worked in different degrees in different parts of the country. One major aspect of the postwar growth has been the trend toward "amenity" regions, particularly the Southwest, California, and Florida.

While these economic and other forces were pulling people out of the small towns, off the farms, and away from the countryside (unless each of these was within commuting distance of a larger city), there were other forces pushing toward decentralization within each metropolitan or urban region. Postwar cars and postwar highways went far toward freeing an urban worker from the necessity of living near his job. He could live nearly anywhere within the urban area and work at any other location, if he really wished to do so. True, there are added costs to some locations as compared with others. Some parts of the total labor force have earnings so low that automobile ownership—and hence travel by car—is difficult or impossible. The cost of housing and zoning restrictions keep low- and moderate-income workers out of the suburbs. But an enormous flexibility in location of home and job has become possible for the majority of households in the United States today.

At the same time, changes under way in industrial plants tended to take them too to the suburbs. Many plants were old at the end of the war. New methods of materials handling required larger areas and were more easily managed on ground level only. In addition, there has been a considerable tendency to build industrial plants with moderately extensive grounds, for aesthetic reasons, for parking, and as a margin for future growth. Location near major express highways is providing advantages that once were associated with location on railroad spurs. As the factories moved from city center out to suburban locations, there was a strong tendency for the labor force to follow. Thus industrial employment has shrunk in the older parts of the city.

The central downtown business district in many cities is no longer as important for manufacturing or trade. Instead, the downtown district is increasingly becoming the location of business, of offices, and of services allied to business. Total downtown employment may remain constant or even rise, but the relative importance of different kinds of jobs changes. New York City illustrates these shifts very well.[3] The shift from manufacturing to office employment in downtown New York has continued, at least until 1965.[4]

Downtown districts of many larger cities have experienced a postwar boom in office building. It is the white-collar workers who commute from suburb to downtown office. The blue-collar worker may live in an older city section and commute to a suburban job or live in one suburb and commute to another.

At the same time, retail shopping stores and districts moved from downtown to the suburbs. The large shopping center, with stores on one or two levels and with ample parking space, has become a major feature in many suburban areas. Movement of customers to the suburbs induced many department stores to open

[3] Raymond Vernon, *Metropolis 1985* (Harvard University Press, 1960).
[4] Regional Plan Association, *The Region's Growth* (The Association, 1967).

suburban branches, and the availability of convenient shopping areas certainly was another force leading families to move to the suburbs.

This combination of shifts in job location, changes in transportation, and development of new modes of communication has led toward a major expansion of the city at the periphery. This expansion conceivably could have been in a relatively solid and blocked-up fashion. It was not—discontinuity and dispersion were its marked characteristics.

FEDERAL PROGRAMS AS A STIMULUS TO SUBURBANIZATION

Since the early New Deal days, the federal government has supported the home-building industry and has helped its citizens to buy homes or to retain homes previously bought. This support to home ownership has greatly stimulated the rate and process of suburbanization.[5]

In the depression of the early 1930s, defaults on mortgages on homes became serious and building of new homes fell to a very low level. As early as 1932, the Federal Home Loan Bank Act was passed.[6] Under the New Deal, assistance in financing of existing mortgages and federal mortgage insurance stimulated home construction. The practice of requiring relatively low down payments (generally 10 to 20 percent of purchase price) and of regular monthly payments for interest, amortization, and taxes became firmly established on a wide scale. The federal government, in return for a small charge added to the monthly payment on the mortgages, insured the lenders against loss from mortgage defaults except for part of the foreclosure costs.

In order to provide such insurance without excessive losses, the federal agencies imposed standards of home building, of home appraisal, and of financial management by builders and lenders which have had enormous impact on home-building over the years. One successful private builder has stated to the author that all his homes must meet Federal Housing Administration standards for loans, even though he has arranged his financing without FHA help, simply because it is too difficult to sell houses which do not have or cannot get FHA loan approval. Thus, the federal standards have tended to become standards for the whole industry, in spite of the fact that FHA loans have financed only about 16 percent of home building.

The slow but impressive resumption of building of housing units during the latter 1930s, as shown in Figure 6, was very much due to these federal aids. A substantial part of this building was in suburban areas. Yet, the number of housing units built during the entire decade from 1933 to 1942 totalled only 3½ million —about two years' output today.

With the end of the war, federal stimulation to house and apartment construction became great and influential. In addition to financing through FHA, a special

[5] I am indebted to Mortimer Kaplan, formerly of the U.S. Department of Housing and Urban Development, for some of the ideas in this section.

[6] A good source for description of these and related programs is Arthur M. Weimer and Homer Hoyt, *Real Estate*, 5th ed., (Ronald Press, 1966). See also Sherman Maisel, *Financing Real Estate* (McGraw-Hill, 1965).

home-buying program for veterans was extended through the Veterans Administration. Down payments were further reduced (sometimes to zero) while guarantees to lenders were increased. Easy money became national policy and further stimulated a flow of capital into the housing industry. The federal programs were supplemented in some states, notably in California and Connecticut, with state programs to help veterans buy homes.

Beginning in 1946, a series of steps were taken to accelerate the rate at which commercial and rental housing property (apartments, particularly) could be depreciated faster under federal tax accounting procedures. One result was the creation of a tax-free cash throw-off, since the depreciation allowance exceeded amortization of principal on the mortgage. These tax arrangements have been particularly stimulating to development of suburban shopping centers and to construction of apartments.

Federal income tax laws, as they apply to the individual, also encourage home purchase. Income tax encouragement to home ownership takes three forms:

1. The imputed rent of the owner's dwelling does not have to be included as part of his income, for federal income tax purposes.

2. Payments for real estate taxes may be deducted from gross income.

3. Interest on home mortgages may also be deducted.

A homeowner receives a substantial part of his income from his own home, in the form of housing, but this income does not have to be included in his income tax return. Slitor has calculated that these three aids to home ownership in 1958 amounted to $3.2 billion, or about $100 per owner-occupied dwelling.[7] These financial advantages to home ownership tend to become more important, even on a relative basis, as personal incomes rise, in part because of the higher tax rates on larger incomes. On the basis of rather typical income and housing conditions, the federal income tax under current income tax rates is reduced by from 14 to 31 percent of the interest and tax payments on the home (Table 4). This is obviously a substantial incentive to home purchase.

The economics of owning vs. renting a home has long been discussed, and obviously depends in part upon economic conditions generally.[8] Shelton argues that, under essentially static economic conditions, the annual net advantage of ownership is equal to about 2 percent of the value of the house.

While Shelton's analysis is quite careful and considers the various components of cost, it greatly understates the advantages of home ownership in the past 25 years, when the general price level was constantly rising. The purchase of a home, especially with a low down payment, provided a hedge against inflation for the full price of the house. While it was true that the seller would have to pay a more or less equally inflated price for any other house he bought, if or when he sold his house, he also received favorable income tax treatment on the nominal capital gain and—more importantly—his previous purchase of a house provided the necessary down payment for the new one.

[7] Richard E. Slitor, *The Federal Income Tax in Relation to Housing*, National Commission on Urban Problems Research Report No. 5 (U.S. Government Printing Office, 1968).

[8] John P. Shelton, "The Cost of Renting versus Owning a Home," *Land Economics* (February 1968).

The effect of these various programs was to stimulate the building of single-family homes for sale to home buyers. The low down payments, low monthly payments (made possible in part because of the low interest rates flowing out of an easy money policy), and the income tax reductions, all combined to stimulate purchase of homes. In total, the scales were steeply tipped toward home purchase, as against purchase of cooperative apartments or as against rental. The single-family home on its separate lot is a voracious consumer of suburban land, and thus the federal measures to stimulate this type of house building indirectly strongly stimulated suburbanization.

It is true that various federal programs also stimulated apartment construction during these same years. There was easy money for apartment construction and also accelerated depreciation, with its substantial tax-free cash spin-off. These programs stimulated the apartment builder, or developer, or owner; but they did not aid the apartment tenant unless the owner passed on these favorable financial arrangements. In a great many cases a family could buy a house with a low down payment and with monthly costs (payments on loan, taxes and insurance, upkeep, etc.) no greater, and often less, than it would have to pay as rental for equivalent space.

The strong demand for houses naturally led to an active home-building industry in the postwar years. There was money to be made in building homes quickly, and concern lest the boom market not continue. Since the builder was typically under some pressure to acquire building sites quickly, he frequently purchased a distant

TABLE 4

EXTENT TO WHICH FEDERAL INCOME TAX PROVISIONS ASSIST HOME OWNERSHIP

	Annual salary before taxes					
	$5,000	$10,000	$15,000	$20,000	$25,000	$30,000
Tax exemption plus deductions[1]	2,900	3,400	3,900	4,400	4,900	5,400
Taxable income	2,100	6,600	11,100	15,600	20,100	24,600
Income tax, 1967 rates (joint return)	306	1,114	2,062	3,160	4,412	5,876
Marginal rate of tax[2]	16%	19%	22%	25%	32%	36%
Net income, after tax	4,694	8,886	12,938	16,840	20,588	24,124
Price of house[3]	9,400	17,800	25,900	33,700	41,200	48,200
Annual payment to lender[4]	649	1,228	1,788	2,325	2,843	3,326
Interest payment first year[4]	423	801	1,166	1,516	1,854	2,169
Annual real estate taxes[4]	141	267	389	505	618	723
Interest and taxes paid, first year	564	1,068	1,555	2,021	2,472	2,882
Reduction in income tax[5]	90	203	342	505	791	1,038
As percent of net income	2	2	3	3	4	4
As percent of income tax	29	18	17	16	18	18
As percent of payments to lender	14	17	19	22	27	31

[1] Assuming 4 dependents at $600 each, plus 10 percent for miscellaneous deductions.
[2] Rate applicable to last income earned.
[3] Assuming double net income after taxes, rounded upward to nearest $100.
[4] Assuming 5 percent interest, 1 percent for amortization and mortgage insurance, for 90 percent loan plus local real estate taxes at $1.50 per $100 full value.
[5] On assumption interest and taxes are net additions to deductions and that marginal rate applies.

site that was immediately available rather than spend time negotiating for a more favorably located one. The sites available were usually influenced by prior use of the land—for example, whole farms now would go on the market. The same booming market for housing encouraged the landowner to hold his land for further increases in price. These forces accentuated the more or less normal tendency for suburban development to move erratically outward, and the result was the sprawl and discontinuity of settlement which has been so widely discussed.

In the postwar years, until nearly 1960, about 80 percent of all housing units built in the United States were detached single-family dwellings. For reasons not entirely clear, the building of apartments then began to accelerate, particularly in suburban areas, so that by 1964, 39 percent of all housing units built were apartments.[9] The changing age distribution (toward more older people), more general purchase of apartments on a condominium basis (so that tax- and inflation-hedge benefits accrued to apartments as well as to houses), and a wider range of sizes and styles were all factors. Neutze feels that some part of the suburban apartment boom was not explained by these factors, and may have been due to a shift in consumer tastes. Some disillusionment with owning one's own home in the suburbs is altogether possible.

Nearly all the major SMSAs experienced this boom in apartment building, including suburban apartments, but with somewhat different timing and at different levels in relation to building of single-family homes. In the Washington SMSA, apartment house building has varied much more from year to year in recent years than has the building of single-family homes. In 1955, apartments were less than a fourth of the total, but in 1965 they were two-thirds of the total.[10] In several SMSAs the apartment boom seems to have peaked in the mid-1960s and to have receded somewhat; high interest rates in recent years have been especially discouraging to the building of apartments as rental property. But activity in apartments seems to have been resumed again in 1968 and 1969.

Economic Bases of the Flight to Suburbia

The postwar suburbanization, with its relatively large demands for land, may be looked at from the viewpoint of those families—typically young couples with small children—who bought homes and settled in suburbs. Why did they buy these homes, rather than live in suburban apartments or in houses or apartments in the older parts of the city?

The statement is commonly made that the postwar rush to the suburbs reflected a different demand for housing, a desire for a different life style, a different set of personal values, than was dominant a generation or more earlier. The role of higher incomes, of the auto as a more flexible individual form of transportation, and above all of a new approach toward life and new demands for a different style of living, are stressed in popular and professional publications. These may well be factors, and the present generation of young married couples may indeed have different

[9] Max Neutze, *The Suburban Apartment Boom* (Resources for the Future, 1968), p. 9.
[10] *Washington Post,* December 28, 1968, p. E 1.

standards of living than their parents and grandparents had. Before one comes to the conventional conclusions on this point, it may be helpful to look at the various factors which seem likely to have influenced the decisions of those locating in the suburbs since the war. The financial terms, particularly to an economist, on which different alternatives are available are significant.

Quite apart from the fact that houses and apartments in older parts of the city were simply not available on a net increase basis, the young couple with children who bought a house in the suburbs found a good many advantages in doing so.

1. The suburban house was new—clean, fresh, full of modern gadgets—although it might be shoddily built and subject to rapid deterioration.

2. It offered a way *out of* the ills of downtown or older residential areas and *into* a congenial community with desirable services, such as schools. The heavy concentration of suburban settlers in the above-average income group, in the young married stage of the life cycle, and with very similar backgrounds might lead to an unbalanced community from the sociologist's point of view. But this very unbalance was often attractive to the new settlers. The reality of suburban life may not have lived up to the dream, but the dream was surely a factor in leading young couples to settle there.[11]

3. The suburban new house could be purchased for a relatively low initial outlay. Down payments and various settlement charges generally were a fourth of a year's income for the purchaser and often less; with high and rising incomes for the salaried class, savings of such magnitude were not very difficult to achieve. The down payment on the house, if spread over five years or even less, would often be no greater than the difference between monthly purchase payments on this house and monthly rentals for similar housing. Purchase of older housing could not be financed so readily. The demand for housing is highly sensitive to the size of the down payment; small reductions in the payment open up the possibility of home purchase to relatively large groups whose incomes are modest or low.[12]

4. The monthly payments were offset to a significant degree by the federal (and usually state) income tax provisions, which permitted deduction of interest and local real estate tax payments. Such subsidies extended to ownership of older homes also, but occupants of such homes were more likely to be out of debt on their home; such subsidies did not extend at all to renters of houses or of apartments.

5. Lastly, purchase of a home was a magnificent hedge against inflation; in fact, for the low down payment, the buyer had a hedge against inflation on the total price of his home. With the steadily rising cost of new housing, the selling prices of older houses often has risen also. A family has been known to buy a house, occupy it for some years, and sell at a price which has meant (in current dollars) that it had cost them nothing to live in the house for several years. Moreover, fed-

[11] Contrasting views of suburban life are presented by John Keats, *The Crack in the Picture Window* (Houghton Mifflin, 1957) and Herbert J. Gans, *The Levittowners* (Pantheon, 1967).
[12] Jack E. Gelfand, "The Credit Elasticity of Lower-middle Income Housing Demand," *Land Economics* (November 1966) shows that the potential market demand in this income class is highly sensitive to size of down payment but only modestly sensitive to either length of mortgage period or to interest rate.

eral income tax policy has treated such capital gains with great tenderness; if another home of equal or greater cost was purchased within six months capital gains tax was postponed.

With these very powerful financial incentives toward purchase of a new separate dwelling in the suburbs, it is no wonder that suburbanization has proceeded rapidly since the war, and that suburbanization has taken a lot of land. In view of these incentives, one may reasonably ask: Just how different are the preferences and the living styles of the present generation of young married couples, as compared with their parents and grandparents? Had the latter enjoyed the same opportunities and incentives, might they not have responded in the same way?

Or, to put it differently had national policy been different, how much of the postwar suburban settlement with its nearly total reliance on purchase of single-family dwellings might have been directed toward rental instead of purchase of living space, or toward suburban apartments instead of suburban houses, or toward building apartments in the older residential areas or the downtown? Suppose, for example, federal income tax law were changed to allow an individual to deduct apartment rental payments from his gross income. What difference would this have made? Suppose that renters had somehow been given a guarantee against inflation, not only in their monthly rentals but of their capital assets, comparable to that which home purchase provided. What difference would this have made? Or, alternatively, suppose that mortgages on homes had been geared to an index of general price level with both principal and monthly payment rising during inflationary periods. Suppose that rehabilitation or rebuilding of older housing had been given substantial financial incentive, operating through the building industry and the householder as contrasted to public urban renewal; or that credit had been as favorable for restoration of old dwellings as for buying new ones. What difference might this have had?

Such questions suggest that the direction, pace, and extent of suburbanization since the war has been, to a substantial degree, an outcome of federal housing and income tax policy. If past suburbanization has reflected past federal policy, then future urbanization might equally be affected by future federal policies.

THE 4 NATURE OF THE URBAN IMPACT
ON THE RURAL COUNTRYSIDE

Since the primary focus of this book is upon the land conversion process at the expanding suburban fringe of the city, it seems desirable to take a brief overall look at the nature of the urban impact upon the rural countryside. Such impact may be general or indirect, on one hand, or more direct but geographically more limited, on the other. The former is all-pervasive, at least in the United States, while the latter is limited to certain areas of land. Admittedly, direct impact shades into indirect, but considerable differences characterize their purer or simpler forms.

A very large city or metropolitan area, such as New York, is virtually worldwide in its economic and social impact. Few regions of the world are wholly immune or oblivious to its influence, and certainly no area in the United States is unaffected by this one large urban concentration, much less by urban centers in general or in total. The Navajo herdsman, the Kentucky hill dweller, the Ozark small farmer, and every other citizen of the United States, however far from cities he may live, is affected in many important though indirect ways by the cities of the United States.

In consideration of the effects of the city on American life today, one should distinguish between those which are due to the city as a form of land use or of life, and those which are due solely to the numbers of people involved.[1] For instance, one could conceive of the entire population of the United States so evenly spread that each square mile had exactly the same number of persons, yet the total demand for food might be unaffected thereby. On the other hand, the city has special manifestations, particularly in terms of information, ideas, and communications, which would be greatly different if the same total population were thinly spread over much larger areas. The real policy issues concerning the future may turn on the *degree* of population concentration rather than on such matters as uniform distribution.

Throughout history, and in the United States today, cities (large cities in particular) have exerted important indirect effects upon rural areas. Among them have been and are these:

1. The city is a market for the food, fiber, wood products, and other output of

---

[1] The literature on the city is voluminous. A few publications that are particularly related to land use are listed at the end of the chapter.

the rural areas. The relative demands of urban consumers for different products have great effect upon what rural people produce, and hence upon their daily lives.

2. The city is the source of an enormous flow of information to the countryside —radio, television, movies, magazines, books, and newspapers. The ideas which shape the social life of rural people originate mostly in the city and nearly all flow from the city to the various rural areas.

3. There are significant flows of money from countryside to city and vice versa, as goods are bought and paid for, loans made, or other financial transactions are carried out.

4. The city provides jobs for the surplus rural manpower. The attraction of a town job, with its higher income and different way of living, has reached into even the most remote rural areas in the United States.

There is an extensive literature which demonstrates that the effect of a city is greatest in nearby areas and declines at varying rates or speeds as distance from the city increases.[2] This is particularly marked for heavy goods of low unit value; sand and gravel for any city cannot be hauled far, while oranges and other specialty foods may be shipped across the continent or the ocean. Radio waves travel far, as do other means of communication. Even if there were no other cities in the United States than those found from Washington to Boston, their influence would probably be all-pervasive in the country today. The influence of modern technological change has been to reduce greatly the resistances and costs of distance and space; the remote rural resident today is more effectively in the urban orbit than was the man who lived near the city a generation ago.

LAND OCCUPANCY FOR URBAN PURPOSES

Cities obviously occupy and use land for a variety of specialized purposes. The area often does not rank high on any national scale of land uses, but the land values, the capital investment, and the numbers of people involved are likely to be important.[3]

Unfortunately, data about urban land use in the United States are very poor. Moreover, the legal city does not conform to the economic or to the social city. The latter may, indeed, be hard to define in a manner that everyone will accept. But part of the problem of obtaining, compiling, and publishing relevant data on urban land use depends on whether one approaches the problem as the urban planner does or as the agriculturalist does. The former is concerned with actual land use for urban purposes, including usually land reserved for various open space uses such as parks; the latter is concerned with the land lost to agriculture. It was this difference in viewpoint which led the author some years ago to differentiate between land "used" for urban purposes and land "withdrawn" from other uses by cities. If the areas of land were approximately the same by each definition, the exact terms of the definition might not matter much; but the estimate for about

[2] Publications that will provide some guidance to the ideas and literature in this field are listed at the end of the chapter.

[3] Several of the many publications on urban land use are listed at the end of the chapter.

TABLE 5

LAND USE IN SAMPLE OF LARGEST CITIES IN THE UNITED STATES, CIRCA 1966

Type of land use	102 cities of 100,000 plus[1]		40 cities of 250,000 plus[2]	
	Percent of land area	Acres per 1,000 population	Percent of land area	Acres per 1,000 population
Total	100.0	130.1	100.0	97.5
Public streets	17.5	22.8	18.3	18.2
Total excluding public streets	82.5	108.3	81.7	79.3
Privately owned, total	67.4	89.2	64.7	57.3
Residential	31.6	44.3	32.3	37.0
Commercial	4.1	5.4	4.4	4.6
Industrial	4.7	6.1	5.4	5.6
Railroads	1.7	2.4	2.4	2.4
Undeveloped	22.3	26.9	12.5	11.9
Public and semipublic (excluding streets)	13.7	15.8	16.2	13.9
Recreational areas	4.9	5.6	5.3	4.6
Schools and colleges	2.3	3.3	1.8	2.1
Airports	2.0	3.1	2.5	2.9
Cemeteries	1.0	1.2	1.1	1.0
Public housing	0.5	0.5	0.4	0.4
Other (by subtraction)	3.0	2.2	5.1	2.9

Sources: Based on data in National Commission on Urban Problems, *Three Land Research Studies*, Research Report No. 12 (U.S. Government Printing Office, 1968). These data come from the section on "Land Use in 106 Large Cities" by Allen D. Manvel. Because data were not available for all items for all cities, estimates are based upon varying numbers of cities, and totals may not always check with items due to this fact.

[1] Out of 130 such cities in 1960 in the United States.

[2] Out of 52 such cities in 1960 in the United States; these 40 are also included in the 102.

1950 was 17 million acres withdrawn and only 11 million acres used, by cities of 2,500 or more population, including their unincorporated suburbs.[4]

As a result of a recent inquiry for the National Commission on Urban Problems, some data on use of land within a sample which includes most of the larger cities of the United States are now available (Table 5). One striking fact is the proportion of the land within these large cities that is publicly owned—about a third of the total, when streets and other public areas are combined. Interestingly enough, this is almost the same percentage in public ownership as for all land in the United States. Another interesting and significant fact is how much land is "undeveloped" even in these large cities. This varies greatly from city to city, depending in part upon whether the city is under-bounded or over-bounded.[5] No data are available on the physical character of this land. Some is undoubtedly expensive to develop or undevelopable at reasonable costs with present techniques, but such information

[4] Marion Clawson, R. Burnell Held, and Charles H. Stoddard, *Land for the Future* (Johns Hopkins Press, for Resources for the Future, 1960), pp. 60 ff. See especially pp. 94 ff.

[5] A city whose legal boundaries are so tightly drawn that much of the economic activity is outside them may be termed "under-bounded." A city which contains much idle land is "over-bounded."

as there is suggests that much of it is quite suitable for many urban uses. This does not, of course, suggest that all other land in the city is used to the limit of its physical or economic capacity. On the contrary, such evidence as we have suggests that a great deal of land could be used much more intensively. It is also noteworthy that housing is the largest single land use, with about a third of the total area used directly for this purpose. If one excludes the undeveloped land and allocates streets approximately to their location, then generally residential areas in these sample cities must have included more than half of the total used area.

Similar data are not readily available for smaller cities, but there is some evidence that land is used much more lavishly there.[6] This seems to be true for most of the major land use categories, especially for residential and street uses.

With comparatively rare exceptions in the United States, a city (or urbanized area outside of city boundaries) is able to bid the land it wants away from other specialized uses or other claimants. Towns overlying valuable mineral deposits may be moved or the expansion of towns over mineral deposits may be halted when mining and urban uses conflict. Some urban uses of land, especially residential uses, may be abolished on land needed for major transportation routes. And a few other exceptions to this generalization can be made. But urban uses nearly always dominate over agricultural uses, virtually always replace forestry or grazing uses, and otherwise are likely to be dominant.

The city (or city-like grouping of population) is an efficient place to put large numbers of people, as far as economy of land area is concerned. Even thinly settled suburbs are likely to have 3,000 or more people per square mile. Larger cities average about 10,000 per square mile, and density may rise well above 50,000 per square mile in a high-rise apartment district. In contrast, rather heavily settled rural areas in the United States usually do not reach 1,000 persons per square mile and usually are far less and range downward to less than 1 per square mile in ranching areas. Astounded at the rapid spread of suburbs, many persons with a rural background have tended to blame the cities for the rapid postwar conversion of land from rural to urban uses. But if the city people had been spread widely throughout the rural countryside and small towns, they would have used far greater acreages for residential and related purposes.

THE SHADOW OF THE CITY

Although all the cities and towns in the United States combined directly use something of the general magnitude of 1 percent of the total land area, they cast their shadow more or less strongly over a larger area.[7] The expectation that land will be converted to some more intensive use at some future date, at a much higher price per acre than can possibly be supported by farming or other rural land uses, has operated in practice to take a good deal of land out of any produc-

[6] Clawson, Held, and Stoddard, *Land for the Future*, p. 94.
[7] Although this aspect of land use has had less attention than the direct urban land uses, yet a considerable body of literature is growing up here also; a few references are listed at the end of the chapter to illustrate the kinds of material available.

tive use and hold it idle, waiting for suburban development of some kind. The processes by which this occurs, and the reasons it is held idle rather than used for some lowered value purpose while awaiting conversion will be considered in more detail in Chapter 7.

Cities cast their shadow into the countryside in other ways also. One of the most obvious is the commuting of small town and rural residents to larger cities for employment. Berry has plotted the commuting field of central cities in all the metropolitan areas of the United States.[8] If one includes all areas that have some commuters, however small a proportion of their labor force, then by far the greater part of the entire United States, except the Great Plains and the Mountain and Intermountain West, lies in the commuting zone of some central city. Even if one restricts the commuting zone to those areas where 5 percent or more of the labor force travels regularly to the central city, the area of this kind of shadow of the larger city is still quite impressive. If only a relatively few workers from a small town commute daily to the relatively distant large city, their earnings add to the economic base of the home community by giving business to the local merchant.

TRANSPORTATION AS A LAND USE

The modern city requires a lot of land, within its borders and between it and other cities, to provide transportation for persons and goods.[9] The acreage, in streets, alleys, rail lines, airports, and other forms of transportation within the city are usually included in acreage figures for the urban land use as a whole but may be separated out in special studies of land use within cities. While their total acreage is often but a relatively small portion of the total urban area, they often exert a marked influence on other land uses within the city. In the suburbs, availability of transportation is one of the factors leading to development of an area, and lack of transportation (or poor quality or low capacity) may inhibit or prevent urban growth in certain directions or areas. The more scattered the suburban growth—the greater the degree of sprawl—the larger will be the acreage of land in transportation usage, compared with the area actually used for other purposes and with the number of people served.

Transportation routes have always been required between cities, but the economy and style of life in the United States today requires more such linkages than were necessary in an earlier day. In particular, the heavy reliance upon the private automobile and the truck requires an extensive highway network, which uses far more land than the railroads or the airways. By the middle 1950s, there were about 15 million acres in road and highway rights of way outside of cities, perhaps 4 million acres in all city streets, less than 2 million acres in all airports, and about

8 Brian J. L. Berry, *Metropolitan Area Definition: A Reevaluation of Concept and Statistical Practice* (revised), Working Paper 28 (U.S. Bureau of the Census, Washington, 1969); Brian J. L. Berry and Elaine Neils, "Location, Size, and Shape of Cities as Influenced by Environmental Factors: The Urban Environment Writ Large," in *The Quality of the Urban Environment*, Harvey S. Perloff, ed. (Washington: Resources for the Future, 1969).

9 Of the many publications concerned with transportation, a few which consider land use explicitly or are directly related to land use are listed at the end of this chapter.

8 million acres in all railroad rights of way, for the United States as a whole.[10] With the expansion of the interstate highway system, the acreage in highway rights of way has increased somewhat. Thus, transportation outside cities uses about as much land as is used for all urban purposes, including streets, put together.

Transportation both responds to urban growth and influences it. As a suburb is developed or a factory located outside of the present city, new forms of transportation are required to serve it. A new road, or a much better road, influences the amount and kind of development. The building of express highways around and into the larger cities has surely facilitated suburban spread because people living at relatively more remote distances can more readily get to downtown employment. Improved transportation reduces the frictions and costs of space and hence tends to spread the effects of the city center more widely.[11]

Recreation as an Urban Impact upon Rural Countryside

A major and rapidly growing urban impact upon rural countryside has resulted from the demand of city-dwellers for outdoor recreation.[12] Some land within each city is used primarily for outdoor recreation—playgrounds, playing fields, parks, zoos, golf courses, tennis courts, and numerous other uses. Such areas are for user-oriented outdoor recreation—the kind of areas that must be close to the users, if they are to serve their purpose and are to be used at all. The acreage of such areas is included in most statistics on urban land area. In addition to these areas within, or closely adjacent to, the city there are other outdoor recreation areas lying in more rural surroundings but used primarily by urban people. These areas vary considerably in location, in size, and in specific activities.

Many urban people seek to use rurally located recreation areas on a one-day basis, leaving their homes in the mornings or early afternoons and returning at night. This is the type of outdoor recreation which has been described elsewhere as intermediate in location, size of area, and function between the user-oriented areas described above and the more remote resource-based areas described below.[13] The intermediate areas must be within reasonable travel time of the users. A family planning to use such a place will not want to spend more than two hours in getting there and will prefer an hour or less. The distance that can be covered in two hours will obviously depend on the nature of the roads. If high-speed limited-access highways are available most of the way to the country park, as much as 100 miles or more can be covered in a two-hour trip.

The urban impact on the rural countryside that grows out of this kind of outdoor recreation, is not limited to the recreation areas themselves. Travellers to such areas require roads; for some cities, the weekend recreation traffic on the highways exceeds the workday commuting traffic. Demands on roads—and hence the land

---

[10] Clawson, Held, and Stoddard, *Land for the Future*, p. 421.

[11] See Colin Clark, *Population Growth and Land Use* (London: Macmillan, 1968).

[12] A few publications from the large and rather rapidly growing literature on outdoor recreation are listed at the end of the chapter.

[13] Marion Clawson and Jack L. Knetsch, *Economics of Outdoor Recreation* (Johns Hopkins Press for Resources for the Future, 1966), pp. 36–40.

area required for them—are affected more by peak rather than by average traffic volume, and recreation is thus responsible for a considerable area of land used for highway purposes.

The third major type of outdoor recreation sought by urban dwellers is resource-based. Here, the qualities of the site are the dominant consideration: mountains, lakes, seashore, and the like. These may be national parks, national forests, or some state parks. Many areas are privately owned and developed for use by other individuals. While some areas of this type may be within one or two hundred miles of some large cities, many lie much farther away—some across the continent. Usage of such areas thus tends to be during vacations; considerable time may be spent in travel to and from them, and at the site. By far the great proportion of all visitors at national parks come from moderate- to large-sized cities. Some visitors to the best-known national parks such as Yellowstone and Grand Canyon come from cities hundreds of miles distant.

Outdoor recreation will almost certainly continue to grow as a use of land and water resources in rural areas. Every study or plan considering this activity has projected a greater future volume. More people, higher real income, shorter work weeks, more paid vacations, and better travel facilities will all lead to a greater attendance at outdoor recreation areas. To this direct impact must be included the indirect impacts of transportation and service to the users of the various kinds of areas.

EXURBIA

Suburbs of cities are usually thought of as being rather closely identified with the cities on whose outskirts they lie. Many suburbanites commute to the central city for employment, some kinds of shopping are likely to be carried out in the city, and, in general, the suburb is an integral though outlying part of the urban complex to which it is physically adjacent.

The term "exurbia" has come to be applied to a less clearly defined type of land use and of living, more remote from the city and less closely integrated with it.[14] There is no sharp, clear line between rather remote suburb and relatively near exurbia, or between suburban living loosely oriented to the city and exurban living much less dependent upon the central city. But exurbia, as a present land use and as a possibility for the future, clearly deserves some attention in consideration of urban impact upon rural countryside.

Exurban developments may arise for several reasons. For some people, such living locations start out as vacation places; millions of acres of land are apparently owned for this purpose and in this way.[15] While the acreage per dwelling unit

[14] In addition to the considerable amount of popular writing on the subject, see Hugh A. Johnson, Jr., J. Raymond Carpenter, and Henry W. Dill, Jr., *Exurban Development in Selected Areas of the Appalachian Mountains*, ERS–111, Economic Research Service (U.S. Department of Agriculture, 1963); and Hugh A. Johnson, Jr., *Rural Residential Recreation Subdivisions Serving the Washington, D. C. Area*, AER–59, Economic Research Service (U.S. Department of Agriculture, 1964).
[15] See David J. Allee, "Changing Use of Rural Resources," *Journal of Farm Economics* (December 1966).

varies greatly, it is nearly always large even by suburban residential land use standards. Hence the land area involved is much larger than the numbers of units would suggest. For some types of occupations or employment, the home may be located at a considerable distance from the place where the paycheck originates. A writer or an artist may live in the country and market his output in the city. A man who travels a great deal as part of his job can be away from a rural home as readily as away from a city one. Some exurbanites with an independent income choose to live in this type of environment, although of employable age. Retired persons choose exurbia for its style of living or in hopes that it will be cheaper than suburban or urban living. There is a noticeable tendency for residences that started out as vacation homes to become year-round retirement homes, as the original purchasers grow older.

The exurban type of settlement clearly has an urban origin. It was in the city that most exurbanites secured enough capital or a sufficient assured income to be able to afford exurban living, and it has been their attitudes toward city and suburban living which have led most people to locate in exurbia. With rising real incomes, more people in retirement who can afford to live where they choose, and perhaps in further rebellion against urban and suburban living, exurban living can be expected to increase in importance and in its impact on rural countryside.

URBAN DEMAND FOR RURALLY ORIGINATED WATER

One direct and often heavy urban impact upon the countryside grows out of the cities' expanding need for water, water which can come only (or most readily) from rural areas. The modern city is a voracious consumer of water, for household, industrial, and commercial uses as well as waste disposal. At the same time, it typically produces less usable water from its own territory than it once did. Paved streets and buildings have covered areas that used to serve as recharge areas for groundwater. The same impervious surfaces accelerate surface runoff. Thus the city's wells produce less yield, and their flow is apt to vary with the sharper peaks of the runoff.

American cities have long been reaching into nearby countryside for water. But the rapidly increasing demands of fast-growing urban areas have necessitated the use of larger and more distant watersheds, sometimes on the far side of mountain ranges. The impact on the areas from which the water comes has been substantial, sometimes crucial for the residents.

The use of a rural area primarily as a watershed for water for use in urban areas presents many difficult technical, economic, and political or governmental problems.[16] Even though the water will usually pass through a city treatment plant, the need to prevent pollution at the source has tended to preclude most local uses.

---

[16] For two general references on this point, see John A. Paul, Paul Opperman, and Norman E. Tucker, eds., *Environmental Engineering and Metropolitan Planning* (Northwestern University Press, 1962); and Advisory Commission on Intergovernmental Relations, *Intergovernmental Responsibilities for Water Supply and Sewage Disposal in Metropolitan Areas* (U.S. Government Printing Office, 1962).

The reservoir will require the displacement of all other users, and often the valley sites most useful for reservoir purposes are also the site of varied other activities. Construction of the pipelines or conduits will inevitably interfere with some other land uses en route. With rare exceptions, the rural watershed will lie not within the legal boundaries of the city but in other counties and sometimes in other states. Not only may fiscal problems of taxes forgone and services required as a result of watershed use of land lead to frictions between the governmental units involved, but more general problems of land use and governmental jurisdiction are likely to arise when one unit of government carries out a program in the territory of another.

The problem of getting water for urban uses is closely related to the problem of disposing of the city's sewage and solid wastes. The water that enters the city water supply must, with limited exceptions, be carried away by its sewage disposal system. The resulting impact upon the rivers, lakes, bays, and ocean downstream from the city, although extremely important, is outside the scope of our study. A more direct impact of the city on rural land use arises out of the disposal of the solid wastes. The volume of such wastes is rising rapidly, under the impact of modern technology in production and consumption. Wastes can be disposed of by burning, with consequent dangers of air pollution; by burying, with the problems of finding adequate land-fill sites; or by flushing down the watercourses, with consequent water pollution hazards. In this, as in many other aspects of modern life, resource use for one purpose or in one way is closely intertwined with resource use for another purpose or in another way.

ADDITIONAL REFERENCES

The literature on the city and on land use there is voluminous. A few publications which have special relevance to sections of this chapter but are not cited in notes as sources are listed below as an aid to interested readers.

A. *The City in General* (Note 1)

Gutkind, E. A. *The Twilight of Cities.* Glencoe, Ill.: Free Press, 1962.

Hatt, Paul K., and Reiss, Albert J., Jr. *Reader in Urban Sociology.* Revised edition. Glencoe, Ill.: Free Press, 1957.

McKelvey, Blake. *The Urbanization of America, 1860–1915.* New Brunswick, N.J.: Rutgers University Press, 1963.

Mumford, Lewis. *The City in History: Its Origins, Its Transformations, and Its Prospects.* New York: Harcourt, Brace and World, 1961.

Saarinen, Eliel. *The City: Its Growth, Its Decay, Its Future.* New York: Reinhold Publishing Corp., 1943.

Schneider, Wolf. *Babylon Is Everywhere: The City As Man's Fate.* New York: McGraw-Hill Book Co., 1963.

Vernon, Raymond. *Metropolis 1985.* Cambridge: Harvard University Press, 1960.

Wilbern, York. *The Withering Away of the City.* University, Ala.: University of Alabama Press, 1964.

B. *Effect of Cities on Rural Hinterlands* (Note 2)

Clark, Colin. *Population Growth and Land Use.* London: Macmillan & Co., 1968.

This book, while listed in source notes, is repeated here because it summarizes a large number of previous studies of the decline in economic activity from the city center outward.

Olsson, Gunnar. *Distance and Human Interaction: A Review and Bibliography.* Bibligrophy Series No. 2. Philadelphia: Regional Science Research Institute, 1965.

Vining, Rutledge. "A Description of Certain Spatial Aspects of an Economic System." *Economic Development and Cultural Change,* III (1955).

Zipf, George K. *Human Behavior and the Principle of Least Effort.* Cambridge: Addison-Wesley Press, 1949.

C. *Land Occupancy for Urban Purposes* (Note 3)

Bartholomew, Harland. *Land Uses in American Cities.* Cambridge: Harvard University Press, 1955.

Clawson, Marion, and Stewart, Charles L. *Land Use Information: A Critical Survey of U.S. Statistics, Including Possibilities for Greater Uniformity.* Washington: Resources for the Future, 1966.

National Commission on Urban Problems. *Three Land Research Studies.* Research Report No. 12. Washington: U.S. Government Printing Office, 1968.

Niedercorn, John H., and Hearle, Edward F. R. *Recent Land-Use Trends in Forty-Eight Large American Cities.* Memorandum RM-3664-1-FF. Santa Monica, Calif.: The Rand Corporation, 1963.

Reps, John W. *The Making of Urban America: A History of City Planning in the United States.* Princeton: Princeton University Press, 1965.

General planning, transporation planning, and special land use planning studies made by or for a great many cities or metropolitan organizations contain much information about urban land uses.

D. *The Shadow of the City* (Note 7)

Blake, Peter. *God's Own Junkyard.* New York: Holt, Rinehart and Winston, 1964.

Clawson, Marion. "Urban Sprawl and Speculation in Suburban Land." *Land Economics,* XXXVIII (May 1962), pp. 99–111.

Gaffney, Mason M. "Urban Expansion—Will It Ever Stop?" In: *Land: 1958 Yearbook of Agriculture.* Washington: U.S. Government Printing Office, 1958.

Harris, Curtis C., Jr., and Allee, David J. *Urbanization and Its Effects on Agriculture in Sacramento County, California.* Giannini Foundation Research Reports Nos. 268 and 270. University of California, 1963.

Schmid, A. Allan. *Converting Land from Rural to Urban Uses.* Washington: Resources for the Future, 1968.

Whyte, W. H., Jr. "Urban Sprawl." In: *The Exploding Metropolis,* by the editors of *Fortune.* Garden City, N.Y.: Doubleday and Co., 1958.

E. *Transportation as a Land Use* (Note 9)

Fitch, Lyle C., and others. *Urban Transportation and Public Policy*. San Francisco: Chandler Publishing Co., 1964.

Mitchell, Robert B., and Rapkin, Chester. *Urban Traffic, A Function of Land Use*. New York: Columbia University Press, 1954.

Owen, Wilfred. *The Metropolitan Transportation Problem*. Revised edition. Washington: The Brookings Institution, 1966.

Zettel, Richard M., and Carll, Richard R. *Summary Review of Major Transportation Studies in the United States*. Institute of Transportation and Traffic Engineering. University of California, 1962.

F. *Impact of Outdoor Recreation on Rural Areas* (Note 12)

Outdoor Recreation Resources Review Commission. *Outdoor Recreation for America: The Report of [the] Commission to the President and to the Congress*. Washington: U.S. Government Printing Office, 1962.

Strong, Ann Louise. *Open Space for Urban America*. Washington: U.S. Government Printing Office, 1965.

Extensive references to other studies are contained in the study reports of the Outdoor Recreation Resources Review Commission and the reports of the Park, Recreation, and Open Space Project of the (New York) Regional Plan Association.

THE DECISION-MAKING PROCESS IN URBAN EXPANSION

The decision-making process in urban expansion is highly complex and diverse. It is incredibly fragmented and diffused among a wide variety and large number of private individuals and organizations and among many public agencies at each of the major levels of government.[1] Some decisions are made more or less by default, in the sense that agreement among the necessary parties cannot be achieved. For instance, a tract may be passed over in the suburbanization process because the owner, the possible builder, and the planner cannot agree.

The size of the unit for which decisions are made varies also. Sometimes the decision unit is a single house, as when a potential buyer is considering purchase of a home or a lending agency is considering a loan to a buyer. Sometimes it is a subdivision or development, as when a builder is contemplating a project or a planner is considering a land use zone. Increasingly, the unit of decision-making is growing larger. Even the home buyer tends to consider the neighborhood as well as, and perhaps as much as, the house itself.

ROLE OF THE DEVELOPER

A description of the decision-making process in urban expansion could begin almost anywhere because it must always get back to the starting place. That starting place seems often to be the developer, though it must be said that he himself starts with a background of personal knowledge or the experience of others in the remainder of the process.

To take a piece of raw land, lay it out into building lots and streets, install needed services such as sewers and water lines, erect houses or apartments, and sell or rent them to occupants is obviously a complex and highly involved process, or series of processes. For simplicity's sake, this chapter will consider these processes as all carried out by a single firm, to be called "developer." But several persons or firms—land assembler, broker, site planner, builder, subcontractor, sales agent among them—might also be involved with the developer. A variety of such specialists might work together on some basis to carry out some or all the processes here

[1] The National Commission on Urban Problems, both in its report, *Building the American City* (U.S. Government Printing Office, 1968) and in its five volumes of *Hearings* and in extensive research reports has assembled and published a great deal of useful information directly relevant to this chapter.

ascribed to the developer. The more firms involved, the greater will be the problems of interrelationship.

A basic consideration, always to be kept firmly in mind, is that private housing development for a private market is first, last, and all the time a business operation, conducted for profit, and the merit of decisions is always judged by their effect upon profit.[2] A great many factors affect the final profit from a housing development. First come the price paid for the land and the cost and availability of credit when needed. Then various skills come into play: skill in minimizing tax liabilities, taking advantage of numerous and often complicated federal programs, and selling the final product. Each of these factors is highly important. A bad decision on any one of them may wholly offset great effectiveness in handling all the others. But it is the interrelationship of these factors which offers the greatest challenge to the managerial skill of the developer.[3] In a great many housing developments, the margin between considerable loss and relatively high profits may be rather narrow. A little extra delay in construction or in sales may lead to losses, while better management or more luck which reduces time involved may lead to high profits. A somewhat higher vacancy rate in apartments than anticipated may lead to losses, while just a little higher occupancy rate may lead to fairly high profits. Abrams, in discussing the rebuilding of older parts of cities, cites some dramatic examples of how this works; the same general relationships exist for new housing in suburbs.[4] In part, the explanation lies in the heavy use of credit and the low equity capital of many developers.

Early in the process of planning a housing development, every builder must make some kind of an estimate of the demand for housing—in general or nationally, for his city, and for the type he wants to build.[5] This estimate may be highly sophisticated or very simple, even impressionistic. It may be based upon various general factors, such as rate of household formation, the state of the national money market, or other general considerations. Or it may be highly localized and personal—a simple judgment that ten or twenty houses of a certain type and price range can be sold in this location over the next year or so. Since the developer is really concerned with the state of the housing market for *his* houses when the latter are ready, he must forecast ahead, often by one to two years, when he is considering undertaking development of a specific tract of land. Obviously, additional uncertainties enter when the future rather than the present demand is concerned.

In order to carry out a housing development, a developer must first have a tract

[2] This aspect of urban development is touched on in: Arthur M. Weimer and Homer Hoyt, *Real Estate* (Ronald Press, 1966); Edward P. Eichler and Marshall Kaplan, *The Community Builders* (University of California Press, 1967); and Charles Abrams, *The City Is the Frontier* (Harper and Row, 1965).

[3] For a book which well describes the business or managerial side of home building, see James Gillies and Frank Mittlebach, *Management in the Light Construction Industry*, publication of the Real Estate Research Program, Graduate School of Business Administration, University of California, Los Angeles, 1962.

[4] Abrams, *The City Is the Frontier*, pp. 87–92. See also Sherman Maisel, *Financing Real Estate* (McGraw-Hill, 1965).

[5] See Glenn H. Beyer, *Housing and Society* (Macmillan, 1965); Preston Martin, "Aggregate Housing Demand: Test Model, Southern California," *Land Economics* (November 1966); and A. H. Schaaf, "Some Theory and Policy Implications of the Postwar Housing Boom," *Land Economics* (May 1966).

of land.[6] He may have in mind his ideal tract, ideal as to size, location, physical characteristics, and price; and he may also have in mind the degree of divergence from the ideal which he will accept if he has to. His decision-making unit is the subdivision of a size for his operation, but this may vary considerably in acreage. In any case, the kind of houses, their price, and their market must be related, in his judgment, to the character of the site. It would be wasteful to put low-priced houses on an expensive tract in a high-class neighborhood. Probably it would be financially disastrous to put expensive houses into a lower-middle-class neighborhood. However definitely the developer has an ideal tract in mind, in practice he may very well have to choose from among a very few tracts, none of which conforms to his ideal. The managerial function consists here, as it does so often in every field, in deciding among alternatives, none of which is wholly satisfactory—a selection of the least-worst, or tolerable, as well as of the best. In the case of sites for building, the developer has a further decision to make: how far ahead to plan and to acquire land for planned building, or how much to take advantage of present opportunities to buy available tracts for future use. There are advantages in having land readily available as needed, but there are also costs in holding land.

Since private housing development is a profit-oriented process, one might expect the decisions about site selection to be carefully calculated on a profit-loss-cost-advantage basis. The rueful comment of Weiss and her colleagues after making a number of such studies is significant in this connection:

> Land development is obviously much more of an *ad hoc* process than we had previously supposed. The unsystematic manner in which developers approach the production of residential lots indicates that most of the decisions made at this stage in the development process are probably made on the basis of their own experience and a general awareness of "what's going on" in the local development industry rather than on the basis of what new techniques and ideas are available.[7]

It may well be that large developers make more closely considered and more carefully researched decisions than do small and medium builders. The latter may not be at a disadvantage, compared with their competitors, if they have bought sites not too far out of line with the general market, even if a site is not ideal from their viewpoint. Rather than insisting upon maximizing the profit possibilities of site selection, the developer may "satisfice," accepting the first site which reasonably meets his standards, so that he may get on with the job.[8]

[6] Some stimulating and insightful research on developers' choices of building sites has been done at the University of North Carolina. The fourth in a series of reports on this subject is Shirley F. Weiss, John E. Smith, Edward J. Kaiser, and Kenneth B. Kenney, *Residential Developer Decisions—A Focused View of the Urban Growth Process*, Center for Urban and Regional Studies, Institute for Research in Social Science, University of North Carolina, 1966. Other references are listed at the end of this chapter.

[7] Shirley F. Weiss, Raymond J. Burby, and Newton W. Andrus, "Lake-Oriented Residential Subdivisions in North Carolina: Decision Factors and Policy Implications for Urban Growth Patterns," *Research Previews*, Institute for Research in Social Science, University of North Carolina (November 1967), p. 13.

[8] "Satisfice" is a word that does not appear in standard dictionaries but is coming into increasing use among economists. It means meeting certain standards or criteria to an acceptable degree but not to a perfect peak. Thus it contrasts with "maximize."

Once a tract has been acquired, the developer has to make some decisions on street and lot layout. A simple and obvious way is to employ straight streets run on cardinal directions and linked in a grid with similar streets in adjacent areas, and to lay out lots of width and depth suited to the size and cost of the houses contemplated. Many suburbs have been so developed, and there is much to be said in favor of such simple layout, in spite of its lack of variety. The curving street, however, has become the symbol of even the modestly ambitious suburban development. It does provide vistas which are likely to be much more attractive than those available to motorist or pedestrian in the grid layout, and houses may have somewhat different directional orientations. A newer subdivision form, with many advantages, is clustering of houses so as to provide larger open space for general use.[9] If well planned, a clustered development will reduce the land area in streets, perhaps yield a few more buildable lots, and yet produce more usable open space than the typical rectangular subdivision. Topography may well dictate a subdivision plan other than the grid.

The developer constructs a house or apartment—a physical structure—for an expected clientele; but, more importantly, he provides something more nearly approaching a total housing package.[10] People who will buy his houses or rent his apartments are concerned with the nature of the community, with the kind and quality of public facilities of every type, with general location, with transportation to the central city and elsewhere, and with other factors, none of which are under the primary control of the developer. He may choose his site with these factors in mind, but as a general rule he must adapt to them, rather than altering them, although he may be able to influence public action with respect to some of them. Considerations of architectural style, variety, and standardization influence the prospective occupant. He is also interested in the household appliances and conveniences installed in the house.

Lastly, the developer must decide whether to sell or to rent the housing unit he builds. Virtually all suburban construction of single-family homes has been for sale; apartments are usually rented but may be sold under a condominium arrangement. Even when the property is rented to the occupant, the developer may sell it to a person or firm who is more interested in investment and more capable of property management than he is.

SUPPLY OF BUILDABLE LAND

In order for the developer to buy and develop a tract of land, someone who owns the tract must be willing to sell at a time and for a price which are attractive or at least tolerable for the developer. The market for suburban land will be ex-

[9] See William H. Whyte, Jr., *Cluster Development* (New York: American Conservation Association, 1964). The National Association of Home Builders has developed a number of plans for clustered development, based on studies of developers' experience, and a film that illustrates the results.

[10] See *New Approaches to Residential Development: A Study of Concepts and Innovations,* Urban Land Institute Technical Bulletin 40 (Washington: Urban Land Institute and National Association of Home Builders, 1961).

plored in more detail in Chapter 7, but it is useful to consider the supply side of the suburban land market briefly at this point.

Many professional and popular writers assume that the seller will be a farmer who decides to quit farming.[11] Sometimes the seller will indeed be a farmer, if the pace of suburbanization has been swift and if farming in that area has been reasonably profitable. Much more commonly, the genuine operating farmer has sold out long ago to someone who bought his land in anticipation of its later development for housing or other urban purposes. There is a notable lack of information as to who these intervening owners are. Indeed, there is a lack of precise terminology to describe them; they are frequently categorized under the usually pejorative term "speculator," but speculation in suburban land may be engaged in by farmer and developer as well. The intervening owners may provide a real service in assembling small tracts into larger ones better suited to a developer's needs; they may be able to buy at lower prices than he could; or they may have a stock of land, in tracts of varying sizes and characteristics, which will enable a developer to find a tract more nearly to his needs.

Holding land for later urban use inevitably involves a considerable degree of uncertainty as to just when it will be in active demand and at just what price. If there were complete certainty on these two points, present prices of land would be inversely proportional to the discount rate. Each present landowner must be on both sides of the land market; that is, he has a reservation price at which he is willing to sell what he owns and another price at which he would be willing to buy additional land. For the dealer, these two prices may be rather close together, so that he would buy and sell whenever a profit prospect arose. For the farmer, his buying price may be much lower than his selling price in an area where he expects urbanization to take land away from agriculture within a few years. Likewise, every suburban developer is on both sides of the land market, willing to buy attractive land when the price is right, willing to sell what he now owns if the price is irresistibly attractive. The developer is primarily on the buying side of the market, the land dealer and farmer primarily on the selling side, but each has a reservation price schedule.

When an opportunity for sale arises, the present landowner must decide whether to sell his land or to hold it. His expectations of future land prices, his present need for liquid capital, his personal income tax position, and other factors will affect his decision. His holding costs are primarily taxes and interest which he could earn elsewhere on the capital he would realize from land sale.

Present land ownership units in the developing suburban areas may or may not be suitable for the developer. In a few cases, the present ownership unit will be larger than the developer can manage or than he wants; and the owner may be reluctant to divide, judging that the ultimate value of the undivided tract will be greater than the sum of the values of several smaller tracts. More commonly, pres-

---

[11] For general reference, see Mason M. Gaffney, "Urban Expansion—Will It Ever Stop?" in *Land: 1958 Yearbook of Agriculture* (U.S. Government Printing Office, 1958); and Curtis C. Harris, Jr., and David J. Allee, *Urbanization and Its Effects on Agriculture in Sacramento County, California*, Giannini Foundation Research Reports Nos. 268 and 270, University of California, 1963.

ent ownership tracts are smaller than the developer wants, and land assembly becomes a problem. This may be done by the land dealer or by the developer himself. With the trend toward large units in the residential construction field, land assembly is likely to be a more serious problem in the future than the past. In older urban areas where redevelopment is considered, land assembly problems may be severe; each and every piece of land may be critical to the design of the whole. In the suburbs land assembly may be less of a problem. As a last resort, a developer may even abandon the area and work elsewhere with less loss.

In the wisdom of hindsight, it is clear that errors of judgment as to timing of development may be made by landowners, land speculators, and developers. There is very little objective information on this point. According to many popular articles, just about anyone can make a fortune speculating in suburban land without risk. In a period of prolonged and massive rise in land prices, like the rise since about 1950, some fortunes have indeed been made and risks have been less. But not everyone who gambled in rising land prices in this period won, and some who sold at a price much above what they paid, may still have realized less profit than could have been made with the same money invested elsewhere.

In the 1920s—earlier in some areas—there was extensive land subdivision and sale to individuals, hopefully as a prelude to actual development. Streets were laid out and paved, sidewalks and curbs installed, water and sewer lines built, bonds floated to pay for such improvements, and taxes raised to pay off the bonds. In a great many instances, such promotional subdivision went very sour.[12] Taxes became delinquent, bonds were defaulted, and titles to land were fouled up. This type of land promotion is less common now, because most residential development includes building construction and sale, but it is by no means unknown today. Experience does suggest that severe losses may arise from suburban land holding and from premature efforts at development, particularly if the whole economy is not moving up briskly.

The time at which a developer bought his land, in relation to the time when he actually began to build on it, may have a substantial effect upon his profits. It can rightly be argued that his opportunity cost for land, when he gets ready to build, is not what he paid for the land but what he could sell it for when he is ready to build. If he bought at a low price, he has a gain from rising land prices, a gain which his own development program may have helped to bring about.

ROLE OF PUBLIC AGENCIES

The agencies of federal, state, county, and city government play a very important role in urban expansion into the rural countryside. The immense diversity among government agencies was dramatized a few years ago by a book about the New York metropolitan region with the expressive title, *1400 Governments*. There

---

[12] See Phillip H. Cornick, *Premature Subdivision and Its Consequences*, Institute of Public Administration, Columbia University, 1938; Ernest M. Fisher and Raymond F. Smith, *Land Subdividing and the Rate of Utilization*, Michigan Business Studies, School of Business Administration, University of Michigan, 1932; and F. T. Aschman, "Dead Land," *Land Economics* (May 1949).

were literally more than 1400 separate units of government in this metropolitan region, "each having its own power to raise and spend the public treasure, and each operating in a jurisdiction determined more by chance than design."[13] Moreover, most of these governmental units had several agencies concerned with one aspect or another of suburban growth. Under these circumstances, obviously, no unit of government has the power or can take the responsibility for guiding urban growth, even on the public, as contrasted with the private, side of the ledger.

Federal Government

The federal government exercises a number of important responsibilities that affect urban impact on the rural countryside. Part of its influence is general or indirect, in the sense of affecting all urban and suburban areas to one degree or another. For the past generation, the federal government has had programs that affect the overall supply of housing—programs to stimulate a high level of economic activity and employment and a reasonable stability of the general price level, programs to make credit readily available for mortgages and to insure the mortgages.

But some federal programs apply directly to specific tracts of land—urban renewal, public housing, housing for military and defense workers, housing programs for the elderly, and others that are localized to particular areas. Some of these have been direct federal activities, such as building housing for military; others have operated through various loan, grant, and guarantee programs, which have offered special incentives to private firms and to local government. As noted in Chapter 3, the effect of the federal programs as a whole has been to stimulate suburban expansion in several indirect but effective ways. Defense activities, aid to highways, and other federal programs have affected urban growth greatly, often in highly localized areas.

Role of the States

The states have generally played a less important role than the federal government in suburban growth. Their primary role has been to provide enabling legislation for local governments. To a considerable degree, this role has been a negative one; that is, legislatures have refused to enact measures which would have better equipped local government to deal with the wave of postwar urbanization. It has repeatedly been pointed out that the states are, to a degree, anti-city in their actions if not in their philosophy. Until recent years, most state legislatures were heavily dominated by rural representatives, men who were often unsympathetic to the needs of the cities and unwilling to provide authority or funds for cities. During the depression years of the 1930s, the cities increasingly looked to the federal government rather than to the states for help, and this trend has continued, at least to some degree, in the postwar period.

[13] Robert C. Wood with Vladimir V. Almendinger, *1400 Governments: The Political Economy of the New York Metropolitan Region* (Harvard University Press, 1961), p. 1.

Nevertheless, states do have some programs which do or could have major effects on urban extension into rural countryside. States provide, with federal financial aid, the major highways leading into the larger cities, as well as those connecting them. Location and capacity of highways obviously affect the direction and rate of spread of suburban areas. States exercise public health powers; if these had been, or were now, stringently applied they would markedly affect many suburban areas which have been or are dependent upon septic tanks for sewage disposal. States have open space programs which have often included local parks. Many states help to fund local schools, and there have been grants for other purposes. These various programs have aided suburbs, but perhaps not more than the older cities.

Regional Governments

In some metropolitan areas—New York, for example—there are various forms of regional government. While the development of all-purpose metropolitan government has not gone very far, metropolitan government for special services is becoming fairly common. Water supply is often a regional function; sewerage may be. Parks, especially the larger ones, are sometimes under metropolitan regional authority. Certain public works, such as bridges or tunnels between cities, may be regional in organization and operation. In an increasing number of metropolitan areas, data collection and analysis and planning are conducted at the regional level. In recent years, councils of governments have been established in several metropolitan areas, typically including all the cities and counties within an SMSA. Their role is consultative and advisory. The councils are often concerned with gathering data and planning for the entire area, but they usually lack statutory power to compel conformity to their plans. These programs, like the federal ones, tend to apply to a whole metropolitan area, rather than specifically to the suburbs.

Local Governments

The cities and the counties have had the greatest impact upon the direction and rate of suburban growth, in ways that have greatly influenced if not determined which specific tracts would be used, for what, and when. Cities and counties should be considered together here, for to a considerable extent they operate as substitutes for one another. When the boundaries of a city are so far-flung that suburban-type development can take place within its legal boundaries, then it is the city which exercises power over residential growth. More commonly, the suburban growth takes place in unincorporated areas outside of any city (in the legal sense), and the legal powers and actions of the county as a unit of government are determinative.

A very large number of local governments exercise various powers with respect to planning, zoning, subdivision regulation, housing codes, and other aspects of urban and suburban development (see p. 98). These functions may be exercised by part-time boards of citizens, often unpaid, as well as by official units of government. Most of these local governments are small—too small in most instances to engage any full-time employees for any of these functions. Those which do hire usually pay low wages. Only the largest of the local governments have top-ranking jobs that pay enough to attract and hold well-trained professional or technical people. Staffing levels in planning and land-use-related activities are low in relation to numbers of persons engaged in the construction activities affected by their work. There is great variation among building and other codes established by such local governments.

Cities and counties have the power to make land use and other plans; develop zoning regulations; promulgate control ordinances over subdivision procedures and methods; develop and enforce building codes; provide a range of public services, which may include water, electricity, and gas, either directly or by power companies under governmental regulations, sewerage, schools, roads and streets, parks, and a host of other services required or desirable for modern urban living.[14] These legal powers are exercised with greatly varying diligence and skill, and for different policy ends. Typically, the areas of fastest and least directed suburban growth have been outside of cities in counties that were essentially rural in economy and society, unaccustomed to the use of their legal powers to direct suburbanization. The men in local government in such counties have often resented suburbanites and been unsympathetic to suburban problems. Moreover, the landowning classes in such counties have often sought to reap their own financial harvests, with little concern for the longer run. Both cities and counties have used federal financial grants for planning, as well as for the provision of some services but, generally speaking, the federal government has exercised little control over the direction and content of such planning, as long as the money was properly accounted for.

Cities and counties exercise their planning, zoning, subdivision, building code, housing code, and similar activities under the broad concept of police power—the power to regulate individual activity in the interest of the safety, health, morals, and general well-being of the whole population. Courts have generally upheld exercise of such powers when the purposes to be served were reasonably clear, the means to the end reasonably defined and relevant, and the procedures in accordance with due process. At the same time, courts have been unwilling to deprive property owners of all rights to use of their land in the name of such general public purposes.

In addition to the police power, local government has several other broad types of legal powers which are or can be used in the suburbanization process. The power of eminent domain enables government to take private property, for a fair compensation, for a public purpose. The definition of a reasonable public purpose has surely broadened over the past several decades—urban renewal and public housing are accepted today, when a generation or more ago they were not—and probably will broaden further in the decades ahead. Government also has the legal power to impose taxes, subject to limitations of fair treatment to all taxpayers, and in some jurisdictions subject to some maximum limit. While taxes as instruments of social policy—i.e., to encourage one kind of land use and to discourage another

[14] Some useful publications from the voluminous literature on planning and zoning are listed at the end of this chapter.

—have generally been illegal, or not upheld by courts, or politically unacceptable, most taxes have some side effects in terms of private actions induced or restrained. Taxes in relation to services rendered, such as sewerage charges to repay costs of new sewer lines, have generally been used and upheld by the courts.

Another power of local government is the power of the purse, or the spending power, especially for public improvements. Cities and counties construct and operate a wide variety of public improvements—schools, roads, parks, sanitary and water facilities. The location and the quality of the service provided can be influential in guiding or inhibiting private land development. In the urban and suburban locations, there has been relatively little use of the direct and conditional subsidy to induce private action, as farmers are given "conservation payments" in return for certain land use practices. One may indeed question the wisdom and the results of the extensive system of private subsidies or conditional grants that has been used in agriculture for a generation, but the technique has major applicability to urban problems which has not as yet been utilized.

In many situations, the actions of city and county government are based on more than one of these general powers. A county builds an improved road and a sewer line into a potential subdivision area which has been planned and zoned for single-family homes; the latter must conform to building and other codes; taxes will be levied on the land and for special improvements; a tract of land is taken over by the county for a park; and so on, as various programs are carried out, under a variety of legal powers. Indeed, it is in the articulation of various programs to a defined goal that the management possibilities in local government are the most exciting and important.

The cities and counties have followed different policies in the exercise of powers which can affect suburban growth—policies which are more often implicit in action than explicit in statement. Wood has pointed out that cities and counties are in competition with one another for people whom they consider most desirable, against people whom they consider less desirable, and for economic developments which will bring employment and taxes but not disrupt the style of life they have or want.[15] Molotch has advanced a similar idea of governments competing for people considered desirable.[16]

Wood found that, in the New York metropolitan region, different units of government manipulate their property assessments and their tax rates so that, with grants in aid from state and the federal government, they can provide the level of government services their citizens want. He has also shown how local governments can attract certain kinds of employment through provision of services essential to such firms; and how certain kinds of residents can be attracted, and others repelled, by such actions as establishment of minimum lot sizes so large that only well-to-do people can afford the kinds of houses that will be built on them.

Within the New York metropolitan region, especially in its New Jersey sections, he found widely contrasting systems of local government. Some units employed a great variety of governmental measures to influence the desired development,

[15] Wood, *1400 Governments*, pp. 65–113.
[16] Harvey L. Molotch, "Toward a More Human Human Ecology: An Urban Research Strategy," *Land Economics* (August 1967).

while others in generally similar circumstances refused to employ any measures for this purpose. Some areas want primarily to be left alone to enjoy the fruits of metropolitan growth and prosperity without any direct disturbance. Other areas have growth complexes and are eager to entice people, factories, jobs, almost anything. Others are more selective, trying for some kinds of people and some kinds of jobs but not others.

Techniques for Control

A number of techniques are available to the city or county seeking to guide or control the kind and speed of its suburban growth.[17] The general land use plan, in itself, is some degree of encouragement to certain kinds of residential and business development, and a discouragement to others. The plan can be backed up by zoning. Provision of public services, especially sewers in areas where septic tanks are not a practical alternative, is a most effective device. As Chapin points out, the tools are generally available; what is lacking is the will to use them. Too often, the groups who would be restrained by these means get control, or partial control, of the mechanisms and hence prevent their use or use them to aid their own purposes.[18]

The lack of a clear and explicit purpose to land planning and control, which would perhaps be fatal to effective action, has been compounded by a lack of efficient and competent methodology in planning.[19] As noted in Chapter 9, a modern city is a complex web of economic interrelationships, each part both competing with and supplementing every other part. The value of each land parcel is created more by other parts of the urban complex than by the parcel in question. Planning, zoning, and other public controls, to the extent they really work, affect the amount and the areal distribution of the economic values arising out of the whole urban complex.

Although difficult in practice, in theory it would be possible to measure the amount, the geographical distribution, and the incidence among persons or groups of the value so created. A priori, one would expect that some pattern of urban growth and development would maximize whatever general goals underlay the land planning and control. The benefit-cost approach used in the case of water development might be applied here, but it should be supplemented by a more careful con-

[17] See F. Stuart Chapin, Jr., "Taking Stock of Techniques for Shaping Urban Growth," *Journal of American Institute of Planners* (May 1963); James G. Coke and Charles S. Liebman, "Political Values and Population Density Control," *Land Economics* (November 1961); and Massachusetts Department of Commerce and Massachusetts Institute of Technology, *The Effects of Large Lot Size on Residential Development*, Technical Bulletin No. 32 (Washington: Urban Land Institute, 1958).

[18] There is a voluminous literature on urban planning, much of it as woozy as the planning. For two different but realistic discussions see: Edward C. Banfield and James Q. Wilson, *City Politics* (Harvard University Press, 1963); and Harvey S. Perloff and Lowdon Wingo, Jr., "Planning and Development in Metropolitan Affairs," *Journal of American Institute of Planners* (May 1962).

[19] For studies critical of city planning and suggesting more efficient approaches, see: Ronald R. Boyce, "Myth versus Reality in Urban Planning," *Land Economics* (August 1963); Nathaniel Lichfield, "Cost-Benefit Analysis in City Planning," *Journal of American Institute of Planners* (November 1960); and William L. C. Wheaton, "Applications of Cost-Revenue Studies to Fringe Areas," *Journal of American Institute of Planners* (November 1959).

sideration of the incidence of the values than is common in water planning. Only rarely has anything like this been attempted in urban land use planning, which more commonly resorts to slogans such as "sound land use principles." At one stage, city planners generally favored the separation of land uses—no factories in residential districts, no houses in factory areas. More recently, it has become apparent that such separation in the large cities of today means that workers must travel long distances to jobs, that low-income workers may be severely handicapped, and that single-purpose areas in themselves have serious disadvantages. This is but one illustration of adherence to rules of thumb with little or no objective testing.

Many land use plans for a city or a county seem to have maximized nothing more than the preconceptions of the planners who made them. Even other planners may not agree. But neither group has had objective facts and analysis to back up its position. Local governments have been unwilling to provide the funds which might have permitted the development of a sounder base.

Bad as the plans have typically been, their implementation has been worse—worse if one assumes they should have been implemented, the better if one assumes it was a good thing that they were not. Although there is a wide variety of techniques for implementation of land use plans, in practice almost total reliance has been placed upon land zoning, with other legal measures such as subdivision control and building codes and such public services as sewers used little or not at all and sometimes in actual conflict with the zoning. Land use zoning suffers from many technical and legal deficiencies, in practice.[20] But its technical or legal difficulties are overshadowed by its political limitations. If zoning is to mean anything, it must prevent someone from doing something he would otherwise do. If zoning is only to sanctify what every individual wishes, then it has no real public purpose. In suburban areas, where local government is weak, zoning simply cannot stand up against the kind of political pressures that inevitably arise. A broader public purpose will go down to defeat against a private interest which seeks to capitalize on growth in the area. But zoning may indeed serve to protect an established residential area from the intrusion of nonconforming and discordant uses, because in such a situation there are countervailing political powers to challenge the intruders and often to rout them.

Neutze has some revealing things to say about zoning in Montgomery County, Maryland, where

> in the 1963–66 period, it seems to have been relatively easy to have land rezoned for apartments. In fact, it appeared that the legal costs of a good zoning lawyer could possibly be regarded as the cost of getting rezoned. Land already zoned for apartments was relatively unattractive because its owners had already put a premium on their selling price, but land zoned for single-family housing or even for agricultural purposes could be bought much more cheaply, even if the purchase was, as quite commonly, conditional upon rezoning being granted. As long as the area could be construed as in some sense suitable for apartments, there would be a good chance of rezoning being

[20] Some publications dealing directly, and critically, with land zoning as applied to suburban areas are listed at the end of this chapter.

granted, at least in the 1963–66 period. It almost appeared that the best way to keep apartments out of an area was for the Planning Commission to take the initiative in rezoning it for apartments—the current owner would then reap the capital gain and the area would be less attractive to apartment builder-speculators. Of course, this was an unstable situation and resulted from the expectation that the liberality of the rezoning policy would not continue. The political opposition to it was ample justification for this belief.[21]

While land zoning in developing suburban areas has usually not been firm enough to implement broad land use plans, it has not been wholly without effect. Rezoning is not invariably accomplished; or it may be so delayed as to create a substantial cost to the party seeking it. Zoning seems to have been much more effective in a negative than a positive way—that is, it can prevent some developments but cannot assure others. Suburbs determined to keep out certain socio-economic groups, or to prevent apartment house construction, can often make zoning to these ends effective. But they may be less successful in achievement of a contiguous suburban development in which development of scattered and distant areas is restrained until a later date. In each case, the politics of the zoning, not its legality, is determinative.

Another major deficiency of land use planning and control is that it has lacked any sense of growth process. Metropolitan, city, or county land use plans are typically developed for a specific future date or for a specific future population with little consideration of the processes of change from the present situation to the goal outlined in the plan and still less consideration to the processes of change after that date. It is true that the city planners frequently state that planning is a continuous process, and land use plans are remade from time to time; but the new plan is equally tied to a future date and a future population.

Perhaps the most important single topic for the social scientists interested in urban affairs is the *process* of change. For instance, how may land now zoned for one purpose ultimately be rezoned for some other purpose, with equity to the landowner, to competing land users, and to the general public? Even a modest acquaintance with the history of any American city reveals that land use has changed over the decades. To cite an extreme example, mid-Manhattan was once the site of vegetable gardens. Change is inevitable; it may be desirable, or may be harmful; and it surely will bring major rewards to some and major penalties to others. A truly competent city planning procedure would provide the means for dealing with change. In practice, land use planning and its implementation have moved in even more awkward jerks than would probably have occurred under a free market.

Urban land use planning, like any other public process, is a political process and, as such, is very much influenced by the positions and attitudes of the electorate within its area.[22] In the developing suburbs, it is primarily the present landowners and the developers who have the most immediate and direct financial stake in the

[21] Max Neutze, *The Suburban Apartment Boom: Case Study of a Land Use Problem* (Resources for the Future, 1968), p. 45.
[22] Some of the major publications about the political aspects of urban land use planning, each of which has further references, are listed at the end of the chapter.

public land use planning process, and consequently they attempt to influence that planning to ends most nearly satisfactory to them. The future residents of the suburbs are not yet on the scene, hence cannot play a role in suburban planning; and even the early residents are apt to be preoccupied with their personal problems of adjustment to the new environment and with securing needed public services such as schools. Most suburban counties have found it very difficult to enlist able, dedicated talent to attack their problems of growth and land use planning, except those people directly financially interested in the matter—primarily present land-owners, real estate dealers, and developers. These people have naturally tended to develop land use plans compatible with their interests, often believing sincerely that they were acting in the general public interest. Their influence on land use plans, zoning, subdivision regulation, and even building codes at the county level has been great. While they are affected by such governmental rules and regulations, they have also markedly affected the governmental action. In no other part of the suburbanization process is the playback from action to actor and back again to action more direct and clear.

Capital and Credit in the Decision-Making Process

The whole process of suburban expansion requires substantial amounts of capital. Developers require capital to buy the land, to erect the buildings, and for numerous related purposes during the construction or building process. Purchasers of housing require capital also, whether they occupy the housing they own or rent it to others. The owners of the capital required therefore inevitably exert a major influence on the whole decision-making process.[23]

Residential builders and developers in the suburbs, like redevelopers in the central city, have relied primarily upon borrowed capital. For several reasons, equity capital in the residential building industry has been low:

1. The typical units in the building industry have been too small and the successful ones have expanded too rapidly to have accumulated much equity capital in relation to their scale of operations.

2. Builders have preferred, probably wisely, to use their limited capital to expand their construction and development operations, rather than to operate more largely on their own resources or to finance what they have previously built.

3. Outside equity capital has not been much attracted to the building and development of residential property in the past, although a few large industrial corporations with ample capital seem now to be considering entering the field.

In general, low equities of developers have meant high risks to them; the prospects or hopes of high returns must be present to justify high risks; and high profits have required using what capital they do possess at high "leverage." Other sources of capital, such as building and loan associations, savings banks, and insurance companies, have made loans for residential development, but perhaps more commonly to finance purchase than construction.

[23] See Charles M. Haar, *Federal Credit and Private Housing* (McGraw-Hill, 1960) and Maisel, *Financing Real Estate*.

Some minimum amount of capital during the development process is necessary for the developer, but a major aspect of his business operations is to arrange financing on profitable terms. His goal is often to get out of a particular development as quickly and as profitably as he can, once the building is complete, the houses sold or the apartments rented, and the management phase of the residential area begun. When the houses are sold, the buyers take over their maintenance and the management, with local government providing the necessary public services. Some apartment houses are built by developers or contractors for sponsoring organizations, whether investment firms or limited profit organizations. But many apartments are built by developers who seek to get out quickly, taking their profit and going on to other building projects. When their apartment is completed and largely or wholly occupied, the builder may own it for a few years or sell it to an investment and/or management firm. Abrams has shown how the redeveloper in the older city strives to get out as quickly and as profitably as he can; the same general process operates for the suburban builder of single-family homes.[24] The buyer of an apartment house seeks to hold it for a limited number of years (usually about eight) to take advantage of the tax-free cash flow from depreciation, and then sells it to someone else, who repeats the process.

The attitudes of lenders toward specific areas, particular types of residential construction, and individual developers are apt to play a decisive role in suburban development projects. If the developer can borrow the necessary funds, he can go forward with his proposed project; if he cannot borrow, then he cannot make the development. Most lenders have been primarily concerned with the "financial soundness" of projects, but the factors they use in measuring such financial soundness are likely to be conservative. In general, such considerations of financial soundness have operated to reinforce tendencies for racial or income segregation.

Role of the Home Buyer and the Apartment Renter

The home buyer in the suburban development and the apartment renter in the city or suburb play a crucial role in the whole urban expansion process, for it is their willingness to spend money and their choices in spending that fuel the whole process described up to this point. The role of the individual purchaser or renter is passive in the sense that he chooses among the alternatives open to him rather than trying to devise and implement those or other alternatives. As a member of a group he may, of course, seek to affect public action in various ways. It is obvious that the real price of housing, especially of suburban single-family houses, has been markedly affected by public programs discussed in Chapter 3, and the choices of housing consumers have surely been affected by the price tags.

If the potential suburban house buyer will not buy a particular type of house or a house in a particular location, then the developer who built that house will fail financially. Even with the booming suburban housing market of the postwar years, some subdivisions have failed. If potential buyers demand and are able to force

[24] Abrams, *The City is the Frontier*, pp. 110–16. See also Maisel, *Financing Real Estate*, pp. 314–26.

substantial concessions in price, or if they buy too slowly, the profit margin from the suburban development evaporates for the developer, whose low equity financing makes him highly vulnerable to any chilly wind. A rapid sale at a price satisfactory to the developer, on the contrary, can make good his hopes of profit.

Housing competes, in the consumer's budget of available income, with all other aspects of modern living. Winger has shown that the demand of a family or individual for housing depends upon his position in the life cycle—single persons have one demand when young, another when old; married couples have one demand before children arrive, another while children are growing up, still another when children are grown, and so on. Demand also depends upon such personal characteristics as education and occupation; upon such broad social forces as the general attitude toward home ownership as contrasted with renting; and upon the region or part of the country.[25] The housing actually occupied at any date reflects past conditions; there is a substantial time lag in adjustment of actual housing to housing demand. Many a widow or widower or older couple whose children are grown and gone continues to live for many years in the house originally chosen for raising the growing family. The time lags probably depend upon the stage in the life cycle; the family whose second baby has arrived will be determined to move quickly out of a one-bedroom apartment.

It seems probable that families buying homes in suburbs or renting apartments there are motivated by one or more of several factors.[26] Location with respect to jobs, shopping facilities, public services of various kinds, and transportation facilities and costs, and time spent in getting to places of employment or shopping, surely are some of the factors. However, since the amenities and the personal satisfactions obtainable from suburban housing are not standardized or equal in all locations, differences in character or "quality" of the suburban development are also factors. And the price at which houses or apartments are available to buy or to rent surely must be a major factor also.

The typical American urban resident has a very limited emotional or psychological attachment to a specific site or location. He lacks the attachment to the site of family history that prevails in some European cities or has been common in many rural locations in the United States. Janowitz has referred to this as "limited liability." If faced with a developing community situation which seems unsatisfactory—such as invasion by a different social, ethnic, or racial class—the typical family is more likely to run away than to try to change the situation or to adjust to it.[27] The small businessman faced with the same situation often cannot escape without much greater financial loss; and as a result, many a deteriorating section of the older city still has the merchants and other small businessmen who estab-

[25] Allan R. Winger, "Housing Space Demands: A Cross Section Analysis," *Land Economics* (February 1962).

[26] For some attempts to measure these factors quantitatively, see F. Stuart Chapin, Jr., "A Model for Simulating Residential Development," *Journal of American Institute of Planners* (May 1965); Willard B. Hansen, "An Approach to the Analysis of Metropolitan Residential Extension," *Journal of Regional Science* (Summer 1961); and John F. Kain, "The Journey-to-work as a Determinant of Residential Location," in *Papers and Proceedings of Regional Science Association*, 1962.

[27] Morris Janowitz, *The Community Press in an Urban Setting* (Free Press, 1952), pp. 210–13.

lished themselves there when the residential community was quite different. Residential mobility in the United States is very high; millions of families move every year to follow or find jobs or to secure housing more adapted to their needs. As a result, there is an enormous market for used housing at prices which range from well above original construction cost in some prosperous communities downward to relatively low prices in deteriorating neighborhoods.

The available evidence suggests that most suburban house buyers are reasonably well pleased with their choice of house and of location.[28] The intellectual community, including many persons who live in suburbs, may be highly critical of the character and quality of the typical postwar suburbs in the United States. Without either joining this chorus of criticism or trying to refute it, one may note that a substantial part of the upper middle class who can afford to own homes in suburbs do in fact live there. While many move from year to year, a large proportion of those who do move, move to another suburb. Many suburbs could be much better than they are, and the fact that people buy houses in them is not proof that the present suburbs are those which the same people would have chosen, had a different set of alternatives been open to them. It is also true that many suburbanites may not have gotten from their suburban home as much as they had hoped for or expected, but a gap between reality and hope is surely not confined to suburban home buying. Rosow concludes that the average person is far less responsive to his environment, assuming that it is not too obviously deficient or uncomfortable, than are the planners and housing specialists.[29]

The kind of new houses that the consumer will buy and how much he will pay for them determine the profit the developer makes out of providing them. The housing consumer as king may be a limited monarch in the sense that he reacts rather than initiates, but he is still a powerful king.

BACK TO THE DEVELOPER

This brings us back to the developer. His decisions on his next new suburban housing development will grow primarily out of his experiences with his last one. These experiences depended upon his own decisions, and those of land suppliers, public agencies, lenders, and home buyers. What worked last time, with some modifications, may well work next time also. Change in the form of suburban development is possible at every stage in this decision-making process. Viewed in this way, suburban residential development has many cyclical aspects; but it is a cycle in which variation is possible. Each participant in the total decision-making process may initiate change or may veto or nullify changes proposed or made by others. There is a constant interplay and feedback.

The developer is critical in this cyclical process because he, more often than

[28] For two publications bearing on this point, see: John B. Lansing and Gary Hendricks, *Living Patterns and Attitudes in the Detroit Region*, Metropolitan Area Regional Planning Commission, Detroit, January 1967; and Basil G. Zimmer and Amos H. Hawley, "Suburbanization and Some of Its Consequences," *Land Economics* (February 1961).

[29] Irving Rosow, "The Social Effects of the Physical Environment," *Journal of American Institute of Planners* (May 1961).

others, is the innovator, the one who starts change. Yet his innovations must be within limits imposed by others, as he perceives or anticipates such limits. Successful innovation in this industry, as in others, may pay handsomely, while failure to change may bring financial failure. Although not all possible innovations are perceived and attempted, and not all decisions are the best possible, no careful observer can fail to see that decision making in urban expansion is a dynamic process.

ADVANTAGES AND DISADVANTAGES OF DIFFUSED DECISION MAKING

Discussion of the decision-making process in suburban growth calls for some evaluation. Since the process is so complex and there are so many actors and parts, an evaluation must be in somewhat general and subjective terms. Looking over the total decision-making process, what conclusions do we reach?

Many writers have been critical of this diffused decision-making process, attributing to it many of the deficiencies in modern suburban development. Deficiencies such as segregation by race and income, lack of new housing for the lower half of the income scale, and excessive costs of the products are readily apparent. No single person can take into account all the factors involved or bear all the costs or realize all the gains. The task, the responsibility, and the gains are shared. It would be miraculous if such a diffused process came out with the same results as one where a single person or group was charged with the whole responsibility and given the means to exercise it. Under the diffused system, actions are often nullified, in part or in whole, by other actions. Opportunities are missed because no one is in a position to capitalize on them.

But it can also be argued that there are advantages to such diffused decision making. Many persons, in different groups, have the opportunity to innovate, to dare new things, to take their own risks, and to gain (and lose) as a result. Participants in the suburban development process have an incentive to think and to try new things. Some will surely come up with actions or procedures superior to those which any single group will devise. The diffusion of decision making may help avoid big mistakes which could arise from a more tightly knit process. There is likely to be neither massive and monolithic perfection nor massive and monolithic failure.

In practice, as suburban land conversion has been carried out in the past twenty years, these alleged advantages of diffusion in decision making seem to have been largely overwhelmed by its disadvantages. Some innovation has occurred, but depressingly little; too often, it had been easier to conform than to innovate. It is true that the people of the United States have been spared an ill-designed domination of local suburban growth by the federal government; but they have also received no integrated policy leadership. One may take what comfort he can from the diffusion that has existed, while at the same time considering the possibility of major improvements. The objective should be to retain whatever real advantages there are from the present diffusion of decision making and at the same time to search for ways to remedy its demonstrated weaknesses.

Diffused decision making in suburban growth is very much in the American tradition of a polycentered economy, social structure, and political organization. Foreign observers are often baffled in their search for the final decision-making point or person, in large part because such final point or person simply does not exist in many situations. In a fast-moving economy, society, or governmental situation, marginal or incremental decisions can often exert great effect, just as a marginal deflection of the airstream on a plane's guiding surfaces can greatly affect the direction of the whole aircraft. Suburban growth is much like industrial, transportation, and other economic activities in this polycentered aspect.

ADDITIONAL REFERENCES

In addition to the publications cited in the footnotes, those listed below have special relevance for sections of this chapter.

A. *Developers' Decisions on Location* (Note 6)

Kaiser, Edward J. "Locational Decision Factors in a Producer Model of Residential Development." *Land Economics,* XLIV (August 1968).

Kaiser, Edward J. *A Producer Model for Residential Growth: Analyzing and Predicting the Location of Residential Subdivisions.* Center for Urban and Regional Studies, Institute for Research in Social Science, University of North Carolina, Chapel Hill, November 1968.

Kaiser, Edward J., Massie, Ronald W., Weiss, Shirley F., and Smith, John E. "Predicting the Behavior of Predevelopment Landowners on the Urban Fringe." *Journal of the American Institute of Planners,* XXXIV (September 1968).

Kaiser, Edward J., and Weiss, Shirley F. "Decision Agent Models of the Residential Development Process—A Review of Recent Research." *Traffic Quarterly* (October 1969).

Weiss, Shirley F., and Kaiser, Edward J. "A Quantitative Evaluation of Major Factors Influencing Urban Land Development in a Regional Cluster." *Traffic Quarterly* (January 1968).

B. *General Treatments of Planning and Zoning* (Note 14)

American Society of Planning Officials. *Problems of Zoning and Land-Use Regulation.* Research Report No. 2. National Commission on Urban Problems. Washington: U.S. Government Printing Office, 1968.

Bosselman, Fred P. *Alternatives to Urban Sprawl: Legal Guidelines for Governmental Action.* Research Report No. 15. National Commission on Urban Problems. Washington: U.S. Government Printing Office, 1968.

Chapin, F. Stuart, Jr. *Urban Land Use Planning.* New York: Harper and Brothers, 1965.

Delafons, John. *Land-Use Controls in the United States.* Cambridge: Harvard University Press, 1962.

Grad, Frank P. *Legal Remedies for Housing Code Violations.* Research Report No. 14. National Commission on Urban Problems. Washington: U.S. Government Printing Office, 1968.

Kramer, Robert, editor. "Land Planning in a Democracy," special issue of *Law and Contemporary Problems*, XX, Spring 1955.

Raymond and May Associates. *Zoning Controversies in the Suburbs: Three Case Studies*. Research Report No. 11. National Commission on Urban Problems. Washington: U.S. Government Printing Office, 1968.

C. *Land Zoning in Suburban Areas* (Note 20)

Babcock, Richard F. *The Zoning Game—Municipal Practices and Policies*. Madison: University of Wisconsin Press, 1966.

Feiss, Carl. "Planning Absorbs Zoning." *Journal of American Institute of Planners*, XXVII (May 1961).

Reps, John W. "Requiem for Zoning" in *Planning 1964*. Selected papers from the 1964 ASPO National Planning Conference. Chicago: American Society of Planning Officials, 1964.

Sussna, Stephen. "Zoning Boards: In Theory and in Practice." *Land Economics*, XXXVII (February 1961).

D. *Politics and Land Use Planning* (Note 22)

Altshuler, Alan A. *The City Planning Process—A Political Analysis*. Ithaca: Cornell University Press, 1965.

Dahl, Robert A. *Who Governs? Democracy and Power in an American City*. New Haven: Yale University Press, 1961.

Gilbert, Charles C. *Governing the Suburbs*. Bloomington: Indiana University Press, 1967.

Kent, T. J. *The Urban General Plan*. San Francisco: Chandler Publishing Co., 1964.

Makielski, Stanislaw J. *The Politics of Zoning: The New York Experience*. New York: Columbia University Press, 1966.

6
THE CHIEF ACTORS IN
URBAN EXPANSION

The purpose of this chapter is to examine, as actors in the process of urban expansion, those groups whose roles in the decision-making process were identified in Chapter 5. A basic assumption is that the personal characteristics of decision makers influence the decisions made. Each reacts to certain objective or measurable aspects of a situation, but the reaction of each is partly conditioned or influenced by personal characteristics. The decisions reached may, in turn, influence the character or nature of the decision maker, at least over the long run.

The fact which dominates this chapter is how little we know about the various actors in the decision-making process. Ideally, one should have information on the personal profiles of the individuals concerned—their age, education, income and wealth, status, and other measurable socioeconomic characteristics. Still more useful would be information on their mental and emotional processes—on what "makes them tick" as far as decisions about urban land use are concerned. There must be many variations among the many thousands of persons who make important land use decisions. Actually, almost no information is available about them. From what does exist, one can draw inferences about the actors themselves but only within wide limits, and one cannot be sure that all important characteristics of decision makers are revealed.

In the process of building new residential suburbs, the various actors work both in cooperation and in rivalry. They must cooperate to some degree, if only unconsciously. To use a simplified example, the home buyer cannot have a home without the builder, who is dependent upon the local planning agency, which in turn is governed by the home buyers. The efforts of many groups and persons interweave in numerous complex and variable ways to produce economic outputs of value to each. But there is also rivalry, since each wishes to gain as much as he can, at the expense of the others if necessary. The owner of undeveloped land seeks to get as high a price as he possibly can; the developer, on the other hand, wants to buy it as cheaply as he can. A tug-of-war ensues over division of the anticipated returns from the residential development; but, if either gets too greedy or if they cannot agree, then the enterprise does not go forward, and each seeks gain somewhere else or in another deal.

In this sort of process, each actor looks at the objective or measurable aspects of the situation, but each also seeks to understand his competitor-rival, and the latter factor may be as important as the former. For example, the builder must estimate the demand for housing, the state of the money market, and other factors; but he also has to know or guess how eager the landowner is to sell, and what his financial interests, objectives, and tax situation are. The suburban land market is far from a competitive one, in the economic theory sense of that term. Its deficiencies are considerable, but at least one is relevant here: the number of actors is relatively small; each must consider the probable reaction of other individuals and of his own actions upon them. It might be suggested that game theory is more applicable than competitive theory. If so, it might be the rules or the practices of a battle royal in which several fighters slug it out in the ring at once, rather than a baseball or other game wherein two teams are matched at a time.

HOME BUYERS

Since residential occupancy is the largest single use of urban land, home buyers should be the first of the actors in the urban expansion process to be described. By far the greater part of the residential land in urban areas has been used for single-family homes, almost all of them occupied by the owners. Public policy has strongly favored ownership, rather than renting, of such properties. But apartments on either a condominium purchase or a rental basis have also become important in residential expansion in recent years.

There is a complex relationship between old and new households on the one hand and old and new housing on the other. The ability of a family to buy a new house may depend in part upon their ability to sell their old house for a good price. Likewise, the rent which a family must pay for an apartment depends in considerable part upon the demand for that apartment by other prospective tenants. The addition of new housing on one side of the equation or of new households on the other side of the equation may mean a far-reaching rearrangement of households within housing space, for new housing is not simply occupied by new households. One can conceive of a situation in which the housing supply was so ample that present homeowners would have great difficulty selling their homes in order to move into new and larger ones, or where present tenants of apartments could force such concessions in rent from landlords that they would not find it worthwhile to move. While such a general oversupply of housing is theoretically conceivable, it is most unlikely to exist for long except in a city where economic activity is declining to the extent that it experiences net population loss.

Home buying or other occupancy of new residential space is a function of population mobility, as well as of population or household growth. Americans are a mobile people, with about a fifth of them moving their residences each year. Many of these moves are from one region or one city to another, but most are from one location to another within the same city or metropolitan area. In many respects, it is these latter which are most significant to this analysis because they are likely to represent residential decisions within the same employment framework.

The house buyer or renter may move for any one or a combination of several reasons:

1. He may be dissatisfied with his present housing, because of its physical characteristics, or its location with respect to job, friends, or recreation, or the social characteristics of the neighborhood, especially changes in such conditions.

2. His family may need more space, largely because of its stage in the life cycle; the apartment that was suitable for the couple is no longer adequate for the children as well.

3. His income may enable him to afford more and/or better space; residential space is a consumer good whose consumption increases as income rises, on the average.

4. If his family has ambitions for higher social status, he may purchase a larger and better house in a more prestigious neighborhood.

5. Another potential house buyer or renter may be forced to seek cheaper housing because his income has been reduced.

6. A change of job, even within the same city or metropolis, may induce a change in residence.[1]

Although there are many reasons to move and American families do move frequently, there are many lags in adjustment of households to the space they would consider ideal. Finding a new and better location requires effort as well as money. If the present housing situation is not too bad, many families will continue in it, although they would not now choose it if they were required to make a new choice. Many older couples or persons stay in housing in which they have lived for some years, in spite of the fact that it may not be ideal for them. Not only is there attachment to the old home, but the effort to find a better one seems not worthwhile. Thus, in any period of time, those who actually move from one residential unit to another are only part of those who might have moved. Almost nothing is known about this group of potential housing decision makers. Some of those who might have moved but did not this year may move next year or the year after.

Home buyers are an extremely diverse lot, so far as we can judge from available information.[2] Certain characteristics of purchasers of houses, particularly of new houses, are as follows:

1. Purchasers of new suburban houses are often young couples with small children, who have outgrown their present apartment and want a better environment in which to raise their children. Home purchase is associated with a stage of the life cycle. It is most common among young and middle-aged adults with children, uncommon for very young adults or those beyond middle age. There is considerable contrast in the age distribution of all family heads and those who move from city centers to suburbs, many to buy homes (Figure 7). These data do not permit a differentiation of those under 25 years of age. The proportion of family heads in the under-35 age group among the movers to the suburbs, is more than double that in the whole population, and the proportion over 65 is very small. In the years 1961 through 1967, when the Census Bureau asked families about plans

---

[1] Newton W. Andrus has nicely summarized these reasons in *Lake-Oriented Subdivisions in North Carolina: Decision Factors and Policy Implications for Urban Growth Patterns*, Part II —*Consumer Decisions*, Report No. 10, Water Resources Research, University of North Carolina, 1968.

[2] In addition to Andrus, the following discussion draws on other publications listed at the end of this chapter.

A. ALL HOUSEHOLD HEADS

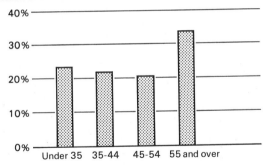

B. HEADS, RECENT MOVERS INSIDE SMSA'S, NOT IN CENTRAL CITY

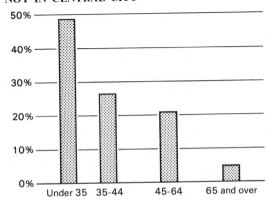

FIGURE 7. Age distribution of family heads, all families and recent movers to suburbs.

to buy a house within 12 months, it found that families intending to buy were mainly young, with the head under 35 years of age.[3]

2. Purchasers of new homes are predominantly white, to judge largely from indirect evidence. A high proportion of new homes have been constructed in suburbs, but Negro and other nonwhite population is relatively much smaller there than in central cities.

3. Buyers of new homes have average or above-average incomes. In 1966, the median total money income of all nonfarm families was about $7,600. Since a reasonable purchase price for a home is considered to be two to two and a half times annual income, it could be said that the average household in 1966 could afford a new house costing $15,000 to $19,000. In 1966, however, nearly two-thirds of all one-family homes for sale were priced above $20,000, while only about an eighth were priced at less than $15,000. Thus, the lower third, if indeed not the lower half, of all families is rather effectively shut out of the new house market.

Other studies have emphasized that the housing needs of the very poor, the

[3] Data from U.S. Department of Housing and Urban Development, *Statistical Yearbook, 1966* (U.S. Government Printing Office, 1966).

elderly, the infirm or unwell, and the racial minorities are very poorly met in nearly every city.[4] Such groups are rarely buyers of new homes. The only way in which they are likely to influence the demand for new houses is by providing a market for old housing.

Many professional and popular writers have decried the social stratification of the postwar suburbs. It is obvious to the most casual visitor that extensive suburbs have been built that cater to white middle-aged or younger couples of at least average income. Children growing up there may be unaware that different economic, social, and racial groups live in the nearby city. It is often argued that the development of new housing in the suburbs for low-income groups is essential to avert the potential consequences of social stratification in antipathy toward the out-groups.

Of a more tangible nature is the relatively great requirement for transportation from middle- and upper-class suburbs, where many workers commute to the city. Nowadays there is a growing volume of reverse commuting by lower-class city residents who have jobs in suburban business, industry, or government organizations.

However desirable it might be to have different groups housed in communities that are integrated socially and economically, and for people to live closer to where they work, it will be extremely difficult to build new houses for the lower-income third of the population. The cost of a new house is materially affected by the cost of land, which has risen markedly in recent years. Interest rates, which affect the size of monthly payments, have risen to new heights.

More significantly, the cost of building a house is rather loosely linked to wage rates, not only of workers in the building trades but also of those who produce building materials—brick, lumber, pipes, and the like. It is true that, with gains in productivity of both classes, not all wage increases are invariably passed along into the price of a finished house.[5] But even if per capita income rises, so that low-income groups have more to spend, the wages of those who build houses and components are bound to go up as part of the general rise. Therefore the cost of building a house is likely to rise also unless productivity per worker increases sufficiently to offset higher wages. Such a comparison would, of course, have to be based on houses of exactly the same type. But it should be remembered that the size and quality of houses have been rising in recent years.

The relationship among variables is shown to some extent in Figure 8. On the average, per capita incomes have risen at just about the same rate since World War II as a standard index of construction costs. Under these circumstances, a rise in income of the lower-income classes at about the same rate as that for the

---

[4] See Nathaniel Keith, *Housing America's Low- and Moderate-Income Families—Progress and Problems under Past Programs—Prospects under Federal Act of 1968*, National Commission on Urban Problems, Research Report No. 7 (U.S. Government Printing Office, 1968). See also the Commission's Research Report No. 8, by George Schirmer Associates, *More Than Shelter—Social Needs in Low- and Moderate-Income Housing* (U.S. Government Printing Office, 1968).

[5] Eichler and Kaplan argue that the cost per square foot of finished house was held relatively constant after 1950 by the larger (though not mass-producing) builders in spite of virtual doubling of hourly wages in the building trades. See Edward P. Eichler and Marshall Kaplan, *The Community Builders* (University of California Press, 1967), p. 146.

higher-income classes may not significantly improve their ability to buy new houses. A rising trend in productivity per hour of labor directly or indirectly used in dwelling construction would modify this conclusion, but there is little evidence of such a trend in recent years. A fall in interest rates would reduce the monthly payments on houses, but the trend in recent years has been in the opposite direction, and the low interest rates of some years ago seem unlikely to return. Thus the conclusion is inescapable that the inability of low-income people to buy new houses is primarily a function of the disparity in incomes among the wage-earning classes, not of the absolute level of their incomes.

A significant effort to improve the housing of lower-income classes must take one of four major directions:

1. A more rapid "filtering down" of a better grade of used housing by an acceleration of other peoples' movement out of such housing and into new housing; or

2. A major technological innovation in construction, which does not now appear on the horizon; or

3. Subsidies in the cost of housing (including subsidized interest rates) or

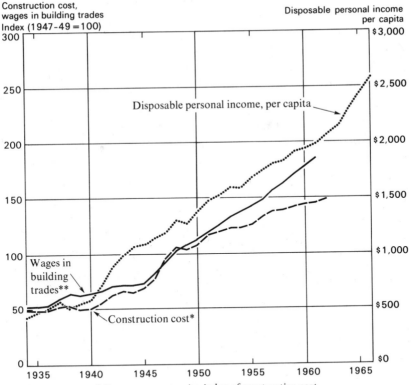

*Department of Commerce composite index of construction cost.
**Index of union wage rates for all building trades.

FIGURE 8. Disposable personal income per capita and indexes of construction cost and of wages in building trades, 1934–66.

through rent supplements, so that lower-income people can afford to buy or rent better housing; or

4. Various programs which would simply eliminate the lower end of the income distribution, such as a guaranteed income and training programs for those unable to work.

THE HOME-BUILDING INDUSTRY

A great many individuals and organizations of widely varying kinds and types build houses in the United States; a continuum from very small to very large, or along any other descriptive axis, is evident.[6] Information about builders—indeed their very grouping into classes—is limited and not always consistent from one source to another. Hence it is necessary to explore this material with care and with attention to sources and definitions. Nevertheless, it is possible to distinguish some rather major types: the owner-builder, the general contractor, the operative builder, and the subcontractor.

The Owner-Builder

The owner-builder is a person who builds a house for his own use, largely with his own labor, often with labor from other members of his family, sometimes with a little hired labor on jobs requiring more than one man, sometimes by subcontracting out specialized jobs for which he lacks the necessary skills. According to Maisel, "these amateurs ordinarily appear in the market only once in their lifetimes."[7] In the San Francisco Bay Area, where Maisel made his study, about two-thirds of the builders in this general group in 1949 had no relation to the house-building industry at all; they were simply amateurs who had read a book (or had a friend with skills) and wanted to build their own houses. The other third of this general group in that area at that time were craftsmen whose jobs and skills were related to the house-building industry in some way—carpenters, building inspectors, and the like who wanted to build their own homes. By using mostly his spare time and by the skills he possesses or can hire under subcontract, the owner-builder keeps his costs low. The kind of house built by this group is often, but not invariably, modest. In 1955, 49 percent of all houses built in nonmetropolitan areas that sold for less than $10,000 were built by owner-builders, compared with much lower percentages in higher-priced houses and in metropolitan areas.[8]

Many people who know that in an earlier day it was quite common for a pioneer

[6] Except as specifically stated to the contrary, this section deals only with the builders of detached single-family houses.

[7] Sherman J. Maisel, *Housebuilding in Transition* (University of California Press, 1953), p. 19. For an interesting study of house-building in Southern California, see James Gillies and Frank Mittlebach, *Management in the Light Construction Industry*, publication of the Real Estate Research Program, Graduate School of Business Administration, University of California, Los Angeles, 1962.

[8] Data in this paragraph and the four following it are from Kathryn R. Murphy, "Builders of New One-Family Houses, 1955–56," *Construction Review* (August-September 1958).

on the farm or in a small town to build his own home might think that this sort of thing had become very uncommon. However, as late as 1949, 34 percent of all houses built in the United States were built by owner-builders; in the metropolitan areas they accounted for only 19 percent of all houses, but in nonmetropolitan areas, for 62 percent. A substantial decline in their importance took place over the next few years, so that by 1955 the percentages were 14, 9, and 31, respectively. The role of the owner-builder has almost certainly shrunk much further in the years since 1955, but it would be a mistake to assume that the building of one's own home has become, or soon will become, extinct.

The owner-builder encounters many problems in getting building permits, in complying with building codes, in coping with new specialized methods of home construction and similar problems that only a specialist in the field knows how to cope with. While it is conceivable that in the future the manufacture and sale of major components would enable the individual to build his own house more readily, on balance the building of one's own home is likely to become increasingly difficult, especially in the larger cities and metropolitan areas, where building codes grow increasingly complex. Conceivably, the rehabilitation of old houses might be done on a larger scale by their occupants, perhaps with stimulation and technical instruction from some public agency. The great assets of the owner-builder are enthusiasm and time; he may or may not have skill, but skill can be acquired or hired.

Although the owner-builder is an increasingly small percentage of the total homebuilding industry, his numbers have been very great in the past and their inclusion in the statistics may readily confuse the picture of the more commercial part of the industry, especially for historical comparisons.

The General Contractor

The general contractor can be defined as one who "builds housing on contract on someone else's land and according to another's instruction. He provides the building service: i.e., he plans and supervises the construction, purchases materials, and hires workmen or subcontracts parts of the job. He may build a multifamily structure for someone who intends to rent or sell the units or he may build single-family houses. In the latter case, the general contractor usually builds for an owner who intends to live in the house, although he may build one or more single-family houses for someone who intends to sell or rent them."

In 1949, the general contractor built about 16 percent of all houses in the United States, in metropolitan and nonmetropolitan areas alike. In 1955, his percentage of the total was about the same, but his share of building in metropolitan areas had declined to 12 percent of the total, while in nonmetropolitan areas it had risen to 24 percent. The latter figure suggests that he had taken over some of the building that otherwise might have been done by the owner-builder.

Maisel subdivides the commercial house-building industry entirely on the basis of the size of the business units, but his "small" category may closely approximate the general contractor category just described.[9] He defines a small builder as one

---

[9] See also Sherman J. Maisel, *Financing Real Estate—Principles and Practices* (McGraw-Hill, 1965) for a general discussion of builders.

who builds between 1 and 24 houses annually, does less than $200,000 total volume of business, employs fewer than 10 men, has less than $100,000 in total assets, or is owned and managed by a craftsman who spends most of his time actually working on the job. Maisel's studies were made in the San Francisco Bay Area immediately after World War II. Hence the monetary aspects of his definition may be out of date with rising prices, but the general character of such builders is probably still much as he described them. Maisel points out that in about 1920 the small builder "*was* the industry." Although his importance has since declined considerably, the small builder is still important in smaller cities and towns and might have an important role even in the larger areas in the future. The small builder has some advantages: his overhead is very low; his direct supervision of operations is a factor for efficiency; he can adopt many new building techniques about as fast as they come on the market. But his disadvantages are also considerable: he cannot be an innovator or undertake research; he cannot purchase materials in large quantities with consequent economies; he cannot hope to compete in the mass housing market where the larger builders have major advantages. The general contractor must seek his continued position in markets which, for some reason, are not attractive to builders of mass housing. This may be the relatively expensive custom-built house. It is significant that in 1955 his share of houses selling for $20,000 and over was twice or more his share of the whole housing market.[10]

A more interesting possibility, as regards suburbanization, is that the small general contractor might evolve into a builder on relatively small bypassed tracts, and hence become a major factor filling in housing on bypassed land. Such tracts would often not be large enough to attract the really large builders and often would present special problems. Possibly the small general contractor might find a way of using this land profitably.

The Operative Builder

Murphy describes the *operative builder* as one who:

plans and executes construction of houses or apartments on his own land (which may range from one or more lots, often scattered, to extensive tracts on which he may develop virtually an entire community), to his own specifications, for sale or rent. Such builders determine the number of units to build and their basic design, size, price, and location; frequently develop the land; hire labor directly or use contractors; and assume the risk of selling or renting the dwellings. They may reduce their risk by building model houses and selling copies on order, usually according to a master plan for utilizing the land. Whether they lay the foundations for all of the units before signing the sales contracts or only as they sell copies from models, they nevertheless produce essentially a ready-made product, in contrast with the custom-type operations of owner-builders and builders operating as general contractors.[11]

[10] Murphy, "Builders, 1955–56," p. 9.
[11] Ibid., p. 6.

Eichler and Kaplan, in describing the operations of the "merchant builder," by which they apparently mean the larger end of the operative builder group,[12] stress the same factors as Murphy but include also market research, land development, permanent sales organization, and other factors which some of Murphy's larger firms probably also include but the smaller ones almost surely do not. Maisel separates firms according to size; his medium and larger firms probably more or less correspond to this definition.[13]

The operative builder, as defined by Murphy, built 41 percent of all houses built in the United States in 1949; in metropolitan areas, his share was 54 percent, in nonmetropolitan areas, only 18 percent. By 1955, his share of building had risen to 70 percent of all houses built in the country, 78 percent in metropolitan areas, and 44 percent in nonmetropolitan areas. Although fully comparable data are not available for a later date, it seems clear that his share has risen further. In 1955, this type of builder virtually monopolized the construction of middle-priced houses in metropolitan areas. His role was somewhat less for the lower-priced houses, where owner-builders were relatively more important, and definitely less for the higher-priced houses where the general contractor's custom building was more important. In each price class the operative builder's share was less important in nonmetropolitan than in metropolitan areas.

Writing in 1967, apparently influenced considerably by experience in California, and speaking in general rather than in statistical terms, Eichler and Kaplan state that the merchant builder has come to dominate the housebuilding indusry.[14]

Maisel considers medium- and larger-size builders in California. His medium-size builder constructs between 25 and 99 units annually, hires between 10 and 99 employees, has a dollar volume and capital assets of corresponding size, and "is owned and managed by an executive who has little or no staff and performs almost all overhead work himself, while also spending a good deal of his time on actual job supervision."[15] So defined, the medium-size builder is primarily a larger version of the small builder—perhaps one of the more successful of the latter. He has some of the small operator's advantages, although he is in danger of developing a higher overhead cost and of spreading his own supervisory efforts too thin; he may be able to buy some materials in larger volume and at better prices; he must pay more attention to marketing his output but he may not be in a position to make specialized market studies. Maisel appears to feel that the medium-size builder runs more risks than the small one, without much greater prospects of profit, and he seems dubious about the future of the medium-size builder. Possibly this builder, as well as small builders, might operate on bypassed tracts of land, thus helping to fill in such areas—on the assumption that such tracts would often not be attractive to the larger builders.

By "large" firm, Maisel means one which builds 100 or more units annually, has 100 or more employees, has a commensurate financial structure, and a large overhead staff.

[12] Eichler and Kaplan, *The Community Builders*, pp. 20–22.
[13] Maisel, *Housebuilding in Transition*, p. 21.
[14] Eichler and Kaplan, *The Community Builders*, pp. 20–23.
[15] Maisel, *Housebuilding in Transition*, p. 21 and ch. 4.

The postwar market, based on the need for housing and the money to get it, produced the big builder. He was the answer to the mass market's demand for mass production. There were 30 housebuilding firms in the Bay area which were able to build a hundred houses or more a year to satisfy the hunger for housing. They represented only 2 per cent of the Bay area builders, but they built . . . 35 per cent of the industry's output. . . .

It may not have been much of a house, measured by some standards, since it was located on newly developed tract land and was meager in quality and detail; some critics thought it had atrocious design. But the builders did not have to worry about design and quality; it was a seller's market and the buyer took what he got. The product sold itself and the firms concentrated on aspects of business other than design, market analysis, or merchandising.

They concentrated, for example, on operating structure. . . . They developed additional functions such as warehousing and production control which increased their total overhead costs but made more than equivalent saving in direct costs. . . . By turning over their capital an average of five times a year and obtaining the highest rate of profit on sales, they received an average 30 per cent return on net worth. The firms with the lowest net worth turned over their capital fastest, made the greatest profits, and did the most expanding.

In financing, all large firms were preoccupied with the necessity of obtaining permanent loans before they could obtain construction advances, and with negotiations for highest possible Veterans Administration and Federal Housing Administration appraisals. . . .

In production, they specialized the functions of their labor force, increased their use of mechanization, took advantage of more precutting and pre-assembling, more laborsaving devices such as patterns and templates. These innovations increased their efficiency, saving 26 per cent in labor costs compared with those of the small builder.

In purchasing, they saved 18 per cent on supplies compared with the small builder, by inaugurating a new distribution system based on direct buying of materials; and saved 21 per cent in subcontracting costs by developing new and more efficient subcontractual relationships. . . .

Through taking advantage of the economies inherent in their greater scale of operations, the large firms averaged 10 per cent profit on sales. The largest firms seemed satisfied with that. Observing that yet further expansion in housebuilding only increased effort, strain, and risk without appreciably increasing net return after taxes, the largest firms showed a tendency to stabilize their capital in housebuilding and to expand in related fields.[16]

This graphic account of the advantages of the larger house-building firms relates to a particular postwar year (1952, approximately) when conditions were unusually favorable for the industry generally, for larger operations, and for operations conducted as largely as possible on credit. In other times, the advantages of the larger firms might not be so dramatic. However, Herzog has shown that the percentage of

[16] Ibid., pp. 131–33.

all houses built by firms building 100 or more annually in Northern California has risen from 32 percent in 1950 (about the time of Maisel's study) to 74 percent in 1960.[17] This would seem fairly convincing proof of the competitive strength of the larger firms. Moreover, he found that the share of the market built by larger firms almost invariably rose when total volume of house-building declined; the smaller firms were shaken out in such unfavorable periods. The average output per large firm rose only slightly during this decade, and mostly ranged from 250 to 325 houses annually.

Units of Decision Making

The unit of decision making varies considerably for builders in each of the three classes. The owner-builder chooses a single site, builds a single house on it; for him, the house is the unit of decision making. The general contractor, or small builder, builds only a few houses annually, not necessarily all in one location. When he builds one or a few custom-designed houses, perhaps the house is the unit of decision making; when he builds several houses in one location, then the small subdivision or tract is the unit. The larger builder, who constructs more than 100 houses each year, often in the same subdivision, where often he builds for more than one year, is concerned primarily with the subdivision as the unit of decision making. He seeks to obtain the advantages of a planned residential development. The largest of the large builders, who construct several hundred houses over a period of two or more years, are concerned with a whole suburb as the unit of decision making. For those few large builders who have sought to build wholly new towns, then of course the town is the unit for which decisions are made.

Subcontractors

Subcontractors perform numerous specialized jobs in home building, for all types of builders. Site preparation, foundations, installation of wiring or of plumbing, air conditioning, specialized flooring, plastering, painting, and numerous other specialized aspects of house-building may be subcontracted. Very little information is available about such subcontractors. In most cases, their businesses are relatively small in scale, usually directed by one man whose personal skills and supervision are critical to the success of the enterprise. It seems likely that they are now less used by the larger operative builders, who often have their own complete staffs of specialized workers, and hence that the subcontractors may have a more difficult time participating in the building of new homes in the future.

Another View of Builders

A somewhat different view of home builders is provided by the periodic surveys the National Association of Home Builders makes of its members. This organiza-

[17] John Herzog, "Structural Change in the Housebuilding Industry," *Land Economics* (May 1963).

tion is the trade association of the home-building industry; it includes most but not all builders of single-family homes and apartments. Each five years, it circulates a questionnaire to its membership; approximately half of them have reported in recent surveys, and these are assumed to be representative of the whole membership.[18]

The significant difference between this source of information about builders and the other sources discussed earlier is that the NAHB surveys show no decline in the proportion of small builders; on the contrary, the surveys seem to show a slight decline in the importance of the large builder. From 1959 to 1964, the proportion of small builders actually increased slightly; from 1964 to 1969, there was no change. In 1969, 65 percent of all builders who reported in this survey built fewer than 25 single-family homes. In terms of the proportion of houses built, the small builder was less dominant; he constructed 17 percent of the homes, while the medium-volume builder (those building from 25 to 100 homes) accounted for 36 percent, and the larger builders (constructing more than 100 homes) accounted for 49 percent.

In 1969, many builders were diversified in their business operations: 32 percent were involved in land development, 22 percent were real estate brokers, 18 percent were commercial and industrial as well as home builders, and other activities were reported, so that 60 percent of those replying to the questionnaire had some business interest other than building single-family homes. Many built garden apartments, some built townhouses, but only a few built high-rise apartments.

One particularly interesting fact reported in the 1969 survey was that builders were increasingly turning to the use of scattered lots; 18 percent reported such building in 1969, compared with only 10 percent in 1964. If this trend continues, it could be a significant force leading to infilling of sprawled suburban areas where land has been bypassed. The 1969 survey reported that the price of finished lots had averaged $2,800 for the nation in 1960, $4,500 in 1964, and $6,200 in 1969. The rising price of land may have been one factor leading builders to seek out scattered lot locations. However, rising cost of land was listed as only fourth in their scale of pressing problems in 1969; high costs in an inflationary period, labor, and financing took precedent.

About half of the builders reporting in 1969 were incorporated; most of the others were individuals or partnerships. Many builders are relatively young; the average age in 1964 of those reporting was 45 years. In these and other aspects, the typical builder as revealed by the NAHB surveys of its members closely approximated the picture arising from Murphy, Maisel, and other writers.

Since the focus of this book is on the expanding suburb and the land conversion process therein, it is not appropriate to devote much space to builders of mobile homes, whose products have often been excluded—or at least are absent—from the typical suburb. However, large settlements of mobile homes—only dubiously mobile any longer—have been established in and around many cities, where local building

[18] 1959 and 1964 data are contained in Nathaniel Rogg, Michael Sumichrast, Norman Farquhar, and S. M. Vinocour, *The 1964 NAHB Builder Member Survey* (Washington: National Association of Home Builders, 1964); 1969 data are given (in preliminary form) in the NAHB *Economic News Notes* (February 1970).

codes or zoning would permit. It may well be in the future that the mobile home industry will play a much larger role in providing housing for Americans, especially for lower-income people, and land conversions to this type of residential occupancy will thus grow in importance.

Summary

This section on the builder as an actor in the urbanization process may be summarized as follows: in land use terms, the size of the typical decision-making unit has shifted from the lot or single house perhaps 40 or 50 years ago, to the subdivision of perhaps block size by the time of the second World War, to the subdivision of perhaps 40 acres or more in size today, with, of course, great variation among builders at each date. In organizational terms, the builder has shifted in the same period from an individual craftsman building on another's land to his client's specifications, to a businessman, often incorporated, building on his own land to his own plans and selling the product to purchasers. Throughout, the builder has had modest capital for the construction and has rarely been in a position to finance the purchaser of the finished home. Although size and type of operations have changed, it is still an industry heavily dominated by the personality of the owner or director of the business unit.

Although reference is made in several of the publications to "large builders," this term needs to be put in some perspective. The average "large" builder in Northern California as reported by Herzog built approximately 300 houses a year circa 1960; at an average selling price of no more than $20,000 this is a gross volume of business of $6 million annually. These are "large" businesses only if they are compared with farms and service stations, although they are slightly in excess of a large supermarket; they are tiny in comparison with most industrial establishments. The home-building industry is evolving toward larger and more sophisticated business operations, but its handicraft ancestry is not far beneath the surface.

Will the typical unit of building decision shift from the subdivision to the whole new town in another generation? Eichler, himself a builder of imagination who started his study with a strong favorable disposition toward the new town, concluded by doubting both the financial feasibility and the social necessity of the new town. Might a wholly new type of builder dominate the industry—vertically integrated in production of building materials, in land purchase and development, in construction, in sales, in financing of the purchase by the purchaser, and operating on a town scale? The few large corporations manufacturing building materials or housing appliances who have begun operations in the house-building field, or have shown some interest in doing so might become builders of new towns or of very large subdivisions.

PLANNERS

Urban planners may be employed by public agencies or by private business interests. They may be either general (comprehensive) in their interests and in the scope of their work, or they may be highly specialized in terms of function—highway, sewer, electricity supply, or others. This section is primarily concerned with those who are public employees and have a broad or general interest and activity.

Nearly all cities of 5,000 and over, about half of the smaller cities, about half of all counties, and about half of the New England townships have planning boards.[19] The total number of all governmental jurisdictions with planning boards in the United States in 1968 exceeded 10,000. However, three-fourths of these planning boards had no full-time employees; as might be expected, these were typically the smaller cities and counties. Nearly all cities with 25,000 or more total population had at least one full-time employee, but many counties and townships with the same population did not. Altogether, the equivalent of 33,000 full-time employees worked for planning boards, although many were not professionally trained planners. In addition, many men (probably many more) were concerned to some degree with planning, usually of a specialized type done for an agency of local government concerned with such matters as transportation, public works, or fiscal management. Pay scales are relatively low for planners, especially in the smaller cities.

The staff of general planning agencies may carry out one or more of a group of related functions: making land use surveys to ascertain present land use; making land use plans to suggest or outline desirable land use at some future date; helping in the development of land zoning regulations, to conform actual land use to the planned use; helping with zoning appeals and applications for rezoning; and many activities not directly connected with land use, such as general public works plans. The relative emphasis upon these various aspects of the general urban planner's job differs greatly from one city to another; some of his frustrations arise out of the need to be concerned with short-term specific tasks when he would like to be working on long-range and general plans.

Development of the Planning Profession

City planning as a specialized and separate professional field is comparatively recent in origin and development.[20] Hardly known as a separate field at the time of World War I, it grew slowly during the 1920's and 1930's, often by conversion of men originally trained in other fields, as well as by the addition of some men specially trained as city planners. Its really major development has come since World War II. Now, there is a substantial body of trained urban planners in the United States. Many, if not most, of them got their training as city planners as graduate students after having had basic training in some allied field as undergraduates.

The professional society of the city planning field is the American Institute of Planners. In a series of major meetings and conferences beginning in 1966, it

[19] Data in this paragraph from Allen D. Manvel, *Local Land and Building Regulation—How Many Agencies? What Practice? How Much Personnel?* Research Report No. 6, National Commission on Urban Problems (U.S. Government Printing Office, 1968).

[20] See Russell Van Nest Black, *Planning and the Planning Profession—The Past Fifty Years 1917–1967* (Washington: American Institute of Planners, 1967); Mel Scott, *History of City Planning in America Since 1890* (University of California Press, 1969).

celebrated its fiftieth anniversary with attempts both to look forward for another fifty years and to appraise the opportunities and challenges for the planning profession.[21] The Institute has emphasized the broad scope of planning, of which planning for land use is only a part.

City planning became firmly established, in a legal sense, with the Supreme Court decision of *Village of Euclid vs. Ambler Realty Co.* (272 U.S. 365, 1926), which strongly affirmed the power of a municipality to regulate use of private land, under defined conditions and with proper procedural safeguards. (In planning and zoning circles, "Euclidean" refers to this decision, not to the Greek mathematician.) A model zoning law was prepared in 1928, under the leadership of Herbert Hoover, then Secretary of Commerce, and became the basis for several state laws on land use zoning.[22] A new model zoning law is reported to be in preparation by the American Bar Association.

The kinds of decisions any professional group makes are dependent in part upon the kind of training it has had and the professional standards or ideals obtained as a result of that training. This is likely to be particularly true in a relatively new field such as city planning, which has expanded so rapidly.[23]

F. Stuart Chapin, Jr., one of the major writers in the field, defines city planning[24] as:

. . . a means for systematically anticipating and achieving adjustment in the physical environment of a city consistent with social and economic trends and sound principles of civic design. It involves a continuing process of deriving, organizing, and presenting a broad and comprehensive program for urban development and renewal. It is designed to fulfill local objectives of social, economic, and physical well-being, considering both immediate needs and those of the foreseeable future. (p. vi)

Land use planning, which is part of the city planning process, is concerned with the location, intensity, and amount of land needed for the various space-using functions of city life. The term "urban land use" is used in planning literature in several ways, Chapin states (p. 3). To some writers, it means the spatial distribution of various city functions. To others, "it means a two-part framework for visualizing urban areas: first, in terms of activity patterns of people in the urban setting and their institutions as they require space . . . and second, in terms of physical facilities or improvements to the land in the urban setting." Still else-

21 Three books have resulted from these conferences, each edited by William R. Ewald, Jr., and published by Indiana University Press, Bloomington. They are: *Environment for Man: The Next Fifty Years* (1967); *Environment and Change: The Next Fifty Years* (1968); and *Environment and Policy: The Next Fifty Years* (1968).
22 See Charles M. Haar, *Land-Use Planning—A Casebook on the Use, Misuse, and Re-use of Urban Land* (Little, Brown, 1959). I have benefited greatly from the opportunity to read an extensive but unpublished paper entitled "Zoning for Open Space in California" which deals with the evolution of zoning, particularly in court decisions, prepared by Gerald D. Bowden, assistant director of the staff for the California Joint Committee on Open Space Land, Sacramento.
23 For a book which traces the development of the city planning field and describes its educational background as of the mid-1950s, see Harvey S. Perloff, *Education for Planning—City, State, and Regional* (Johns Hopkins Press for Resources for the Future, 1957).
24 Chapin, *Urban Land Use Planning* (Harper, 1965).

where, it implies attention to the role of value systems in regulating space-using activities.

Theoretical research in planning seeks to use relevant materials from fields related to city planning, such as anthropology, architecture, economics, geography, human ecology, social psychology, and sociology. In this country, the first systematic attempts to frame a theory of land use came from such writers as Burgess, Hoyt, McKenzie, Harris and Ullman, and Firey. To quote Chapin again:

> As these explanations of land use have developed, each in a theoretical system of its own, city planning, in slowly maturing as a professional field, has been more directly concerned with the applied aspects of land use arrangements. . . . it has had little occasion until recently to engage in fundamental research, particularly of a kind aimed at defining a theoretical frame of reference for urban planning. Such a theoretical framework is urgently needed. (pp. 3–4)

Urban land use policies, as Chapin defines them, are:

> . . . a series of guides to consistent and rational public and private decisions in the use and development of urban land. They are maxims to guide land development decisions in principle. They give direction to the urban planning process, but they also become conditioned by the findings and proposals developed from the planning process. . . .
>
> Perhaps the highest order of policy decision could be viewed as a choice between urban development stabilized at a certain level (measured in terms of economic development, employment, population, land area in development, and so on) and urban development proceeding on an indeterminant and noncontainment basis. . . . A second level of policy decision might relate to the basic orientations in the way land development and transportation systems are to be accommodated. . . . a third-order series of policy decisions might relate to homogeneity versus heterogeneity of development among functional use types and among various activities within each use type. (pp. 349–50)

The "progressive planning approach," says Chapin, can be phased into the kinds of policy making described above. Progressive planning analysis requires the planner to take six steps:

> 1. Develop a first estimate of existing conditions and significant trends in the urban area. . . .
> 2. Determine the principal and most pressing problems and needs, briefly evaluate them, and develop an interim program. . . .
> 3. Formulate a detailed program indicating priorities for undertaking component studies of comprehensive plans. . . .
> 4. Carry out detailed plan studies according to program and priority. . . .
> 5. Integrate various plan studies into comprehensive plan. . . .
> 6. Revise plans as conditions alter their applicability. . . . (pp. 351–52)

Major Issues Faced by Planners

Given the background and training indicated in the foregoing paragraphs, and faced with many difficult problems of application of planning in various cities, city planners—or at least some of them—have been troubled by one or more of a group of interrelated philosophical, policy, or operational issues.[25]

One important issue is the extent to which a city plan should try to be comprehensive, in the sense of including all aspects of city activity, or be concerned with specific aspects of urban living such as transportation, waste disposal, or schools. Closely connected is the question of whether the planner should work for the interests of the general public or those of some particular segment of it. Although it might be argued that the comprehensive-specialized and the general-particular interest issues are separable, in fact they tend to be associated. One rationale for the general urban planner is that he can or should take into consideration a far wider range of subject matter and of social consequences than the specialized planner can or does. But this is far easier said than done. Time and again, the general city planner bumps into the more extensive and detailed knowledge about some subject which the specialized planner has acquired from longer experience. The general planner may realize that building a sewer line will do much to direct suburban growth, while the specialized sewer planner either does not realize it or does not care. But the specialized sewer planner can raise a host of real or imagined engineering problems to which he has answers and the general planner does not. Unless the general planner can establish a close working relationship with the mayor or the city council or can build powerful citizen support, he is likely to be frustrated by the specialized planner. So he is wise to establish a working partnership with the specialist.

The matter of general interest vs. specialized interest is also difficult. In the sewer example, the general planner may realize full well that where the sewer is placed has important consequences for the values of private land—that someone will be rewarded at the expense of a public investment. The sewer planner may be less aware of this result, or fully committed to the enrichment of the individuals concerned, or indifferent to the income-generating and income-distribution effects of his decisions. Protection or enhancement of a general public interest is not made easier by the fact that most of the general public is sound asleep when its interests are being despoiled, waking up much too late if ever.

On both the comprehensive-specialized and the general-special interest issues, the problem of the general planner is more difficult because of a serious lack of objective criteria, standards, and measures. It is all very well to say that the general plan must be based upon "sound land use principles," but this is about equivalent to the old advice, "in doubt, do what Caesar would have done." Is it sound land use to establish an industrial district in one location or not in another, or to permit high-rise apartments in one district but not in another? There has been much support for separation of land uses; carried to the extreme, this means very long journeys to work that may be extremely burdensome to lower-income workers who

---

[25] The next several paragraphs draw heavily, but without direct citation, from several books listed under "City Planning" at the end of this chapter.

cannot afford their own cars. The general city planner may argue that his land use plan is best, but he often cannot produce any quantitative estimate of the values it produces as compared with any other plan. There is nothing in city planning comparable to the benefit-cost calculations that have become standard in many types of public investments.

Given these situations, the general city planner is often forced to rely on personal judgment, upon assertion rather than upon proof, upon rhetoric or personal persuasion. Frequently he is unable to win sufficient support for his plan or can do so only by use of tactics which are more political than professional. In any case, he often faces a difficult personal situation.

A second major issue which the general city planner faces is his relationship to the political power structure of his city or county. Shall he seek to serve the dominant political figures and forces, helping them to solve their problems as they see them, quite possibly being useful and well-appreciated in the process? Or should he seek to play a more nearly independent role, developing plans which in his professional judgment are in the general public interest, trying or hoping to persuade the political leaders to accept or support such plans? If he works on matters of direct concern to political figures, this is likely to mean work on matters of small size and immediate urgency, while the broader, longer-range general planning issues go by default for simple lack of time and manpower. But general plans may not arouse much interest, unless it is opposition, from political figures. Such plans seem too remote, too general, to be understood and valued.

Banfield and Wilson have emphasized how little political muscle most city planners have, and how little political "sex appeal" a general city plan is likely to have with the whole electorate.[26] On the other hand, a broad-gauge political leader at the urban level (who might or might not be the mayor or a councilman) could well use the city plan as the source of ideas and even of guidance for dealing with current issues as they arise and for initiating new programs. Many planners have sought to keep their offices somewhat aloof from the political machine, fearing— often rightly—that close involvement would leave them no time or opportunity for genuine planning. Kent, on the other hand—speaking, probably, as a practical politician as much as a professor of planning—has emphasized that the planner's chief client is the city council and the mayor, rather than the general public.[27] In any case, the city planner has often found himself in situations where his professional training offered few answers and may have raised some serious obstacles to his accommodation to the political scene or his ability to modify the latter to his needs.

A third major issue facing city planners has been their relationship with the general public. Typically, indeed almost universally, planners have developed land use or other plans to what they considered a final and defensible stage and only then sought public understanding and support. Rarely have they sought to involve the public in the actual development of the plan; possibly because it would have been difficult to interest an uninformed or indifferent citizenry. Planners of sub-

[26] Edward C. Banfield and James Q. Wilson, *City Politics* (Harvard University Press, 1963).
[27] T. J. Kent, *The Urban General Plan* (Chandler, 1964), pp. 22–25. Kent served as councilman and then mayor of Berkeley, California for several years.

urban developments have rarely sought consultation with land speculators, developers, and merchant builders in land use planning, perhaps because these groups might well have sought to take advantage of anything they learned by consultation with planners. Yet, in the end, the planner's land use plan must run the gauntlet of landowners' criticism, usually without the help of those who might possibly have supported it if they had been involved in its development. Relationship with the general public during the planning process is an issue which many planners have not recognized as a problem. They have resolved it in terms of their operations as professional planners without public interference until the plan was "ready" and often have been disappointed at the public reaction.

The city planning process could be used, much more than it typically has been, to emphasize the positive values that could be created by joint or cooperative action, as compared with those likely to arise under unguided private enterprise. City planning has often been used in a more restrictive or defensive sense—to limit what could be done, to impede new and nonconforming land uses, to preserve values in established areas. Its use to emphasize the creation of positive values would involve a consideration of positive externalities. In any event, a city plan has, or should have, economic implications greater than are generally realized.[28] The potentialities of rigorous and dependable economic analysis for testing alternative city plans are great, although the difficulties are great too. Planners are taking some initial steps to include economics, law, and other disciplines in their planning, and economists and other professional groups need to modify and extend their analyses to cope adequately with city planning problems.

Advocacy planning is a special kind of urban planning of relatively recent origin.[29] Various citizen groups in a metropolitan area have sought to establish their own planning organizations. These may be racial minorities or low-income groups from the older city; they may also be middle- to higher-income people from suburban areas. In each case, the group feels that its interests are not properly taken into account in the public planning process; it seeks to have a planning machinery which will serve its own ends and help to defeat those aspects of public plans that it does not like. In this motivation, such planning bodies are more akin to private industry planning organizations of earlier periods than to the typical public planning body today. The latter seeks, with variable success, to develop plans that serve all citizens to a reasonably satisfactory degree. Industry and advocacy planning seek to serve the interests of their organizations—interests that may be narrower than those of the public as a whole.

City planning as a profession is gradually moving toward consensus as to content, objectives, methods, standards, and the like. The city planner will surely play a larger role in the suburbanization process in the future than in the past.

Somewhat similar comments could be made about related activities. As shown in Table 6, more than three-fourths of all local governments have one or more of

28 Werner Z. Hirsch and David L. Shapiro, "Some Economic Implications of City Planning," *UCLA Law Review* (August 1967).

29 See the issues of the *Journal of the American Institute of Planners* for March 1968, September 1968, and July 1969 for various articles which discuss this relatively new development.

TABLE 6

NUMBER OF LOCAL GOVERNMENTS IN THE UNITED STATES WITH PLANNING, ZONING,
AND BUILDING REGULATION ACTIVITIES, 1968

Coverage group	Governments with—					
	Planning board	Zoning ordinance	Subdivision regulation	Building code	Housing code	Any building regulation[1]
Total[2]	10,717	9,595	8,086	8,344	4,904	14,088
Within SMSAs	4,963	5,199	4,509	4,527	2,780	6,264
Outside SMSAs	5,754	4,396	3,577	3,817	2,124	7,824
County governments	1,596	711	886	415	211	1,796
Municipalities	6,673	6,880	5,297	6,484	3,976	8,905
1960 population of:						
1,000 or more	6,167	6,140	4,894	5,770	3,470	7,827
Under 1,000 (in SMSAs)	506	740	403	714	506	1,078
New England-type townships	2,448	2,004	1,903	1,445	717	3,387
1960 population of:						
1,000 or more	2,359	1,815	1,827	1,356	666	3,273
Under 1,000 (in SMSAs)	89	89	76	89	51	114

Source: Allen D. Manvel, *Local Land and Building Regulation: How Many Agencies? What Practice? How Much Personnel?*, National Commission on Urban Problems, Research Report No. 6 (U.S. Government Printing Office, 1968), p. 23.

[1] These figures cover units reporting any of the other specified types of activity *or* a local building-permit system.

[2] The "total" relates to governments subject to sample survey representation, and thus omits (a) all municipalities and townships of less than 1,000 population located outside of SMSAs; and (b) township governments located in states where these governments lack municipal-type powers.

the following: a planning board, zoning ordinances, subdivision regulations, and building or housing codes.[30] About three-fourths of these have planning boards, with smaller numbers having one or more of the other activities. The functions other than planning, such as zoning and subdivision regulation, may be performed by planning personnel, or by others, or partly by each. Both zoning and subdivision regulation involve legal considerations, which may be handled by planning personnel or by legal personnel. Building and housing codes may involve engineers, fire department personnel, health department personnel, and others, as well as planners. Frequently, political and other considerations have led to substantial divergence between actual practice and the law. If housing codes were strictly enforced, much housing for low-income groups would have to be abandoned, for restoring it to a level where it could pass the inspection would be more costly than its subsequent worth would justify. If health regulations were rigidly enforced against septic tanks, a great many suburban subdivisions would have a hard time qualifying.

In this section on the public agencies as actors in the suburban land conversion process, a brief word should be said about the courts, for many land use zoning controversies wind up there. By and large, most judges are neither interested in

[30] Manvel, "Local Land and Building Regulation," p. 23.

nor informed about law relating to land zoning and use. Although many courts have upheld zoning based upon solid land use plans, clear criteria, and proper procedures, other courts have acted in ways that have seemed arbitrary or capricious to many observers.[31] This book is not primarily concerned with the legal aspects of land use changes. The point is raised to make it clear that here is an important and difficult field that merits careful attention from those interested in the law, as contrasted to the economics, of suburban land conversion.

LENDERS

In 1960, more than 40 percent of all homeowner properties had no mortgages, although today 85 to 90 percent of newly built houses have mortgages. Few buyers can afford to pay for their houses in cash. Indeed, most purchasers would be unable to buy without a mortgage. Houses are resold at 8 to 10 years, on the average, and most such sales also are financed in part by mortgages.[32]

In 1962, a third of all residential mortgage debt was held by savings and loan associations, whose primary or sole purpose is to stimulate individual savings and to channel them into home buying. About a fifth was held by life insurance companies, which accumulate very large sums of capital that must be invested somewhere. About a sixth of the total was held by mutual savings banks—organizations with considerable similarities to savings and loans associations. Thus, these three types of savings-investment organizations held over two-thirds of the total mortgage debt for single-family dwellings. Commercial banks, individuals, and "others" held the rest. In the ten preceding years, the share of the savings-investment group had increased from just a little over half, while the share of the commercial banks and individuals had shrunk substantially.

The federal government too is heavily involved in financing the construction of houses, chiefly through mortgage insurance. Over a third (35 percent) of all residential mortgage debt in 1962 was insured by the Federal Housing Administration or the Veterans Administration. However, many of the prime lenders who finance home mortgages (mainly commercial banks and savings and loan associations) are themselves under a degree of federal supervision because deposits are guaranteed up to stipulated sums by federal deposit insurance.

While the role of the federal government is largely indirect today, the home-financing program initiated in the 1930s to rescue homeowners, lending institutions, and the construction industry have greatly affected the mortgage business. Prior to that time, mortgages were typically short in term, with few provisions for monthly amortization, no escrow provisions to cover taxes and insurance, and no guarantees. Down payments as a rule were far larger than they are today. The experience under federal mortgage loans for homes and farms greatly stimulated the development of new and larger private lending operations.

[31] See Richard F. Babcock, *The City Planning Process* (University of Wisconsin Press, 1966), Ch. VI, especially pp. 101–11.

[32] This section draws heavily on Maisel, *Financing Real Estate.* For an excellent earlier reference, see Charles M. Haar, *Federal Credit and Private Housing* (McGraw-Hill, 1960).

With the exception of individuals who lend money on home mortgages (who form a minor part of the total mortgage supply), mortgage lenders are rather large-scale business enterprises, with institutionalized or formalized procedures and methods, somewhat impersonal in their operations. Yet competition for business is keen among them, at least at some stages of the building cycle or when the demand for housing is high. The methods of appraising residential property are reasonably well standardized; appraisers have their trade associations and their manuals of procedure, and emphasize the objective nature of their work. Likewise, legal and administrative forms and procedures are fairly well standardized. The concern of each firm is not to loan above the "market," yet competition forces it to make loans on generous terms as to interest rates, fees, length of loans, and the like.

Lenders play a major role in financing the builders as well as the buyers of houses. Some observations by Maisel reveal the nature of this lending, and hence the role that lenders play:

> All phases of the construction process tend to be equity-poor. The great majority of the firms in the industry are compelled to stretch their capital to the utmost. Typically, the leverage in the industry is large. In theory, lending contracts for construction oblige the builder to furnish equity to 20 percent of the finished value. In practice, by careful timing and judicious scheduling of work and bills, contractors can cut their equity requirement by more than half. . . .
> Subcontractors, material suppliers, and labor may all furnish credit to the builder. . . .
> A builder who finances all his own work has of necessity a very low capital turnover rate. Conversely, the higher his borrowing, the more work he can perform and the greater his potential profits. Most builders attempt to maximize turnover. While these are the compelling forces behind the desire to borrow, the availability of the property for security enables large loans to be made. An old saying claims that many builders can borrow $20,000 to build a house who could not borrow $50 to buy a suit.[33]

Conversations with builders confirm Maisel's statements, and some even suggest that he was too conservative. Many builders manage to get loans so that, when the housing is sold subject to a theoretical 90 percent or other high mortgage, they have in fact got out all their investment. Instances are not unknown in which a house buyer found he was stuck with materials supplier's, subcontractor's, or labor liens against his house and had to pay, in effect, double for the house, since the developer had borrowed more than 100 percent of the value and lacked assets to pay off liens.

As Maisel emphasizes, the typical builder lacks equity capital and his profit prospects are much enhanced by operating as heavily in debt as he can obtain credit. Such operations, of course, are highly vulnerable to adverse economic conditions, even to a mere slowing in sales rates for finished houses. One strongly sus-

[33] Maisel, *Financing Real Estate*, pp. 315–16.

pects that many builders' decisions are taken in light of credit availability, rather than in light of other economic analysis.

Lending institutions as a group would strongly deny that they make land use plans or that they influence land use policy. They would instead emphasize their concern over "sound loans," no higher than the value of the assets and the repayment ability of the borrower will support, and at as reasonable rates as the general state of the money market will permit. All of this is true enough, and yet the kinds of loans lenders will make—and, perhaps even more, the kind they refuse to make—have greatly influenced the use of urban and suburban land. When developers and home buyers can get loans for some particular type of residential development, that type of development will be built. If they cannot get loans for some other type or location of development, it will not be built. A major part of the income-racial segregation of most suburbs rests firmly on lending policies of financial institutions.

INTERACTION OF PRIVATE PARTIES AND PUBLIC AGENCIES

The many actors in the suburbanization growth process may be grouped into four general categories, and there are numerous interactions among and between them. In the upper left hand corner of Figure 9 are the landowners or land speculators, those who own developable land but do not themselves intend to develop it into residential or other suburban land uses. In the lower left is the considerable category of private businesses, all operating in search of a profit, each performing some function in the process of converting raw land into suburban development. In the lower right is a group of nonelected public officials and public employees who are not selected by the voters but are appointed by some person or group with authority to do so. These include the members of the planning board or zoning board, if these are separate; members of sewer or water commissions or other similar boards; and employees of various public agencies, with professional

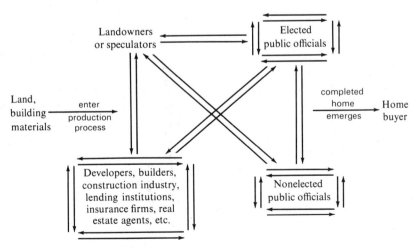

FIGURE 9. Interactions among various actors and interest groups in the suburbanization process.

standards and criteria as well as technical expertise. In the upper right are the elected public officials—members of county councils, city councils, and any others who are chosen by the voters. The dividing line between some groups is clear. The elected officials obviously stand apart, as do the nonelected officials, in their official capacities, although the same individual may be a member of this and other groups as well. But it may be hard to draw the line between other groups, such as land-owners and developers—for one man may be playing both roles at the same time.

These various interacting groups take raw land, building materials of various kinds and construction equipment, and hire skilled labor to produce a final product, which we assume is a dwelling in this figure—all this with an eye to the final home buyer, whose willingness to buy is essential to the success of the whole enterprise.

Landowners, Speculators, and Dealers

Of all the groups involved in the process of suburban growth, least is known about the landowners, speculators, and dealers—and, considering how little we know about some other groups, that is a strong statement. Such evidence as does exist suggests that members of this group, in addition to buying land from farmers or others who used it for production and selling it to developers, may buy and sell land among themselves.

The greatest asset of this group is not land itself but information. Its members seek to be highly knowledgeable about urban plans—real ones, which may or may not be the same as the official plans—and about public programs such as sewer construction. They seek to be well-informed about which developer paid what for which piece of land and why, and what may be the demands for land in the very immediate future, and by whom and for what. Although the daily or monthly turn-over of land may be small, the role of the trader is very similar, whether he trades in land, commercial stocks, or wheat. The land trader or dealer profits primarily by his superior knowledge and by his ability to take advantage of that knowledge; if everyone knew what he knows, his role would be greatly diminished. It is not surprising, under these circumstances, that this group has not been anxious to tell outsiders everything about its operations.

Members of this landowning group surely try to influence public action. They do not quietly wait for zoning or a new sewer line to drop a plum in their lap but shake the tree vigorously to help the decision drop where and when they want it. It seems reasonable to suppose that they try to exert influence upon elected public officials through promises of political support, contributions to campaigns, or more direct financial reward. Bribery of elected county officials in land zoning cases is surely not unknown.

Members of the landowning group almost certainly attempt to influence the actions of nonelected public officials. Landowners may get themselves named to the board itself. This has been the case in the Washington Suburban Sanitary Commission, operating in the Maryland section of the Washington metropolitan area.[34]

[34] Francis Xavier Tannian, "Water and Sewer Supply Decisions: A Case Study of the Washington Suburban Sanitary Commission," unpublished doctoral dissertation, University of Virginia, June 1965.

Infiltration by the supposedly regulated onto the board of the regulators is an old American practice, and one should not be surprised that it arises in suburban development.[35] Landowners and speculators plead their cases before planning and zoning personnel, informally as well as formally, trying to adduce new facts or new viewpoints which will produce a decision favorable to them. In this respect, they are not different from lobbyists for various interest groups who appear before Congressional committees or other legislative bodies. Trying to influence public action in directions favorable to oneself is not necessarily illegal or improper, although illegal or improper methods may be used.

In the operations of the landowning group, as of the developer group, the role of the lawyer is often critical. Some lawyers have great success in getting zoning and rezoning for their clients or in otherwise obtaining favorable public actions. Such lawyers are sometimes on public boards or have close connections with board members.

The landowning group is in rivalry but also in cooperation with the developers. The two are in cooperation to the extent that each has much to gain from any public or private actions which will make profitable a new use of the land in question—zoning, public services, other private construction. They are in rivalry in that each is struggling to get the largest possible share of the expected gain. If the builder pays "too much" for the raw land, his profits are reduced and his prospects of a profitable operation may be dimmed.

Substantial sums are involved in appreciation of land value from its use for farming until it is converted to suburban housing. On the basis of Schmid's data on land prices and on estimates of the area converted annually from rural to urban uses, the writer believes that the total annual gain in land prices in converting raw land to suburban residential use may be on the order of $13.5 billion annually—a not insignificant sum even in modern America.[36] The gains for any one tract of land are distributed among numerous landowners and over several years. According to Schmid's data, farmers get nearly half of this gain, land speculators or dealers the other half. To the gains from new residential use should be added increases in value of land developed for commercial and other non-residential purposes. This often involves a change in land use and rezoning; the annual acreages are unknown—surely very much smaller than the acreages taken for residential use, but the gains in value per acre are surely very much greater. Possibly the total appreciation in this type of land may equal that for land converted to residential use. With sums of anything like this magnitude at stake, it would be miraculous if owners of and dealers in this land did not seek to influence those public actions which affect the value of their land.

There is a more depressing aspect of appreciation in land values to landowners and speculators. The price of raw land is likely to increase, as public agencies spend money to provide public services. If the marginal costs of public services

[35] For an interesting and graphic example of how "public" boards are created but privately staffed to insure their impotence, see Harold Swanton, "The Mad Harbor Party," in *Cry California* (Summer 1968).

[36] A. Allan Schmid, *Converting Land from Rural to Urban Uses* (Resources for the Future, 1968).

were directly and immediately assessed against the land, in such a way that the new owner realized what he was paying for, then raw land prices would presumably not be affected by the extent of public services. Their cost would create an equal value in the land, which the purchaser would pay, leaving the raw land price unaffected. In fact, the costs of such public services are spread over existing as well as new suburban developments, and the pricing arrangements are such that the new settler neither pays the full cost he creates nor is even aware what it amounts to. Over a long period of years, he may indeed pay sums equal to the costs properly chargeable to his settlement, as he is assessed to help pay for similar public services to other new subdivisions. This matter is discussed more fully in Chapter 8.

Developers, Builders, and Other Profit-Motivated Participants

In the lower left corner of Figure 9 are grouped the developers, builders, and others in the suburban building process whose chief motive is profit from their operations. They are distinguished from the landowners and speculators in that the builders and others in this group hope to make their profits out of actions, while the landowning group hopes to profit from superior information and from the passage of time. Actually, the group including builders is a highly diverse one, with many separable interests and many crosscurrents; intragroup relations are possibly quite as important as are those between groups.

The builders, for example, are highly dependent upon sources of borrowed funds. Builders not only expect to sell the houses or other structures they build, at prices which enable them fully to recoup their money shortly, but they also usually operate on borrowed funds in the building process itself.

The developer may be his own construction firm, or he may contract or subcontract. In the latter case, he obviously has numerous and complex relations with other firms. In either case, the conditions embodied in union labor agreements or working rules are extremely important, in terms of the building methods he can use. The merchant-builders normally have their own sales agents; but smaller builders may utilize the services of real estate agents, at least to some degree. The developer requires insurance for his properties under construction and numerous other services, all of which involve relationships with other firms of this same general group.

The developer often takes the initiative in assembling land and in putting together a "deal." A common practice is to take an option on a piece of land, the completion of the deal and the price dependent upon getting the desired zoning or rezoning, assuming that the land is not already zoned as desired. This promptly brings the developer and/or the landowner into contact with the nonelected professional staff of the zoning authority first, then with the zoning board, and possibly with the elected county governing board if the latter has appeal power over the zoning board. But equally important are the public services available to the tract of land in question, and this brings the developer and/or the landowner to the sewer authority, the water authority, the highway authority, or others. In each case, the developer seeks public actions which he believes are in accord with the rules governing such actions, but he often may have to persuade the public officials that they are in fact in accord with such rules.

Of less immediate but perhaps of greater long-range importance are the relations between builders and those units of local government which establish building, safety, and health codes. These matters are less immediate because they can ordinarily not be changed for a single subdivision, but they may be more important because they very much set limits to what a builder can build. Building codes are widely attacked as unnecessarily restrictive and backward-looking, as inhibiting new methods of construction; but they are a tool by which the public can prevent dangerous or shoddy construction. If the health inspectors had taken a much stricter view of septic tanks, many of the scattered subdivisions would not have been constructed during the past 20 years. It is widely believed that building and health inspectors do upon occasion turn a blind eye toward subdivisions that would not meet their standards if strictly enforced.

The developer-builder group utilizes lawyers to a major extent, particularly in zoning and rezoning cases, but also for help in various agreements and negotiations. Lawyers often play a critical role in such cases, because of special knowledge, special bargaining skills, possibly because of special influence with public officials, and possibly as legal means of payoffs from one group to another. This is a phase of the suburban-building process about which there is much gossip and virtually no hard evidence.

Elected Public Officials

Each city and county has an elected governing board with general governing powers, which has different names in various parts of the country. In theory, such a board has complete control over the actions of the nonelected officials, both those on appointed boards and the public employees. In theory, the general governing board should set policies and can develop consistent programs to carry out such policies. In practice, the general governing body may be quite unable to exercise these broad powers. They may be so smothered in detail bucked up to them by their employees, or so captive to special political groups within their city or county, or so incapable of controlling various specialized nonelective boards and commissions, that in fact they are able to exercise very little power at all. Perhaps even more serious, often the members of the general governing group are themselves the representatives of special interest groups, and their real function is to prevent any public action inimical to the group they really represent.

One might well ask why a citizen should want to seek election to a general governing board of a city or county. In any active suburbanizing area, the demands of such a board upon the time of the members is heavy—frequent evening meetings, often lasting quite late, frequent daytime conferences. What is, in theory, a part-time job is, in practice, often a full-time one—and not confined to 40 hours per week either. These jobs are poorly paid, often less than a fourth of what the people holding such positions would consider reasonable pay for a private full-time job of comparable complexity. Moreover, it is by no means uncommon for a candidate for such a public office to spend as much money—some his own, some donated— in getting elected as he can hope to collect as salary during his tenure. Electioneering is a particularly demanding consumer of time. These public offices invariably subject their holders to criticism for their official actions, often to a glare of publicity on their private lives.

Given all these undesirable aspects to these public offices, as members of the general elected governing boards, why do men and women seek such offices, nearly always in numbers that produce real competition for the offices? Various alternative explanations are possible:

1. Some men are undoubtedly public-spirited, anxious to obtain good government for their city or county, and convinced (often rightly) that they can contribute to that end. Such men are likely to be members of informal or formal groups with similar objectives, which urge them to run and offer support. In a general skepticism over such local governing bodies, one should not underestimate the power and motivation of such groups.

2. The office on the local governing body may be a stepping stone to a higher, better-paid, more prestigious public office—possibly in the state or federal legislature. In many areas of the United States, there is a considerable tradition of progressive public service, from local to state to national office, and service on a local governmental body may thus be considered a capital investment in the man's political future.

3. The payoff may be direct, in actual cash in extreme cases, but more commonly in terms of better business deals for himself or his associates. A great deal of this sort of thing is suspected, gossiped about, or actually charged in political campaigns, in newspapers, and elsewhere. Only occasionally are formal charges brought, and these do not always result in convictions. One may assume that illegal acts are much less common than legal acts whose result may be an equal betrayal of the general public interest. There are undoubtedly many legal ways to help one's friends; it is here that lawyers can provide valuable services.

One major interrelation between the builder-developer group and the elected public officials arises at this point. A builder-developer, or the lawyer serving such businesses, may well find it worth his while to seek public office and to devote to the affairs of the public body the time it requires; the direct financial gain to him and his interests may fully repay any time and effort ostensibly devoted to the public business. In many suburbanizing counties, it is not easy to get participation in the public political process except by those who have some direct financial gain from so doing. Many officials in such counties are landowners, anxious to sell at the best prices, or builder-developers anxious to build with minimum public restrictions and with maximum public help, or are lawyers or other agents of these groups.

Nonelected Public Officials

The nonelected public officials must be divided into two quite different groups: members of appointed boards of various kinds; and employees of the general and specialized local governmental agencies.

In many parts of the United States, extensive use is made of the appointed board—sometimes advisory, often actually governing or operative. There are highway commissions, fish and game commissions, park and recreation boards, water control boards, water pollution boards, and many others at state levels and sometimes at county levels also. Members of such boards may receive a small salary, but often only their expenses are paid. Many boards are innocuous—their origins lost in antiquity or serve merely to provide a degree of public recognition to outstanding private citizens. However, in some instances such boards have real governing power and exercise it. The best defense for such boards is that the members serve overlapping terms which provide continuity, stability, and some measure of protection against irresponsible elected bodies. Some at times seem almost out of control of the general elective governing body.

The Washington Suburban Sanitary Commission is one of the latter.[37] Created in 1918 partly because of outbreaks of water-borne diseases, it has become not only the construction agency to build public water and sewerage systems but also to control the building and operation of systems it does not build. At the time of this study, the six members of its board of directors were appointed by the governor of Maryland for four-year terms and are eligible for reappointment. Two members were appointed from each of the two counties served (Montgomery and Prince Georges), from a list submitted by the county governing board; but two members were appointed by the governor without such limitation. The board has great latitude in use of the revenues it collects and may issue bonds for further construction without the necessity of approval by any other body or the electorate. By 1965, it was spending about $65 million annually. The legislation authorizing the Commission does not establish clear policies or objectives. Board members are paid small salaries. While they do not have to run for office, they have been the recipient of much public criticism, some in quite virulent terms. In recent years, the county councils in Montgomery and Prince Georges counties have sought with only limited success to control the Commission through review and approval of its construction program and its budget.

Why should anyone seek appointment to the WSSC board? In fact, there are always many candidates for positions on it. Tannian offers four possible reasons:

1. Direct personal income. The Commissioners have the power to set their own salaries, but salaries have been so low that this clearly cannot be the reason.

2. Economic efficiency, as an objective for public business. Tannian offers evidence that the operations of the board have been highly inefficient, in the economic sense, and hence he rejects this explanation.

3. Expansion of influence of the board and, by implication, of its members—operation of a large enterprise, with size an objective in itself. While Tannian thinks this had had some significance, he believes it has not been the prime factor.

4. Special interest for oneself and one's friends. This, Tannian believes, has been the chief motivation. He cites numerous newspaper accounts from the 1950s and early 1960s, of occasions when WSSC board members took official actions which could not help rewarding them as private individuals. A member, and after

37 Tannian, "Water and Sewer Supply Decisions."

his retirement an employee, of the board was president of the bank in which were deposited most of the WSSC funds. Members have represented private landowners or builders in zoning and rezoning cases. They have owned land that would be served by extensions of water or sewer lines they voted to extend.

To the extent that the Washington Suburban Sanitary Commission is typical, it is evident that the members of the nonelected boards and commissions have numerous, often intimate, relations with members of the landowner-speculator, developer-builder, and elected official groups. Moreover, no small part of the power of a group like the WSSC is to withhold action favorable to some landowners while extending it to others. Hence its relationships to other groups show as great variation as among the individuals in each.

Public Employees

The employees of public agencies include planners, engineers, architects, and others. In each instance, it may be assumed that their basic desire is to do a "good job" as they define it, to earn a reasonable income, and to occupy a respectable place in the social hierarchy of the community. Each is conditioned by the nature of his professional training. Engineers are likely to be concerned with "good engineering" and be proud of the nonpolitical nature of their work, as they conceive it. As noted earlier in this chapter, planners have typically received education that has implanted certain ideals of sound urban and land use planning in their minds. As professional persons, with professional standards, such men are employable in other governmental units. If conditions are too unsatisfactory they can, and probably will, move. One result has been to impose some minimum level of performance, including honesty, on all units of local government.

Babcock has described some of the problems of the planner. "The intolerable position of the planner is underscored by his suspicion that the final decisions will not be his."[38] The planner is constantly caught in a struggle between advocating what he thinks is best from a broad social viewpoint and what he thinks the community—and more specifically the planning and/or zoning board—will accept. Altshuler develops the same general point, from the study of planning he made in the Minneapolis-St. Paul area.[39] In each case, the planner lacked objective tools of analysis such as the engineer uses, tools which often have a spurious objectivity in which both the engineer and the public can take refuge. Moreover, city or county plans are often intended to achieve objectives, such as exclusion of certain income or racial groups, which the governing body will not make explicit and which many planners reject as suitable objectives.

In a great many situations, the planner or zoning employee is under considerable pressure to give in to some individual or group that wants some public action to its particular profit. In such situations, the planning or zoning employee often has no

[38] Richard F. Babcock, *The Zoning Game—Municipal Practices and Policies* (University of Wisconsin Press, 1966), p. 65.

[39] Alan A. Altshuler, *The City Planning Process—A Political Analysis* (Cornell University Press, 1966).

political ally and only political opposition—it is no wonder that he loses so many such contests. Meyerson and Banfield think that many planners have actually sought to be overwhelmed in detail, as a means of seeming to be important while at the same time evading the really difficult and demanding issues of general planning.[40] They further suggest that the selection process for planners and the processes within agencies by which planners advance or at least remain, are such as to bring to the top those planners who will consider only the more detailed actions.

A different division of power between planners and elected officials is conceivable; the planner may develop sufficient political strength to overcome the political forces that may be arrayed against him. Kaplan suggests that this is what happened in slum clearance in Newark. A powerful and astute housing authority was extremely successful in getting federal grants and managed to stay largely out of the control of the city governing body.[41] However, in this case one may say that the nonelected public official has in fact usurped a role which properly belongs to other groups.

In any case, it is evident that the salaried employees of the public agencies in a suburbanizing county or city have numerous contacts with the elected public officials, with nonelected officials, with the private developing-building industry, and with the landowning-speculating group. The salaried employee normally has limited political strength, but his knowledge and his position in the governmental process nevertheless nearly always make him a useful and sometimes vital part of the whole process.

ADDITIONAL REFERENCES

In addition to the publications cited in the footnotes, those listed below have special relevance for sections of this chapter.

A. *Characteristics and Demands of Buyers* (Note 2)
   Lansing, John B., and Hendricks, Gary. *Living Patterns and Attitudes in the Detroit Region,* a report of the Detroit Regional Transportation and Land Use Study. Detroit: Detroit Metropolitan Area Regional Planning Commission, 1967.
   Rossi, Peter H. *Why Families Move: A Study in the Social Psychology of Urban Residential Mobility.* New York: Free Press of Glencoe, 1955.
   Seeley, John R.; Sim, R. Alexander; and Loosley, Elizabeth W. *Crestwood Heights: A Study in the Culture of Suburban Life.* New York: Basic Books, Inc., 1956.
   Wheaton, William L. C.; Milgram, Grace; and Meyerson, Margy Ellin, editors. *Urban Housing.* New York: The Free Press, 1966. See especially articles by Maisel and Winnick and by Kristof.

[40] Martin Meyerson and Edward C. Banfield, *Politics, Planning and the Public Interest— The Case of Public Housing in Chicago* (Free Press, 1955).
[41] Harold Kaplan, *Urban Renewal Politics: Slum Clearance in Newark* (Columbia University Press, 1963).

Winger, Allan R. "Housing Space Demands: A Cross Section Analysis." *Land Economics*, XXXVIII (February 1962).

Zimmer, Basil G., and Hawley, Amos H. "Suburbanization and Some of Its Consequences." *Land Economics*, XXXVII (February 1961).

B. *City Planning* (Note 25)

American Society of Planning Officials. *Problems of Zoning and Land-Use Regulation*. Research Report No. 2, National Commission on Urban Problems. Washington: U.S. Government Printing Office, 1968.

Raymond and May Associates. *Zoning Controversies in the Suburbs: Three Case Studies*. Research Report No. 11, National Commission on Urban Problems. Washington: U.S. Government Printing Office, 1968.

THE 7 SUBURBAN LAND MARKET

As an urban area increases in population, it expands territorially at the margin, and this expansion invariably requires sales of land by previous owners and purchases of land by new owners. Thus a market for suburban land is necessarily created. This market has many peculiarities, and the following pages will deal with some of them. The thesis here is that the form of the market in itself has a considerable effect on the kind of land use and the type of suburb which is developed. The chapter will therefore attempt to measure how far and in what ways the nature of the market determines or affects the kind of suburbs which emerge, and how far and in what ways the market might yield to public efforts to change the outcome.

DEMAND FOR SUBURBAN LAND IN GENERAL

The economic concept of demand concerns the relation between the quantity of any good or service purchased or consumed and its price or some other variable. An important part of this basic concept is the idea of elasticity, or the relative change in quantity associated with a relative change in price or other variable. When changes in quantity are relatively great in response to a small change in price and total expenditures increase as price falls, the demand is said to be relatively elastic.

The economic concept of demand was originally applied to price-quantity relationships. In its simplest or purest form, a demand schedule or relationship assumes that *all* factors other than price and quantity remain unchanged. If this latter condition is met, the quantity purchased or consumed increases as price falls, without—as far as we know—any exception. Hicks has distinguished between the substitution and the income effects of price changes.[1] If the price for commodity A falls, then some or all consumers will buy more of it and less of commodity B, to the extent that these two commodities are in any way substitutes for one another. At the same time, the reduction in price of commodity A increases the real income of the consumer; he has to spend less money to buy the old volume of that commodity, while leaving unchanged his volume of purchases of all other commodities.

The income effect of a price change may under some circumstances have effects different from the price-substitution effects. If income increases significantly because

[1] J. R. Hicks, *Value and Capital—An Inquiry into Some Fundamental Principles of Economic Theory* (Oxford University Press, 1939), pp. 26–37.

111

the price of some major commodity drops, then this income effect must be corrected for, in order to ascertain the pure price effect.

The price-quantity aspects of demand are frequently supplemented, these days, by a consideration of income-quantity or income-price relationships. As the income of buyers or consumers rise, they will usually buy more or pay higher prices—or both buy more *and* pay higher prices—for many commodities or services. For some commodities and services this may not be true; their quantity or price or both decline, as consumer incomes rise. These are economically inferior goods. As family income rises, the housewife may buy fewer potatoes and less bread, and more fruits and vegetables, or less of the poorer cuts of meat and more of the better cuts. The income elasticity of demand may be greater or less than the price elasticity, or may be in the opposite direction. Thus, in a very poor country, a fall in the price of wheat or rice would surely be a stimulus to more consumption because of the price substitution effect, but the income effect of this price decline might lead many consumers to spend more for other foods, thus leading to a decline in the consumption or to a further decline in the price of the grain whose price fell initially.

It has become apparent in recent years that economics must include consideration of the credit elasticity of demand also. Any purchase item whose cost is large in comparison with periodic (daily, weekly, semimonthly, or monthly) income receipts must be paid for out of accumulated cash reserves or from loans. Nearly all owner-occupied housing in the United States today is purchased on a down payment and monthly payment basis, with down payments ranging from zero to 25 percent or more, length of loans ranging from 15 to 30 years, and interest rates ranging from $4\frac{1}{2}$ percent upward to perhaps 8 percent and more. But many consumer durables such as automobiles, television sets, and other household items are often bought "on time"—which means on loan. Often it is not the *cost* of the credit which influences such purchases—many purchasers are wholly ignorant of and unconcerned about the costs they are paying—it is the ease of getting the loan which counts. The demand for housing is particularly sensitive to the availability of credit, to the size of the down payment, and to a lesser extent to the interest rate or cost of the credit.

The long-run demand for raw suburban land is derived from the demand for improved building sites in suburbs, where streets have been laid out and built, where water supply and sewer lines have been installed, where other services are available in the community, and where the land has been subdivided from larger tracts or assembled from smaller tracts, in either case into units suitable for the proposed new use. The demand for improved building sites is, in turn, derived from the demand for housing, for retail and wholesale trade, for factories, and other potential suburban land uses. The demand for raw suburban land is thus derived from a demand which in turn is derived from a consumer or user demand. The decision-making unit for the buyer is the house; for the developer, the subdivision.

If various intermediate goods must be combined in fixed proportions in order to produce a consumer good, then obviously the quantity of each intermediate good varies proportionately with the quantity of the final good bought or consumed.

If the quantity taken of the consumer good changes, then the prices for the various intermediate goods will shift in inverse proportion to their elasticities of supply. Those goods whose supply is highly elastic will change in volume in proportion to the change in volume of the other inputs, but their prices will change relatively little; such input commodities will either be shifted to other uses or simply will not be produced at all. On the other hand, those inputs whose supply is highly inelastic must also shift in quantity in the same proportion as the other inputs, but their prices change greatly. If some input accounts for 20 percent of the total cost of some final commodity, and if all the other inputs have an infinite elasticity of supply, so that their volume can be reduced or increased without any change in their price, then reducing the price of the final product from 100 to 95 would be associated with a price reduction of this input from 20 to 15 or 25 percent (and similarly for an increase). The assumption of infinite elasticity for the other inputs may seem unrealistic, but different inputs do have different price elasticities. Labor under union contract, where the wage scale is fixed and the volume of employment varies as demand changes, is perhaps as nearly an example of infinite elasticity of supply of an input as one can find.[2]

In many cases, the proportions of the various inputs can be varied, at least within some limits. A shift in demand for the final product is reflected back to the various inputs differentially, not only as to their price but also as to their volume. To the extent that variations in input combinations are possible, differential shifts in their prices tend to encourage shifts in quantities of each used.

Demand for Housing

As far as we can ascertain, there have been few published studies which estimate the pure price elasticity of demand for housing, *all other factors remaining constant or unchanged*.[3] Several studies, referred to below, have dealt with income or credit elasticity of demand for housing, but none has considered the effect of price of housing upon quantity consumed or purchased. Other studies have been concerned with the income elasticity of expenditures for housing; expenditure is influenced by quantity and price combined. A number of reasons may underlie this apparent neglect, of which three reasons seem most important.

1. It would be extremely difficult to devise a significant measure of the "quantity" of housing bought or rented; and "price" without a quantity dimension is ambiguous or meaningless. The number of rooms is clearly not a suitable measure of quantity. Even disregarding factors such as variations in room size, or definitions of what constitutes separate rooms, a mere count of room numbers makes no

---

[2] Although expressed somewhat differently, these are basically the same ideas set forth by Alfred Marshall in *Principles of Economics* (8th ed., Macmillan, 1920). It will be recalled that Marshall drew some of his examples of derived demand from the building trades.

[3] Margaret G. Reid, *Housing and Income* (University of Chicago Press, 1962), explores in considerable detail the relationships between consumer income and expenditures on housing, and cites numerous references. Her treatment of the price of housing is brief. She concludes that such evidence as she can marshal suggests that the price elasticity of housing is not above —1.0 and is probably somewhat lower.

allowance for differences in quality of housing, differences which are very great indeed. A five-room tumbledown house is vastly different from a five-room luxury apartment. One measure of "quantity" of housing is the price paid for it. But one obviously could not use price as a measure of quantity of housing and then relate this to price paid; the correlation would be perfect but nonsensical. If the price of housing declined 10 percent or some other figure, all other factors remaining unchanged, by how much would the average family increase its "quantity" of housing purchased or rented? This is a question to which very little research has been directed.

2. The market for housing exhibits several peculiarities which make prices more unreliable for studies of demand than prices usually are for commercially traded products. There is little turnover; the stock of housing is large, annual additions are small, and even annual turnover in older housing is not large. A small rate of turnover would not, alone, invalidate the market price as a reliable measure. In the grain exchanges or on the stock exchange, for instance, the volume of turnover daily is small relative to the total volume of grain or of stocks; but every holder of grain or of stocks is also a buyer, to the extent that his reservaton price is at least as high as the market price. He may not sell, but he knows he could do so and what price he would receive. But many owners or occupiers of housing occupy their space for reasons of sentiment or inertia, or because they do not know the cost they might incur elsewhere for equal or better housing, or the price they could receive for their house if they decided to sell. The imperfection in the housing market or the lack of standardization in housing is a major factor here. One cannot seriously argue that the present dwelling space for most occupiers represents closely reasoned choice based on cost or price and of quantity purchased or consumed. Many racial groups have been denied the opportunity to buy housing they were willing and able to pay for.

3. It seems highly probable that the pure price elasticity of demand for housing is overwhelmed by income elasticities. The amount of space a family needs and the best location for that space depend greatly upon family size, stage in the life cycle, and other sociological factors. Housing is a major item in almost all family budgets and must compete with food and clothing as well as with many other lesser but often insistent items. All of these factors might well be much more powerful than any purely price-quantity relationships in housing demand, even if such price-quantity relations could be measured accurately.

In contrast to the paucity of studies on the net relationship between price of housing and the "quantity" consumed, there have been many studies of the relationship between income and housing expenditures. It has long been recognized in the formal economic literature as well as in more popular writings that low-income people pay a relatively high percentage of their income for housing and that, as income rises, the total amount paid annually for housing also rises but usually less than proportionately to the income changes.[4] There is also reason to believe that poor people, especially blacks, pay more to rent housing in relation to what

---

[4] See William L. C. Wheaton, Grace Milgrim, and Margy Ellin Meyerson, editors, *Urban Housing* (Free Press, 1966), particularly chapters by Maisel, Winnick, Guttentag, and Rapkin.

they get for their money, than do higher-income people. Their range of choice is less, and their bargaining power is weaker. If the percentage spent for housing remained constant at all income levels, this would imply a unitary income demand elasticity for housing; each proportionate change in income would be matched by an equal proportionate change in amount spent for housing. It is wholly conceivable that the proportion spent for housing might rise as income rose; this would mean an elasticity greater than one. In fact, the opposite seems to be the case. To the extent that housing is a necessity, expenditures for it may be highly inelastic, whether one considers either price or income. To the extent that high-quality housing is something of a luxury, then the price and income demand for it may be relatively elastic.

In this connection, some economists have differentiated sharply between actual income at any time (as annually) and the family concept of normal or permanent income. Friedman, the originator and most explicit advocate of this approach, contends that people spend, at least for many items, in terms of their expected future normal income, which he believes is but poorly correlated with their present or short-run income.[5] Reid points out that the various studies of the relation between income and housing have come up with elasticities ranging from nearly zero to more than 3.0. "The coefficients are relatively low where the income of [individual] consumers is the explanatory variable and relatively high where the average income of subsets is the explanatory variable."[6] She believes that housing expenditures are little affected by short-run changes in family income, whereas most income data report primarily such relatively short-term variations in income. She further believes that the income elasticity of demand for housing, if one uses some measure of long-term normal income or some approximation to Friedman's permanent income, is relatively high—at least 1.5 to 2.0, perhaps higher. To estimate the latter, she makes comparisons between different areas or places, recognizing that this in turn may introduce other complications.

Another way of looking at somewhat the same phenomena might be to distinguish between a gross or net income elasticity of demand for housing. The gross relationship would be simply the observed relation between family income and expenditure on housing, with no allowance for other factors. A net relationship might be estimated by comparing families of the same size, race, stage in the life cycle, education, occupation, and otherwise generally similar; the relation between their incomes and their expenditures on housing would thus remove the effect of these other variables.

Winger has done something akin to this.[7] His analysis states that an increase of $1,000 in annual income per adult equivalent member of the family is associated with an increase in number of rooms per such equivalent adult, as follows: for married couples over 65 years of age, .05; for married couples 45 to 65 years of age without children, .072; for couples of the same age but with children, .074; for

[5] Milton Friedman, *A Theory of Consumption* (Princeton University Press, 1957).

[6] Reid, *Housing and Income*, p. 375. By "subsets" Dr. Reid means averages of groups of consumers.

[7] Allan R. Winger, "Housing Space Demands: A Cross Section Analysis," *Land Economics* (February 1962).

married couples of less than 45 years age with no children, .132; for couples of the same age, with children under six years, .168; and for couples of the same age, with children over 6 years, .131. These data suggest that older couples and child-less couples are rather unresponsive to income changes, as far as housing is concerned; frequently, they prefer to continue where they are, even though they could afford something much better. On the other hand, younger couples, especially those with children, tend to expand their housing space when they can afford to do so. Winger's analysis uses annual income data, not any estimate of normal or permanent income. It uses number of rooms as a measure of housing, which may be a very poor measure of housing "quantity." Further, the form of Winger's equation requires a constant income elasticity of demand for each group, which may not be the case if income elasticity varies over the income range. However, his results do seem reasonable and important.

4. It is also obvious to anyone with even a moderate acquaintance with housing that the credit terms on which housing is available greatly affect the demand for it. Gelfand, in studying family budgets and housing preferences, imposed limitations of ready capital equal to the required down payment and ability to meet monthly payments without exceeding 24 percent of monthly income, in deciding what proportion of his sample was able to buy houses under other differing conditions.[8] When the down payment was lowered from ⅓ to ⅒ of the cost of the house, other factors remaining unchanged, the proportion of the families who could and would buy houses almost doubled. In contrast, lowering the interest rate from 6¼ percent to 3 percent, other factors remaining unchanged, increased the proportion of families who could and would buy houses by roughly 10 percent for those families who could manage the ⅓ down payment, up to as many as ¼ of those families who could manage only a ⅒ down payment. Lengthening the mortgage period from 25 to 40 years had still more modest effects upon the proportions of families who could and would buy houses. All of this suggests that the credit elasticity of demand for housing is moderately high.

All of the foregoing discussion in this section has related to housing—that is, to the structure and its site as a unit. It would be very useful for our purposes if we knew the houseowner's demand for *land* separately. How much more is he willing to pay for a large lot than for a small one, the structure being identical in each case? Some writers have argued that one way in which the higher incomes of suburbanites are used is in the form of greater "consumption" of land, or larger lots in relation to size and cost of house.

Once a family has bought a house, it can very seldom increase its acreage of land. This would be possible only if the land on one side were vacant, as would rarely be the case. Even in those rare instances, it may be impossible to buy only a small or marginal addition to the present area. When a family is buying a new house, it may be able to select among houses with lots of different sizes but with the same physical structure and with the same neighborhood characteristics. More commonly in practice, however, the more expensive structures tend to be on larger lots and in different kinds of neighborhoods, and a family might find it difficult

[8] Jack E. Gelfand, "The Credit Elasticity of Lower-Middle Income Housing Demand," *Land Economics* (November 1966).

to choose on the basis of lot size, all other factors being constant. Under these circumstances, it would be extremely difficult to measure the buyers' preferences for land as such. It might be argued that the size of lots used by the builders for houses of different size and cost reflects their estimate of buyers' demands for land; but this is at least doubtful. There has been virtually no research on the demand for suburban lot size, separate from the demand for suburban houses of different sizes and costs.

DEDUCTIVE DEMAND FOR SUBURBAN LAND

We do not know exactly the position and shape of the price, income, and credit demand curves for housing, nor do we know their elasticity exactly. It seems highly probable that there is not a single curve representing the relationship between each of these variables and the quantity of housing built or sold each year, but rather a family of such curves. Other factors, such as stage in the life cycle or size of family, may affect position, shape, and elasticity of each of these curves.

However, on the basis of generally accepted economic theory of rent, we can make some logical deductions as to the relative elasticity of demand for housing, for improved building lots, and for raw suburban land (Figure 10). These deductions flow out of the earlier discussion of the nature of derived demand. This is all built upon the theory that rent is, in effect, a residual—inputs other than land must be paid for at some incentive or alternative opportunity price, whereas land requires no incentive to be made to produce and that the residual income above other costs accrues to the owner of the land. The following section will show that this simple theory of rent is not adequate for raw suburban land whose ultimate development into one form or another of urban use seems probable.

The upper third of Figure 10 deals with the demand for housing. On the left is the relation between the quantity of housing (however this may be measured) and its price. On the right, the relation between income of prospective housing purchasers or renters and the quantity of housing, and also between the liberality of credit terms (without defining these further) and the quantity of housing. The price demand curve is moderately elastic through most of its range, but the degree of its elasticity is not critical to the analysis which follows.

On the income or credit demand curve, the response in terms of quantity is roughly twice the change in income or credit. The general shape of each curve seems reasonable, in light of such research as has been published; but the discussion which follows could readily be modified to accommodate any reasonable revision in these curves. The decision-making unit is the house, and the decision maker is the house buyer. While each might go elsewhere than the particular area or house under consideration, this would not necessarily change the shape of the curves. They may be as applicable on a whole suburban basis as for a particular subdivision.

The middle third of Figure 10 is concerned with the demand for improved building lots, without buildings but with streets laid out, graded, and paved, water and sewer lines installed, and other necessary improvements made. The cost of improved

I. DEMAND FOR HOUSING

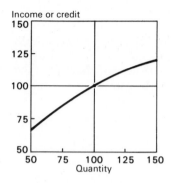

II. DEMAND FOR IMPROVED LOTS

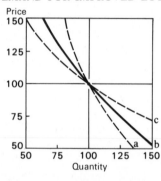

III. DEMAND FOR RAW SUBURBAN LAND

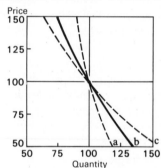

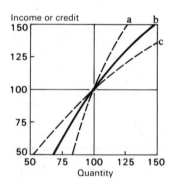

FIGURE 10.   Demand for housing, improved lots, and raw suburban land (deductive basis).

building lots has usually run between 12 and 20 percent of the price of a new
house and lot. A price relationship of this general order is assumed in this section
of the chart, but the chart would not be changed by modest differences in such
relation. Line c on both the left and the right parts of the middle section of the
figure is the same in position, shape, and elasticity as the demand curve in the
upper part of the chart. Line a in each half is drawn on the assumption that the
other inputs into the building of a house—labor, building material, etc.—are highly
but not completely elastic in supply. If they were completely elastic in supply,

Line a would be very much steeper in each case than it is shown on the figure. In each half of the middle third of the chart, Line b has been drawn approximately midway between Lines a and c. Line b could be somewhat steeper or somewhat flatter than is shown, as long as it falls between Lines a and c, without in any way disturbing the discussion which follows. Here and in the following paragraph, the decision-making unit is probably the subdivision and the decision maker is the builder.

The lower third of Figure 10 shows the demand for raw suburban land before the improvements noted above have been installed. In practice, the average cost of such improvements is approximately two-thirds of the value of the improved lot, but the discussion is not dependent on the precise magnitude of this difference. The costs of improvements are more or less constant, regardless of land prices. Again, Line c has the same position, shape, and elasticity as the intermediate demand curve (Line b) from the middle part of this chart. Line a is built on the assumption that the inputs required to convert raw land into improved lots (again, labor, machinery, materials, etc.) are more elastic in supply than is the land itself; and Line b is intermediate. As in the middle section, the precise position and shape of these curves is not critical to the discussion as long as their relative positions remain as in the figure.

On deductive grounds, a good case can be made for the position that the supply of the other factors that must be combined with raw land to produce improved lots, or must be combined with improved lots to produce houses, is relatively elastic. A major part of the costs in each case is labor, either directly or indirectly. To the extent that the wage scale tends to remain fixed or to move upward over a period of years, but not to vary readily upward and downward in response to short-term variations in demand, the volume of employment is the variable. Although prices of building materials vary and costs of using machinery also vary, each tends to be rather sticky, with more adjustment made in volume than in price of each.

The significant relationship in Figure 10 is that the demand for improved lots is more inelastic than the demand for housing, and that the demand for raw suburban land is more inelastic than that for improved lots. This relationship is inherent in neoclassical rent theory or in rent theory derived from it. As already noted, the exact relationship on each part of Figure 10 could vary considerably without disturbing this general conclusion; with perhaps equal logic, considerably more inelastic relationships might have been chosen. This analysis assumes that workers or the producers of other inputs must be rewarded for their efforts and that their labor or materials would not be forthcoming otherwise. This puts the bulk of the fluctuation in demand for the output (housing or improved lots) upon the price of the land (whether improved or raw).

Neoclassical rent theory assumes that land is used. This assumption is reasonably correct for agricultural land, as long as current operations produce any net rent; and neoclassical rent theory was originally developed for agricultural land. If an agricultural output is not secured each year from the land, that opportunity is gone forever; in this sense, agricultural output is "perishable." The owner and the renter may have expectations about future income and future rent which differ considerably from present income and present rent, but such expectations about the future do not affect present agricultural land use or its present rent. Undeveloped suburban land produces little or no current output of goods or services; its "output" is an expectation of a greater future value due to a different land use. If those expectations are realized, then the land is "producing" annually even if idle. It may, in fact, be producing more than if occupied, because idle land may be the more readily transferred to a new use. The postponability of the land use conversion introduces a new element into the demand for suburban land.

This analysis may be described as the demand approach to the pricing of suburban land. If this were the only lot of factors to be considered, then the general relationships shown in Figure 10 would probably be found in practice. One would not expect the quantities of raw land drawn into the development process to change much more than proportionately to changes in the total volume of new housing, but one would expect the prices of such land to vary widely in response to variations in the volume of housing (annually or for other moderately short periods of time). Even a casual acquaintance with the suburban land market is enough to reveal that this is not true. Hence it seems clear that other factors are operative to modify the simple relationships shown in this figure. The fact that other factors must be considered does not invalidate the demand curves; it simply says that, alone, they are insufficient. In order to provide a more nearly complete explanation of the market for raw suburban land, we must consider the structure of that market, and how the various operators in it actually react.

STRUCTURE OF THE MARKET FOR SUBURBAN LAND

Sales of land from previous owners to developers are a necessary part of suburban growth and development. The developer, in turn, sells the same land plus the house he has erected on it, to the home buyer. In the very simplest case, an operating farmer might sell his land to a developer who would build upon it. Unfortunately, there have been very few studies of transactions in suburban land. However, it seems probable that this type of simple land transfer is relatively uncommon. Much more typically, the land is sold by the farmer to a land dealer—who may be described by various terms, usually not well defined, of which "speculator" is a common one—and he in turn may sell it to other intermediaries, until at last it is sold to the man or firm that actually builds upon it. We have virtually no information as to the percentage of suburban land which goes through one, two, three, or more such transactions, on the volume of sale by typical operators or on who such people are. More, but still very little, information is available on the prices at which suburban land is sold at different stages in different metropolitan areas. Although purchases and sales of suburban land are an extremely important aspect of land use in the United States today, very little dependable information is available about them.

The size and shape of landownership units in suburban areas, prior to actual development, is largely a historical accident.[9] All land in the United States was once the property of some unit of government—colonies or proprietors for some

[9] Marion Clawson, "Urban Sprawl and Speculation in Suburban Land," *Land Economics* (May 1962).

Atlantic Coast states, the federal government for most of the country, and in some areas, states which received their land by federal grant. Such governments disposed of the land to private individuals under a wide variety of arrangements. The dominant use of those acquiring land on the first (government-private) transaction was for agriculture, although in some areas forestry was important. The economics of a frontier country, with ample land, scarce capital, and scarce manpower, led to the establishment of family-size farms on which the owner and a man or two could perform all the labor. There were many exceptions to this pattern, such as plantations in the South and larger ranches in the West; but the vast latifundia of Latin America have had little parallel in the United States. The essential point here is that the size of the landholdings which resulted from the original disposal from public to private hands, and the subsequent ownership history, would only by accident produce landownership units appropriate for the suburban land developer. When they are too small for an efficient housing, commercial, or industrial development, then a problem of land assembly arises; when they are too large, there is a problem of land subdivision. In either case, there is a definite role to be played by a dealer in land.

For suburban land, there is no organized market where tracts of land are bought and sold over a counter or in an organized exchange; nothing is remotely comparable to the stock exchange or to the various commodity exchanges. There is no "futures" market for land. The nearest approach to a futures market is the optioning of land by one individual from another; but this lacks most of the essential features of a true futures market. It is, indeed, hard to imagine how such an organized land exchange might operate, largely because land is not a standardized commodity. One tract of land may be a reasonably good substitute for another for some purposes, but more commonly each tract has peculiar characteristics which make it a wholly different commodity from another tract. Not the least of these peculiar characteristics is location; two tracts which are physically similar in other respects may differ greatly in value because of location.

Another factor which would inhibit the operation of a formal market for suburban land is that turnover in suburban land is relatively slow. From what limited information is available it can reasonably be argued that the time a tract is owned by each owner is usually to be measured in years or months, not in days or hours as in some exchanges. Partly because of the lack of standardization in land, but partly for other reasons as well, a sale-purchase of suburban land often takes some weeks or months to consummate; a quick forced sale is likely to bring a much lower price. A comprehensive theory of the suburban land market would have to include time as one variable.

Operators in any suburban land market may have a pretty fair idea of how much land is being sold, by whom and to whom, and at what price, although rumor and gossip are more prevalent than hard facts. Almost no information is readily available to the public on transactions in suburban land in any particular suburban area, let alone on a national basis. One suggestion for improving the suburbanization process, indeed, is for the compilation and publication of such information about suburban land transactions as can be obtained, including the making of outlook analyses on probable future demand.[10]

[10] Ibid.

The housing or other developer in a suburban area seeks a tract of land suited to his needs, in terms of size, location, price, installed public facilities, and zoning.[11] Different suburban house builders have different styles of operation, catering to different markets as well as operating on different scales. Hence, a suburban tract might be a good bargain to one developer but unsuited to the needs of another. Different suburban parts of a metropolitan area have different reputations as to social character, and this fact affects the price of the land as well as the kind of a house that will sell to best advantage. While one might expect that developers would make careful choices of sites, with rather close and exact calculations of costs and probable returns, Weiss and associates found that a considerable element of randomness seemed to enter into such decisions.[12] This may not be as irrational as it sounds. It may be that the developer "satisfices" rather than optimizes. That is, any tract which reasonably meets his needs may be satisfactory, with other elements of his business largely influencing his profits. The time and difficulty involved in trying to estimate which tract is absolutely best may not be worthwhile; the advantage of selecting a reasonably good tract and getting on with the job may more than offset any small disadvantage incurred by choosing something less than the very best.

If the actual developer represents the demand side of the suburban land equation, then the landowner represents the supply side. The most important single cost of landownership is the interest which could be earned by investing elsewhere the money that could be realized from the sale of the land. Another cost of landownership is taxes; there may be additional costs, such as upkeep of fences. If suburban land is actually farmed, then its owner has presumably not forfeited any income from the land, but is obtaining as much from it as economic and natural conditions will permit, but probably less than its holding costs. Even if the suburban land is idle, its owner may not have forfeited any income by its idleness; farming operations in many suburban areas simply do not pay, in part because suburban conditions impose many extra burdens on farmers. The income from forestry, as a use of land, is negligible in most suburban conditions. On the other hand, there are several advantages to the landowner in a suburban situation in keeping his land idle, the chief of which is that he is in a position to take quick advantage of a good opportunity to sell his land.

The extent of the tax cost on suburban land (idle or not) depends to a large extent on local millage rates and local assessment practices, particularly on the frequency of reassessment, a factor which is extremely important in a rising market. Some states, like Maryland and California make special legal provisions for assessing farm property at its use value for farming rather than at its full market value, if the latter includes some element of prospective future urban value. Aside

[11] F. Stuart Chapin, Jr. and Shirley F. Weiss, *Factors Influencing Land Development*, Institute for Research in Social Science, University of North Carolina, Chapel Hill, 1962. See also the various references in Chapter 5 above to Kaiser, Burby, and others working at the university.

[12] Shirley F. Weiss, Raymond J. Burby, and Newton W. Andrus, "Lake-Oriented Residential Subdivisions in North Carolina: Decision Factors and Policy Implications for Urban Growth Patterns," *Research Previews*, Institute for Research in Social Science, University of North Carolina (November 1967).

from these exceptions, all land—indeed all property—is supposed to be assessed at some specified fraction of full market value, the precise fraction varying from state to state. There are, however, wide variations in assessment procedures, not only as between governmental units but also as between properties within the same unit. Farm property and vacant or idle land is significantly under-assessed as compared with urban property.[13]

Millage rates for real estate taxes vary widely, from perhaps as little as 1 percent to 4 percent or more of assessed value, which in turn is a percentage of full market value. While this may seem a small amount in comparison with the value of the property, real estate taxes, as Netzer has pointed out, may amount to from 20 to 35 percent or more of the annual income from the property. If real estate taxes were levied as a tax on property income or rentals, it would be apparent that they are very high indeed. In the case of idle suburban land, where income is zero or negligible, then of course the real estate tax is infinite in comparison with income, even though modest in comparison with value. Real estate taxes on idle suburban land, even on the basis of full assessment, would not force such land into use immediately, but they could be a significant force over a period of years.

The appropriate interest charge on the realizable capital from the land depends on the opportunity cost of other investments, which in turn depends in large measure upon the owner's personal situation. If he is in a high-income tax bracket, he is anxious to secure capital gains, taxed at 25 percent, rather than pay a tax of 50 percent or more on other personal income. Thus a net return of as low as 3 or 4 percent on his investment may be rational for him. In this respect, ownership of suburban land may be similar to ownership of tax-exempt state or municipal bonds. On the other hand, if he is an operating farmer short of capital, who must practice capital-rationing, then an interest rate of 12 to 15 percent may be equally rational for his landholding operation. For most investors, capital in suburban land should earn 8 percent or more. Long-term investment in the stock market, with no more risk and with greater liquidity, can produce a return this high from current dividends and value appreciation, and much of such return would be capital gain with its attendant favorable tax treatment.

A suburban landowner is faced with carrying costs of such landownership on the one hand, and with the expectation of a future sale at a higher price on the other. He cannot be sure when he can sell for actual development or to another land dealer, or at how high a price he can sell. Different individuals may well have different expectations about the future date and future price; some may be much better informed than others, and some may simply be more optimistic. Some simple illustrations are shown in Figure 11. The low-holding-cost line is based upon a 3 percent interest rate and taxes at 0.5 percent of full value, with reassessment every 10 years. The high-holding-cost line is based upon interest at 6 percent, taxes at 2 percent of full market value, and reassessment every 5 years. It would not be irrational to use illustrations with still higher holding costs. Even at the low holding cost, the owner's investment nearly doubles in 20 years, and nearly quadruples in

[13] Dick Netzer, *Impact of the Property Tax—Effect on Housing, Urban Land Use, Local Government Finance*, National Commission on Urban Problems, Research Report No. 1 (U.S. Government Printing Office, 1968), p. 46.

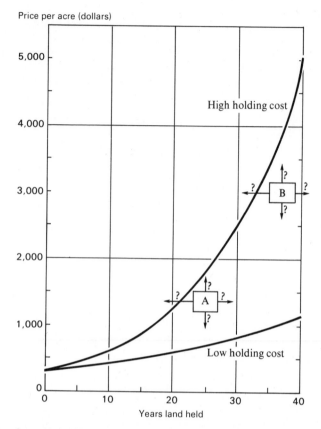

FIGURE 11.   Landowner's holding costs under alternative assumptions, and average prices received by farmers (A) and average prices paid by developers (B), raw suburban land.

40 years. At the high holding costs, investment is more than 4 times in 20 years and nearly 17 times in 40 years. By far the greater part of these investment costs are not out-of-pocket cash costs, but rather earnings forgone on the same investment if made elsewhere—but they are not less real for not being cash costs. If this land could have been farmed at a profit, then the holding costs would be reduced by the extent of the earnings attributable to land from the farming operation.

Schmid used $300 per acre as a reasonable estimate of the alternative use value of suburban land in farming. This is nearly double the average value of all farmland in the United States, but most cities are located in regions where farmland has a higher-than-average value.[14] He estimated that the average sale of suburban land for subdivision use, out of the farmer's hands, was at $1,332 per acre in 1961. The real question is, when can the farmer expect to make such a sale? Figure 11 shows this sale by the Block A, with the arrows and the question marks showing the uncertainty of both timing and price. If a farmer actually acquired land at $300 per acre, then he could bear the high land holding costs if he could sell for

[14] A. Allan Schmid, *Converting Land from Rural to Urban Uses* (Resources for the Future, 1968).

the price assumed in Figure 11 in 20 years; or he could bear the low holding costs for 40 years, if at the end of that time he could sell at the assumed price of Block A. These low holding costs are unlikely for most farmers, unless their farm operations are fairly profitable, since a rational interest rate for most farmers is well above 3 percent.

Schmid found further that the average price paid by developers for raw unimproved land was $3,030 per acre in 1964. If the land dealer who bought from the farmer at the average price of $1,332 per acre could sell this land at the average price of $3,030 per acre in 12 years, then the high holding costs could be met. The timing and price of sales to developers is shown in Block B in Figure 11, with arrows and question marks again suggesting its uncertainty. If the land dealer can operate on the low holding costs, then he can break even or better on a much longer period of holding. The costs shown on Figure 11 are cumulative costs at each date. The landowner, in deciding whether to sell or to hold, should consider only his marginal costs for the year or other period which he is considering in his calculations and weigh this against prospective price changes in that interval. The figure shows his profit and loss possibilities for the whole period.

Figure 11 suggests that holding suburban land for a rise in price may not be rational investment policy, at least not in all cases. The fact that the land is ultimately sold for *much* more than was paid for it is no evidence at all that it was a probably a losing one. A major consideration must be how long the land must be profitable deal. On the contrary, unless a great deal more is obtained, the deal was held to produce any specified gain in price per acre.

It seems fairly clear that the suburban land holder has a reservation price, below which he will not sell his land. It may be hard to ascertain just what this reservation price is; even the owner may not know until he has a firm offer in hand and time in which to think it over. The typical suburban landholder expects the price of his land to rise over time. This expectation has been met for nearly all metropolitan areas since World War II, and the likelihood is high that it will continue to be met for the indefinite future. The situation surely varies greatly from one SMSA to another and within SMSAs. The owner always has the option to hold his hand as well as to sell it if an offer is made by someone. Holding land is far from costless, if he takes account of his alternative opportunities; but his cash costs of holding are relatively low. Few suburban landholders are sensitive to short-run downward fluctuations in demand for their land. If housing demand is down, and thus what the developer could reasonably pay for raw land is down, most landholders will not accept a lower price but will simply hold for the day when they can get their price. It is the volume of sales which fluctuates in response to changes in demand, not the price of raw suburban land. A few landholders, it is true, may be overextended, having used short-run credit for land speculation, and they may be shaken out if demand for land is down. But the average suburban landholder is able to weather such periods of reduced demand. On the other hand, he may well respond to short-run increases in demand for housing and for buildable land by selling at what he considers is a good price.

The developer who must buy suburban land for his operations is in a relatively far weaker position. Many developers try to hold an inventory of some buildable land, perhaps enough for a year or two of operations, so that they are not at the mercy of landholders if demand does rise sharply. But, as noted previously, many developers have limited capital resources, and as an industry the residential builders operate primarily on credit rather than on equity capital. Hence, it often pays them better to use what capital they have in their building operations rather than to have it tied up in idle land. Moreover, holding land costs money; most land which a builder might hold for operations in the next few years is already at a relatively high price level, so that interest and tax costs are likely to be high. As a result, a large proportion of all developers are in the market for buildable suburban land more or less constantly, or at least frequently. With a construction organization, a labor supply, a sales organization, contacts with the public, and a general business momentum which must be maintained, they cannot well pause for a year or more to let the suburban land market settle down. If the demand for housing is strong, they are under considerable pressure to pay for buildable land whatever is necessary to buy it, and hope to pass the costs along to the home buyer. Schmid has noted that the cost of the lot as a percentage of the price of the finished house and lot rose from about 12 percent immediately after World War II to about 20 percent by the mid-1960s.[15] Within a considerable range, therefore, developers have been successful in passing higher land prices along to home buyers.

It was noted earlier that the accepted rent doctrine emphasized that land as a factor of production does not have to be rewarded in order to be used, that land tends to be the residual claimant of income after other inputs have been paid at their alternative use prices. This theory implicitly assumes the land will be used as long as rent is positive. We may amend this statement, for suburban land, to say that land may not need to be rewarded but the landowners must be. Suburban land need not be "used"; it may be appreciating in value as fast if idle as if used. As long as the landholder has a reservation price, which he has a reasonable expectation of achieving at some future date, he will not sell unless his price is met. In the past 20 years, prices of raw suburban land have reflected landowners' reservation prices far more than they have reflected year-to-year variations in demand for that land.

It should be clearer now why suburban land prices tend to ratchet upward. Landowners have reservation prices, below which they will not sell, but they are prepared to take advantages of higher prices. Developers will pay higher prices, perhaps reluctantly, rather than cease to operate, especially during periods of high demand for housing. The pressures are all upward, with no effective pressure leading to a reduction in land price. The uncertainty lies in how rapidly the upward pressures will be effective. The upward spiral of suburban land prices in the past was inevitable given the structure of the market; but the market structure, especially the tax factor, could be changed and a similar continuing rise in suburban land prices is no longer inevitable.

The nature of public services and the general role they play in suburban growth and development are discussed in Chapter 8. At this point it is sufficient to note that the public services provided—or the expectation that they will be provided—

15 Ibid., p. 8.

and the pricing methods for such services greatly affect the prices for developed suburban lots and for raw suburban land. One means of influencing prices of raw suburban land is in providing (or withholding) various public services and in pricing them.

SOME EMPIRICAL FINDINGS

At various points earlier in the chapter, reference has been made to a lack of information. But it would be a serious mistake to suggest that no studies have been made. Some indeed are available, although they do more to whet the appetite than to satisfy the desire for a reasonably complete understanding of the suburban land market.

It has long been accepted economic doctrine that land values within and adjacent to a city are partly a function of distance from the city center. The reason is primarily to be found in transportation costs. As land near the city center becomes fully utilized, people are forced to go farther and farther out; travel to the city center costs money and takes time; and one can afford to pay more for a closer site in order to avoid the travel costs. This theory is simpler and more accurate for older single-centered cities than it is for modern multi-centered cities. A considerable number of studies, theoretical or empirical or both, have dealt with this subject.

In such studies, as in virtually all others dealing with urban and suburban problems, the grain of the inquiry tends to affect the nature of the results. Stated in another way, the results depend in part upon the size of the area averaged within each measure of land value. If the values are for census tracts or larger areas, as is the case in some of the studies noted below, then a certain amount of "smoothing" of variations in land value has already occurred. If the values are by land parcel or tract, as in some of the other studies, then the extent of smoothing is very much less. A relatively coarse grain, or the smoothing of land values by relatively large areas, tends to iron out many of the variations within local business districts or within blocks.

Colin Clark, in a recent book, has summarized a large number of such studies in many cities around the world.[16] Almost without exception, they reveal the tendency for land use density and land value to decline with distance from the city center. Clark presents many numerical measures of the slope of this decline and of factors which affect it, as well as of the height of the central value. His review of numerous studies, including many which are not easily available to most researchers, is quite impressive evidence of the universality of this tendency. In the great majority of the studies, a single-centered city was studied and/or the formula for study required a single-centered city for measurement. The focus of nearly all these studies, and of Clark's review, is within the city, including its suburbs, rather than with land at or beyond the suburban fringe, which is the main focus of this inquiry.

[16] Colin Clark, *Population Growth and Land Use* (St. Martin's Press, 1968).

Muth used census tract data to establish a housing density gradient (and hence, inferentially, a land value gradient) from city center outward.[17] He found that such gradient was less when transport costs were low, when employment in outlying areas was high, and when city centers had deteriorated seriously. But he also found many variations between cities not accountable for by such an analysis. Seyfried, using assessed land values, found that land rents declined from the central core outward to the periphery in Seattle.[18] Brigham, using assessed land values, found that values per square foot along three rays or lines extending outward from the city center of Los Angeles declined with distance, although amenities, topography, and land use history were also significant factors.[19] Hoyt, in his classic study of the history of land values in Chicago, found that land values tended generally to decline as one moved outward from the city center, although there were many subsidiary centers where values were also relatively high.[20]

Wingo has developed a transportation-urban-land-value model and applied it to data for some cities.[21] He particularly introduces considerations of transportation technology and its effects upon travel time, translating data about travel time and costs (including value of the time of the persons concerned) into calculations of rational economic rent. This study is particularly useful in providing a theoretical and mathematical model for analysis of variables, especially transportation, which clearly have some role to play in land values.

None of these and certain similar studies was directed specifically toward land values in suburbs or in the outer suburban fringe. However, the same logic that underlies the relation between land prices and distance within a city should apply to surrounding lands. This is not to say that distance, even when measured in time rather than in miles, is the only, or even the chief, determinant of suburban land values. But it may well be one factor, sometimes a highly important one. If all other factors were equal, presumably anyone would prefer a closer-in location to one farther out, and the difference in transportation cost would presumably be a good measure of the difference in preference.

However, all factors other than distance are rarely equal. For one thing, as cities grow and subsidiary centers develop in the suburbs around the periphery, it is not clear to which center the distance factor should be referenced. In an older day, when employment and most shopping was downtown, the relationship was clearly from dwelling place to city center. But nowadays employment, shopping, and other attractions may also be in the suburbs. In any case, factors other than distance have always affected the desirability of location—the character of the neighborhood, various natural advantages of different sites, and the like. Moreover, in more recent times, distance as measured in miles has become less correlated with time and

---

[17] Richard F. Muth, "The Spatial Structure of the Housing Market" in *Proceedings of the Regional Science Association,* 1961.

[18] Warren R. Seyfried, "The Centrality of Urban Land Values," *Land Economics* (August 1963).

[19] Eugene F. Brigham, "The Determinants of Residential Land Values," *Land Economics* (November 1965).

[20] Homer Hoyt, *One Hundred Years of Land Values in Chicago* (University of Chicago Press, 1933).

[21] Lowdon Wingo, Jr., *Transportation and Urban Land* (Resources for the Future, 1961).

inconvenience of travel; beltways, expressways, and other improved travel facilities may make the more distant location closer in time than the area that is geographically closer. Furthermore, the much higher incomes of suburban residents in recent decades have almost surely made them less sensitive to relatively minor differences in travel costs between one location and another. For example, the difference in travel costs between a subdivision and one a mile farther out may not be decisive or even significant.

Moreover, it is not *present* conditions of travel, amenity, distance, and the like which are decisive in undeveloped suburban land values, but rather the consensus of informed expectations about *future* conditions. The present land price is the expected future land price, discounted back to a present price, with differing expectations of future date, future price, extent of risk, appropriate discount rate, varying costs of land holding, and other factors weighted according to the willingness of various landowners and dealers to put their money on the line to support their expectations. In one sense, of course, all property value is expected future value, for if we really believed the end of the world was tomorrow, no property would have much value. But the role of expectations, as contrasted with the role of presently enjoyed fruits, is greater for undeveloped suburban land than for most real estate.

Trends in suburban land values since World War II must be judged against the larger economic framework. This has been a period in which all property values have moved upward dramatically. Total values of all stocks traded on the organized exchanges, for instance, have moved upward irregularly but to a truly major extent in the postwar years. Personal incomes have also moved upward. For many purposes, it would be highly significant whether the movement in incomes had been greater than the movement in property values or vice versa. For our present purpose, it is not necessary to make such a comparison but only to state that each has moved upward greatly. Some of the increases in current prices merely reflect a changing value of the monetary unit, an inflation, but some is "real."

Using data collected by the periodic census of government on assessed values of property, corrected to an estimated full-value basis, Manvel has calculated that the market value of all real estate in the United States increased by more than 80 percent in the decade 1956–1966, measured in current dollars.[22] The rate of annual increase varied somewhat by type of property, averaging 6.9 percent. For "acreage" and farms, the comparable figure was 6.1 percent, and for vacant lots within urban settings it was 7.6 percent. The rise in land prices was somewhat greater than the rise in prices of structures on land. If adjusted for changes in the general price level, these increases would be substantially less, of course, but still significant.

Data on the value of farm land and buildings per acre, collected annually by the U.S. Department of Agriculture, reveal a continued and rather steady rise in prices beginning with 1955.[23] In only one year from 1955 to 1968 was the increase below

[22] Allen D. Manvel, "Trends in the Value of Real Estate and Land, 1956 to 1966" in *Three Land Research Studies*, National Commission on Urban Problems, Research Report No. 12 (U.S. Government Printing Office, 1968), pp. 1-2.

[23] See discussion in Marion Clawson, *Policy Directions for U.S. Agriculture: Long-Range Choices in Farming and Rural Living* (Johns Hopkins Press for Resources for the Future, 1968), pp. 233 ff.

4 percent, and in four years it exceeded 6 percent. This record is the more remarkable because this was a period of approximately constant total national net farm income, one in which the prospects for higher farm incomes in the future were not bright. The factors responsible for this marked and continued rise in prices of farm real estate need not concern us at this point.

The rise in suburban land values has a parallel in the rise of land prices in designated federal and state recreation or park areas.[24] Designation of any area for public acquisition as a park or recreation area invariably sets off an active land market, often with multiple sales and purchases of the same tracts. Purchasers know that the public agency will ultimately buy the land at the market price, whatever the latter may be; and the land often acquires a large increase in value for private ownership and occupation because of the park development. The cited report describes several instances of rapidly rising land prices in or adjacent to federal recreation and park areas. The rise in value of recreation land is in large part a function of the rising incomes, increased leisure, and improved mobility of population, the same basic factors which underlie much of the postwar suburban residential development.

The postwar changes in suburban land prices in the United States must be evaluated against this general background of rising general property values and rising land prices in general. It is not enough to note that suburban undeveloped land prices have risen. The critical question is: Have they risen more or less than other land prices and other property values? Unfortunately, practically none of the studies cited in the immediately following paragraphs faces this issue of rise in suburban land prices as compared with rises in other property values, but the data quoted may make such comparisons possible for others.

Two additional comments may be made here.

1. The rise in suburban land prices has often been a major factor in the rise of land prices for long distances away from the city. One farmer sells his land to a land speculator or dealer at a relatively high price, and with that capital is able to bid successfully for a farm, perhaps a larger and better one, somewhat farther away, and the farmer from whom he buys in turn is able to bid for still another farm in a still more remote location if he chooses to do so. Like ripples in the water created by dropping in a stone, the initial increase in land prices in a suburb or for purchase of a new park or a reservoir site tends to spread outward, diminishing in force but nevertheless noticeable for some distance.

2. Federal income tax provisions have often tended to stimulate dealings in suburban land. It is not only that increases in land values are usually capital gains, subject to a lower rate of taxes than many high-income individuals experience on some other types of income. Sellers often want to receive only part of the purchase price at the time of sale, because they can further reduce their tax liability in this way. But a modest down payment and time to pay the balance is obviously helpful to the purchaser also, and surely tends to increase the price he is willing to pay for the land.

Czamanski has shown that land values in Baltimore are related to past public

[24] Bureau of Outdoor Recreation, *Recreation Land Price Escalation* (U.S. Department of the Interior, 1967)

investments, among other factors, and that future public investments, in mass transit or other features, will have major effects upon private land values.[25]

Schmid has made a study dealing explicitly with the conversion of rural land to urban uses, including a consideration of land values, using such data as he could find.[26] The average market value of a building site for single-family homes, according to data from the Federal Housing Administration, rose from $761 in 1946 to $3,725 in early 1967; as a proportion of the total price of house and lot, these prices of building sites rose from 11.5 percent to 20.2 percent during the same years. The index of consumer prices rose from 68 to 108 (1957–59 base), and the average value of farm real estate rose from $54 to $157 per acre. The price of residential building lots rose more than construction costs of such buildings, more than the general price level, and more than the rise in farm real estate prices. While part of this rise in price of building sites for dwellings was due to somewhat larger lots in later years, and to somewhat greater costs of improvement, by far the greater part of the increase was due to increases in the price of raw land. Although a number of factors seem to be involved in such price rises, Schmid concludes from special studies which he summarizes that there seems to be "a large and growing residual land value contributing to high lot prices which is not explained by agricultural opportunity costs, lot size, improvement costs, or general inflation." He suggests that some of the differences in lot prices were related to differences in buyers' incomes.

Using admittedly imperfect data, Schmid calculates appreciation in value of suburban land over value of farmland plus costs of lot improvement; he concludes that it has been significant and is apparently increasing. In 1960, the farm value per lot was only $70, on a national average; improvement costs were estimated at $2,435 per lot, and appreciation at $351 per lot; the average selling price was $2,857 per lot. In 1964, farmland value per lot had risen to $84, improvement cost per lot was still estimated at $2,435, but sale price per lot had risen to $3,874, for an average appreciation of $1,356 per lot. Although the data are not perfect, great changes had almost certainly taken place, and there was great variation from city to city.

After reviewing all the available data, Schmid summarized the land price situation at various stages, as shown in Table 7. These data show that the total appreciation in land value above farmland value plus improvement cost of the lots, averaged $3,441 per acre, or a third of the selling price per improved lot. While these data had to be built up from various estimates, the general relationship seems correct.

Schmid was further able to obtain estimates of market prices of new lots as of 1950, and market prices for 10-year-old lots (as of 1960), for a number of cities. Assuming that prices at the latter date had been correctly foreseen in 1950, then the 1950 price should have been the 1960 price discounted back to the earlier date; or, alternatively, assuming that the 1950 price was a realistic one, the 1960 price would have represented additional holding costs for the decade. In fact, however, the

[25] Stanislaw Czamanski, "Effects of Public Investments on Urban Land Values," *Journal of the American Institute of Planners* (July 1966).
[26] Schmid, *Converting Land from Rural to Urban Uses.*

TABLE 7

LAND PRICES AT VARIOUS STAGES IN THE CONVERSION PROCESS: A COMPOSITE

	(Dollars per acre)
Farm land value (1964)	300
Price farmers received for subdivision use (1961)	1,332
Price paid by developers for raw land (1964)	3,030
Improvement cost ($2,435 × 2.6 lots/acre)	6,331
Selling price of improved lots (1964) ($3,874 × 2.6 lots/acre)	10,072
Total appreciation above farm land value (less improvement costs)	3,441
Percentage appreciation above farm land value	1,147%

Source: A. Allan Schmid, *Converting Land from Rural to Urban Uses* (Resources for the Future, 1968), p. 26. For sources of data see the original text.

1950 price plus carrying costs (6 percent interest) was realized in 1960 in nearly all cities and far exceeded in most of them. It would appear that, on the average, landholders in 1950 were not sufficiently optimistic about the trend in future land prices. Given this type of experience throughout most of the nation, the firm adherence of suburban landholders to a relatively high reservation price is wholly rational.

Harris and Allee made a study of the conversion of farmland to suburban land uses in Sacramento County, California.[27] Various parts of the county experienced rapid suburbanization after World War II. The timing of development in each area was due in part to the development of improved transportation into the capital city. Once development seemed imminent, land began to change hands rapidly and at sharply rising prices. Land dealers or "speculators" bought land from farmers, sometimes sold it among themselves, and ultimately sold it to actual developers at very much higher prices than had been paid to the farmers. The study covered a relatively short period from late 1958 to early 1961, when most of the sales were concentrated in one locality south of Sacramento. Construction of the last links in a freeway and of a lateral sewer line were at least partially responsible for the boom in land prices.

The authors were impressed with the fact that many sales took place which did not accurately represent land "values" in the sense that some seemed unrealistically high and others unrealistically low, each in view of the longer prospects for the area. Many land sales included a lot of credit, and prices were then higher than for cash sales. Access of tracts to improved highways and a few other observable facts accounted for some of the variation in prices received, but at least half of the latter were unexplained by any of the variables examined. Under these circumstances, data on price averages must be used with great care. However, on the average the net price increased about 16 percent per year.

In a very detailed study of the suburban land market, Milgram and Mansfield examined the suburbanization of an area of northeastern Philadelphia in the post-

[27] Curtis C. Harris, Jr., and David J. Allee, *Urbanization and Its Effects on Agriculture in Sacramento County, California: 2. Prices and Taxes of Agricultural Land*, Giannini Foundation Research Report No. 270, California Agricultural Experiment Station, University of California, 1963.

war years. At the close of World War II, about two-thirds of the area was in open land, mostly in tracts of 10 acres or more, but two-thirds of them less than 50 acres in size. The authors judge that most of the tracts studied were adequate for residential building operations without the necessity for land assembly. In 1945, most of the land had been acquired by its owners over a considerable period of years. During the postwar years, public transportation facilities were improved, trunk sewers were extended into the area, two new shopping centers were built. The area was ripe for development, and in fact development did proceed relatively rapidly. However, the proportion brought into active use in any year varied from 2 to 4 percent of the remaining open land, and in no year did it exceed 7 percent. Although a few large builders tended to dominate this development, a considerable number of smaller builders built at least some houses. Professional land dealers bought and sold a good deal of land, at one time owning as much as a fourth of all the open land. Although many dealers exchanged information and perhaps otherwise cooperated among themselves, yet there was a substantial degree of competition among them. Development proceeded somewhat irregularly, but throughout was most active in the undeveloped area on the fringe of the more intensively developed city.

Some of the open land, particularly that in various forms of institutional possession, did not turn over at all during these years; at least a quarter of the areas involved in sale and purchase were in transactions by other than the ultimate purchaser; and the average turnover per tract was 120 percent. Land approaching development was transacted in the same year or the year immediately prior to the beginning of construction at an annual rate of approximately a third of its acreage; in the period 2 or 3 years preceding development, the rate of transaction was one-quarter annually and in earlier years about one-sixth each year. Although some developers held land in reserve, many tended to buy land as they needed it.

For the whole period, prices for all land rose from $1,030 to $13,300 per acre, measured in terms of current prices. However, about half of this rise was due to a rising general price level, and some was also due to improvements placed on the land by owners. By means of multiple regression analysis, it was estimated that land, with individual land improvements in effect held constant, showed an annual increase of 13 percent in deflated dollars. The authors state that

> . . . the greatest increase in value was produced by the possibility of more intensive use, with land zoned for twin housing almost double and that zoned for row housing more than double the price of single-family land. Land with access to sewers similarly was just short of double the price of land without access.[28]

These latter comparisons make it clear that the value of public improvements was largely capitalized into private land values.

Mittelbach estimated an average annual increase of 10.7 percent in prices of raw land utilized for tract housing in the Los Angeles general area from 1946 to

---

[28] Grace Milgram, with the assistance of Christine Mansfield, *The City Expands: A Study of the Conversion of Land from Rural to Urban Use, Philadelphia, 1945–62.* (U.S. Government Printing Office, 1968), p. 7.

1959.[29] Maisel found an average annual increase in the value of raw land in the San Francisco region of more than 10 percent, for the 1950 to 1962 period, with the most rapid rate of increase near the end of the period.[30]

This section may perhaps be summarized briefly. Prices of suburban land have moved up briskly in the postwar period. The extent of the advance has apparently varied considerably from one SMSA to another and has probably varied much more from one tract of land to another within an SMSA. Much publicity has been focused on the cases of rapid rise in land prices, and the research has tended to focus on such situations. We know far less about the situations in which the rise in suburban land prices has been slow or halting. In general, it seems that the prices of suburban undeveloped land have moved upward somewhat faster than prices of all real estate or of all property—perhaps in the range of 10 to 15 percent annually as contrasted with 6 to 10 percent.

SPECULATION IN SUBURBAN LAND

In the United States, land has always been traded as if it were a commodity; speculation in land is deep in the American tradition and practice. Indeed, one primary motive for early colonization was the hope of major gains from land speculation, and throughout the era of massive land disposal in the 19th century, dealing in land and land speculation was rife.[31]

One may emphasize the pervasiveness of dealings and speculation and at the same time recognize that many people owned land primarily for other purposes and that their attitudes toward land were far different. Many farmers and others acquired land for homes as security, as well as to make money from use of such lands. The powerful appeal of free or cheap public land drew many immigrants to this country. Many people regarded land as something quite different from a commodity to be bought, sold, and speculated with.

In one sense, everyone who owns, buys, or sells land (with or without improvements) is a speculator. Land prices may go up or down, greatly modifying the value of the assets of the person concerned. Even if land prices rise over a period of years, if the rise was fairly well foreseen by many operators in the land market, an investment in land may not have been profitable because the purchase price at any date had already capitalized within it the expected future rise in price. Moreover, there have been many examples in American history when land prices fell, and still more examples when they rose too slowly to make an investment in land profitable.

[29] Frank S. Mittelbach, "Residential Land Values in Los Angeles County," *Appendix to the Report on Housing in California*, Governor's Advisory Commisson on Housing Problems, 1963.

[30] Sherman Maisel, "Background Information on Costs of Land for Single-Family Housing," in the same report.

[31] The literature about land settlement and disposal is very extensive, but two recent books deal at length and revealingly with speculation in public and other land on the frontier: Malcolm Rohrbough, *The Land Office Business—The Settlement and Administration of American Public Lands, 1789–1837* (Oxford University Press, 1968); and Paul W. Gates, with a chapter by Robert W. Swenson, *History of Public Land Law Development*, Public Land Law Review Commission (U.S. Government Printing Office, 1968).

In spite of its ubiquity, "speculation" has always had an emotional or moralistic connotation in the United States, and has been widely condemned in many aspects of life. Legislation against or for control of organized gambling has been enacted in most states and by the federal government. Legislation has also been enacted to regulate the various commodity markets (wheat, other grains, cotton, and so on) and the stock exchange and other security markets. Even land dealings have been regulated to a degree. In most states, real estate dealers must be licensed, and many types of actions are forbidden or are subjected to scrutiny of public agencies. But there is a widespread feeling that the land speculator reaps where he has not sown, that he benefits from public actions which enhance the value of the land in which he deals.[32] Throughout our history, there has been a good deal of moralistic disapproval of land speculation, even though it was very common.

Putting aside such moralistic concerns with speculation, and using the word very sparingly, we may examine briefly the roles of different landholders or dealers. At one end of the suburban land conversion process, there are farmers, forest landowners, and others whose primary motive in landownership is the use of the land as part of a productive process to earn a living. At the other end of the land conversion process, there is the homeowner whose motive in land and dwelling ownership is primarily the satisfactions that come from occupancy of the home. Each of these has some speculative aspects, but the primary motive is the flow of goods and services from production or consumption processes in which land is a critical part. Between these two ends of the suburban land conversion process lie a number of landowners and dealers, about whom we know very little. For at least some of them, the primary purpose of landownership is the possibility of gain from a rise in price of the land; but others own land primarily as part of a production process, such as the construction of dwellings.

Intermediate landowners as a group may perform one or more of a number of functions, although perhaps few if any individuals perform all of the following:

1. They communicate demand signals, from production or consumption sectors which demand land, to present landowners. They do this by bidding up land prices. They seek to buy cheap and sell dear, but this is the age-old role of the dealer in every commodity. By bidding up the prices of farm and other land, they facilitate its conversion to other uses.

2. They help to ration land (in the economic sense of the term) to its highest and most valuable use. They do this by making the land too costly for anyone to use it for less valuable uses. While the dealers' actions may seem harsh to those

[32] Two recent publications, each representing the views of influential groups, have emphasized this point anew, and as applied to suburban land. The National Commission on Urban Problems, in its final report, *Building the American City* (U.S. Government Printing Office, 1968), emphasizes in Chapter 6 that "land value results largely from social and governmental factors" and recommends studies aimed at public capture of some of the values so created; and the statement of supplementary views by four members of the Commission goes much further. *Nation's Cities* (March 1969) has a long article representing the position of the National League of Cities on this matter, stating (p. 37) that " by definition, the value of unimproved urban and suburban land is created not by anything the owners have done to improve it, but by an enormous investment of other peoples' money to build the community around it and an enormous investment of other taxpayers' money to provide the infrastructure," and going on to propose ways in which some of the increases in value could be captured for public benefit.

who would like to build lower-cost housing on cheaper sites, this type of rationing is widespread through the economic system, and it is easy to develop an economic rationale for it. For example, if some land has real value as the site for a new shopping center, this type of bidding up of land values will prevent its use for single-family housing.

3. They may assemble several small tracts into one larger one or divide a large tract into several smaller ones, in each case trying to change an unsuitable land-ownership pattern into one more suitable for the new use. In many types of land use situation, as well as in growing suburbs, the specialized land dealer has been able to assemble or subdivide land more efficiently than either the old or the new owners could do.

4. Land dealers may provide a ready stock of land, from which the developer or other person needing land may select what he needs, in the same way that any wholesaler provides a stock for retailers.

5. The land dealer may bear some risks or some uncertainties involved in suburban land development. As previously noted, the time at which land will be taken into use and the price at which it will be sold for that use are or may be most uncertain. A specialized land dealer may have a better idea than either the present landowner or the future owner; his bids for land, or his willingness to sell land he owns, may help greatly to determine the price. Presumably, the price which best reflects the future income stream from the land is determined by economic conditions of various kinds, but the dealer may help translate those conditions into a price per acre. In this risk-bearing role, both the specialized land dealer and others are handicapped by the lack of any organized market in land futures.

Even if one accepts the proposition that the land dealer performs useful functions, and if one is not morally or ideologically opposed to speculation in land, still it is both possible and proper to raise a number of questions about the land conversion or transfer process and the role which land dealers play in it.

1. Does the present system work reasonably well, given its own ends and given the general economic and institutional structure within which it operates? Does land get transferred efficiently from those who have owned it to those who can best afford to pay for it? Is suburban development facilitated or retarded by the operations of the suburban land market, in which land dealers are an essential part? Is the final form of the suburban development adversely affected in any way by the operations of the land market, as such?

2. Does the present system reward antisocial or devious acts, such as bribery, fraud, and the like? As noted in Chapter 5, there is a marked playback from the private regulated sector in suburban development to the public land-regulating mechanism. There is a widespread belief that land dealers attempt to influence zoning and other decisions of public bodies, and bribery certainly is not unknown. Are these illegal or undesirable actions so common as to constitute a serious deficiency in the land market as such? Or do they require such strenuous efforts at detection and prevention as to incur unreasonable costs?

3. Is the present suburban land market too costly, in the sense that too much manpower is engaged in its operation in relation to the results it achieves? Even if one concedes that specialized speculators are productive, it does not follow that

all of them or all of their actions are productive enough to offset the real costs involved.

4. Would some other system or structure for the suburban land market work better? Might there be extensive public operation of the suburban land market, with some governmental unit or corporation buying and selling land? Or might something different work still better?

5. Is there some way that the gains in land value, arising out of public investments and public actions, might be captured for the same general public?

The two latter points will be discussed in later chapters, and alternative ways of guiding or influencing future urban growth will be considered.

Direct Public Intervention in the Suburban Land Market

All of the foregoing analysis is concerned with an essentially private market in suburban land. Various public actions, such as the provision of roads, schools, and sewers, or the establishment of a mortgage discount rate, may affect land prices in that private market, and there will be limited direct public intervention, to purchase school sites or parks, or in other ways. But these indirect and small direct interventions do not essentially reduce the basically private nature of the market for suburban land.

Suppose, however, that some public agency or public body intervened in the private market for suburban land by buying substantial acreages of land which might be used to provide permanent open space or leased or sold to private parties for development. Major economic consequences would flow from such public acquisition of land.

1. The price of the land purchased would rise, compared to its preprogram price or compared to appraised land prices. The public body buying land would be a new force in the demand side of the equation for suburban land. The precise effect of the public purchase program would depend upon how much land was bought, when it was bought in relation to suburban land conversion, how rapidly the program moved, how urgently the public agency moved to bid up and acquire land, and other factors. It is easy to conceive of circumstances under which the effect of the public purchase program would have a major effect on the prices paid for the land bought. This effect of public purchase upon land prices is often responsible for the fact that the final costs of a park or other public land purchase programs is so much higher than the original estimate. Escalation in final costs over initial estimates is often cited as evidence that the original appraisals were too low; but, even when they were quite correct, the very fact of the public purchase pushed up land prices.

2. The prices of land *not* bought by the public agency will rise too. This is inherent in the concept of a market—transactions in one part of it are quickly felt in other parts. As the public purchase program takes some readily available land off the market, private purchasers must bid higher for what is left to induce other landowners to offer their lands. The expectations of the landowners as to the future course of land prices will change and as a consequence their reservation

prices will rise also. Since the market for suburban land is not perfect in the economist's sense of the term, the impetus from public purchase might spread somewhat erratically to the private sector. The full effect of the public purchase might not be felt immediately, but rumors might well lead to exaggerated expectations about the course of future events and even small public purchases might have a very large effect on private land prices. It is conceivable, but generally improbable, that public purchase of land on one side of a metropolitan area would lower land prices on another side because people would regard development here as less probable. But the overall effect of public land purchase on prices of land not bought would always be positive.

A crucial question here is: What is the elasticity of demand and of supply for buildable suburban land? Will taking 5 percent of the potential supply off the market affect the price per acre of the remaining supply by more or less than 5 percent? At this stage of national knowledge, we must simply say that we do not know. Intuitively, one would expect that both the demand for and the supply of suburban land are rather highly inelastic. The fact that the demand for raw suburban land is derived from a derived demand would surely suggest this. The fact that land, even at present levels of cost, is still only one component of finished house prices, suggests the same.

3. The assessed value of undeveloped land not purchased by the public agency *should* rise proportionately to the increase in sales prices and in reservation prices for such land. After all, assessed values are supposed to be some fraction of market values; and, if the latter rises, so should the assessed value and in the same proportion. Whether assessed values of undeveloped land will actually rise at all, or by this amount, depends upon the structure of local government and its assessment procedures, which are notoriously variable from one unit of local government to another and typically result in underassessment. Even underassessment, if constant, would not preclude increases in assessed values. It has been suggested that the law of constant cheating is widely applicable and that the divergence from standard may not be greater at one time than at another.

To the extent that assessed values of remaining privately owned undeveloped suburban land did rise, the local government would benefit from higher tax revenues from such land. If the elasticity of demand for undeveloped suburban land is no greater than -1.0, and if the rise in market prices is carried over into new assessed values, then the local government might secure as much revenue as before, although now from a smaller acreage. In such a case, local government revenues would not be affected by public land purchase on any scale. It might well be, of course, that elasticity would approach unity for some ranges of a public land purchase program but would be less at other ranges. If the demand for undeveloped suburban land is highly inelastic, then it is possible that the increase in tax revenue would amortize the land purchase program over a period of years, so that in the long run the purchase of land by a local jurisdiction that taxes real estate would be costless. These comparisons illustrate the policy significance of estimates of the elasticity of demand and of supply for undeveloped suburban land.

4. The program for making the publicly purchased land available for private development might be crucial, not only in terms of the direction and character of

suburban development but also of land prices. The scale of the public purchases, in relation to the total suburban area, would be highly important. At one extreme, public purchase and release of land for private development could dominate suburban land conversion; at another scale, its effects would be less, perhaps not really important. The acquired land could be released to private developers on long-term leases or by sale. Many important policy issues here are explored more fully in Chapter 18. It is altogether possible that public purchase and sale to private developers could have a net dampening effect upon land prices, if that were desired; or the public agency could seek to disturb the private land market as little as possible and to obtain a profit from its land operations. In any case, the land purchase side of its operations must be viewed in combination with the land disposal aspects.

It is certainly within the range of possibility that a unit of local government, with power to levy taxes on real estate and with competence to appraise such land at a high and constant proportion of full value, even when the latter rises rapidly, and with access to the capital markets for funds at reasonable interest rates might be able to acquire substantial areas of undeveloped suburban land essentially without cost to it in the long run. This possibility of gain is more or less independent of the issue of whether the land so acquired is to be permanent open space or whether it is to be later sold or leased for private development, in which case the unit of government would benefit from prices paid by private developers. A unit of local government might employ such a program as suggested here to prevent private development in certain areas, thereby forcing it to proceed elsewhere within the same SMSA. This might well lead to substantial savings to society as a whole, in the provision of public services for more fully settled areas.

A study along this line has been made of the San Francisco Bay region, with some very interesting results.[33] The costs of acquiring all recommended open space areas would approach $2 billion. This estimate was based on present appraised values and probably is too low, for as any public agency began to buy, land prices would probably move upward. Savings in the installation of gas, electricity, water, and telephone services alone would amount to more than 40 percent of the estimated acquisition costs, since development would be somewhat more clustered and somewhat less sprawled. Savings in government operating costs, plus revenues from leasing the acquired lands for uses compatible with their permanent open space role, would offset large additional amounts of the land cost. The San Francisco study made no effort to measure the impact of the purchase program on the prices of land not bought or on tax revenues arising out of such increased land prices, but these would be substantial, quite possibly enough to offset much or all the acquisition cost of the land. The study did explore other means of retaining the desired lands in permanent open space—a combination of purchase and zoning, possibly with compensable zoning arrangements. The real significance of the study is its demonstration that open space produces benefits as well as costs, and that net costs may be low or negative. It illustrates how such matters can be studied and quantitatively appraised.

[33] People for Open Space, *Economic Impact of a Regional Open Space Program* (San Francisco: People for Open Space, 126 Post Street, 1969).

This illustration has been carried forward in terms of public purchase of a fee simple ownership of undeveloped suburban land. But the same general relationships would exist for the purchase of development rights to such land. There would be additional complexities to such a program which would be extremely important in practice but do not affect the analysis here. If development rights were purchased for land nearly ripe for development, then the price per acre would presumably be high but the effect of purchasing such rights for a given acreage would be relatively great. If the development rights were purchased for land unlikely to be developed for a long time, then the cost per acre would be much less and the effect on the remaining private lands would be much less. If a system of compensable zoning were inaugurated, the effect on values of land unaffected by such zoning would depend in large part upon the areas and precise terms involved.

The essential point of this section is that direct public intervention in what is otherwise basically a private market for suburban land has various economic consequences. There are values to be gained, as well as costs to be paid, and no one can say in advance, without detailed specification of the nature and scope of the public intervention, how the costs and values will compare.

What Difference Does It Make?

The way in which the various factors in the suburban land market are combined results, almost inevitably, in hit-or-miss suburban development with consequences that may be both esthetically and economically undesirable. This kind of market is associated with, if it does not directly contribute to, the form of land use known as urban sprawl. A good many observers have found the results less than lovely. Moreover, spotty development leads to higher costs for public services, since sewers and the like must cross idle land between settlements.

Probably the most serious consequences of the form of the suburban land market are social. The market tends to push up the price of raw land dollar by dollar as more and more speculation occurs, to levels beyond those explainable in terms of alternative use values of the land plus costs of development. The home buyer, of course, must buy the whole package, including the lot on which his house is built. If the lot price inches up, the kind of house that can profitably be built on it rises even faster, since the cost of the site is only a fifth or a fourth of the total sales price of the finished house. The climb in the cost of suburban housing that comes from rising land costs thus helps to price it out of the reach of low-income families.

Esthetic, economic, and social consequences of the form of the suburban land market will be evaluated in Part III of this book.

PU8LIC SERVICES FOR
SUBURBAN AREAS

The purpose of this chapter is to explore the nature and the role of public services needed or demanded by new residents of suburban developments. The following pages will do so in more detail than was possible earlier in the book.

KINDS OF PUBLIC SERVICE

The term "public service" is used here to mean any kind of social or economic service to a suburbanite which is frequently, but not invariably, provided by some unit of government. Schools are one form of public service, although of course there are private schools. The services considered can nearly always be provided most economically for units far larger than the individual household. For example, there are great economies of scale in a sewer system, but a septic tank can be used to dispose of a single family's sewage. Likewise, household water supply can often be provided most economically for a whole suburb or for an even larger urban complex, yet some householders are served by individual wells.

Waste Disposal

Waste disposal is a basic requirement for all residents in a suburban area. At least three major kinds of waste must be disposed of: water-borne household wastes, solid wastes, and natural waste waters. In the typical modern American home, each member of the family wants to flush down the toilet or down the sink any kind of waste that can be accommodated physically, whenever he desires to do so. This includes personal and household wastes of many kinds. The volume of such wastes per capita is rising rather sharply. Indeed, the amount of wastes a community has to dispose of is one index of its level of living. Health regulations, as well as the personal tastes of the average householder, require such wastes to be carried away quickly, though what happens to them once they are out of sight is often ignored.

The average American home also has a substantial volume of solid wastes to dispose of. Newspapers and magazines may easily amount to a ton a year in many homes. Other household paper, primarily wrappings or containers of various kinds,

141

must also be got rid of. Then there are many food containers—the nonreturnable bottle adds greatly to the weight and volume of such solid wastes—and garbage in the strict sense of the term—food scraps, inedible portions of purchased foods, and the like. In the average suburban single-family home, the volume of yard trash—cuttings from shrubs and trees, grass, weeds, and the like—may be substantial. The average suburbanite is unhappy if his vegetation does not grow; but when it does grow, he energetically cuts it back and expects someone to pick up the cuttings promptly. All of this must be hauled away from the individual home to be disposed of elsewhere.

In nearly all suburban sites in the United States, even those in arid areas, there will be waste water to be disposed of during and after hard storms. The rate at which rain falls in the United States is so rapid, in comparison with the British Isles or most of western Europe, that not all the water can infiltrate the soil as fast as it falls. The surplus water disposal problem is always more serious here, even in a completely undisturbed watershed. The process of urban growth means that a substantial proportion of the land surface—a third or more, in some cases—is rendered impervious because it is a paved street, a rooftop, or similar surface. The whole water regime is changed as a result; peak flood flows are increased greatly and must be carried off to prevent local damage. This type of public service is essential in nearly all suburbs. Sometimes neglected in the design and initial construction, it must be provided later, often at high cost.

Water and Other Utilities

Water supply is another essential service in suburban areas. Water is essential in many household uses, as well as for drinking. Wastes are often carried away by running water. The family requires water to bathe in, to wash clothes and dishes, and for many other personal uses. A substantial volume may be used to sprinkle yards, especially in dry climates. Americans demand that the entire water supply be suitable for drinking, in spite of the fact that only a very small percentage of it is used for this purpose. The water must not only be safe, in the sense that it must be reasonably free of pathogens, but it must also appear attractive. Some years ago, when detergents were typically "hard"—i.e., nondegradable—and persisted in water for long periods of time, water might foam somewhat as it came out of the faucet. Very minute amounts, less than 1 part per million, of such detergents would cause foaming. Many people objected, some rather violently, to such foaming water in spite of the fact that the public health authorities were unable to measure any adverse effect from drinking it, although it did kill the bacteria needed to decompose materials in septic tanks.

Other utilities, such as electricity, gas, and telephone are also essential for modern living and are in demand in new subdivisions. All of these utilities except gas are nearly ubiquitous in the United States today.

Transportation Facilities

As noted many times in earlier chapters, transportation facilities are critical to suburban development. The suburb, almost by definition, is not an economically self-contained area, and transportation is economically necessary. Within the subdivision, the transportation facilities include paved streets, curbs and gutters, and sometimes sidewalks. While there was a time in recent history when a family might move into a new suburb before the streets were paved, today a builder would be seriously prejudicing his sale of houses if he failed to pave the streets before putting his houses on the market. But transportation is needed from the subdivision to the suburb of which it is a part, as well as from the latter to other suburbs and to the city center.

Transportation facilities differ greatly in the speed and comfort with which they can be used and in the volume of traffic which they can handle. Reasonably accessible public transportation, usually in the form of busses, is an asset to a new residential subdivision but hardly an absolute requirement in the United States today.

Schools

Facilities for education are necessary for modern suburban living, since a large share of all families who locate in suburbs have children of school age. Schools at the elementary and secondary levels must be available. Ideally, the system should include higher education, adult education, and education for special groups—the retarded, the handicapped, and the gifted. But it is not enough to have a high school. Does it offer Spanish, Russian, and Chinese, as well as the traditional French?

The location of the school in reference to the home is critical. The school need not be within the subdivision, but an elementary school should be within easy walking distance or within a reasonably short bus ride. The higher the level of the school, the farther away it can be from the homes of students, but even the high school should not be too distant. Colleges within commuting distance are being developed increasingly, primarily to serve those who cannot afford to leave home to get a college education.

Recreation

Recreation in several different forms is a valued public service in most suburban areas. Playgrounds, at the schools or elsewhere, are needed for children; so are various kinds of organized recreation activities, especially in summer; so are swimming pools, close enough to home that children can walk to them. Local parks, even if small, may add considerably to the amenities of life in a suburb or subdivision. City, metropolitan, and regional parks are also valuable, but would normally be so located as to require travel from the subdivision. The character of local transport facilities, and hence the travel time required, are more important for such areas than their exact location. The requirements of vacation recreation areas are even more flexible.

Public Safety and Health Services

Fire protection is another public service essential for a new subdivision. This usually means a fire station not too far away, which in turn has working arrangements with other fire-fighting organizations for help in emergency situations. The ready availability of fire hydrants and the existence of ample water at adequate pressure are also factors in fire protection. The character of the fire protection service is likely to be reflected directly in the rates for fire insurance, which usually are part of the monthly payment on the suburbanite's house.

All of the foregoing public services needed by a new resident in a new subdivision tend to have sharp locational characteristics; to be useful, they must be available just where needed. There are differences among them, of course; the water supply and waste disposal services must be available within every house, while the school may be a few blocks away. For other public services that are necessary for modern living locational requirements are not so strict, since travel to them would be necessary in nearly every case and a little additional travel might not be important. These include health services—hospitals and clinics as well as access to private practitioners. Distance and convenience of travel to such facilities are not so important as with fire protection, except in emergencies. Police protection too is necessary, but it can be provided from a central headquarters some distance away from the subdivision. Such governmental functions as tax assessment and collection, public welfare, maintenance of land records, courts, and others are also essential to a subdivision but may be located at some distance from it. The occupant of the new subdivision will almost surely have one or more automobiles and can travel modest distances for such services.

WHO PROVIDES PUBLIC SERVICES?

It is usually assumed that whatever agency provides a public service decides when and how it shall be provided. Who actually makes the decision, and what influences it, are much more complicated matters. This section will consider the roles which various governments or groups play in providing the services discussed above.

There is considerable variation, from one metropolitan area to another, in the unit of local government which performs different public service functions of the type discussed in this chapter.[1] These services have been ranked according to the degree to which they are customarily local as contrasted to areawide in provision (see Table 8). For any given function this depends upon the economies of scale in its performance, and upon various political factors such as competency and legal powers of the different governments, according to this analysis.

[1] See two publications of the Advisory Commission on Intergovernmental Relations: *Intergovernmental Responsibilities for Water Supply and Sewage Disposal in Metropolitan Areas* (U.S. Government Printing Office, 1962), and *Performance of Urban Functions: Local and Areawide* (U.S. Government Printing Office, 1963).

TABLE 8

RANK ORDER OF URBAN FUNCTIONS ACCORDING TO LOCAL-AREAWIDE CRITERIA

	Rank	Function
	1	Fire protection
	2	Public education
	3	Refuse collection and disposal
Most	4	Libraries
local	5	Police
	6	Health
	7	Urban renewal
	8	Housing
	9	Parks and recreation
	10	Public welfare
	11	Hospitals and medical care facilities
	12	Transportation
Least	13	Planning
local	14	Water supply and sewage disposal
	15	Air pollution control

Source: John C. Bollens and Henry J. Schmandt, *The Metropolis—Its People, Politics and Economic Life* (Harper & Row, 1965), p. 312. Based upon data and discussion in Advisory Commission on Intergovernmental Relations, *Performance of Urban Functions: Local and Areawide* (U.S. Government Printing Office, 1963).

The Householder

The householder can do very little to supply any of these "public services" for himself. If local regulations permit or require him to do so, he may burn some of the burnable household wastes on his own premises, thereby relieving any public agency of responsibility for collection, but at a real cost of a considerable air pollution. He may have his own septic tank for disposal of household flushable wastes and/or his own well for water supply. But these actually reflect the decisions of the builder and local governments, for they are almost always installed before the house is offered for sale. The typical suburbanite will own his own car—probably more than one if he lives in an outlying area where public transport is not available—which can be operated only on the streets and roads provided by someone else. A householder might develop yard and home recreation, to offset in some degree a lack or shortage of public recreation facilities in the community. But, all in all, the role that the householder can play in providing the range of services under discussion is very small.

The Builder

The builder of the suburban development can play a larger but still somewhat limited role in the provision of public services. Increasingly, builders are urged or required to provide transportation facilities within their subdivisions by grading and paving streets, by installing curbs and gutters, and by building sidewalks (if the design calls for them). The cost of constructing these transport facilities is included in the purchase price of the house and lot and hence is paid for by the new purchaser; but the decision to build and the specifications of the works are the decision of the builder, subject to ordinances and regulations of local government.

If the area relies upon septic tanks for disposal of flushable wastes and/or upon wells as a source of water, the builder ordinarily decides to install them. In most subdivisions, he will be required to connect the house to the nearest public sewer and water lines. If these lines run up the street of his subdivision, then installation is a simple matter; but if they lie at the edge or beyond the boundaries of his sub-division, then connections are more expensive to make. In large but relatively dis-tant subdivisions, the builder may construct his own sewage treatment works under regulation of appropriate government agencies. The buyers of homes in sub-divisions usually pay, in one way or another, for sewer installations. The builder may be required by local government to install storm drains and storm sewers to take care of excess water, but in many subdivisions he seems to have evaded this responsibility, leaving the construction of such facilities for later, when the need has become painfully apparent, to be done by some unit of government.

Finally, the builder may construct an artificial lake as an amenity attraction for his subdivision and as a place of recreation for its residents. Such lakes have been quite popular in many areas. But there is grave danger that a buildup of plant nutrients will lead in time to a growth of foul-smelling algae, so that the lake which started out as an attraction becomes a nuisance.

Utility Companies

Utility companies normally provide the electricity, gas, and telephone service desired by the new suburbanite, although sometimes these are provided by local government or by cooperatives. These private companies, which are monopolies in their service areas, operate under public regulation. Today, such companies are eager for new business and readily extend their services to new subdivisions. The suburbanite pays for these facilities in the long run through the rates he pays, although it is by no means clear that the new outlying customer pays all the extra costs of his service.

General Local Government

General local government provides many of the public services needed by the new suburbanite. If the subdivision is within a legal city, the unit of local govern-ment may be the city, but in many instances the subdivision lies beyond the bound-ary of any city. In New England, the unit of local government may be the "town," which includes much open country as well as the built-up area. Often the unit of local government will be the county.

Such local governments will almost surely provide transportation facilities (streets and roads) outside of the subdivision, and they may also provide streets and associated works within it.

They may or may not provide educational facilities, but these are more generally provided by a type of special governmental district which is considered subsequently. Similarly, sewerage and water supply may be provided by general local government or by special districts. Cities own their sewer and water systems more frequently than do counties. Counties are likely to supply local types of recreation and local parks. They may operate a recreation department, often for the children and youth of their area. Public parks physically within the legal limits of a city are nearly always owned and managed by the city. Some cities have parks outside of their legal boundaries. Some state parks are located within suburbanizing counties. The general local government will almost surely provide police and fire protection for the new suburbs, although the fire department may be manned largely by volunteer firefighters.

Special Districts

Special districts for the provision of one or more of these public services exist, and in fact are proliferating in urban areas generally, including suburban areas. Wood calls the formation of these districts "the outright creation of new governments. Essentially, this amounts to a double-tapping of the same revenue base by simply establishing another governmental layer. The usual form is the special district established to provide a single public service, and the revenue source may either be property taxation or a user charge."[2]

The Committee for Economic Development, using census information, says of special districts:

> Of all forms of local government, special districts have grown most rapidly in numbers in recent years. Many metropolitan area residents live under six or more layers of special districts, each with an independent government. They may receive water from one, have sewage collected by another, obtain health services from a third, support parks through a fourth, pay for street lights to still another, and gain protection against mosquitoes from a sixth. Between 1942 and 1962, the number of special districts more than doubled [to more than 18,000]. . . .
>
> Most special districts were formed to provide urban services in unincorporated areas. Some were created to solve problems extending over several political jurisdictions. Others were established coterminously with an existing unit, where legal or financial restrictions prevented performance of a particular function by that unit. Almost half of these special districts have taxing powers and many have the right to issue bonds, but most of their revenues come from service charges, sales, rents, and tolls.
>
> The advantages of special districts in overcoming political and financial limitations are generally offset by each district's preoccupation with a single

_____

[2] Robert C. Wood, with Vladimir V. Almendinger, *1400 Governments: The Political Economy of the New York Metropolitan Region* (Harvard University Press, 1961), pp. 72–73.

function. Resulting fragmentation complicates coordinated development of the entire area. Other obvious weaknesses are absence of broad legal authority and lack of political responsiveness due to appointment or ex officio composition of many governing bodies.[3]

The 35,000 school districts in the United States are about equally divided between "dependent" systems, where the school board is an administrative agency and funds are furnished by some other governmental unit, and independent school districts, which not only administer school systems but levy taxes and raise revenue. The number of school districts has declined considerably on a national basis in the past 30 years or so, but many very small districts yet exist. In fact, as the CED pointed out "over 3,000 independent school districts do not maintain schools, having no children of school age or sending their few to other districts on a tuition basis. Such districts exist primarily to avoid or minimize school taxation."[4] Most school districts are concerned with primary and secondary education, although development of local junior colleges is increasingly done by such districts.

The schools provided by school districts, like those provided by counties, serve far more than new suburban subdivisions, of course; but the need to serve such additional areas creates difficult problems for the school system. In particular, new capital investment is required to provide additional school facilities; frequently, this is raised by bonds or taxes which are obligations of the entire school district or county and not merely of the new subdivision or new suburb.

States

States provide some public services of direct value to new settlers in new subdivisions. The state normally provides the major transportation network between cities and also within them. States supply a considerable part of the higher education available within their boundaries. They are likely to provide much of the intermediate type of outdoor recreation and some of the resource-based type. (See Chapter 4.) Many functions of general government are provided by the state. The state tends to operate on a broad geographic basis, not distinguishing the services it renders to new subdivisions from those it provides for older urban and rural areas; in this regard, its activities contrast sharply with those of the builder, for instance.

Thus far, attention has been directed primarily to the agencies which actually provide public services. Responsibility for financing may be much more widely spread. Federal grants are available to states, cities, and other units of government for some of the services discussed here, and state grants are available to cities, counties, and school districts for some services. Sometimes a service agency obtains grants from both federal and state governments. Such intergovernmental transfers of funds present formidable problems to cost analysis, problems too complicated for treatment here.

[3] Committee for Economic Development, *Modernizing Local Government* (New York: The Committee, 1966), p. 32.
[4] Ibid., p. 30.

Costs of Public Services

How much do these necessary or desirable public services cost? Attempts to measure costs of public services in any meaningful way, particularly to permit comparisons between areas or types of suburbs, are hampered by many problems. The financial data are themselves not entirely clear. Uniform accounting is not always practiced, distinctions between capital outlays and annual operating expenses are sometimes not made or not logically made, and such data are often confused by intergovernmental transfers of funds. However, other and more basic problems exist.[5]

First of all, it is not easy to measure the output or quantity of public services provided, although naturally it is easier for some services than for others. Hirsch has shown how the volume of garbage collection service can be measured in terms of number of full refuse containers collected annually. A measure of the volume output of an educational system may be either the number of pupils enrolled or the number graduated annually. For some other services, similar tangible measures of output can be provided. However, it is difficult to reduce these measures of output for different services to a common denominator. In two urban or suburban areas where the mix of services differed—and they would generally differ to some degree—it would be hard to arrive at an overall measure of governmental output.

But considerations of volume of output quickly get into the matter of the quality of the service rendered. Just how good is the education provided to the students enrolled or graduated? Are some of them still functionally illiterate even though they have graduated? Just how good is the garbage collection? Hirsch has shown that costs vary according to whether the garbage is collected once a week or twice a week, and according to whether the garbageman picks it up at the rear of the house or from the front of the house where the householder has put it. But even this does not face the issue of how much garbage the collector scattered on the ground and failed to pick up. In some instances, indexes of quality of service can be prepared. Sometimes, as in the case of education, expenditures per unit (as per child) are used as a proxy for quality of service. The assumption here is that good quality is not attainable without larger expenditures and that the latter do measure better quality. But large expenditures may measure inefficiency in service or high factor costs—high wages, in particular.

Many studies of costs of public services, or of the expenditures by local government for such services, have concluded that the single most important factor affecting such costs is the ability of the local area to finance them.[6] In this respect, public consumption is not unlike private consumption; a major factor in individual expenditures for many consumption items is the income of the person concerned.

[5] For two articles which discuss these problems in a rather inclusive manner and include many references to other studies, see Werner Z. Hirsch, "The Supply of Urban Public Services" and Julius Margolis, "The Demand for Urban Public Services" in *Issues in Urban Economics,* Harvey S. Perloff and Lowdon Wingo, Jr., eds. (Johns Hopkins Press, for Resources for the Future, 1968). For an earlier work which develops data (essentially on an engineering basis) on various factors affecting the costs of municipal services of various kinds, see Walter Isard and Robert E. Coughlin, *Municipal Costs and Revenues Resulting from Community Growth* (Wellesley, Mass.: Chandler-Davis, 1957).

[6] This is essentially the position taken by Wood and Almendinger in *1400 Governments.*

If any analysis is to be made of the comparative costs of public services provided in suburbs and in cities, or in two forms of suburban settlement, then it must be based upon a strictly comparable quantity and quality of public services, or the raw data must be corrected for differences in such quantity and quality. Moreover, it is entirely possible that the cost differentials might run in one direction for public services of low volume and/or low quality and in the opposite direction for services of high volume and/or high quality. It may prove impossible to eliminate completely all differences in quality. How much is it worth, for instance, for children to be able to walk to school, rather than having to take a bus?

With all this cautionary background, some data on average costs of public services per capita are provided in Table 9. These are presumably expenditures by the governments concerned, eliminating transfers of funds between levels of government, but one cannot be entirely certain that this is the fact. The amounts listed here are incomplete in some respects for the services included. For instance, there is nothing for parks and recreation except by local government, in spite of the fact that some state and federal park and recreation areas are used primarily by people from these metropolitan areas. In some urban areas, the important contributions to municipal water supply made by state and federal agencies are not included. Nor are many federal and state general public service programs operat-

TABLE 9

PER CAPITA EXPENDITURES FOR ESSENTIALLY LOCAL PUBLIC SERVICES,
38 LARGEST SMSAs, 1964–65

Kind of service	All local governments	States	Federal government	Total[1]
Education	$123.65	$25.82	$ 5.42	$154.89
Highways	19.85	43.30	*	63.15
Public welfare	25.13	7.45	*	32.58
Health and hospitals	18.17	9.49	11.91	39.57
Police protection	17.27	*	*	17.27
Fire protection	9.87	*	*	9.87
Sewerage	10.20	*	*	10.20
Sanitation, other than sewerage	6.34	*	*	6.34
Parks and recreation	9.04	*	*	9.04
Water supply	15.34	*	*	15.34
Other utilities	19.22	*	*	19.22
Interest on general debt	11.54	*	*	11.54
General control	7.27	*	*	7.27
Other general public expenditure	42.87	*	*	42.87
Postal service	*	*	27.00	27.00
Housing and urban renewal	*	*	4.89	4.89
Total[1]	$335.76	$86.06	$49.22	$471.04

Source: Data from Julius Margolis, "The Demand for Urban Public Services," in *Issues in Urban Economics*, Harvey S. Perloff and Lowden Wingo, Jr., eds. (Johns Hopkins Press for Resources for the Future, 1968), pp. 528–29.

* No data available in source.

[1] Of reported items only.

ing within urban areas. However, by far the greater part of the costs of the kinds of public services under discussion is included, and the data give a reasonable idea of the magnitude of such costs and the relative importance of different items.

These costs may be put in perspective. They average nearly $500 per capita annually—perhaps, if the omitted items were included, they would be fully $500. For a family of four persons, this is $2,000 a year. Some of this will be paid by means of real estate taxes, some as sales taxes, some as user charges or fees, some as income tax, and some by companies or other private business firms which in turn collect from the individuals with whom they do business—often in terms of prices for their services or products which are necessarily higher because of the taxes paid. The listed services by no means include all the services financed out of taxes paid by the average taxpayer; in particular, they include only a minor fraction of the costs of the federal government, toward which he is likely to have contributed relatively large sums via the personal income tax. A suburbanite who bought a new home a few years ago for $22,000 may have had to pay down $2,000. His monthly payments on the mortgage—for interest and amortization, fire insurance, and local real estate taxes—are likely to run about $180, or $2,160 annually, perhaps higher if real estate taxes have risen much. A suburbanite paying the same price in 1970 would have higher monthly payments because interest rates are now very high. Local real estate taxes might well run $500 out of the figure given. If this is omitted, the servicing and amortization of the home loan will be $1,620 annually, or about 80 percent of the cost of these public services. This situation might vary greatly from one area to another and somewhat from one time to another. However, it may be said that the annual cost of these various public services is in the same general order of magnitude as the cost of acquiring a reasonably good home.

These costs are average for the large SMSAs of the country. They might well run higher in newer suburban areas, where people of above-average income demand better-than-average services. Moreover, these are costs to the units of government which supply the services; the settlers in a new suburb may or may not bear all the costs of such services.

In spite of the relative size of these costs of public services, especially as compared with the costs of individual homeownership, it seems likely that the average suburbanite is less responsive to the costs of public services than he is to their quality. He may be annoyed if the monthly garbage collection fee rises from $4.00 to $5.00; but he will be outraged if the garbage is not collected and piles up on his back porch. He may protest if the millage rate rises because of increased school enrollment, so that his total local real estate tax bill rises from $450 to $500 annually; but if the local school is put on double shifts, so that his children have to go especially early in the morning or have to stay unusually late in the afternoon, he is likely to protest vehemently. He may indeed protest service of poorer quality or smaller volume than he would like and at the same time protest the increased taxes necessary to provide such service—and see nothing inconsistent in his actions. Moreover, there may be differences in viewpoint among different residents of a suburb. Everyone, for instance, wants "good" schools, for a reputation for good schools is an important part of the value of each residence. But those who have children in school are likely to be willing to spend more to get good schools than those who do not have children of school or preschool age.

Suburban Settlement Pattern and Cost of Public Services

The foregoing discussion is all in terms of average costs per capita of public services for the whole of an SMSA. What about per capita costs of public services in suburban areas and, particularly, costs of public services for different suburban settlement patterns? In this connection, it may be helpful to recall Chapter 2, which distinguished major ways in which suburban settlement patterns differ: (1) subdivision contiguity or discontiguity; (2) lot size, or the distance between houses on the land; and (3) floor area ratio, which includes both proportion of lot covered by buildings and building height. To these might well be added clustering of houses within a subdivision, as a special form of grouping of houses in one part of the subdivision in order to provide more open land in other parts of the same subdivision.

Ideally, there would be studies measuring the effect of various alternatives within each of these major categories upon both public and private costs and benefits. The net effect of various settlement patterns could probably best be estimated by a series of engineering or socioengineering studies, which would estimate carefully both costs and benefits for each settlement pattern. The costs would include both investments and annual operating expenditures—and should include all costs associated with each settlement pattern—regardless of who actually bears such costs. The benefits, in addition to savings in costs, should include any differences in satisfactions from living under different settlement patterns—an admittedly difficult matter to measure. Such ideal studies would also show who bears the costs in each case, who gets the benefits, and how far costs and benefits are associated. Even a casual review of the typical suburban situation suggests that many new settlers get benefits they do not pay for.

No studies have been made which conform to this ideal, which are comprehensive for all costs and benefits, and which cover a wide range of alternatives. Some studies have indeed been made, as noted below, and their results are highly suggestive but not definitive. One field in which much more research is needed, and which should yield some useful results at a relatively early date and for modest outlays, is in this matter of costs and benefits of different suburban settlement patterns.

Gains from Cluster Development

The clustering of houses *within* a subdivision provides some economies.

Good aesthetics, it is said, makes good economics. Cluster development . . . is one instance where the thought is demonstrably true. Whether considered from the community's interest or the developer's or the homeowner's, the factors that make cluster developments look better are the same factors that make them more economical.[7]

[7] William H. Whyte, Jr., *Cluster Development* (New York: American Conservation Association, 1964), p. 16.

TABLE 10

Cost Estimates for a 300-Acre Subdivision Development, Ville Du Parc, Wisconsin, under Conventional and Clustered Development Plans, 1962

Items	Conventional	Clustered
Sewer and water	$ 439,770	$ 258,490
Streets	104,000	68,120
Storm drains	220,140	56,600
Engineering, etc.	41,178	26,725
Sidewalks, hydrants	51,160	10,672
Land	360,000	360,000
Total development cost	1,216,248	780,607
Cost per lot	4,807	2,891
Fee for no park space* (courts, recreation areas)	50,600	275,000
Total cost per lot	5,007	3,987
	(253 lots)	(270 lots)
Lot sales price	6,000	8,000
Estimated gross return	1,518,000	2,160,000
Net return on lots	251,152	1,104,493
Percent return on investment	19.8%	104.6%

Source: "New Ideas in Land Planning—Cluster Plan Cuts His Costs by One-Third," *Journal of Homebuilding* (May 1962), p. 76.

* If no park space is provided in the overall site plan, the developer must pay the community $200 per lot.

An illustration of this fact is provided in Table 10, which gives cost estimates for a subdivision in Wisconsin. In this case, total development cost under cluster was estimated at less than two-thirds that under conventional subdivision, as a result of savings in each of the improvements (sewer and water, streets, storm drains, and sidewalks and hydrants) which the developer is expected to provide. Even with the same number of lots as a conventional subdivision, the saving is considerable. In addition, the cluster's developer gets some additional lots out of the same tract, so that the cost per lot to him is less than 60 percent as great as under conventional subdivision. At the same time, it is estimated that the sales price per lot can be a third more, thus making the subdivider a handsome profit from cluster development. If the difference in price per lot represents a real increased value to society, then the community at large has benefited both from savings and from increased value. This example ignores any possible savings outside of the subdivision. The National Association of Home Builders, which published the estimates in Table 10, has developed many examples with the same general conclusion, namely that clustering of houses within a subdivision is good business both for the developer and the home buyer.

A comprehensive study has been made of the potential savings through clustering of suburban settlement in Howard County, Maryland.[8] A general land use plan had been made for the county. When the "new town" of Columbia was begun within the county, its land use plans opened up new perspectives for settlement patterns that were both possible and acceptable to the public.

[8] *Howard County 1985*, Comprehensive Planning Section, Howard County Planning Commission, April 1967.

A new plan employed a population projection for 1985 and set up three alternative patterns of settlement to achieve this population growth. Model I assumed a continuation of the scattered settlement which had characterized the county prior to the beginning of Columbia; it is, in fact, designated the "trend" model. This model in effect assumes that Columbia will not be completed. Model II assumes, in contrast, that Columbia will be completed as planned, but that all other settlement in the county will be on a dispersed basis. Under this model, roughly half of the settlement is rather considerably clustered in Columbia, while about half is widely dispersed. Model III assumes that nearly all additional settlement in the county, up to 1985, will be on the pattern of Columbia—i.e., rather clustered. Columbia clearly involves subdivision contiguity and also some degree of residential clustering on a finer scale.

Cost estimates for land and for major public services for the 1965–1985 period were estimated. (Table 11) The savings in land area are large; Model III requires somewhat less than half as much land for the major land uses as does Model I. The value of these land savings has been estimated on an extremely modest basis, with prices per acre at much less than $2,000, which is very low even for raw land some years in advance of settlement. The value per acre of the land used is somewhat higher for Model III than for Model II and this in turn somewhat higher than for Model I, so that the monetary savings for land are proportionately less than the acreage savings. But the cost of land under Model III is still $30 million under Model I for the 20-year period. Savings in land are a private gain but also a social one, since the land may be used for other purposes.

Much larger savings are estimated for the provision of public services. Water supply costs are half, sewer costs and road costs less than half for the clustered than for the open-settlement pattern. Only the costs for recreation and park land and their development are higher for the clustered settlement pattern, on the assumption that more public park and recreation areas would be required where private homes were clustered. Other public services provide large proportionate savings, but their total value is relatively low.

Since all three models are based on the same population projection, the estimated savings can readily be reduced to a per family basis for the additional families to be settled. Contrasting the fully clustered with the fully open-settlement patterns, the per family saving is $600 for land and over $2,400 for investment in public services. The latter may not be absolutely complete, since some minor items are omitted, but it is nearly so. If one assumes that these savings (mostly in capital outlay) could earn an interest return of 5 percent or more, then the annual saving per family is about $150, or nearly $40 per capita. To these savings in investment should be added some saving in annual operating costs of public facilities, for a geographically more compact system would surely provide some economies in operation which were not included in the estimates. These comparisons take no account of private savings from settlement pattern; for instance, private travel costs might be much lower in Model III than in Model I. Neither do they include such secondary benefits as reduced air pollution due to much less automobile traffic in Model III than in Model I. Public transport becomes possible with more consolidated settlement, as it is not with badly scattered settlement. Thus the calculations in Table 11 understate the advantages of Model III.

Model I is improbable, now that Columbia has been started and seems likely to proceed. Model III is also improbable, in the sense that some scattered settlement will almost certainly occur, even if other planned and clustered large settlements similar to Columbia are undertaken. However, the cost estimates do provide a measure of the possibilities. To the extent that some clustering occurs, some savings are probable. Model II shows savings more or less intermediate.

TABLE 11

LAND AND PUBLIC SERVICE COSTS FOR ESTIMATED DEVELOPMENT
BY 1985, HOWARD COUNTY, MARYLAND

Cost item	Model I— sprawl[1]	Model II— partly sprawl, partly clustered[2]	Model III— closely clustered[3]
Area of land: (acres)			
Residential	49,000	33,900	22,400
Commercial	3,150	2,750	2,450
Industrial	9,000	6,575	4,750
Total	61,150	43,225	29,600
Cost of land: ($1,000)			
Residential	59,710	44,610	33,110
Commercial	3,850	3,450	3,150
Industrial	11,000	8,575	6,750
Parks and open space	2,922	4,006	4,888
Road right-of-way	5,338	3,570	2,265
Subtotal, land	82,820	64,211	50,163
Water utilities installations	65,011	47,110	32,068
Sewer utilities installations	83,941	62,777	38,693
Road installations	54,745	38,072	25,746
Road maintenance, 1965–1985	20,548	14,773	10,509
County acquisition of parks and open space	534	1,689	2,384
County acquisition of school sites	3,412	2,250	800
School bus operation, 1965–1985	23,965	15,254	9,031
Subtotal, services	254,245	181,925	119,381
Total	337,065	246,136	169,544

Source: Howard County 1985, technical report prepared by Comprehensive Planning Section of the Howard County Planning Commission, April, 1967, pp. 38a, 99a. All estimates based on 68,276 dwelling units in 1985, compared with 13,600 in 1965, or an increase of 54,676 in the 20-year period.

[1] Model I assumes that 88 percent of the housing added in Howard County over the 20 years will be in the same dispersed pattern (sprawl) which existed up to 1965; this in effect assumes that the "new town" of Columbia will not be completed.

[2] Model II assumes that Columbia will be completed as planned, but that all other new housing in the county will be on a sprawl basis.

[3] Model III assumes that 88 percent of the additional housing in Howard County in this period will be built on the same density as planned for Columbia.

The impressiveness of the potential savings from Model III, as contrasted with Model I, depends upon how one looks at them. A potential saving of almost $170 million seems very large, even for a 20-year period and even for a whole county. Surely it would make a considerable difference to the county, either in terms of public services that could be afforded or in terms of the tax rate, or both. If one looks at the per capita annual savings of $40, the savings may appear small. Certainly, they are only a small part of the total cost to the householder of acquiring a home in this county.

Settlement Patterns and Sewer Costs

Downing has analyzed sewer costs for suburban areas of differing density and varying location with respect to treatment plants and has considered collection, transmission, and treatment costs separately.[9] His groupings according to density apparently reflect, predominantly, differences in lot size; they range from 0.4 to 512 persons per acre (256 to nearly 33,000 per square mile), or from very sparse to very high (using the terminology of Table 2 in Chapter 2). Distances from sewage treatment plants largely reflect subdivision contiguity or its lack, and they range from 5 to 30 miles. Downing makes estimates on two bases, high and low, but only his high estimate series is presented here.

Annual sewage treatment costs at the plant are constant on a per capita basis, at $2.07; it does not matter how far the sewage has traveled. Annual collection costs within the subdivision are constant, regardless of how far it may be from the subdivision to the treatment plant, but vary according to density from $0.16 to $33.60 per capita. The annual transmission cost varies with both density and distance, from a low of $0.80 to a high of $736 per capita. The latter is for the lowest density, of less than 256 persons per square mile, and the longest distance, of 30 miles from the subdivision to the treatment plant.

These costs are summarized in Table 12. The economies of higher density within the subdivision are very great at all distances from the treatment plant: the lowest costs are from 1 to 2 percent of the highest costs; but within a more modest range in density (from 4 to 16 persons per acre) which conforms to a range of lot sizes from 1 to ¼ acres, the costs per capita fall by half or more. The economies of distance, which more or less conform to the economies of subdivision contiguity, are very great at the very lowest densities, and gradually decline both absolutely and relatively for higher densities. But, at the usual suburban subdivision densities, subdivision contiguity seems to reduce costs to a fourth or a third of costs with the greatest degree of distance. At this range of density, annual sewer costs alone may be $25 to $70 per capita higher for distant than for closer-in subdivisions.

This study covers only one public service, though an important one. Significant in themselves, the results are also suggestive of what might be done for other services. Downing reports some interesting figures on the costs of installing septic

[9] Paul B. Downing, "Extension of Sewer Service at the Urban-Rural Fringe," *Land Economics* (February 1969). See also his book, *The Economics of Urban Sewage Disposal* (Praeger, 1969).

TABLE 12

MARGINAL ANNUAL COST PER CAPITA OF SEWAGE COLLECTION AND TREATMENT
WITH DISTANCE AND DENSITY—HIGH ESTIMATE

(1957–59 dollars)

Density (people per acre)	Distance from subdivision to treatment plant—miles					
	5	10	15	20	25	30
0.4	$158	$282	$404	$531	$649	$772
1	66	115	164	213	262	301
4	23	38	52	67	81	96
16	12	16	21	26	31	36
64	5	7	9	11	13	15
128	4	5	7	8	10	11
256	3	5	6	7	8	9
512	3	4	5	6	7	8

Source: Paul B. Downing, "Extension of Sewer Service at the Urban-Rural Fringe," *Land Economics* (February 1969).

tanks which later have to be replaced by sewers. An investment saving of $740 per lot is estimated for the Los Angeles area, if sewers are planned and installed at time of development before streets are paved, as compared with costs that must be incurred if septic tanks are installed initially but later must be replaced by sewers.

Savings from an Open Space Program

A study of the economics of open space preservation in the San Francisco Bay area produced some interesting estimates of the economies of more closely spaced settlement.[10] The open space plan had been proposed on the basis of the desirability of the lands concerned, not for the primary purpose of achieving economies of settlement pattern. If the open space program is implemented, it will help to confine suburban development and thus lead to a somewhat greater, though not complete contiguity of subdivisions. Without the open space program, it was estimated that the urban service area of this region would include 1,441 square miles; with it, development would be confined to 1,114 square miles, a saving of 327 square miles or 23 percent as a result of the open space program.

By some careful estimates prepared in cooperation with the public utility agencies, it was estimated that the savings per square mile, in investment cost, would be as follows:

Water	$1,000,000
Electricity	480,000
Gas	270,000
Telephone	137,000
Total	$1,887,000

[10] *Economic Impact of a Major Open Space Program* (San Francisco: People for Open Space, 126 Post Street, 1969).

For the 300 square miles of urban service area conservatively estimated as saved by the open space program, this would amount to a total saving in investment of $566 million; and for the 7.3 million people projected for this area by 1990, this would be an investment saving of $78 per capita. Some savings in annual maintenance costs are also estimated, amounting to $9 million, or $1.23 per capita, per year. This, together with interest on the saved investment, brings the annual savings to about $5 per capita. In addition, some savings in ordinary costs of government would result from the more compact urban area. No calculations were made on possible savings in transportation network.

These amounts are not large on an annual per capital basis, although they are sizable in terms of an initial investment. But it should be emphasized again that this plan was not designed to maximize savings from settlement pattern. If it had been, the savings might well have been several times greater.

Some Observations

None of these studies include any private operating costs of residents of scattered versus contiguous subdivisions or of other forms of settlement pattern. It is altogether possible that a more compact suburban settlement pattern would reduce transportation costs considerably. Nor do these studies include any allowance for reduction in air pollution that might be possible because of less auto traffic.

Full subdivision contiguity would reduce idle land from the third-to-half of total land area which now prevails in many suburban belts to a very small fraction, and thus produce significant savings. Public investment costs could be reduced up to a half, judging by the Howard County study; annual savings could easily run to $40 per capita, or $150 per family. Downing's estimates would seem to suggest much larger savings. In the modern affluent American society, these are hardly overwhelming sums, yet they could spell the difference between a good school system and an excellent one; or they could be passed on to residents, enabling them to spend more for private consumption. Presumably, few people would find offsetting disadvantages in subdivision contiguity; their location with respect to their own neighbors would be unaffected.

Further savings could be realized by higher densities within subdivisions. These could be attained by smaller lot sizes, more use of row houses, walk-up apartments, and high-rise apartments. It is risky to estimate the amount of such savings, but it seems probable that they would equal or exceed the savings from subdivision contiguity. Often these measures would introduce greater changes in the pattern of suburban living than would subdivision contiguity and hence might not be as acceptable. Private savings might also be significant for some patterns of settlement. The most impressive, and depressing, aspect of the whole situation is how little we really know about it and how little research is directed toward it.

Some writers have argued that the extent of the idle land in a suburb at any one moment is not significant, as affecting public and private costs that might arise out of scattered settlement, since the idle lands will be developed or filled in shortly and thus disappear. Lessinger has even argued that scatteration is a positive good, since he thinks it will simplify the replacement pattern of old houses when this becomes necessary.[11] Serious doubt may be expressed about this claim, since renewal may be for large tracts, and diverse ages of housing might be a handicap in site assembly. The rate of infilling in many suburbs is very slow; much land lies vacant for decades, not merely for years. Where infilling is slow, it may never reduce the costs of public services below what they would be under scattered settlement. If the initial construction of public works, such as sewer lines, is on a scale adequate for the initial scattered settlement only, then additions to capacity when infilling does occur may be as expensive as for scattered settlement, since in effect the new developments are scattered. If initially the scale of the public works anticipates the later infilling, then the substantial excess capacity that exists until the infilling occurs is costly too.

This section has been concerned only with savings that are more or less measurable in dollar terms. No attempt has been made to face the more difficult, and probably more important, issues of the aesthetics and the social values of various settlement patterns. People may choose something other than the lowest-cost settlement pattern. However, the choices people have made have been limited by the alternatives open to them, and that these have not, by and large, included clustered settlement. Hence it is an error to say that they have chosen sprawl.

PRICING POLICIES FOR SUBURBAN PUBLIC SERVICES

Now that we have considered the kinds of public services supplied to suburban residents, their general costs, and the effect of the settlement pattern on these costs, it is time to consider who pays the costs and how he pays.[12] A basic assumption is that each actor in the subdivision and settlement process is influenced by the costs *he* pays in relation to the benefits *he* gets, and is influenced little or not at all by any general benefit-cost comparison.

There are two rather different aspects of the problem of who bears costs and how: some costs are incurred to provide public services for additional population in any unit of local government, irrespective of where those people are located; and, conversely, some costs of public services depend upon the population distribution or the specific location of the new arrivals.

When the population of a city, a suburb, or a county grows, more school facilities are likely to be needed, and this requires capital outlays and increased annual operating outlays. As noted earlier, something on the order of one-third of all public service costs is for education. Additional costs are involved for more schoolchildren, irrespective of suburban settlement pattern; but costs may be higher for

[11] Jack Lessinger, "The Case for Scatteration—Some Reflections on the National Capital Region Plan for the Year 2000," *Journal of the American Institute of Planners* (August 1962)
[12] For a general discussion of the rationale of different methods of financing costs of various public services, see William W. Vickrey, "General and Specific Financing of Urban Services" in Howard G. Schaller, ed., *Public Expenditure Decisions in the Urban Community* (Resources for the Future, 1963).

one pattern than for another. Typically, the school administrative organization (city, county, or school district) floats a bond issue to raise the necessary capital and imposes taxes to raise the necessary annual revenue for operation and to meet the charges upon the bonds. The assessed value of all property within the taxing unit is likely to grow because of the added population and the increased associated private investment; but usually the increase in assessed value is insufficient, and the tax rate must be raised. Every property owner in the tax-levying unit must pay taxes to help pay for these additional school facilities and their operation, even those owners who live where existing school facilities are adequate.

In defense of this allocation of costs, it may be argued that each generation inherits a structure of public services, that each must help to expand its own services as the need arises, and that each must leave an improved and enlarged structure of public services for the next generation. Clearly, in this illustration, the added cost of the new schools is not borne by the new people within the taxing unit alone. Indeed, given the population mobility which characterizes modern America, it would be extremely difficult to assess these added costs against the new settlers alone. In many urban areas, the inmigrants locate in older parts of the urban area, where schools and other public services exist—though their quality may be poor—while the new suburbs are partly composed of migrants from the central city.

The same general relationship exists for all the other public services at least to some degree. Transportation facilities outside the subdivision, main sewers and sewage treatment plants, main water supply systems, parks, and other facilities are paid for in large part by the older settlers as well as by the new ones, whether the facilities were built before or after the new settlers arrived. The same is largely true for privately provided services such as electricity and telephone. The new settler simply does not pay for all the added costs he creates. In time, he does pay part of these costs and also part of the costs for additional subdivisions created later; but at no time are his payments linked to the costs he created.

Increasingly in suburban subdivisions, the builder or developer is required to bear some of the costs of public services within the subdivision and sometimes some costs outside of it. Presumably the builder passes these costs along to the home buyer, in the total price for the house and lot and all its amenities, for he could scarcely be expected to absorb them out of his profits. Perhaps the buyer may vaguely realize he is paying for these services, but he is unlikely to know how much they are, much less to have made a conscious decision to buy this much, and no more, of the services in question, at the cost (price) involved.

A great many of the public services the new suburban resident requires are located outside the subdivision and perhaps outside of the suburb, or are not paid for by the developer, or both. This would normally be true for schools, to use but one example. But it would also be true for the collector sewer lines and the sewage treatment plant in most cases. Here, the situation is exacerbated by the typical pricing arrangements for such new public services. Generally speaking, the new resident in a subdivision does not bear the full costs—indeed, sometimes any of the costs—caused by his particular location. The prices he pays for various public services are the same, or almost the same, regardless of where he locates within a general suburban range. The most extreme case is postal rates. Postal rates are the same within any class of service at any point in the United States; no matter how far the postman must walk or drive to reach an outlying house, the rate is the same. From this fact has come the designation of a flat rate as a "postal" rate. Telephone, electricity, and other "public" services provided by private companies nearly always use postal rates for a given general service area; rates are not higher for more distant than for closer customers. For water and sewerage lines, the new customer is often permitted to hook onto existing lines with little or no charge for mainline services, and certainly for charges far less than he would encounter if he were to build his own line to the treatment plant. The charge is usually not greater if he is at the end of the line than if he is much closer in. The economies of scale in the whole system are often granted to the new customer, irrespective of where he lives. In the case of the Washington Suburban Sanitary Commission, serving the Maryland suburbs of Washington, the charges for water and sewerage service are unrelated to distance, and no charges are made for intervening idle land which is serviceable from the lines as extended.[13]

The new settler in a subdivision may or may not bear all the costs for public services for works physically within the subdivision, such as street grading, street paving, water lines, sewer lines, and the like, but he rarely is charged any significant part of the costs of services outside of the subdivision, to the extent these costs are a function of his location. That is to say, the charges he is required to pay are mostly unrelated to the location of his subdivision, being neither greater for a distant subdivision nor less for a closer one. Under typical pricing arrangements, the new settler or the prospective settler has little incentive to locate in a sub-division closer to the suburb in order to reduce the cost of service. As noted, the costs to the whole community are much greater for sprawled than for compact settlement, at the subdivision scale as well as within the subdivision; but the costs to the new settler do not reflect any of these differences in community costs. Naturally, in choosing where to live the settler ignores those costs which he does not bear. The pricing system for "public" services, whether these are provided by a unit of government or by a private firm, thus tends to encourage sprawled settlement, or at least not to discourage it. Although the pricing of public services might not, in itself lead to sprawl, pricing policies surely reinforce the trend toward sprawl.

The pricing system for public services affects the private market for land. We may assume that the price paid by the purchaser of a new suburban home reflects his demand for lot, building, and public services combined. The developer almost surely puts a price on the house which reflects demand for the volume of houses produced; if demand is higher, more houses are built, and if it is lower, fewer are built. If the house purchaser (1) paid for all the public services associated with his house, in cash at the time of purchase, or (2) paid for them fully over a period

[13] Francis Xavier Tannian, "Water and Sewer Supply Decisions: A Case Study of the Washington Suburban Sanitary Commission," unpublished doctoral dissertation, University of Virginia, June 1965.

of years in taxes or service charges levied against him and at the time of purchase *realized that he would have to do so,* or (3) any combination of these alternatives, then the cost of the public services would have to be deducted from his purchase price to get the price paid for house and lot, the cost of constructing the house would have to be deducted to get the price of the improved lot, and the cost of improving the lot would have to be deducted to get the raw land price.

To the extent that the house purchaser evades any costs of public services to his property, the raw land price will be higher than if he had to pay them. The house purchaser will have gained little or nothing by evasion of these costs, nor will the builder have gained. Virtually all of the gain from costs evaded by the purchaser will have passed on to the owner of the raw land. To the extent that the house purchaser does not pay all the costs associated with his property, some other tax-payers will have to pay them.

The situation is not much different if the house purchaser has to pay these costs over time but at the time of purchase did not realize that he would have to do so. If he was uninformed or blithely optimistic, then he probably paid as much for house, lot, and services as he would have paid if he had known he could evade the costs of the services. In the end, he pays double.

Moreover, in this situation, the greater the degree or extent of the public services, the more marked is the situation and the higher is the raw land price, other factors being equal. A unit of local government which extends a wide range and high quality of services to newly developing suburban areas may find that it is primarily benefiting the raw land owners.

Sequence of Public Services and Settlement

A complex interrelationship exists between jobs and housing. The development of additional employment opportunities in a general area is a strong inducement to the development of housing reasonably accessible thereto, but employers tend to locate their businesses where adequate labor force exists. Something roughly analogous to this exists for public services and new subdivisions. A new sewer line is a strong incentive for the establishment of new subdivisions in the area served by it; but the demand for new subdivisions provides a strong rationale for the construction of new sewer lines. The same statements may be made about most of the other public services we have discussed. The public services are, however, much more place-dominated than are the new jobs.

The sequence in which public services are provided to a subdivision, compared with the construction of houses within it, may be considered as ideal, customary, or the minimum tolerable from the settler's viewpoint. Before he can start living in a new house, he absolutely must have some means of disposing of flushable wastes, some source of water, electricity, and a minimum road to get his car in and out. Where the soils and underlying geology are favorable and the public health authority will permit, the flushable wastes may be disposed of to a septic tank; otherwise, connection to a central sewer system is an absolute must. The construction of sewers is often the key step in development of a new subdivision. The water supply may be from wells if there is enough groundwater and if public health authorities permit its use; otherwise, connection to a central water supply system is absolutely necessary. Electricity is equally necessary to modern living, but because electric lines are ordinarily extended into new subdivisions without delay, this service is less likely to prove the critical factor in a new subdivision. Likewise, some minimum road facilities within or adjacent to the subdivision will almost surely exist or can be created by the developer. Major highways from suburbs to city centers or between large suburbs are often significant attractive forces to suburban land conversion. Anything less than these four essentials will render a proposed subdivision intolerable for prospective settlers.

Ideally, the new settler wants every public service ready when he moves in, at a fully adequate scale and quality. Customarily, public services exceed the minimum tolerable but fall short of the ideal. Schools for the children of the new settlers in the new subdivision may be inadequate in size, and badly located for these children, but they exist somewhere. Indeed, the state has imposed compulsory education, and the settler could not avoid sending his children to school even if he wished to. The existence of a school somewhere can be assumed, even if its quality may be unsatisfactory to the settler; and it can also be assumed that local school authorities can be influenced to provide better schools, when the demand is strong enough.

The officialdom or the bureaucracy of special governmental districts often have a direct interest in extending their services widely. As professionals, they want to construct and to provide good services; as individuals, they often attain popularity and political support for such a position. Likewise, the various private interest groups, such as the land speculators and land dealers, have interests in the development of certain public services, especially sewer lines. As noted in Chapter 6 there are interactions and playbacks between private and public groups. Thus calculations of general benefits and general costs do not explain the motivations and actions of important actors in the suburban development process.

It should also be recognized that people who settle in new subdivisions want more than maximum economy. They may be less interested in the cheapest garbage collection than they are in adequate collection. These new settlers have generally not borne the full costs of the typically sprawled subdivision pattern, but some of them might well have located just where they did even if they had been forced to pay all the costs associated therewith. It is incorrect to say that they chose this pattern of suburban development, for in many cases there was no meaningful alternative and no price tag was put upon such alternatives as there were.

Provision of Public Services as a Tool of Public Policy

Since some public services are absolutely essential for the development of a subdivision, and others are highly desirable, it would seem that the provision or the denial of service and the terms or costs on which a service was made available could be influential if not fully determinative of the location of subdivisions.[14] However, for a number of reasons this has *not* generally been the case. Chapin states that "techniques [for shaping urban growth] in use in urban areas today are a curious patchwork of devices, many an outgrowth of special-purpose efforts to meet particular problems and needs of their time, and many bearing the mark of the fragmented governmental situations [that] have prevailed during the period when the techniques evolved."[15] He then goes on to describe five major techniques that might be used, preferably in combination, to shape urban growth:

1. A general plan for a metropolitan region which is imaginative, practical, and feasible, and technically sound while at the same time reflecting the general desires and wishes of a majority of the population for their city some years in the future;

2. Urban development policies instruments, consistent with the general plan, for the use of various units of local government, all directed toward the common goals of the general plan;

3. Metropolitan area public works programs, for transportation, sewerage, schools, and the other services discussed in this chapter, to carry out the plan and the policies;

4. An urban development code, including zoning, subdivision regulations, building codes, health ordinances, and other devices, all integrated to achieve the broad objectives of the general plan; and

5. An informed metropolitan community, which has participated in preparation of the general plan and is prepared to defend and support it.

Chapin develops in moderate detail the ideas which are here simply listed, and shows what might be accomplished, and how, by this broad use of many techniques in concert. But there are major problems to his approach which he recognizes; these may be broadly grouped as administrative or governmental, as political, and as legal.

A metropolitan area simply has too many units of government, from federal to state to metropolitan to city to county to special district levels, for a coordinated approach to the use of public techniques to be easily successful. No single body has the responsibility for consistent and coordinated action, in regard to suburban development. Even where some body, such as a county council, nominally has much

---

[14] Public services of the types discussed in this chapter have been influential in affecting the direction and timing of suburban development. The point here is that they have rarely been *consciously* used for this purpose. Several writers have shown how particular public services or combinations of them have influenced suburban development. Grace Milgram and Christine Mansfield, *The City Expands—A Study of the Conversion of Land from Rural to Urban Use, Philadelphia, 1945–62* (U.S. Government Printing Office, 1968) show how transportation lines, sewer, and other public services affected rate of development in this area; F. Stuart Chapin, Jr. and Shirley F. Weiss, *Factors Influencing Land Development* (1962) and *Some Input Refinements for a Residential Model* (1965), each published by Institute for Research in Social Science, University of North Carolina, show that governmental services such as water and sewerage affect rate and direction of suburban growth; and Kenneth B. Kenney, *Pre-Development Land Ownership Factors and Their Influence on Residential Development*, Center for Urban and Regional Studies, Institute for Research in Social Science, University of North Carolina (1965) includes sewers and transportation routes as items helping to explain timing of suburban development.

[15] F. Stuart Chapin, Jr., "Taking Stock of Techniques for Shaping Urban Growth," *Journal of the American Institute of Planners* (May 1963).

of this power, in fact it is often unable to exercise it. Not only is fragmentation the order of the day, but there are powerful forces anxious to keep it that way so that there will be no unit of government strong enough to take coordinated action on suburban development.

There are serious political problems in applying available governmental powers and techniques to control or strongly influence suburban growth. Governing boards of cities, counties, and special districts may appear to be nominally independent of special interests, but frequently they lack the political courage and/or political muscle to take a truly independent line. It must be recognized that many individuals and groups have strong financial incentive to move contrary to any general plan for suburban development. Any general plan will propose some kinds of developments in some areas and not in others, and those who own the omitted areas will seek to change or destroy a general plan which seems to leave them in the cold. More often, the governing body or board is heavily infiltrated with the very interests it would have to control if any control over suburban growth were to be effective. Land speculators and developers have major advantages to gain by being on the governing bodies of cities, counties, and special districts, and they are willing to devote time, energy, and other resources to getting on such boards and to working as members. All of this is to say that there are serious limits to what any *local* government can do to control suburban development within its area.

Legal questions may arise as to what local units of government are empowered to do to control private use of land. Such objections are often raised by those who resist control; the powers of such governments are usually rather broad, if they take the necessary procedural and other precautions.[16] It would be an exaggeration to say that legal objections are phony, but sometimes they are. And local governments are often unaware of their powers. However, in many cases, even if they were sure of their legal powers, they would not act effectively for political reasons or could not be effective because too many other units of government also had important powers in this field.

The federal government may exercise some influence on local public services through the requirements of its grant-in-aid programs on sewers, water quality, open space, highways, and the like. However, such influence is more upon general standards and general procedures, than it is upon specific programs in particular areas. Indeed, were the federal agencies to get into such matters, there would almost surely be an outcry from states, cities, and counties.

This chapter should not end on a note of unrelieved gloom. There are real possibilities for controlling the form of urban growth and development. Such possibilities are considered in some detail in Part III below. But any effort to change the existing order is likely to be successful only if the difficulties are clearly understood. Hence they are brought forward here in an effort to be realistic, an effort that hopefully pervades the entire book.

---

[16] John W. Reps and Jerry L. Smith, *Control of Urban Land Subdivision*, Division of Urban Studies, Center for Housing and Environmental Studies, Cornell University, 1963, reprinted from *Syracuse Law Review* (Spring 1963).

EXTERNALITIES AND INTERDEPENDENCIES IN URBAN LAND USES AND VALUES

The use and value of any tract or parcel of land within a metropolis (city center and suburbs) is affected more by the use and value of other tracts or parcels of land than it is by what takes place on the tract itself. The modern metropolis is vastly complex, with multitudinous economic, social, political, and spatial interrelationships among its various parts. The individual has wide latitude to arrange his personal life within this complex, including the right to locate where he chooses, within his capacity to pay for location. But his job, his dwelling, his purchases, his play activities, and many other aspects of modern life involve other people—as a rule, relatively large numbers of other people—and also involve many different parcels of land in many different locations. Value which accrues to land is created by these manifold and complex interactions in land use. The purpose of this chapter is to describe some of these interrelations and interdependencies and to relate them to the matter of growing suburbs.

GENERAL THEORY OF EXTERNALITIES

An externality in economic values arises when the actions of one person or group bring costs or values to another, costs which the person initiating the actions does not have to bear or values which he is unable to capture. Interdependencies in economic values may be considered as simply a generalized example of externalities. The latter have typically considered the relation between two individuals or two groups, whereas the interdependencies might be extended to include all groups affected by, or affecting, the individual concerned, as far as his land use activities are concerned.[1] In this chapter, references to externalities apply to interdependencies as well, except where the contrary is specifically noted.

Externality is often illustrated by the case of a factory pouring out smoke, which creates damage and inconvenience to others. Another common example has been

[1] Much of the recent analysis of externalities stems from A. C. Pigou, *The Economics of Welfare*, first published in 1920, though antecedents can be found in many places, including the work of Alfred Marshall. For articles describing recent writing on externalities, see E. J. Mishan, "Reflections on Recent Developments in the Concept of External Effects," *Canadian Journal of Economics and Statistics* (February 1965); and Ralph Turvey, "On Divergences between Social Cost and Private Cost," *Economica* (August 1963).

the individual or firm which dumps its wastes into a stream or other water body, to the inconvenience and damage of others. Economists have been most inventive and imaginative in finding real situations or inventing imaginary ones to illustrate the many complexities of externalities. They have also been imaginative in suggesting some of the ways in which these problems of disassociation between costs and benefits might be ameliorated or solved, but actual solutions have been carried out much less extensively.

Externalities involve two rather different, though frequently intermingled, types of consideration which may be labeled simply as efficiency and equity. On the efficiency side, it is usually recognized that economic production (and consumption) by one person or group often involves some interference with the productive or consumption activities of others. If a factory is to produce goods, it may require the opportunity to do so in ways that produce smoke, and if consumers are to have its products, they may have to put up with some of its smoke. The social welfare argument then takes this form: In which way—no smoke and no goods, or smoke and goods, or some of each—is the total welfare of the whole population the greatest? This is the efficiency argument or range of considerations.

In its starkest form, this argument ignores equity. The economist can show, for instance, that the same action program results whether the polluter is taxed by an amount which exactly measures the cost he creates to others or if those damaged pay him an amount exactly equal to their costs not to create the pollution in the first place. In either case, exactly the same balance is achieved between goods and pollution, and the total social welfare is maximized. Equity considerations, in contrast, are concerned with who should bear the cost—in this example, the polluter or the group suffering the damages.

By and large, economic literature does not clearly distinguish the efficiency and equity considerations. Economists have been concerned primarily with efficiency— how resources should be used to produce the greatest total net product—and have often considered equity only insofar as it affected the efficiency argument. Law and the courts, which have often been involved in situations of external effects, have tended to emphasize the equity aspects—who damaged whom, who should pay, how much, and the like. But each has given some consideration to the other range of arguments. Coase, for instance, cites court cases where the decision nominally turned on the equity of damages but the deciding factor really was the effect the decision would have upon future land use in the area, or the value of land (an efficiency type consideration) in the future, under one decision as contrasted with the other.[2] In land use zoning, allowance typically must be made for prior nonconforming land uses, but this does not seem to be the case in damage suits between parties. How far should the prior user, if lawful, be protected against later actions by others? Times change, and arrangements desirable at one period may not be desirable at another. But where does equity lie, as between the established user and the newcomer?

Most of the examples used by economists and almost all the court cases involv-

[2] R. H. Coase, "The Problem of Social Cost," *Journal of Law and Economics* (October 1960).

ing externalities are two-party adversary cases. One man or group takes an action to his or their benefit, while another person or group suffers a consequence. Moreover, most cases in economic literature and before the courts involve negative externalities—costs or damages inflicted by one party upon the other—although a minor part of the economic literature explicitly deals with external benefits. Much of the economic literature tends to generalize, explicitly or implicitly, from the specific case to the whole of society. Court cases may have the same effect, by setting precedents, although they generally do not consider the longer-run effect of specific decisions. Since the typical case is a two-party adversary affair, the implications, if any, for the much wider circle of people who are indirectly affected, tend to be overlooked or minimized.

Relatively little of the economic theory and court cases deal explicitly with land use in a broad way, still less with the special problems of the growing suburbs with which this book is primarily concerned.[3] It is true that many of the illustrations or cases involve specific land uses, but only as these involve a certain type of conflict, rather than as part of land use planning generally. If one seeks to use either economics or law as the theoretical basis for dealing with the land use problems of a whole urban complex, he must undertake a major effort to translate the theory and the court cases into terms adequate to deal with his problem.

Neither economics nor law has given much attention to practical effectuating mechanisms or institutional arrangements whereby either the adverse or helpful secondary effects of one set of actions could be assessed against or credited to their originator. Economists have talked about levying a tax upon the polluter to pay the damaged persons by exactly the amount of the damage; and courts have frequently imposed damages. But the former would be extremely difficult to administer fairly without creating as many problems as it solves, and the latter is, at best, a very crude redress for losses incurred. Economists have also talked about the need "to internalize the externalities," that is, to make the person who takes the decision bear all its consequences. This is a fine principle, but often difficult to apply, and, in the case of urban growth, probably impossible of application. Currently both theory and practice are inadequate as practical guides to ways in which beneficial effects can be maximized and harmful effects minimized, so far as urban land use is concerned.

Overview of Externalities and Interdependencies in Urban Land Use and Value

A city undergoing a prolonged economic depression with considerable unemployment and perhaps some outmigration will surely experience falling prices for its residential real estate. A boom oil or mining town is at the opposite end of the spectrum—housing is scarce and not easily expandable, and available houses sell for prices far above their original investment cost.

[3]Emery N. Castle, "The Market Mechanism, Externalities, and Land Economics," *Journal of Farm Economics* (August 1965) discusses externalities specifically for natural resources and cites several books and articles. One sentence suggests that "urban expansion [will] provide many additional examples [of external effects]," but the point is not pursued further.

All illustrations of externalities and interdependencies for residential property find a counterpart in situations affecting commercial centers. The value of a single property in a shopping district, or of the whole shopping district, depends upon the number and average income of its customers and upon the nearness and character of rival shopping districts, among other factors. The same general kinds of externalities exist for each other major kind of urban land use.

Externalities in urban land uses and land values might be classified, in an economic sense, in one of several ways.

1. There are positive effects and negative ones, as far as a particular tract or land use is concerned. One may gain, or one may lose, by uses and activities on neighboring land areas.

2. Some externalities concern different areas within the same land use, while others are between different types of use. The relations between one dwelling and other dwellings or between one store and other stores are intrause, while relations between dwellings and stores are interuse.

3. Externalities might be grouped as complementary, or competitive, or destructive—the latter being, perhaps, only the extreme of competitiveness.

These systems of classification of externalities are not mutually exclusive. There may be some similarity between them, in the sense that many examples would fall into a similar grouping within each.

Externalities apply to the older city, both as it now exists and as it existed when it was the only part of the present metropolitan complex. But they have particular significance for city-suburb relationships. The suburb is, by definition, part of a larger urban complex, drawing economic strength from the older city and contributing to it; providing workers but dependent upon the older city for many jobs; the home of customers who shop in both older city and suburb; and in countless other ways both dependent upon and contributing to the older city.[4]

These varied externalities among land uses and land parcels are taken account of, perhaps subconsciously, by buyers of homes, by owners of commercial establishments, and by other individuals in deciding where, if at all, to locate within a particular city or suburb. The home buyer has an image in his mind of the kind of residential community he wants to live in, as well as restraints in the form of limited capital and income; and, similarly, the prospective store owner or operator has an image of what he wants. In their locational decisions, these factors may loom large.[5] Moreover, in any appraisal of the value of property, these factors are taken into account, explicitly or implicitly; considerable weight is likely to be given to the "character" of the residential neighborhood, for instance.[6] Some types of lend-

[4] Two published studies which illuminate some of these numerous and complex relationships but are not specifically concerned with land are: Benjamin Chinitz, ed., *City and Suburb: The Economics of Metropolitan Growth* (Prentice-Hall, 1964); and Harvey S. Perloff and Lowdon Wingo, Jr., "Planning and Development in Metropolitan Affairs," *Journal of the American Institute of Planners* (May 1962).

[5] For an important and ambitious effort to reduce some of these factors to quantitative terms, see T. R. Lakshmanan, "An Approach to the Analysis of Intraurban Location applied to the Baltimore Region," *Economic Geography* (October 1964).

[6] This can be illustrated by any book which deals with urban real estate, or by any urban appraisers' manual. See, for example, Arthur M. Weimer and Homer Hoyt, *Real Estate* (Ronald Press, 1966).

ing institutions will make no loans in certain kinds of areas, irrespective of the characteristics of the particular property, because they consider the neighborhood as a whole too risky.

It would be possible, at least in theory, to measure the economic strength or importance of the bonds between interrelated land uses. In practice it would be difficult to do so, and very few attempts have been made to do so empirically. The interrelationships are so numerous, the flow of values is so often not simply one-way but also reciprocal, and so many other factors affect land uses and values that the influence of any single pair of uses or any single pair of tracts of land would be very hard to identify. However, to the extent that measurable and predictable patterns of human behavior are involved, careful study should make it possible to form some idea of the quantitative importance of the value streams. The process is closely similar to that employed in benefit-cost analysis of specific public programs or of urban land use development projects in general. Lichfield has shown the applicability of cost-benefit analysis for city planning and as a tool in urban decision making. Wheaton demonstrates its applicability to the narrower question of public revenues and public costs involved in suburban expansion. And Lichfield has applied this idea to a specific urban development and redevelopment problem, introducing both monetary and nonmonetary advantages and disadvantages. Rothenberg has applied both the concepts of benefit-cost analysis and of externalities to urban renewal.[7]

Externalities in the urban land use structure are both *ex ante* and *ex post*. The home buyer looks for a congenial neighborhood with convenient and satisfactory shopping facilities, good schools, parks, and other public facilities. In this way, he takes account of externalities *ex ante*. After he has bought his home and lived in it for some time, he may find that all these factors worked out to his expectations, or he may find that the location fell short in various degrees and ways—the next-door neighbors may keep him awake by playing the record player at full volume, or the stores in the shopping center may have poor choices or high prices or both, the schools may have poor teachers or may be overcrowded, or any one or more of scores of other disadvantages may be discovered. In these various ways, the *ex post* externalities and interrelationships may differ from those *ex ante* in either a positive or in a negative direction and by almost any imaginable amount.

When the *ex post* reality of land use externalities is much less favorable than the *ex ante* expectations, the land user (owner or occupier) is faced with a difficult decision. Shall he sell or move, salvaging what he can from the situation, perhaps hoping that the buyer will place a different set of values upon these externalities and interrelationships, or that he will not appreciate their true condition? Or shall

[7] Nathaniel Lichfield, "Cost-Benefit Analysis in City Planning," *Journal of the American Institute of Planners* (November 1960), and "Spatial Externalities in Urban Public Expenditures: A Case Study" in Julius Margolis, ed., *The Public Economy of Urban Communities* (Resources for the Future, 1965) ; Lichfield and Margolis, "Benefit-Cost Analysis as a Tool in Urban Government Decision Making" in Howard G. Schaller, ed., *Public Expenditure Decisions in the Urban Community* (Resources for the Future, 1963) ; William L. C. Wheaton, "Application of Cost-Revenue Studies to Fringe Areas," *Journal of the American Institute of Planners* (November 1959) ; Jerome Rothenberg, *Economic Evaluation of Urban Renewal* (Brookings, 1967).

he stay, making the best of it? These are personal decisions, dependent in large part upon the new expectations of the future. Perhaps he will hope that the noisy nextdoor neighbor will move or the member of that family responsible for the noise will go off to college. The problem of sunk investment and of reality differing from expectations is, of course, widespread in economic life and in personal relations.

These relationships are enormously complicated for urban and suburban areas by the normally long life of buildings and of urban infrastructure generally and by the tendency to reconstruct both buildings and infrastructure incrementally. Even if all the *ex ante* hopes and expectations in a suburban development were fully realized by every land user initially, the basic land use pattern so established will endure, with only modest changes, over many years or some decades. Many specific or detailed changes will occur, within the area and outside of it but strongly affecting it over the years. The question may well be raised: How can externalities in urban and suburban land use possibly change in such proportionate and harmonious ways as not to cause unavoidable losses in value to the individual landowner? The possibility of windfall gains should not be ruled out, but seems much less probable. The salvage value of a home in a deteriorating neighborhood may be low, regardless of the building's physical characteristics. Land use planning may seek successfully to maintain property values and the human satisfactions implicit in such values, in the older as well as in the newer areas; but the magnitude of the task should not be underestimated.

While externalities are usually discussed in primarily economic terms, some effects may more properly be termed social. Many residential neighborhoods at some point in their history had a marked ethnic and/or religious cast which drew many people to them. Such a neighborhood may change in ways that do not involve economic loss, or at least not loss in property values; yet the persons involved may feel a loss of personal values. Firey has shown how various nationality groups stubbornly clung to locations in Boston, when a strict economic analysis might have suggested that they would have been better off elsewhere.[8] One of the major problems in urban renewal in slums is that it disrupts social arrangements, some of great value to the persons concerned. One might indeed argue that any social arrangement which people value has economic value, but it seems better to describe such relationships as primarily social rather than as economic.

EXTERNALITIES AND INTERDEPENDENCIES WITHIN LAND USES

The United States is characterized by relatively extensive areas given over wholly to residential land use. The intermingling of the small shops, that is common in those parts of the world where the housewife walks to market and carries her purchases home, is becoming rare in this country, especially in the newer suburbs. Schools must be located within residential areas, although many urban children, like most rural ones, may be transported by bus to rather distant schools. Local

[8] Walter Firey, *Land Use in Central Boston* (Harvard University Press, 1947).

parks should be found in residential areas but often are not. There are numerous suburban areas in the United States today where no other use than residential (and associated local transportation) can be found for a mile or more in any direction. In the older residential areas, and especially around their fringes, other kinds of land use are more commonly intermingled.

Within exclusively residential areas, the externalities and interrelationships *intra* residential use are extremely important. Various residential areas have reputations, deserved or not, which greatly affect the value of houses within them.[9] The quality of the individual houses, the extent to which they have been physically maintained, the type and income class of residents, the nature of public services and amenities (which gets into *inter*-land use relationships), and similar factors greatly affect the prices people will pay to buy homes in such neighborhoods. Houses which are physically identical will sell for very different prices, depending upon the kind of neighborhood in which each is located. Perhaps one measure of the economic importance of externalities, *intra* residential areas, might be the differences in value of structures which are essentially identical physically but differently located.

Housing units, like families, have life cycles, though not so definite and subject to lengthening or shortening by human decision. The new house can be physically well maintained for many years, but ultimately it gets out of style, lacks what are considered modern amenities, and begins to drift downhill in a physical sense. Although exact data are lacking, it appears that relatively few dwelling units in the United States last as long as 100 years, and that their disappearance is particularly rapid around 80 years of age.[10] Only time will tell whether houses built recently will be serviceable for longer or shorter periods.

The life cycle of the family and of the housing unit are not always in harmony. The new detached house is typically for the family with children and may serve well until they leave home. Many older couples hang on in the same house sometimes long after it ceases to be suitable for their needs. As the house goes downhill physically and/or the neighborhood deteriorates socially, lower-income families often take over; and often they subdivide the large old houses into a number of small and poorly designed apartments. In time, the old house may be cleared away, to be replaced by an apartment which is best suited to single individuals and childless couples. Throughout this life cycle, the various kinds of housing units provide a housing complex with numerous and sometimes complicated externalities and interrelationships among the various kinds of housing.

In commercial land use, similar *intra* externalities exist. Stores selling the same product are in competition with one another, but two or more stores of the same kind in reasonable proximity to one another may attract enough additional customers who appreciate the opportunity to shop and to compare values that each store is actually better off with competition than without it. Generally speaking, stores selling different products are complementary to each other; having several

[9] Homer Hoyt, *The Structure and Growth of Residential Neighborhoods in American Cities* (U.S. Government Printing Office, Washington, 1939), a report prepared for the Federal Housing Administration.

[10] Marion Clawson, "Urban Renewal in 2000," *Journal of the American Institute of Planners* (May 1968); Raymond W. Goldsmith, *The National Wealth of the United States in the Postwar Period* (Princeton University Press, 1962); and John W. Kendrick, "The Wealth of the United States," *Finance* (January 1967) use closely similar estimates or residential life.

stores in one place attracts customers to the benefit of each store. The modern American suburban shopping district is built on this relationship. The most stringent competition now is often between shopping centers, as commercial complexes, rather than between shops within each such complex. The private auto plays a major role. All shopping areas are accessible to most customers only by driving, and, once one is in the car, a few extra miles may make little difference. Thus, the externalities among and between tracts of land used for commercial purposes may extend over considerable distances. The value of land used for commercial purposes depends primarily upon the volume of trade at its stores, which in turn is related to the numbers and average incomes of its customers.[11]

Commercial areas often have a life history too, but often a less regularly predictable one than that of the dwelling or of the family. Some stores and shopping areas in the older parts of large cities have been well maintained over long periods of time. Others decline with age or are supplanted by newer, more attractive, and better located stores.[12] The movement of higher-income customers from urban residential areas to newer suburbs has forced many of the older downtown stores to establish suburban branches. In the old downtown, the failure or removal of a major store weakens those which remain.

Externalities in land use and value exist *intra* industrial land use also. Industrial firms differ considerably in their degree of vertical integration. Even highly integrated firms are likely to have a number of specialized productive plants, often physically separated from each other. The less-integrated firms buy their inputs from—and sell their outputs to—other specialized firms under different ownership and control and often separated geographically. Technologically and in business organization these different productive units within industry have a high degree of interrelationship, which naturally shows up in externalities in land use and land value.

A generally similar situation exists for "business"—the variety of financial, insurance, and related firms which are growing in importance in the American economy. Since World War II, the downtown sections of many American cities have become largely a concentration of offices, with factory operations moving to the suburbs or to smaller cities or even to open country. A dominant characteristic of this "business" community as a whole is the high degree of specialization of its parts. All large banks, for example, make loans, but some banks specialize in certain types of loans. Many of the industrial firms have offices in the same general part of the city. An indispensable part of this specialization in office location is the exchange of information among persons within each firm and among firms. The more specialized a business is, the less able it is to exist out of the main stream. It might be argued that modern communication technology would make it possible for such firms to locate much farther apart and communicate by modernized communication devices. But the facts have been the reverse since World War II; the value of face-to-face contacts has increased and their number has multiplied greatly.

[11] Roger Noel Harris, "Determinants of Central Shopping and Residential Land Values," North Carolina State University, 1965.
[12] Brian J. L. Berry, *Commercial Structure and Commercial Blight* (University of Chicago Press, 1963).

Such interrelationships among businesses also involve interrelationships among tracts of land. Each office building is in competition to a degree with every other office building for the occupancy of prime business tenants. But each office building also tends to strengthen the role of every other office building by providing an indispensable part of efficiently functioning business downtown.

Externalities in land use are evident in the use of land for transportation by air, rail, water, and highway and also within each mode of transport. The express highway moves large volumes of traffic quickly only as long as there is an efficient system of collector streets and highways which enable people to get onto the highway and only as long as there is an efficient system of local streets, once cars and trucks move off the through highway. Moreover, unless adequate parking space is provided at destination, the flow of traffic can be seriously impeded. These interrelationships among modes of transportation involve different tracts of land, and the use and value of each tract is determined primarily by other parts of the transportation system.

Externalities are especially marked in land use for outdoor recreation. Parks and other outdoor recreation areas come in many different sizes, in different locations, for use with leisure at different times of the day, week, or year; together, they form a system, even when they have not been consciously designed as such.[13] The same youth may play in the local playground after school, go on weekend picnics with his family, and participate in a family vacation at a distant seashore or mountain resort. Some kinds of areas are in rather direct competition with each other, while others are not effective substitutes for another type. The direct competition between the local playground and the distant national park is small indeed; but a chain or hierarchy of intermediate areas exists, and use can be diverted from one to another under various impetuses, so that a degree of indirect relationship exists even for the physically most remote areas.

Externalities among Various Land Uses

Inter-use externalities and interdependencies can be treated more briefly because they so closely resemble the *intra*-use ones. The use and value of any particular parcel of land now or in the near future depend upon the use and value of other pieces of land used for different purposes but in an interrelated pattern. The decision maker, when considering whether or not to buy a parcel of land or to erect improvements upon it, looks at how all the surrounding land is used and has been used, and then makes those moves which he conceives as likely to be most to his advantage. In the process, he usually reinforces the trends under way and sets the stage for new actions by others.[14] In every case, the decision maker creates some

---

[13] Marion Clawson and Jack L. Knetsch, *The Economics of Outdoor Recreation* (Johns Hopkins Press for Resources for the Future, 1966).

[14] For two interesting general approaches to this process, see Donald M. Hill, "A Growth Allocation Model for the Boston Region," *Journal of the American Institute of Planners* (May 1965); and Alan M. Voorhees and Associates, *An Approach to the Analysis of Intraurban Location Applied to the Baltimore Region*, Research Document No. 10 (undated, but after 1963).

values for others which he is unable to capture for himself and often imposes some costs on others which he is able to avoid.

Residential location depends primarily upon income and its housing preferences.[15] As noted earlier, racial minorities and low-income people are effectively excluded from most suburban areas. Purchasers of houses are strongly influenced by transportation facilities, times, and costs to their job locations; and by public services such as schools and by other amenities in the new location. In each case, they are paying for the investment in new house construction; but, as pointed out in Chapter 7, they are also paying for the site value of the land, which in turn is likely to include much of the value created by public action and by other landowners in the creation of services and amenities.

As noted in the preceding section, there is usually considerable competition among shopping centers, as well as between stores in each.[16] The extent of the shopping area and the value of land within it depend more upon the income of people in the surrounding trade area, the transportation to the shopping area, and the location and character of rival areas, than they do upon the decisions and actions of the store managers within the shopping center itself. Thus the *inter* land use externalities and interrelations are great.

Transportation greatly affects the uses and values which develop on other land. New transportation facilities have repeatedly led to unexpected volumes, directions, and kinds of traffic, which in turn have helped to create new land uses. Building new or improved transportation facilities creates new values, often of very substantial size, on lands served by such facilities. In the past, these added values have been only partially captured by taxation, with substantial values accruing to the landowners. Conversely, new transportation facilities to one area may decrease land values elsewhere.

Reducing the Adverse Effects of Land Use Externalities

Externalities and interdependencies in land use often have negative effects, in the sense that the actions of one person or group bring losses to other persons or groups. The distinguishing characteristics of externalities are that the market does not reflect the second-person costs and benefits to the initiator of the action. Hence, extra-market devices are used to deal with them.

Land use zoning is the classical approach to dealing with negative land use externalities. The public establishes rules to govern the individual as to what land uses are permissible and what are not. New zoning regulations usually except established nonconforming uses, although they may prohibit rebuilding, improvement, or restoration of buildings in such uses. Zoning is a legal tool, with heavy political overtones or commitments; its economic effects are usually placed in a secondary

---

[15] John D. Herbert and Benjamin H. Stevens, "A Model for the Distribution of Residential Activities in Urban Areas," *Journal of Regional Science* (Fall 1960) ; and Bernard J. Frieden, "Locational Preferences in the Urban Housing Market," *Journal of the American Institute of Planners* (November 1961).

[16] David L. Huff, "A Probabilistic Analysis of Shopping Center Trade Areas," *Land Economics* (February 1963).

position or may be wholly submerged in the public decision-making process.[17] Land use zoning works rather effectively to prohibit or to inhibit land use changes which will have adverse effects on other land users in areas where land use is pretty well established. A proposal to convert a lot in a residential area to a service station will surely encounter strong resistance from neighbors. As someone has observed, a residential area has to decline a very long way before homeowners will agree to see an old mansion converted to a funeral parlor. In older areas the effectiveness of zoning in inhibiting change is due to the existence of significant countervailing political power; the proposer of change is opposed by those who stand to suffer losses or think they will.

On the other hand, land use zoning has not been very effective in keeping out land uses incompatible with plans for the development of new suburban areas. Reps has gone so far as to propose abandonment of zoning as a tool in developing areas, on the grounds that it simply cannot deliver what it seems to promise.[18] Planners develop plans for suburban growth, implicitly taking into account externalities and interdependencies in land use and value. Regardless of whether their plans are sound and desirable, there is high likelihood that such plans will not be implemented by land use zoning. In this case, there are likely to be landowners, developers, and others who see gains they could make from land uses different from those planned and zoned. Those who would lose as a result of their actions are not yet resident in the area, or do not realize their probable losses, or are not adequately organized politically. The deficiency is thus basically political, although it often has legal aspects.

There are some exceptions to this general ineffectiveness of zoning in developing suburbs. If there are some residents or landowners, as well as public officials, who wish to keep out lower-income classes, especially lower-income blacks, zoning to establish very large lots, on which only quite expensive houses will as a consequence be built, may be effective politically.[19] With this exception, land use zoning in developing suburbs rarely has enough political muscle to withstand assaults by landowners or developers who think they have something to gain by forcing a change in the zoning.

Subdivision control in developing suburbs is very similar to zoning, and often is a part of it. Often adopted for the same purpose of keeping out certain income classes, it exhibits similar weaknesses.[20]

In older residential and other areas, inspection to enforce housing codes could be, but usually is not, an effective instrument for reducing the kind or character of land use which brings adverse effects upon surrounding land users.[21] Housing

[17] Richard F. Babcock, *The Zoning Game—Municipal Practices and Policies* (University of Wisconsin Press, 1966).

[18] John W. Reps, "Requiem for Zoning" in *Planning 1964* (Chicago: American Society of Planning Officials, 1964).

[19] James G. Coke and Charles S. Liebman, "Political Values and Population Density Control," *Land Economics* (November 1961).

[20] John W. Reps and Jerry L. Smith, "Control of Urban Land Subdivision," *Syracuse Law Review* (Spring 1963).

[21] Frank P. Grad, *Legal Remedies for Housing Code Violations*, National Commission on Urban Problems, Research Report No. 14 (U.S. Government Printing Office, 1968).

codes rest basically on public concern over health. Codes can ban nuisances of various kinds, can require adequate basic sanitation, can control fire hazards, and in other ways prevent the deterioration of existing structures to substandard conditions. Although they extend to many types of urban land use, they are primarily directed at residential land use, especially at rented property, and often have their greatest impact upon apartments rather than upon houses. But, by and large, housing code inspection is more honored in the breach than in the observance. It undoubtedly has some effect in forcing repairs of substandard housing or in preventing some housing from becoming substandard, but—if literally interpreted and unhesitatingly enforced—the slums which characterize every city could not exist. Full enforcement of strict housing codes would force some very poor housing out of use. This, plus costs of compliance, would raise rents somewhat on the poorest qualities of housing, and probably force further doubling up of poor people in such housing. To say this is not to suggest that the rents on deteriorated housing are now at a fair and reasonable level, but only that they would likely be higher if housing codes were fully complied with. Yet such compliance could surely operate to prevent or postpone some of the deterioration of housing which comes with age, and to encourage if not require an earlier replacement of housing which did deteriorate to unacceptable levels. Raising rents, even though housing quality improved, would surely impose hardships on very low-income families who cannot afford to pay even the present rents.

The citizens improvement association is sometimes an instrument to prevent adverse external effects from land use, by bringing social pressure from neighbors to bear upon the individual land user who neglects his property. Such an approach is perhaps most effective in an older residential neighborhood which has or had a reputation for high-quality housing. Laggards may be induced to "paint and fix up," thereby reducing the adverse effects of neglect. Citizens improvement associations have had only modest trial in older areas but conceivably could be more effective instruments in the future. In new residential areas they have had dubious success.

INCREASING THE POSITIVE EXTERNALITIES IN LAND USE

The adverse effects of externalities in land use have been widely discussed, yet from the viewpoint of social welfare it may well be that increasing the favorable externalities offers greater promise. Economic literature primarily discusses the adverse effects, though sometimes briefly suggesting that the treatment is symmetrical and that changing just a few words would make the discussion equally applicable to favorable effects. Legal cases rarely involve anything but adverse effects; indeed, it is hard to imagine how favorable effects could get into a law case. One may sue his neighbor to stop a nuisance or for damages, but both judge and jury would throw out a case in which one sought to make a neighbor help pay the cost of transforming one's dreary backyard into a lovely garden, however much the improved view might increase the neighbor's enjoyment of life. A public agency may restrain a violation of a building code, yet not consider at all how someone who made a major improvement which lifted land values in the whole neighborhood could recoup any of his costs from the beneficiaries. However, if the positive effects of land use externalities are anywhere near as universal and as important as the earlier discussion suggests, there must be ways to increase such effects.

Perhaps a basic consideration is that of good design, both for individual buildings and for larger areas. There is far from complete agreement among architects and others as to what is good design and what is not, and there is still less evidence that well-designed areas and buildings increase present satisfactions of users and viewers or that they maintain their values better over time. Nevertheless, it seems probable, to one not a specialist in urban design, that good design is frequently valuable beyond the additional cost it requires and that its values do endure.[22] Perhaps the most an economist can say is that short-run considerations of cost alone should not limit design, as unfortunately they sometimes seem to have done.

Public agency planning for land use should be a major instrument in increasing the favorable aspects of land use externalities and in minimizing the adverse effects. Hopefully, the arrangement of uses proposed in the comprehensive land use plan maximizes the external aspects of land use; one must say "hopefully," for this is usually implicit rather than explicit and rests upon rather shaky analytical grounds. (See comments in Chapter 5 on the deficiencies of urban planning.) The official land use plan can provide government itself with a guide to public improvements and other actions and also serve as a guide to citizens who wish to fit their programs into those of their neighbors.[23]

Another device, of great potential value but used relatively little thus far, is that of cooperative citizen planning for urban land use. Only rarely have citizen planning groups attempted to develop plans without official planning support; the technical difficulties and time required are obstacles, of course. There have been some notable exceptions to these generalizations.[24]

It is hard to see why the role of the citizen planning group should not be immensely strengthened and extended in spite of the difficulties. The basic weakness of every official land use plan is its weak rooting in popular understanding and support and its lack of clear policy direction. If there were more general prior agreement as to direction and end result, the technical aspects of the plan could be developed readily enough. If somehow landowners and users could be made to see their interdependencies and the extent to which the actions of each could be made to aid and strengthen all the others, then coordinated approaches to land use should

---

[22] For a selection from the many recent publications on urban and housing design, see the list at the end of the chapter.

[23] Every textbook or major work on urban planning discusses these questions, not always as explicitly as might be desired but often in much detail. In addition, a few recent works may be illustrative and perhaps helpful: Kenneth J. Schlager, "A Land Use Plan Design Model," *Journal of the American Institute of Planners* (May 1965); U.S. Department of Housing and Urban Development, *Improving the Quality of Urban Life* (U.S. Government Printing Office, 1966); and President's Temporary Commission on Pennsylvania Avenue, *Pennsylvania Avenue* (U.S. Government Printing Office, 1964).

[24] Some significant examples are listed at the end of the chapter.

be possible. The whole of a suburban area might be planned as a unit in spite of divergences in interest among landowners; or the revitalization of an older district could be approached on a group basis. Frieden has made a strong case for the gradual but purposeful rebuilding of older city areas, as contrasted with more drastic clearance and rebuilding such as is often involved in urban renewal.[25] Melamed has pointed out the existence of a substantial volume of excess housing, of just the type needed to meet the needs of lower-income sectors of the population, that could be shifted over to their uses.[26] In each case, citizen involvement on a vastly larger scale than has been customary may be an essential ingredient of success. Perhaps urban planners should be lifted from their drawing boards and offices and urged to roam the city in greater contact with its citizens. This was the intended effect of the citizen participation in planning under the Model Cities program.

The great difficulties in organizing citizen groups for action and for planning are of course widely known. If the objective is plans-carried-out, rather than plans-made, citizen participation on a large scale may not be inefficient. Plans can be made more quickly and in greater technical perfection without the distractions of interest groups from the public; but they are too likely to remain just plans. Rosow has argued that most people are far less responsive to their environment, assuming that their personal housing is reasonably good, than are the professional planners.[27] This may indeed be true, and if so, it is a severe obstacle. But the same indifference exists whether one seeks to involve the public in the planning process or to get public approval of his plans. One should not assume there is an easily ascertainable "general welfare" to which all groups will agree; divergence is far more probable. The recent rise of advocacy planning was noted in Chapter 6.

A common suggestion of economists is to internalize the externalities; in the land use field, this can be accomplished, at least to a degree, by enlarging the area under single ownership or control. The trend toward larger subdivisions and larger operations by the typical suburban developer, noted in previous chapters, is a step in this direction.[28] Some of the larger developers today have substantial areas of land under their control and seek to cultivate a particular "image" for their development. In some cases, their area is large enough to include a shopping district as well as residential areas. Street layout and other features can be planned on a larger basis and perhaps capture some values that would escape the smaller developer. But the problems of assembling large tracts of land and the cost of holding such tracts while development takes place are undoubtedly obstacles to operation on a large scale.

[25] Bernard J. Frieden, *The Future of Old Neighborhoods* (MIT Press, 1964).

[26] Anshel Melamed, "The Gray Areas: Unutilized Potentials and Unmet Needs," *Land Economics* (May 1965).

[27] Irving Rosow, "The Social Effects of the Physical Environment," *Journal of the American Institute of Planners* (May 1961).

[28] The National Commission on Urban Problems in its report, *Building the American City* (U.S. Government Printing Office, 1968) stresses this point and makes some recommendations for its implementation.

Role of Urban Planning in Land Use Externalities

The basic role of urban planning, in economic terms, is to maximize the favorable land use externalities and minimize the adverse ones.[29] The individual decision maker is assumed to make the best possible choice for his own interests on the basis of such costs and benefits as he can take into account. The difficulty is that he may escape many costs which others must suffer and that he may create values which he cannot capture because these costs and values are externalities in the economic sense of the term.

Urban planning, as typically practiced in the United States today, is seriously deficient in solving these problems of land use externalities. Wheaton has sharply criticized typical metropolitan planning as being intuitive, as lacking in real analysis and criteria, and as not presenting real alternatives to citizens of the area.[30] These criticisms come from a practicing planner, a recognized leader in the field, who is not rejecting urban planning in toto but is both pleading for improvement and suggesting ways in which this can be done. In this article, he suggests how data could be assembled and analyzed, using a cost-benefit approach, to provide empirical tests of various plans for an urban area. Feiss, another working planner, has sharply criticized urban planning and land use zoning, as typically practiced, primarily because of their negative approach.[31] In his opinion, a more positive approach, with more emphasis upon development possibilities, is now called for. Other critical voices have been raised from within the urban planning profession.

Use of the Econometric Approach

It may be useful to suggest briefly how minimizing adverse externalities and maximizing favorable ones could be tackled as an econometric problem. An adequate econometric solution would require production or transformation functions, by which land and other inputs could be translated into values and satisfactions of various kinds, for each of the many uses of urban land. It would also require demand curves or functions, theoretically for every land user but acceptably for groups of land users with similar tastes and capacities for the products or services of land and—most difficult of all—cross-elasticities or inter-use transformation equations to show the effect that one use or user had upon other uses or users. A fully adequate model would be incredibly complicated. At least 10 and probably as many as 100 different land uses would have to be considered. There would be some hundreds or thousands of user groups in a fair-sized city. Scores of production and transformation functions would be involved, and cross-elasticities and inter-use

[29] Werner Z. Hirsch and David L. Shapiro, in "Some Economic Implications of City Planning," *UCLA Law Review* (August 1967) have carried this idea further and more explicitly than any other source known to this writer.

[30] William L. C. Wheaton, "Operations Research for Metropolitan Planning," *Journal of the American Institute of Planners* (November 1963).

[31] Carl Feiss, "Planning Absorbs Zoning," *Journal of American Institute of Planners* (May 1961).

transformations would run into the thousands. Moreover, the equations and relationships established for one period of time might not remain stable for the future—and planning is by definition concerned with the future. An adequate model would thus require many thousands of equations and an enormous volume of data. Nothing remotely resembling such data exists even in cities where elaborate transportation, land use, and other plans have been formulated with the aid of modern computing equipment. Most of the models to date at best "explain" part of what has happened in the past, when adverse externalities have been far from minimized and favorable externalities far from maximized. Although enormous progress has been made in the devising and use of more and more complicated models in a way that would have been totally impossible two or three decades ago, even the most advanced model now available is a far cry from being fully adequate to deal with the externality problem. Of course, this situation might well change in the next decade or two.

A fully econometric approach would encounter difficulties in addition to the lack of data and of all the equations needed. It seems almost certain that any "solution" will involve costs or losses to some persons or groups, as does indeed the operation of the land market. An attempt to measure the net gain of any proposal thus inevitably includes balancing the gains of some people against the loss to others—the interpersonal utility comparison which economists have typically avoided as unsolvable within their frame of reference. Does the gain to the higher-income suburban family, from not having its children's education impaired by the introduction of less well-prepared children into their schools, more than balance the loss which the low-income family from the less desirable parts of the city suffers because its children are condemned to a school where all children are educationally retarded to a significant degree? Does the gain to the relatively wealthy sub-urbanite, from not having factory smoke pollute his air, more than balance the losses which lower-income sectors must suffer from a concentration of factories near where they live? These are but examples of the kinds of choices that may have to be made.

Perhaps a still more basic objection could be offered to the econometric approach to minimizing adverse land use externalities and maximizing favorable ones. If the choices were made on the basis of individual demand or preference curves or schedules, as usually would be the case, would the result necessarily be sound public policy? A great many citizens in a metropolitan area will choose to "solve" their problems by condemning others in the region to an inferior position. In particular, they will try to keep "undesirable" low-income, racial, ethnic, or other groups of the population out of their suburb or neighborhood. They will seek to include within their local taxing unit the clean factories and the best tax revenue producers while at the same time avoiding as much of the public costs for welfare as possible. Actions of this sort are prevalent now in many suburbs; there is good reason to think that many suburbanites, if allowed to choose freely, would go still further. Such persons meet their problems only by worsening the problems of other groups, and perhaps only by worsening the problems of the whole metropolis. There are times when the long-term general public interest requires an overriding of the localized popular will.

On balance, therefore, it seems necessary to reject the econometric approach to minimizing adverse land use externalities and maximizing favorable land use externalities, at least for the present, on both practical grounds (lack of data and technical transformation functions) and on theoretical grounds (interpersonal comparisons). But this does not mean that urban planning could not be revitalized and modernized to meet these difficult economic problems.

The Ideal Planning Process

An ideal urban planning process would include several steps:

1. Planning that deals with major land use in the whole of an urban area should be on a metropolitan or SMSA scale since land use planning for only part of an economic area is inevitably only partial in its answers. This does not deny that some problems are local or that planning for their solution cannot be local.

2. Urban planning should try to set forth honestly, succinctly, and in readily understandable terms the goals it seeks to reach. One reason why so many city or suburban plans have been so unclear is that many city planning organizations have been unwilling to state honestly what they hoped to accomplish by their plans.

3. The plans should face frankly the secondary effects that will probably result if the plans are carried out. The secondary effects of separating residential and industrial areas and of large-lot zoning and low-income workers are prime examples.[32]

4. The city plan might strike a balance sheet, as quantitatively as possible but in expository terms where figures are not available, as to the gains and losses, and compare them with the gains and losses of other possible plans.

5. In very frank terms, the plan might measure or describe the gains and losses to different groups within the whole urban area. It is absurd to pretend that everyone is better off with any plan that can be devised.

These very general and perhaps utopian suggestions would of course be difficult to implement for a major urban area. A master plan for almost any urban area can muster little political support when faced with opposition from specialized interest groups.[33] But general political support can never be mustered for plans of too circumscribed interest and applicability. Part of the problem is the serious gap between planning and plan implementation.

The basic difficulties with land use planning as a mechanism for increasing the positive externalities are political rather than economic. On the one hand, it is hard to get the total public interested and concerned, and it is hard to dramatize the general values that can be created by imaginative and sound general land use plans. On the other hand, the various special interests usually see clearly their stake

---

[32] See Massachusetts Department of Commerce and Massachusetts Institute of Technology, *The Effects of Large Lot Size on Residential Development*, Technical Bulletin Number 32 (Washington: Urban Land Institute, 1958).

[33] Edward C. Banfield and James Q. Wilson, *City Politics* (Harvard University Press and MIT Press, 1963).

in particular land use proposals or uses, which may be quite contrary to the overall plan. The landowner who wants zoning to sell his parcel to a merchant who will develop a store in an area planned for single-family homes has his counterpart on a larger scale in the suburb which wishes to exclude lower-income families irrespective of the overall metropolitan land use plan. Not infrequently, a particular group or individual has much more to gain by violation of the general plan than by conformity to it. Interest groups have sought, with considerable success, to man the planning and control mechanisms that might operate to their disadvantage. They can be active and aggressive; it pays them to spend time and effort serving on committees or attending planning or zoning hearings. Many proposals for improvement of suburban land conversion founder on the rocks of local politics.

Experience has shown rather conclusively that land use controls alone are insufficient to guide and direct suburban land use.[34] But a wide variety of governmental techniques exist (some of which were considered in Chapter 8) whose combined force can greatly influence if not fully direct suburban land use development.[35] The major deficiency has been the lack of purpose and the will to use these techniques.

Federal, state, county, and city governments are all deeply involved in urban and suburban land use activities, often times inadvertently or incidentally producing effects which they did not intend. A retreat to a completely free and uninhibited market for land in urban and suburban areas is now impossible. All groups concerned must recognize that some actions affect some land values adversely—if not in absolute terms, then by comparison with what the owner dreamed he was going to obtain. The politics and the law on land use controls and plans must follow the economics and the actual practice if the results are to be reasonably consistent.

A full understanding of externalities and interdependencies in urban land use requires both improved economic analysis to define and to measure them and new law to make their realization possible. The relationships described here generally need to be defined much more sharply and to be measured quantitatively. If I have an interest in your maintenance of the quality of your home, just how important is this in monetary terms? It will be far from easy to measure the values involved. But economics has shown a capacity over the years to grow and develop to meet new problems, and one should not despair that it cannot be done here also.

The economic values that arise out of externalities and interdependencies are property—property of a different kind than that represented by a deed to a piece of land, but property nonetheless. New law must be developed to define the property rights involved, to protect them where they exist, and to make possible their creation where they do not now exist but might do so. To a nonlawyer, these tasks appear even more difficult than the clearly difficult economic analysis to measure the values concerned. However, one should not despair of man's ability to devise new institutions and new law to meet new problems and new situations.

[34] John Delafons, *Land-Use Controls in the United States* (Harvard University Press, 1962); and Reps, "Requiem for Zoning."
[35] F. Stuart Chapin, Jr., "Taking Stock of Techniques for Shaping Urban Growth," *Journal of the American Institute of Planners* (May 1963).

LOCATION OF LAND VALUES ARISING FROM EXTERNALITIES

Regardless of the degree to which urban plans and actions maximize land use externalities, all public actions (including not only planning and zoning but also subdivision controls, building codes, health codes and inspections, and public services of all kinds) affect the geographical distribution of such externality values. Such programs are not, and cannot be, neutral in their effect. Some lands will certainly gain more in value than other tracts; others may lose relatively. Some tracts of land may actually lose value absolutely, in the sense that some program makes them less valuable than they were before. A new highway may open up so much potential suburban subdivision land, for instance, that older vacant lands nearer to the city actually fall in price. It is hard to establish datum planes to measure comparative changes in land value. By and large, in modern times in the United States, it is hard to imagine a tract of urban or suburban land actually falling in value, in an absolute sense, as a result of any public action. To the extent that zoning deprived the owner of opportunity for profitable use of his land, the courts might well not uphold the zoning. Declines in price from what one hoped for may be vastly more common.

Public investments in public services affect private land values, and disproportionately between one tract and another. This point (developed in more detail in Chapter 8) need be brought up here only briefly. Czamanski has shown that various kinds of public improvements, especially those affecting accessibility, have affected land values in Baltimore in the past, and that mass transit would have a marked effect upon land values in the future.[36] Zoning and sewers were two of the most important factors affecting the differences in rate of rise in postwar land prices in suburban Philadelphia, according to Milgram's study.[37] Knetsch has shown that land values in suburban areas are affected by availability of parks.[38]

Zoning almost certainly affects land values, often greatly. The strenuous efforts made by developers, land speculators, and others to get zoning changed are sufficient evidence of the monetary gains to be achieved from rezoning. Real estate developers recognize that the kind of zoning (commercial as contrasted with residential) as well as specific zoning provisions, especially such matters as density of use and height of buildings, greatly affect the value of a tract of land. Some properties can be developed under one set of regulations but not under others, if the price asked by the present owner of the land is to be paid. The building and developing trade is fully alert to the importance of zoning as affecting land values.

At the same time, the effect of land zoning upon land value is often obscured. Zoning for a particular use is meaningless if there exists no demand to use the land for that purpose. Merely zoning a piece of open country as commercial or indus-

---

[36] Stanislaw Czamanski, "The Effects of Public Investments on Urban Land Values," *Journal of the American Institute of Planners* (July 1966).

[37] Grace Milgram, with the assistance of Christine Mansfield, *The City Expands—A Study of the Conversion of Land from Rural to Urban Use, Philadelphia, 1945–62*, a report prepared for the Department of Housing and Urban Development (U.S. Government Printing Office, 1965).

[38] Jack L. Knetsch, "Land Values and Parks in Urban Fringe Areas," *Journal of Farm Economics* (December 1962).

trial does not give it the value per acre or per square foot ordinarily associated with commercial and industrial land if in fact there exists no demand to use it for these purposes. On the other hand, the present zoning of a tract to a "lower" use, such as single-family dwelling, may not deprive a tract of much value for industrial, commercial, office, or high-rise apartment use, simply because virtually everyone assumes, often rightly, that the present zoning can be changed when demand requires. Both present landowner and prospective buyer value the land at its potential use minus such costs as may be involved in its rezoning and perhaps minus a small risk factor that the rezoning effort will fail.

For these reasons, the correlation between zoning and land value at any particular time and area may be low. Milgram found that zoning was one important variable. On the other hand, Crecine and associates found little correlation between zoning and present value.[39] The significant comparisons would be between tracts of land for which there was real demand for another use and for which zoning was really firm, and tracts which lacked demand or firm zoning or both. Such comparisons have not been made on a research basis, so far as the writer knows. Indeed, they would not be easy to make, because it would be hard to measure either "firmness" in zoning or demand for other uses.

But it is virtually certain that rezoning often creates substantial values on the land rezoned. Unless one assumes that developers and others are wholly irrational, it seems improbable that they would go to the lengths they often do to obtain rezoning without being convinced that there was something in it for them.

Zoning and other public actions in effect collect economic values from some lands where they would be otherwise and concentrate them upon certain parcels of land. The owners of the latter obtain economic benefits, sometimes amounting to large sums of money, for values essentially created by others and collected by others for concentration on their land. It was considerations of this kind which led the writer to ask, "Why Not Sell Zoning and Rezoning? (Legally, That Is)."[40]

The first reaction might well be that it would be unreasonable to sell zoning and rezoning of land. The argument might run that planning should be the basis on which land use changes were made, and that to sell zoning would be to negate the planning process. Some planners might consider it immoral or at least degrading to their professional judgment. But it seems unlikely that a case can be made that a particular tract of land is desirable or suitable for a commercial or other more intensive land use, while at the same time arguing that no neighboring or nearby tract could possibly be suitable. It is highly doubtful if planning is or can be so precise in its locational dimension. Planners might well decide that some acreage of land was needed for commercial or high-rise residential development within some more or less closely defined locality or neighborhood. Sale of zoning could then be a means of identifying the specific tract of land within the defined locality.

[39] John P. Crecine, Otto A. Davis, and John E. Jackson, "Externalities in Urban Property Markets: Some Empirical Results and Their Implications for the Phenomenon of Municipal Zoning," Graduate School of Industrial Administration, Carnegie Institute of Technology, Pittsburgh (undated, but after 1965).

[40] Marion Clawson, "Why Not Sell Zoning and Rezoning? (Legally, That Is)," *Cry California* (Winter 1966–67).

The establishment of "floating" zones in some local governmental units is a kind of response to this situation, but one to which other objections have been raised.

If a unit of local government that had zoning powers decided to sell land zoning or rezoning, it would establish the total acreage which would be rezoned and define the limits of the area within which rezoning would fall. It might require bidders to own, or to have options on, acreage within the defined locality equal to any bids they submitted. This would reduce the number of potential bidders, but it would ensure that the full price of the rezoning was paid to the public body. Then the rezoning would be sold by competitive bidding, either written or oral. Sale of public property by bids is an established practice, and there would seem no insurmountable problems here.

The advantages of competitive sale of rezoning are several:

1. It would bring the rezoning process fully into the open. It would remove, or at least reduce, the opportunity for collusion between public officials and private parties and for perversion of the whole zoning process. Of perhaps equal importance would be its effect in lowering public suspicions about such collusion and perversion.

2. It would give everyone concerned a more accurate idea of what the monetary values of the rezoning actually are. Most of the general public today has only the faintest idea of what is at stake in many rezoning cases. Since the auctions would be public, they would attract public attention, including that of news media, and the values created by rezoning would be clearly evident.

3. It would award the rezoning in a particular locality to the person or group best able to take advantage of it. The market has an efficient and impartial capacity to choose among potential users.

4. It would capture a substantial proportion of the publicly created land values for the public which created them. This is an equity argument to complement the efficiency argument of the preceding point.

Competitive sale of rezoning would not be perfect. Merely calling it competitive would not necessarily make it so. Collusion among potential bidders and between them and public officials would not be impossible, merely difficult. The competitive sale of rezoning in any locality would not be better than the planning which decided to offer such rezoning in that area. If unwise decisions were made, the bidding might or might not reveal them. While no cure-all for the ills created by present zoning practice, competitive sale of rezoning has many possibilities which deserve careful study.

Interest of the General Public

A discussion of externalities and interdependencies in land use and value, even if in general terms and much more so if in mathematical terms, is likely to seem rather esoteric to the average urban dweller or even to the average professional worker living in an urban complex. But externalities and interdependency in urban land use are the very stuff of which the good urban life is made. Urban living at its best includes pleasant residential neighborhoods where all the houses are well kept and well maintained; good shopping districts, attractive in appearance and conveniently located; good public services such as schools, also conveniently located; adequate recreational areas, also conveniently located; good transportation facilities from home to work and elsewhere as one may wish to travel; and other related features. But every one of these represents an externality to every other one.

The general public has or should have a real interest in the maximization, in the algebraic sense, of positive externalities in urban land use and value. A basic problem is to make the public aware of its interest and of its stake in the outcome, to develop ways of organizing such interest to practical ends and ways of translating such interest into specific actions. Though the discussion may seem esoteric, the problem is real and the stakes are high.

Additional References

In addition to the publications cited in the footnotes, these listed below have special relevance for sections of this chapter.

A. *Urban Design and Housing Design* (Note 22)

Fagin, Henry, and Weinberg, Robert C., editors. *Planning and Community Appearance.* New York: Regional Plan Association, 1958.

Spreiregen, Paul D. *Urban Design: The Architecture of Towns and Cities.* New York: McGraw-Hill Book Co., 1965.

Tunnard, Christopher, and Pushkarev, Boris. *Man-Made America: Chaos or Control?* New Haven: Yale University Press, 1963.

B. *Citizen Participation in Planning* (Note 24)

Institute for Environmental Studies, University of Pennsylvania, and U.S. Geological Survey. *Plan and Program for the Brandywine,* 1968.

Green Spring and Worthington Valley Planning Council. *Plan for the Valleys.* Towson, Md.: The Council, 1966.

Paley, William S., chairman, The Mayor's Task Force. *The Threatened City.* New York: City of New York, 1967.

Regional Plan Association. *Public Participation in Regional Planning.* Bulletin 106. New York: The Association, 1967.

———. *The Lower Hudson.* New York: The Association, 1966.

———. "Basic Issues of the Second Regional Plan." *Regional Plan News,* Number 86, October 1967.

part II

THE NORTHEASTERN URBAN COMPLEX IN THE UNITED STATES

The preceding chapters which form Part I of this book have been concerned with the general process of suburban land conversion in the United States—general in the sense that they deal with the whole country and use data and illustrations from any city or region for which appropriate information is available. Existing literature about suburbanization has been reviewed and set into an analytical framework designed to provide a better understanding of the various kinds of information than has hitherto been possible. Such understanding is essential to any assessment of suburbanization as one of the most important movements in contemporary America, with significant implications for economic, social, and political life in the United States.

Part II, in contrast, deals with a specific region of the country, the Northeastern Urban Complex, and with a specific period, the years since World War II. This is the oldest and largest grouping of population in the United States, important in its own right and perhaps as a forerunner of what is to come in other urban regions, both here and abroad.

As far as available information will permit, the following chapters make explicit and quantitative what was discussed in more general terms in Part I. Here data are drawn from several sources, including original investigations of three areas within the Complex. Even so, the analysis is hampered by lack of fully comparable and relevant data, especially over a period of time. The sample area studies are utilized to throw light on the region as a whole. Summary discussion of other metropolitan areas within the Complex will, it is hoped, help to facilitate understanding of suburbanization.

AN 10 OVERVIEW OF THE COMPLEX

A s used in this book, "Northeastern Urban Complex" means all the Standard Metropolitan Statistical Areas from just north of Boston, south to Washington, D.C., together with all more or less directly intervening rural counties. The Complex includes 34 SMSAs, 78 counties, and 109 cities with 25,000 population or more in 1960. Within its 31.5 thousand square miles, 34.2 million people lived[1] (Figure 12 and Appendix Tables 2 and 3).

This analysis includes the whole of any county which was partly included in one of the 1960 SMSAs, as well as intervening more or less rural counties where urbanization is likely to extend in the next few decades—where it is actually extending now, in several cases. The defined area thus includes one county in New Hampshire, all of Massachusetts except the extreme eastern and extreme western portions, all of Rhode Island and Connecticut, the southeastern corner of New York, nearly all of New Jersey, southeastern Pennsylvania, part of northern Delaware, some of Maryland, the District of Columbia, and a little of Virginia. The area, thus defined, is relatively inclusive as far as total population, employment, income, housing, and other measures of urban life are concerned; that is, it would be necessary to extend its boundaries a great deal farther to include substantially more people. This area includes much more than the direct urban land use zone. This was intentional, as well as almost inescapable because of the nature of the data. Let us begin by looking at land use within the whole area and then gradually narrow down our focus to deal in more detail with the strictly urbanized parts of the whole area.

Any study of urbanism in the northeastern United States inevitably invites comparison with Gottmann's *Megalopolis*.[2] Gottmann states that this term was first applied to a Greek settlement which its founders hoped would become the largest of all Greek cities. Their hopes were not realized, and the term has now come to mean any very large city. Gottmann seems unaware that Lewis Mumford

---

[1] As noted in Chapter 2 above, the Bureau of the Census followed county lines in defining SMSAs in 1960, except in New England, where towns were used. Since 1960, additional counties or towns have been added to some of the original SMSAs, and the 1970 Census will include these and possibly additional areas. However, in this chapter the 1960 definitions are used, partly because much information in the 1960 Census is not available in sample censuses or other sources for the period since 1960.

[2] Jean Gottmann, *Megalopolis—The Urbanized Northeastern Seaboard of the United States* (Twentieth Century Fund, 1961).

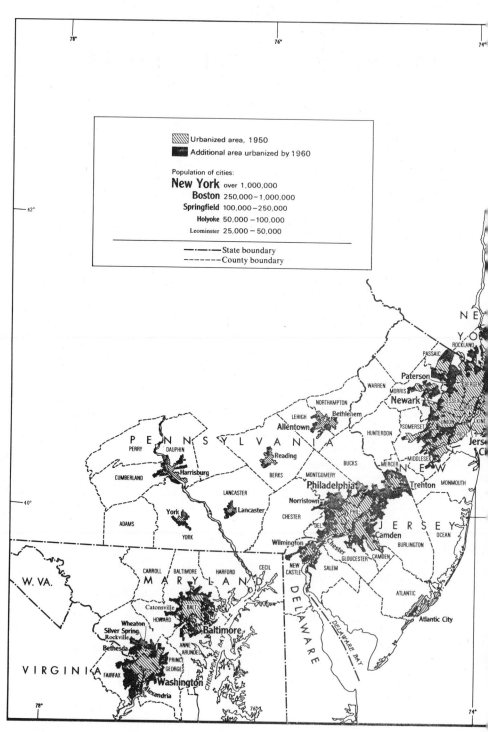

FIGURE 12.   Standard Metropolitan Statistical Areas in the Northeastern Urban Complex.

had used the term more than 20 years earlier, to refer to city population groupings of the largest size and greatest complexity.[3]

Gottmann gave "megalopolis" a special meaning in its application to the northeastern United States and by his dramatic description of this urban region. He includes "the chain of contiguous counties having a metropolitan economy in 1950." The base area varies somewhat in his maps and tables. But, to judge from the map in the end papers, his Megalopolis is somewhat more inclusive than the Northeastern Urban Complex as defined here. He includes (and this study excludes) the Manchester, Pittsfield, Scranton, and Wilkes-Barre SMSAs, and rural areas across the north, along the western boundary, and along the Atlantic Ocean from the north to the southern tip of Maryland. But a great deal of the Northeastern Urban Complex is the same as his Megalopolis, especially in its highly urbanized core. Published in 1961, his book was able to make only modest use of the 1960 Census, only five out of his 227 maps referring to 1960. Total population and such associated measures as employment and housing are rather similar for the two studies, although Megalopolis includes more essentially rural land than the Northeastern Urban Complex.

The difference between the present study and that of Gottmann lies more in approach and in use of statistical data than in area included. He used primarily county data which dominated his findings and led to the widely quoted opening sentence of his book: "The Northeastern seaboard of the United States is today the site of a remarkable development—an almost continuous stretch of urban and suburban areas from southern New Hampshire to northern Virginia and from the Atlantic shore to the Appalachian foothills." From that sentence many a careless reader has concluded that all the land within Megalopolis is fully used for urban purposes, and some have stated that no land is left for urban expansion within the region. Gottmann's maps, which show most of the counties in Megalopolis to be "urbanized"—i.e., to have more than 1,000 persons per square mile average for the whole county—contribute to this misunderstanding. Gottmann made modest use of census data for minor civil divisions and limited use of sample area land use surveys for small districts. But his results are largely dominated by the use of county data, which is a relatively coarse grain of inquiry. Had he relied more upon a finer grain, or had he been more aware (and made the reader more aware) that the coarse grain of county data affected his results, his conclusions—or at least his statements of them—would have been different. A careful reader of Gottmann's book gets a different impression than that conveyed by the opening sentence or many of the maps based on county data.

This book uses different levels of inquiry, or different grains of study, and explores the use of land in more detail, at least for sample districts. SMSA and county data are used at some points simply because nothing better is available. Wherever possible, however, data on a finer grain are used. Perhaps more important than an analysis in detail is the necessity of always keeping in mind the importance of grain of study as to the conclusions reached about land use. (See Chapter 2.) It may be impossible, at times, to obtain data on as fine a grain as one would wish.

[3] Lewis Mumford, *The Culture of Cities* (Harcourt, Brace, 1938). Mumford in turn acknowledged his debt to Patrick Geddes, who used the term as early as 1915.

But at least one can avoid drawing conclusions which are inappropriate to the grain of his inquiry, and one should always warn the reader of the grain and of its effect on the conclusions.

Pickard and Pushkarev, in separate but related papers prepared for the same conference, use a much more inclusive definition of "Atlantic Metropolitan Region," both for historical analysis and for a projection to the year 2020.[4] They include a much larger area to the north, west, and south of the northeastern urban complex and go to the Atlantic on the east. While this quadruples the gross land area of the complex, it adds only 13 percent to the 1960 population, thus demonstrating anew the fact that the core of the northeastern urban area is fairly obvious and will be included in any serious study of the region or of the problem. Differences may arise as to the outer boundaries, but these are more significant for land area than for population or employment. There is logic in using an inclusive definition for population, employment, and similar data; but the northeastern urban complex already includes a great deal of rural land, as this chapter will show, and it seems undesirable to include a great deal more of such rural land. In the analyses which follow, however, it should always be borne in mind that other definitions of the region have included much more land.

None of the studies deal with the total economic, cultural, social, financial, and other influences of the urban areas in their respective regions. Indeed, the area of that influence would include the whole of the United States and even the whole of the world. "Influence" is relative—large nearby, growing weaker with distance. Yet few people in the world are unaffected to some degree by the political decisions of the United Nations and the United States, by the markets of the large American cities or the financial decisions made there. The concern in this book is with land use, and definitions of the region and ways of using data are evaluated in terms of their effect upon the description of land use within the region.

The Pickard-Pushkarev analysis was adopted with an eye to probable developments over the next 50 years. Others have emphasized the probable growth of great urban complexes. Kahn and Wiener have referred to Boswash, the area from Boston to Washington, which they think will include almost a quarter of the total population of the nation in 2000; to Chipitts, the area from Chicago to Pittsburgh, including Detroit, Buffalo, and Rochester, which may have an eighth of the population in 2000; and to Sansan, the area from San Francisco to San Diego, which may have a sixteenth of the population.[5] A Montreal-to-Chicago metropolitan complex (including Toronto, Pittsburgh, Detroit, and other large cities) was recognized in a report made in 1964.[6] In his planning studies of the Detroit metropolitan area,

---

[4] Jerome P. Pickard, "If Present Trends Continue," and Boris Pushkarev, "The Present Situation—Its Implications," papers presented at Conference 2020, arranged by a large group of eastern utilities, states, cities, foundations, and chapters of the American Insitute of Planners and held in New York City, January 30–31, 1969. Pushkarev's revised paper, "The Atlantic Seaboard: Development Issues and Strategies," has since been issued as the September 1969 issue of *Regional Plan News,* published by the Regional Plan Association, New York City.

[5] Herman Kahn and Anthony J. Wiener, "The Next Thirty-three Years: A Framework for Speculation," *Daedalus* (Summer 1967).

[6] *Change/Challenge/Response—A Development Policy for New York State* (Albany: Office for Regional Development, 1964).

Doxiadis has made much of the possibility of a Great Lakes megalopolis, which he thinks will closely parallel the Atlantic megalopolis with a lag of about 20 years.[7]

The "Coffin Area" of Britain—so named because its outlines suggest a coffin shape—is a major urban complex. From London and environs in the southeast, it extends diagonally across the country to include Liverpool and its environs at its northwest end. Whereas our Northeastern Urban Complex includes 31.5 thousand square miles (20 million acres) and 34.2 million people, the Coffin Area includes from 24 to 31 thousand square miles (15½ to 20 million acres), depending upon the exact definition, and from 34 to 38 million people.[8] The close similarity in total land area and in total population is evident; the total-population/total-area densities (measure No. 1 in Table 1) of the two regions are closely similar. However, there are substantial differences in the distribution of population. The U.S. sprawl in the suburbs contrasts with the more tightly bounded city in Britain, and the very high-rise apartments in our largest cities contrast with lower ones in Britain. Their structure of government differs from ours; for instance, in Britain there are no states intervening between central and local government. Moreover, while our Northeastern Urban Complex includes roughly a fifth of our national population, the Coffin Area includes from 74 to 82 percent of the comparable figure for Britain. Nevertheless, the similarity of total area and of total population in the two regions invites comparison as to the differences in public and private programs for urbanization.

The Complex in International and National Perspective

In the modern world, any large urban aggregation of people will necessarily have complex relationships with large numbers of people in other parts of the world. This generalization surely holds with respect to the Northeastern Urban Complex.

Gottmann has well pointed out how the Atlantic Coast of North America—and more particularly the northern part—during colonial times was the "economic hinge" between Europe and the Atlantic Ocean, on the one hand, and the interior parts of what is today the United States, on the other. Settlement was made first along the coast and waterways leading inland from it. In the north, fishing and sea trade were from the first as important to the economy as agriculture and other land-based activities. As settlement extended inward, the port function of the seacoast towns grew in importance. As industry developed, it tended to locate in these same towns or a little inland. The development of rail and water transportation to the interior stimulated economic development in these cities and their immediate hinterlands.

Today the cities along the Atlantic Coast still exercise an important hinge function between the United States and the rest of the world, especially Europe. Not only do these cities have trade and business relations with the rest of the world, but

---

[7] C. A. Doxiadis, "The Prospect of an International Megalopolis," in *The International Megalopolis*, Mason Wade, ed. (University of Toronto Press, 1969); and *Emergence and Growth of an Urban Region, The Developing Detroit Area, Volume I: Analysis* (The Detroit Edison Co., 1966).

[8] Data provided by Ray Thomas, Political and Economic Planning, London.

important governmental and international activities are also located here. Washington, as the seat of government for the United States, attracts many business, professional, and other special interest groups. It is also the location of important international and regional organizations, such as the International Bank for Reconstruction and Development, the International Monetary Fund, the Organization of American States and its various branches, the Inter-American Development Bank, and others. New York is the home of the United Nations, as well as other major international activities. All of these give the Northeastern Urban Complex a major world role.

This region also plays an important role in the domestic affairs of the United States. Governmental activities in Washington affect the whole country. New York has long been the major national financial center. A large part of the insurance companies of the United States have their central offices in this region. Major educational institutions, and the research and development work so often associated with university centers, are also located here. So are important manufacturing and related processes. The large urban population of the region, with average income per capita somewhat above the rest of the United States as a whole, means that major consumer markets are located here. Agricultural products from all over the United States and other countries are shipped here for consumption. In all of these, and in numerous more detailed and specialized ways, the Northeastern Urban Complex is a major part of the total U.S. economic, social, and political life. Gottmann has done a superb job of tracing these relationships in detail.

The Northeastern Urban Complex includes less than 1 percent of the total land area of the United States—slightly more than 1 percent if Alaska is excluded from the base. (Figure 13) But nearly one-fifth of the American people and of the labor

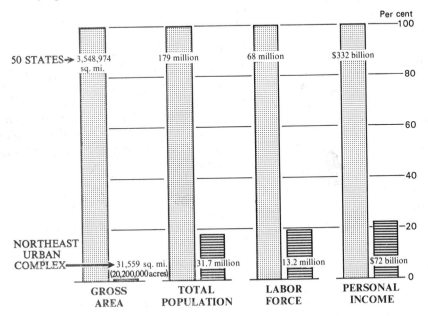

FIGURE 13. Northeastern Urban Complex in relation to the whole United States, 1960.

force live there—18 percent and 19 percent respectively. The fact that this fifth of the American population receives more than one-fifth (22 percent) of total personal income in the country means that income per capita is high in this region. It must be remembered, however, that although the Northeastern Urban Complex is highly important in the national economic and social life, it is still a fraction of the total.

Natural Environment of the Complex

There is space here for only a brief discussion of the natural environment of the Northeastern Urban Complex. Anyone interested in pursuing the subject further would be well advised to read Gottmann, whose training as a geographer makes him particularly sensitive to the relationships between the socioeconomic aspects of urban life and the natural environment on which it is based.

To summarize or oversimplify: the natural environment of the Northeastern Urban Complex has been moderately, but not extremely, favorable to the development of a large urban complex. Such disadvantages or limitations as the region imposed can be and have been overcome without excessive cost. The great strength of the region in a physical sense has been its location with respect to other regions of the world. Indeed, urbanization within the Complex has depended far more upon global locational factors than upon any features internal to the region itself.

The climate of the Complex is highly variable, not only from season to season but also in terms of day-to-day change. The summers are hot, the winters cold. The climate is somewhat milder along the coast than inland, and hence there is a longer frost-free growing season along the coast. Generally speaking, precipitation is ample not only for agriculture but also for urban purposes. However, droughts do occur with moderate frequency, and an ample supply of water at all seasons of every year requires the larger cities to have storage capacity and to reach some distances inland for a source of water. The region gets hurricanes. In fact, contrary to popular belief, the probability of damaging coastal storms or hurricanes is greater in New England than it is in Florida, although Florida storms are more likely to cause severe damages.[9] For modern urban living, residential quarters must be heated in winter and should be air-conditioned for summer, yet living can be pleasant and comfortable in this climate. Air pollution in the region has already become serious—owing in part to industrial wastes and in part to fuel consumption —and is likely to grow worse in the future unless much more effective control measures are undertaken.

Almost the entire region was heavily forested when Europeans first came. Forest types varied within the region, but all provided building materials and fuel to the early colonists. Later, extensive lumbering and other forest operations were carried out. Today, any idle land within the region reverts to trees in time, although the resulting tree cover may not be a productive forest. Cut over many times, the forests today are seriously degraded in the forester's sense of that term. Produc-

[9] Ian Burton and others, *The Shores of Megalopolis: Coastal Occupancy and Human Adjustments to Flood Hazard* (Elmer, N. J.: C. W. Thornthwaite Associates, Laboratory of Climatology, 1965).

tion of wood and wood products is limited and not very profitable, nor is it likely to become profitable in the foreseeable future. Yet wooded lands are very extensive today and play a very important role in the economy and social life of the region. Many urban dwellers own tracts of rural forested land, with or without structures on them, for recreational or other uses.

The soils of this region are highly variable in their adaptability for agriculture. Some were excellent for agriculture in the colonial period, and those not removed from agriculture by conversion to urban use are still well suited for it. Others, especially some of the coastal sandy soils, were naturally rather infertile and not easily usable in an earlier day but now respond well to fertilizer and can often be used profitably. Still other soils were once used for agriculture but have been abandoned because farming on them cannot compete with more fertile and more nearly level lands farther west. Many of these abandoned acres could be used for agriculture, if the pressure of population on land in the United States were so severe as to require their output; but they are not profitable under today's conditions nor are they likely to become so.

The region contains extensive swamps and other poorly drained land along the coast and the rivers, which have never been suitable for agriculture and offer great obstacles to urban development. An example is the "Jersey meadows" across the Hudson River from downtown New York City, which, despite many proposals for filling, remain essentially unused. However, the tidal swamps and similar areas often perform useful roles. They may form an important recharge area for underground water basins, they may provide an overflow area to lessen the impact of floods, and they may provide important food for fish which are later caught in ocean fisheries.

The topography of the Northeastern Urban Complex is also variable. The extensive coastal lowlands are relatively flat, often with sandy soils. Except where swamps or other poorly drained areas occur, this land form is very well suited to intensive urban development. In most of this region, a fall line occurs where the rivers leave the uplands and emerge to the coastal plain. Water power developed at such sites was an extremely important factor in the early industrialization of this region. The fall line marked the end of water navigation by oceangoing vessels, even the very small vessels of the colonial period. The rolling upland areas above the fall line are also generally well suited for intensive urban use. Some land has steep slopes which are costly to build upon and subject to erosion. In some locations bedrock is near the surface and costly to excavate. With these exceptions, the upland areas are nearly all suitable for urban use. Differences in elevation and in slope often offer attractive vistas for residential and recreational use of land. With new technologies for earth-moving and for building, many sites are buildable today which were not usable in an earlier era.

The region's minerals and fuels were important in its early industrial development. At present, relatively limited use is made of mineral resources (except for such common building materials as sand, gravel, and clay), for larger and more readily exploitable deposits of minerals and fuels are found in regions farther west.

The most important of all physical attributes of the Northeastern Urban Complex is its location on the world's surface. The sea on one side, with relatively extensive penetration of the interior by navigable rivers and bays, is highly important. In addition to fisheries, it provides access to the whole world, especially to Europe. The Complex also has relatively easy access to the great agricultural heartland of the United States and to the industrial complexes which have grown up from Pittsburgh to Chicago, with all that these have meant to business in the major cities of the region. The inland route from New York, by canal and by rail at relatively very favorable grades, has possibly been as important as the superb natural harbor of New York. Even if natural conditions within the Northeastern Urban Complex had been much less favorable for agriculture, mining, industry, and general urban development, such development would almost surely have taken place, simply because of the strategic location of the area in world terms. Favorable natural environment helped, especially in the earliest decades, and even today in terms of relatively low costs for urbanization, but unfavorable environment could hardly have prevented urbanization of this region.

Census Data on Population, Employment, Housing, and Income

The Northeastern Urban Complex includes about 31.5 thousand square miles, or slightly over 20 million acres (Figure 14 and Appendix Table 3). In 1960, of this total, about 6 percent—just under 2,000 square miles or about 1.2 million

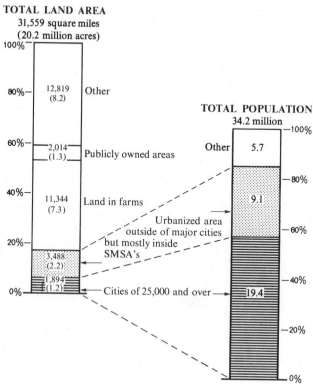

Figure 14.   Land use and population in Northeastern Urban Complex, 1960.

acres—was within the legal boundaries of cities with 25,000 or more inhabitants, though not all of it was in use in 1960. Within these cities, 19.4 million people lived, in the sense of customarily sleeping there; in addition, others worked there, commuting to and from their homes; and others shopped or conducted business there. The domiciled population of these cities was 57 percent of the whole population of the Complex, and 11 percent of the total U.S. population.

The urbanized areas outside of these larger cities, nearly all of which are within an SMSA, in 1960 included 3,488 square miles (about 2.2 million acres) or about 11 percent of the total area of the Complex. In these urbanized areas lived some 9.1 million people, 27 percent of those in the Complex or 5 percent of those in the whole United States. Many of them were dependent upon the central city for jobs, goods, or services, but many of them also worked and shopped in their own zone.

These data clearly indicate a marked concentration of people *within* the Northeastern Urban Complex. As we have seen, the Complex as a whole is a high concentration of people within the United States, but the degree of concentration within it is great also. Pushkarev has made some interesting comparisons on this very point, as follows:[10]

	Percent population	*Percent area*
Atlantic region (214 counties) related to North America	22	1.3
"Core" of Atlantic region (104 counties) related to conterminous U.S.	19	1.4
Municipalities with densities over 10,000 persons per square mile within the more heavily settled 150 counties in the Atlantic region related to total Atlantic region	40	1.2

The more inclusively one defines the Northeastern Urban Complex—or whatever else this collection of urban centers is called—the more extreme becomes the relative concentration of people, since the more inclusive definitions take in disproportionately more rural or lightly settled land.

Agriculture in the Complex

In 1959, the farms located within the Northeastern Urban Complex, as defined here, had more than twice as much land in total as the whole urbanized area had in 1960. About 36 percent of the whole Complex was in farms in 1959. Of this farmland, less than one-half was harvested cropland; about one-fourth was woodland, a little of which was grazed; about 10 percent was other pasture, some of which was improved but some not. This leaves nearly a fourth of the total farm

[10] Pushkarev, *The Atlantic Seaboard*, p. 17.

area in miscellaneous categories, including idle and unused. The picture of farm land use, therefore, is one of concentration of activity on part of the land, presumably the more productive land types, with a low level of activity on the remainder.

The forests of this region are in general not highly productive in their present state. Having been cut over repeatedly, they lack an adequate volume of good-quality growing stock. Moreover, there are few good markets for the pulpwood, posts, firewood, and other products which these forests are capable of producing, due to the species with which they are currently stocked.

A small area of land in the Complex is publicly owned, for parks, forests, wildlife refuges, and similar uses. The available data are found in Table 17 later in this chapter. There is some acreage in city parks, which may be included in the total acreage of cities, and hence to this extent there is double-counting.

The most striking aspect of the total land use picture of the Northeastern Urban Complex, as revealed by these census data, is the very large area—more than a third of the total—which is not accounted for in any of the foregoing categories. It is neither city, farm, nor public land use area. Much of this remaining third is covered with forest of the same general low productivity as those within farms. Inventories made by the U.S. Forest Service and cooperating organizations show that virtually all of it is privately owned, mostly in relatively small tracts—less than 500 acres in nearly all cases, often in tracts of less than 100 acres. Some of it is abandoned farmland. Much of it is owned for reasons other than direct immediate financial return. Some is owned in hope of a rise in prices, but often the reasons are personal—the desire to own land in and for itself, for recreation, or similar motivations. Relatively little is known about this land, its owners, and their reasons for land ownership.

The decennial censuses of agriculture throw some light on changes in farming in the Northeastern Urban Complex. (The 5-year censuses of agriculture are ignored here in the interests of simplicity of exposition.) The changes in agriculture in this highly urbanized region have been remarkably parallel to national changes in agriculture (Table 13). The number of farms declined by half from 1940 to 1959 in the Northeastern Urban Complex, only a little more rapidly than the national decline; farms in the Complex declined only slightly as a proportion of all farms. All land in farms in the Complex declined considerably, while nationally a small increase was reported; likewise, the Complex had a larger proportionate decline in cropland harvested than did the nation.

Farmland abandonment is an old story in New England and the Middle Atlantic regions. Much land that is stony, hilly, or of low fertility, often on small fields not suitable for mechanization, was once farmed and produced at least tolerable, though low, incomes. Today, with stiffer competition from better land in westward farming areas, and with higher standards of what constitutes acceptable farm income, it is no longer even marginal.

The decline in total farm area from 1940 to 1959 in the Northeastern Urban Complex was about 3 million acres, and in cropland harvested a million acres. These contrast with an increase in urbanized area between 1950[11] and 1960 of

[11] There are no data on urbanized areas for 1940.

about 1¼ million acres. These figures might suggest that the area going out of farms was about equal to the area going into city use. However, the relationship is not as simple as this, for the extensive areas of land within the Complex which are in neither use permit many other types of land use changes.

The Northeastern Urban Complex experienced some decline in numbers of dairy cows in each decade of the 1940–1959 period, but proportionately less than the national decline; and the proportion of U.S. dairy cows in the Complex rose over the 20-year period. Dairying is one type of agriculture relatively well-suited to this general region; the presence of the large urban markets stimulates dairy production, though feed grains must usually be shipped in from more distant cropping regions. In terms of total value of all agricultural commodities, the Northeastern Urban Complex experienced a great gain during the decade of the 1940s, largely because of the steep rise in prices of farm commodities, but it also experienced a small rise during the 1950s when the national index of prices received for such commodities was relatively stable or drifting slightly downhill. The gain within the Complex was relatively less than that achieved nationally, so that its proportion of the national total declined somewhat, especially in the 1940s.

In summary, one can say that the high degree of urbanization of the Northeastern Urban Complex has not yet meant the end of agriculture in these urbanized countries. Rather, farming has persisted amazingly well and in some respects actually been strengthened by the urbanization. Outside of the Complex, but within the New England and Middle Atlantic regions generally, agriculture has certainly had a stimulus from urban growth and very little direct interference from it. Agriculture in these general regions is undergoing major changes, similar to but more marked than the changes underway in U.S. agriculture generally. The declines in farm numbers, in total acreage in farms, in cropland harvested, and in numbers of dairy cows, have continued since 1960.

TABLE 13

AGRICULTURAL CHANGE, NORTHEASTERN URBAN COMPLEX, COMPARED WITH U.S. TOTAL, 1940, 1950, AND 1959

Item	Area	Unit	1940	1950	Percent change 1940–50	1959	Percent change 1950–59	Percent change 1940–59
1. Farms	NE	1,000	146.2	123.1	−16	74.9	−39	−49
	US	1,000	6,096.8	5,382.2	−12	3,703.9	−31	−39
	NE/US	percent	2.4	2.3	*	2.0	*	*
2. All land in farms	NE	mil. a.	10.2	9.4	−8	7.3	−22	−28
	US	mil. a.	1,060.9	1,158.6	+9	1,120.2	−3	+6
	NE/US	percent	0.96	0.81	*	0.72	*	*
3. Cropland harvested	NE	mil. a.	4.2	3.9	−7	3.2	−18	−24
	US	mil. a.	321.2	344.4	+7	311.3	−10	−3
	NE/US	percent	1.3	1.1	*	1.0	*	*
4. Milk cows	NE	1,000	668	647	−3	573	−11	−14
	US	1,000	24,926	23,853	−4	19,527	−18	−22
	NE/US	percent	2.7	2.7	*	2.9	*	*
5. Value of all farm products sold	NE	mil. $	336	803	+139	880	+10	+159
	US	mil. $	8,343	28,461	+241	33,511	+18	+302
	NE/US	percent	4.0	2.8	*	2.6	*	*

Source: Censuses of Agriculture.
* = not applicable.

Population

The gross area of all SMSAs within the Noreastern Urban Complex increased only a little (11 percent) from 1950 to 1960, or from 19,466 square miles (12.5 million acres) to 21,564 square miles (slightly less than 14 million acres). This increase in gross area was due primarily to the addition of Fitchburg-Leominster, New London-Groton-Norwich, and Meriden as SMSAs, although there were relatively minor changes in some other SMSAs. But this increase in total SMSA area of about 11 percent is overshadowed by major land use changes within the SMSAs.

The urbanized areas (mostly, but not wholly, within SMSAs) are reported in the 1960 Census to have increased exactly the same as the SMSAs in absolute acreage, from 3,283 square miles (2.1 million acres) to 5,382 square miles (3.4 million acres), a rise of 64 percent. The location of the urbanized areas in 1950 and the additions between 1950 and 1960 are shown in Figure 15. The 1950 urbanized areas were largely concentrated around large cities; however, their extent in some areas was greater than the population of the area would have led one to expect. The extensions between 1950 and 1960 were generally outward from the 1950 areas, but unequally so for different urban areas and unequally by direction for most such areas. Particularly notable are several relatively large extensions in New England. The latter are due largely to the practice in 1960 of including whole towns which were largely but not wholly urbanized. Other relatively large extensions of urbanized area occurred between Philadelphia and Trenton and west of Philadelphia and also south of Washington in Virginia. Large extensions also took place around New York, particularly on Long Island and on the northwestern edge of the 1950 area.

The comparability of the urbanized area data for 1950 and 1960 may be judged by examining apparent changes in density. The average number of persons per square mile (on a total-population/total-area basis) for all urbanized areas dropped from 7,325 in 1950 to 5,300 in 1960, or from 11½ persons to 8¼ persons per acre. While it may be agreed that average density in urban areas—however measured—probably dropped in this decade, a comparison between the added acreage and the added population for all urbanized areas results in a total-population/total-area density figure of about 2,200 persons per square mile (3½ per acre). In the terms used in Table 2 (see Chapter 2), this is at least "very low" density of residential settlement, not much above "very sparse" density. Even this comparison might not seem conclusive. However, it seems probable that some of the added population in 1960 was located on land vacant or idle in 1950 but included within 1950 urbanized areas; to the extent that this was true, the average density in the urbanized areas created between 1950 and 1960 would be lower.

Still further light is thrown on these average data for the whole Northeastern Urban Complex by looking at what is reported for some urbanized areas. In the case of Lawrence, Worcester, Fall River, and New Bedford, the reported increase in urbanized area from 1950 to 1960 is so great, and the reported increase in population so small, that an average total-population/total-area density of about 500 persons per square mile (less than 1 per acre) results for the additional area. This is about one-half the "very sparse" density. In the case of Lowell, Boston,

Hartford, New Haven, Bridgeport, Trenton, Reading, and Lancaster, the reported increase in added area from 1950 to 1960 divided into added population results in an average density of roughly 1,000 persons per square mile (less than 2 per acre), which is still sparse. In contrast, the added population of the greater urbanized area divided by the 1950–1960 increase in acreage produces apparent total-population/total-area densities ranging from 2,500 to 3,800 persons per square mile (4 to 6 per acre) for the urbanized areas of the New York–Northeastern New Jersey area, Philadelphia, Baltimore, and Washington. Actual densities in these added areas would be still lower to the extent that some of the increased population is located within the 1950 urbanized area. There seems no reason to believe that actual patterns of land use change between 1950 and 1960 were as drastically different between the various urbanized areas as these data would suggest.

This analysis for the Northeastern Urban Complex, based entirely upon data from the Census Bureau, clearly supports the conclusion reached in Chapter 2 that census data on urbanized areas do not mean what the published reports say they mean. In fact, it was the analysis of data for the Northeastern Urban Complex which led to the discovery of the general lack of comparability of 1950 and 1960 urbanized areas. The situation may be somewhat worse in the Complex because of the inclusion of a number of New England towns under a "special rule," but it is a national rather than a regional phenomenon. As noted in Chapter 2, the Census Bureau's definition of "urbanized areas" included the statement that, in general, "the urbanized areas of 1950 and 1960 are based on essentially the same concept and the figures for a given urbanized area may be used to measure the population growth of that area." The first half of this statement is in error. The second half may be true so far as population is concerned, though one may express some scepticism. But the implication that changes in urbanized areas between 1950 and 1960 reflect actual changes in land use is clearly wrong, judged by evidence from the census itself. As far as land use is concerned, the concept of urbanized areas, as actually applied in 1960 was clearly different from the concept as actually applied in 1950. Some of the reported increase in urbanized area is a statistical rather than a land use phenomenon. It is most unfortunate that the same term was used to describe different concepts, since the unwary are led to make untenable conclusions—and the Bureau of the Census statement on the subject further tends to confuse the issue.

Data from the studies of three metropolitan areas which are summarized in Chapter 11 show that substantial proportions of the 1950 urbanized area were still vacant in 1960 and that still larger proportions of the urbanized area added between 1950 and 1960 were vacant in 1960. Moreover, the studies of the National Commission on Urban Problems have shown that there are substantial amounts of vacant land within even the larger cities. Of cities within the Northeastern Urban Complex, the proportion of vacant land ranged from 1.8 percent of total land area for Cambridge, Mass. to 27.9 percent for New Bedford, Mass., with 12.5 percent for greater New York.[12] These comparisons emphasize again that data

---

[12] Allen D. Manvel, "Land Use in 106 Large Cities" in *Three Land Research Studies*, National Commission on Urban Problems, Research Report No. 12 (U.S. Government Printing Office, 1968), pp. 28-55.

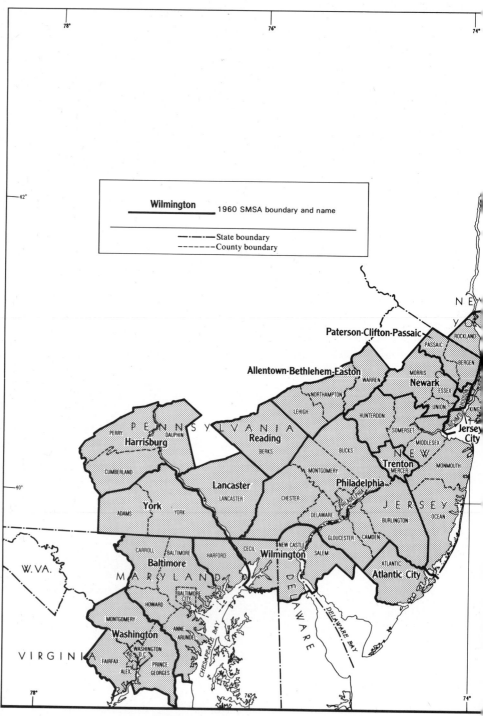

FIGURE 15.   Urbanized areas in 1950 and 1960, Northeastern Urban Complex.

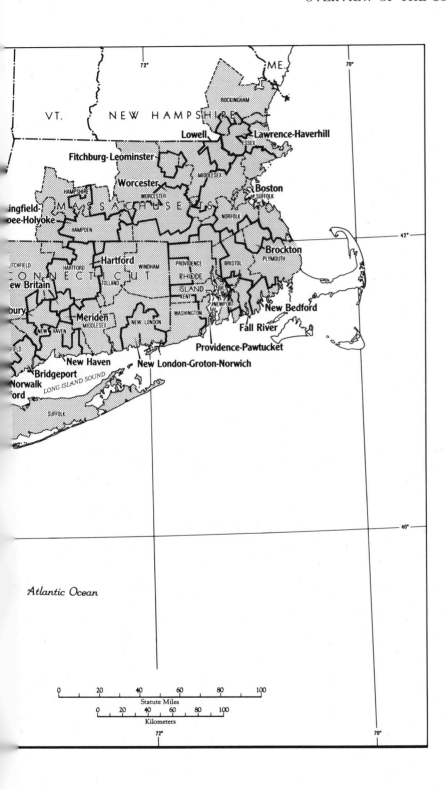

for cities, urbanized areas, SMSAs, or other areas may have one relevance or accuracy for population and employment and quite a different meaning for land use.

The total population of the Northeastern Urban Complex and of its SMSAs has increased since 1940 at a rate almost equal to that of the United States as a whole (Table 14). Nearly a fifth of the whole population of the nation was in the Complex in 1960; well over 90 percent of the population of the Complex was in the SMSAs; 90 percent of that was in the urbanized areas; and the larger cities (25,000 and over) have well over half of the Complex total. The only significant change since 1940 has been in the relationship between larger city and remaining urbanized area. In 1940, three-fourths of the SMSA population was in the larger cities; by 1960, this had shrunk to about 60 percent. Total population of the larger cities rose slowly from 1940 to 1950 and thereafter declined slightly; most of the net growth in population of the Complex occurred in the urbanized areas outside of, but close to, the larger cities. All of these comparisons are based upon cities as legally defined at each date. The extension of city boundaries which was common in the country as a whole has been relatively less important in the Complex than in most regions, largely because many cities already extend to the boundaries of neighboring cities.

The net change in total population in the Northeastern Urban Complex between 1950 and 1960 was 5 million persons. (Appendix Table 4) This was a 17 percent increase over the decade, compared with an 18.5 percent increase for the whole nation in the same period. Of the increase in the Northeastern Urban Complex, only 24 percent was due to net migration into the region, and 76 percent was due to excess of births over deaths. This was a much lower rate of increase due to migration than was experienced in such fast-growing states as Florida, California, and Arizona. It was, of course, higher than that in certain states with heavy out-migration, such as some of the Plains and Southern states.

There was some difference between the northern and southern ends of the Complex in population increase. The northern SMSAs gained relatively least from net migration; the counties from northern New Jersey to the northern end of the Complex contained about two-thirds of its population in 1950 yet they gained only about one-fourth of the net migration. The Washington-Baltimore group of coun-

TABLE 14

TOTAL POPULATION, BY PARTS OF THE NORTHEASTERN URBAN COMPLEX, 1940, 1950, AND 1960

(millions)

Area	1960	1950	1940
United States	179.3	150.7	131.7
Northeastern Urban Complex	34.2	29.3	
SMSAs within it	31.7	26.9	23.7
Their urbanized areas	28.5	24.0	n.a.
Their cities of 25,000 and over	19.4	19.5	18.2

Source: Censuses of Population.
n.a. = not available.

ties gained almost as much from migration, although their population in 1950 was not much more than 10 percent of that of the northern group of counties.

Since World War II, most of the population increase in the Complex has come from its own excess of births over deaths. Perhaps this will continue to be the case, but there will be a substantial rate of population increase. For this region has a significant demographic momentum from its present population which will carry it to larger future total population almost irrespective of migration.

Density of Population

Since the Census Bureau provides data on total acreage and on total population for different kinds of areas, it is possible to calculate total-population/total-area ratios for different kinds of areas within the Northeastern Urban Complex. (Table 15) The whole Complex had an average density of 1,084 persons per square mile (1.7 per acre) in 1960 and 927 per square mile (1.5 per acre) in 1950. The larger cities in the Complex averaged somewhat in excess of 10,000 per square mile (16 per acre) in both 1950 and 1960, with only a very slight reported drop in average density. The urbanized areas outside of these larger cities show an apparent drop in average density, from 3,150 to 2,622 per square mile from 1950 to 1960; but the lack of comparability in definition of urbanized area in 1960 and in 1950 makes this comparison of dubious meaning. Outside of urbanized areas, whether in SMSAs or outside of them, the average density was very low but apparently rising slightly.

The discussion in Chapter 2 about the relationship between different measures of land use density should be recalled. We have been speaking here of total-population/total-area density. Density per square mile or per acre of "developed land," to use Bartholomew's term, would generally run somewhat higher in cities and might easily be double these figures in urbanized areas outside of cities. Within each category there might be as much undeveloped as developed land. Densities in residential areas, whether "gross" or "net" would be still higher, of course.

TABLE 15

DENSITY OF POPULATION (TOTAL-POPULATION/TOTAL-AREA BASIS), BY PARTS OF
NORTHEASTERN URBAN COMPLEX, 1950 AND 1960

Area	Population per square mile		Population per acre	
	1960	1950	1960	1950
Northeastern Urban Complex	1,084	927	1.7	1.5
All its SMSAs	1,475	1,384	2.3	2.2
NUC outside of SMSAs	250	196	0.4	0.3
All urbanized areas	5,300	7,325	8.3	11.5
SMSA area outside of urbanized area[1]	197	179	0.3	0.3
All cities of over 25,000	10,230	10,527	16.0	16.5
Urbanized area outside of cities	2,622	3,150	4.1	4.9

Source: Calculated from census data.
[1] On the assumption (nearly but not strictly accurate) that all urbanized areas lie within SMSAs.

Some further light on this matter of population density is thrown by a consideration of the variations in reported total-population/total-area density among the SMSAs, urbanized areas, and larger cities of the Northeastern Urbanized Complex (Figure 16). Only one of the SMSAs (Jersey City) reported a density in excess of 5,000 per square mile; even the New York metropolitan area as a whole was slightly under 5,000. The mean and the median density for all SMSAs are each close to 1,500 persons per square mile, but a considerable dispersion relative to this central tendency is evident.

When one shifts to the urbanized areas, a wider absolute range in variation is evident. For urbanized areas, the Bureau of the Census groups the three northern New Jersey SMSAs with New York. On this basis, four urbanized areas have

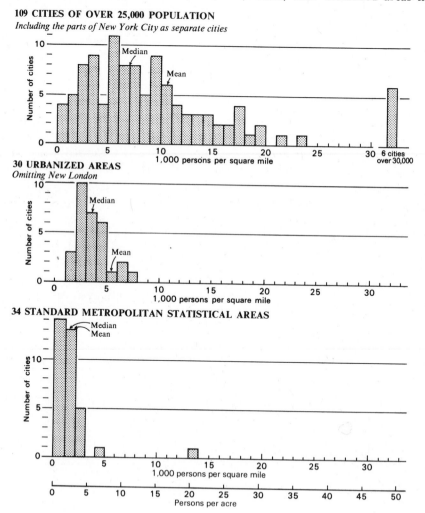

FIGURE 16.   Number of cities over 25,000, of urbanized areas, and of Standard Metropolitan Statistical Areas, according to total-population/total-area density, Northeastern Urban Complex, 1960.

densities in excess of 5,000 persons per square mile. Particularly noteworthy is the way the mean and the median have separated. The median is at slightly over 3,000 persons per square mile, while the mean is over 5,000. The urbanized areas in all of the larger SMSAs—the New York–New Jersey group, Philadelphia, Boston, Baltimore, and Washington—have gross densities in excess of or close to the mean, while the urbanized areas in most of the smaller SMSAs have much lower densities. This strongly suggests that the area of unused land is relatively large in the urbanized areas of many of the smaller SMSAs.

The widest range in gross densities is found among the larger cities. Several have total-population/total-area densities under 3,000 persons per square mile, many are under 5,000, and the median is about 7,000. In contrast, the mean is slightly over 10,000 and a number of cities are over 30,000. The most extreme is Manhattan, with over 77,000; some smaller but closely hemmed-in cities in the New York–New Jersey group also have relatively high densities. These data demonstrate again the degree to which legal boundaries of cities are historical accidents—some cities are tightly bounded and others are greatly overbounded.

Further light on this matter of population density and extent of unused land is obtained by examining population changes during the decade of the 1950s for the larger cities (25,000 and over) in relation to their reported total-population/total-area densities in 1950. (Table 16) Many factors other than land availability affect population growth or decline. The available data relate to legal cities, which may be smaller than the economic cities or may be relatively large, containing a good deal of idle land. An examination of the relationship between population density in 1950 and population growth for the 1950–1960 decade for individual cities showed only a modest correlation.

However, three-fourths of all the cities with more than 10,000 persons per square mile in 1950 decreased in total population over this decade, while less than

TABLE 16

NUMBER OF CITIES 25,000 AND OVER, IN NORTHEASTERN URBAN COMPLEX REPORTING
SPECIFIED CHANGES IN POPULATION, 1950–60, IN RELATION TO
TOTAL-POPULATION/TOTAL-AREA DENSITY IN 1950

	Number of cities reporting, 1950–60					
			Population increase of:			
Total-population/total-area density (persons per square mile) in 1950	Decrease in popu-lation	No change in popu-lation[1]	Less than 10 percent	10 to 20 percent	Over 20 percent	Total
Under 5,000	3	1	4	11	16	35
5,000–9,999	12	1	8	3	9	33
10,000–14,999	16	0	3	1	0	20
15,000–19,999	8	1	2	0	0	11
20,000 and over	9	0	0	0	0	9
Total	48	3	17	15	25	108

Source: Census of Population.
[1] No change when data at each date rounded to nearest thousand.

a fourth of those with lower densities lost total population. All of the cities reporting an increase of more than 20 percent in population had less than 10,000 persons
per square mile in 1950, and all but one reporting a gain of over 10 percent were
in this same density group. These data do not indicate how much land was actually
available in 1950 for further residential use. Even when densities were low, this
may have been due to a low-density residential development, or to other uses of
the land, or to the fact that some land was undevelopable or developable only at
very high cost, so that none was readily available for further residential use. Moreover, a city with land available for residential use may have lacked an economic
base for growth. In spite of these reasons for a low conformity between density
and growth, the fact remains that a considerable relationship did exist.

These data strongly suggest that, at some point, a large city is "full" in the sense
that all the land is used for business or other nonresidential uses and that the existing stock of housing fully uses all the land available for residential use. It would
appear further that this point exists when total-population/total-area density is
about 10,000 persons per square mile (16 persons per acre). The concept of
"pivotal density" has been used by some writers, notably Colin Clark, in much
the same sense as the term "full" is used above. Robin Best has estimated for
Britain that pivotal density occurs at about 72 acres of land per 1,000 population,
or nearly 9,000 persons per square mile.[13] The figure would probably be higher
in Britain than in the United States because there is much less idle land within
generally urban areas; but it would be higher in the United States because our
apartments are often higher than theirs. Thus, the two factors seem more or less
to balance out.

The comparisons are rough, at best, and probably do not apply to individual
cities, but they may be broadly indicative. Obviously, if there were strong economic
incentive for growth and if additional land simply did not exist for any reason,
more people could be crowded into the same already "full" city. This concept of
"fullness" is more sociological or psychological than architectural or engineering.
When faced with high densities at some level, people have chosen to move outward,
even when this meant longer travel distances to the city center. A complex of factors has underlain this suburban migration, but the lack of land available for additional residential units seems clearly to have been one reason.

Labor Force, Income, and Housing

As far as the available data on numbers of families, labor force, personal
incomes, and housing permit comparisons, the various parts of the Northeastern
Urban Complex are more striking in their similarities than in their differences.
(Table 17) The more rural parts of the SMSAs, beyond the urbanized area, have
somewhat larger families and a slightly lower participation in the labor force than
the other areas. The cities report a somewhat higher participation in the labor
force than does the urbanized ring. Manufacturing employment is relatively least

[13] Personal communication, September 29, 1969. Presumably this is overall residential density.

in the cities and relatively highest in the more distant outlying areas, beyond urbanized areas, but the difference is only 5 percentage points. Personal income per capita and per family are about 20 percent higher in the urbanized ring than in the cities, and per capita they are lowest in the more outlying areas, where families are largest. Differences in housing, as far as numbers of housing units per family or number of persons per housing unit are concerned, vary only by about 10 percent from highest to lowest ratios.

A Finer-Grained Look at Land Use

A detailed land use map for 1966 compiled by the Regional Plan Association of New York from aerial photographs and large-scale maps, shows clearly how urban land use is closely concentrated in and around the larger cities. (See the end papers of this book.) There are some medium and smaller cities, and this outstanding mapping and reproduction achievement enables one to distinguish residential subdivisions in more or less open countryside. In general, the scale of mapping permitted the identification of moderately small subdivisions; separate units of 40 acres are shown on the map. This is a vastly finer grain than SMSAs, cities, or urbanized areas. But the extent of the undeveloped white spaces on this map is far more impressive than the extent of the development; particularly if the boundaries of the Atlantic Region are used or if the whole of the Northeastern Urban Complex (which is smaller but still rather extensive) is considered. But it is also true if one

TABLE 17

POPULATION, 1960 AND 1950, LABOR FORCE, PERSONAL INCOME, AND HOUSING, 1960,
BY PARTS OF NORTHEASTERN URBAN COMPLEX

Item	Unit	Whole SMSAs	Whole urbanized area	SMSA outside of urbanized area	All cities	Urbanized area outside of cities
1960						
Total population	mil.	31.7	28.4	3.3	19.4	9.0
Families	mil.	8.1	7.4	0.7	5.0	2.4
Persons per family	no.	3.9	3.9	4.2	3.9	3.9
1950						
Total population	mil.	26.9	24.0	2.9	19.5	4.5
Families	mil.	7.0	–	–	–	–
Persons per family	no.	3.9	–	–	–	–
1960						
Total labor force	mil.	13.2	12.0	1.2	8.5	3.5
Labor force in manufacturing	mil.	3.9	3.5	0.4	2.4	1.1
Labor force in manufacturing	percent	29	29	33	28	31
Population in labor force	percent	42	42	36	44	39
1960						
Personal income, total	bil. $	71.8	65.3	6.5	41.9	23.4
Personal income, per capita	$	2,265	2,295	1,970	2,160	2,590
Personal income, per family	$	8,835	8,860	8,350	8,350	10,040
1960						
Housing units total	mil.	10.2	9.2	1.0	6.5	2.7
Housing units per family	no.	1.26	1.26	1.28	1.30	1.16
Persons per housing unit	no.	3.09	3.09	3.05	2.97	3.35

Source: Censuses of Population.
Note: Per capita and per family figures calculated from unrounded data.

considers only the band reaching from Boston to Washington, where there is still a very large proportion of the total land area undeveloped and the region has the physical capacity to house a vastly larger total population than it now has.

There is no map with similar detail which shows the distribution of population and perhaps it would be impossible to construct one. The concentration of people is much greater than the concentration of land use. In the heart of the larger cities, density is high, whereas in the sprawling suburbs it is often relatively low. The range in intensity of use would be extremely difficult to portray accurately. Nor is there a comparably detailed land use map for any earlier date. The map reproduced as end papers is invaluable in the picture it presents for the present, and as a basis for measuring land use changes in the future. One may accept it gratefully and at the same time wish that maps of both population distribution and land use change were available.

LAND USE AND LAND-POPULATION RELATIONSHIPS SUGGESTED BY TRANSPORTATION STUDY

The diverse nature of data about land use in the United States was noted in Chapter 2. The oldest source, the Census of Agriculture, obtains information about "farms," which are carefully defined in each census, with changes in definition made only as changing economic and social conditions require. One item of inquiry relates to land, including not only crop and pasture land but also woodland and other land within the farm boundaries. Efforts are made by the Bureau of the Census to include all farms which meet its criteria, but even if all farms are included, this does not by any means include all rural land, since some land is outside of farms. For the 48 contiguous states, about 60 percent of the total land area is currently within farms. If the extensive federal land holdings are excluded, about 75 percent of the remainder is within farms. It is evident that a substantial area of land is not included within farms, and the proportion differs considerably by regions.

City, county, and regional planning agencies have frequently collected information about current land use, as the basis for the development of a general plan or a transportation plan for the area concerned. Data on land use collected by such agencies have several serious deficiencies for the purposes of this study.

1. The various surveys have used different definitions of land use, so that, for example, "residential" in one survey is not necessarily equivalent to "residential" in another. In particular, the amount of idle land included within a use category varies considerably.

2. Surveys differ greatly in the degree of detail obtained about the various land uses. One may include all industrial use in a single category, whereas another may subdivide it. Particularly bothersome is the divergent treatment of local transportation uses, such as streets and parking areas, and also office space, which may be shown separately or included with the kind of business activity to which it is attached.

3. The unit of observation or of analysis of land use differs greatly from one

survey to another, ranging from the individual lot or parcel of land to relatively large areas of land with common use. This is the matter of "grain," to which reference has been made.

4. This type of land use survey has typically not been kept current or updated, so that it does not provide a historical data series on changing land use.

In spite of these deficiencies, land use surveys by local planning agencies do contain a great deal of valuable information. With rare exceptions, such data have not been centrally collected and analyzed or published but have been used only in local areas. Their lack of comparability is a major obstacle to wider use.

The growing urbanization of the northeastern United States has already led to difficult intercity transportation problems, which will almost certainly grow worse as population, economic activity, and travel increase in the decades ahead. In recognition of this problem, a special study of intercity transportation in this region has been organized within the Department of Transportation, a study known as the Northeast Corridor Transportation Project. One aspect of the transportation situation is land use, current and projected. The project has obtained all the data on land use which it could get from city, county, and regional planning agencies.[14] The project included 166 counties in its study, as compared with the 78 counties in the Northeastern Urban Complex. Twenty-one of the 166 counties had no land use data, and it was necessary to make estimates, at least in part, in 20 others. However, fortunately for the purposes of the present study, data were available or have been estimated for all the counties included in the Complex.

The kinds of land uses shown separately in data from local sources varied considerably. Although some counties had as many as 20 land use categories, others had only four. The divergences in definition and in detail were so great that inter-county comparisons are limited to four land "uses": residential, commercial, industrial, and public-semipublic. All land not reported in one of these four broad classes is listed as "other." Appendix Table 5 presents a summary of these data for all counties in the Northeastern Complex. In addition, the table includes data on land use within farms, taken from the Census of Agriculture.

The meaning of these terms for broad land use classes is not clear; and analysis suggests that the definitions used were probably not always uniform. Indeed, given the origin of the data, completely uniform definitions are most unlikely.

The "residential" land use category in Appendix Table 5 presumably includes the internal transportation network of streets (and alleys, if any) of the generally residential neighborhoods, although this is not certain. But how much other land, such as the sites of neighborhood schools, local parks, and small neighborhood stores, and other uses associated with residential living, may also be included? In particular, how much idle land within generally residential neighborhoods may be included? Do the data include the interspersed vacant lots, the larger leapfrogged areas, and the more extensive idle tracts within or just outside of the urban fringe itself, which may be of considerable width? Does "residential" include all farm-

[14] The report of this study has been published as *Northeastern Corridor Transportation Project Report* (U.S. Department of Transportation, 1970), but the data used here have not been published. The cooperation of project officials in making them available is greatly appreciated.

houses and other open-country residences, within each county? What was the grain of the land use survey from which the data resulted? Information on these matters is lacking, but there is probably considerable diversity among the counties for which land use data are available.

Somewhat similar questions may be raised about "commercial" land. Do the data include only the major shopping districts, or are all local stores also included? Are parking lots adjacent to, or part of, shopping districts also included? What about streets internal to or bordering on commercial uses? Is warehousing and storage of goods included, as well as places of actual sale to customers? What about offices of commercial business—are they included when part of the same building, or when separate? Are wholesale as well as retail activities included? What about junkyards and similar commercial activities? The matter of grain of survey is perhaps even more important here than for residential areas, since some commercial land use occurs in separate or isolated small tracts, as well as some in larger districts.

Somewhat similar questions might be raised about "industrial" use of land. One question may relate to idle or reserve land owned by industrial firms as sites for possible later expansion. Many industrial firms have moved from city center to suburb in recent years, in order to have larger quarters and to get more of their operations on a single floor; and many of them have acquired reserve area, to permit later expansion if this becomes desirable. Is such land included as industrial land "use" or is it considered idle?

The name of the "public-semipublic" category reflects ownership rather than use of the land. Does it include all parks, all schools, all wildlife areas, all public forests, and all other publicly owned lands, regardless of the unit of government which owns them? Special surveys were conducted by the Northeast Corridor Transportation Project to determine whether national, state, or major regional parks or campgrounds were located in each county. How broadly is "semipublic" defined? Are all publicly owned streets, alleys, highways, and airports excluded, or are some or all of them included under this category? Again, definite information is lacking on these definitions.

The "other" category in Appendix Table 5 is simply the difference between the sum of the four named "uses" and the total area within each county; it has no meaning for actual land use. Part of this "other" category, as reported by the local land use surveys, can be accounted for by data from the Census of Agriculture; and any acreage not included in this census has been listed in Appendix Table 5 as "unaccounted for." There is always some danger of error or discrepancy in putting together data from different data sources. Indeed, in Lehigh County, Pennsylvania, the "unaccounted for" item is negative, meaning that more area was accounted for than actually exists. In all other counties, some residual acreage remained unaccounted for, the proportion of the total acreage varying considerably.

These data from local land use surveys relate to various years from 1957 to 1966, but more than 75 percent of the data reflect the land use situation for the 1959–1962 period.

The most impressive fact demonstrated by Appendix Table 5 is how little we know for certain about land use. In Table 18 below, detailed data from counties

TABLE 18

LAND USE BY MAJOR PARTS OF NORTHEASTERN URBAN COMPLEX, CIRCA 1961

(1,000 acres)

State or SMSA[1]	Land use data, NE Corridor Study						Land in farms, Census of Agriculture, 1959[2]					
									Woodland			
	Total area	Residential area	Commercial area	Industrial area	Public-semipublic area	Other area	Total	Cropland harvested	Pastured	Not pastured	Other pasture	Unaccounted for[3]
New Hampshire, Mass., Rhode Island	4,746	368.3	34.9	52.9	329.9	3,960	1,075	276	77	310	73	2,884
Connecticut	3,135	265.6	16.5	21.7	87.7	2,744	884	237	88	260	110	1,860
New York SMSA	1,375	418.1	31.3	67.7	227.3	631	130	75	4	17	5	501
New Jersey[4]	2,648	611.3	16.9	52.5	195.8	1,771	569	276	7	89	29	1,203
Philadelphia SMSA	2,271	300.7	26.3	35.8	221.8	1,687	913	468	9	119	88	774
Other Pennsylvania[5]	3,809	308.9	21.9	27.8	198.9	3,252	2,363	1,376	36	298	201	888
Wilmington SMSA	729	40.2	3.8	7.6	20.0	657	390	184	7	58	38	268
Baltimore SMSA[6]	1,444	99.1	7.9	33.6	92.9	1,210	719	302	20	118	132	491
Washington SMSA	966	104.6	5.8	8.3	88.6	758	356	108	15	83	49	402
Total	21,123	2,516.8	165.3	307.9	1,462.9	16,671	7,399	3,302	263	1,452	725	9,272
Percent	100.0	11.9	0.8	1.5	6.9	78.9	35.0	16.6	1.2	6.9	3.4	43.9

Sources: Unpublished data from U.S. Department of Transportation's Northeast Corridor Transportation Project; and 1959 Census of Agriculture.
[1] See Appendix Table 5.
[2] The enumerated subclasses do not include all land in farms, hence do not add to total.
[3] Difference between "other," from NE Corridor study, and the total in farms.

[4] Except Warren, Burlington, Camden, Gloucester, and Salem counties, which are included in their SMSAs.
[5] Includes Allentown-Bethlehem-Easton SMSA, and Berks, Lancaster and Adams counties, York SMSA, and Harrisburg SMSA.
[6] Including Harford county.

in the Appendix Table have been summarized by groups of counties more or less conforming to SMSAs or groups of SMSAs. Here we see that nearly half (43.9 percent) of the whole area falls into the "unaccounted for" category, and this amount is larger than that for any single defined-use category, including all agricultural uses. The acreage in the "unaccounted for" category is large in each of the major parts of the Complex shown in Table 18 and in nearly all of the component counties. For reasons implicit in the foregoing and subsequent discussion, it seems highly probable that the land use acreages are exaggerated. Some data —perhaps all—must include substantial acreages of vacant land and/or land in other uses. The reported "unaccounted for" is thus probably less than the area actually falling in this category.

Within the counties of the Northeastern Urban Complex, about a seventh of the total area is used for residential, commercial, and industrial purposes. Probably some additional area is "urban" in some sense; parks, schools, transportation, and other land uses may be in addition to those specified, although the questions raised earlier as to the meanings of these categories should be borne in mind. About a third of the area of these counties—which are basically urban in character and include the big cities of New York, Philadelphia, Boston, Baltimore, and Washington, as well as many smaller cities—is in farms, but less than half of the farm acreage is used for crops. It is interesting to note that, overall, the acreage used for residential, commercial, and industrial purposes in these highly urbanized counties is less than that used for crops.

A substantial but unknown part of the "unaccounted for" acreage is in woods that are not part of farms or managed intensively for forest production but are owned for recreation or other personal reasons. Such wooded land, plus physically similar wooded land within farms, is not used intensively for the most part. Some of the total reported land area is swamp or overflowed land or is otherwise unsuitable for residential development. Although some land included in these counties is as intensively used as any land in the United States, yet a substantial part of the total area is very lightly used, by almost any measure of intensity of land use.

The broad groupings of counties shown in Table 18 have considerably different patterns of land use. In the New York SMSA and the northern New Jersey area a much higher than average proportion of the total area is used for residential purposes. In the New England and Connecticut groups of counties, a much smaller than average proportion is used for this purpose. There is also considerable variation in the proportions of the total area included in farms.

The total urbanized area in the Northeastern Urban Complex, as shown in earlier tables taken from census data, was about 3.4 million acres in 1960. The total of residential, commercial, and industrial use as shown by these local land use surveys was about 3 million acres. The two sources of data seem to differ somewhat but not grossly; it is impossible to say whether their agreement is close enough for each to help verify the other.

These data on acreages of land reported in each use may not be particularly meaningful in absolute terms, but relating them to some measure of activity on the land may be more helpful. (Appendix Table 6) The number of persons per reported residential acre varies from less than 2 (less than 1,280 per square mile) in two counties to over 270 (about 179,000 per square mile) in New York County (Manhattan), and averages 13.6 per acre or 8,700 per square mile. In spite of the fact that major uses other than residential should be excluded from this category, great variation in reported density of use still remains. (Figure 17) These data are presumably somewhere between "gross" and "net" residential density, as the latter was defined in Table 1 above. To the extent that all nonconforming uses are excluded but only internal transportation systems are included, the data are "net." To the extent that nonconforming uses—and especially idle land—are included, they are more nearly "gross." It can be seen that 90 percent of the counties have a residential density of less than 20 persons per acre (12,800 per square mile), but a few counties go very much higher. Nearly all the latter are the central cities of Boston, New York, Jersey City, Baltimore, and Washington. Parts of other counties may well run fairly high also in the apartment house areas.

The typical suburban county has a density of 5 to 15 persons per acre of residential land (3,200 to 9,600 per square mile). This raises a question about the 14 counties which report a density of use for residential land of less than 5 persons per acre (less than 3,200 per square mile of residential land). By the standards outlined in Table 2, this is a "low" density of residential land use. There surely must be some parts of towns and cities in these counties where residential density runs far higher. One concludes that there must be a considerable acreage of idle or

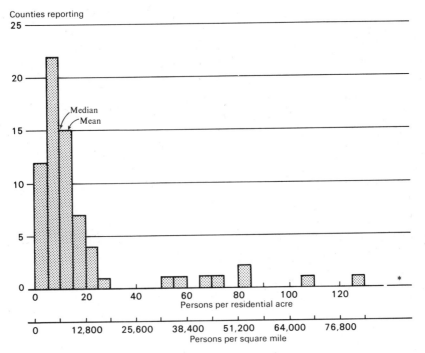

One county in 270–275 interval.

FIGURE 17.   Number of counties reporting various densities of residential land use, Northeastern Urban Complex, circa 1960.

nonconforming land included within the residential category in these counties, and/or that they have very large lot subdivisions for a substantial part of their entire residential area.

There is also considerable variation in the volume of retail sales per acre of commercial land. (Figure 18 and Appendix Table 6.) Some of this may be due to the fact that some of the commercial land is not used for retail purposes but for wholesaling, warehousing, or other storage. About half of the counties had retail sales of less than $200,000 per acre of commercial land, but Washington, D.C. had sales of over $3,000,000. Curiously enough, Washington reported retail sales per acre of commercial land nearly 40 percent higher than did Manhattan. The weighted average for all the counties was $252,000 per acre.

If the intensity of use of residential land in a county is plotted against the intensity of use of commercial land (as measured by retail sales per acre) in the same county, there is some correlation but not a close one. Counties which are the central parts of the large metropolises like Boston, New York, Jersey City, Philadelphia, Baltimore, and Washington have a high intensity of land use for each purpose; but the correlation of use intensities is not high within this group. Likewise, counties of small population tend to have low intensity of land use for each purpose, but the correlation within such counties is not high.

There is also a considerable variation among counties in the number of manufacturing employees per industrial acre. (Figure 19 and Appendix Table 6.) About half of all counties had less than 10 employees per industrial acre and about 70 percent had less than 15. In contrast, Manhattan had over 210, Boston had over 90, and Philadelphia had over 75. The average number of employees per industrial acre was 12.7, close to the average number (13.6) of residents per residential acre.

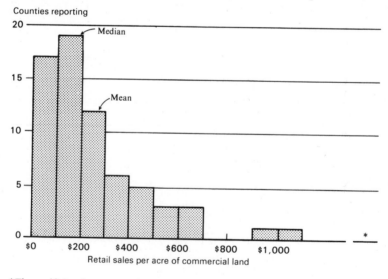

Three additional counties at $1,460, $2,321, and $3,260.

FIGURE 18. Number of counties reporting various volumes of retail sales per acre of commercial land, Northeastern Urban Complex, circa 1960.

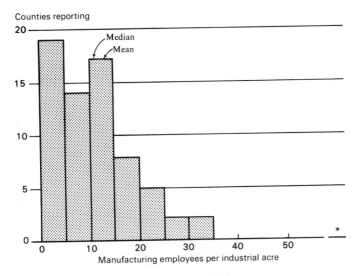

Counties reporting

*Three additional counties at 75.7, 91.6, and 210.9.

FIGURE 19. Number of counties reporting various numbers of manufacturing employees per industrial acre, Northeastern Urban Complex, circa 1960.

Again, there is some correlation, but not a close one, between intensity of land use for residential and commercial uses and that for industrial uses, among the various counties of the Northeastern Urban Complex.

These considerable variations in reported density of land use within broad categories raise more questions than they answer. The differences are considerable between counties that one would expect to be similar. The possibility surely exists that the data are not fully comparable. More than mere formal definitions are involved—rather, the manner of application of definitions may be equally important. As noted earlier in this chapter, the formal definition of "urbanized area" as used by the Bureau of the Census changed only a little from 1950 to 1960, but the application of the definition in practice changed so much that the results are not comparable. It is also possible that some of the reported differences in intensity of use actually exist, using any reasonable definition. Time and resources available for this study did not permit a detailed examination on the ground of these differences in reported land uses; it may be that other factors would account for some of them.

SUMMARY OF LAND USE IN THE COMPLEX

This chapter has unavoidably been long, detailed, and concerned with an appraisal of sources as well as with significance of data. Given the generally unsatisfactory character of the data available, the fact that more than one kind exists, and the further fact that data do not always mean what they purport to say, it is necessary to consider carefully what those available do indeed mean. It is possible to summarize briefly the main points which emerge from this chapter as follows:

1. The Northeastern Urban Complex is a small part of the United States, in a geographic sense, including less than 1 percent of the total area, but it is far larger in terms of population or personal income, including about 20 percent of each in 1960.

2. The population *within* the Complex is highly concentrated, with 83 percent located within its urbanized area, which includes only 17 percent of the regional acreage.

3. Only a small part of the Complex is used for urban purposes, by any reasonable definition of the latter. The census classification shows 17 percent as urbanized, and the local land use surveys suggest a slightly smaller area. Whatever the exact figure, and whatever the precise definition, urban land area is only a relatively small fraction of this region which in turn is less than 1 percent of the U.S. total area.

4. Postwar changes in agriculture within the Complex have been remarkably similar to changes in U.S. agriculture as a whole. Despite its urban character, this region still has considerable agriculture.

5. Various measures of intensity of land use, or of population density in the case of residential land use, are possible and equally accurate if adequately defined and properly understood. By any reasonable measure of intensity of land use, a great deal of variation is apparent between different counties of the Complex. Using total-population/total-area as a measure of intensity of land use, the following mean intensities were found for the whole Complex in 1960:

| | Persons per | |
	Square mile	Acre
Whole Northeastern Urban Complex	1,084	1.7
All SMSAs	1,475	2.3
Entire urbanized area	5,300	8.3
All cities of 25,000 and over	10,230	16.0
All suburbs (urbanized areas outside of larger cities)	2,622	4.1

Since these figures are based upon total acreage within the respective kind of area, they are lower, by varying amounts, than the intensities on the lands actually used; or, to put the same point in different words, varying acreages of idle land are included in the different areas. For the land reported as used for residential purposes, the median density was about 10 persons per acre, or about 6,400 per square mile, whereas the mean density was 13.6 persons per acre or about 8,700 per square mile.

6. The Northeastern Urban Complex can absorb a very large number of additional people without any basic change in urban form and on lands well suited to urban uses of various kinds. Some number can be absorbed on presently idle lands within the various use categories, including urbanized areas; later chapters will provide the basis for a better estimate of idle land and hence of the capacity to absorb additional people within such areas.

If all urbanized areas with average total-population/total-area densities of less than 3,000 persons per square mile in 1960 were brought up to this level, nearly

1 million more people could be accommodated. If all with less than 4,000 per square mile were brought up to that level, more than 3 million additional persons could be accommodated. If all with less than 5,000 per square mile were brought up to that level, the present urbanized areas could accommodate 4 million additional persons. And if all 1960 urbanized areas had been brought up to 7,300 persons per square mile (the mean for 1950), then 14 million additional persons could be accommodated. The latter, at least, would have required higher residential densities than existed in much suburban land fully used for residential purposes. However, if only lands now vacant or unused within urbanized areas were brought into use at average densities of presently used areas, substantial numbers of persons could be accommodated, although data are lacking for a precise estimate. If the whole 31,500 square miles of the Northeastern Urban Complex were developed at the reported density of the urbanized area in 1960 (5,300 per square mile, which is too low because it includes so much idle land), a total of 170 million people could be accommodated.

Some of the land within the Complex is physically unsuited for residential or other urban use. If urbanized areas were to expand to occupy all physically suitable lands within the Complex, present average intensities of land use would permit the accommodation of at least 50 million—more likely 100 million—additional people. Still larger populations could be placed on surrounding areas included in the Pickard-Pushkarev "Atlantic Metropolitan Region" but excluded from the Complex as here defined.

Substantial further capacity to absorb population exists if use is made of various devices for increasing intensity of land use; and planned efforts to increase intensity of land use might still retain substantial areas of open land. Population increase within the Northeastern Urban Complex will not be hampered by a lack of land for several generations, if ever. It should, of course, be clearly understood that in thus calculating physical capacity of land to provide sites for people, there is no endorsement of the wisdom of a social policy which encouraged such concentrations.

11

LAND USE IN THREE STUDY AREAS
OF THE NORTHEASTERN
URBAN COMPLEX

As a major part of this inquiry into suburban land conversion, three Standard Metropolitan Statistical Areas were studied in some detail. Findings are summarized in this chapter and the next.

The three SMSAs studied were Washington, D.C.; Wilmington, Delaware; and Springfield, Massachusetts. The fact that Washington is the national capital gives it special economic characteristics. It is the fourth largest SMSA in the Northeastern Urban Complex—bigger than Baltimore, but smaller than Boston and, of course, much smaller than Philadelphia and New York. It is also the most southerly SMSA in the Complex. Since World War II the Washington SMSA has had the fastest growth rate among the major SMSAs of the Complex.

Wilmington is about an average-size SMSA, whose rate of growth in the past two decades has been rather rapid. It is the headquarters of some of the largest American industrial firms; some of their manufacturing plants are in its metropolitan area but outside the central city.

Springfield is a relatively old city. Its SMSA was slightly larger than the Wilmington SMSA in 1960, but its growth rate has been low in recent decades.

Each of these SMSAs has climate, topography, and soils common to the whole Northeastern Urban Complex as described in Chapter 10, although there are variations which locally are highly important. Washington was located at the head of navigation on the Potomac River, but the river is more important today as a source of water than as a means of transportation. Wilmington is located on the Delaware River, where transportation was once highly important and is moderately so today. Springfield is on the Connecticut River far above significant water transportation, but water power from the river was important in its early industrial development. All have air, rail, and highway transportation services of varying quality today.

Washington draws official visitors and tourists from over the nation and from other parts of the world, but it makes and exports few goods. The other two SMSAs produce goods of various kinds which are shipped to other urban areas in and outside of the Complex. While each of these SMSAs is physically distinct from others, each is closely interrelated with many other urban areas in economy and culture.

CHANGES IN AREA AND IN POPULATION, 1950–1960

Two of the three SMSAs and all of their central cities remained unchanged in acreage from 1950 to 1960 (Springfield SMSA increased), but the urbanized area of each nearly doubled, largely as the result of the redefinition of the term (Table 19). Total population of the central cities declined modestly in Washington and Wilmington but rose slightly in Springfield. The SMSA and urbanized area were the real sites of population growth, the population rising by nearly half in Washington, by less in Wilmington, and least of all in Springfield. Not only is this difference in overall rate of growth responsible for differences in amount of land used for urban purposes, as will be shown in this chapter, but it also affects the suburbanization process, including the decision-making process, as discussed in Chapter 12. Population densities for the central cities (on a total-area/total-population basis) paralleled the modest changes in population numbers; those of the SMSAs all rose, also paralleling the change in total population; while those of the urbanized areas all declined, by varying proportions.

Figures 20, 21, and 22 show the urbanized area of the three metropolitan areas in 1950 and 1960. Expansion of the urbanized area in Washington and Wilmington follows the expected pattern, including areas adjacent to those previously developed. However, in Springfield, the entire town of Enfield, Connecticut was added. The practice of including entire New England towns—i.e., geographic areas—as urbanized area without regard to actual land use tends to have misleading results. Since these areas do not meet the density criteria for selection, comparisons with other SMSA urbanized areas is difficult. It is also interesting to note that even though Enfield was added in 1960 to the SMSA (and its urbanized area), it was dropped in a redefinition by the Bureau of the Budget in 1964. At that time, the

TABLE 19

CHANGE IN URBANIZED AREA, POPULATION, AND POPULATION DENSITY,
STUDY AREAS, 1950 AND 1960

	Washington		Wilmington		Springfield	
	1950	1960	1950	1960	1950	1960
Area (*sq. mi.*)						
SMSA	1,488	1,485	787	787	333	429
Urbanized area	178	341	47	81	167	239
Central city	61	61	10	10	33	33
Population (*thousands*)						
SMSA	1,464	2,002	268	366	407	479
Urbanized area	1,287	1,808	187	284	357	450
Central city	802	764	110	96	162	174
Population density[1] (*per sq. mi.*)						
SMSA	984	1,348	341	465	1,223	1,116
Urbanized area	7,216	5,308	4,012	3,506	2,133	1,883
Central city	13,065	12,442	11,261	9,778	5,123	5,271

[1] Total-population/total-area basis.

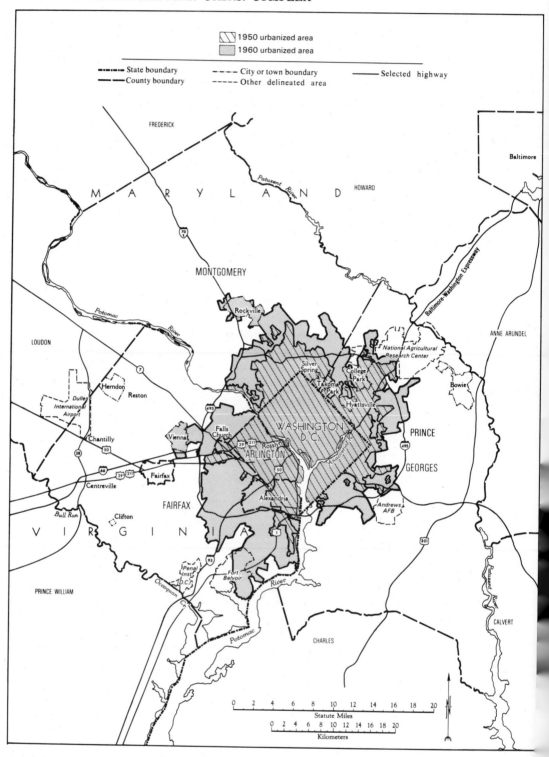

FIGURE 20.   Urbanized area, 1950 and 1960, Washington SMSA.

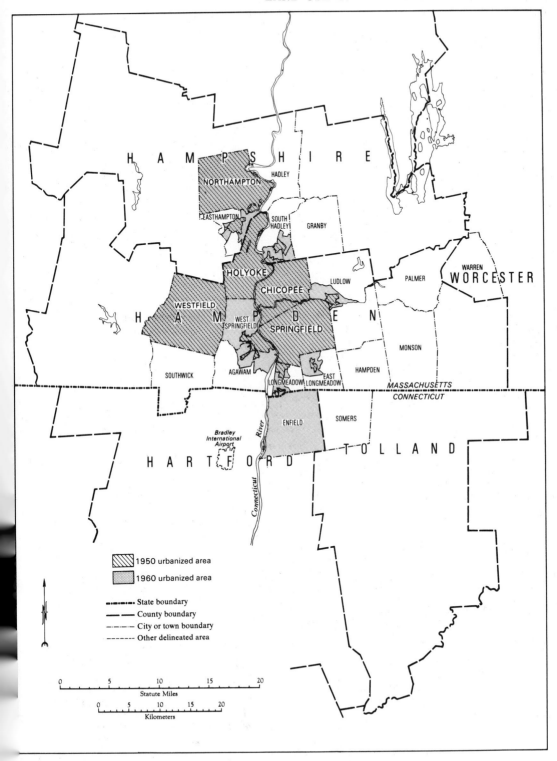

FIGURE 21.   Urbanized area, 1950 and 1960, Springfield-Chicopee-Holyoke SMSA.

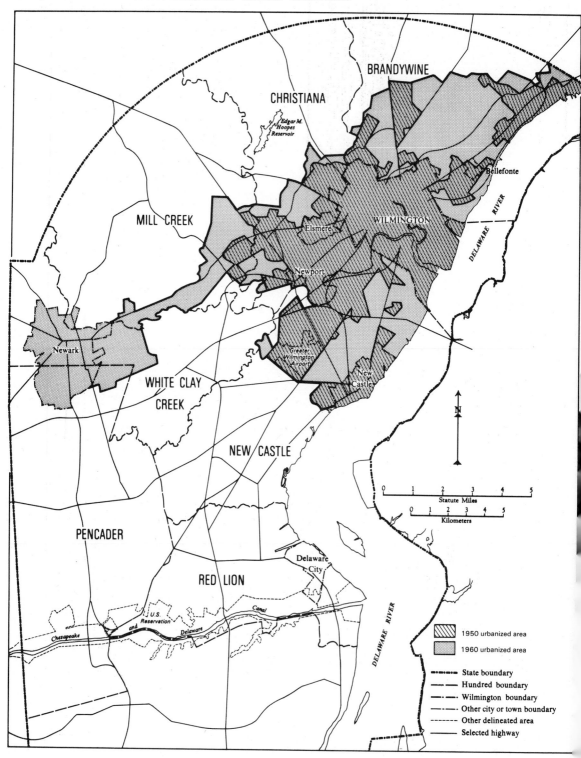

FIGURE 22.   Urbanized area, 1950 and 1960, Northern New Castle County, Delaware.

town of Somers, Connecticut (nonurban) was added. Such redefinitions of SMSAs and urbanized areas reduce the historical comparability of data.

One thing becomes clear immediately in terms of the land use in the study areas: on the average, the population density is low in each SMSA. Even Washington, with the highest density, had an average of only about two families per acre. Much of the area is obviously much more densely populated than these average figures indicate. (In the central cities of Washington, Wilmington, and Springfield, densities were 12,442, 9,778, and 5,271 per square mile respectively.) A considerable quantity of "urbanized" land is not developed but is vacant at the present time.

The population density on land outside the urbanized areas but included in the SMSA is very low—270 per square mile for Washington, 116 per square mile for Wilmington, and 153 per square mile for Springfield in 1960.

In 1965, there was a substantial amount of land available for development in the urbanized areas. In Fairfax County, of the 51 tracts added to the urbanized area from 1960 to 1965[1] only about 10 (16 percent) had less than a third of their land classified as vacant. At the other extreme, 23 of the tracts (38 percent) had over two-thirds of their land so classified. Large parcels of land often strategically located within the settlement pattern were idle. The Wilmington SMSA showed a similar situation, with the urbanized area as defined in 1950 containing 62 percent open land. This area still contained 37 percent open land in 1964. The urbanized area added between 1950 and 1960 contained 42 percent open land in 1964. Similarly, 76 percent of the Springfield SMSAs urbanized area in 1950 was classified as open land, forest, or wet land. This had decreased to less than 60 percent by 1965. Land within this SMSA but not included in the urbanized area as defined by the Census was 94 percent open, forested, or wet land in 1950 and still slightly over 78 percent in these categories in 1965.

Land Use

Comparisons of selected land uses in the three metropolitan areas are shown in Table 20. Relatively more land was in residential use in Springfield than in Washington, which in turn used more for this purpose than Wilmington. Commercial and industrial use of land was also greatest in the Springfield area. Washington had more land in public ownership, as would be expected, followed by Springfield and then Wilmington. These figures indicate that Wilmington has used land for its residential, commercial, and public uses more sparingly than has either Washington or Springfield. Agriculture is much more important in Wilmington and Springfield than in the Washington area. Land unaccounted for in any of the above categories was greatest in Washington and least in Springfield, but even here was nearly three-fifths of the total.

In spite of the fact that there is a considerable amount of vacant land available for urban development within the urbanized areas of each SMSA, much of the

[1] The 1965 urbanized area was not established officially by the Bureau of the Census, but unofficially by the Fairfax County Planning Commission. However, the same definition was employed.

TABLE 20
PERCENTAGES OF LAND IN SELECTED USES IN STUDY AREAS, CIRCA 1965

Area	Resi- dential	Com- mercial	Indus- trial	Public	Cropland	Other
Washington SMSA	10.8%	0.6%	0.9%	9.2%	11.2%	67.3%
Wilmington SMSA	5.5	0.5	1.0	2.7	25.2	65.1
Springfield SMSA	12.8	1.1	2.5	7.1	17.9	58.9

land conversion is taking place outside of these areas. In addition, an important change is occurring in the intensity with which the land is being used. The density in the urbanized area added to the Washington SMSA between 1960 and 1965 was lower than the average density of the total SMSA urbanized area. This indicates that the density in the developing suburban areas is lower than has historically been the case. The same trend is present in the Springfield area where density of the developed urban areas declined from 5,083 per square mile in 1950 to 3,204 per square mile in 1965.[2] The city of Holyoke in the Springfield area had an absolute decline in population, but had a 50 percent increase in the amount of land used for urban purposes between 1950 and 1965. In the Springfield area as a whole the population increased about one-sixth, while the developed urban area increased 1½ times.

Wilmington, however, has shown an opposite trend. Its population density in the developed areas increased from 1,768 per square mile in 1937 to 3,924 in 1964. The density of dwelling units per acre of approved plats in suburban northern New Castle County during the period 1945–1967 varied from a high of 8 per acre in 1949–50 to a low of 1.5 per acre in 1959–60. The average was 3 dwelling units per acre for the entire period. The high density was due to the influence of apartment construction, while the low density reflected subdivision platting for 2½ acre lots.

Apartments provided almost half of the new dwelling units in northern New Castle County from 1964 through 1967 but consumed less than 400 of the 3,200 acres of land authorized for residential development. The efficiency of multiple-unit housing relative to land use is obvious. Data from the Springfield study support similar conclusions—i.e., single-family units averaged 3.5 and 2.1 per acre of residential land in the central cities and the suburban towns respectively, as compared with 33 and 20 multiple-family dwelling units per acre respectively.

Differences in the patterns of development among the study areas are obvious. Not only is the efficiency of suburban land use in Wilmington greater than in the other two areas, but it is being improved by considerable infilling of previously bypassed idle land. Almost all development has been conducted on the basis of full-fledged subdivisions. The Washington area is also being developed by full-fledged subdivisions, but large areas of land are being bypassed as the subdivisions are built beyond the existing suburban communities. Much of the bypassed land continues to lie idle. The pattern of recent Springfield development has been con-

[2] The data for Springfield were obtained from aerial photographs.

siderably different. Some subdivisions have been developed, but much of the development has taken place in previously rural areas in the form of single-family custom-built homes on lots located on or near an access road. With this pattern of development, large blocks of land are being surrounded by single or double rows of houses but are remaining in the same land use.

IDLE LAND

There is a great deal of land available for development at the present time within the boundaries of the study areas, especially land outside the urbanized areas. Even within the urbanized areas much open space remains. (In these studies all land permanently set aside for open space was classified as "used" rather than "idle.") Choice-located unused land is scarcer than idle land nearer the suburban fringe. There are possibilities for using currently idle land more efficiently through infilling rather than allowing the urban development to sprawl beyond the boundaries of the present developed areas. Infilling this presently idle land could be done with a very low level of public expenditures for providing public services, since these services are already available. Good planning would set aside some of the presently idle lands as permanent open space, i.e., permanent park and recreation space. Those which are not so preserved for public use should be developed along the lines of the best present development techniques. Opportunities for doing so exist in all of the study areas.

The use of the term "idle" implies that the land can be, but has not been, brought into development. Related to this concept is a very important consideration—that of buildable land. Land may be idle but not buildable. Land development technology was not sufficiently advanced prior to World War II to develop marshland and steep woodlands economically at the prices for developed lots which then existed. Thus, the idleness of such land was not really in question. Recent advances in land development technology and effective consumer demand has made feasible the development of essentially all idle land.

In northern New Castle County in 1937 there were 36,000 acres of idle land, which comprised 28 percent of the total open land (including agricultural and undeveloped nonagricultural land) outside of Wilmington. By 1960 this classification of idle land had declined to 31,000 acres, but forest land and marsh land, which could now be developed economically, added another 18,000 acres to the idle land. Thus 49,000 acres, or 53 percent of the total remaining open land, were classified as idle in 1960.

Land idled owing to the abandonment of farms (crop and pasture land declined from 42 percent to 28 percent of total land) was developed for urban uses at only a slightly faster rate than all open land: that is, 21 percent from 1937 to 1964 as compared with 18 percent for all open land in northern New Castle County outside of Wilmington during the same period. There was a marked tendency, however, to develop more quickly the abandoned farm land located near the city than that located farther out. Thus 42 percent of the abandoned farm land in New Castle hundred, located near Wilmington, was developed during the period 1934–1964 compared to only 6 percent in Red Lion hundred, located farther from the city center.[3] This compared to the percentage of total open land developed—23 percent in New Castle hundred and 13 percent in Red Lion hundred.

Some infilling is taking place in the Wilmington area as indicated by the increased density of the urban population between 1950 and 1960. Several plots of land bypassed in the original development were studied. The reasons for their nondevelopment included misjudging the housing market, battling over changes in deed restrictions, lack of water, objections of surrounding home owners to the types of developments proposed, and the existence of long-standing trusts.

Institutional Framework

The institutional environment within which the land market operates in the study areas does not very closely fit the traditional competitive model. Numerous levels of government—federal, state, county, and local—have enacted legislation which prevents the unencumbered operation of the land market. Basically, land itself is not transferred but rather a set of rights is transferred to utilize land in certain ways. Use may be limited by federal laws concerning what crops can be grown on the land, federal and state statutes regarding conservation, public health, public safety, condemnation for public use, and the like. State, county, and local laws prevent certain uses to protect public health, safety, morals, and welfare. These normally take the form of comprehensive plans, zoning ordinances, subdivision controls, and building and housing codes.

Under these circumstances, some land remains idle in the suburbanization process since the conflict between high expectations of development on the part of owners and low prices that developers are willing to pay creates an impasse. The Delaware study identified one parcel of land with fair development potential that had been held for sale since 1902. This situation can be partially explained by the cost of developing different tracts of land. A 10-acre tract of land with "excellent" development potential was estimated to require $41,750 to develop, while a tract that was similar in size but had "poor" development potential would require $71,500 in development costs. Assuming a uniform market for the developed lots, the developer could pay about 5½ times as much for the raw land in the "excellent" tract as for the "poor" tract. Speculative landholders sometimes do not understand why they cannot get their "price" and thus continue to hold the land.

The price of "raw land" as purchased by builders in the Wilmington area increased from $3,091 per acre in 1960 to $5,250 in 1964 or by 70 percent. Raw land prices also increased 70 percent in the Springfield area during the same period, rising from $800 per acre to $1,356 per acre. This difference in absolute level of land prices indicated the lower demand in the slow-growth Springfield area.

The studies reveal many factors which affect land use change and the pattern of land conversion. One of the most important is the rate of growth which is occurring in a given area. In both the Washington and Wilmington areas the population

---

[3] The "hundred" is a minor division of land in Delaware, historically of importance as a unit of local government but now only a statistical reporting area.

increased between 75 and 80 percent from 1950 to 1967. However in the Springfield area, the population increased only about 20 per cent in the same period. Related to this is the out-migration occurring from the central cities to the suburbs. Thus the "net" population gain which occurred in the suburbs from 1950 to 1965 (in addition to the natural increase) amounted to 70 percent in the Washington suburbs and 60 percent in the Wilmington suburbs but only 30 percent of the gain in the Springfield area. This differential in the rate of growth has been reflected in the demand for land for suburban development in the different areas.

EMPLOYMENT AND SUBURBAN GROWTH

Economists have long raised the question as to whether the people follow the jobs or the jobs follow the people. The Delaware study emphasizes the impact of a rapid rate of economic growth and labor mobility upon suburban land conversion. In the Wilmington area, entrepreneurs have developed the jobs, and people have moved into the area to fill them. Similarly, the rapidly expanding influence of the federal government has been the major factor in the Washington SMSAs growth.

In Springfield, on the other hand, employment failed to expand rapidly enough to absorb the natural increase in the work force, although the area has a long history of industrial activity, a broad manufacturing base, and access to a large portion of the U.S. market. The natural expansion of a skilled work force is not a sufficient condition to induce expansion of employment even in a generally expanding national economy. In the Washington SMSA, approximately 84 percent of nonagricultural employment was located in Washington, D.C. in 1950. By 1966 this proportion had decreased to 66 percent. Manufacturing was low in the region in both periods comprising just over 4 percent of the total nonagricultural employment in 1966. In 1960, 78 percent of the employed people living in Washington, D.C. worked there; while just short of 11 percent worked in the suburban ring. In contrast almost 44 percent of the employed persons living in the suburban ring worked in downtown Washington, while approximately 50 percent worked in the suburban ring.

Total employment in the Wilmington area showed a quite different pattern. In 1940, 66 percent of the SMSAs total jobs were in Wilmington. This had decreased to 31 percent by 1960, with almost 53 percent of the jobs in Wilmington being held by persons living outside the central city. Thus 25 percent of the total suburban labor force commuted into Wilmington, and 19 percent of the Wilmington labor force commuted to the suburban ring for employment. Wilmington was much more dependent upon manufacturing, which furnished over 38 percent of the total employment.

Employment has always been concentrated in the central cities in the Springfield area, which still furnished approximately 80 percent of the total employment in 1965. In 1960 over 61 percent of all persons employed lived in the central cities and 84 percent of these worked there. Six and one-half percent worked outside the central city but within the SMSA. Thirty-nine percent of the employees lived outside the central cities and 31 percent of these worked in the central cities while

57 percent worked in the suburban ring. Manufacturing was most important in the Springfield area, furnishing approximately 40 percent of the total employment in 1965.

The major reasons for the different locations of employment is that Washington, D.C. is the center of the federal government, the major employer. In Springfield, manufacturing developed in the central cities early, and the factories are still located there. With its slow growth, only a few new firms have moved into the suburban areas. Wilmington's pattern of development has been quite different, with many of the industries having their headquarters in the central city but locating their plants and research development facilities in the suburban areas. Almost all of these new locations since World War II have been in the suburbs. Since development has taken place rapidly during this period, it has tipped the balance of employment heavily into the suburban locations.

An analysis of the concentration of employees per industrial-commercial acre in Springfield indicated that in 1965 there were over 20 employees per industrial-commercial acre in the central cities and only 12 per acre in the towns, in the New England sense of that term. The concentration on the industrial acres was much higher than on the commercial acreage, averaging approximately 54 employees per acre on the industrial land in the central cities. The higher density in the cities than in the suburbs has an obvious significance. As industrial locations shift to the suburbs, the Springfield study shows that the suburban industrial developments are two to three times as land-consuming as historically has been the case in the central cities. This characteristic is being encouraged by present zoning regulations and also is dictated because of the large minimum size of commercial and industrial lots.

Residential Patterns

Although consumer demand for residential environment was taken as implicit in the Washington and Wilmington studies, it was treated as an explicit factor in the Springfield study. Several factors which affected consumer demand were isolated and examined relative to their location within the central cities and suburban towns. It was found that the characteristics of the suburban consumer himself are considerably different from those of the central city consumer. The head of the suburban household is likely to be over 25, but less than 65, usually 35 to 45 years of age. He has a slightly larger household, and his children are mostly less than 15 years of age. He is well educated, holds a white-collar job, and earns an income considerably above the median of the SMSA. He lives in those areas of the suburbs that are growing the fastest, on a one-half acre lot in a single-family dwelling unit. His neighbors are very much like himself, and thus, the neighborhood is quite homogeneous.

The central city dweller is older, on the average. He lives in a smaller-sized household, is not as well educated, probably holds a blue-collar job, and earns less income than the suburban householder. He lives in a more densely populated area with a one-quarter acre lot if he lives in a single-family dwelling unit. He may well live in a multiple-family unit with densities of 10 to 33 dwelling units per acre.

He is more likely than the suburbanite to be less than 25 or over 65. Thus the central city community is overall more heterogeneous, perhaps containing a wide range of quite homogeneous neighborhoods. This heterogeneity of neighborhoods within the total central city makes the urban problems more complex than those in the suburbs.

Persons moving to the suburbs in the Springfield area are building more expansive homes than those in the central city. Where 68 percent of the new homes built in the central cities between 1960 and 1964 were valued at less than $20,000, almost 56 percent of the new homes built during the same period in the suburbs were valued at more than $20,000, with almost a fourth valued at over $25,000. This is consistent with data showing the value of housing by income group calculated from the U.S. Census of Housing in 1960. These figures show that almost 70 percent of all homes valued at over $20,000 in that year were owned by persons in households earning incomes of over $10,000. Thus, the higher-income people moving to the suburbs are building the higher-value houses at the present time. These houses are likely to be on relatively large lots and thus to be quite land-consuming.

The data from the Delaware study show similar trends. The highest average construction cost per unit of new single-family houses since 1945 was encountered in suburban Brandywine hundred ($15,000) while the lowest average cost was in close-in New Castle hundred ($9,300).

Factors which consumers in the Springfield area thought were important in determining where they lived were access to good educational facilities at all levels and living in a community which is well-kept and attractive and provides many parks and recreational activities. These three factors were considered to be much more important than any others. Other factors deemed to be important were the general quality of government, the provision of public services, and access to shopping centers, hospitals, and cultural facilities. The opportunity for inexpensive living with a good tax rate was also expressed as being important. Of lesser importance were a high level of ownership of single-family homes; access to churches and public transportation; zoning which excluded industry from residential areas; and a scenic setting.

Northern New Castle County's suburban residents rated convenience to work, convenience to shopping and other activities, nice appearance, reasonable cost, good schools, no traffic or parking problem, closeness to family and friends, and convenience to public transportation in that order as being the best features of their communities.

Access to employment might prove to be important in Washington with its larger population and more intense traffic congestion than would be the case in either Wilmington or Springfield. Also the importance of open space and recreational areas might be greater in Washington than in the more rural settings of Wilmington and Springfield. In contrast, the presence of hospitals, shopping centers, and cultural facilities might be more important in the more rural areas. All of these factors which make up consumer demand for residential housing and environmental quality are subject to change with the changing family cycle, changing level of income, differing amounts of leisure time, and the age distribution of the residents in the household.

Urban-Suburban Interrelations

Most economists would agree that development decisions should be made on the basis of marginal costs to the person or group making the decision. As pointed out in earlier chapters, the present decision-making system does not include all of the suburban development marginal costs borne by society as a whole. Many of the externalities, diseconomies, and other costs which arise in the process are not included in the decision-making framework for the persons or groups who make the decisions.

In many cases the residents of the older city center are subsidizing the development of the suburbs. The Delaware study, particularly, points out the types of subsidization which occur because of central sewage treatment facilities, the provision of downtown parking, and the building of access highways to allow people to commute more easily from the suburbs to the central city. The Springfield case also provides evidence of externalities whose costs are borne primarily by the central cities, such as traffic congestion caused by commuters and air and water pollution by industries which furnish employment for the suburbanites. Washington subsidizes the suburbanites from the standpoint of traffic congestion. It also provides low-cost housing and other public services for low-salaried, blue-collar employees needed to service the high-salaried, white-collar jobs generally held by the suburbanites.

The framework within which suburban land use decisions were made undoubtedly had a considerable impact upon the resultant developmental pattern. A different public decision-making framework might have resulted in a different pattern. Decisions on rezoning proposals, different physical characteristics of soils relative to their ability to "absorb" effluent from septic tanks, problems of pollution control, allocation of areas for public facilities, and public open space in the overall plan for the development of an area—all had an impact upon the development pattern. The organization of the decision makers in and outside of government also was important.

In slow-growing Springfield, the major expansion took place along the existing access roads, with a minimum amount of full-fledged subdivision development. Whereas much speculative building has been done in both Washington and Wilmington, little housing has been built in Springfield except on a presold or custom basis. The larger relative proportion of the development in Springfield has been of the intra-SMSA type—i.e., people moving from the central city to the suburban towns. Thus the pressure to obtain housing has been much less, since the people moving to the suburbs have had a place to live while their new residence was being built.

In the Springfield area, access to sewer systems has had little influence on the pattern of development in the suburban area. In fact, seven of the suburban towns do not at present have sewerage. Others have sewers and interceptor systems but not treatment plants. Most of the remainder of the area is served by plants that provide only primary treatment. Thus extensive development has taken place without consideration of this public service.

If the new homeowners had been required to have access to a sewer system, the pattern of development would probably have been considerably different. At present they can use septic tanks, and many get water from their own wells. If areas developed in this way are eventually forced to provide a sewer system, the cost to both new and old residents will be much higher than if sewers had been constructed initially.

The development of suburban land in the Wilmington area appears to have been the result of two major factors. First, development seems to have followed the extension of trolley lines and roads in the years from 1900 to 1930. This type of development caused the development of satellite cities surrounding the central city of Wilmington. Later, access to sewer systems seems to have had the major impact on the development pattern. As the entire county was sewered fairly early in the urbanizing process, development tended to follow the major lines of the sewer system and considerable infilling occurred among the previously scattered development. By 1963 less than 10 percent of all residences in northern New Castle County were dependent on septic tanks. All of the remaining were tied into the sewer systems.

PLANNING, ZONING, AND SUBDIVISION CONTROL

Planning had been done to a different extent in all of the study areas, and they all had problems in carrying out master plans or comprehensive plans. The problems arose primarily from the fact that the planning designation always has some impact upon the development of an area and the price of any specific parcel of land. The development of a master plan for a community tends to change the price of land of a similar type merely by specifying different land uses. Land zoned for industrial, commercial, or high-density residential use is likely to acquire a development price several times that of adjacent land zoned for agricultural use. This price effect is in large part independent of the fact that demand for the more intensive use is too weak to bring all the land to development, and also of the fact that the planning board may lack power to implement its plans. Even though more than an adequate amount of land is classified in the master plan in each use category, applications to change the particular use category are always forthcoming.

A survey of 9,300 acres of land in the Springfield area zoned for industrial uses indicated that only 4 percent of it had been developed for industrial purposes between 1955 and 1964, 7 percent had been developed for other uses, and 89 percent was still undeveloped. Because of the high expectation values held by owners of industrially zoned land, the entrepreneurs had found it to be less expensive to purchase land zoned for less intensive use and have it rezoned than to purchase land already zoned industrial. It will be recalled that Neutze found a similar situation on land zoned for apartments in suburban Washington.[4] While it is true that master or comprehensive plans must be approved by a majority of the voters in a town in Massachusetts, this does not mean that the results will be accepted by all the affected landowners. Individuals will set out to change the basic idea of the

[4] G. Max Neutze, *The Suburban Apartment Boom* (Resources for the Future, 1968).

master plan by attempting to change plan designation or the zoning of their particular parcels of land.

Zoning was the major tool used in each of the three study areas to control land use, and in all of them it was found to be an imperfect instrument. Land use decisions were frequently made and carried out that were in conflict with the zoned uses. In Fairfax County, Virginia, a comprehensive county plan was adopted in 1958 which was in general accordance with the "Policies Plan for the Year 2000" for the Washington metropolitan area. Basically, this plan called for the accommodation for new growth in corridors radiating out from the District along the major arterial highways. Within these corridors, urban development with different densities was planned. Between them, very low-density development and recreational areas were to be maintained. However, the rapid growth of the Washington area brought unforeseen and unimagined pressures for urban development upon the county. Land suitable for urban development diminished rapidly, and rising land prices made it unwise economically for owners to develop areas at densities specified in the 1958 plan.

A zoning ordinance had been adopted in 1959 to carry out the 1958 plan. However, thousands of rezoning applications were filed in the few years that followed. Thus by 1963 there was little resemblance between the 1958 comprehensive plan and the then current zoning maps.

The experience in Wilmington was somewhat different. Suburbia was well along when the New Castle County zoning code was enacted in 1954 in an attempt to prevent misuses of land in the urbanizing process. However, zoning has not changed the privately intended use of land for most individual owners, since 73 percent of all rezoning petitions in New Castle County between 1954 and 1964 were approved. In 1956 there was several times more land zoned in each of the land use categories than was actually in that use. Between 1956 and 1958 the zoning map was substantially amended, mainly to permit more high-density residential, commercial, and industrial land use. Nevertheless the demand for rezoning proved to be insatiable and almost a thousand zoning cases came before the County Levy Court between 1954 and 1964.

In the Wilmington area there was also another problem. Although zoning was adopted in 1954, there was no comprehensive plan for New Castle County until 1958. Thus the zoning decisions during most of the period were not made within the framework of a comprehensive plan.

Several of the towns in the Springfield area have used zoning as a tool for guiding growth patterns. Certain types of development determined to be undesirable in the suburban towns have been zoned out of existence. Large-lot zoning has also been used in an attempt to channel growth into areas zoned for smaller lots. This was not felt to be discriminatory but rather to be in conformity with sound planning practices. Some communities have used large-lot zoning to exclude all residential growth but are being challenged in court by the home builders.

In all of the study areas the personalities of the individuals responsible for rezoning cases had a definite effect on the outcome of the cases. In Springfield arbitrary actions by members of zoning boards have maintained some towns as almost 100 percent residential—or even single-family dwelling unit residential—while other towns have developed the commercial and industrial capacity to support the employment of persons residing in the residential towns. Such actions have been challenged and in a recent case one of the zoning appeal boards has been indicted by the grand jury for irregularities in its proceedings.

Fairfax County had a somewhat similar problem. Several of their county supervisors were indicted and convicted of bribery conspiracy in the approval of rezoning applications. In Wilmington there was considerable evidence that pressure was constantly applied to the Levy Court in zoning appeal cases, but no evidence was found that the public officials succumbed to this pressure in any illegal way.

A third method of directing development of suburbs is subdivision control. Massachusetts law specifies that subdivision control is "to protect the safety, convenience, and welfare of the inhabitants of the cities and towns . . . by regulating the laying out and construction of ways in subdivisions providing access to the several lots therein . . . and insuring sanitary conditions in subdivisions and in proper cases, parks and open areas." The general objective of subdivision control in other study areas is similar. Subdivision controls, together with building and housing codes, exert tremendous influence on the cost (and resultant value) of dwelling units. Building and housing codes are based on the proposition that the community cannot afford to have situations develop which are injurious to the public health, safety, and welfare if the community is later forced to take aggressive and expensive action to overcome these deficiencies. Building and housing codes assure minimum standards in construction for long life and proper maintenance of buildings which serve as a property tax base for all communities. They assist in stabilizing the valuations which are the source of financing local government and in carrying out the physical aspects of the master plan. Since a high proportion of local revenue comes from taxing the assessed value of real property, housing which will have a low assessed value will have a marked impact on the welfare of the community.

In Fairfax County, the county board of supervisors has the power to approve comprehensive plans and to adopt zoning ordinances and zoning maps and any changes in them. It also rules on all rezoning applications on a case-by-case basis. The board adopts site plans and subdivision control ordinances and considers any variances to them. Setting the assessment ratio and the property tax rate are also within the province of the board. These decisions are all made on the town or city level in the Springfield area.

In Delaware the Levy Court has responsibilities far beyond acting on zoning cases. Since it has fiscal responsibilities in budgeting and appropriating funds, the Levy Court is in a good position to analyze the fiscal impacts of any zoning changes. Since most zoning changes are intended to place the affected land in a more intensive use, zoning benefits the petitioner by increasing the value of his assets and the local government by increasing the tax base. However, increased tax revenues must be used at least partially to offset the increased cost of services demanded by the development of the rezoned property. In practice, the petitioner seldom mentions the added services which will have to be provided.

Public Service Costs

Costs of alternative patterns of urban development can be grouped into three general categories: (1) private costs incurred by the residents who move into the area; (2) public costs borne by the various levels of government and paid from public receipts obtained from the taxation of real property and other assets; and (3) social costs borne by society as a whole and not usually quantifiable in the monetary sense in any way similar to private and public costs.

The differences in per capita public costs of living in the suburbs and those of living in the central city were examined in Springfield. The tax rate, per capita assessed valuation, per capita tax levy, and per capita debt had all increased more in the towns than in the central cities from 1956 to 1967. The absolute level of assessed valuation, tax levy, and debt was higher in the towns, while the tax rate was higher in the suburbs.

The public revenues from taxes and commercial receipts (licenses, fees, etc.) were also examined for the central cities and the towns. Per capita increase in total taxes, property taxes, total commercial receipts, and receipts from public service enterprises was greater in the towns than the central cities, but the absolute levels of receipts were higher in the central cities than the towns except for property and poll taxes in the latest period, 1964. (Tables 21 and 22.)

While property and poll taxes comprised 82 percent of the total central cities' tax receipts in 1951, they had decreased to 66 percent by 1964. The towns' depen-

TABLE 21

PERCENT OF CHANGE IN PUBLIC COSTS, CENTRAL CITIES AND TOWNS, SPRINGFIELD SMSA

Item	Period	Central cities	Towns	Cities as percent of towns, 1967
Tax rate	1956–67	+31%	+37%	121%
Per capita assessed valuation	1956–67	+17	+93	60
Per capita tax levy	1950–65	+130	+218	98
Per capita debt	1950–67	+270	+830	77

TABLE 22

PERCENT OF CHANGE IN PER CAPITA REVENUE SOURCES, CENTRAL CITIES AND TOWNS, SPRINGFIELD SMSA, 1951–64

Revenue source	Central cities	Towns	Cities as percent of towns, 1964
Per capita total tax	+144%	+175%	106%
Per capita property and poll tax	+97	+157	98
Per capita commercial receipts	+120	+184	186
Per capita public service receipts	+113	+265	340

dence upon property and poll tax declined from 80 percent in 1951 to almost 75 percent in 1964, relatively less than in the cities. Further, the ratio of total taxes to total commercial receipts was about 2 in the central cities in 1964 while it approached 4 in the towns. This indicates that the towns are much more dependent upon property taxes as a source of revenue than are the central cities. The overall impact of the tax levy was a 9 percent higher average tax cost for homeowners in the suburbs than in the central cities of the Springfield area.

Social costs are closely related to public costs except that they are usually of a type that cannot be captured in the marketplace. Thus costs related to destroying the visual environment with small lots, single-family, grid-type housing development, or by the erection of unaesthetic high-rises, impose a social cost on everyone viewing these developments. Upsetting the ecological balance of a given area by expanding the urban development also produces social casts. Presently some of the more serious types of social costs are being borne in the areas of water pollution, air pollution, and noise pollution. While these degrade the general living environment, perhaps even pose health problems for the general population, no way has been found to charge these costs to those responsible for them. Social costs can be either positive or negative depending upon the particular situation involved.

The incidence of private costs undoubtedly differs between the various study areas, although they were not directly quantified. The cost of land is much higher in the Washington area than in either the Wilmington or the Springfield areas, because there is a strong demand for urban land in Washington and the people purchasing these lots have high incomes and desire a low-density development. Although land prices in Springfield are lowest on a per acre basis, the tendency is toward large-lot zoning which offsets the lower land prices to some extent. The private cost of providing a water system is probably significant only in Springfield, where many of the developing areas do not have access to public water systems. The private cost of septic tanks is probably similar in the sense that sewer systems are usually a prerequisite for building in both Wilmington and Washington but not in the suburban towns of the Springfield SMSA. Commuting costs would probably be higher in Washington, since it is a bigger city and the new developments are further from the city center which still provides the majority of the jobs. Commuting may be least costly in the Wilmington area, where much of the industrial employment is dispersed within the suburbs.

The public costs of providing the various public services probably would not be too different in the three areas except as they are affected by natural conditions such as drainage and the economies and diseconomies of size inherent in the system. Thus providing sewers to some of the small towns in the Springfield area might be fairly costly on per-capita-served basis relative to the large system in New Castle County. A similar situation might exist in the provision of water and public transportation. School systems enjoy economies of size up to around 30,000 enrollment and thus the systems in the towns of the Springfield SMSA are likely to be higher-cost than those in the Washington area.

The social costs of air and water pollution may be more serious in the Springfield area than in the other two study areas primarily because of the autonomy of individual town units of government, which has prevented the development of county-wide sewer systems and has encouraged each town to go its own way. Hence the rivers and streams in the area are badly polluted. Several towns provide no sewage treatment at all. Air pollution has similar impacts, with the factories in the central cities emitting smoke which drifts into the surrounding towns.

Traffic congestion can be expected to be worse in Washington because of the heavier traffic flows. Damage to the visual environment is probably least in Springfield because it has no full-fledged subdivisions, which tend to destroy entire blocks of the natural environment in the process of development. The same is probably true in terms of the destruction of the existing ecology, with Springfield being the least affected at the present time because of the slow rate of growth. All of the central cities in the study areas suffer high unemployment, relatively high crime rates, and the inability to provide safe access for their citizens to all areas within their boundaries at any time of the day or night.

A social benefit which accrues to the Washington area more than to Wilmington and Springfield is access to cultural amenities. The presence of art galleries, museums, legitimate theater, occasional opera and ballet, and major political gatherings provides a cultural environment which is unavailable in the other study areas. In turn the outlying suburbs of Springfield may provide a visual environment unavailable in the other areas. Easier access to the ocean is among Wilmington's assets.

All in all, each area offers some social benefit unique to itself and provides some benefits not available in the other areas. It was not possible to equate these factors in this study.

12 DECISION MAKING IN SUBURBANIZATION OF THE THREE STUDY AREAS

One major purpose of this book is to explore the decision-making process in suburban growth and development. Only by better understanding of the process as it has worked and as it currently operates, can one seek to change and hopefully to improve it.

This chapter attempts to review, and to a degree to interpret, the findings of the three case studies as regards the decision-making mechanisms in suburban growth and development. Thus it complements Chapters 5 and 6, where the decision-making process and the actors were considered in general.

Part of the decision-making process is public; part is private. Each part is divided among a number of actors—government agencies, industry groups, and the like—and many individuals within each group. While each actor plays a role, it is their interaction which is most important. None operates in isolation, but rather each takes his cues from others and in turn provides them with cues to their roles. The multiplicity of decision-making units and the fragmentation of the process are its most striking aspects.

Expositional necessity requires the description of the role of each unit in turn; but, wherever one starts, he comes back at the end to the group with which he began. The role of the public agencies is perhaps the most obvious, and there is more—but still not enough—information about them than about the other units. Their actions are subject to a greater degree of public scrutiny, supervision, and reporting than those of various private groups. Hence, the discussion here starts with the public agencies, not because they are in any sense more important. In a process where many actors are essential to the final result, it is difficult indeed to single out any as more important than any other.

A major hypothesis emerges from these three case studies: The nature of the decision-making process in suburban growth and development depends to a considerable extent upon the rate of that growth and development. Where growth is very rapid, as in Fairfax County, the process takes on certain characteristics; where growth is slow, as in Springfield, the process is quite different. This is not to deny the importance of local governmental and private institutions but merely to say that their effects are subordinate to larger economic and demographic forces. An interesting intellectual exercise, in its nature inconclusive and unsolvable, is to

speculate on how suburban growth would have taken place under the town government system of Massachusetts, had growth there been as rapid as it actually was in
Fairfax County; or to estimate how it would have been in Fairfax County, had
growth been as slow as it actually was in Springfield. These "might-have-been"
speculations can be more than a stimulating intellectual diversion, for they do try
to separate the effects of different variables which were, in fact, combined in the
three case studies.

ROLE OF THE FEDERAL GOVERNMENT

The federal government may seem rather remote from the decision-making
process in suburban growth and development, yet it is basic and underlies all the
local activities. The federal government plays both an indirect and a direct role in
suburban growth and development.

Perhaps the foremost indirect role is the maintenance of a high level of economic
activity. Private economic activity in the United States operates within a framework and under conditions established by the federal government. The three case
studies provide some historical depth, the detail depending in large part upon the
availability of information, but they are almost wholly concerned with the years
since World War II. The Wilmington study is something of an exception, for it
does have more analysis of the prewar periods, but even it focuses on the recent
past. Within the postwar period, each study is more concerned with the 1960's than
with earlier periods. Availability of data as well as a desire to consider current
affairs and procedures was responsible for this emphasis. But these were years of
high economic activity. It is not asserted that U.S. economic output in every postwar year or in every year since 1960 was as high as it reasonably could have been.
But there has been no massive depression like that of the 1930s, or even major
recurrent business cycles with large declines lasting several months, such as seemed
"natural" and inevitable before 1930.

Springfield grew more slowly in employment and population and presumably in
total metropolitan income than either Wilmington or Washington. Yet even in
Springfield a substantial number of new dwellings has been constructed in recent
years, primarily single-family dwellings in suburban areas. Total population increased by 18 percent between 1950 and 1965, yet total area used for urban purposes increased 136 percent in the same years. The economic force was there to
fuel suburban growth and expansion.

Another indirect role of the federal government that was important in the three
case study areas is in the tax field. The distinction between capital gains and "ordinary income" and the difference in tax rates applicable to each have had major
impact on suburban growth. Other provisions of the tax law make it useful to
receive only part of the sale price from land in one year, so that total tax liability
from the sale of land is spread over several years. Such provisions encourage land
sales on a deferred payment plan, with the land seller in effect financing a major
part of the increase in land price. On a rising land market, the seller takes little
risk in so doing, and his actions are important in stimulating land transactions.

One interesting aspect of federal taxing power is that it gives the federal government both the authority and the motive to investigate local business dealings which are illegal or suspected of being so, because such activities nearly always include tax evasion. In Fairfax County, it was the federal investigations of possible tax evasions which uncovered the frauds involved in land zoning, or at least triggered the state and local investigations leading to the same end. One cannot know, or even reasonably estimate, how much the federal tax investigation power has kept local citizens from taking advantage of the great potential for gain from local governmental actions which affect suburban land values, but one can suspect it has been a major force.

The federal government has played an indirect role in its measures to facilitate home ownership, as described in general in Chapter 3. Even where neither Veterans Administration nor Federal Housing Administration financing or guaranteeing of loans is directly involved, the standards set by these agencies have vitally affected suburban expansion. In Fairfax County, for instance, FHA refused to approve loans in the area directly affected by flight patterns from Dulles International Airport. While it might have been possible for some builder to build, sell, and finance the construction of homes from his own resources, in practice the position of the federal government was effective in largely preventing home construction in this area. The similar effectiveness of FHA in limiting or guiding development was noted in some of the infilling examples described for the Wilmington metropolitan area.

In addition to these indirect roles, the federal government operated more directly in the three case study areas. In each, it paid 90 percent of the cost of building major highways. In the Wilmington area, highways had a direct effect on land prices. In the other two areas, the accessibility provided by such highways has surely been a major factor in their growth.

The federal government has provided some direct subsidies for sewers, schools, open space, and other purposes; a variety of such programs have been enacted in the past decade. In Fairfax County, the federal government built the Dulles interceptor sewer, to provide service to Dulles International Airport.

The federal Water Quality Control Act of 1965 required the states to develop, or promise to develop, water quality standards at least equal to the federal standards by June 30, 1967 or have the federal standards become effective. The direct effect of this legislation to date is hard to measure in the three case study areas and may well be insignificant. However, the federal legislation is surely the handwriting on the wall. It has already led to stiffer state standards and may well lead to still stiffer ones in the future; and this, in turn, will lead to stronger pressures on local governments to enforce water quality standards and pollution control.

In Fairfax County, the federal government has been a major force in providing the economic climate for suburban land development. The physical growth of Washington in the postwar years, as indeed earlier, has been an expression of the growing economic importance of the federal government, which is both the largest single employer in the Washington metropolitan area and also the stimulus for a great deal of other employment. Federal workers required a place to live; suburban development in several directions, including into Fairfax County, was the result.

The pace of growth was swift for the whole metropolis, and for the growing suburbs it was extremely rapid. In this sense, the Washington experience is unique—the direct role of the federal government in its seat of government can be felt only in one metropolis. But federal employment has been a major factor in several smaller metropolises—Denver, for instance, or in war industry cities like San Diego, or near major military bases.

Role of the States

The role of the states in suburban growth and development varied considerably among the three case study areas, yet in none of them was it dominant or even as large as that of the federal government. In all states, a considerable part of the major highway system was constructed and maintained by the states, some with state funds, some largely with federal funds. The three case studies did not explicitly explore the effect of such highways upon suburban land conversion; there is nothing to indicate that the states consciously employed highway construction as a tool to influence the direction or the pattern of suburban growth. But the accessibility that highways provided to the city centers of Springfield, Wilmington, and Washington almost surely was a factor in the growth of the suburbs.

States provide some help to local schools. This is most marked in Delaware, where most of the cost of local schools is paid by the state. In Springfield, state funds are also important, less so in Fairfax County. However, state school funds were not used consciously to affect rate or direction of suburban growth; rather they were used to help both older city and newer suburban schools, wherever these were located. It may be that this apparent neutrality of state school funds actually served to facilitate suburban growth, but the case studies do not provide evidence for or against this view.

Something similar is true with regard to park and recreation areas. Each of the states concerned has a park program; and state parks are an important asset to residents of both older cities and newer suburbs who can afford to travel to them. But there is nothing in the three case studies to indicate that state parks were used as a tool in guiding suburban growth or that they had a major effect in this direction.

States have important legal powers for public health, and in each of the three case study areas the state might have been a major factor affecting suburban growth, by strictly regulating the use of septic tanks. Without such septic tanks, the form of suburban growth in Springfield would have been very different, for there would have been strong financial incentive to build in areas served by sewers instead of stringer development along roads. This assumes that there are situations in which septic tanks have had, or will have, adverse effects upon public health sufficient to warrant their control. Massachusetts has exercised very little control over septic tanks in the past. In Delaware, the issue has not been important, largely because the county extended sewer lines so widely and so far ahead of actual settlement that there was much less incentive for use of septic tanks. In Fairfax County, septic tanks were reasonably well controlled, and sewers had to meet health standards. However, the state water control board pursued a somewhat less than clear and unequivocal policy course regarding the discharge of more or less treated sewage effluent into Bull Run, which was the source of city water for the City of Alexandria. Had the state water control board taken a much stronger position, and insisted upon it, the construction of small sewage treatment plants in the Centreville and Chantilly areas would have been very difficult or impossible; development on those localities would have had to wait for the major sewer system previously planned, and the whole course of suburban development in the county would have been much different. The case study of Fairfax County does not throw much light on the way the state water control board conceived of its job or the processes by which it reached its decisions. There was some reason to believe that the board "did not want to get involved in local politics" but actually did affect local development materially.

State law permits the local governments to carry out certain functions and thus implicitly forbids—or at least does not permit—other functions. But the laws are often general and apply to all counties alike. Fairfax County has the same powers as other Virginia counties, although many are rural, whereas Fairfax encounters severe problems because of the rate of its growth. While states, as governments, perhaps should not be held responsible for all the sins of action and inaction by local government, the states cannot avoid a large measure of responsibility for what happens at local levels, because they have provided a permissive legal framework.

The states concerned in these case studies filled this role in various ways. Massachusetts has provided both the authorization for "towns" to have planning boards and has required that towns above 10,000 population prepare a master or land use plan. However, the state has provided virtually no supervision or guidance and towns have done pretty much as they pleased. Delaware likewise has provided authority for counties to enact zoning ordinances but without either help or guidance in performing this function efficiently. Delaware has intervened directly in some local situations, as when it passed an act incorporating the single-tax community of Arden. The local service functions budget for New Castle County, Delaware, is a recent major attempt by the state government to restore the fiscal balance between cities and suburbs by requiring the suburbs to pay fully for the services they get. Fairfax County sought to control suburban development in the Centreville and Chantilly areas, until areas closer in were more nearly fully developed. To achieve this end, the county proposed not to construct sewers and other public services earlier than the plan called for and to rezone these areas for large residential lots only. The courts of Virginia upset this effort, stating that such action was arbitrary and did not promote the public health, safety, morals, and general welfare. The state did nothing to try to clarify the situation or to provide the county with the necessary legal authority to implement its plans.

In these three case study areas, the role of the states can be described as aloof, indifferent, or unconcerned. There was little or no effort to deal with the problems of suburban growth and development directly by state action or indirectly by providing local government with a full kit of tools. Many people, perhaps a majority of the electorate, would have endorsed the role the states actually played; to such people, suburban growth is simply not a proper subject for state action. Others would decry the lack of authority at local levels and lack of help to local government as abdication by the state of its responsibilities in a major modern problem. At the least, it should be recognized that state charters to local government were nearly always enacted in an earlier period, when suburbanization was not such a vital local process.

It might not be easy for states to exert some real direction over local government in its efforts to affect suburban growth and development even when this is clearly within state legal powers. Massachusetts experience with towns in their handling of sewage effluent may be instructive. As the Springfield study points out, several of the towns have long dumped untreated raw sewage into the handiest local stream; others have provided a degree of primary treatment, which has by no means removed either the health hazard or the aesthetic offense. The state has begun tentatively to prod these towns into effective sewage treatment, in part under the shadow of federal control. But some of the towns have made it clear that they intend to stall as long as they can; they now get rid of their sewage cheaply, and someone else suffers the consequences. If states are really going to affect suburban growth and development, they must be prepared to develop effective legal and governmental tools and to apply them with vigor and courage.

Role of Local Government

The role of local governments in suburban growth and development had far more attention in the three metropolitan case studies than did either the federal or the state role. The character of these "local governments" varied considerably. In each case, there were cities—legal entities, usually established some decades ago, with rather complete legal and governmental powers for the area, property, and population resident within their boundaries. They can assess property, levy and raise taxes, construct a wide variety of public works, and perform governmental functions such as planning, zoning, operation of schools, and others. The main difficulty in each case is that the legal city no longer conforms to the actual or economic city; the suburbs are, with few exceptions, outside the central legal city. Some of the suburbs are also legal cities, able to undertake governmental programs and develop employment centers and business districts of their own. The central city performs some functions which benefit suburbs, but it cannot recoup its costs from them. Many people work in the cities and obtain some services from them but reside in the suburbs, to which they are more loyal. So far as the three case studies reveal the situation, the legal powers of the central cities are reasonably comparable and reasonably adequate within their boundaries but quite inadequate for the larger metropolitan area.

There were counties in each of the case study areas, but their powers differed greatly. The county is an unimportant unit of government in Massachusetts, as in New England generally; its governing board meets only quarterly, its budget must be approved annually by the state legislature, and its powers are severely limited. The county in Delaware has more powers; in particular, it has been the general governing body for suburbs lying outside of any city. The county engages in general planning, enacts zoning and other controls, and carries out a considerable number of functions. Its taxes are not high, in part because the state pays most of the cost of schools and roads—the two most costly items in the budget of most local governments. The county has constructed sewer lines into many parts of its territory.

In Virginia, Fairfax County has equally great, or even greater, legal powers. In particular, its planning and zoning powers are considerable; it constructs public works, such as sewer lines and schools. Only a comparatively small part of the actually urbanized area of the county is within any city, and for the rest, the county serves as the unit of local government. In Virginia, when territory is annexed to a city, it ceases to be part of the county—cities and counties are mutually exclusive. The county has had its difficulties in carrying out its functions. Fairfax, like many other rapidly urbanizing counties, has needed to make large investments in public improvements, thus necessitating bond issues to raise the needed capital.

In Massachusetts, as in the rest of New England, the significant unit of local government is the "town." A town is simply a small city; or, as New Englanders would probably say, a city is simply a large town. The town was the unit of settlement in New England in colonial days; a selected group of settlers was allotted a sizable piece of land, on which they located a settlement and cleared fields for farming. Today both towns and cities include extensive surrounding rural areas so that during recent decades agriculture decreased as much in the towns as in the cities. The average town in the Springfield study area included 23.22 square miles of land. Had this all been developed at urban density (say 4,000 persons per square mile), it would have had about 93,000 people. The fact that the average town had only 11,000 residents suggests how far it was still rural in its land use. But it is the town (or city) which makes the general plan, enacts the zoning and subdivision controls, makes many of the improvements, operates the schools, and dumps its raw sewage into the stream that flows past the neighboring town. In terms of powers and functions, the town might be designated a minicounty. The towns of Massachusetts, and elsewhere in New England, are governed, in the last analysis, by the annual town meeting; all else, in the form of local government is derived or delegated from that town meeting. All citizens are eligible to attend, to speak, and to vote—and many do. To its admirers, this is true democracy in action. The fact that many of the towns are too small for efficient government is unimportant to them.

Each of the three case study areas had special local districts, but of different kinds and with different powers. In Delaware, the county might use a special district to operate its sewer system, but such districts were simply an arm of the county. In Virginia, on the other hand, special sanitary districts were established by action of the affected landowners, who dealt directly with the Circuit Court in establishment of districts and presented them to the county as a fait accompli which the latter could do little more than ratify. These sanitary districts can be established so as to effectively thwart or circumvent the county's general plan. Such special districts, with relatively little control by either county or state, are able to levy taxes, sell revenue bonds, and construct public improvements. They can, and in Fairfax County during the period of study they did, go far to thwart the plans and programs of the county.

Many of the towns in the Springfield study area, the major county in the Wilmington study area, and Fairfax County each had a professionally manned general planning organization. In substantial part, these are financed out of federal planning grants authorized by Section 701 of the Housing Act of 1954, but some local money goes into them too. Every self-respecting local government must have a planning office. It is a status symbol—and sometimes not much more. The staff is often ill-paid, as noted in earlier chapters; but the men are almost surely professionally trained, and it would be a serious mistake to underestimate their competence or, indeed, their long-run influence upon the thinking of local officials. Nevertheless, these professional planners have distinctly limited power.

For one thing, the professional planners are sometimes not held in high esteem by the political governing body. The first professional planner in New Castle County, Delaware, did not enjoy a harmonious relationship with the Commission; his tenure lasted 15 months. The Commission placed little reliance upon his suggestions. This may have been rather extreme, yet in the other areas, especially in Fairfax County, the governing body repeatedly took action contrary to the recommendations of its planners or acted without serious consideration of its planners' reports and recommendations. A county board may want a planning office, partly because state and federal agencies seem to put stress on their existence, partly because it may be a necessary condition to getting federal grant funds, and partly because it is considered "a good thing" to have. But at the same time the governing board will feel little hesitation in rejecting the views of its planners, especially when they conflict with "practical" advice from some other source.

Perhaps even more serious is the demonstrated incapacity of local general governing bodies to think in overall, general, and policy terms, and to take specific actions in accordance with general plans. At a single meeting, the Fairfax board of supervisors would approve or agree to some general policy or plan and then immediately take a specific zoning action that negated the general plan, sometimes on motion of the same supervisor. One could readily, but probably wrongly, attribute this to insincerity and cynicism. A more probable explanation is that the logical consequences of such a general principle or plan as filling up much of the partly developed eastern third of the county before allowing any significant suburban development in the western end simply were not apparent. County supervisors are not the only people in this world who see nothing inconsistent in mutually contradictory actions. In each of the three case study areas, general plans were proposed, approved, and translated into general zoning ordinances, with greater or less skill and detail, only to be substantially undermined in later specific zoning actions.

Another factor greatly limiting the powers of the specialized planners in each case study area was that the various public works agencies simply did not feel themselves bound by the general plans. The division of sanitary engineering in Fairfax County certainly did not have the same objectives as the county planning department. The engineers did not oppose the building of sewers at any place within broad geographic boundaries established by the board of county supervisors, if builders were willing to construct and pay for them and if the sewer charges collectable in the reasonably near future would more or less pay for operating costs. If a developer or builder wanted a sewer, by all means let it be constructed and never mind what happened to the overall settlement pattern in the county and to costs of other governmental services affected by that settlement pattern. Not only were lines built where the planners did not want them, but lines located in accordance with their plans were often built at larger sizes than called for by the plan, thus making possible developments not originally planned for. While this divergence between planners and sewer builders was perhaps the most serious, in terms of settlement consequences, the same general relationship existed in all areas and for all functions. The professional planner is simply not the real planner in too many cases. The role of the general governing board is critical here, for it could back up its planners far more than it does.

Counties in Washington and Wilmington and towns in Springfield have the legal power to enact zoning ordinances. As noted earlier a zoning ordinance is the legal means to carry out the objectives of its enactors; it specifies what may be done and directly or indirectly specifies what may not be done, on particular tracts of land or in particular zones—the kinds of uses, the intensity of use (as measured by floor area ratio, for example) and similar matters. Ideally, a zoning ordinance should:

1. be based upon a general- or land-use plan for the urban area or part thereof which is covered by the ordinance, and be one of the means of translating such a general plan into action;

2. include more than a single property or single tract of land; and

3. have some degree of permanence and specify the conditions for deviating from it.

These ideals for zoning ordinances were not met in the three case study areas. In New Castle County, Delaware, a zoning code was enacted in 1954 but no comprehensive plan was adopted until 1958, and that one was in rather general terms. In Fairfax County, a general plan was adopted in 1958 and the entire county zoned in accordance with it, but subsequent rezoning did more to undo the plan than to carry it out. In the Springfield area, zoning powers were used by all the towns even though six of them had no general plan, and some of the others employed zoning some years before they had adopted a general plan. But even where the general plan preceded the zoning ordinance, the plan seems to have been only one factor affecting the zoning ordinance; here too local government bodies found nothing inconsistent in taking specific actions contrary to their own general actions.

Zoning ordinances seem to have little or no sound economic base. In the Wilmington area, the acreage zoned for low-density residential use was more than four times the area actually used for this purpose, commercial zoning was equally generous, and industrial zoning even more so. Likewise, in the Springfield case study area, far more land was zoned industrial than was used for this purpose in the postwar years. In Fairfax County, far more land was zoned for various types of development than was actually developed in the ensuing two or three years. By having more land zoned for a use than is needed immediately, potential users have a choice, and present landowners do not have a monopoly. But, with such generous acreages available in each category, zoning obviously was not very influential on the location of each type of development. Unless zoning actually prevents some development which would otherwise occur, one may well question its meaningfulness. Why, by zoning, permit what will not in any event take place?

The actual zoning actions taken in the three study areas were on a case-by-case basis, although often more than one application was acted upon at a given meeting, and the various cases were more or less linked in the minds of the zoning authority. It linked cases together, perhaps as much as anything else to avoid public criticism for inconsistent and discriminatory action. The three case studies, especially the one for Fairfax County, are full of illustrations of such case-by-case action. The zoning authorities, by so acting, were planting (or cutting) trees one by one, but in the process created (or destroyed) a forest—a forest which they might, or might not, have wanted had they really thought about it as a forest, but apparently were unable to conceive of as such. It is doubtful, for example, that the towns of the Springfield metropolitan area really chose "string town" settlement along their roads, yet this is what their separate zoning actions created.

In each of the three case study areas, existing land use zoning was really not effective in preventing nonconforming use. Existing zoning might have to be changed, and this constituted something of an obstacle to development of a particular type but not necessarily one that could not be overcome. Rezoning was an irritant to developers, but apparently not much more; time and cost were involved but the outcome was usually not in doubt. Each case study recognized that it was difficult to test this point, and that the number of zoning and rezoning applications rejected was not a valid test, for proposals that were likely to be rejected were simply not made or were withdrawn without prejudice if opposition arose. Each study emphasized the key role of certain attorneys or of certain leading political figures. In Springfield zoning variances and special permits seemed to be almost universally approved for certain members of the community while a more restrictive attitude was taken toward other members of the community. Thus, a prominent member of an old New England family who happened to hold land which he wished to have rezoned might make a conditional sale of this land based upon successful rezoning, apply for the rezoning permit in his name, and immediately transfer it to the new owner when the rezoning was accomplished. This type of resident seemed much more likely than a land purchaser new to a community to get his rezoning approved.

In New Castle County, Delaware, only six attorneys presented 39 percent of the petitions submitted, indicating that some attorneys specialize in zoning cases. Three attorneys handled 26 percent of the petitions and received favorable decisions 80 percent of the time. The more successful attorneys employed several tactics in obtaining favorable decisions. First of all, they refused to handle petitions that they felt would be unfavorably received. Actually the attorney made a decision at this point which saved the time of Zoning Commission and Levy Court members at a later date. Experience in Fairfax County also emphasizes the role of key attorneys and others who know the ropes and have useful political and personal connections. While such people may encounter delays and difficulties in getting all the rezoning they seek, they know pretty well both what is possible and what is not, and they are also fairly effective in achieving their objectives.

The zoning process, and the role of the zoning authorities, is like the conquest of a lady of easy virtue. She must be approached by the right man, properly dressed, bringing suitable gifts, and the language must follow established patterns; but in the end, she yields, as everyone, including the lady herself, knew from the beginning that she would. If one retains the right lawyer, dresses up his rezoning proposal in attractive language, perhaps makes a gift of land for schools or parks or otherwise appeases some local opposition, properly emphasizes the employment potential of an industrial zoning and the favorable tax aspects for any zoning, the result is really not in doubt. The costs of such concessions and gifts, and the delays of getting favorable action, are less predictable and may prove onerous. But it seems clear that local zoning in an expanding urban or suburban area is not really an effective barrier to most kinds of development.

Perhaps the most striking aspect of local government, more noticeable in Fairfax County than in the other two case study areas, was the degree to which the nominally governing authorities, supposedly the protectors of the general public interest, intervened in the governmental processes for their own financial benefit or that of their clients. In Fairfax County, members of the board of supervisors owned land and traded in land at the very time when they were taking public action which affected its value. In zoning petitions involving land owned by a board member, he did not participate in the actual vote; but his presentation of the case, and the fact that he might well be expected to vote on another occasion on the petition of a fellow board member, hardly separated his influence as a public official from his benefit as a private citizen. Much of the work of the county government is to accommodate members of the private sector. At the same time, county officials are charged with protecting the interest of the public at large. Problems arise, however, in achieving a consensus on just what these interests are. Contrary to one popular view, not all of the trump cards are held by the private sector. In Fairfax County, the governing body has considerable power to guide growth and shape the urban pattern. The willingness and ability to exercise this power, however, is another matter. Certainly, there are opportunities for immoral (and perhaps illegal) use of this power, when the makers of public decisions are at the same time private participants in the business of land conversion.

There is little evidence from the public record that several former supervisors had the interests of the general public foremost in their minds while they were devoting so much effort to issues pertaining to Sanitary District 12. Yet these men have some prominent support. For example, one county official stated that Supervisor X believed that growth was good for Fairfax County as a whole, whether it took place in the Centreville district or anywhere else, and that he rarely voted against a rezoning or other matters promoting growth. For this reason, it was difficult for this official to understand why anyone would bother to bribe the supervisor or how he could ever have been involved. A former member of the Board expressed the opinion that this supervisor and the others did nothing illegal in supporting the activities in behalf of Sanitary District 12. Even if these activities are viewed in terms of some ethical standards, this official felt that their constituencies were adequately served. When it comes to defining public interest, matters of ethics, and constituencies, the distinctions are fine indeed in Fairfax County.

LAND CONVERTERS OR DEVELOPERS

The three case studies provide some information about the buying, selling, and related processes of converting rural land to urban uses. None of the researchers was able to obtain as much information as he would have liked, but these studies provide more than has been available elsewhere. Two tentative conclusions stand out: a variety of people, under a variety of names, are at work, at least in some areas; and the number and variety of such land agents, assemblers, converters, or whatever one wishes to call them, and their activities, depend in large part upon the pace of development within the metropolitan area.

As elsewhere a number of more or less separable processes were involved between a farm or other tract of completely undeveloped land and a completed dwelling or other structure. The unit of decision-making was the subdivision for residential building. In some cases, there was a function of land assembly, when the raw or agricultural land ownership was more finely fractured than the area desired by the builder or other user.

Sometimes the opposite process was involved; land needed subdivision from relatively large to smaller tracts more suitable to the needs of the builder of residential property. Another, and major, function was to obtain rezoning of the tract and the approval of a proposed subdivision plotting. Construction of some improvements, often limited to access roads or to a rough street layout, might also be part of the land agent's or dealer's job. Perhaps more important, he might be able to stimulate the building of necessary public improvements, of which sewers were often far and away the most important.

In the Springfield metropolitan area, the pace of growth and of land conversion was so slow that most of these functions were readily performed by builders themselves, by real estate agents as an auxiliary to their other business activities, or by a few others. In sharp contrast, in Fairfax County dozens of people performed one or more of these functions. It was impossible to ascertain exactly how many persons were involved in one way or another, but clearly the number was high. Many retired professional or other persons, including housewives, were in the land market. Several individuals would form a loose pool or partnership to buy a tract, often with a rather high debt-to-value ratio, and then seek to take whatever steps would make it possible to sell the tract to an actual builder. Tracts were sold and resold, sometimes with rezoning added, but sometimes with no apparent change. One tract apparently advanced by more than a third in price in just 18 days, without any rezoning or physical improvement; others advanced far more over a longer period, as rezoning was obtained. Sometimes it was impossible to know just who was behind such land transactions, for some of them were carried out by corporations or in trust, and hence it was hard to tell whether they constituted arm's-length bargaining. But the land market in Fairfax County had many of the attributes of an active commodity market anywhere, with many operators and various specialized functions. The Wilmington area was apparently somewhat intermediate to the other two; although the pace of development was faster than in Springfield, there was an abundance of suitable buildable land and hence there was a less frantic market than in Fairfax County.

To some extent, the possibilities for profits or high rewards to the various agents in the land conversion process depend upon their perversion of general governmental processes and actions. That is, an area planned and zoned for one kind of development has a value which, in part at least, reflects the zoning; if the latter can be changed, especially in ways not contemplated in whatever general plan may exist, the person or group who can force the change is rewarded more handsomely than the group which conforms to the plan. A conspicuous example was the formation of Sanitary District 12, in Fairfax County. The District was contrary to the general plan for the county; so was much of the subsequent rezoning. The individuals who were able to form the sanitary district, guide the $1.7 million sewer bond referendum to a successful conclusion, and either build on the land or sell it to a builder, secured some large increases in price. Some had not been so successful, by the time the study had to be concluded. There is no evidence that the price of any tract of land went down; some may not have risen, or risen much, at least for some periods. Moreover, as holding land involves costs, such as interest on the capital involved, merely selling at a higher price than was paid is not evidence of real profit. It was impossible in Fairfax County—and probably would be in any study—to learn much about actual profits from land dealings. It was hard enough to estimate sales prices of land, without regard to holding costs. In the other two case study areas, the rise in land prices was apparently less because the demand was less than in Fairfax, and the profit was less in rezoning or otherwise going contrary to the general plan.

BUILDERS IN THE CASE STUDY AREAS

The three case studies did not give much explicit attention to the role of builders in the process of suburban growth and development, but such information as was obtained in them agrees closely with the more general discussion in the earlier chapters of this study.

The dividing line between developers and builders is not a sharp one. In the Springfield area, where the rate of growth was slow and the pressure to convert land from rural to urban uses correspondingly less, the builders were to some extent also developers. A builder would have a client for a house or would wish to erect a few houses in anticipation of a clearly perceived demand; he would deal directly with a landowner or with a real estate agent who owned a piece of land or was in contact with an owner. There were no great problems in locating and obtaining a suitable piece of land on which to build.

In Fairfax County, the active developers sought to interest an actual builder in the development of a tract which they had assembled and/or gotten rezoned and which as a consequence was hopefully ripe for development. But larger builders were also their own developers, at least to a degree. Levitt and Sons, Inc., participated in attaining sewer facilities for a large tract of land in Sanitary District 12 for later development into one of the large suburban communities for which this builder is well known. In Fairfax County, it would appear that developers were the active or initiating agents; that is, a group of persons would form some type of syndicate, acquire land by purchase (almost invariably with high debt-value ratio) or by option or both, seek rezoning to the use they thought likely to be most profitable, and then seek a builder or builders who would actually carry the development forward. Such developers almost never had the capital, desire, and management ability to build, even with the customary borrowing that most builders used. As intermediaries, they were interested in acquiring the land, improving it without building, and disposing of it. They sought out both builders as buyers and landowners as possible sellers. But it is also possible that builders were, to a degree, the innovators; they might let a developer or a group of developers know of their interest in a particular tract or in any tract that would meet their general specifications.

In the Wilmington case study area, the role of builders seems to have been somewhat intermediate to that of Springfield and of Fairfax County. Sometimes builders bought land zoned for the use they wished to make of it; it may be presumed they paid, perhaps generously, for such zoning as an element in the land's value. In other cases, the builder had to acquire for himself the necessary zoning; this was generally the case if he sought to build anything different or unusual. A group of builders trying to develop a model community at Pike Creek Valley in the Wilmington area encountered delays in securing the zoning and had to make some modifications in their plans. In several of the cases reported in the three study areas, builders were more or less forced to donate land for public uses or modify building plans in order to forestall opposition to their zoning application.

Although comparatively little information was obtained directly on the subject in the three study areas, it seems that builders there, as elsewhere, operate on a very low equity and a very high debt, expecting to recoup all their investment when the property is sold. Their rate of operations was closely limited by the availability of loan funds.

HOME BUYERS

Several of the same things can be said about home buyers in the three case study areas as were said about builders. They were not the subject of much explicit study in the three areas, but the situation there largely confirms the general discussion of Chapters 5 and 6 above, where it was shown that home buyers are an essential, and at times a critical, part of the suburban land conversion process. In each area, it was the number of potential home buyers who established the pace of suburban growth—slow in Springfield, where there were relatively few such home buyers, and very rapid in Fairfax County, where there were, at least potentially, a very large number. The general rate of economic growth and the incomes of young married couples with small children are likely to be critical for the rate of suburban growth and hence for much of its process. When loan funds for house purchase are scarce and/or costly, the rate of purchases will slow down, the rate of building new houses will also slow down, and this puts a damper on the activities of the developers and traders in land.

The generally rising trend in land prices to actual builders, and the consequent rise in price of the average house built was noted in each of the three study areas for recent years. The kinds of houses built were those which only families with average or higher incomes could afford to buy, even with minimum down payments and with long-term mortgages. As a result, in the three study areas, the new suburbs were not the homes of lower-income families. However, there was a modest range in prices of houses and, as a result, in "character" of the communities, from fairly high income to about average income, usually with occupational stratification paralleling the income stratification. The willingness of potential buyers to buy and pay for houses of different or unusual types is probably critical. Though there was little direct evidence on this point in the case studies, in several communities or subdivisions the builder or developer made much of the fact that it was a "planned community," without ever precisely defining the term, which seems to have had some sales appeal to purchasers. Although precise evidence is lacking, one may hazard the guess that potential home buyers are more venturesome than zoning authorities and at least as venturesome as builders. In these three areas, as in other metropolitan and suburban areas, potential home buyers have only a limited range of choices. They can, and do, react to what is offered, but they cannot by themselves innovate.

In the Wilmington area, a survey of the attitudes of suburbanites toward their communities revealed a rather high degree of satisfaction with the kinds of communities into which these people had moved. By statistical analysis in the Springfield area, it was possible to suggest that people placed a very high value on "good schools," in their selection of a home site—without any precise definition of what that term really means.

The Wilmington case study did present some interesting analysis on the effort to use community citizens' associations as a substitute for local government. In the postwar years, several suburban developments took place outside of any city, where the only formal local government was New Castle County. In two of these places, Brookside and Ashbourne Hills, the developer-builders promoted community organizations of all families to assume certain highly local community or governmental functions, such as the operation of parks and playgrounds, maintenance of architectural standards, policing against nonconforming uses, and the like. Each suburban development was promoted as a planned community and much was made of the local self-government. Without direct measurement, it would appear that this was a selling point for houses in these communities. Buyers were undoubtedly hopeful that taxes would be lower outside of the cities; they probably largely ignored the fact that governmental services might also be less; and there may well have been a vague but nonetheless important general "anti-government" bias to their thinking. Americans seem often to long for some supposedly simpler society where government is less onerous, less demanding, and less costly but fully as effective.

The general verdict in these two cases is that the citizen community organization is an extremely poor substitute for effective local government and that it will become increasingly so in the future. Where the community organization has no legal power to compel local residents to pay dues or other charges or to conform with rules about uses of property (including such matters as trash dumping), the organization is ineffective from the beginning and gradually grows more nearly powerless. Initial enthusiasm may carry it along for a time, but new residents of the community must continuously be "sold" on its merits, and participation in its activities declines with the passage of time. A considerable part of such participation as can be aroused is spent in merely keeping the organization alive. If the community organization has legal powers, either by some sort of special act of state legislature or county government or by covenant running with the land that binds homeowners to pay dues and to conform to community association rulings, then its effectiveness depends to a considerable extent upon the exact nature of the legal powers. It still must face internal politics; sometimes it is difficult to bring the force of reasonable law to bear on a neighbor. To the extent that a community citizen group has strong legal powers, it approaches a unit of local government; but, at the best, it falls short, and perhaps seriously so.

In Fairfax County, citizen groups seem to have been quite effective in influencing specific actions of local government. The Fairfax County Federation of Citizens' Associations has over 140 member associations. This group has been vocal in trying to obtain public actions in directions it desires. County officials, recognizing such groups as blocks of political support or political opposition, take them seriously. However, there is a major difference between citizen organizations thus seeking to influence public action, and citizen organizations actually trying to carry out local governmental functions, as in Brookside and Ashbourne Hills. In the former role, they can be effective; in the latter role they have severe limitations.

ROLE OF FINANCIAL INSTITUTIONS

It was not possible, in the three case studies, to get detailed information about the role of financial institutions in suburban expansion and growth, but some information was obtainable. Where the rate of suburban development is rapid, the locality requires a net inflow of capital from other areas; where the rate of growth is slower, the metropolitan area may generate enough savings or other investment funds for its own needs. Thus in the Wilmington area there has been a more or less continued flow of investment capital from outside sources into residential development. The amount has varied somewhat from year to year, depending in part upon the attractiveness of other competing investments. A state limitation of maximum interest rate on such loans in Delaware has handicapped local builders and homeowners in securing loans and hence has inhibited the rate of suburban growth in recent years. Although precise data are lacking, there must have been a substantial inflow of capital into Fairfax County to finance dealings in land and development of residential and other areas. In this case, local lending institutions often acted as agents for outside sources of capital.

Banks and some other sources of capital are reluctant to finance purchase of land unless this is part of a definite development project. However, they often find construction loans highly profitable.

In the three study areas, as elsewhere, most actual builders operated primarily on borrowed funds; their own equities were usually small, and they sought to get all their money and all their profit out of a project when the houses were sold. They were not interested in, or capable of, financing the purchase of their product by its buyers. But some sources of capital, including some building and loan, or savings and loan, associations were willing to help finance land deals, as the record in Fairfax County makes clear. In a generally rising land market, the equity of the "buyer" is often considered unimportant; a rise in price of the land improves the lender's security, even though he has not reduced the loan. In Fairfax County, some tracts of land were sold and resold with apparently little or no repayment of loans and with higher mortgages at each sale. If there should be a decline in land prices, then of course this type of operation could quickly get into serious trouble. A dead or sluggish land market, perhaps growing out of capital scarcity and/or high cost for residential or other building, could well mean trouble to short-term borrowers with thin equity, when stronger holders could ride through such difficulties.

A major source of capital to finance dealings in unimproved land is the present owner of such land. His personal income tax situation is improved if he receives no more than 30 percent of the purchase price in cash at the time of sale. Down payments of this magnitude, in a rising land market where the annual increment in land price may easily average 15 percent or more, mean that in effect he gets his profit or price enhancement in cash while retaining a mortgage or other claim more or less equal to a price of his land only a year or two earlier. The seller, under these circumstances, is helping greatly to stimulate the rise in land prices from which he also gains.

In the study areas the lending institutions were not the innovators in suburban land development. They did not seek out tracts of land, get it rezoned, find a developer or builder, arrange for construction and sale of houses, or arrange for construction of shopping districts. Indeed, if some lending institution performed one or more of these functions, it would have been operating in a different role than as a lender. However, it also seems clear from the case studies that some source of capital is often involved rather early in the development process. A developer, having found a land tract, having gotten it rezoned or confident that he can do so, and having some plans for development and use of the land, is likely to have to find an adequate source of capital before he can go much further. At this stage, the role of the financial institution may become critical.

DISPERSION OF DECISION MAKING

At various points Part I of this book emphasized the dispersion of decision making in the processes of suburban land conversion. A number of actors participated in making the decisions, with no single one in control or calling the tune. The experience as reported in the three case studies reinforces this emphasis upon dispersion in decision making. The surface manifestations of the bargaining, dealing, arranging, negotiating, and decision making in Fairfax County, among numerous public officials and private groups were considerable and what is evident on the surface to the outsider is probably only a fraction of the total activity. Likewise, in the Wilmington area, the description of various zoning struggles strongly suggests that there must have been a great deal of behind-the-scenes bargaining and arranging. Even in Springfield, where the pace of suburban growth was relatively slow, a number of actors seem to have participated in the process.

Although each case study area had some kind of a general planning organization, the latter really did not make overall plans that became the major basis for public and private action. In the suburban development process with its numerous actors, there was nothing remotely resembling the architect with his blueprint for the building or the conductor with his score for the orchestra. Each actor "did his thing," taking the existence and the actions of the other actors as part of his environment within which his decision making operated.

A GLANCE AT OTHER METROPOLITAN AREAS IN THE NORTHEASTERN URBAN COMPLEX

13

The strength of the case study approach lies in wealth of detail that can be accumulated and the understanding that may be arrived at. A close look at a situation may lead to conclusions quite different from those that result from a broader look or from more generalized data. The weakness of the case study approach is that the cases chosen for study may not be broadly representative of their class but, instead, unusual or special in critical aspects.

The present chapter briefly reviews the situation in several SMSAs of the Northeastern Urban Complex that were not studied in detail, partly for the sake of better understanding, partly as a means of testing or examining the case studies in a broader framework. The bases for this chapter are census data and special planning studies made for the selected areas. Neither the data nor the analysis purport to be original. But the chapter does draw together in convenient form a great deal of information from scattered sources, some of which are not readily available except to a specialist in urban affairs.

MIGHTY NEW YORK

"New York" is a term with many meanings. To some, it means Broadway, the theater, glamorous actresses, and all the rest; to others, it means Wall Street, national and international finance, with many millions of dollars involved in many transactions; to others, it is the United Nations, with all its colorful international costumes, personnel, and activities all over the world, and so on. Anyone who first sees the great manmade canyons of the downtown and midtown office buildings cannot be indifferent to their emotional as well as to their intellectual impact. Some speak of New York in great admiration; the Tri-State Transportation Commission expresses it thus:

> The Tri-State Region leads all metropolitan areas throughout the world in the size of its population . . . the world's wealthiest. . . . contains the financial capital of the world, and since the establishment of the United Nations, its political capital as well. . . . the Port of New York is one of the busiest in the

world. . . . the world's most prosperous market area; . . . one of the world's leading centers of the arts and entertainment.[1]

Others speak of the huge city with horror, looking at its slums and its crowding, feeling that life there must be intolerable and that the future can only be worse than the present. But the old bromide, "an interesting place to visit, but I would not want to live there," obviously does not apply to the many millions of people who, in fact, do live there, and from choice.

Defining the City

These different viewpoints of New York lead to a specific question: what does one mean when he speaks of New York? One of the oldest and most common meanings is really Manhattan, where Broadway, Wall Street, the UN, and other internationally known aspects of New York are to be found. This island includes only 14,000 acres (22 square miles), but 1.7 million people lived there in 1960, and large additional numbers worked there but lived elsewhere (Table 23). This gives a total-population/total-area density of about 77,000 per square mile (about 120 per acre) in spite of the fact that only a third of the total floor space is residential.

The next larger area to which the term "New York" can be applied is the legal city, consisting of the five counties of Bronx, Kings (Brooklyn Borough), New York (Manhattan Borough), Queens, and Richmond. As a legal entity, with an elected government whose powers extend to the city but not beyond, it obviously has great importance. Its area is about 200,000 acres (315 square miles), its population in 1960 was about 7¾ million, giving a total-population/total-area density of nearly 25,000 per square mile (39 per acre). This includes 12.5 percent of the city area that is "undeveloped" as well as substantial open areas in the form of parks or other public service areas.[2] A great deal of land is also used for offices, manufacturing, and trade. The density in residential areas thus averages far higher than this overall figure.

But the legal city of New York is obviously far less than the economic city of New York, and this fact underlies many problems of definition. The Standard Metropolitan Statistical Area includes Long Island (Nassau and Suffolk counties), Rockland County, and Westchester County (Figure 23). The area included in the New York SMSA remained unchanged from the 1950 to the 1960 Census, and is likely to remain so in future censuses for the simple reason that neighboring SMSAs include any territory to which the New York SMSA might otherwise expand. (Other SMSAs adjoining or near the New York SMSA include Newark, Paterson-Clifton-Passaic, Jersey City, and several more remote areas in New Jersey, as well as several in Connecticut.) The total population of the New York SMSA rose from about 9½ million in 1950 to about 10½ million in 1960, in spite of a small decline in New York City as a whole.

[1] Tri-State Transportation Commission, *Regional Development Alternates* (New York, 1967), pp. 5–6, 8.

[2] Allen D. Manvel, "Land Use in 106 Large Cities," in *Three Land Research Studies*, National Commission on Urban Problems, Research Report No. 12 (U.S. Government Printing Office, 1968), p. 45.

TABLE 23

TOTAL AREA AND POPULATION, 1960, FOR DIFFERENT DEFINITIONS OF NEW YORK

Source of information and definition of area	Population (thousands)	Total area	
		Square miles	1,000 acres
Bureau of the Census:			
Manhattan	1,698	22.0	14.1
City of New York (5 boroughs)	7,782	315.1	201.7
New York SMSA (boroughs plus Nassau, Rockland, Suffolk, and Westchester Counties)	10,695	2,149.0	1,375.4
New York urbanized area (includes northeastern New Jersey)	14,115	1,891.5	1,210.6
New York-Northeastern New Jersey Standard Consolidated Area	14,759	3,748.0	2,398.7
New York Regional Plan Association:[1]			
1922 definition of region	15,822	5,528.0	3,537.9
1947 region (22 counties)	16,139	6,907.0	4,420.5
1965 region (31 counties)	17,624	12,748.0	8,158.7
Tri-State Transportation Commission:[2]			
Intensively developed area	16,300	3,663.2	2,344.4
Entire region	18,100	7,886.5	5,047.4

[1] Basic data from Regional Plan Association, *The Region's Growth* (New York, 1967), pp. 81–82.
[2] Tri-State Transportation Commission, *Measure of a Region* (New York, 1967), pp. 5, 9. Slightly different population data are used in other Commission reports. Those used in this table are for 1963, and hence are not fully comparable with the 1960 data from the other two sources.

Recognizing that SMSAs included a good deal of essentially nonurban territory because they were drawn on county lines for the most part, the Bureau of the Census in 1950 compiled data for "urbanized areas." In 1950, the New York urbanized area, which included northeastern New Jersey, had about 800,000 acres of land and 12¼ million people. The much more inclusive 1960 definition of "urbanized area" increased the New York urbanized area about 50 percent to 1⅕ million acres, but the total population was only 15 percent greater. The concept of "urbanized area" was still not wholly satisfactory for the New York region and hence, beginning with the 1960 Census, data have been reported for the New York Standard Consolidated Area, which is about twice as big as the urbanized area but has only 5 percent more population.

In the meantime, other organizations were using still other definitions. The Regional Plan Association, one of the oldest private research and planning organizations in the country, has been a pioneer in the development of concepts relating to cities and in the making of studies and plans for the New York area. In making the first regional plan in 1922, the association tried to develop a meaningful concept or definition of New York as an economic city (Figure 24). This city reached somewhat into Connecticut and well into New Jersey. This attempt to define an economic city antedated the concept of Standard Metropolitan Statistical Area by about 20 years. The 1922 New York region, as defined by the Regional Plan Association, included more acreage than the total area of the 1960 Standard

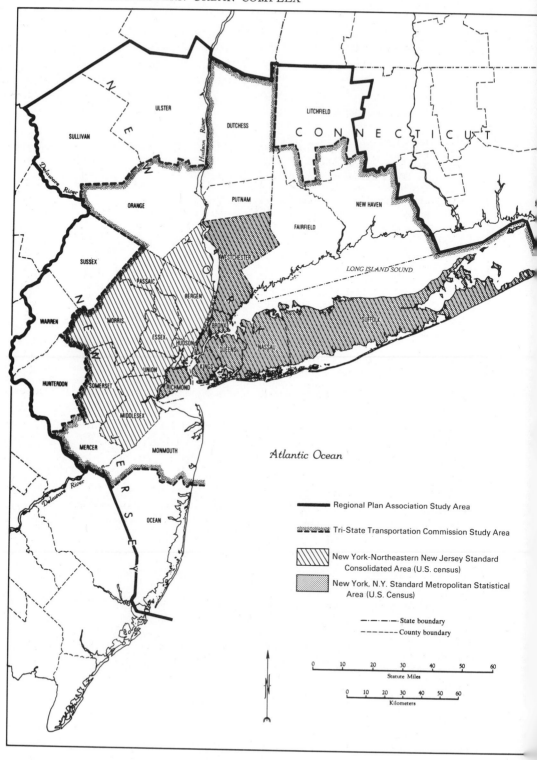

FIGURE 23. New York Region definitions by various agencies.

Consolidated Area, although it was not more inclusive in every locality. By 1947, the Regional Plan Association decided that its definition of the region was too restrictive and adopted a new one that was 25 percent larger. In 1965 it again expanded the boundaries of its region, this time by 85 percent. Each of these extensions included relatively more acres than people.

The Tri-State Transportation Commission was established by legislative action of Connecticut, New York, and New Jersey in 1965 as a study and planning group. Its region includes somewhat more acreage than the Regional Plan Association region of 1947 but much less than the latter's 1965 region. Since the Tri-State Commission's region is based upon legislation, it is "official" in a sense that the Regional Plan Association regions are not, but the Commission has no legislative, administrative, or fiscal powers.

This history of efforts to define an economic city of New York, and the varying definitions now existent, lead to a few specific conclusions:

1. By any reasonable standard, the economic city of New York today far exceeds the legal city of that name.

2. The economic city is not easily or unequivocally defined. In this connection, it is noteworthy that all the more inclusive definitions include Trenton, New Jersey which the Penn-Jersey studies (to be considered later) include in the Philadelphia region. As economic cities grow, they may compete for tributary or satellite cities lying between them.

3. The differences between the definitions are not particularly great in terms of the numbers of people involved; nor, if data were presented, would they be found greatly different in terms of employment, trade, and the like.

4. But the differences between definitions *are* large in terms of land. How much of the essentially rural countryside should be included in the definition of the economic city? In this connection, the matter of grain of inquiry comes up once again. Most definitions are based upon county or other relatively inclusive lines. Were information readily available on land actually used for various urban purposes, on a fine grain, different data would result. Even the census "urbanized area," which deviates considerably from county or other governmental lines, nevertheless includes a considerable area of vacant or idle land, especially in 1960, in part because it too uses legal as well as land use boundaries.

There is no fully satisfactory criterion for delimiting the economic city, for New York or any other large city. Data on numbers of workers commuting to the city center are often used, and this is an important measure. But where does one cut this off? The point where not more than 2 percent of the labor force commutes to the city center is an arbitrary answer often given. But other economic and social forces may be more important than employment in defining the economic city. Whatever the measure used, the results are almost sure to be more inclusive than the land directly used for urban purposes.

Physical Growth of the City

New York has had an interesting history, which in many respects parallels the history of the United States as a whole. In 1615, the New Netherlands Company built a storehouse, a fort, and some dwellings on the south end of Manhattan

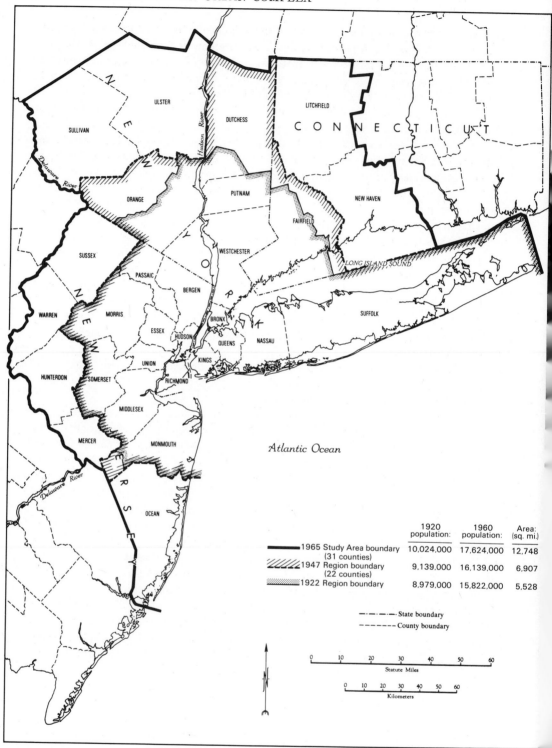

FIGURE 24.   Regional Plan definitions of the New York Region, 1922, 1947, and 1965.

Island. The settlement grew slowly as a colony of the Netherlands. In 1664, the British peacefuly took possession and renamed the settlement as New York. In 1665, they extended the city limits to include the entire island of Manhattan. By 1760, the city had about 14,000 residents and was a metropolis of the New World. A great deal of military and political action centered in and around the city during the Revolutionary War; by 1784, total population had risen to about 24,000 and thereafter grew rapidly.

In 1811, the first comprehensive street plan for the city was laid out as far north as 155th Street, on essentially the lines which have developed to the present. Up to this time, a great deal of land on Manhattan was owned by the municipality but was sold to private interests. The city's population had grown to about 120,000, most of which was concentrated south of Houston Street. By 1871, the city reached a total population of one million. In 1874, its corporate limits were extended beyond Manhattan for the first time, to include about 13,000 acres across the Harlem River in the Bronx. In 1883, the Brooklyn Bridge was opened to traffic, thus greatly stimulating population growth in Brooklyn. In 1895 there was a further extension of city boundaries. The city got a new charter from the state in 1897, and in the following year the five boroughs were united to form Greater New York—or, as we more commonly say today, New York, meaning the legal city.

Population Changes

The Regional Plan Association has analyzed population growth by major sectors of its larger study area, divided into Core, Inner Ring, Intermediate Ring, and Outer Ring (Figure 25). These are now the functional parts of the larger area, but in much earlier times the more remote parts of this larger region were perhaps no more closely tied to its center than they were to other urban areas. By presenting data for this larger area over a long period of time, the Association does permit a ready analysis of the population changes for a consistently defined area.

The Core includes all of New York City except Richmond County and also includes Hudson County, New Jersey. It has the largest population of any of the zones or areas established by the Association, 46 percent of the total in 1965, but it was once far more dominant in the larger New York region (Figure 26). At the time of World War I, nearly two-thirds of the population of the larger region lived in the Core; since 1930, and more markedly since 1950, its population has tended to level off at 8 to 9 million. Within the Core there have been substantial relative shifts in population over the decades. In 1850, Manhattan was 70 percent of the Core; as late as 1880, it was half; but today it is only 18 percent. The population of Manhattan peaked in 1910, at 2⅓ million, and today is down a third from that peak. But the intensity of use of its residential land today must be far higher than in 1910, for the loss of residential land to other uses in the past 50 years has been greater than the loss in population.

The Inner Ring, as the Association uses the term, includes Richmond and Nassau counties and the southern part of Westchester County in New York; and Bergen, Essex, and Union counties in New Jersey. Total population in this area

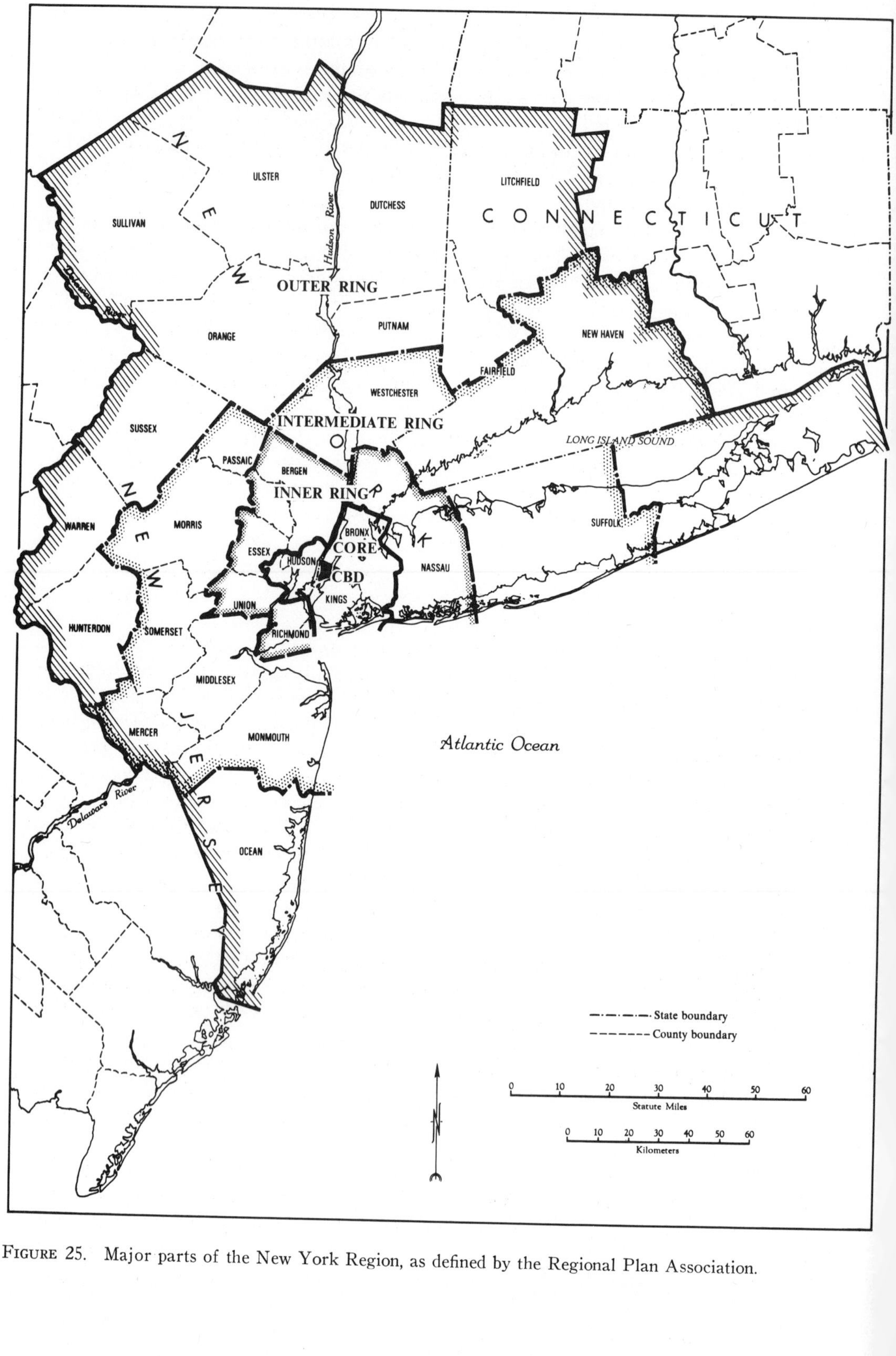

FIGURE 25. Major parts of the New York Region, as defined by the Regional Plan Association.

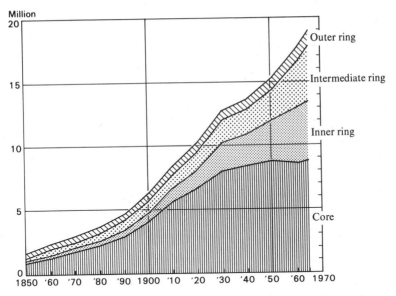

See Figure 25 for definition of areas.

FIGURE 26.   Population by major parts of the New York study area (as defined by Regional Plan Association in 1965), 1850–1965.

has increased steadily over the 100-year span, but the demographic importance of the region increased greatly after World War I, as did the degree of its interconnection with the Core. Today, the Inner Ring has about 25 percent of the total population of the region, over half that of the Core.

The Intermediate Ring includes part of Suffolk County, all of Rockland County, and the northern part of Westchester County in New York; Fairfield and New Haven counties in Connecticut; and Morris, Somerset, Middlesex, Mercer, and Monmouth counties in New Jersey. This area was comparatively important in 1850, with 2½ times as many people then as were in the Inner Ring, owing largely to independent cities such as New Haven and Trenton, which then were but loosely related to New York City. The Intermediate Ring has also grown steadily in population since 1850, but its real demographic takeoff has come only since World War II. During these later years the area has been increasingly related to New York City. The total population of the Intermediate Ring fell behind that of the faster-growing Inner Ring in 1930, and in spite of rapid growth in recent years, the Intermediate Ring has not yet caught up. It seems obvious, however, that this part of the region has a great future growth potential.

The Outer Ring includes the remaining part of Suffolk County and all of Putnam, Dutchess, Ulster, Sullivan, and Orange counties in New York; Litchfield County in Connecticut; and Sussex, Warren, Hunterdon, and Ocean counties in New Jersey—the outermost portions of the region, in all directions. This part of the region is still relatively remote, still largely rural in its land use, and its inclusion in the New York region is justifiable only in terms of its future growth possibilities. In 1850, the total population of the Outer Ring exceeded that of the

Intermediate Ring and of the Inner Ring, but the area was very remote from New York and only loosely connected with it economically. The Outer Ring has grown steadily in population (except for the 1910–1920 decade, when it lost slightly), but growth has been very slow. Today it has less than a third the population of either the Intermediate or Inner Rings. It may be argued that this part of the region is on the verge of takeoff and that the next generation will see rapid population growth here; but this remains to be proven.

The larger New York region, as defined by the Association, grew somewhat faster in total population than did the nation as a whole from 1850 to 1930, when its percentage of the national population more or less steadily increased from 6.7 to 10.3. Since 1930, its share of the national total has not increased, and in fact by 1960 it had slipped below 10 percent. In recent decades, by far the greater part of the population growth of the region was due to an excess of births over deaths; inmigration accounted for less than 25 percent of the population increase of the 1950's. Like most other parts of the Northeastern Urban Complex, New York has a demographic momentum which will increase its population in the decades ahead without net migration from other regions.

People and Jobs

This book has not considered the relationship between population and employment in detail and has referred only briefly to the important question of whether population movement follows job opportunity, or industry and other employment follows labor force. But, for the New York larger region, the matter of people and jobs is so important that a brief discussion of the essential facts seems necessary.

First of all, the geographic distribution of residences and of jobs is very different within the region. (Table 24) In the central business district of Manhattan in 1956, there were four times as many jobs as there were residents. For all of Manhattan, in both periods, there were about 1½ times as many jobs as residents. The ratios for the several parts of the region ranged from 41 percent to 43 percent, so that there were about four times as many workers in all of Manhattan as its population would suggest. The other workers commute in each day; in fact, gross movement of workers is probably higher than this, since there are some unemployed in Manhattan and there is some reverse commuting to outer areas. The Core as a whole, which includes Manhattan, had some surplus of jobs in 1956. Although many workers lived in its densely developed residential areas, they did not fully offset the number of jobs, and thus there was net inmigration daily to the Core as a whole. The Inner, Intermediate and Outer Rings had very similar proportions of jobs to people, below the regional average. Although the area definitions are not identical for the two time periods, it would appear that there was little shift in the relationship between resident population and jobs in the decade between 1956 and 1965.

The makeup of employment has also been shifting. Manufacturing employment has been relatively stable in Manhattan since the latter 19th century and has

TABLE 24

POPULATION AND JOBS, BY PARTS OF THE NEW YORK REGION, 1956 AND 1965

Area[1]	1956[2]			1965[3]		
	People (1,000)	Jobs (1,000)	Ratio	People (1,000)	Jobs (1,000)	Ratio
Manhattan, CBD	620	2,475	4.00			
Manhattan, all	1,811	2,718	1.50	1,565	2,406	1.54
Core	8,236	4,302	0.52	8,757	4,453	0.51
Inner Ring	4,573	1,572	0.34	4,655	1,568	0.34
Intermediate Ring	2,566	826	0.32	4,280	1,339	0.31
Outer Ring				1,290	407	0.32
Total	15,375	6,700	0.43	18,981	7,796	0.41

[1] These areas are not strictly comparable for the two sources and time periods; their definitions are as follows:

	1956	1965
Core	Manhattan, Hudson, Brooklyn, Queens, Bronx	Manhattan, Hudson, Brooklyn, Queens, Bronx, City of Newark
Inner Ring	Richmond, Essex, Bergen, Passaic, Westchester, Union, Nassau	Richmond, Essex West, Bergen, Passaic South, Westchester South, Union, Nassau
Intermediate Ring	Middlesex, Rockland, Morris, Monmouth, Somerset, Fairfield, Suffolk, Orange, Putnam, Dutchess	Fairfield South, Middlesex, Suffolk West, Mercer, New Haven, Rockland, Monmouth, Morris, Westchester North, Somerset, Passaic North
Outer Ring		Fairfield North, Suffolk East, Dutchess, Ocean, Warren, Putnam, Hunterdon, Litchfield, Orange, Ulster, Sussex, Sullivan

[2] Edgar M. Hoover and Raymond Vernon, *Anatomy of a Metropolis* (Harvard University Press, 1959), p. 8.

[3] Regional Plan Association, *The Region's Growth*, p. 112.

increased only slowly in the Core in that period. The kinds of manufacturing have also changed, with those types requiring large areas of land shifting out of the older cities into more peripheral locations where adequate space was more easily obtainable. All of the Ring areas show continued growth in manufacturing employment. The various kinds of office employment have risen in the central cities, offsetting the decline in manufacturing. From 1940 to 1964, blue-collar employment in the entire New York region rose only 18 percent.[3] During the same period, white-collar employment rose 73 percent, and employment in the service activities by 14 percent. Other shifts in employment were also under way in these years.

[3] Regional Plan Association, *The Region's Growth*. "Blue-collar includes craftsmen, foremen, and kindred workers; operatives and kindred workers; and nonfarm laborers. White-collar comprises professional, technical, and kindred workers; managers, officials, and proprietors; clerical and kindred workers; and sales workers. Service workers include attendants in hospitals and other institutions; personal and protective service workers; and household workers." (p. 93)

Natural Features

The natural features of the New York region have favored urban deveolpment. First in time and in importance have been the water areas—the ocean, Long Island Sound, East River, Hudson River, and others, and the fine harbors which these bodies of water provide. The water areas made easy transportation from Europe, among the colonies, and to a degree with the interior of the country, especially in the colonial and early national years when transportation was mainly by water. No small part of New York's economic development is due to these water bodies.

The physiography of the region has also been favorable for urban growth. Some swamps and wet areas have not been suitable for development. Much farther away, on some steep and rocky hills and mountains, development is more difficult and more costly, although superior residential sites can often be developed. Between these lie extensive areas of plains or flatlands and of rolling terrain where development is relatively easy. New York, especially Manhattan, has been blessed by deep rock formations which are not inordinately expensive to excavate and are strong enough to bear the largest buildings and to facilitate the construction of subways and other underground transportation. If the gravity vacuum tube becomes the truly high-speed method of transportation of the future, it will be possible to construct the necessary tunnels here much more easily than in some other metropolitan areas. Although not all forms of urban development have been equally easy on all land in the New York region, the acreage of readily developable land, within reasonable distance has been ample, at least until now.

Land Use

For the entire New York region as defined by the Tri-State Transportation Commission (which, it will be recalled, is more inclusive than any other definition except that of the Regional Plan Association in 1965), only slightly more than 1½ million acres was in urban use in the early 1960s. (Table 25) This is equivalent to a square with about 50 miles on a side; several national forests in the United States contain more land than this. According to the Commission data, almost half of this area was in residential use and more than a sixth in streets, many of which served residential areas exclusively. The total area in commercial, industrial, and related uses was less than 10 percent of the total, or only about 150,000 acres. Limiting these data to the intensively used part of the region reduces the total area in urban use by only 23 percent and does not greatly change the percentage use of the various categories. Other definitions of the region, whether more or less inclusive, would presumably not change the acreage in use by large amounts. Even for the intensively developed part of the region, "vacant" land is three-fourths as large as the developed area, and for the whole region is about double the developed area.

The use distribution in the sample of large cities studied for the National Commission on Urban Problems is considerably different, with much less land in residential use. These data are not strictly comparable, because "undeveloped" land is included in the data for large cities, which may or may not be comparable to the "vacant" land for the region. However, the large cities generally contain more employment centers and less residential uses, while the larger suburban areas which are included in the regional totals are primarily residential in land use.

It is not easy to show the geographic intermingling of different land uses for an urban region such as New York in a fully satisfactory way. The map used as the end papers in this book shows the "developed land" of the region and its environs, as mapped very carefully by the Regional Plan Association from aerial photographs and other detailed sources. While this is highly valuable in showing the general geographic distribution of land in more or less active use and thus the interspersion of vacant lands, no such map can convey an idea of the great variations in intensity of land use. But it is obvious to any observer that an acre of land in downtown Manhattan has a very different meaning from an acre in some distant suburb.

Substantial areas are land publicly owned or committed to various open space uses. There are some large city parks, of which Central Park in New York is the largest and best known. Other reserved areas are mostly along the seashore or in the mountains. While travel is necessary for residents of this region to reach such parks and other open land, all of these areas lie close enough to permit day use.

As the New York region has grown in population, it has naturally spread out (Figure 27). About a hundred years ago the present New York City complex was largely Manhattan and nearby Brooklyn and Jersey areas. Elsewhere in the region there were relatively small and isolated cities. Substantial increases in area of land more or less fully used for urban purposes had taken place by 1900, and much greater increases by 1935. The really big increases in land use for urban purposes took place between 1935 and 1962, when transportation by private automobile really began to dominate expansion. Figure 27 is broadly accurate and expressive. However, on this scale and with this method of analysis, it is not possible to show a great deal of the vacant, idle, or undeveloped land which the previous statistics

TABLE 25

LAND USE IN THE NEW YORK REGION AND IN SELECTED LARGE CITIES

| | New York region[1] | | | | Sample cities—percent of city area[2] | | | | |
| | Intensive developed area | | Entire region | | | | | | |
Land use	1,000 acres	Percent	1,000 acres	Percent	Jersey City	Newark	New York	Paterson	Yonkers
Residential	681	53.8	819	49.9	21.7	20.7	–	34.7	31.8
Streets	221	17.6	299	18.4	15.6	15.8	30.1	29.3	18.1
Public[3]	230	18.2	371	22.3	7.4	38.9	26.5	9.6	23.8
Commercial	50	4.0⎱	153	9.4	3.7	10.1	–	10.0	4.4
Other[4]	81	6.4⎰			32.9	8.5	–	–	6.8
Undeveloped	–	–	–	–	18.7	9.4	12.5	4.0	15.1
Total, urban use	1,264	100.0	1,642	100.0	100.0	100.0	100.0	100.0	100.0
Vacant	940	–	3,145	–	–	–	–	–	–
Swamps, watershed	143	–	260	–	–	–	–	–	–
Total land	2,347	–	5,047	–	–	–	–	–	–

[1] Tri-State Transportation Commission, *Measure of a Region.* Data are for an unspecified date, apparently 1962.

[2] Allen D. Manvel, "Land Use in 106 Large Cities" in *Three Land Research Studies*, National Commission on Urban Problems, Research Report No. 12 (U.S. Government Printing Office, 1968). Data are for different years circa 1965. Dashes indicate that data do not appear in the report.

[3] "Public open space and public buildings" for Tri-State data; "public, semipublic" for sample cities.

[4] "Transportation, manufacturing" for Tri-State data; "industrial, railroads" for sample cities.

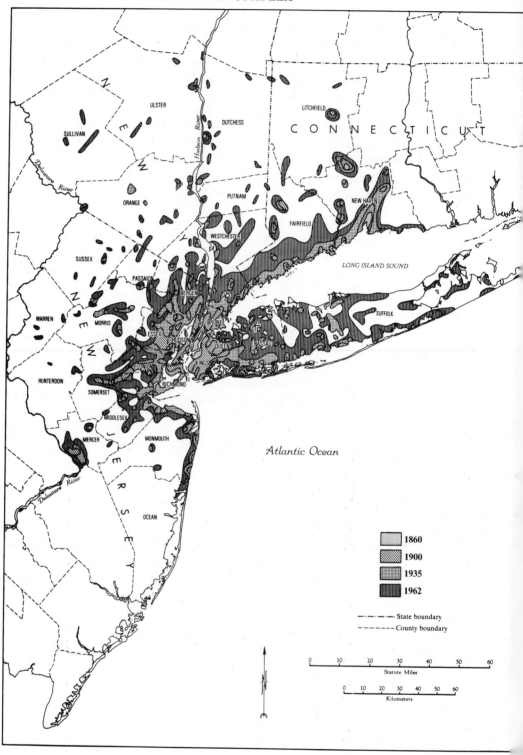

FIGURE 27.   Growth of the New York Region, 1860–1962.

and the end paper map show. Figure 27 does show that, at a radius of perhaps 50 miles from downtown New York, dominantly undeveloped lands exceed the largely developed lands.

Various measures can be used to describe the intensity of land use within the New York region. One is the extent to which the wetlands, as they existed in 1900, have been filled for manmade land in 1966. Extensive areas along many waterfronts have been filled, and the process is still going on. The role of marshes and swamps as sources of food for marine life is coming to be appreciated, and increasing efforts are being made to prevent more landfill. However, it is true that some highly valuable lands have been created in this way, often well located with respect to the various urban centers. In a large city there are considerable possibilities of using landfill for disposal of solid wastes or of using wastes to create landfill.

Another measure of intensity in land use is the area of floor space. The Tri-State Transportation Commission, which has made extensive use of this measure, has collected a lot of information about floor area of buildings. Floor area can be increased either by covering more of the land surface with buildings and/or by using more than one level, either downward or upward. The Commission feels that travel and other activities are more closely related to floor space than to land area used for various purposes. While floor space may be an excellent measure, it also seems probable that there are differences in the intensity of floor space within buildings, just as there are differences in intensity of land use.

For the entire New York region, as defined by the Tri-State Commission, there were about 9 billion square feet (the equivalent of 206,000 acres) of floor space of all kinds, in the period around 1962 (Table 26). Nearly two-thirds of this was for residential use. The area of floor space is equal to 18 percent of the whole for the intensively used area; since many dwellings are two stories in height and others are higher, especially in the apartment house areas, this would suggest that the land surface actually covered by buildings in residential areas was much less, quite probably below 10 percent.

TABLE 26

MEASURES OF INTENSITY OF LAND USE IN THE NEW YORK REGION, CIRCA 1962

	Intensively developed area				Entire region			
Land use	Land area (1,000 acres)	Buildings (million sq. ft.)	Floor space as percent of land surface	Floor space per unit of use[1]	Land area (1,000 acres)	Buildings (million sq. ft.)	Floor space as percent of land surface	Floor space per unit of use[1]
Residential	681	5,348	18	328	819	5,735	16	317
Public buildings	56	872	36	54	73	959	30	53
Commercial	50	966	44	42[2]				
Transportation	46	346	17	13[2]	153	2,346	35	–
Manufacturing	35	889	58	44[2]				
Total[3]	1,264	8,419	15	–	1,642	9,040	13	–

Sources: Reports of Tri-State Transportation Commission, particularly *Measure of a Region* and *Regional Development Alternates,* both 1967.

[1] Units of use defined as follows: for residential and public buildings, total population, use per person; for commercial, retail sales, square feet per $1,000 sales; for transportation, trips per person, square feet per trip; for manufacturing, value added, square feet per $1,000 value added.

[2] Estimated from data for entire region, on basis of ratio of total population in intensively developed area to total population in entire region.

[3] Includes streets and public open space, but excludes vacant land, and swamps-watershed.

A ranch-style house, basically of one story, may have 1,000 to 1,500 square feet of floor area. Since the half-acre lot on which ranch-style houses are customarily built has about 22,000 square feet, this type of house might well have much less than a 10 percent ratio of floor area to land area. But most other single-family dwellings would have a higher ratio, and apartment house ratios would be higher still. Manufacturing and commercial establishments have floor areas approaching or exceeding half of the land area, but this seems low because many such structures are undoubtedly more than one story in height. However, land area probably includes parking areas for many plants and sometimes includes land reserves held by the same company for later expansion. On the average, there was over 300 square feet of floor space per person in residential buildings, over 50 feet per resident in public buildings, and varying other amounts in relation to use for other activities. The calculations in Table 26 will become more meaningful if or when comparable data are available for other cities and other dates.

The amount of vacant land is another measure of land use intensity (Figure 28). In general, vacant land is inversely related to the area of land in use. But the striking thing about this figure, and about any other data on vacant land within urban areas, is how much vacant land there is *within* areas or neighborhoods that are generally developed. As noted at several points in this book, urban development does not proceed smoothly and fully as it goes outward from the older city center but instead jumps over many tracts of land, some of which are "infilled" by later development, some of which stay idle for many years. There are many reasons why development bypasses a tract of land; but it seems probable that, if the pressure for suitable land were stronger, less land would be bypassed. The extent of bypassing is therefore one measure of land use intensity, even on the lands actually in use.

Transportation and Public Services

Still another measure of land use intensity is the number of trips ending, per square mile, in various areas. For each square mile of midtown Manhattan there were more than 800,000 trips per 24 hours. In downtown Brooklyn, the comparable figure is about 150,000 and for New Haven or Jersey City, about 60,000. One remarkable aspect of this situation is the relatively constant amount of travel by auto. The role of various forms of public transport increases nearer the high-density areas and reaches its peak for rail and subway only in the more intensively used parts of downtown New York.

About 90 percent of the region's population is served by a public water supply system; the exceptions are primarily the most outlying areas of scattered settlement. About 80 percent of the population is served by public sewers, though large suburban areas, including much of Long Island, are not so served. Many communities begun on a septic tank basis are now finding that central sewer systems are required.

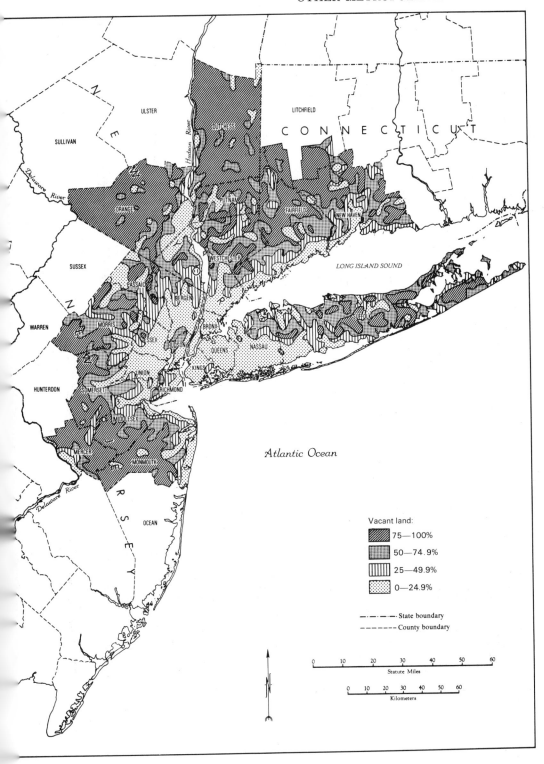

GURE 28.   Vacant land in the New York Region, circa 1962.

Decision Making

Finally, a few words may be said about decision making as it affects urban growth and development. Sayre and Kaufman have considered the problems of government in New York City, where a multiplicity of economic, social, ethnic, and political forces combine with a complex governmental structure to make these problems very difficult of solution.[4] Some other writers have gone so far as to suggest that New York City is really ungovernable. The New York City government is not directly concerned with the matter of urban expansion; but indirectly its actions may greatly affect the attractiveness of the city as a place to live or work, and may influence the rate of rebuilding the older deteriorating housing or the rate of expansion on the suburban fringes.

Wood assembled a great deal of information on the fragmentation of local government in the New York region, showing how different units of government were in competition with one another for the kinds of residents and of tax base which each wanted and how they utilized various measures to discourage the kinds of residents and industries that they did not want.[5] One effective means of raising more tax revenue was to establish a special unit of government with legal or political revenue-raising power which a general-purpose unit of government would not have. Much of the action taken by local governments is designed to offset the effect of other actions by other units of local government.

Under such circumstances, planning and action programs for the whole region are very difficult. The Regional Plan Association has provided a regional viewpoint for more than four decades that undoubtedly has been very influential. The creation of the Tri-State Transportation Commission in 1965 was official recognition of the need to face at least some problems on a regional rather than on a local scale.[6]

Future Development

A brief review of the Regional Plan Association's analyses and plans for the future of the New York metropolitan region is appropriate as a conclusion to this

[4] Wallace S. Sayre and Herbert Kaufman, *Governing New York* (Russell Sage Foundation, 1960).

[5] Robert C. Wood and Vladimir V. Almendinger, *1400 Governments* (Harvard University Press, 1961).

[6] There is perhaps no more outstanding planning organization, public or private, in the world than the Regional Plan Association, and certainly none with a longer record of outstanding performance. Over a period of more than 40 years, it has made a large number of important studies; its 100th report was issued in September 1962; a recent one in May 1969 is number 113. In recent years, it has had several outstanding planning directors—Henry Fagin, the late Stanley B. Tankel, and now Boris Pushkarev. The range of its interest, the imagination it has brought to its various studies, and its skill in presentation of results have all been notable. In 1967 the American Institute of Planners gave it one of their Special Fiftieth Anniversary Awards. A full listing of all its reports is inappropriate here, but those of particular relevance to this study include: *People, Jobs and Land 1955–1975* (1957); *The Law of Open Space* (1960); *The Dynamics of Park Demand* (1960); *Nature in the Metropolis* (1960); *The Race for Open Space* (1960); *Spread City* (1962); *The Lower Hudson* (1966); *The Region's Growth* (1967); *Waste Management* (1968); *Public Services in Older Cities* (1968); *Urban Design Manhattan* (1969); and *The Second Regional Plan* (1970) and some localized applications of it in *The Future of Orange County, The Future of Nassau County,* and *The Future of Bergen and Passaic Counties.*

section. In its 1962 report, *Spread City*, the association analyzed the municipal zoning ordinances of 509 municipalities in the region which had such ordinances; 42 cities had none. In attempts to zone out tax users (lower-income families with children) and to zone in tax providers (industry), many municipalities had increased the minimum size of lots substantially. For the vacant land in the region at the time of this study, the average lot size for single-family dwellings was two-thirds of an acre. The study projected an increase in regional population of 6 million, from 16 to 22 million, in the 1960 to 1985 period—and on the basis of no net inmigration after 1975. If this population increase actually takes place, on the basis of the municipal zoning as it existed in 1960, then the total built-up area of the region would double by 1985—a 37 percent increase in population, a doubling in land area.

The result would be a "spread city," a widely dispersed urban area, largely lacking in urban centers, too dispersed to use public transportation, too dispersed to have strong shopping and other centers, and with housing on large lots too expensive for couples with young children. "By spreading and scattering rather than concentrating jobs, goods, services and homes, we fail to build communities, and we have poorer access to and so less choice of jobs, friends, recreation, goods, services, types of housing and modes of travel." (p. 3) The report does not criticize the fragmentation of local government as Wood does, and as this writer does, yet clearly such fragmentation underlies the situation analyzed in the report. Each unit of local government, working toward its own ends in its own way, produces an overall pattern of land use and land control which it is highly doubtful if any one group charged with responsibility for the whole area would have chosen.

As an alternative to Spread City, the Association developed *The Second Regional Plan*, which has been supplemented by various reports for different parts of the region, all of which have been used as a basis for wide-ranging discussions with community leaders.

> To change the amorphous spread of urbanization into genuine metropolitan communities capable of supporting high-quality services in health, retailing, the arts, entertainment (including professional sports), libraries, and adult education (including job training) and to provide a real community framework for civic and political action, *The Second Regional Plan* proposes the creation of about two dozen partially self-contained metropolitan communities within the region. . . . (p. 10)

Thus, the plan involves a large degree of concentration of population, with integrated outlying suburbs where densities would be lower. The Plan is developed in the areas of housing, jobs, services, and transportation.

To supplement this overall Plan, the Association in 1969 gave major attention to downtown Manhattan, reported in *Urban Design Manhattan*. A small increase in residential population is projected for the central business district to 2000, and a modest increase in jobs, especially office jobs, is also projected. Large-scale office construction will be required, both to house the new workers and to replace many substandard office buildings. While the increase in offices would be large in relation to present office space, the land area requirements are not especially difficult to meet. The important point is that downtown New York will undergo substantial building and rebuilding over the next generation, and it can be designed to produce an aesthetically interesting and highly livable city—an exciting one, to people who like cities—if the decisions about building are directed to that end.

Staid Old Boston

As with New York, Boston is a word with different meanings. The legal city, or the old town of Boston, is small in area—about 31,000 acres—thus somewhat larger than Manhattan, but of course less intensively used. The Boston SMSA includes 20 times as much area, about 619,000 acres; while Boston city had about 700,000 people in 1960, Boston SMSA had about 2.6 million. If one includes the Lawrence, Lowell, and Brockton SMSAs, then the total area rises to 906,000 acres and the total population to 3.1 million. A land use survey in eastern Massachusetts included about 1.5 million acres. (Table 27) This survey provided no population data, but the area surveyed included 1.03 million dwelling units. As in the New York region, the more inclusive definitions of the Boston region involve a great deal more land but add comparatively few more people.

The Boston region, however defined, is a relatively slow-growing one. The four SMSAs increased in population only 8 percent in the decade of the 1940's as com-

TABLE 27

LAND USE IN THE BOSTON REGION, CIRCA 1962, ACCORDING TO DIFFERENT DATA SOURCES

(1,000 acres)

Land use	Four SMSAs[1]	Five counties partly within these SMSAs[2]	Eastern Massachusetts Regional Planning Project area[3]
Residential	–	188	214
Commercial[4]	–	21	16
Industrial[5]	–	17	18
Public	–	114	114
Streets and roads[6]	–	–	86
Other developed[7]	–	–	29
Other[8]	–	1,225	1,052
Total	906	1,566	1,529

[1] From Appendix Table 3—Lawrence, Lowell, Boston, and Brockton.
[2] From Appendix Table 5—Essex, Middlesex, Suffolk, Norfolk and Plymouth.
[3] Vogt-Ivers and Associates, *Comprehensive Land Use Inventory Report*, made for state and federal agencies concerned with the Eastern Massachusetts Regional Planning Project; data from their 24-category system.
[4] Retail, wholesale, and services for eastern Massachusetts study.
[5] Manufacturing and mining-quarry for eastern Massachusetts study.
[6] Includes parking areas for eastern Massachusetts study.
[7] Includes transportation and construction for eastern Massachusetts study.
[8] For five counties, is simply difference between total area and enumerated uses (which are not defined precisely); for eastern Massachusetts study, "vacant land, forest; agricultural; swamp; and water."

pared with a U.S. average rate of 15 percent. In the 1950's, these SMSAs increased 12 percent in spite of considerable additions in land area while the U.S. average rate was 18 percent. In Appendix Table 4, it is clear that the counties making up this region suffered a loss of about 49,000 from net migration; births exceeded deaths, but some of the natural increase moved elsewhere.

Of the different sources of data on land use, the inventory made for the Eastern Massachusetts Regional Planning Project includes the largest area and the most detail. About 477,000 acres were in some sense "developed" in 1963. Of this developed area, 45 percent was residential, 24 percent in public areas (including recreational), and 18 percent in streets and roads, leaving only 13 percent of the developed area for all other uses. More than two-thirds of the surveyed area, however, was undeveloped. The other data for five counties include almost exactly the same total area, and employ somewhat different (and not precisely defined) categories. A general similarity is evident, although there are some large differences in acreages and the five-county data do not include streets and roads separately.

The land use survey of eastern Massachusetts includes no population data, and hence it is not possible to make any comparisons of population density per acre or per square mile. This survey does, however, include information on numbers of single-family, two-family, and multiple-family dwelling units. Boston and the closer-in towns have a high proportion of multiple-family residential structures, the towns surrounding Cambridge on the west, north and east have the highest proportion of two-family structures, and the outlying suburban towns in all directions have high proportions of single-family structures. As a consequence, the number of dwelling units per net residential acre ranges from above 8 in Boston and surrounding towns, especially to the north, to less than 3 in nearly all the suburban towns, and to less than 1.3 for some of the latter.

Aerial surveys made in 1952 enabled a partial reconstruction of the land use situation then and changes between 1952 and 1963. The area used for residential purposes increased about 49,000 acres, an increase of about 30 percent in the area used for this purpose in 1952, but population for the four SMSAs increased only 12 percent from 1950 to 1960. While these data are not strictly comparable in time or area covered, they do suggest that the increase in area was much greater than the increase in population—a relationship which has been found in all the other SMSAs studied. In general, the pattern of residential development during the 1952–63 period followed closely the 1952 pattern—that is, the new units were generally apartments in the towns where apartments were already dominant and generally single-family homes in the towns where such residences predominated. The areal location of the residential development shows an interesting pattern. (Figure 29) There was comparatively little development in Boston and neighboring towns and cities, simply because almost all the land was already developed. This being the case, there was less development in proportion to land area in the outlying towns, simply because they were remote from the center. In percentage of total land area, the area added for residential purposes increased most in a ring of towns lying from 10 to 20 miles from downtown Boston. For several of these towns, more than 5 percent of their total area went into residential use in this 11-year period.

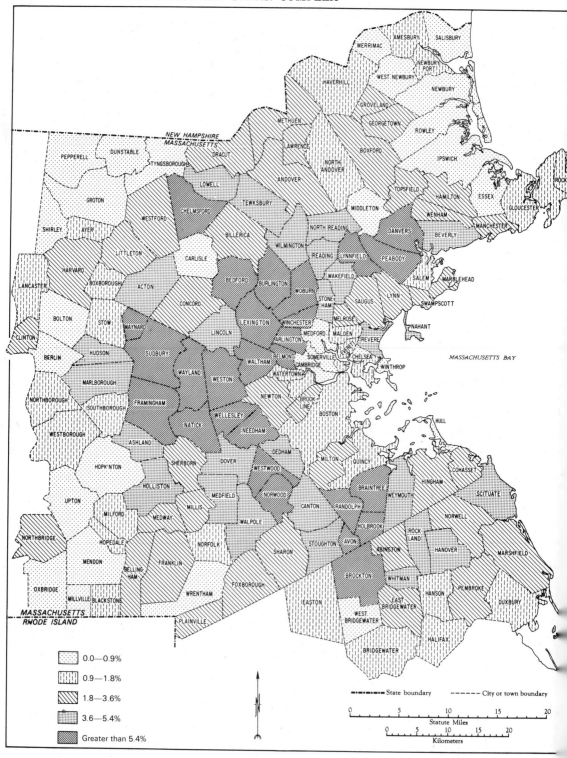

FIGURE 29. Net residential acres developed between 1952 and 1963 as percentage of total acres, Eastern Massachusetts.

During the 1952–63 period, the area used for commercial purposes apparently increased by slightly over 3,000 acres, or about 24 percent of the area used for this purpose in the earlier year; for manufacturing, the comparable figures are about 5,500 acres, or 30 percent; and for streets and highways, about 13,000 acres, or 16 percent. In each case, these acreage changes are greater than the total population change in the four SMSAs, suggesting that all activities are coming to use more land. It may also be significant that the area converted to streets and roads was relatively less than the additions to any of the other uses. Either there was unused capacity in the streets and roads at the earlier period, or there are now economies of scale in the use of streets and highways, or both.

In 1963, there were 873,000 acres classified as "vacant," including forests and agricultural land, in the eastern Massachusetts survey. Of these, 217,000 acres were classified as "Prime I Vacant Land" defined as "most suitable for future (urban) development" with good surface drainage and slope of less than 12 percent, bedrock below footing levels for slab construction. There were 544,000 acres classified as "Prime II Vacant Land," that is, "high in development potential" but "somewhat less favorable" than Prime I—possibly with some flooding hazard and shallow bedrock but with slopes of less than 12 percent. Only 112,000 acres were classed as "marginal vacant land," less suitable in some way for urban development. If one contrasts these acreages with the approximately 71,000 acres developed in the 1952–63 period, it appears that there is enough vacant land suitable for urban uses to accommodate urban growth for 100 years at a rate similar to that of the period studied. The possibility that land now classed as unsuitable will become "buildable" with the passage of time, as it did in the Wilmington area, should not be overlooked.

As might be expected, the amount of vacant but developable land was relatively small (less than 15 percent of total land area) near Boston, but in a few towns further out such land was more than 60 percent of total land area (Figure 30). Still further out, it exceeded 75 percent and even 90 percent of total land area. One must conclude that there is no shortage of buildable land in the Boston region for the foreseeable future.

In its planning projections for 1990, the Metropolitan Area Planning Council estimates a population increase that will require 641,000 new owner-occupied residential units, which will require 334,000 acres of land. Other land uses are projected to require 110,000 acres, or 444,000 acres in total, which is slightly more than 50 percent of the vacant and developable land within the region.[7] In view of recent history, these estimates seem high, but even they can be satisfied with the land available.

Municipal water supply is available for nearly all this area and public sewerage for the larger communities, which include more than 85 percent of the total population.[8] However, in 1965 only about a third of all the sewage received even primary

[7] Metropolitan Area Planning Council, *Guides for Progress—Development Opportunities for Metropolitan Boston* (Boston, 1968), pp. II–4 and II–8.
[8] Metropolitan Area Planning Council, *Inventory of Water and Sewer Facilities* (Boston, 1967).

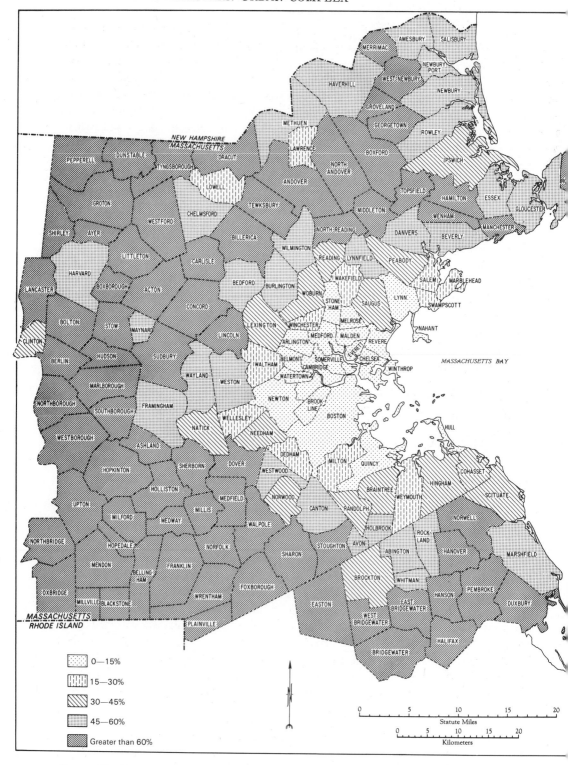

FIGURE 30.   1963 vacant acres as percentage of total acres, Eastern Massachusetts.

treatment, and the rest was discharged raw. Projects now under way should improve this situation.

PHILADELPHIA

Philadelphia is, and always has been, an important city. Once the largest of the colonial cities, it had been exceeded in total population by New York by the time of independence, was passed by Chicago in the Census of 1890 and by Los Angeles in the Census of 1960. It is still in fourth place among American cities. As with any other major urban area, there is the legal city of Philadelphia, neighboring or not too distant other legal cities, urbanized area, and SMSA. Although Philadelphia as a legal city is located wholly within Pennsylvania, the Philadelphia SMSA, like many another in the United States, includes parts of two states—in this case, a rather extensive area in New Jersey as well as substantial areas in Pennsylvania. The interstate character of the SMSA has shaped the form of its public planning in recent years.

Planning Activities

A substantial body of information has been assembled and regional plans have been prepared for the Philadelphia SMSA by two regional planning organizations. The Penn-Jersey Transportation Study was organized in 1959 to study and plan for transportation. Its governing body included representatives of Pennsylvania and New Jersey, the federal Bureau of Public Roads, the city of Philadelphia, the Pennsylvania counties of Bucks, Chester, Delaware, and Montgomery, and the New Jersey counties of Camden, Burlington, Gloucester, and Mercer. Its primary concern was with transportation. A large and well-qualified technical staff engaged in some of the most sophisticated and ambitious metropolitan regional planning studies that had been undertaken in the United States. A great deal of information was assembled on existing transportation facilities, travel patterns and behavior, land use and development, the economy of the region, its population, and its government facilities and services. From these studies, the project published three major reports.[9]

In July 1965, the Penn-Jersey Transportation Study was succeeded by a new metropolitan agency, the Delaware Valley Regional Planning Commission, which included also the cities of Chester, Camden, and Trenton. The scope of planning was enlarged to include (in addition to transportation) land use, open space and recreation, water supply, sewage and solid waste disposal, housing, utilities, and airports. The new agency inherited Penn-Jersey's staff and facilities, its huge data bank, and its planning experience. The Delaware Valley plans are a logical

[9] *PJ Reports: Volume 1, The State of the Region* (1964); *Volume 2, 1975 Projections, Foreground of the Future* (1964); and *Volume 3, 1975 Transportation Plans* (1965), all published by Penn-Jersey Transportation Study, Philadelphia. Numerous technical papers were circulated during the course of the study.

TABLE 28

TOTAL AREA AND TOTAL POPULATION OF PHILADELPHIA-TRENTON SMSAS, PENN-JERSEY
CORDON AREA, AND PHILADELPHIA-TRENTON URBANIZED AREAS, 1960

Item	Philadelphia-Trenton SMSAs[1]	Penn-Jersey Cordon area[2]	Philadelphia-Trenton urbanized area[3]
1. Units included	Bucks, Chester, Delaware, Montgomery, and Philadelphia counties, Pa.; Burlington, Camden, Gloucester, and Mercer counties, N.J.	Central portion of the nine counties, including the most heavily urbanized parts of the total region, plus those which can be expected to become urbanized in the near future.	
2. Gross land area (*1,000 acres*)	2,490	752	443
3. Total population (*1,000*)	4,609	4,351	3,877

[1] This is also the total planning region of the Penn-Jersey and Delaware Valley Planning Commission studies and plans.

[2] Penn-Jersey Transportation Study, *The State of the Region* (Philadelphia, 1965).

[3] See Chapter 2 above.

continuation of the work begun by its predecessor. The DVRPC has issued a number of major reports.[10]

All of these plans are advisory only, for the regional planning organization has no legal power to carry them out. However, the advice is directed largely to the members of each commission; for example, the Commission advises what the future transportation plan should be, but the Pennsylvania Department of Highways and the New Jersey Department of Transportation are members of the Commission. Moreover, by the range of data and the thoroughness of analysis and of projections, the plans will almost surely carry some weight—perhaps a great deal—with other units of government and with private organizations. However, the land use plan must be translated into zoning ordinances and other controls, the open space plan must be translated into programs of public acquisition of land, the water pollution control plan must be translated into specific sewer building programs, and so on. This type of metropolitan regional planning can be effective, as is the work of the New York Regional Plan Association. The Philadelphia plan has the added advantage of participation by all the major affected units of government. Such regional planning is a pragmatic attempt to overcome the severe handicaps of a fragmented political structure which does not conform to the economic reality of a metropolitan area.

[10] DVRPC Plan Report No. 1 (1967), *1985 Regional Projections for the Delaware Valley*; *Supplement* to the foregoing; Technical Supplement to Report No. 1, *The Construction of an Urban Growth Model*; DVRPC Plan Report No. 2 (1968), *1985 Regional and Use Plan*; Plan Report No. 3, Technical Supplement (1969), *1985 Interim Regional Open Space Plan*; DVRPC Plan Report No. 4 (1969), *The Regional Water Supply and Water Pollution Control Plans*; Plan Report No. 5 (1969), *1985 Regional Transportation Plan*; and Plan Report No. 5, Technical Supplement, *1985 Regional Transportation Plan*; all published by Delaware Valley Regional Planning Commission, 1317 Filbert Street, Philadelphia.

The Penn-Jersey and Delaware Valley Regional Planning Commission studies include not only the Philadelphia SMSA but the Trenton, New Jersey SMSA as well. These two SMSAs included five counties in Pennsylvania and four counties in New Jersey in 1960, with a gross land area of about 2.5 million acres and with 4.6 million people. (Table 28) It is interesting to note that the New York Regional Plan Association and the Tri-State Transportation Commission also include Trenton in their definition of the New York region, facts which illustrate the general point that definition of meaningful metropolitan regions is far from easy or unequivocal.

Most of the analysis in the PJ studies was in terms of a "Cordon Area," which was defined to include all the urbanized area in 1960 plus additional area that is expected to be urbanized "in the near future." The Cordon Area included about one-third of the land but 94 percent of the population of the two SMSAs; it was nearly double the size of the urbanized area, but included only 12 percent more people. As later discussion will show, all of these areal distinctions are somewhat arbitrary, in the sense that there is a continuum in degree of development from the city center to the outer rural area, with considerable idle land in all parts.

Growth of the Area

The development of cities and urban patterns of land use in this region exhibit some characteristics common to the growth of many cities in the United States, as well as some differences (Figure 31). In 1800, urban development was still closely confined to the Delaware River, which was the main artery of transportation. The total area of land in urban use was miniscule by modern standards, yet the present pattern of urban use may be seen in that beginning. As late as 1850, most settlement was still close to the river, although railroads were beginning to push settlement outward, especially to the west of Philadelphia. By 1900, the pattern had begun to change. Although much of the urban development still lay close to the river, substantial outliers had been built, especially to the west. By 1960, the total urbanized area had expanded manyfold—and in some new directions. Substantial development had now occurred east of the river, near Camden and Trenton particularly, and also along the river between these two cities. Development had spread up the river on the west side and moved much farther to the west in a more or less contiguous fashion, with large outliers still farther west. The small-scale maps demonstrate well the general scope and direction of urban growth in this area, but at each date there was almost surely some vacant or idle land within the apparently developed areas; and, of course, area does not alone indicate the intensity of land use.

The Penn-Jersey region has grown in population at almost exactly the same rate as the nation. In every census year since 1880, the population of the nine counties has not been less than 2.58 percent or more than 2.70 percent of the national total. Thus, Philadelphia, Camden, Trenton, the other cities and their suburban parts as a whole have grown more slowly than many cities in the United States, especially in the Far West and in the South, but faster than some other cities and most of

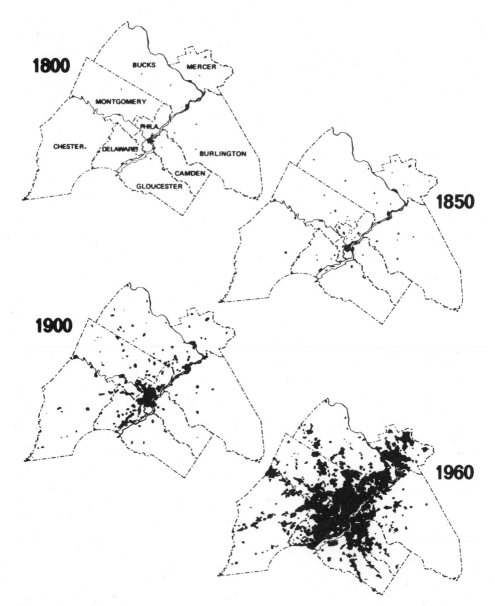

FIGURE 31.   Urbanized area, Philadelphia and Trenton SMSAs, 1800–1960.

the rural areas of the country. Since 1930, net migration to this area has accounted for slightly more than one-third of the growth, with a regional excess of births over deaths accounting for nearly two-thirds. Although Philadelphia has had some blacks since colonial days, like most other northern cities it has had an influx of blacks since World War II; the nonwhite percentage rose from 10 percent in 1940 to 15½ percent in 1960.

These nine counties have a relatively high employment in manufacturing, as compared with the national average, and the manufacturing is highly diversified, thus providing a good economic base. This region is one of somewhat above-average unemployment, expecially during periods of above-average unemployment everywhere.

Physical Characteristics

The physical characteristics of the nine-county area are in general highly favorable to urban land use. Past urban expansion has largely reflected the judgments of private builders as to the suitability of land for urban use. However, in this metropolitan region there has perhaps been as much awareness, on the part of government and university personnel, of the environmental limitations on urban land use, as in any other metropolitan region of the nation. The DVRPC has compiled and published a map showing areas not well suited to urban development. These areas are of two major kinds: flood plains, which have important ground water recharge values as well as flooding risks; and steep slopes, where building would often be difficult or expensive and would usually result in accelerated erosion or accelerated runoff or both. In addition, some heavily forested areas have scenic and recreational values that make their development for residential uses undesirable (Figure 32).

There is some swampy land near the Delaware River, and some areas are subject to flooding, but they are not extensive. In the southwestern part of the Cordon Area particularly, but to a lesser extent elsewhere, there are steep lands (with 15 percent or more slope), which are not highly adaptable to urban development. However, such steep lands often offer unusually good sites for high-grade residential settlement if density is kept very low. By far the greater part of the nine-county region is well suited to almost any type of urban development. For the 1945–1960 period, 93 percent of the development was on land with little or no slope, and 72 percent was on land whose soil was classified as good or excellent for urban use. Further urban growth in this nine-county area will not be impeded for several decades, if ever, by unfavorable soils or sites. In this connection, it should be remembered that "developable land" is a dynamic concept, as technology and economics change. (See Chapter 11 on the Wilmington area.) As time goes on, some land not now favored for development may become more readily developable than it is today.

Patterns of Land Use

In 1960 it was possible to show a few major patterns of urban land use for the Cordon Area. By far the most extensive, with much intermediate vacant or idle land, was the residential class, with less than 10 dwelling units per acre. (Figure 33) Closer in to each city center was a relatively large area of more intensively used residential land, with more than 10 dwelling units per acre. The total area used for industry, offices, major transportation facilities, and the like was much smaller

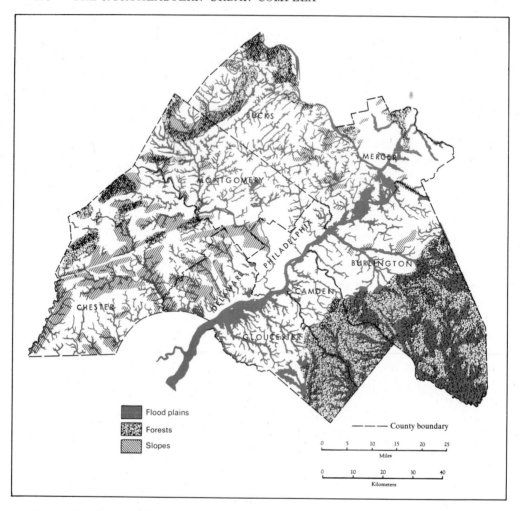

FIGURE 32.   Stream valleys, woodlands, and slope areas in the Philadelphia Metropolitan Region.

and tended to be concentrated in a few locations. At the scale of this map, streets and other localized transportation facilities, small nonconforming uses within each major category, and idle land cannot be shown. The map, while accurate in its general picture, thus may suggest a degree of orderliness in land use which does not, in fact, exist upon the ground.

These data may be reduced to statistical totals. (Table 29) As noted earlier, in 1960 the Cordon Area was nearly double the urbanized area, but more than half of the former was entirely undeveloped (from an urban point of view). In the developed half of the Cordon Area, residential land use took slightly less than half of the total. Streets and highways are shown separately; if we assume that *all* of these were so listed separately, then a substantial part of their area lies within the residential areas. Even within this so-called developed area, nearly 10 percent was vacant lots and land reserves. If these are dropped out, then the actual used area as reported by the PJ studies was less than three-fourths of the urbanized area as

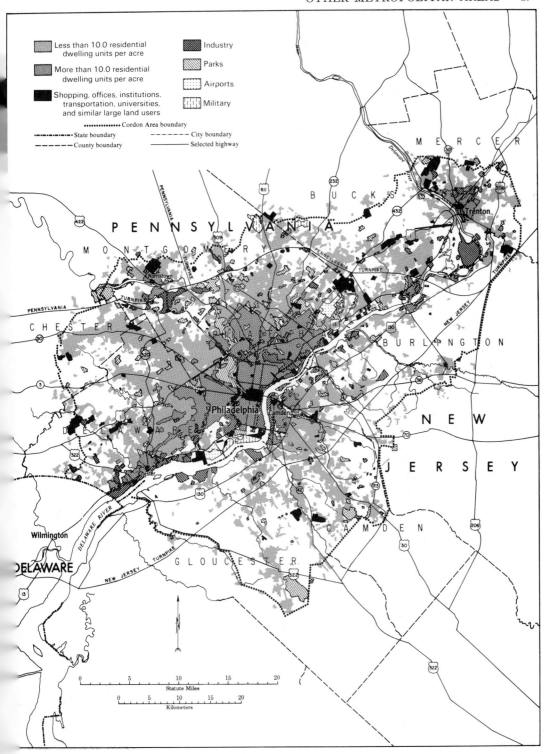

FIGURE 33.   Generalized land use within the Cordon Area, Philadelphia Region, 1960.

TABLE 29

AREA OF LAND, BY MAJOR USE CATEGORY, PENN-JERSEY CORDON AREA, IN 1945,
CHANGES FROM 1945 TO 1960, IN 1960, AND PROJECTED FOR 1975

(1,000 acres)

Item	1945[1]	Changes from 1945 to 1960[2]	1960[3]	1975[4]
Urbanized area, Philadelphia and Trenton, as defined by Census	–	–	443	–
Cordon Area:				
Residential use	91	77	168	230
Nonresidential uses	79	22	101	
Vacant lots and land reserves	–	1	31	–
Streets and highways	43	10	53	62
Subtotal, developed	–	110	354	–
Undeveloped	–	–	398	–
Total, Cordon Area	–	–	752	–
SMSAs, Philadelphia and Trenton	–	–	2,490	–

[1] Estimated from data in next two columns.
[2] Penn-Jersey Transportation Study, *The State of the Region*, p. 42.
[3] *Ibid.*, pp. 35–36.
[4] Penn-Jersey Transportation Study, *1975 Projections, Foreground of the Future* (Philadelphia, 1964), p. 66.

reported by the Bureau of the Census. If comparisons were made for the same total area, then presumably even more idle land would be shown in the urbanized area. The general land use picture as shown by Table 29 for the Cordon Area is generally similar to that presented in Table 5 for a sample of the larger cities in the United States.

Substantial changes in land use in this Cordon Area occurred between 1945 and 1960. Land used for residential purposes increased substantially, though by less than double, while the area for nonresidential and street uses each increased less than one-fourth. The "developed" area added in the 1945–60 period was more than 40 percent of the developed area in 1945, but still was only 15 percent of the Cordon Area and only 4 percent of the SMSAs' area. In general, the 1945–60 land conversions took place on the margins of the land already used for urban purposes. (Figure 34) Some infilling took place, so that areas previously unused appeared used in 1960, at least at this scale of mapping. But in a great many cases, the new conversions from rural to urban land uses were sprawled out at the margin, so that in 1960 it is highly doubtful if any reasonable measure would show less sprawl than 15 years earlier. It should also be stressed that this is the more densely settled part of the two SMSAs. If the more outlying parts were included on this same basis, additions to sprawl outside of the Cordon Area would almost surely be evident.

The DVRPC studies estimated land use, by categories, for the whole metropolitan planning region in 1960 and projected these uses to 1985. (Table 30) The planning region is slightly more than three times the size of the Cordon Area, but the area "used" (including "recreation other than parks") was only a little more

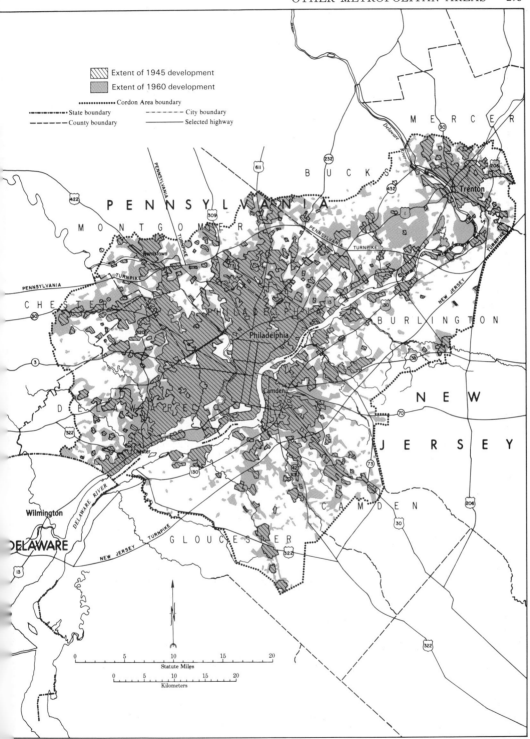

RE 34. Land development, Philadelphia region, 1945–60.

TABLE 30

AREA OF LAND BY USE CATEGORY, 1960, AND PROJECTED FOR 1985, FOR ENTIRE
PHILADELPHIA METROPOLITAN PLANNING REGION

(1,000 acres)

Land use	Used in 1960	Projected for 1985	Percent increase
Residential land	237.2	388.7	64
Hotel, motel, and apartment hotel[1]	2.9	3.4	17
Offices[1]	9.1	17.3	90
Retail trade and services[1]	10.9	14.7	35
Manufacturing, mining, and wholesale[1]	28.5	36.2	27
Passenger transportation[1]	3.2	5.2	62
Construction, storage, and freight transport[1]	11.7	14.8	26
Education and institution[1]	42.3	49.2	16
Recreation other than parks	143.0	145.9	2
Total	488.8	675.4	38

Source: Delaware Valley Regional Planning Commission, *1985 Regional Projections for the Delaware Valley* (Philadelphia, 1967), Appendixes II through X.

Note: The Philadelphia metropolitan planning region is the same as the Philadelphia and Trenton SMSAs in Table 28.

[1] These figures exclude land used for these purposes in central business districts of major cities in this region.

than a third larger. Almost half of it is for residential use; it is hard to make comparisons of the other reported uses with the categories used in other urban land use studies. A 40 percent increase in population between 1960 and 1985 is projected; land for residential purposes is projected to increase considerably more than this, in part because of continued shift to the suburbs where density is lower than in the older cities. Some other uses are also expected to increase relatively more than population, but the overall increase is just slightly less than the population increase because the use of land for "recreation other than parks," which was a major use of land in 1960, is not expected to increase much. If the projected increase in land use to 1985 occurs, the developed land will still be only a little more than a fourth of the planning region and will be less in total than the Cordon Area, although some of the development will surely be outside of it.

Intensity of Land Use

These data on land use may be combined with other data on population to obtain some measure of intensity of land use by zones or parts of the Cordon Area. (Table 31) The PJ studies distinguished the large cities of Philadelphia (part only, omitting the section northeast of Tacony Creek), Trenton, Camden, and Chester; some small cities, which are not important in either total area or total population; and the suburban area, or the Cordon Area outside of the cities. Even in 1945, three-fourths of the residential area was in the suburban area; the large cities had less than one-fourth of it. The additions to residential area from 1945 to 1960 were even more extreme, with 95 percent of the land added in the suburban area.

TABLE 31

LAND USE, POPULATION, AND DWELLING UNITS, BY LOCATIONS WITHIN PENN-JERSEY CORDON AREA, PHILADELPHIA REGION, 1945, 1960, AND PROJECTIONS FOR 1975

Item	Large cities	Small cities	Suburban area	Total, Cordon Area
1. Land use in 1945 (*acres*):				
Residential	19,800	1,700	69,400	91,000
Nonresidential	–	–	–	54,430
Streets	–	–	–	43,750
2. Land use changes, 1945–1960 (*acres*):				
Residential	3,000	700	73,700	77,400
Nonresidential	3,200	300	18,800	22,300
Streets	–	–	–	9,510
3. Land use in 1960 (*acres*):				
Residential	22,800	2,400	143,100	168,400
Nonresidential	–	–	–	76,020
Streets	–	–	–	53,260
4. Land use projected for 1975 (*acres*):				
Residential	–	–	–	229,900
Nonresidential	–	–	–	91,390
Streets	–	–	–	62,300
5. Population (*1,000*):				
1930	2,152	122[1]	762	3,036[1]
1960	1,991	132[1]	1,900	4,023[1]
1975	2,004	141[1]	2,661	4,806[1]
6. Total dwelling units (*1,000*):				
1945	590	20	258	868
Added, 1945–1960	48	4	273	326
1960	638	24	531	1,193
Projected 1975	–	–	–	1,351
7. Dwelling units per residential acre:[2]				
1945	30	–	3.7	9.5
Added 1945–1960	16	–	3.7	4.2
1960	28	–	3.7	7.1
Projected 1975	–	–	–	5.9
8. Population per residential acre:				
1960[2]	87.4	–	13.3	23.9
Projected 1975	–	–	–	20.9

Sources: Data from, or calculated from, Penn-Jersey Transportation Study, *The State of the Region*, pp. 47, 48, and 51, and *1975 Projections, Foreground of the Future*, pp. 18, 35, 42, 66.
Note: Nonresidential data exclude land used for recreation.
[1] Includes three small cities outside the Cordon.
[2] Calculated from data in this table.

It seems probable that there was simply no land within the larger cities that was not already used for residential or other purposes. Thus, in 1960, 85 percent of the residential land, but only 45 percent of the population, was in the suburban area. Conversely, the larger cities, with less than 14 percent of the residential land, had 50 percent of the population. Assuming that the data in this table are accurate, they show rather dramatically how much expansion in population and in residential area is possible with limited increase in street and highway acreage. Residential land area increased by 85 percent from 1945 to 1960 with an increase of only 22 percent in street and highway acreage. It is also significant that a similar trend is projected for the 1960–75 period—an increase of 36 percent in residential area and of only 17 percent in street and highway acreage. These data would suggest considerable unused capacity in streets, or considerable economies of scale in use of transportation acreage, or both.

In 1945, there were 30 dwelling units per acre of residential land in the larger cities; in the added area and added population of 1945–60, there were only 16 units per acre; so that in 1960 the number of dwelling units per residential acre in the larger cities had declined to 28. Population data are lacking for this same period, but it seems likely that the average size of household also declined for this period for these larger cities, as more and more single-person households were formed. If so, population density within the larger cities declined somewhat in these postwar years.

In marked contrast, density of use of residential land in the suburbs remained exactly constant over these years, but at a much lower level than in the cities. This would seem to indicate that average lot size had not changed over the 1945–60 period.

Because the mix of suburb and city shifted considerably over the period, the average density for all residential land dropped, and is expected to drop even further in the period up to 1975. Later DVRPC projections to 1985, made by a different statistical procedure, contemplate a further reduction in average residential density for the same reason.

Average density per residential acre for the whole Cordon Area in 1960 was 23.9; if the average density is calculated on the basis of the total "developed" land area, then it falls to 11.4; if the total area in the Cordon Area, developed and undeveloped, is used in a total-area/total-population density calculation as discussed in Chapter 10, then the figure falls further to 5.4. For the whole SMSAs, the corresponding figure would be only 1.6. As noted several times in this study, each measure is accurate and each may be useful, if one understands what each means; each is a form of land use intensity or density, but defined quite differently.

Special interest attaches to the category, "vacant and agricultural" land. (Figure 35) Available data were analyzed per quarter square mile, in units one-half mile on a side and containing 160 acres. For some of the more intensively used parts of the Cordon Area, less than 5 acres per quarter square mile (less than 3 percent) of the land was vacant. For large residential areas, shown on Figure 33 as the less intensive residential areas, more than 5 but no more than 75 acres per quarter square mile (3 to 47 percent approximately) were shown as vacant or agricultural —a very wide range probably indicating considerably different degrees of land idleness or undeveloped land. For other areas, mostly lying farther out and mostly in low-intensity residential use, the proportion of vacant and agricultural land rises to more than 90 percent.

To some extent, of course, the vacant and agricultural land category is the inverse of the land use categories previously shown in Figure 33. Perhaps the most impressive aspect of Figure 35 is the highly interspersed picture of vacant

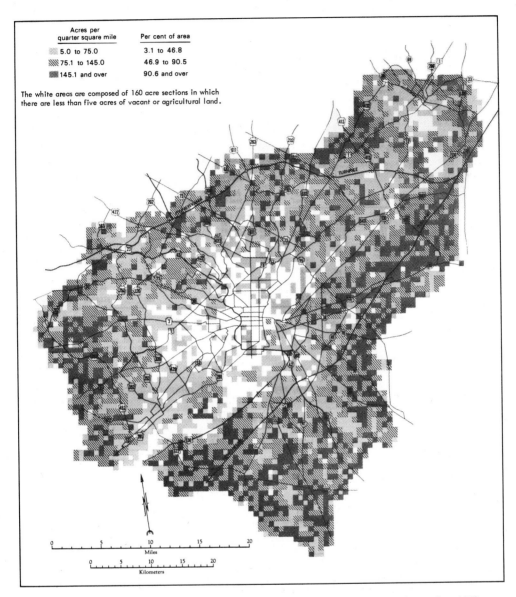

FIGURE 35.   Vacant and agricultural land within the Cordon Area, Philadelphia Region, 1960.

and agricultural land. Moreover, it must be borne in mind that the process of compiling data per quarter square mile is in itself a form of averaging or rounding of data. A very large-scale land use map would almost surely show an even more interspersed character of vacant and agricultural land. These two figures show again the necessity of keeping clearly in mind the limitations of the scale or grain of inquiry; the importance of idle land seems to change as the degree of detail of the inquiry increases.

Water Supply and Sewerage

The water supply and sewage disposal situation within the Cordon Area reflects the nature of its residential growth. The DVRPC reports provide a great deal of information on this subject. The larger cities have both central water supply and central sewerage; the more outlying areas, especially to the west, tend to have central water supply but to rely on septic tanks. Water is not easily obtained from wells in this western area, hence the need for central water supply. On the Jersey side, in contrast, groundwater is easily obtained from rather shallow wells. Throughout the entire Cordon Area, it has seemed relatively easy to utilize septic tanks. However, if the experience of other suburban areas is repeated here, as seems highly likely, these tanks will ultimately have to be replaced by sewers in order to avoid health hazards. In many such areas, septic tanks have proved satisfactory under low-intensity land use or for the first few years under other circumstances, or both, but have had to be replaced at a much greater cost than would have been necessary if sewers had been installed at the beginning. The sewerage problem in the Cordon Area is not so severe as in Fairfax County, for example, and hence it has had less of a limiting effect on suburban development.

Decision Making

The PJ and DVRPC studies did not explicitly consider decision making in the process of urban growth and development. The studies themselves are notable examples of cooperation by federal, state, and local agencies. They do, however, point up the great number of agencies and organizations at work in the area. Penn-Jersey's first report, *The State of the Region,* emphasizes the need for continued planning studies in the region. A rather rueful footnote comments:

> While there are twenty to forty major transportation agencies in the region, depending on the definition used, there are not less than five hundred major public agencies who have direct control of land utilization through zoning, or indirect influence through taxing powers. (pp. 19–20)

It is obvious that decision making in the urban growth process is highly fragmented here, as elsewhere.

Penn-Jersey's reports do not deal with the role of private decision makers—the landowners, the developers and builders, the financial institutions, the home buyers. The number of such private decision makers must be very great indeed.

BALTIMORE, "REGION OF PLENTY"

The metropolitan regional planning organization for the Baltimore SMSA is now known as simply the Regional Planning Council. Formerly its name was "Baltimore Regional Planning Council." Reports have been issued by both organizations. Baltimore, like Boston, is a metropolitan region which falls within one state, although one major city and several counties are included in the SMSA. In this respect, these two metropolitan regions are unlike New York, which includes parts of three states, and Philadelphia, which includes parts of two states. Although every SMSA has numerous difficult problems, in theory at least it should be easier to get coordinated public programs if only one state is involved.

The Regional Planning Council has described its region as one of "plenty," apparently meaning that it has plenty of natural resources for economic growth and pleasant urban living. The region has, indeed, good transportation facilities, including access to the seas and thus to other parts of the United States and of the world; it has ample land resources for future growth; and it has good water resources for industrial and other urban uses. Without attempting to appraise further the natural resource endowment in this metropolitan region, we may simply adopt the Council's term to describe it.

What is now the city of Baltimore began in 1729 as a town on the north side of the Patapsco River. Although other settlements were founded on the Chesapeake Bay, this one was destined to grow into a large metropolitan center because it was the best place where the Bay intersected the Piedmont Plateau. It had access to deepwater navigation, firm land close to the waterfront where wharves and other facilities could readily be constructed, and water power from various falls. The city was primarily an agricultural supply and export center until about 1815, although there were some textile mills and metal-working plants. American railroading more or less began in Baltimore, when the Baltimore and Ohio Railroad was chartered there in 1827. Before the Civil War, the city had developed as an industrial center, largely as a result of the stimulus of railroading and steamboating. Although it early had iron works, the smelting industry nearly disappeared in the 1870's as a result of western competition. But by 1887, a new steel industry began operations, using imported iron ores—from Cuba, at first. Since then, Baltimore has become more and more an industrial city.

The Baltimore region may be defined in various ways. (Table 32) In 1950, the Baltimore SMSA included Baltimore City, Baltimore County, and Anne Arundel County; Baltimore City is a separate legal entity, not a part of Baltimore County. By 1960, Carroll and Howard counties had been added to the SMSA, increasing the area by more than 50 percent but adding at that time only about 5 percent to the SMSA population. An urbanized area delineated in 1950 included 14 percent of the area but 87 percent of the SMSA population. In 1960, it was increased in area by 45 percent in line with the general redefinition of urbanized areas but with a far less than proportionate increase in population. In 1940, the population of Baltimore City was nearly 80 percent of the SMSA, but by 1960 population in other areas had increased so much that the city had little more than half of the total. The Regional Planning Council chose a somewhat larger region than the SMSA, adding Harford County to it. Table 32 illustrates once again the fact that an urban region may be defined in more than one way, with only small effects on population but with major effect upon land area and land use.

A more detailed picture of the increase in population is presented in Table 33 and Figure 36. Baltimore City has increased only modestly above its 1920 population; between 1950 and 1960, its population decreased slightly, as did the popula-

TABLE 32

TOTAL AREA AND TOTAL POPULATION OF BALTIMORE REGION, BY VARIOUS
DEFINITIONS AND VARIOUS DATES

Area, data source, and date	Area		Population (1,000)
	Square miles	1,000 acres	
SMSA, Census:			
1940[1]	–	–	1,083
1950	1,106	707	1,337
1960	1,807	1,154	1,727
Urbanized area, Census:			
1950	152	97	1,162
1960	220	141	1,419
Baltimore City, Census:			
1940	–	–	859
1950	79	51	950
1960	79	51	939
Baltimore region, Regional Planning Council, 1965[2]	2,260	1,448	2,013

[1] Although SMSAs were not established until after World War II, the Bureau of the Census, in presenting data for 1950, also presented population data for the same area in 1940. The Baltimore SMSA in 1950 included Baltimore City, Baltimore County, and Anne Arundel County; in 1960 Carroll and Howard counties were added.

[2] Felix J. Rimberg and Alan M. Voorhees and associates, *Projections and Allocations for Regional Plan Alternatives*, Baltimore Regional Planning Council (Baltimore 1965). The region is the 1960 SMSA plus Harford County.

TABLE 33

POPULATION OF THE BALTIMORE REGION, BY SUBAREAS, 1920–65, AND PROJECTIONS TO 1980

(1,000)

Year	Subarea						Total
	Anne Arundel County	Baltimore County	Baltimore City	Carroll County	Howard County	Harford County	
1920	43	75	734	34	16	29	931
1930	55	124	805	36	16	32	1,068
1940	68	156	859	39	17	35	1,175
1950	117	270	950	45	23	52	1,457
1960	206	492	939	53	36	77	1,804
1965[1]	267	579	955	58	64	90	2,013
1980[2]	487	884	967	79	186	160	2,763

Sources: Reports of the Baltimore Regional Planning Council. Projection for 1980 is from its *Projections and Allocations for Regional Plan Alternatives*, p. 59.

[1] Estimated.

[2] Projected.

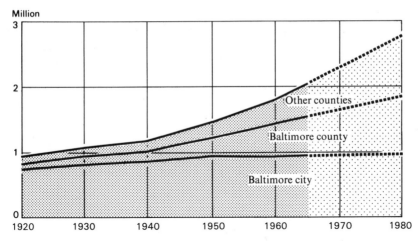

FIGURE 36. Population of Baltimore Region (as defined by Regional Planning Council), by parts, 1920–65, and projection to 1980.

tion of many other large cities (if only the legal city is considered). The Council's projections are that its population will not change much in the future. In some sense, the legal city is "full" of people, at least on a residential basis. The most dramatic changes to date have taken place in Baltimore County, which nearly surrounds the city, except for a small distance on the southeast where the city borders Anne Arundel County. From less than a tenth of the region's population, Baltimore County has increased to well over a fourth today and is projected to rise to over a third. But the other, and generally more distant, counties have also risen in population, less in absolute terms but greatly in proportionate terms. This pattern of decentralization or growth of the outlying areas is, of course, a typical one for all major cities in the United States in the past generation, but these data give it quantitative expression for Baltimore.

The Baltimore SMSA has grown more rapidly since World War II than have most other SMSAs in the Northeastern Urban Complex. (Table 34) Its growth rate has been clearly less than that of Washington. In 1940, the city and the SMSA of Baltimore exceeded the respective units of Washington by 30 percent and 12 percent; but in 1960 the situation was reversed as far as the respective SMSAs were concerned, although Baltimore city was still larger than the city of Washington. Among the dominantly manufacturing SMSAs, Baltimore's growth rate has been equalled or exceeded only by Wilmington, Paterson-Clifton-Passaic, and Hartford. The vigor of growth in the postwar period suggests a larger relative role for Baltimore among the SMSAs of the region in the future.

As noted, Baltimore is largely an industrial city. In 1960, the Baltimore SMSA had 30 percent of its labor force employed in the manufacturing sector, compared with 23 percent on a national basis. Among its manufacturing, heavy or durable goods are dominant, with nearly two-thirds of the manufacturing labor force so employed.

Two sources of data on land use in the Baltimore region do not agree. (Table 35) One is the land use studies of various counties, as reported by the Northeast

TABLE 34

RELATIVE CHANGE IN POPULATION, 1940–50 AND 1950–60, FOR LARGER SMSAS
IN NORTHEASTERN URBAN COMPLEX

SMSA	Percentage population increase	
	1940–50	1950–60
Boston	9	9
Springfield	11	18
Providence	9	11
Hartford	21	47
New York	10	12
Paterson-Clifton-Passaic	22	35
Jersey City	−1	−6
Newark	14	15
Philadelphia	15	18
Wilmington	21	37
Baltimore	23	29
Washington	51	37

TABLE 35

AREA OF LAND, BY TYPE OF USE, AND BY PARTS OF BALTIMORE REGION, CIRCA 1962

(1,000 acres)

Kind of land use	Subarea						
	Anne Arundel County	Baltimore County	Baltimore City	Carroll County	Howard County	Harford County	Total
I. Northeast Corridor Transportation Study[1]							
Residential	22.8	42.3	16.4	4.4	3.9	9.3	99.1
Commercial	2.0	1.4	2.4	0.3	0.6	1.6	7.9
Industrial	7.3	14.8	7.3	0.8	1.9	1.5	33.6
Public	25.1	36.1	9.3	8.5	7.2	6.7	92.9
Other	209.7	294.5	15.6	275.9	146.5	268.1	1,210.2
Total	266.9	389.1	51.1	289.9	160.0	286.7	1,443.7
II. Baltimore Regional Planning Council[2]							
Residential and streets	26.7	56.3	26.0	14.4	8.8	15.7	147.9
Nonresidential	32.2	31.5	14.9	4.2	4.6	53.7	141.2
Vacant	151.6	228.7	5.7	203.2	118.7	149.4	857.3
Undevelopable	36.3	91.3	4.7	70.8	36.5	47.6	287.2
Total	266.4	390.1	51.4	297.3	155.7	286.8	1,447.6

[1] See Appendix Table 5.
[2] *Projections and Allocations for Regional Plan Alternatives,* p. 28.

Corridor Transportation Study and summarized in Appendix Table 5 of this book. As noted in Chapter 10, the definitions used by the various counties probably differ and often are not available. The definitions used by the Baltimore Regional Planning Council are contained in their reports; but the data published by this organization do not include much detail according to land use. Although these two sources of data do not agree, yet there is some similarity between them. The area shown as residential and streets by the Regional Planning Commission is about 50 percent greater than the area shown as residential in the Northeast Corridor study. Possibly the areal difference might be accounted for by the necessary street acreage. The differences in data for this category between the two sources are not constant, either in absolute or relative terms, for the different counties. The data from Appendix Table 5 for commercial, industrial, and public (including semi-public) land uses correspond generally with the data on nonresidential land use as reported by the Regional Planning Commission. But, when the comparison is made by counties, there is very poor correspondence, with no consistent direction to the differences. The "other" category from Appendix Table 5 is simply a catchall or difference, hence nearly meaningless. The Regional Planning Commission data separate "vacant" from "undevelopable." The latter is probably contingent upon present technology and present costs and values, as was found to be the case in Wilmington. In either case, the amount of land *not* used for urban purposes is very large, compared with the area so used—more than three-fourths of the total for the whole region and for each county, though less for Baltimore City. But even in the city, more than 10 percent is reported vacant.

As might be expected, a map of land use in 1965 shows a concentration of commercial land near the city center, with residential land use density higher there and lower toward the margins of the region, and with the larger industrial areas located along Chesapeake Bay and streams where water transportation is available. (Figure 37) This map shows a considerable dispersion of tracts or areas developed for relatively low-density residential use, with large undeveloped areas interspersed among the smaller developed areas. It may be doubted whether this map shows the full extent of this interspersion or has some degree of rounding or smoothing which reduces the degree of interspersion of idle land. But even this map makes it clear why the available statistics show so much undeveloped land in the region. The public and quasi-public areas are also scattered; the park and recreation areas have taken advantage of special sites useful for these purposes but not always in high demand for other purposes.

The Baltimore Regional Planning Council and the National Capital Regional Planning Council in 1960 developed some estimates of residential intensity of land use, related to location or distance from the city center.[11] (Table 36) On what their report calls "neighborhood density," the density declines in Baltimore from about 100 persons per acre in the inner city to under 4 in "rural" areas; the latter must exclude vacant or undeveloped lands, as the definition suggests, for one-acre lots would produce this density. The Baltimore Regional Planning Council refers

[11] Baltimore Regional Planning Council and National Capital Regional Planning Council, *Land Use and Transportation*, Baltimore-Washington Interregional Study, Technical Report No. 7 (Baltimore, 1960).

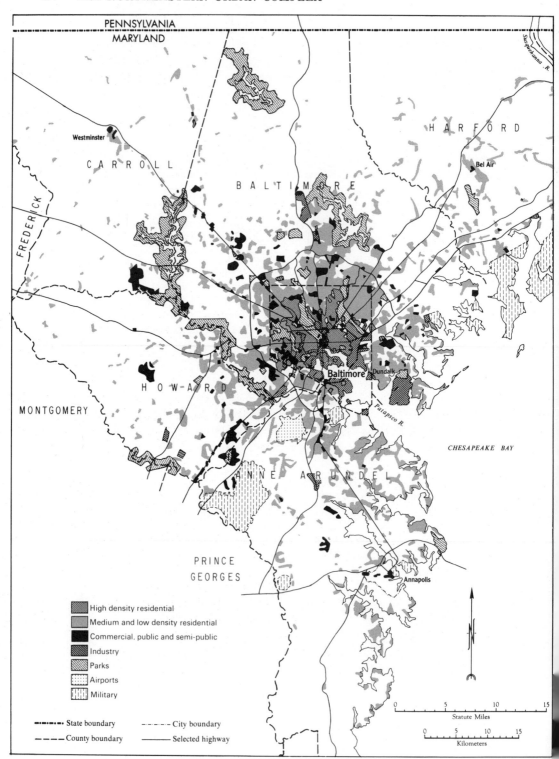

FIGURE 37. Land use in the Baltimore Region, circa 1962.

TABLE 36

RESIDENTIAL DENSITY GROUPS, BALTIMORE-WASHINGTON REGION, LATE 1950s

Density group	Neighborhood density[1]		Net residential density[2]			Gross development density[3]		
	Range	Average	Average lot size per dwelling unit (sq. ft.)	Persons per acre	Dwelling units per acre	Persons per acre	Acres per 1,000 persons	Persons per square mile
Inner city	50–120	–[4]	1,000 or less	120 or more	40 or more	20 or more	50 or less	13,000 or more
Outer city	21–50	30	2,400	55–65	16–18	18	55	11,000
Inner suburban	12–21	15	6,000	20–25	6–7	8	125	5,000
Outer suburban	4–12	7	16,000	9–12	2–3	4	250	2,500
Rural	under 4	3	40,000	4–5	1–2	2	500	1,200

Source: Baltimore Regional Planning Council and National Capital Regional Planning Council, *Land Use and Transportation*, Baltimore-Washington Interregional Study, Technical Report No. 7 (1960), p. 58.

[1] Persons on land devoted or to be devoted to residential use, divided by the acreage of said land, including residential streets and local neighborhood facilities.

[2] Density as applied only to strictly residential land, in the units as indicated, exclusive of streets, neighborhood facilities, etc.

[3] Density as applied to all land developed or to be developed in relation to the resident population, in the units as indicated.

[4] About 100 persons per acre in Baltimore City; about 75 in the District of Columbia.

to "net residential density" and to "gross development density." The relationship between distance from city center and number of persons per acre is generally similar for each of the three measures used; however, the level of intensity differs considerably. If "gross development density," the lowest of the three, is taken as the base mark, then "net residential density" generally runs about three times as many persons per acre, and "neighborhood density" runs somewhat less than twice as high. These data illustrate again how different measures of land use intensity must be defined carefully in order to be meaningful; each is equally accurate if properly understood, but they simply measure different things.

CONCLUSIONS

Materials presented in this chapter and in the two preceding it lead to these conclusions:

1. Data on land use in and around the larger cities are very poor. There are no consistent definitions of land use categories, no consistent units of land for which data are collected, and no consistent units of area for which the available data are summarized and analyzed. The situation is bad enough within each SMSA or planning region for any particular date, but especially bad if one seeks to compare information for different dates for the same SMSA or to compare different SMSAs. For many SMSAs, data on land use prior to some planning study of the mid- or late-1950's can charitably be described as rudimentary.

2. Although improvement has taken place in land use data, serious question may be raised as to its adequacy. In the reports available for use in preparation of this chapter, each SMSA or planning region had tackled the problem of data improvement alone, with no evidence of a data system inclusive of different SMSAs and different time periods. On the basis of these reports, one has to conclude that the urban land use data systems of this region are still seriously deficient. These

studies generally preceded publication of the *Standard Land Use Coding Manual* and of *Land Use Information,* which may lead to some basic improvements.[12] Several of the studies emphasized the need for continuous collection of data on land use, or at least for rather frequent updating of such data, but question may well be raised as to how far these good intentions have been translated into action. Data collection is often a dreary and tiresome job; while its ultimate rewards may be large, the worker may not see them or indeed share in them.

3. Data on people in urban areas (their numbers, age, race, sex, employment, income, and other useful items of information) are vastly better than data on land use in the same areas. This conclusion is valid for today, and it is clearly true for earlier periods. The United States has had decennial or more frequent censuses of population or economic activities since 1790, which include a great deal of information about people and their activities, but much less about land and land use.

4. Although the legal or political city is readily definable, the socioeconomic city is not. Even more difficult than defining the whole city is the definition of socio-economically meaningful parts or subsections. Still more difficult is the question of whether it is better to retain constant areal definitions or boundaries over time in order to permit comparisons among constantly defined but changing areas, or whether areas should be redefined in order to reflect changing situations. This chapter has shown that there is not yet a clear consensus on this issue among urban specialists; the problem is likely to grow more acute, as urban complexes continue to grow and change.

5. Decentralization of population within each urban complex and the creation of lower residential density land use on the periphery seems universal, on the basis of the studies reported in this chapter. As suggested in Chapter 10, at some level of density the older cities are in some sense "full" of people, even though there is some idle or unused land within the older city and even though much of the residential area of each older city could be rebuilt to house a great many more people. But it has been both easier and more congenial to many Americans to accommodate more people by horizontal expansion at the periphery rather than by intensified land use nearer the center. The definition of "full," in the foregoing sense, seems to vary from one city another, being a much higher density for large cities than for smaller ones. There emerges no clear evidence that the density of land use is changing *within* each of the major parts of large urban complexes (core, inner ring, intermediate ring, outer ring, etc.); but the mix of parts is changing for most large urban complexes, and the lower densities in the growing areas tend to lower average densities for the whole. One notable fact is that the definitions of residential density or other measures of land use intensity are especially bad and confusing.

6. These studies show clearly that there exists today a great deal of vacant, unused, idle, or undeveloped land (whatever term one wishes to use) *within* each of the major SMSAs or planning areas, where future population expansion may

[12] Urban Renewal Administration and Bureau of Public Roads, *Standard Land Use Coding Manual* (U.S. Government Printing Office, 1965) ; and Marion Clawson and Charles L. Stewart, *Land Use Information—A Critical Survey of U.S. Statistics Including Possibilities for Greater Uniformity* (Resources for the Future, 1966).

occur. (There may indeed be some SMSAs or planning regions which are so hemmed in by others, that this statement is not true; we know that there are some cities closely hemmed in by others.) The idle land is dominantly but not exclusively on the margins of presently developed areas; land in choice locations is scarce and always will be. But the large urban areas reported in this chapter have a great deal of land capable of future development. Even at the low densities or intensities of land use at the periphery, population growth for many, many years can be accommodated within them, often within their presently "urbanized" areas. Since there is reason to think that some presently used land will be more intensely used in the future as the total size of the urban complex grows, the capacity to absorb more people is still greater than calculations based upon presently undeveloped or unused land suggest. Moreover, much land now considered "unbuildable" is likely to be used in the future, as techniques of building and of land development change.

7. The planning studies used in this chapter do not deal explicitly with decision-making in urban growth and expansion, but they do contain some information which bears on this subject. On the basis of the information included, there is no reason to believe that the decision-making in them is any less dispersed or less diffused than was found to be the case in the three case studies reported in more detail in Chapter 12, or than was discussed in general terms in Chapter 5. Certainly the multiplicity of governmental agencies and units concerned with urban expansion is as great here as in the other areas, and it seems probable that the multiplicity of private forces is also as great.

14

THE EMERGING REGIONAL URBAN COMPLEX

The Northeastern Urban Complex, as defined in this study, is clearly highly *urban* in its concentration of a large population within a limited area and in its style of living. It is equally clearly a *complex* of cities, SMSAs, and urbanized areas. But is it, in any meaningful sense, an integrated region or integrated regional megalopolis? Is it anything more than a large collection of urban centers within a region which is moderately small on the U.S. geographical scale? The degree of unity or of integration of the geographic area is the subject of this chapter.

Gottmann first applied the term "megalopolis" to this region, and hence it is desirable to study what he meant by the term.[1] Did he view the region as primarily a large collection of cities (or SMSAs or urbanized areas) within a limited geographical space, with obvious and natural interconnections between the various centers? Or did he view it as something more—an integrated regional megalopolis, set apart in some way or to some degree from other urban areas of the United States and the world, with a unity and a character beyond that of a mere collection of urban centers?

Unfortunately for the present purpose, the more one studies Gottmann, the less sure one can be as to exactly what he does mean. The problem is perhaps partly one of semantics. Just what meaning and connotations attach to such words as "megalopolis," "complex," "integrated"? Perhaps the problem is more difficult. The kind of population pattern along the northeastern seaboard is, Gottmann asserts with logic, in some degree unique in the world's history. Hence one neither fully understands it nor finds words that exactly portray his meaning.

Many of Gottmann's statements lend support to the idea that he conceived of the Northeastern Urban Complex as a regionally integrated megalopolis, something more than a mere collection of urban areas. He refers to "the enormous and powerful concentration of people and activities now achieved" in the region (p. ix). The opening chapter declares that:

> . . . the processes of urbanization, rooted deep in the American past, have worked steadily here, endowing the region with unique ways of life and of land use. No other section of the United States has such a large concentration

---

[1] Jean Gottmann, *Megalopolis—The Urbanized Northeastern Seaboard of the United States* (New York: Twentieth Century Fund, 1961). Mumford and Geddes, who used this term earlier, did not apply it to this region.

of population, with such a high average density, spread over such a large area. And no other section has a comparable role within the nation or a comparable importance in the world. Here has been developed a kind of supremacy, in politics, in economics, and possibly even in cultural activities, seldom before attained by an area of this size. (p. 3)

Other phrases suggest integration—"unique cluster of metropolitan areas" (p. 7) and "an almost continuous system of deeply interwoven urban and suburban areas" (p. 4). The key to most questions involved in his study, he declares, "lies in the interrelationships between the forces and processes at work in the area rather than in the trends of growth or the development of techniques" (p. 9). Finally, it may be noted, he states that Megalopolis is "characterized by concentration of a great variety of phenomena—in short, by *manifold concentration*—and by a *polynuclear structure*" (p. 25, emphasis in the original).

On the other hand, a great deal of Gottman's book is taken up with the presentation of rather detailed data showing the differences within this complex of a great many factors. He certainly recognizes, as only a geographer can, the large spatial differentiation of activities. He is fully conscious of city center, suburbs, and hinterland, and the variations in this pattern for the major SMSAs. He does not deal explicitly with the issue of regional integration. Much of his analysis bears upon it, but not in a way that makes it clear just where he stands on this issue of collection of urban areas versus integrated urban region.

Some aspects of the situation in the Northeastern Urban Complex seem to be generally accepted by most students of the region.

1. There are a lot of people (about 32 million in 1960) in a fairly concentrated area (20 million acres) living in a generally urban form of settlement on the land and in a clearly urban life style.

2. The Complex is geographically somewhat set apart from other major urban centers or metropolises. One can go northward into Maine, New Hampshire, and Vermont for long distances, without adding many people to the regional population. Similarly, but not in quite so marked a fashion, one can go westward in New York and Pennsylvania, encountering only small cities until he reaches the Great Lakes. Or one can go southward from Washington to Richmond and Norfolk, a considerable distance, to add only a small fraction to the regional population. This is why the Northeastern Urban Complex may be defined in any reasonable alternative way without much affecting the number of people involved. Alternative definitions differ primarily in land area included.

3. There are substantial interactions among the individuals and the urban groupings of population in economic, social, political, and communications terms. The various urban centers compete for labor force, for raw materials, for capital, and for markets for their output; but there are important complementary and supplementary relationships among them also.

4. Although the urban form of life is dominant, urban use of land is discontinuous, with large gaps between many urban centers and with large acreages of idle land within SMSAs, urbanized areas, and cities. This point is by no means generally recognized. The previous chapters have documented it thoroughly and

provided some quantitative estimates of the areas involved. Data from other sources were utilized but the analysis is in some degree new.

5. The nature of each urban grouping (city, urbanized area, SMSA) is changing. The center is often decaying physically and usually decaying economically too. It has become the home of the lowest-income classes and a few of the highest-income people and the site of office buildings. Manufacturing, trade, and the middle- to upper-income classes have fled from center to suburbs; and the suburbs are spreading outward. The process has racial overtones that are disturbing to any thoughtful person.

A number of arguments may be marshaled against the idea that the Northeastern Urban Complex is a regionally integrated megalopolis, but rather is only a collection of large and small cities within a geographically defined area:

. . . All people everywhere in the world today, and all large collections of people everywhere, live primarily by interactions with other people. If man ever lived in isolation, that day has gone, and the degree of interaction with others increases as the world grows smaller in a human use sense. Other factors remaining constant, the closer one group is to another, the greater the degree of those interactions. Or, stated differently, the distance-decay function is ubiquitous, although its slope varies for different functions and under different conditions. Thus, heavy raw materials of low unit value, such as sand and gravel, move only short distances; people move much farther and more readily, in their personal interrelations with other people; and communications such as radio and TV move farthest, fastest, and easiest. Transport and communication facilities also affect interactions. Since there are relatively a lot of people within a modest geographic area in the Northeast, one would expect many interactions among individuals and among groups of people, regardless of the degree of regional integration. Thus, while it is easy to show that there is a substantial flow of goods and services between the various urban centers and metropolises of the Northeastern Urban Complex, this alone is not proof of regional integration.

. . . Many parts of this "region" are not closely tied together in any meaningful way. One can as easily go from Washington to Los Angeles or San Francisco as to Springfield or Providence; Wilmington may be as closely integrated economically with Pittsburgh as with Boston. There are many other examples of a lack of integration among parts of the "region."

. . . The "region" has no political structure or power. It is, of course, part of the United States, and the cities are parts of their respective states. There are a lot of votes here and hence some political power, but there is no regional political or governmental mechanism, no regional government, even for limited functions. To the extent that there is anything resembling a regional approach, it has been conducted—even forced upon the area—by the federal government. The Northeast Corridor Transportation study, for instance, or river basin studies, have been federal in entrepreneurship and in financing. There is no overall governing body for any SMSA, although there are some functionally limited activities that include the whole of some SMSAs.

. . . The economic, political, and social problems of the SMSAs of the Northeastern Urban Complex closely resemble those of other SMSAs all over the country. The Complex simply has more SMSAs within shorter distances than do other parts of the United States. There is nothing unique to the region or common among its parts that is not shared by SMSAs elsewhere.

On the other hand, proponents of the idea that the Northeastern Urban Complex is to some degree a functionally integrated region may cite these arguments in support of their position:

. . . There is a substantial internal flow of goods, services, people, and communications within the region among the various cities and SMSAs. Although very little data on this point have been provided here, it can be documented from many sources. While this alone is not proof of regional integration, it is suggestive of integration. Individuals, firms, and groups in one part of the region are tied to individuals, firms, and groups in other parts of the region by numerous bonds of common interest and mutual exchange. If something happens to disturb one part of the region, other parts are quickly and seriously affected also. The massive electric power failure of 1965 directly affected only part of the region but indirectly affected all of it—and, indeed, a much larger area as well.

. . . At the margins between several pairs of SMSAs, some workers commute daily to one SMSA, while neighbors go to another. Hence at the margin the two are closely united and in direct relationship. In some parts of New Jersey, some workers commute northward to the New York urban complex, while others commute south to Trenton; and in other parts of New Jersey, some workers commute north to Trenton while others commute south to Philadelphia. There are many other such pairs of cities or urban complexes. One could quite possibly find a chain of interacting urban areas from the northernmost to the southernmost part of the "region," just as a squirrel finds interlacing branches that enable him to travel blocks without touching the ground. To the extent that workers may actually choose between different SMSAs or urban groupings for their employment, without changing residence, there is an equalizing or leveling economic influence between such areas. However, a closer look at such data shows that the areas of overlap are largest if only 1 percent of the labor force go to other SMSAs, much smaller if 5 percent of the labor force is the cutoff point, and largely absent if it is as much as 20 percent.

. . . The SMSAs, urbanized areas, and cities of the "region" are growing toward their neighbor SMSAs, urbanized areas, and cities, so that formerly clear dividing lines are becoming blurred. There has been a great deal of popular and semi-popular exaggeration on this point. Washington and Baltimore are *not* a single city or metropolitan area now, nor are they likely to be so for many decades. Still less is Baltimore united with Philadelphia, Philadelphia with New York, or New York with Boston. The major SMSAs are still quite distinct, especially if one uses properly disaggregated data. If one uses county data—as many unwary writers do—then there appears to be a merging or blurring of SMSAs which simply does not exist on the ground. However, within the larger SMSAs, the line between formerly distinct cities has frequently vanished, and there is little physical evidence as to where one begins and the other ends. The economic (and frequently the social) "city" no longer conforms to the legal or political one. While this may be marked in the Northeastern Urban Complex because there are so many cities, which often are rather small geographically so that a growing one quickly touches another, yet this situation is by no means unique to this part of the country.

The future of urban growth and development is considered in Part III of this book, but it may be useful at this point to speculate a little on the future of regional integration. Whatever merit there now is to the arguments that regional integration exists will probably be stronger several decades hence. Further population growth seems nearly inevitable, and most growing areas will be on the fringes of the present urban areas. Cities, urbanized areas, and even SMSAs will increasingly grow toward each other. Larger populations, with higher incomes, will have increasingly diversified demands for goods and services of all kinds, and transactions among people in different parts of the Complex will surely increase. One might even speculate that the growing complexity of living in this broad geographic area will force some form of regional government, probably by compacts of some kind, almost certainly without eliminating any existing units of government. If one is sceptical about regional integration now, he may continue to be sceptical about it a generation from now, but almost certainly the forces leading toward close regional integration will be stronger then than now.

The need for transportation of people and of goods within the Complex, and the problems of providing transport on the scale that will be demanded, may force a greater degree of integration upon the region in the future. Since World War II, movement of people has shifted from rail to air and to private automobile; but the limits of capacity of these modes is within sight. Since 1967, the capacity of the air to sustain plane travel seems to have been reached at some seasons. Larger planes may increase air capacity, but ground transportation problems to the airfields will increase. When planes get stacked up over one airport, its airspace holding area tends to merge with that of neighboring metropolises. More multilane superhighways can be built at a significant cost in money and in land area, but their impact upon city centers may be disastrous. So much land may be taken up with the highway and the parking areas that little is left to provide the services which attract people to the city. A revival of rail transport, or the development of wholly new surface or subsurface transport such as the gravity vacuum tube might well open a wholly new dimension to intermetropolis travel, even though problems of getting to stations might remain serious. Problems of air and water pollution, of water supply, and of recreation will also increase in regional importance and be a factor pushing toward some form of regional action. Any development in these directions will require some form of regional effort, probably one led by the federal government.

This brief chapter may close with a reference to other regional urban complexes, existent or emerging. As noted previously, Herman Kahn has used the term ChiPitts to describe the complex of cities, urbanized areas, and SMSAs from Milwaukee, past Chicago to Detroit and Cleveland, and on to Pittsburgh. His term SanSan describes the emerging California complex from north of Oakland (or San Francisco, from which his first "San" comes) to San Diego on the south. Other groups could be cited, as in Texas. Doxiadis has made much of an emergent Great Lakes Megalopolis which, in his more expansive moments, stretches well into Canada. But it seems fairly clear that as of now, and probably for some time to come, each of these is even less an integrated region than the Northeastern Urban Complex. In each, total population is now less, and total area is much greater than in the Northeast. While careful quantitative studies are lacking, any comprehensive measurement of the degree of regional integration is likely to show that each is much less integrated economically—and still less integrated socially and politically—than the Northeast. There surely is no more political unity anywhere else, even in the California and Texas groupings. Rival metropolitan centers may pull apart quite as much as they pull together. But the economic bonds within each of these so-called megalopolises may be little if any stronger than their economic bonds with other urban groupings.

The Northeast is indeed an Urban Complex. But it is surely debatable whether or not it is an integrated region.

part III

POSSIBILITIES FOR THE FUTURE

The following chapters, which form Part III of this book, are concerned with the broad possibilities for and the directions of change in the suburban land conversion process. They present neither a detailed plan nor a program for legislation or other action, public or private. A basic assumption is that substantial improvement in suburban land conversion is both urgently necessary and possible. The major problem is to agree on policy issues and directions for change. If agreement can be reached on these points, then specific steps can be taken, though they may be far-reaching and difficult.

As noted in the opening pages of this book and many times since, the primary focus here is on land use at the expanding edge of the city—its suburbs—the process, actors, and results of the process. Of necessity some attention is given to the problems of the city as well as its suburbs. But the suburbs are an important part of the city, land use is an important part of suburban growth and change, and the process of suburban land conversion is significant in its own right.

The primary concern in Part III is to outline ways in which the process of land conversion at the suburban growing edge of the city might be different in the future in order to remedy or to reduce some of the shortcomings of the process and to produce results which seem more desirable for society. Consideration of this central topic involves getting into problems of urban renewal in the older city, for what is done there—or not done—greatly affects the demand for land in the suburbs. Likewise there is some discussion of poverty, for a great deal of suburban land conversion has rested, directly or indirectly, on the inability of the poor to afford new housing or good housing in good neighborhoods. And the possibilities for reorganization of local government are considered, since efforts to reshape suburban land conversion will quickly come up against the deficiencies of local government as an enabling mechanism. All of these forces, and others discussed in these chapters, will help to shape the future of the suburbs which are now so important a part of American life.

A SUMMARY APPRAISAL OF SUBURBAN LAND CONVERSION

At various points in the preceding chapters, judgments as to the efficiency, desirability, or general working of the process of postwar suburban land conversion have been expressed or implied. This chapter will make such judgments explicit.

It is impossible to judge suburban land conversion simply and unequivocally—to say that it is "good" or "bad" or describe it by using some other single and unqualified term. The process is much too complicated for that. Almost anyone who carefully studies what has been going on since World War II will find some aspects which he would evaluate favorably and other aspects which he would regard less favorably.

This chapter seeks to characterize the suburban land conversion process briefly and sharply, and then state its chief advantages and its chief disadvantages as they appear to the writer. Weighing the advantages against the disadvantages is left to each reader.

Characteristics of Suburban Land Conversion

As one recalls the detail of the foregoing chapters, a few major characteristics of suburban land conversion seem to stand out.

1. Decision-making in suburban land conversion is highly dispersed and fragmented. There is a considerable number of actors, each playing a particular role. Each operates to gain his own ends, within the means which he is able to muster; each "does his thing," seeking his own gain. No person or organization is responsible for the final result or for the whole job, and it is altogether possible that none of the actors would have chosen the final result, if the choice were his. There are, indeed, general planning organizations which try to visualize the final course of development in their city or metropolitan area, but they almost invariably lack the means to carry their ideas into operation.

2. Some actors seek to thwart the actions of others. Some suburbs have sought to attract some types of settlers or some types of economic activities and to repel others, irrespective of the effect upon the larger metropolitan area. Some real

estate developers have sought to develop subdivisions contrary to the official plans for the areas concerned. In most if not all such cases, action which ran counter to a larger plan has proven profitable to those who were able to carry it off.

3. The suburban land conversion process has left a great deal of land unused at any particular time within the generally urban environment. Even within the "urbanized areas" as established by the Bureau of the Census, there is much vacant land; and within the Standard Metropolitan Statistical Areas, far more land is vacant than is used for urban purposes.

4. The market for suburban land is highly imperfect, in economists' terms. "Land" is not a homogeneous commodity; to a substantial degree, each parcel or tract is unique. Its location is fixed in a physical sense, though its location vis-à-vis other land can be altered by improved transportation and communication facilities. Land (in suburban areas and elsewhere) is rarely available in incremental pieces; instead, it is bought and sold in tracts, which are often large compared with the final use. The unit of suburban transaction is really the subdivision rather than the house lot, and the subdivision itself is highly variable in size. There are typically only a few buyers and a few sellers in the market at any particular time. Information about the suburban land market, including particular transactions and prices, has not been assembled on a reliable basis readily available to any interested person. The public processes of planning, zoning, and subdivision control are designed to bring some order into this land market. But it appears that they introduce uncertainty, increase the risk of land holding and development by making the form and the date of the land use conversion less predictable, and hence increase rather than diminish the imperfections of the market.

5. Partly as a result of these market imperfections, the price of suburban land is high and has been rising steeply, and there seems to be no suburban land whose rent or price is at an agricultural alternative level. The suburban land market is far from a fully competitive one, and the prices of land established in it have serious repercussions in terms of the kind of housing that is built.

6. A great deal of both private and public investment is made in growing suburban areas. As a rule, the cost of the public investment is inequitably divided, with the older areas (in both cities and suburbs) often subsidizing newer suburban areas to a substantial degree.

7. The older legal cities are typically today not the full economic city of which they are a part; the economic city far exceeds the borders of the established legal cities. Thus there is typically a discrepancy between economic interest or responsibility and political power.

8. Urban and suburban growth and change create economic values which are external to the particular properties. Interdependencies in use and value dominate the uses and values confined to or arising from the tract itself. These externalities and interdependencies have been imperfectly measured, and generally there is no legal measure or recognition of value corresponding to the flows of economic values.

Other characteristics of the process of suburban land conversion could be cited, but these seem to be the major ones. What are the advantages and disadvantages of this process?

Advantages

The suburban land conversion process, as it has operated for the past 20 years or more, has had several strong advantages.

First of all, it has been a process of great vitality. Many private persons and organizations have directed their energies and their capital toward the building of new residences, new shopping districts, and new industrial plants in suburban areas. Many public agencies have directed their energies and capital to the same general end. The postwar years have been generally a period of economic growth, possibly not as rapid as could have been achieved but still high as compared with many past periods. They have been years when people migrated to cities from rural areas and small towns. Many people and much industry and trade have moved from the city center to the suburbs. Millions of homes and hundreds of shopping districts have been built from this public and private energy. The vitality of the whole process seems clearly to have been a major national asset.

Secondly, the process of postwar suburban land conversion has produced a lot of rather good housing and a lot of rather pleasant neighborhoods. Millions of families have found comfortable housing, some of it rather gracious, with modern conveniences and gadgets. Schools, churches, and other community institutions have also been developed. A whole generation of postwar suburbanites has grown up, to whom this was the norm of modern living. When the criticisms of these suburbs are raised, one must always bear in mind that after all, a great deal of pretty comfortable housing and associated developments were built.

Thirdly, though dispersion of decision-making inevitably leads to inconsistent results wherein one part of the process works against other parts, dispersion may avoid massive errors. Dispersed decision-making may miss some opportunities, but it also avoids the big blunders. A multiplicity of groups, each striving for its own interest, may produce somewhat inconsistent specific decisions; but each group, seeking its own advantage, is quick to capitalize on the errors of others. This is the idea of the competitive market applied to the complex of economic, social, political, and other decisions made in suburban land conversion. A central planning agency might produce a far better coordinated plan; but it might also go astray in a truly massive way. Dispersed decision-making may fail fully to achieve the favorable potentials of a situation, but it is also likely to avoid the major unfavorable possibilities. The danger of an overly centralized urban planning process leading to a program carried into operation on a city-wide scale which later proved to be undesirable seems to be remote in the United States.

Disadvantages

Several major criticisms have been directed at the postwar suburban land conversion process and associated urban changes and developments, of which the following stand out.

In the first place, the costs have been too high for the kinds of housing produced. Firm information, applicable to the average suburb, has been hard to come by. Studies cited in Chapter 8 indicate that the direct public costs of scattered suburban sprawl are in the neighborhood of $150 per family per year. This is a very tentative figure which excludes, among other things, the direct or indirect costs imposed upon the suburban dweller as an individual, such indirect costs as increased air pollution because of increased dependence upon private automobiles each typically carrying but a single rider to and from work, and the increased costs of a more extensive road network in suburbia. Moreover, this is the cost of subdivision noncontiguity—of sprawl on the subdivision scale. It does not include costs imposed by reliance on the single-family detached house rather than row houses, apartments, and other denser forms of settlement. Considering the fact that there may be 10 million suburban households to which such a figure applies, and that it is an annual figure, it seems that the costs of suburban sprawl are significant even in this age of affluence.

Moreover, postwar suburban expansion has been wasteful in its use of land. Land use (including parks and other permanent open space as "used") may have been lavish in the sense that different forms of housing would have required far less land. But the area of land not in any recognizable use has been substantial, often as much as was actually used for urban purposes. Land has gone out of farming, is not used for purposeful forestry although perhaps supporting a stand of trees, and has no recognizable or measurable use; but it has not yet gone into any form of urban use. Such land may be called idle, vacant, or undeveloped. The area of such land within "urbanized areas" as defined by the Bureau of the Census is considerable, and there are additional but less clearly defined idle areas more remote from the city. Some of the land idle or vacant at one point in time will be drawn into more definite use later, as infilling takes place. But infilling seems to be slow and in any case may not reduce the public costs involved in the initial sprawl. If facilities such as sewers are built initially with capacity to accommodate the later infilling, then the cost of idle capacity is large. If such facilities are built originally to accommodate only the developed areas and later expanded as development proceeds, then the economies of scale are lost. If the idle or vacant lands were taken over for some form of permanent public open space, the density of residence would not be changed, but the land would no longer be idle, as the term is used here.

Many critics have decried the kinds of residential suburbs built as lacking in aesthetic value; and the intermixture of idle land and developed suburbs have been especially criticized. One may argue that aesthetics is a matter of individual taste and that suburban housing has met the standards of those who live in it. But others will point out that many of the purchasers of this housing really had little choice, because little else was available. Whatever one thinks of the inside of suburban houses, the land on which they were placed has typically been denuded of all vegetation during the house-building process, after which the new owner struggled for years to grow lawn, shrubs, and trees—hoping that the latter would get big enough to swing a hammock from by the time the mortgage is paid off. Some efforts at different use of land have been undertaken, some with great success, but many zoning authorities have resisted such efforts.

Most serious of all its disadvantages is the fact that the suburban land conversion process in the postwar years has not produced housing for a full half of the population; its costs have simply been too great. Frequently, the suburban governmental unit has intended that the cost of new housing should be beyond the reach of middle- and lower-income groups, for such people were simply not wanted. The imperfections in the suburban land market, plus other factors, have led to land costs per dwelling unit that were high and rising. Houses built on such lots have had to be high-priced, if the total package of house and lot was to seem reasonable in price in relation to its characteristics. Housing construction costs have in any case trended upward as rapidly as income per capita, because a large proportion of such costs have been directly or indirectly for labor. As long as there is a fraction of the population with incomes less than half of the median, that fraction is unlikely to be able to afford to buy new houses. But the overall economic and social consequences of a suburbanization directed toward the upper half of the income scale have been very great. Total urban population is becoming increasingly stratified by race, income, and occupation, creating or exacerbating severe social stresses and strains. It may well be that suburban land conversion should not be charged with full responsibility for what has happened, since some of it arises out of deeper and more pervasive social and and economic forces, but surely the land conversion process as such must bear at least part of the responsibility.

These shortcomings of the suburbanization process grow directly out of the form of the suburban land market if indeed they are not caused by it. The structure and functioning of the market, in turn, is partly a matter of public action. As long as the suburban land market continues to operate so as to ratchet land prices upward, stimulated by favorable tax concessions and other public programs and policies, then discontiguous suburban settlement and high-priced houses will result. No significant change in results can be expected unless major changes are made in the market.

Some of these disadvantages occur because too much manpower and too much entrepreneurial talent have gone into suburban land speculation, into working out arrangements for suburban residential and other construction, and into wheeling and dealing generally—and such efforts have been rewarded more generously than necessary. One has only to read the accounts of the three area studies reported in Part II, to see that a great deal of time and ingenuity went into land deals there. Some entrepreneurial input, to secure the best combination of factors of production such as land and labor, would have been needed in any case. But the imperfections of the suburban land market and the rising prices of land offered a fertile field for the "operator," who typically took advantage of the opportunity. Any country which imposes price controls or marketing restrictions quickly finds that a substantial amount of time and talent of its citizens goes into efforts to circumvent such controls or restrictions. As noted earlier in this chapter, the rewards of thwarting plans and controls have frequently been greater than those of conforming to them, and so a lot of effort has gone into such thwarting.

While so much money, energy, and maneuvering were producing a high rate of activity in suburban land conversion, very little progress was made in rebuilding the decaying residential areas of the city. Under private auspices there has been a limited amount of converting such areas into commercial buildings or luxury housing. Under public auspices there has been some renewal of old residential areas and slums for continued, though different, residential uses. But the vast bulk of older and generally substandard housing has not been replaced and has been improved to only a limited degree. The amount of effort directed toward improving the older housing has been minuscule in comparison with efforts to build new suburbs, and for the very good reason that more money was to be made by keeping older areas unimproved and harvesting tax depreciation allowances than by improving them. Perhaps one should not charge suburban land conversion with the short-comings of renewal in older areas, but both have been part of the total urban processes in the postwar years.

And finally, programs such as control of air pollution and development of co-ordinated regional transportation, which must necessarily be undertaken on a metropolitan scale, have been made difficult, if not nearly impossible, by the fragmentation of government in metropolitan areas. Such fragmentation has taken place largely because each suburban community wants to be "independent" in some sense. The physical and economic city has outgrown the legal and political one with the active aid of suburbs. While this is not the direct result of the suburban land conversion process alone, both have been the result of settlement patterns and attitudes of people in suburban areas.

Ideal Standards and Practical Improvements

An evaluation of suburban land conversion by some ideal standard is unrealistic from various points of view. There is almost sure to be a lack of full agreement as to the standard. Moreover, in a complex process which necessarily involves many individuals and groups, shortfall in some respect is inevitable. It can be argued, of course, that measurement against an unrealizable standard is still worthwhile; that the degree of approximation toward the ideal is more significant than whether it is actually attained.

But it might also be useful to consider ways of seeking some practical improvement. Could the process of suburban land conversion be better, in some sense of the term, than it currently is? In what directions might improvement be sought? Some may argue that progress is not possible unless there are clearly defined common goals toward which action can be directed. But many situations arise in the world where people of quite different philosophies or ideologies can nevertheless agree on pragmatic steps to remedy an admittedly imperfect situation. Communist, socialist, and private enterprise societies may unite on a world health program, for instance. One may be struck by the similarity of specific proposals, once the ideological statements have been made for the record. Chapter 17 will explore some of the ways in which the process of suburban land conversion can be changed to move toward goals which will be widely accepted.

ANOTHER GENERATION OF THE PRESENT SUBURBANIZATION PROCESS

I f the present processes of suburban land conversion continue to the year 2000, what results are likely? What reason is there to expect that the cities and suburbs of 2000 will be anything but more of the same that we have now? To what extent might processes of the recent past and of the present lead to something different in the future, owing to changing elements in the system and in the whole economy and society?

Some changes, of course, are inevitable; nothing stands still for long in a dynamic world. But the process of suburban land conversion has changed only gradually since the war, and the changes have not been significant. For the present, let us assume that something like the postwar rate of change will continue, without attempting to specify what it may include.

This chapter is written in recognition of the serious social, racial, economic, and related problems which afflict most American cities, especially the larger ones and especially their older centers. It can reasonably be argued that the United States faces as divisive a situation as at any time since the Civil War. Any thoughtful citizen must have been gravely disturbed at some of the events in the larger cities during the past decade. In this total urban situation, the lily-white suburb is surely a major part and must bear a major part of the responsibility for the whole situation. Urban problems must engage the most earnest attention of governments at all levels and of citizens of both political parties and of many economic and social groups. Any program to improve this situation will almost surely have some repercussions on suburban land conversion. However, urban problems go far beyond suburban land conversion, if the latter be defined with any clarity.

Suburban growth and suburban land conversion, if considered only as a means of providing new homes for the upper half of the income scale, do not face a real crisis. The processes and the results we now have are not the best attainable, but there has not been and there will not be a real breakdown in the process. The United States can continue a process of slow evolution in its city-growing mechanisms, and probably will do so. The results will not be perfect or even as good as reasonably attainable, but neither will they be chaos. Findings of this study show that there is plenty of land in suburbs to accommodate urban expansion for another generation. Implicit in the findings is the fact that life in the suburbs is not intolerable but rather pleasant, and that the suburbs are well-regarded by those who live in them. This too does not deny the possibility and the desirability of improvement, but it does deny imminence of disaster for the people who can afford suburban housing.

METHODOLOGY AND APPROACHES OF THE CHAPTER

In any projection of the future, it is possible to set up a formal model with equations and numbers and to explore the effect of alternative coefficients and numbers. A model is not necessarily more accurate simply because it is more formal, and a formal model may mislead the unwary into assuming that it has an accuracy that in fact it does not possess. The critical factors for both formal models and less formal procedures are the formulas or relationships between various variables and the results. In the suburbanization process, there are many such relationships, some of which are imperfectly known. Many of the past relationships might be changed in the future, or at least the possibility of change must be considered. The opportunity for conscious choice is assumed to exist; the relationships, past or future, are not unchangeable.

For the present purposes, exact figures for projections of the future are probably not necessary. We must consider, for example, the total population numbers at any future date as part of any projection. It is impossible, or past experience would so suggest, to make exact population projections for a relatively distant future date, but a general increase in population of the United States seems fairly certain, barring some catastrophic war. If a particular figure is projected for the year 2000, it may not matter much whether it is realized in 1995 or in 2005, or a little earlier or a little later. General relationships, general directions of change, general rates of change may be more important than specific figures; a "ball park" range may be quite adequate.

For the foregoing reasons, and partly as a matter of personal style in research, a formal model of suburban land conversion has not been set up, though it may be a desirable next step in research. Discussion in this chapter is based upon a more informal analysis.

The concern of this book is primarily with the spatial arrangement—city vs. suburb, or one part of a suburb vs. another—of whatever population is projected, and the effect of that spatial arrangement upon living styles, costs of and returns from living, and the like. These aspects of urban life are not easily measured or quantified, and most econometric projections have omitted them.

Many aspects of the national society and economy are relatively unaffected by the settlement pattern. For instance, it seems probable that the total population at any future date is not a function of the degree and form of suburbanization. People will have children and old people will die, almost irrespective of where they live. It is true that families with small children may move to the suburbs, but these same families might have had just as many children, and no more, if they lived in the central city. Their style of life would have been different, to some degree, but not the number of their children. Similarly, average income per capita may not be affected much by where people live, although it may affect where they can afford to live and will live if given a choice. It might be argued, of course, that people are more productive when they live in one place than in another, but one would be hard pressed to defend or measure such differences.

A great deal of the totality of a national society and economy is related to total population and to average income per capita. For present purposes, it is assumed that these are determined by sociological, technological, and other factors so that they are "givens" for this study of suburban growth and development. The concern here is to consider the settlement pattern under assumed population and income conditions.

GENERAL SHAPE OF THE ECONOMY AND SOCIETY

For specific data on future total population, number of households, and average disposable income, this book draws on the studies of others. (Table 37) Pickard, utilizing census data, has made population projections in total and for the metropolitan areas of the United States and of different major regions. His work was published in 1967, which means that the latest data available to him were those for 1965. If done today, it is possible that slightly lower population projections would be made, in view of the marked downturn in birth rates in the past few years. However, the general pattern of his population projections seems reasonable: an increase of about a third in national population from 1960 to 1980; a slightly smaller relative increase from 1980 to 2000; the rate of increase in his Atlantic Metropolitan Region (which is somewhat more inclusive than our Northeastern Urban Complex) slightly lower than for the United States as a whole in each period; an increasing proportion of the total population within metropolitan areas;

TABLE 37

POPULATION, HOUSEHOLDS, AND DISPOSABLE PERSONAL INCOME PER CAPITA, UNITED STATES AND THE NORTHEAST, 1960, 1980, AND 2000

Item	Unit	United States			Atlantic Metropolitan Region		
		1960	1980	2000	1960	1980	2000
Population, total	million	179	240	314	43	56	71
Portion metropolitan	percent	68	74	79	88	89	90
Households	million	53	70	92	12½	16½	21
Disposable personal income per capita	index	100	153	220	–	–	–

Sources: Total population and portion metropolitan: Jerome P. Pickard, *Dimensions of Metropolitanism,* Urban Land Institute, Research Monograph 14 (Washington: 1967), p. 32. Households: data for 1960 for United States from Hans H. Landsberg, Leonard L. Fischman, and Joseph L. Fisher, *Resources in America's Future* (Johns Hopkins Press for Resources for the Future, 1963), p. 517. Other years and other areas assume same average household size. These give minimum figures for the future, since the number of households has risen faster in the past than has the total population (the ratio of households to population rising nearly a fourth from 1900 to 1960) and is likely to continue to do so. See L. Jay Atkinson, "Long-term Influences Affecting the Volume of New Housing Units," *Survey of Current Business* (November 1963). Disposable personal income per capita: *Resources in America's Future,* p. 551.

and the proportion in such areas at each date higher for the Northeast than for the nation. Without accepting his figures as precisely right—and equally, without rejecting them as in error—we can say that the general relationships they reveal seem reasonable and pertinent to the present purpose.

The number of households may change somewhat differently from the total population, if the tendency toward single-person households (both younger and older people) should continue. But, on the basis of the same average household size in 1980 and in 2000 in the Northeast as in the United States (which gives a minimum figure in relation to total population), the numbers nationally increase by 17 million from 1960 to 1980 and by 22 million from 1980 to 2000, and by 4 and 4½ million, respectively, in the Northeast. Disposable personal income per capita is expected to rise by about half in each 20-year period, or to more than double by the turn of the century. Again, without either accepting this precise figure or trying to estimate a different one, we may accept this change as probable.

A doubling of real personal income in a generation will obviously have significant effects upon expenditure and consumption patterns. Several will have special relevance for land use. The trend in expenditures for recreation of all kinds, and for outdoor recreation in particular, as percentages of disposable income seems to be upward. If a larger percentage of a larger average income per person for a growing total population is spent on outdoor recreation, then a substantially larger total expenditure will be made for this purpose. This will require additional areas for outdoor recreation and additional transportation capacity to get people from their homes to the recreation areas and back again. Thus it will have an impact upon land use, suburban and other. An increasing proportion of the people will live in metropolitan areas and probably within relatively urbanized portions of those metropolitan areas; the outdoor recreation areas may lie in the more remote parts of the same metropolitan regions, or elsewhere, but in any case likely to require travel. The weekend traffic jam is likely to continue to rise in comparison with the weekday work-home traffic.

With higher real incomes, people will almost surely spend more for housing, even if the percentage of their income going to this use should decline modestly. Some of this spending will be for more expensive and more luxuriously equipped houses; some for larger yards; some for more luxurious apartments with no private yards; and some, perhaps a good deal, for a second, a third, and even a fourth alternative housing unit. The family that has wanted a vacation home but could not afford one may both be able to afford it and decide to acquire it; the family that has had a summer vacation home may decide to get a winter one as well, and other combinations of multiple homes may arise. All of this will have its impact upon essentially urban uses of land. More land will be required, both directly for more housing units (and perhaps larger average land areas per housing unit) and also for shopping districts, and the like.

The future is likely to see some developments in travel technology that could be highly important for land use. The automobile is already widely spread, yet ownership among the residents of downtown larger cities, especially among the poor, is relatively low. More of these people will have money to buy a car, and more affluent people may buy more cars per family. Mounting air pollution problems in the larger cities could curtail automobile use; more probably they will force changes in the kind of power unit in the auto so as to produce less air pollution. More automobiles and greater mileage per auto will require much more capacity in highways, and this in turn will require somewhat more land. The private automobile will continue to be a major force for spreading of the suburban pattern. If one must in any case drive to work, to shop, to play, then an extra mile or two may not be important. In this respect, the most likely trend in travel technology is to reinforce the suburban land use trends of the recent past.

The one travel technology now under discussion which might have a major impact upon the pattern of urban and suburban development and upon the relationship between metropolitan areas is the gravity vacuum tube.[1] This would require relatively deep tunnels built in the form of long arcs curving downward away from each point and upward toward the next point, so that the acceleration of gravity could be utilized in the first part of the journey and the deceleration of gravity in the second part. Without discomfort to the riders, the vehicle could attain speeds which would be impossible on level tract. By using near-vacuum within the tunnel, trains could move with a minimum of resistance and hence a minimum of power required. Attainable speeds would be partly a function of distance between stops, but would greatly exceed anything now available for surface or subsurface transportation. With a maximum attainable speed of 420 miles per hour, an average speed of 175 miles per hour could be achieved for stops 16 miles apart; 142 miles per hour for stops 7 miles apart; ranging downward to only 45 miles per hour for stops 1 mile apart. With 12 intermediate stops, travel time for downtown New York to downtown Washington would be 1 hour and 12 minutes; with 6 intermediate stops, just over 50 minutes travel time. Comparably short times between other major points are estimated for this method.

A gravity vacuum system of rapid transport would have some serious problems. Its costs would be relatively high, although new methods of digging might lower these considerably compared to past tunnelling. The fact that its tunnels would be deep would mean minimum interference with surface activities. The problem of getting people to, and away from, its major nodal points by any system of surface transportation would surely be serious. The technology would be financially feasible only with large volumes of people, yet these would create more difficult congestion problems around its nodes. It is impossible to provide a firm estimate of the date when such a transportation system might be placed in operation. Yet it is surely a new technique more or less on the horizon. If something like this were to come into use, it would be a powerful force tying the various metropolitan areas of the Northeast into a system, and also tying people into their own metropolitan area.

A brief consideration of natural resource problems in general is warranted in connection with discussion of the suburban land problems of the next generation. More people and higher real incomes per person will obviously produce a greater demand for natural resources. However, the impact of these greater demand factors upon the supply of natural resources is not as great as one might expect. The resource component of gross national product has been declining and promises to

[1] Lawrence K. Edwards, "Urban Gravity–Vacuum Transit System," *Transportation Engineering Journal* (February 1969).

continue to decline, primarily for two reasons: more of our GNP consists of services and relatively less of goods; and the extent of processing of raw materials increases more or less steadily, so that value added per unit of raw materials increases. Moreover, technological and other changes have led to more efficiency in use of many raw material inputs and to the substitution of more common for the scarcer materials—e.g., plastics for metals. Thus it appears that scarcity and/or high prices of raw material inputs will not be a serious factor affecting the well-being of the American people for at least a generation and probably for much longer.[2]

But the quality of resources that will be available in the future is a far more serious problem than their quantity. There may be enough water for urban and industrial uses, but how badly polluted will it be? There may be ample land for suburban expansion, but will it be degraded by unsightly commercial advertising or other developments? Will its forest cover have been stripped off needlessly, or will erosion from suburban land be silting up our streams?

Planned and integrated programs for construction and management of the urban and suburban environment are likely to become both necessary and possible for the next generations. Mere prevention of spoliation will not be enough. Ways now exist or can be developed to make presently unattractive areas (vacant land, highway borders, occupied building sites, and many others) very much more attractive. This will require investment of capital and entrepreneurship; more importantly, it will involve the matter of externalities and interdependencies considered in Chapter 9. If I fix up my land, so that it is attractive to every beholder, I gain only part of the increased "output." Likewise, if my neighbor improves his land, my value is thereby enhanced. Regardless of whether suburbs evolve "naturally" as we assume in this chapter, or whether major social measures are taken to influence the pattern of suburban growth, programs to improve and to manage the urban and suburban environment seem highly desirable for the future, indeed almost indispensable. The problems are large, and they are more social and organizational than technical. But the potential rewards are considerable. Still, it does seem that the continued evolution of suburbs along the present lines is not likely by itself to produce improved suburban resource management.

HOUSING AND SUBURBAN EXPANSION

If total population and number of households expand as suggested in Table 37, then significant additional amounts of housing will be required. By definition, a household is a separate housing unit. As noted in Chapter 3, formation of new households is a function of income levels as well as of total numbers of people. If incomes are low, some persons live with others—children remaining with parents, sometimes even after marriage, older parents living with adult children, two or more adults sharing apartments, and the like—while many of these same persons

---

[2] This is an oversimplified statement of the research by Resources for the Future reported particularly in Hans H. Landsberg, Leonard L. Fischman, and Joseph L. Fisher, *Resources in America's Future* (Johns Hopkins Press for Resources for the Future, 1963).

would have established their own households if they could have afforded to do so. Under the assumptions of Table 37 as to rising real income per capita, we may assume that the number of persons who share living quarters with others because they cannot afford separate space will decline, but it is unlikely to vanish.

At a minimum, then, the nation will require 17 million new housing units between 1960 and 1980 and 22 million between 1980 and 2000, just for the increase in number of households. But this is far below the real requirement. For one thing, much housing is now substandard; since substandardness is partly a psychological matter, as average incomes rise, some housing which might have been passable at one stage will no longer be acceptable. For another, some housing now tolerable is almost certain to deteriorate further from age alone, and thus become substandard even when it is not so today. Some of the nearly 8 million housing units that were more than 60 years old in 1960 would be considered substandard now, even if they were new, for they lack plumbing, heating, wiring, or other features considered essential today or have rooms that are too small, or were built by construction methods no longer acceptable. And age has certainly not improved them. Some older houses are excellent, of course. But some built since 1900 were unattractive or unacceptable in 1960. And another 40 years of aging is unlikely to improve any of these houses. More than 12 million housing units built before World War I and still existing in 1960 must be removed by 2000 as well as nearly an equal number of more recent vintage. To these estimates of housing removals and net additions to housing stock to accommodate additional households, must be added some allowance for more than one housing unit per household.

All of this adds up to a total "need" for *new* housing units of the general magnitude of 60 to 65 million between 1960 and 2000—39 million for additional households, 24 million as more or less minimum replacement, plus something for vacation or other second homes making more than one unit per household. This compares with 58 million housing units of all kinds (houses, apartments, etc.) in 1960. This is the basis for a common statement that dwelling unit construction from 1960 to 2000 must double the number of existing units as of 1960. For the present purpose, the precise figure is not critical. It is hard to see how it can be much below 60 million units, which would provide no real up-grading of the housing stock; and it might rise to 70 or more million if housing standards really improved. The significant thing is that it is *large* compared with 1960 conditions. A great deal of the urban housing of 1960 must be rebuilt, and a great deal of new housing must be added. We now have both the opportunity to direct the pattern of urban and suburban growth and change, and the necessity of doing so.

From several points of view, it would be helpful to examine this matter of housing "need" or housing "demand" more fully, and to seek numerical expression of the effect of different factors. However, some of the policy issues or alternatives may be considered without making a detailed empirical inquiry. First of all, how much, if any, of the new housing will be available to people in the lower half or lower fourth of the income distribution? Virtually no new unsubsidized housing in the past has been within the capacity of the lower-income people to buy; and the trend seems away from them, not toward them. In particular, the trend toward higher land prices in suburban areas, and thus the trend toward larger and more expensive homes, has been away from the purchase of new suburban homes by lower-income people. It might appear, at first glance, that the rising average incomes, projected in Table 37, would improve the situation of the lower-income people, as far as buying new houses is concerned. However, rising real incomes per capita are likely to be paralleled by rising wages in the construction and related fields, so that the cost of new houses is apt to move up about as much as the income of the lower-income sectors of the population. Thus, if suburban land conversion in the next generation goes forward more or less as it has in the past generation, then it is doubtful if much new housing construction will be purchasable by lower-income people unless it is heavily subsidized.

The improbability of new housing construction for lower-income people focuses attention on the "filtering down" process. In the past, low-income people have bought or rented "used" housing, as they have often bought used automobiles, used furniture, or other partially depreciated consumption items. This process can be criticized on economic, sociological, psychological, and other grounds, but it has played a large role in American housing. Moreover, it affects people who sell used houses as well as people who buy them; a market for a used house may be as important to the family that wishes to upgrade its housing as the market for used automobiles is to the family that contemplates purchase of a new car.

In the past, unfortunately, "filtering down" has all too often been synonymous with "running down," as far as housing was concerned. Well-maintained housing in well-maintained neighborhoods has often kept its value, and in the postwar years, it has generally increased considerably in value. This is fine. But it has also meant that only the housing and/or the neighborhoods which were declining in "quality" were available for filtering down to lower-income people. One interesting possibility is to explore ways in which the physical and aesthetic quality of housing and of neighborhoods can be maintained and yet produce a decline in the price of the housing sufficient to make it available to a lower-income group. The rate at which new housing is built and thus releases old, so that the latter filters down, is not invariable; perhaps some means could actully be devised to speed up the filtering down and at the same time retard the running down. To the extent that the construction of new housing is stimulated, the supply of new houses rises and the price of used housing must fall. Conversely, to the extent that the construction of new housing is retarded or depressed, the supply of new houses is reduced and the filtering-down process is slower. Thus, the ultimate incidence of a reduced rate of new construction, because of higher interest charges or for other reasons, may well be upon the consumers of the most filtered-down housing units, those at the margin of acceptance. It is well known that low-income people often pay more rent in proportion to what they actualy get than middle- and higher-income people, for their alternatives are often more limited.

All of this has an important racial dimension. Much of the filtered-down housing has been occupied by blacks, Puerto Ricans, and other minority racial or ethnic groups, in part because their incomes were lower. Because the filtered-down housing is generally also badly run down, these groups have often occupied poor or substandard housing; and they have often paid prices for it which were quite excessive, for its quality. An acceleration of filtering down of housing is thus of particular concern to such minority groups. Any program which could maintain the quality of such housing but still make it available is of particular importance to them. The rate at which new housing is built in the suburbs, and the prices at which it is available, may have significant effect upon the cost and the quality of the filtered-down housing in the older city areas. This is one of the ways in which the future of the suburbs and the future of the older city are directly interrelated.

Aging Phenomena

The one factor that may make the suburban expansion process of the period around the year 2000 markedly different from the past, even if one assumes no consciously designed and operated programs for change, is the aging process in general. Every building in 2000 will be 30 years older than it was in 1970, if it still stands, just as every man in 2000 will also be 30 years older than he was in 1970, if he is still alive. Time runs continuously and at the same real speed, despite occasional science fiction and the common tendency to think that somehow it is running faster than it once did. What might the aging process of established cities and suburbs actually do that would change the suburban land conversion process in 2000?

Of the 58 million dwelling units enumerated by the Census in 1960, more than a fourth had been built after 1950, and nearly 40 percent had probably been built after World War II. (Table 38) More than 13 percent of the housing units had been built before the turn of the century, and about a fourth before World War I. Many of these older units were on farms or in small towns; some have been abandoned since 1960, partly because they are no longer habitable, partly because the farm was no longer operated as a separate unit or because the village itself was

TABLE 38

HOUSING UNITS REMOVED AND REMAINING, BY DECADES

(*millions*)

Period built	Number in 1960	Estimated number remaining in				Estimated number to be removed in decade of			
		1970	1980	1990	2000	1960s	1970s	1980s	1990s
Before 1890	2.9	1.6	0.5	0.1	0.0	1.3	1.1	0.4	0.1
1890–1899	4.9	4.0	2.3	0.6	0.1	0.9	1.7	1.7	0.5
1900–1909	5.4	4.9	4.0	2.3	0.6	0.5	0.9	1.7	1.7
1910–1919	5.6	5.2	4.7	3.8	2.2	0.4	0.5	0.9	1.6
1920–1929	8.6	8.1	7.5	6.8	5.5	0.5	0.6	0.7	1.3
1930–1939	5.6	5.4	5.1	4.7	4.3	0.2	0.3	0.4	0.4
1940–1949	9.3	9.0	8.6	8.2	7.6	0.3	0.4	0.4	0.6
1950–1959	16.0	15.5	15.0	14.4	13.6	0.5	0.5	0.6	0.8
Total	58.3	53.7	47.7	40.9	33.9	4.6	6.0	6.8	7.0

Source: Marion Clawson, "Urban Renewal in 2000," *Journal of the American Institute of Planners* (May 1968), p. 175.

slowly being abandoned. But a great many of them were in cities, nearly always in the more central part, if not the actual "downtown," of the older city. Some of the latter were single-family homes; many were apartments. Our information about housing, by type, location, and other characteristics, and also by age, is very poor. Even Table 38 had to be constructed by methods which make the results an approximation rather than an enumeration.[3] It is difficult to obtain reliable information on building age, in part because present occupants simply do not know how old their residences are, but a fruitful line of study of the future of various areas within cities would be to accumulate information on the age of structures and on the rate at which they are replaced because of age.

On the basis of estimated past rates of housing replacement, it was estimated that virtually all of the housing units constructed before 1900 would be replaced by 2000 and that very few pre-World War I units would still remain. (Table 38) Replacement of the relatively large numbers of units built in the 1920s would be begun by 2000, although more than half of these units were estimated to remain in use after 2000. Some replacement of still younger units was estimated, in part because of fires, other natural causes, shifts in population, and obsolescence.

Will housing replacement rates in the next 30 years average the same as they have in the past 60 years or more? For a housing unit to be replaced, its former owner or a new purchaser must conclude that a new unit will be more profitable than the old one; he must have or be able to borrow the necessary capital to finance the replacement; he must be able to obtain a site of reasonable area (not necessarily the same as the present site size); and necessary permission must be obtained from zoning and building authorities. This is a formidable list of conditions. Many old and relatively degraded residential rental properties (apartments, usually) are still profitable to the owner, in part because he can charge off depreciation based on the price he paid for the property, and thus obtain a substantial cash flow not subject to income tax. As noted earlier, the optimum holding period for any owner for such property is about eight years; after that, he can often sell at a price which yields him a profit and enables the new owner to repeat the process, as long as the property can meet health and housing standards and is habitable by someone who will pay rent. While these relationships underlie the estimates of housing unit replacement in Table 38, it is by no means clear that they will operate at the same speed in the future as in the past, especially if average incomes rise as estimated in Table 37.

A substantial infusion of new capital is needed to rebuild deteriorating housing, whether apartments or single-family homes. Present owners may not have the capital and may be unable to borrow it. It is here that some of the externalities discussed in Chapter 9 are likely to come into play. A single property owner is unlikely to rebuild or to find it profitable if he did; the whole neighborhood, community, or district may have to be rebuilt. The unit of area for rebuilding may be quite different from the present ownership units; generally, much larger sites

[3] See Marion Clawson, "Urban Renewal in 2000," *Journal of the American Institute of Planners* (May 1968).

are required, and this means a problem in site assembly. The potential rebuilder and the planning and/or zoning authority must agree on the type of housing to be built, if the residential area is to be rebuilt to residential uses; and what seems most desirable from a public viewpoint may not be most profitable from a private one, and vice versa.

Nevertheless, the rate at which older residential areas of cities are rebuilt during the next generation may be a major factor affecting the demand for suburban building. While there are many variables in the situation, the further aging of presently rather old and substandard residential property is inexorable and may well have a significant effect on suburban growth in the future.

The other area in which aging might have a significant effect is for the more modest suburban areas built immediately after World War II. In the rush to meet the pressing housing situation of that period, many single-family houses were built that can most charitably be described as mediocre—some with substandard design or construction methods, some in poorly designed neighborhoods, some with other deficiencies. Housing built from 1947 through 1955 will be from 45 to 53 years old in 2000. While many houses of these ages are still in good physical shape, and many neighborhoods of this age are still highly attractive, yet much of the more mediocre housing will definitely have passed its peak. Jerry-built houses will be seriously on the down grade; many neighborhoods will be moving downward also. Neighborhoods and houses of this age category will vary greatly in their original character and in the degree to which they have slid downhill. Some will have been fine homes in good neighborhoods, both well-maintained over the years, but others will have been poor to begin with and poorly maintained, with still others in intermediate conditions.

Might some of these suburbs in a decade or two from now have deteriorated to the point where they are ripe for a take-over by low-income racial or ethnic groups? In the past, such take-overs in older housing areas have more often followed than preceded a decline in neighborhood quality. Far from depreciating property values, such changes in neighborhood character have often helped to sustain property values that were already on the decline. Ethnic and racial take-overs have been common in older sections of most large cities, in the postwar period (earlier, in some cities). Might such take-overs spread to suburbs, in a large way, in the next generation? Until now, zoning, social pressures, limitations on credit, and other measures have often operated to prevent blacks and other minorities from moving into suburbs, and especially to prevent an influx of lower-income people. Such people have viewed—and rightly viewed—the suburbs as generally hostile to them. But might not these barriers be overtopped, so that there might be a major migration of lower-income racial and ethnic groups from older city areas into suburbs? Much will depend upon the attitudes of the groups concerned. But the inexorable aging process is creating a suburban situation ripe for a late 20th century migration of low-income blacks and other minority groups from the older cities to some of the poorer suburbs. If such a migration once began, it is hard to know where it might stop. Is it conceivable that some day the present black-core/white-ring relationship might be completely reversed?

Alternatives in Urban Expansion

Still retaining the assumption of no major or designed changes in past suburban land conversion processes, it is possible to consider a number of alternatives in urban expansion over the next generation. If an econometric model were constructed, several alternative ratios or numbers could be used at various strategic points. As noted just above, the rate of rebuilding aging and other residential properties would have an effect upon suburbanization rates and processes. Table 38 contemplates that nearly 25 million housing units will be replaced between 1960 and 2000, more than 42 percent of those existing in 1960. This estimate is based on past rates of replacement of older housing units. It is not difficult to imagine situations under which the replacement rate might be much slower or much faster. The difficulties of renewing decaying older sections of cities have been described; private efforts at such renewal have been relatively ineffective in the past. On the other hand, even the assumed rate of renewal would leave nearly 13 million housing units of 60 years and over, in 2000, of which some might be good or even superior housing but many would surely be marginal or substandard. A total renewal of housing units from as few as 15–18 million units to as many as 30–35 million units, is within the bounds of possibility for the 1960–2000 period.

A part of the area now used for the housing to be replaced would be in demand for nonhousing purposes—stores, offices, etc. We lack any information on the area of land now occupied by these older dwelling units. On the basis of the data in Appendix Table 5 for the Northeastern Urban Complex, a release of 40 percent of the residential land (if, indeed, the 40 percent of the dwelling units likely to be removed now occupy 40 percent of the residential land) would provide six times the present commercial acreage and more than double the present commercial and industrial average. Consequently it seems probable that most land cleared of old residential units could not find a use for such purposes; rebuilding of housing, though perhaps of a different form (apartments instead of single-family houses, for instance) would be necessary for most of it. Would the rebuilt housing accommodate the same number, or more, or fewer people than the housing it replaced? Probably more, for apartments would more often replace single-family homes than the reverse, but it is hard to say how much more. If we assume that housing units of average occupancy are replaced, such units had from 45 to 107 million people in 1960; if the total population in 2000 is 314 million as suggested in Table 37, then from a seventh to a third of the population in 2000 would be housed in replaced housing, assuming all replaced housing went back into housing and at the same average occupancy rate. These are obviously the crudest kind of estimates, given simply to suggest the possible ranges. If we assume further that some part of those not accommodated by replaced housing would otherwise move to the suburbs in search of new housing, the implications for suburban land conversion start to emerge.

Of the increasing population who may settle in the suburbs between now and 2000, how many will choose to live in suburban high-rise apartments and how many will choose to live in single-family houses? This is the kind of a question on which the experience of the past few years yields quite contrasting answers. As Neutze has pointed out, up to about 1960 nearly all the new residential units in suburbs were single-family homes; but in the early 1960's, the portion of housing units with two or more units per structure rose to over 40 percent nationally and in some suburbs has risen to well over half.[4] In the fairly early postwar years, many observers of the urban scene were convinced that there was a strong, even an over-powering, desire on the part of most families to own their own house in a suburban location; the experience up to that date supported such a view. However, as noted in Chapter 3, a complex of factors was operative in those years, and the desire of people to have a single-family house in the suburbs may have been much over-estimated. The suburban apartment boom of the 1960's suggests the possibility that suburban development over the next generation will be a mixture of single-family houses and apartments. However, will the mixture be 90 percent single-family houses with 10 percent apartments, or will it be 50–50? Since the residential density might easily differ by a factor of 10 or more, the assumption on this point obviously will affect total land requirement greatly. Recent experience with apart-ments in suburbs suggests the possibility that in the future this form of housing might be accompanied by use of large areas of land attached to each large apart-ment structure for the recreation and other enjoyment of the occupants, so that the average density per unit of land area might be considerably different from that associated with apartments in the past. In all of these ways, different assumptions might be introduced into an econometric model, even one which assumed no major changes from the past suburban conversion of land.

Whatever may be the proportion of future suburban dwellers who live in single-family houses, how large will be the average lots or what will be the average density of residential areas? Past experience is somewhat varied on this point, ap-parently, and in any case may not be a reliable guide for the future. In some metro-politan areas there has apparently been no trend toward larger average lots. Indeed, in the Wilmington area there seems to have been a trend toward smaller suburban lots. In virtually all metropolitan areas, average lot size is larger in the suburbs than in the older cities, so that the average density for the whole metropolitan area has been declining; but we are less sure how general, or how great, this has been *within* the suburban areas.

But lot size is not primarily within the decision-making scope of the suburban dweller or even of the suburban builder. Zoning regulations typically specify lot size. While zoning can be changed, and often is, yet the desire of many suburbs to exclude lower-income families and the use of large lot sizes as a tool to this end is a rather firmly held position. The situation around New York City, as described by the Regional Plan Association in *Spread City*, has been discussed in Chapter 13. Briefly, existing zoning in undeveloped suburban areas would require a much lower density of suburban development than now exists in typical suburbs. If such large lot zoning persists, its effect upon suburban land requirements will be con-siderable. However, if the effective demand is for suburban apartments, the power of local developers to get zoning changed in directions that are profitable to them surely should not be underestimated.

[4] Max Neutze, *The Suburban Apartment Boom* (Resources for the Future, 1968), pp. 9, 100.

Another factor is the extent to which infilling of previously bypassed tracts takes place. This book has emphasized, with data from different sources, how much land lies idle within the generally urbanized areas of the United States. Very little information is available on the rate of infilling of land idle at any given date. Such information as came out of the three case studies suggests that infilling proceeds slowly. There were generally powerful reasons why a tract of land was not developed earlier. Sometimes conditions change, including new estimates of its present and probable future worth, which make development possible, but the time lag between development of land around a particular parcel and the development of that parcel may be very great.

It may be argued that total land requirement for suburban expansion is not affected by the rate of infilling. This may, or may not, be true as regards land actually *used* for various suburban purposes, including parks and other permanent open space. But the extent of the physical outreach of suburban areas is directly affected by the speed of infilling. If past patterns of idle land within generally urbanized areas persist, then the gross extent of suburban land conversion will be much greater than if more infilling takes place, though much of the land will be idle within the outer suburbanized boundary. Again, any econometric model should provide for alternative estimates on this matter.

One estimate of the number, acreage, and population of the larger urbanized areas in the United States and as projected for the future is shown in Table 39.

TABLE 39

NUMBER OF MAJOR URBANIZED AREAS, THEIR AREA, AND THEIR POPULATION, 1920, 1940, 1960, AND PROJECTIONS FOR 1980 AND 2000

Item	Unit	1920	1940	1960	1980	2000
1. Urbanized areas of over 100,000 population each						
Number areas	number	70.0	98.0	160.0	194.0	223.0
Land area	million acres	3.4	5.7	13.8	24.6	38.8
Population	million	34.6	52.4	91.0	148.0	220.5
Density[1]	persons per square mile	6,580.0	5,870.0	4,230.0	3,840.0	3,732.0
2. Urbanized areas of 50,000–99,999 population						
Number areas	number	61.0	92.0	109.0	–	–
Land area	million acres	0.7	1.0	1.7	–	–
Population	million	4.3	5.7	7.7	–	–
Density[1]	persons per square mile	4,050.0	3,740.0	2,940.0	–	–
3. All urbanized areas						
Number areas	number	131.0	190.0	269.0	–	–
Land area	million acres	4.0	6.7	15.4	–	–
Population	million	38.9	58.1	98.7	–	–
Density[1]	persons per square mile	6,160.0	5,560.0	4,090.0	–	–

Source: Jerome P. Pickard, *Dimensions of Metropolitanism*, Research Monograph 14 (Washington: Urban Land Institute, 1967), pp. 48–53.

[1] Calculated in original source from unrounded data; total-population/total-area density.

Pickard has tried to apply the 1960 definition of urbanized area, as used in the census, to earlier periods.[5] The number of both the larger and the smaller urbanized areas, as he defines them, grew from 1920 to 1960; the population of these areas increased somewhat faster than the number, and their acreage grew even more rapidly. As a result, the population per average area has risen, the acreage per average area has increased more, and the density (total-population/total-area) has declined. At each date, some additional urbanized areas were included, as some areas increased enough in population to fall within the definitions used in this study. If the 1960 definition of urbanized areas were indeed used throughout, it seems probable, on the basis of other studies, that a third of the urbanized area was vacant at each date. However, this might not affect the trend in urbanized area much, if any.

Using a method of ratio-trend projection, Pickard estimated the number, population, and total acreage of the larger urbanized areas in 1980 and 2000. These are projections, based upon certain assumptions as to future trends, rather than predictions of what will most probably occur. In addition to projecting a marked rise in number, population, and total acreage of the major urbanized areas, a somewhat lower density was also projected for the future. However, the decline in density projected from 1960 to 2000 was relatively modest.

A number of variables entered into these projections, which cannot be considered in detail here. It is not unlikely that estimates differing by as much as 25 percent up or down could have been obtained by modifying some variables.

The number of people outside of urbanized areas (as defined by Pickard) rose only a little from 1920 to 1960 and from 1960 to 2000 is projected to change hardly at all. Thus, the total area used for all site purposes in the United States probably rose only slightly more than the increase in area shown in urbanized areas from 1920 to 1960, or proportionately rose less rapidly than shown in the table. And because the areas outside of the urbanized areas are almost surely used at a much lower average density, the decline in density of use of all site land in the United States has been proportionately less than shown in the table. Likewise, the projections to 2000 include a modest decline in density within urbanized areas; but, since these areas form a rising proportion of all site land and are probably used at a higher density than areas outside of urbanized areas, the national average density of land use may remain more or less constant in the future. While the density of land use has been falling *within* urbanized areas, it is still higher there than in the smaller towns and open country outside of them. In looking at the increasing use of land for site purposes, it has been the rising total population which has been the chief factor, not the declining density of land use.

EFFECT OF NEW TOWNS ON SUBURBAN LAND CONVERSION

There is a great deal of interest in the United States today in "new towns." Hence it seems desirable briefly to consider how much, if any, they are likely to affect the process of suburban conversion of land during the next generation.

[5] Jerome P. Pickard, *Dimensions of Metropolitanism*, Research Monograph 14, (Washington: Urban Land Institute, 1967).

It is essential to distinguish two quite different ideas which have each been labelled "new towns."

First are the self-standing or "independent" new towns or cities, generally with 50,000 or more residents, in which would be provided jobs for most residents and from which would be drawn most of the labor force for the employment located within the town. Such towns would of course trade with other parts of the United States, drawing raw materials from other areas, exporting and importing various finished products, and having a substantial flow of services back and forth. But there would be relatively little commuting into or out of this type of new town.

Second is the primarily suburban type of new town, closely dependent upon and closely interrelated with a larger and older city reasonably close by. These towns might vary widely in size, but most would fall in the 10,000–50,000 range. There would be considerable commuting from this new town to the older city and probably some commuting from the city to the suburb. The new town might have considerable employment within itself, but there would not be a balance of employment and labor force in total or by kinds of jobs. This type of dependent new town would be large enough to have its own shopping centers and to provide at least part of its own cultural requirements.

There might be a continuum of new towns between these two major types, rather than a sharp dichotomy. Nevertheless, there are basic differences and hence it seems useful to separate them. In particular, the outlook for building new towns differs greatly between these two types.

The primarily suburban new town seems to have real possibilities for the next generation. The planner-developer of such a new town could go far toward internalizing some of the externalities of new suburbs because of the size of the town. In many ways, it can be viewed as a giant subdivision, a logical extension of the single house/small subdivision/large subdivision progression which has taken place over the past generation or two. The planner-developer of such a town could take advantage of the commercial possibilities that its residents would create; he could build into the town many advantages and attractions that would help sell the houses and apartments. The great advertising appeal of the "planned community" in present suburban development is evidence that this type of new town would find considerable consumer acceptance.

There would be great difficulties in bringing off a new town of this type successfully, particularly if it were large enough to internalize a significant part of the externalities. Its developer would require an adequate tract of land—usually from two square miles upward—and, in order to capture the external values he would create, he would need complete ownership of all land within its borders. Moreover, he would have to acquire this land at a reasonable price, in part because development of the town would at best be spread over several years and holding costs would be serious. The land requirement alone will limit the number of such new towns. The developer will require a great deal of capital, either equity or long-term borrowings at reasonable interest and repayment. There will be important problems in design of the new town—its major structures and its public facilities in particular. There will be difficult problems of providing reasonable balance among its residential, commercial, public service, and other parts both during the growing years and at its ultimate development. Government of such a new town will necessarily be in the hands of its developer until a significant resident population is in place, but then transfer of power from him to the citizens may be difficult. In all of these ways, and perhaps in others, new towns of this type will encounter difficult problems. But, assuming that they are reasonably located with respect to an established and economically healthy larger city, their economic base is likely to be adequate.

Although new towns of the basically suburban type are likely to play a larger and perhaps significant role in suburban land conversion over the next generation, it hardly seems possible that they can be the dominant type of suburb for the next two decades. The scale of suburban development required to provide residences for the growing population, the vitality of the smaller developers, and the difficulties of building such new towns would seem likely to limit their role.

The problems of a free-standing new city, of 50,000 or more residents, are much more difficult of solution. Such new towns would face all the problems of the suburban new towns—adequate land base at reasonable cost, large capital requirement, outstanding design, balance among parts during growth and at ultimate scale, transfer of political power, etc.—and at a very much greater and more difficult scale. In addition, lacking an economic base of their own and (by definition) located where commuting to older cities was impractical for a significant part of the labor force, they would face the basic but very difficult problem of developing jobs and housing in approximate coordination. It would be hard to attract residents unless there were jobs, and hard to attract employers unless there were a labor force—and not merely in total, but houses of types and prices demanded by workers actually employed, and workers of the skills and specialities required for the businesses established. Decisions to move to such new towns would be in different hands for the many possible workers and for the various possible employments, and coordination would be extremely difficult.

The financial requirements of self-standing new towns of 50,000 or more people will be very high; the net cash flow will be outward for many years; and the ultimate profit prospects are not bright. It seems highly dubious that private capital alone will undertake many self-standing new towns; public help in acquiring land and holding it until needed would improve the prospects for private development of new towns of this type, but would not guarantee it. Self-standing new towns might be innovative, although there would be powerful forces operating toward conservatism in town structure and functioning, in order not to alienate potential residents and employers. Their construction, especially if successful, might stimulate builders of suburban-type new towns and smaller suburbs to innovate also. In other ways too, the self-standing new towns, even if there should be only a very few of them, might exert a considerable influence. However, it seems quite unlikely that such new towns can provide the locus for more than a very small fraction of the new resident population of the country or for more than a very small fraction of the new jobs.

Investment and Land Values

A considerable investment will be necessary if we are to construct 60 to 70 million housing units over the 40-year period, 1960–2000, to accommodate the additional households that are being formed and to replace the housing which will become substandard in that period. It seems highly probable that the average housing unit will cost more in the future than today, even measured in terms of constant prices, because it is likely to include many additional features. For the whole period, if we assume that the average housing unit costs $25,000 in terms of today's prices, we project an investment of $1,500 billion in housing units alone, including such fixed furnishings as stoves and refrigerators. The investment in social infrastructure such as roads, schools, parks, sewer systems, water systems, and the like, and in necessary business services at the local level, such as stores and other service establishments, might easily run to a similar sum. A total investment of $3,000 billion over a 40-year period means an average of $75 billion a year invested in housing and associated amenities, omitting investments required for jobs and production. The rate would be lower at the beginning of the period and higher toward the end, since the amount would be related to the increase in population in that year. This is a large sum, even for an affluent United States, over the next generation. However, it is not an impossible one, for it is equal to about 5½ percent of the average annual gross national product in those same years, or to about a third of the projected average annual private domestic investment.[6] If fewer housing units, or less expensive ones, or fewer or less costly public and private infrastructure are built, then the average annual investment is proportionately lower. The higher the investments for these purposes within the capacity of the economy to bear them, the greater the impetus to the economy in terms of more employment and higher wages.

If the basic assumption of this chapter—namely, no major changes in the suburban land conversion process—is accepted as a starting point, then it is difficult to see how land prices in suburban areas can be lower than they are today. Indeed, they are more likely to be higher. The present land pricing process has capitalized into it the expected future increases in suburban land prices. Any consensus that prices of land to be converted in the future from rural to urban uses would not be relatively high would pour cold water on present land prices, even of land some years away from a development process. If the land market continues in the future as it has in the past, land prices will continue high and probably rising—surely rising, as between a rural use or rural idle status and an urban development status, but possibly also rising at about the same stage in a development cycle. No attempt is made here to estimate how large these increases in land values will be, or who will gain them. High and/or rising land prices will certainly stimulate the construction of higher-priced houses in the future, as they have in the past; and the higher-priced, because more luxurious, houses will make the higher land prices at least bearable. Either way, new housing for the lower-income half of the population will be difficult or impossible to achieve.

[6] Data on gross national product and private domestic investment taken from Landsberg, Fischman, and Fisher, *Resources in America's Future,* p. 529.

Summary

The present and preceding chapters may be summarized very briefly, in an interpretative way, in this fashion:

A continuation of the process of suburban land conversion, without major efforts to change it (natural evolvement) will lead primarily to much more suburban development of basically the same kind as we have had since World War II. Suburbs will continue to spread outward, with a great deal of idle or vacant land intermingled among the developed subdivisions; costs of public services and of some private activities will be higher than necessary because subdivisions are not contiguous. Prices of undeveloped land are likely to continue upward, though possibly at a slower rate than in the past and with no certainty that they will advance fast enough to be profitable, when allowance is made for alternative investment opportunities. Housing in new suburbs will be too costly for people in the lower half of the income range to buy new houses; such people will be unable to buy new housing, except as it may be heavily subsidized for them. The exact figures on number of people, numbers of new housing units, prices of land, prices of new houses, and the like are relatively unimportant; the direction of the development and the general nature of the result are highly important.

The major factor which might produce something significantly different from the postwar developments is the inexorable aging of existing housing. Housing that is now old and frequently deteriorating should be, and may be, replaced; but at what rate and to what extent cannot be determined at present because both are subject to influence by a number of public and private actions. There is the possibility that before 2000 the lower-income minority groups now concentrated in the central cities might break out, particularly into some of the less desirable suburbs built in the early postwar years. More extensive mobile home colonies might also be built in the suburbs to accommodate some of the lower-income half of the population. If such developments occurred and were coupled with a rebuilding of the central cities into higher-priced housing, we might ultimately see a reversal of the present black, low-income cores and white, upper-income suburbs into white, upper-income cores and black, lower-income suburbs.

17 ALTERNATIVES FOR PLANNED MODIFICATION OF THE SUBURBAN LAND CONVERSION PROCESS

How can we go about improving the process of suburban land conversion? The broad objective of change is to cure or at least reduce the disadvantages of the present process, while at the same time not losing any or much of its advantages. If one seeks social change, one must state the nature of the change desired. Here the focus is on the social mechanisms which can produce change. There is little gain in stating goals which are wholly unattainable; the capacity or means of attaining goals is inevitably a factor in statement of the goals themselves. There has been a considerable amount of popular and semipopular writing about the shortcomings of modern suburbs, but rhetoric alone will produce few improvements. Many of the proposals for improvements strike the present writer as impractical in the sense that, even if adopted, they would not produce the results desired.

In laying out a wide range of specific possibilities in this chapter, I do not wish to give the impression that all are wholly new or original, or that nothing is now being done about them.[1] For example, various efforts are under way to improve the skill of suburban land planning, but the proposal here is for a greatly accelerated effort, that would so change the rate of progress as to constitute a major new measure. It is my hope that the wide range of possible measures discussed in this chapter will provide a perspective for analyzing and judging possible improvements in suburban land conversion.

In outlining a considerable range of possible measures to improve suburban land conversion processes and the whole suburban-urban development process associated therewith, this chapter begins with measures most easily described, most easily visualized, and involving the least drastic change from the past. It proceeds toward measures that are newer and very different, hence less easily described, less easily visualized, and probably less likely to gain popular support, at least in the short run. Almost every one of these measures could be considered and used inde-

---

[1] In this chapter only a few references are cited, and those mostly to my own writings, where the points concerned have been developed more fully. All the preceding chapters and the references cited therein are source materials here. This chapter represents a more or less personal synthesis and interpretation of the earlier parts of the book.

pendently of all others; however, there are major interrelationships among them, and some would importantly complement others if adopted concurrently; near the end of the chapter, we explicitly deal with this matter of interrelationships among various measures. We also consider briefly who might initiate change. Programs might be undertaken in some states, urban areas, or regions, but not necessarily everywhere. The various measures outlined in this chapter do not constitute a specific program of suburbanization reform; far more study and discussion is needed for that. The objective here is to stimulate discussion, debate, and consideration.

A special word of caution is required about environmental management, ecology, reduction of air and noise pollution, and related matters. These are extremely important concerns for the future. They may well require setting aside extensive areas of land specifically for these purposes and the establishment of urban and suburban land settlement patterns accordingly. In the terminology of this book, land planned for these purposes and specifically reserved for them is "used," not idle or vacant. The idle lands with which this book has been concerned are the substantial areas of land between new subdivisions, which may or may not be filled in later. Whether or not later filled in, these idle lands lead to higher costs for many public services and for private activities than are necessary.

MEASURES TO MAKE THE PRESENT PROCESSES WORK BETTER

Unlike the preceding chapter, where it was assumed that the present process of land conversion would continue without significant change, this chapter assumes that research, discussion, and political action will lead to major changes for the better in tools and procedures now used in suburban land conversion. Much will turn, of course, on what one calls "major." But certainly the conversion process could be made more effective and equitable through better planning, zoning, research, timing and location of public improvements, and assessment of their costs.

Planning

The planning of land use and other aspects of suburban growth and development could be improved considerably by cities, counties, metropolitan planning agencies, metropolitan councils of government, and states that are concerned with suburban planning. One needed improvement is to sharpen the economic analysis in the plans; i.e., to estimate more precisely the benefits of a particular plan and its costs, and to present much better evidence that the proposed plan maximizes the benefit-cost ratio (or absolute margin of net benefit) rather than merely asserting that the ratio is positive or favorable. Some of the better urban and suburban planning is moving in this direction, but substantial further sharpening of economic analysis is possible in most cases. To the usual benefit-cost calculations should be added estimates of the incidence of benefits and costs—who (specifically, by name) gains, and who loses, and by how much? In the three case studies it was clear that some of the participants in the suburban land conversion process were acutely aware that they would gain from that process. Neither benefits nor costs are distributed smoothly over the whole population, nor do either occur randomly. On the contrary, the benefits often accrue to a small and rather easily identifiable group of individuals; the costs may be more widely dispersed. The general public, which is expected to give or to withhold its political endorsement of the plan, rarely understands who benefits and who loses from it. Such information therefore seems as important in reaching judgments as the estimates of cost or the design of particular features.

Urban and suburban land and other planning might be modified through more cooperation during the preparation of the plans with the private sector—the real estate dealers, the developers, the banks, the public utility companies, chambers of commerce, prominent industrialists and merchants, and citizen groups. Urban planning has traditionally held aloof from such groups until the plan was developed, and at that point endorsement was sometimes sought. Close interaction with such groups during the planning process will greatly complicate it. People will seek to modify the draft plans to their advantage. But there would be large advantages in such involvement in the planning process: help could be obtained in estimating benefits and costs, reactions to planning proposals could be obtained before the plans seemed to be final, and support for the final plan could be engendered. To some extent, it might be possible to realize some of the positive externalities; that is, various groups within the community could see that each would gain if the others did certain things, and an interdependent and mutually reinforcing program of development might thus become feasible.

If the planners seek involvement of private groups during plan formulation, such involvement should be on as wide and representative a basis as possible, both to avoid advice or reactions which represent only some of the views within a community and also to provide the maximum countervailing pressures among the private interests. If the planner consults only one group, he may be in the position of having to oppose its ideas; if he consults several groups, different ones may offset others, leaving him with greater professional freedom. Complete agreement on plans is not only unlikely but also undesirable, for various groups have divergent interests which no amount of consultation will erase. But differences in political position might be more clearly defined and extraneous matters cleared away.

Urban and suburban planning might get more involved in the political process of the respective governmental area.[2] In the past, many planners who tried to hold themselves above the political process have found it nearly always impossible to do so, and sometimes the results were disastrous. An urban or suburban land use or general plan is a political document adopted by a political process; political attitudes, personages, and processes may be ignored during the process of preparation but must be faced before adoption or during implementation of the plan. As noted in the case study areas, the real planners in some suburbs are not the official

[2] For a thoughtful article that discusses this subject and gives many references, see Willard B. Hansen, "The Expanding Domain of Metropolitan Planning," *Newsletter*, Bureau of Community Planning, University of Illinois (Spring 1969).

planners but the sewer builders or the highway engineers or someone else in the government or quasi-government structure. Important moves toward more public and official involvement have been taken in much planning in recent years, but much further progress in these directions is possible. There are, admittedly, dangers in political involvement; but there may be greater dangers in political aloofness. The real issue may be how to maximize the advantages and minimize the disadvantages.

Zoning

Chapters 5 and 6 explicitly criticized the land zoning process as it works in urban and suburban areas, and the case studies provided significant illustrations of those shortcomings. It is clear, at least to this writer, that the time has come for a new standard or model zoning act or ordinance. The model bill developed in the U.S. Department of Commerce in the 1920s under the personal leadership of Herbert Hoover, was a great step forward and has had immense influence over the years. But it has become increasingly out of date in spite of many (and not always consistent) amendments. A new model bill could be developed by a federal agency, the Council of State Governments, the National League of Cities, the American Bar Association, the American Institute of Planners, the American Society of Planning Officials, or some combination of these and other organizations. A model bill would be ineffective unless adopted by states, but the very fact that it existed would be a powerful help in securing adoptions. And the debate and discussion which would precede formulation of a model measure of any real stature would be extremely valuable.

The model bill should make a basic change in zoning authority by requiring that the responsible unit of local government must adopt a general land use plan for the area before it can zone land. Some of the most serious abuses of zoning recounted by Babcock and others arise where there is no accepted land use plan; individual zoning actions are then ad hoc, often inconsistent, sometimes contradictory, perhaps irrational. It is hard to plot a course without a map and a compass. The model bill could further provide that zoning action could be taken only in accord with the general land use plan; the latter could, of course, be amended or changed by appropriate and defined procedures. Since most units of local government, or important interests within them, gain major advantages by zoning which prohibits undesirable changes in land use, a requirement of general land use plans as a condition to a grant of authority to enact zoning would be a powerful incentive to planning. It would not, of course, guarantee that every plan was professionally competent, wise, and in the general public interest; but it would come near to guaranteeing that a general plan existed in nearly every urban and suburban area.

Another change in zoning that would get at the present serious weakness of divergent and conflicting zoning actions in different units of local government would be to provide some form of appeal from local action to a unit of government at a higher level—possibly a special court, a metropolitan planning or other agency, or a state agency. The important thing is that it be outside of the unit of government which exercised the zoning authority. To reduce the volume of cases, prior appeal to the local government might be required. Appeal to a higher authority might be open to the planning agency which had been overruled, as well as to the private person or group affected directly by the planning. It might, under carefully defined conditions, be available also to citizen groups, and apply to situations in which zoning was granted as well as cases in which it was denied. Something of this kind would greatly reduce the divergences and disparities in zoning enacted by local governments in a single urban or metropolitan area. The practice and the experience in appeals on federal land management programs would be very suggestive here.

Land use zoning needs to become more credible to land buyers and sellers and to tax assessors. As the case studies illustrated and as much literature has described, transactions in suburban land conversion do not take present zoning seriously. Sometimes land is traded subject to a rezoning; often it is traded on the assumption, nearly always realized in practice, that zoning can be changed as desired. Land is supposedly assessed according to its highest and best use—in practice, most suburban land is seriously under-assessed—and this takes little or no account of present zoning. If idle land is zoned for some type of extensive use but so located as to have real possibilities for intensive development, its market price will reflect the latter, and the assessment should reflect the market price. Achievement of credibility will not be easy nor quick; some of the other changes suggested in this and other sections could be significant in such a development.

Unless some means is devised to avoid creating major windfall gains when properties are rezoned, the zoning body will always be subject to such severe political pressures as to jeopardize its independence and to compromise its reputation. The illegal actions of Fairfax County supervisors which led to indictments were possible only because certain types of rezoning created very large windfall gains. As long as this kind of gain is possible, the temptation to slick, even illegal, acts will be great, yielded to at times, and suspected frequently. If local officials, especially planning officials, wish to appear, as well as to be, above suspicion of illegal or improper acts, then some means must be found for removing the windfall gains from rezoning. It was this situation which led the writer a few years ago to propose selling rezoning by a competitive bidding process.[3] This is not the only answer or perhaps the best one, but the overriding importance of the issue must be stressed.

One innovation that deserves trial is the idea of compensable zoning.[4] Briefly, under this any landowner who can demonstrate that the loss of development rights by zoning action has resulted in a loss in property value can require the local government to recompense him for his loss. The administrative difficulties, especially the determination of the amounts to be paid, may be serious; also, it may in some

[3] Marion Clawson, "Why Not Sell Zoning and Rezoning? (Legally, That Is)," *Cry California* (Winter 1966–67).

[4] Jan Krasnowiecki and Ann Louise Strong, "Compensable Regulations: A Means of Controlling Urban Growth through the Retention of Open Space," *Journal of the American Institute of Planners* (May 1963).

instances be cheaper to buy the land involved than to pay for the loss of development rights. Nevertheless, as part of a comprehensive program of suburban land development, such compensable regulations may have real usefulness.

Research

There is comparatively little research under way in the United States on the complex physical, economic, social, political, and other problems of the modern city. Excellent research is being done in a few universities and special research institutes, but the volume of their combined efforts is far too small. The amount of such research is not remotely comparable with the research effort on national defense, on health, or on agriculture.

There are limitations to what research on urban problems can accomplish, especially in the short run. Difficult policy issues must be settled irrespective of the amount of research. But, with good research, policy issues can rest more solidly on a factual and conceptual base and be less a matter of hunch and bias. Research is obviously not a task for the action agency, such as a county or metropolitan planning department; but there should be good communication between research agencies and action or planning organizations.

It would be extremely helpful if there were a national system of urban research organizations, roughly comparable to the land grant colleges in the agricultural field. It would be especially helpful if every metropolitan region had a competent multidisciplinary independent research institution to explore, define, and suggest answers for major urban problems.

Control over Public Improvements

Extension of various public improvements, such as roads, sewer lines, water lines, schools, and others, and even such privately provided services as electricity, gas, and telephones, in coordinated fashion into suburban areas ripe for development, could be a powerful tool affecting the location and rate of such suburban development. The power to extend such services in some areas implies the power to refuse it elsewhere. There seems considerable doubt about the legal powers of counties to refuse such services even though they would be in contradiction to the overall land use plan, and still more doubt as to their political power to do so. Owners of undeveloped suburban land feel not only that they have a basic political right to develop the land as they choose but also that they have a right to publicly constructed improvements which will give their land its maximum value.

If the general governing body of counties or some other unit of local government seeks to use control over location and timing of public improvements as a tool for controlling suburban development, then a first step is to gain, or regain, political control over many of the specialized agencies of government. As the case studies well illustrated, in some counties the sewer authority proceeds on its own, building sewers pretty largely when and where it wishes; and other specialized agencies of local government have done the same sort of thing. Unless and until the various kinds of public improvement programs are brought under unified control, this potentially powerful tool for affecting suburban development will be largely impotent.

Pricing of Public Services

A closely allied line of improvement in local governmental control over suburban land conversion is better pricing of the services so provided. If the costs of services were charged more accurately to the beneficiaries, the latter would have a more dependable basis for making locational choices. As it is, a suburbanite gains from various public improvements without necessarily bearing the costs proportionately, indeed often without realizing what costs he does bear. These costs can be classified as those which are inherent in any suburban location and those which are specific to a particular location.

As suburban settlement grows, expenditures for public improvements are necessary; for example, schools must be built. These are general costs of suburban growth. It would probably be unwise to try to assess them exactly to the beneficiaries. School costs should be assessed against all property, even that owned by bachelors and childless couples, not merely property owned by families with children. But it might be possible to assess all or part of the cost of the basic public services needed by the new suburb if settlement is to go forward, against new residences there. A capital levy might be made which could be added to the mortgage and amortized over the same period; taxes equal to the difference between the use value and the market value of the land could be deferred for some years but come due when the property is developed; or other devices could be used. If something like this were done, at least some of the costs associated with new settlement would be obvious to the persons involved. It should become plain that some of these costs might well be avoided if older areas were rebuilt.

A different approach would be to make every subdivision bear all the costs arising out of its particular location—the added costs of longer sewer lines, longer water lines, more roads, longer power and telephone lines, longer mileage for school busses. Such information as is available strongly suggests that the average suburban immigrant does not bear the full costs of his location; "postal" or broad zonal pricing removes any incentive to locate where such costs are less. It might well be that many suburbanites would prefer a relatively distant location, even bearing all the costs that such location entailed. But, if they do not bear such costs, then one cannot say that their locational choices were completely considered and rational. The material presented in earlier chapters suggests that the difference in costs, depending upon precise location, might be considerable.

Summary

The measures to improve present processes of local government described in this section could be quite important in suburban land conversion and related processes. To some extent, suggestions that local governments do "better" than they have customarily done is a little like advice against sin and in favor of virtue —easier given than taken. But, even if local governments did take all the steps suggested above, it may be doubted if the results would be adequate to meet the problem. Improvement in present local governmental process is not enough, *alone*, to bring major changes in suburban land conversion. It is not sufficient in itself; it may not even be necessary; but it would surely be helpful. In particular, it would be helpful if supplemented by other measures.

MEASURES TO IMPROVE THE FUNCTIONING OF THE SUBURBAN LAND MARKET

The imperfections of the suburban land market have been emphasized in earlier chapters. A relatively large number of persons deal in suburban land, especially in an active suburban area such as Fairfax County. Many of these people speculate in land "on the side," being employed or occupied at some other activity most of the time. The operations of the market are not clear to outsiders—or, one suspects, at times to insiders. There are no accurate data on volume of transactions, average prices, or credit use on suburban land deals. There is nothing remotely approaching, for suburban land, the data which the U.S. Department of Agriculture has collected for many years on farm land transactions. The Federal Housing Administration maintains a series of prices for the site value of developed lots used for new single-family homes with FHA-insured mortgages. Valuable as these data are, they include only a portion of residential lots and do not cover suburban land for other uses or land at earlier stages in the long progression from farmland to developed lot.

Improving Market Information

There would be many difficulties in collecting and summarizing meaningful and reasonably accurate data on transactions in suburban undeveloped land. In many instances, neither buyer nor seller would be willing to reveal information about a transaction. On the other hand, some aspects of such transactions are public; deeds and other instruments must be recorded, and revenue stamps on such transactions give at least an approximation to prices paid. A major difficulty arises in knowing whether the transaction is bona fide and what are the credit or other terms of the sale. The zoning status of the land and the prospects for rezoning surely affect its value. Nevertheless, it would be possible to obtain and to publish more data on suburban land prices than now exists. Such data, to be meaningful, would have to be grouped according to the city, the general location within each urban complex, and in other ways. For example,

> . . . this type of reporting on transactions made could be supplemented by demand and outlook studies of the type long established in agriculture. Given the best possible forecasts of population growth in a city or metropolitan area, how much land will be needed annually, and over the next 10 years? How does the amount required compare with the area presently available?

Several past studies have shown platted and subdivided land adequate to accommodate 20 or more years' anticipated growth in a city. The ratio of land available to average area developed has varied greatly from time to time though perhaps nearly always far in excess of a rationally optimum area. . . . Information of this type would at least help actual developers and builders to avoid some speculative traps and excesses and should exert some stabilizing effect on speculation.[5]

Improving information about market transactions is an old and highly effective means of improving the efficiency of markets. When trustworthy information is readily available to the public, private operators need not spend as much time and energy collecting information for themselves. Thus they can devote more time and energy to actual buying and selling and to activities related to the commodity. The range between asked and bid prices typically narrows. There are fewer opportunities for profits (and losses) due to the disparity in information between one operator and another. The price received by the seller rises, or the price paid by the buyer declines, or both. With such information available, it would be possible to narrow the wide spread in price between the farmer who sells to the first land dealer or speculator and the actual developer.

Changes in Tax Laws

Improved information would not by any means take all the steam out of land transactions (speculation) in suburban areas, particularly for a growing area such as Fairfax County. The federal income tax laws might be changed to remove increases in law land prices from the capital gains category and transfer them to ordinary income. There are now some circumstances in which such increases in price are treated as ordinary income—for one who is a land dealer, buying and selling land, rather than an "investor." Such provisions of the law might be extended to all sales of unimproved land, or the time period which land had to be held to obtain a capital gain might be increased greatly. In either event, the result would be to raise the effective rate of interest for land speculators and dealers and thus to reduce the tendency to hold land for speculative purposes and shorten the length of time such land was actually held.

The federal income tax laws might be changed in a different direction with a substantial indirect effect on suburban land conversion. The owner of rental residential property is allowed to charge depreciation on it at the price he paid for it; during the first years of ownership the depreciation charges markedly reduce, if not eliminate, the net income from the property, hence he has a substantial cash inflow tax free. After about eight years of ownership, it ordinarily pays him to sell the property to a new owner, who can repeat the process, basing depreciation on what he paid for the property; and so on, to a third, a fourth, and more owners, at intervals of about eight years. This type of property is often delapidated if not actually a slum, and the occupants may pay rents very high in relation to the poor

[5] Marion Clawson, "Urbal Sprawl and Speculation in Suburban Land," *Land Economics* (May 1962).

housing they get, largely because they simply do not have the money to rent something better.

If the income tax laws were changed to permit the original cost of such property to be depreciated *once only*, this would greatly affect the profitability of holding older property. For the case where the original owner held the property until it was fully depreciated, there would be no problem; he would charge off the entire original cost as depreciation and thereafter no depreciation could be charged off by him or any subsequent owner. If this original owner charged off only some fraction of his original cost—say half—the next owner could be allowed to charge off up to half of what he paid for the property, regardless of its relationship to the original cost, and so on for later purchasers. But once 100 percent of depreciation had been charged off, no further depreciation would be allowed.

With the tax-free cash flow thus cut off, each owner would be forced to look at the property and decide whether net income was higher with the old building (depreciated, for tax purposes) or with a new one from which he could again collect depreciation. On balance, the clearing of old buildings and the construction of new ones would be accelerated; but the degree of speed-up would depend on many other circumstances, including the demand for the kind of property that would be built. It is not so clear what this would do to rents. To the degree that more new and better housing was constructed, then rents would decline; but, to the degree that new housing could not be built at the old rents, there would be less housing and rents would rise. In either event, the older residential areas would be rebuilt faster, there would be relatively more reasonably new and good housing, and the relative over-pricing of slum and near-slum apartments might decline.

Local real estate taxes could also be modified in several ways so as greatly to affect suburban land conversion. First of all, more of the local real estate tax could be shifted to land, with the tax on improvements correspondingly reduced. This would clearly provide some incentive to replace old buildings at an earlier date. It would be possible to *defer* some taxes on undeveloped suburban land, the actual tax paid each year based on the use value of the land, and the total tax based on the market value. If such deferred taxes came due when development took place, this could provide some of the capital funds for public improvements to serve the area. Several states have enacted tax laws providing for reduced taxes on farm land or idle land in suburban areas. Except in California and perhaps a few other states, the landowner assumes no obligation to keep his land open, and he can—and often does—sell when a profitable offer is made. This is tax relief for land speculators that encourages them to hold land idle a little longer but produces no open space in the longer run.

In many suburban counties, it would make a lot of difference if assessed land values for idle land were adjusted quickly to market price changes and to rezoning of the land. The case studies strongly suggest that idle suburban land is assessed at only a small fraction of its full value, compared with the assessment ratio for improved property. If land rezoned from single-family dwelling to commercial use were reassessed promptly on the basis of a commercial value, then some of the pressure for rezoning would be lifted.

Lastly, various federal inducements could be utilized to encourage states, counties, and local tax-assessing governments to change the basis of the local real estate tax, in the directions just outlined. Elsewhere, the writer has suggested how this might be done.[6] Various forms of federal grants could be made to local governments or to individuals, conditional upon changes in the local real estate tax. While such grants would not force any state to change its laws or any local government to change its practices, they would provide an incentive for doing so.

Reducing Profits from Speculation

All of the measures discussed in this section, and probably others, would have the intent and the effect of reducing the profit from speculative holding of land or other property. In particular, the profitability of holding idle a bypassed tract of suburban land, in the hope that development around and beyond it would raise its price materially, would be considerably downgraded. Taxes on idle land in proportion to its sale value and including its present zoning would provide a strong incentive to sell it. But the profitability of holding any suburban land or of holding older rental housing would also be diminished, with consequent effect on renewal of the latter and of building on the former.

The concern here is not to abolish profits. But the question may be asked: What did the recipient do to earn the profits? What effect does his earning them have upon his actions, or the actions of others? And are these effects in the general public interest? Looked at from this point of view, the profits and the earnings of land and real estate speculators and dealers must rate rather low, and reduction of their profits might well have socially beneficial results.

REORGANIZATION OF LOCAL GOVERNMENT

It is now a truism to say that many, if not most, areas of the United States have a great number and variety of local government units which often work at cross-purposes. Earlier chapters have indicated how this situation affects land conversion at the suburban fringe. We now turn to reorganization of local government as a method of improving the suburban land conversion process. Three general lines of approach, which might be taken independently or concurrently, would markedly affect land conversion in the suburbs.

Abolition of Very Small Units

First of all, units of government below some minimum size might be either abolished or severely curtailed. It can be demonstrated that, in the modern world, a unit of government below a given size experiences high costs for the services it performs, is unlikely to do a good job irrespective of costs, and cannot attract and hold competent personnel. The federal and state governments might refuse to

---

[6] Marion Clawson, "Urban Renewal in 2000," *Journal of American Institute of Planners* (May 1968).

disburse grant funds to local governments which were below some minimum size. For instance, an announcement that no federal program or any program using federal funds could be administered out of an office which could not serve at least 30,000 or 50,000 persons, would effectively work toward the consolidation of smaller counties. Or the state might refuse to grant legal powers for tax-raising and disbursement and for zoning to municipalities or fiscal grants to school districts, unless each had some minimum population. Many other proposals of this kind could be suggested. They would be violently attacked in many quarters as unreasonable interference with the wishes of local people. But it might be asked, how far is the state or the federal government required to subsidize inefficiency, special interest, and downright incompetence in the name of local autonomy?

Any reorganization of local government which reduced the number of such units and increased their average size, might have significant economy effects. In the area of suburban land conversion, the most important effect would be to reduce the possibilities for zoning and other restrictions which benefitted a local area to the disbenefit of larger adjacent areas. More consideration would have to be given to problems of larger scope, simply because the units of local government were larger.

Developing Metropolitan Government

A different direction for change in local government is the promotion of much larger units of government of metropolis-wide scope. Unless some unit of government has the responsibility for planning and action on problems which involve the whole metropolitan area, such problems will simply go unattended. Proposals have been made to replace city governments by metropolitan governments; but, with few exceptions, they have not been accepted by the electorate in the United States. It may, in fact, be questioned whether a single general governmental body is needed to perform all functions of local government for a whole metropolitan area. Many tasks of government within a metropolis are local, or at least less than metropolitan in nature. In the past few years, for instance, it has been argued that public schools need not be administered on a city-wide basis, in order to attain all or most of the economies and the quality of education possible under a larger system, and that there are some advantages in having more localized control and greater local participation in school government. But the problems of air and water pollution and of solid waste disposal must be faced on a metropolitan basis; so, ordinarily, must the problem of water supply; transportation has major implications for the whole metropolis.

If a single general-purpose metropolitan government is unacceptable, as it seems to be in most American metropolitan areas, an organization to carry out one or a few functions for the whole metropolitan area seems more acceptable. A water supply authority, or a sewer authority, or a park authority, or some other agency is often set up to provide one or more services on a metropolitan basis. This device has the advantage of geographical consistency and economy; the danger is that it exacerbates the functional inconsistencies at the same time. The park authority might work at cross-purposes with the transportation authority, and vice versa, or other pairs of inconsistencies might develop. So far as the writer knows, no metropolitan area has established a metropolitan land zoning authority. However, the state of Hawaii zones all land within its borders.

A development of recent years has been the establishment of a Council of Governments in metropolitan areas. Generally speaking, these Councils have had very limited powers—data collection, general planning, perhaps a few others. They seem to have had an important role in encouraging the officials of local government to confer together, to look at the problems of the metropolis from a wider viewpoint than that of a particular local government, and perhaps to provide some incentive to take fewer local actions contrary to the interests of the whole metropolis. They have been stimulated by various federal programs. It is probably too soon to evaluate these Councils. Possibly they will serve a limited but useful purpose; possibly they will prove in time to be the first stages in the evolution of a metropolitan government of limited powers. Their present direct effect upon suburban land conversion is small; it is hard to evaluate the indirect effect.

Sharing of Revenues and Costs

The third direction for reorganization of local government in metropolitan areas is a wider sharing of revenues and costs of local government. To some extent, federal and state grants of funds to local government for schools or any other purpose operate in this way; the funds are raised by a unit of government with broader jurisdiction and are spent in areas that do not conform to the areas from which the revenues were raised. This type of thing could go much further; the federal government might take over all responsibility for welfare payments, on the grounds that poverty is a national and not a local problem; or the state could finance all the costs of schools, on the grounds that there is a broad interest in having everyone reasonably well educated; and so on. This type of grant is not without its own problems. Not infrequently, as with matching grants, funds are available on terms which enable the richer local governments to take maximum advantage of them, and thus the area in which the grant money is spent may not be much different from the area in which it is raised. The higher level of government simply serves as the collection agency.

It would be possible, but improbable, to have some actual sharing of local revenue and local costs within a metropolitan area. For instance, all tax revenues, regardless of which unit of local government collected them, might be put into a common fund for the whole metropolis; and all costs of local government could be paid out of such a pool. It is simply to avoid such an arrangement that many people have moved to suburban areas and defend so stoutly their local government; their devotion to local democracy seems to have a price tag on it. If anything of this kind were done in any metropolitan area, its implications for suburban land conversion would be considerable. The prospects of avoiding costs of central cities and of sharing political power in approving governmental costs would no longer be a motivating force to suburban sprawl. Short of a complete sharing of costs and revenue, special taxes might be levied on a metropolis-wide basis to finance activities which must be metropolis-wide.

LARGE-SCALE PUBLIC PURCHASE OF SUBURBAN LAND

Measures to make the present suburban land conversion process work better, to improve the functioning of the suburban land market, and to reorganize local government might well have considerable importance. But could they be sufficient, without public acquisition of land, even under the best of circumstances? In the judgment of this writer, they could not. If we wish really to cure the major deficiencies in the suburban land conversion process, public land purchase must be initiated and carried out on an adequate scale.

Legal Basis for Land Acquisition

Public purchase, well in advance of actual settlement of land, that will later be used for public purposes, has been shown repeatedly to be sound public administration. But there would also be great advantages to extensive public purchase of land that will be sold or leased for long terms to private developers for residential, commercial, industrial, or other purposes. Acquisition of sites for later public use could have some effect in guiding private land conversion; e.g., the probability of a school or park might enhance the private prospects. But large-scale public purchase for disposal by sale or long lease is a wholly different order of public participation in suburban land conversion.

Among the broad powers possessed by the federal and state governments, most urban land planning has been based primarily on one: police power. Certain activities are forbidden, restricted, or controlled because they threaten the public health, safety, morals, or other aspects of the public welfare. This has been the logical or philosophical basis for land zoning. Where it cannot be shown (or convincingly argued) that zoning operates to this general end, the courts have often overthrown the ordinances and the actions. In Fairfax County, for example, an extremely important zoning action aimed at trying to promote the reasonably full development of the eastern end of the county before settlement spread widely in the western end and thus to achieve significant economies, was overthrown by the court on the grounds that no clear connection between the zoning action and the public health, safety, or welfare had been demonstrated. While court philosophy has changed greatly over the past generation, so that actions which once would have been struck down are now supported, zoning rests upon a rather narrow legal philosophy which will always limit what can legally be done. And the political limitations of zoning as a means of directing suburban land conversion may be far more restrictive than the legal limitations.

But federal, state, and local governments have far more broad powers than the police power. They have the power of eminent domain—to take privately owned land for public purposes, on payment of fair compensation. This power was long used for roads, public buildings, and the like. Within the past generation, courts have upheld the power of government to condemn land for urban renewal, which was accepted as a public purpose in the 1930s as it almost certainly would not have been in 1900. Indeed, concepts of public purpose will probably continue to change as the growing size and complexity of the modern metropolis requires actions which would not have been considered in the public interest before. The power of eminent domain has been used, and will be used, in suburban land conversion, and it might be used much more widely.

But government at every level also has the power of the public purse—the power to levy taxes and to expend revenues. Taxing power has been limited in various ways to exclude punitive actions or favoritism, but it has been upheld, at least in some instances, when its purpose was to effect economic or social changes. Certainly, almost every tax has some economic or social effects, whether so intended or not. Public funds are spent today for a wide range of purposes, many of which would not have been considered proper in an earlier era. Public improvements— roads, schools, sewers, and the like—which surely have an effect upon land use, are the result of the use of the power of the public purse.

In urban and suburban areas, public funds have been used in some instances to directly affect private use of land; purchase of slum areas, clearing the site, and sale (usually at a discount) to a private builder has been one such use. But use of public funds to induce private action has been much less common in urban than in rural areas. In the past generation, a wide variety of federal programs have become firmly established, by which public funds are used to induce private landowners (farmers and forest owners) to carry out land management practices deemed in the public interest. Such programs have had their critics, and one need not endorse them fully to point out that they have been widely used and generally accepted by the electorate. The precedent for the use of public funds to control or to influence the use of private land has been accepted, politically and legally, and it could be utilized in urban and suburban land programs far more widely than it has been used. The people of the United States have rather clearly expressed their willingness to have public funds used to induce private actions when they have not been willing to forbid contrary actions by the same private parties.

It is proposed here that some unit of government should buy substantial areas of undeveloped or largely undeveloped land in advance of suburban settlement and development, and later make this land available to private parties for development under carefully specified terms.

Such a program would have to buy the land from present owners at the present market price, whether the purchase was by negotiation or by condemnation. The present market price of the unimproved land includes a consensus of informed judgment as to its future date of conversion to some other use and as to the price at which such conversion will take place. Moreover, if any unit of government began actively to buy land, even if its purchases were limited to parcels offered to it, the action would push up the average price of land within the general area. Present prices of unimproved land represent a balancing of demands by buyers and potential buyers with offerings by present owners; a new buyer, especially a large one, would upset the balance and push land prices upward.

How could any unit of government buy land at the market and later dispose of it, again at the "market," without suffering a loss—or, at the best, merely breaking even? As compared with the private land dealer, the unit of government might possess either or both of two major advantages: its interest rate, hence its real holding cost, might be lower, especially if the private gains from increases in raw land prices were to be treated as ordinary income rather than as capital gains; and it should be in a position to reduce the risks of timing and kind of development. The private land speculator inevitably runs some risk as to the timing of development, the kind of development on a particular tract, and the exact land price at which development occurs. The price he is willing to pay, some years before development occurs, reflects these risks. A unit of government, on the other hand, especially a unit of government which planned and directed suburban development, would have much less risk. It could designate an area for single-family homes or for a shopping center for development within a given time period, with far greater likelihood of making this designation come true, through its other actions, than could the private landowner.

One argument against public purchase of land for later suburban development is that the land so purchased would no longer be on the tax rolls. However, on closer examination the loss-of-tax argument falls apart. To the extent that the public purchase of suburban land for later development pushed up the price of the land not bought, which it would do to some degree, and to the extent that the tax assessment procedures in the unit of local government really kept pace with changes in market prices of land, the public purchase of some land would be accompanied by a rise in tax assessment and in taxes paid on the remaining privately owned land. Depending upon the elasticity of demand for privately owned suburban land, and also upon the sale and leasing policies of the unit of government, it is entirely possible that a substantial public purchase of land would result in no loss of tax revenues. In fact, there are circumstances under which tax yield from private land would actually rise with public purchase of land.

The publicly purchased land need not remain idle. If there is a profitable use for suburban land in private ownership, that use can be continued under public ownership and lease to private parties. A great deal of suburban land is, in fact, idle. It is often hard to use it profitably for farming, forestry, or other uses; and there are advantages in having it idle so as to be in a position to take immediate advantage of an opportunity for a quick sale. But there are many extensive yet rather transitory uses for suburban land—as a golf driving range, for instance—which may be profitable. There is nothing in public purchase of land which needs to exclude profitability from current land use.

Must the unit of government or the public agency which buys undeveloped or largely undeveloped suburban land for later sale or lease to private developers have, or use if it has, the power of eminent domain to condemn tracts that the owner does not wish to sell on a negotiated basis? With the power of eminent domain, any desired tract can be bought. But use of the power of eminent domain is not simple. When used against a reluctant seller, it involves at the minimum a court case. A great deal of time and trouble may go into preparation and handling of such a case. The purchasing agency can by no means be sure what price will be awarded by the court; the price of that unit may be unreasonably high, and this in turn may become the basis for higher asking prices on other tracts. The political problems of using the power of eminent domain may be still more serious if adverse public reaction to the whole program is engendered. A taking action based on the power of eminent domain is as much a matter of public relations as of law. An agency may be able to enlist public support to acquire one or a few held-out tracts that are critical to some popularly supported program, but it runs the grave danger of being cast by the press and other media in the role of the grasping and hard-hearted impersonal government oppressing the poor citizen.

The really important thing that this legal power does for such an agency is to make serious negotiation possible. If the agency can point out to a reluctant seller that it does in fact have the power to take his land against his will, then he may be more willing to talk reasonably about sale; he too may wish to avoid the costs and the turmoil of a court case. But might there not be other ways in which public agencies could bring some pressure on private owners of undeveloped land, either to sell to the public agency or to develop the land privately? One of the prime costs of holding idle undeveloped land is, or should be, real estate taxes on the land. A great deal of such land is greatly underassessed, partly because the market price is often far from clear. If the public agency buying land for later subdivision and development makes an offer for any parcel of undeveloped land, then this offer is clear evidence that the market price is as high as the offer. If the offer is refused, the market price, at least in the mind of the owner, is higher. If tax assessment were responsive to offers to purchase, then taxes on idle land should be at full value or that fraction of value imposed by law. Moreover, as public purchase tended to push up the price of privately owned land not bought, taxes on held-out tracts would rise even further.

Granting the power of eminent domain to the agency that was buying undeveloped suburban land would surely, and probably rightly, arouse considerable public opposition. There would be fears that the agency would use the power to take land away from private owners unnecessarily and unfairly; there indeed might be some danger that the agency would be less considerate in its dealings with private landowners than was desirable. To the extent that the same general ends can be achieved in other ways, there is argument against granting such power. If one were the director of a suburban land purchase program, it would be very helpful to have the power of eminent domain; but one would be politically wise to use it sparingly. If a director were denied this power, he might find that he could manage without it.

What Share of the Market?

The power of eminent domain leads directly into another question: Should the agency purchasing suburban land for later private development seek to have a monopoly on all the developable land within the area of its operations? How could the agency control development unless it owned all the developable land? If the purpose of public land purchase is to cure the deficiencies of the suburban land conversion process, how could the agency do so unless it has *all* the developable land? There would be some advantages to the agency, and to the public, if it indeed had monopoly on developable land; for the ensuing development would thus be under the control of the agency. But there would be serious disadvantages to a monopoly position and, on balance, the disadvantages would seem greatly to out-weigh the advantages. It will be recalled that one of the major advantages of the postwar suburban process has been that the dispersion of decision-making has avoided major blunders and has enlisted the judgment of many persons. A public agency with a monopoly on developable land could readily fall into serious errors. If it really had a monopoly, there would be no private market to provide a measure and a corrective. A bureaucracy with a monopoly would be under strong tempta-tion to fall into unprogressive, insensitive, and inefficient ways of operation. Even if it did not yield to this temptation, it would always be under public suspicion of having done so. Moreover, if it did have a monopoly on developable land, it would be forced either to deal with every applicant or to defend its reasons for not so doing. If, on the other hand, there were still private undeveloped suburban land, it could always require an applicant to go there. A public agency operating in the environment of—to a degree in competition with—a private real estate market would be forced to meet any standards that private market could develop. A gov-ernment monopoly may be no more desirable than a private one.

If the public agency buying suburban undeveloped land does not have a monop-oly, how large a share of the market should it aim for? How large a stock of land should it have? And how far ahead of actual development should it buy land? These are difficult questions, not susceptible of easy or simple answers. Nor can it be said that one figure is adequate while a slightly different one is not. As first approximations, one may suggest that the agency should seek to have 60 percent or more of the land in the general area within which it operates, and that it should seek to acquire land for more than five years ahead, generally for more than 10 years ahead, and often for up to 20 years ahead. How many acres this would require would vary from one metropolitan area to another. There is no objective test by which to judge these or any other guidelines. But these figures are large enough to enable the agency to have a major, if not dominating, role in suburban development in the area, and yet small enough to have a private land market that would help keep the public agency on its toes. These proportions would also be small enough that the public agency would feel no compulsion to deal with every difficult personal situation which might develop; if some owner fights public purchase, let him retain his land, but subject to the full costs of doing so.

Capital Requirements and Conditions of Sale

How much capital would a program of public land purchase of this kind require? A very crude answer would be: Quite a lot. In a county with little developed prop-erty but a great deal of land that might be developed in a decade or two, application of the foregoing general rules might easily lead to an investment equal to 20 per-cent or more of the total assessed value of private property in the county. This is perhaps an extreme case, since a county with more developed land would have a higher tax base, as would a city or metropolitan government, and of course a state would have vastly more total property within its borders. But the total cost could run into many millions, even in a fairly small metropolitan area.

Where could sums of such magnitude be raised? Many states and local units of government now have debt up to, or close to, their legal maximums. Perhaps special districts could be established, or special financial powers of established units of government used, to raise capital on revenue bonds; the undeveloped land, if wisely bought, would surely provide security for such bonds. However, since a considerable period of land purchase might precede the period of active land sale, revenues might be insufficient for some time to pay interest on bonds. The whole problem of raising enough capital for land purchase is a difficult one, to be studied in light of the legal powers, fiscal situation, and other characteristics of the governments concerned.

One possibility is federal loans. The federal government has long constructed irrigation works, whose cost the water users were supposed to pay back in 40 installments (after an initial 10-year grace period) without interest; in practice, many districts have taken far longer. The federal government has long made nonrecourse loans on certain crops. A farmer could put his corn in his own corn crib, have it sealed by government inspector, and get a loan at essentially the market price. If the price went up, he paid off the loan and pocketed the profit. If the price went down, he asked the government agency to come and take its corn out of his crib. And in neither case did he pay interest. Why should not federal loans be available on some such terms to local governments to buy undeveloped suburban land? The federal irrigation and crop loans have been severely criticized as no longer serving a broad public purpose; but, regardless of their present soundness, the possibility of generally similar loans for an important present and future public program surely should be considered.

The conditions and the methods of sale or lease of the acquired land are important matters, if the public acquisition of undeveloped suburban land is to achieve its objectives. Two major issues are involved: What is the purpose to be sought by the sale or lease? To whom shall the lease or sale be awarded? The latter is, in some ways, the simpler problem. In general, one may suppose that leases and sales will be made by competitive bid. This is a practice long established for public lands and resources, and indeed it is hard to think of a better method. But it is by no means as easy or as simple as it may seem. Merely calling a sale or a lease "competitive" does not in the least ensure genuinely competitive action. Even in the absence of collusion—which certainly cannot be ruled out as unlikely— the number of bidders may be so few, and each may be so concerned with his relation to the others in this or in subsequent sales, and the characteristics of the tract may be so particular, that the competition is limited, if not missing altogether. It may be assumed that the unit of sale will be the subdivision or something approximating the present subdivision; the bidders will be developers, rather than individual home buyers. Nevertheless, even the motions of a competitive bid allow the entry of the potential bidder about whom no one knew anything; and a competitive bid may well produce genuine though limited competition.

The purpose of the sale of the property or the lease on it presumably is the furtherance of the long-range plan for the area. If the planning agency and the land acquisition agency are one, or are branches of a common government, then coordination of the sale and the plan should be possible. In the absence of a general plan, the land acquisition agency could not well avoid making one to determine how much land is to be sold each year, where, for what purposes, with what public improvements installed or promised, and the like. The relative role of the public land agency would be critical here. If it owned virtually all the developable land, then its sales offerings would set the pace of suburban development. If it owned less, then its sales offerings would almost necessarily have to be coordinated with those of private landowners.

The sale of the property or the lease would presumably specify not only the uses to which the land would be put but also any design or other conditions. It could also specify the time period within which development would be required. Such conditions could be made part of the bidding process and of the contract given to the successful bidder. Since the successful bidder would enter the contract by his own free choice, there would be no legal reason why the terms of the sale and of the contract could not specify virtually anything relating to future land use, rather than being limited to matters which the courts have upheld as reasonable in zoning cases. As in many other aspects of suburban land conversion, the legal limitations will almost certainly be less confining than the political ones.

Although realization of a maximum price for the public lands sold, *within conditions specified in the sale*, is a reasonable objective, those conditions need not be established to produce the maximum sale price. In particular, public purchase and sale of land or leases may be the only way in which housing for lower-income people can be developed in the suburbs, at least for some years. A tract of land could be sold, subject to the condition that the lots and the houses built on them would be offered for sale at not to exceed some stipulated price. The price would be set low enough to meet the capacity of some income group to buy. Although generally a price without a quality specification is nearly meaningless, this would not be the case here. If the builder were to move his property promptly—and, unless he did, his chances of making a profit would be very slim—he would have to offer a reasonably good buy. Subject to that price for finished house and lot, the builder or developer would be required to bid for the land; his maximum price might be high or low—conceivably, even zero. He would take the risk that his houses would not sell at profitable prices, just as he would reap the profit if they did.

To the extent that the public land agency chose, or was directed, to pursue ends other than maximizing the sale price of its land, then those objectives would have to be justified in other terms—generally in social rather than in economic terms. Without at this point getting into a discussion about the social wisdom of certain objectives, it may be said that this process of public purchase and disposition of undeveloped suburban land could insure development along any lines chosen—indeed, may be the only way to achieve some objectives, such as building of housing within the capacity of the lower half of the income scale to buy. This should not be interpreted to mean that the public land agency can ignore economics. It could not sell land for a shopping center if the profit prospects of such a center were nil, nor could it work other economic miracles. But it could use the economic rent of any site it sold to achieve social purposes which it sought, and this degree of achievement in suburban land conversion is now rarely attained.

Which Agency?

Discussion thus far has referred simply to a public agency that might buy land. Which one? It might be some unit of general government—a city, a town, a county, or conceivably the state. It probably could not be the federal government, more for political than for legal reasons, although the federal government might provide much of the financing. Cities would generally not include within their boundaries the kind of undeveloped suburban land suitable for public purchase, although a few cities in the United States are so overbounded that they do include a great deal of such land. More counties have the geographical extent and also a great deal of undeveloped land. If there were a metropolitan government with adequate legal powers and political strength, it would be a logical agency to undertake such land purchase. Indeed, land purchase might be one of the functions for a general- or special-purpose regional government.

There would be great advantages in forming a special district for land purchase, with or without other developmental duties.[7] Such a district could be bounded to meet the problem; it could enlist those units of government interested in and capable of action in this field; it could even include private interests, as well as public ones. Focused upon the land acquisition and development process, it might well do a better job than an agency with wider responsibilities. There is no reason why it could not have the same legal and financial powers as any unit of government.

The matter of choosing the most appropriate agency to carry out a program of acquiring undeveloped suburban land and selling or leasing to achieve desired objectives, is an important one. The choice will depend a good deal upon powers and traditions of various government units. It is almost impossible to visualize the county undertaking such a role in Massachusetts, but in Delaware, Virginia, or Maryland the county might be the logical unit.

One last question about public acquisition of undeveloped suburban land, and its sale or lease, must be considered. What reason is there to hope or to think that *any* agency can do this job measurably better than the units of local government have done the zoning job, which has not been done very well? If the county supervisors lack the vision, the moral courage, and the competence to put the general public interest above the private interests, then what reason is there to think that the public land agency would do better? One of the traps many analysts of public action fall into is to observe and analyze the deficiencies of existing governmental arrangements and then to propose something they assume will not have the same deficiencies or new and worse ones. The competence of the public agency to buy undeveloped land and to dispose of it to further a broad social purpose may well depend upon the particular agency and its relation to the whole governmental structure, which might vary from place to place.

Without attempting a general political judgment on the capacity of unspecified local governmental agencies to do this job, at least one aspect of the situation requires mention. One major reason why planning, zoning, subdivision, and other

[7] See Marion Clawson, "Suburban Development Districts," *Journal of the American Institute of Planners,* (May 1960) ; and Henry Bain, *The Development District* (Washington: Center for Metropolitan Studies, 1968).

controls at the local governmental level do not now produce more socially acceptable results is that decisions are typically made on a case-by-case basis, with the general issues often hidden behind some personal issues applicable only to this case. The developer, promoter, builder, or other person seeking rezoning can afford to spend time working up a proposal and seeing it through, for he stands to gain substantially if he gets the rezoning he asks for. The citizen who has a broader interest in mind, whether he speaks for himself or for a group, is either unaware of such detailed cases, thinks they are not important because the areas are small, or is simply unable to give the time to appearances before zoning boards and other units of local government. Moreover, he may win his battle with a developer a dozen times, yet the latter has only to win once, and the issue is then, to all intents and purposes, closed.

The public land purchase agency might operate, or be made to operate, very differently. Some of its negotiations with present owners of undeveloped land might have to be more or less private, but its acquisition objectives and general strategy would have to be public. Presumably it would sell its land (or leases thereon) in relatively large blocks—subdivision size, not building size. Such sales would have to be conducted publicly by competitive bid or otherwise. They would attract public attention in newspapers or other communications media; persons objecting to them could make a fight on a general basis, not lot-by-lot. The whole operation would be subject to continuous public scrutiny in a way that zoning has not been. Whether or not this would be sufficient to make socially responsible public officials out of persons who otherwise would not be, it is hard to say.

Housing for the Poor

From a social point of view, the most serious shortcoming of the suburban land conversion process as it has operated in this generation is its failure to provide housing for the poor. Indeed, it can be said that the growth of suburbia has been based on large-scale poverty in the cities, or at least that it would have been much slower in the absence of such poverty. Middle- and upper-income groups have been able to buy suburban housing because the very poor were available as a market for housing they left behind on their way to the suburbs. What can be done to remedy this shortcoming, or at least to ameliorate its worst results?

Abolition of Poverty

The past few years have seen a series of small flank attacks on the problem of poverty. Now it is being realized that the attack will have to be mounted on a much wider front if it is to succeed. Several methods have been proposed to change the present distribution of personal income in the United States. This is not the place to examine the merits of the negative income tax or the guaranteed annual wage or other methods of getting more money into the hands of the lowest income strata. It may be useful, however, to examine here what the present income distribution means to housing and how redistribution might affect it.

Today the poor are typically housed in old and substandard housing in neighborhoods that are drifting steadily downhill. Housing has filtered down from well-to-do people to low-income people to the very poor, and in the process of filtering down it has typically run down. The stratification of the city is largely based on income, and it has marked racial overtones. The problem is not so much with the absolute level of the lowest incomes but rather with its comparative status vis-à-vis that of other income groups. As noted earlier, some rise in the absolute incomes of the lower third of the income distribution might do little or nothing to help them buy or rent suburban housing as long as wages and other components of the costs of housing keep rising as a part of the general income-raising process. Even the most generous treatment of low-income people now envisaged would leave them with incomes far below the average.

What, then, would the "abolition" of poverty do for housing the very poor and for suburban land conversion? A guaranteed minimum income might provide enough money for a poor family to rent, or even buy, much better housing in the city than they typically occupy today. Most of the housing would probably still be filter-down, but the filtering process might be speeded up, and housing of the poorest quality might be abandoned as no longer in demand even by the poorest people. Redistribution of income might speed up the present invasion of the shoddier postwar suburbs by poor blacks. Combined with public programs, such as public purchase of suburban land for low-income housing or urban renewal within the cities, redistribution of income might have profound effects on housing and on the process of suburban land conversion.

Urban Renewal

It cannot be too strongly emphasized that it is impossible to consider the future development of the suburbs of American cities without considering the future of the older parts of those cities. Much of the housing in the city centers is substandard, as everyone knows. But far more serious is the substandard condition of the neighborhoods in which such housing is located. By and large, these neighborhoods have trended downhill, not only physically but sociologically.

It does not pay any individual to fix up his house or apartment unless many, perhaps all, other owners or occupiers do so too. This is externality with a vengeance. It brings to mind the old story of the law which prohibited either of two trains meeting at a crossing to move until the other had passed. If no one can fix up his house or apartment until others have done so, nothing will happen. Most of the housing occupiers in such neighborhoods lack both will and ability to restore either physical property or neighborhood; their economic capacity is low, and their attachment to the area or to the housing unit is low. The owner of rental housing in such areas is not interested in maintenance, much less in improvement, of his property, and his interest in the neighborhood is minimal.

There are many obstacles to restoration of decaying housing and deteriorating neighborhoods. Indeed, it will often be cheaper to abandon the housing that exists and build new housing, in the process building new neighborhoods in the social sense of the term. The physical restoration of very old housing is likely to be more costly than the building of new housing of similar character; those parts of the old houses that can be salvaged are not highly valuable, and restoration usually makes use of labor-saving methods impossible. Experiments with restoration of old housing have generally not produced cheaper housing. There may be aesthetic or other values in the old facade with a wholly new interior, but not economy.

The rebuilding of deteriorating residential areas presents many obstacles. Over the past generation, many public projects of urban renewal have been undertaken whose results have been the subject of much criticism and also spirited defense. The program may well continue, but it seems highly doubtful if public funds will be available on a scale sufficient to remove present structures and to build new ones, for the extensive areas of now decaying housing and for the still larger areas of old housing that almost certainly deteriorate in the next two or three decades. If such areas are to be rebuilt on a large scale, then private efforts will be needed, and means should be sought to facilitate private urban renewal.[8]

One major problem in private renewal of deteriorating residential areas is the assembly of a site sufficiently large to be economic. It is nearly always much cheaper to build a considerable number of units than to build a single house or a single apartment house. More importantly, if the builder seeks to have a major impact on the neighborhood, either by building on so large a scale as to constitute a neighborhood of its own or by inducing others to restore or to rebuild, then a substantial area is required. The external economies require a large site, one to be measured in blocks rather than in lots within a block. The larger the area, the harder it is to assemble all of it for rebuilding; and, unless all of it can be obtained, the whole enterprise is jeopardized. Real estate men and developers have many horror stories of would-be builders who got all of a site but one or two properties, only to be held up for fantastic prices or for long periods of time or both, to get the remaining tract or tracts.

Urban renewal during the past generation has met this problem in part through use of a governmental unit's powers of eminent domain to acquire a substantial site, which is then sold to one or more private developers, often at a substantial write-off. Private urban renewal would be advanced by giving to private developers the power of eminent domain under strictly controlled conditions, a power which is now granted by most states to railroads and utilities. To obtain the power of eminent domain, a private developer might be required to meet various conditions; but three seem to be logical.

1. The developer must have acquired by purchase or option most of the area he wishes to redevelop, perhaps as much as 80 percent of it. His power of eminent domain would then protect him from the holdouts.

2. The area he acquires in this way should have some reasonable natural boundaries—streets, water bodies, highways, city boundaries, for example. That is, he

[8] See Clawson, "Urban Renewal in 2000."

should not be able to use an acquired or optioned area as a base from which to reach out for property not really related to his project.

3. The use which he proposes to make of the land, and to which he should be bound as a condition of the right of eminent domain, should be in conformity with the public plans for the area.

The earlier comments about power of eminent domain for units of local government to buy undeveloped land in suburbs apply here also. This legal power is not a magic wand; one still has to pay for the property purchased, often at prices which seem very high in relation to the market; and often extended and expensive legal proceedings are involved. But it does make serious bargaining possible, and it does provide the developer with some assurance that he will not be wholly frustrated by one or a few holdouts.

Site clearance is not difficult, once the properties have been acquired, but it does cost something. One possibility would be to accumulate a significant sum for this purpose only for each housing unit. A small overriding charge could be placed on every house or apartment loan, to accumulate a fund which would always stay with the property and be usable by any owner only for site clearance purposes. As little as 0.1 percent added to the loan charge would ordinarily suffice to provide a sum fully adequate to clear the site by the time the house was too old for economic restoration. The same thing could be accomplished by a special tax levied on the property. In either case, the existence of a sum which could be used only to clear a site would be a considerable impetus to site clearance.

It should also be remembered that a change in the federal income tax laws so as to make possible the depreciation of rented residential property only once in its lifetime would be a strong force leading to removal and rebuilding. Changes in local real estate taxes, to put higher taxes on the land or site and less upon the improvements, would also operate in the same way.

Stimulating Migration to the Suburbs

In the past, the removal of downtown or midtown older housing, whether it was replaced with housing or with other forms of use, has meant displacement of lower-income residents, of whom many were blacks. "Urban renewal is Negro removal" has been a criticism of the public urban renewal programs. But perhaps one might pose the question: Why not concentrate public efforts to help them get established elsewhere? Perhaps the answer to their need for decent housing at prices they can afford lies more in a faster filter-down process elsewhere than it does in rebuilding in the same spot. Some of the postwar suburbs are now, or will be in a decade or two, prime areas for migration of lower-income people. Over past decades, many ethnic and cultural groups have shifted their locations within cities, although there is often a strong emotional attachment to a particular neighborhood. Low-income black neighborhoods in many cities are of relatively recent origin. Might not some of the residents of such areas shift to new neighborhoods where existing housing is far better and cheaper than new housing on the old site could ever be? Might not a renewal which adds higher-income groups, whether white or black, be part of a general program of breaking up the very large areas of single-class residential districts that now exist? Perhaps the efforts of public-spirited citizens might be directed more toward the conversion of presently middle-income areas for low-income people, rather than an attempt to replace substandard old housing with austere new housing aimed at the same income groups as now occupy the area.

STIMULATING SOCIAL INTEGRATION

Another measure, or group of measures, that might greatly affect the processes of suburban land conversion would be large-scale and effective programs to promote social integration within large metropolitan or city areas. As noted earlier new suburbs tend to be highly segregated by age, income, family stage, and even occupation. Very few are for nonwhites, and there is also segregation within the white group. As a result of segregation in the new suburbs, the older parts of the city tend also to be segregated by different age, income, family stage, and occupational groups—and by race as well, so that many suburbanites are almost totally unaware of the existence of other groups because they do not see them in their daily lives. Many observers of the urban scene have been disturbed at the long-run social consequences of this type of segregation. In an earlier day, some parts of the cities were rather closely segregated, but the scale was so much less that people in different areas were not so completely isolated from one another.

Various efforts might be made to establish neighborhoods of lower-income non-whites in suburban settings; or various programs might be undertaken in the hope of luring higher-income whites back to the central city. Either would promote some degree of mixing by age, income, race, and other characteristics.

If anything like this were to be attempted, the unit of area to be included would be a significant issue. Should one seek to promote the migration of relatively large numbers of people from one location to another, so that a new "colony" or group would be formed in the new location, within which many of the social externalities could be internalized? Would this form of social integration accomplish the broad objectives so well as integration on a house-by-house basis?

One should not minimize the difficulties of trying to promote greater social integration in residential areas, both those in the older city and in the newer suburb. People in each kind of area will resent and oppose any direct efforts to persuade them to move. But time may bring changes in present neighborhoods—if only the continual deterioration of aging housing that will in itself encourage or force population migrations. It might be possible for public leaders to give some encouragement and direction to the population movements that are highly probable in any case.

INTERNALIZING EXTERNALITIES

Within the modern city and suburb, the use and the value of each tract of land depends more upon what is done on other tracts within the same urban complex than it does upon anything which can be done on the particular tract. (See Chapter 9 above.) There are complex flows of value from one tract to another within the same general kind of use and between one kind of use and another. The value of my house depends in large part upon what you do to and with your house, and vice versa.

There has been much concern over the negative externalities—the damages one person or group inflicts upon another. A factory discharges smoke into the air which damages people downwind for considerable distances. Or a town discharges raw wastes into a convenient stream, as some of the towns in the Springfield study area did, with consequent hazard to people downstream. Such negative externalities are rather obvious, and many people will feel that a fair treatment to those damaged is called for. Pollution regulations or standards may be established that forbid certain activities altogether or require that pollutants be reduced below some tolerable level. One of the promising lines of attack, especially for water-borne pollution, is to impose charges upon those making the pollution, in proportion to the seriousness of it. This leaves to the polluter the choice of whether, or how, to reduce his pollution; and a public body has the opportunity to clean up the pollution, and perhaps the revenue to do so. While pollution is not the only negative externality, it offers a relatively obvious example, and others are generally similar.

Far less attention has been given, thus far, to positive externalities, yet in the long run they may prove the more important. The use of land in an established city depends upon external factors; more particularly, the possibility of economically uplifting a deteriorating part of an older city depends upon external factors. How do we get *all* property owners to restore or improve their properties, so that each gains from the improved neighborhood aspect? How do we get those community or area facilities and activities which may not be very profitable to anyone but which are nearly if not entirely indispensable to the whole area? Building design, traffic flow, open space, and visual amenity are involved. Each property can contribute; none can do the job alone.

In a new suburb too, positive externalities are extremely important. The buyer of a suburban house wants not only a good house for his family, but a good neighborhood, good schools, good and reasonably convenient shopping districts, and other amenities. To some extent, he may get these in a subdivision, if it is large enough to have many or most of these amenities within itself and if the builder has been concerned enough and skillful enough to develop them well. But many subdivisions are too small for this, to say nothing of the building that occurs with only a few houses at each location.

The positive externalities between suburb and central city are the most difficult and yet most important. If the older city is reasonably "full," as discussed in Chapter 11, so that there are few if any sites for additional residential construction, then new housing must be built in the suburbs. But the latter are rarely fully self-contained. Some of their residents commute to the central city to work, some of their shopping is done there, the central city may offer many cultural advantages, and increasingly the central city is the home of part of the labor force which works in the suburbs. As noted many times above, some suburbs have sought to have the best of both worlds—to be separate, to avoid taxes for programs necessitated by poorer people, to have the pleasant living conditions, yet to work in and to obtain needed services from the city. The cities have been unable to play a constructive role in suburban development beyond their legal borders.

Faced with some of these situations, many analysts have talked of internalizing externalities—making the consequences of decisions the responsibility or the burden of those who make the decision. This is a sound general idea but, like many another sound idea, difficult to put into practice. On the intellectual side, as far as urban and suburban problems go, there seem to be three main tasks.

1. To devise clearer, stronger means of measuring the flows of value. Intuitively, as one observes the urban scene, one senses that complex flows of value do exist. One good home helps another, a good shopping district is an asset to both, a good school is part of the neighborhood strength, and so on. But just where do these value flows begin and end and, above all, how large are they in quantitative terms? These are economic problems to which relatively little time and talent have been devoted thus far. They are extremely difficult problems. If externalities are as nearly ubiquitous as they appear to be, it will be very difficult to contrast a situation of no such externalities with one where they were more clearly evident. But the problem is not beyond solution, given enough time and thought. The conceptualizing and measuring aspect of the problem must be attacked with adequate mental resources.

2. To devise legal measures to define the property rights that such flows of value from externalities create or encompass. If I have an economic interest in the appearance of my neighbor's house, then there exists a property value or aspect to that appearance, and there is or should be a legal right commensurate with the economic value. How can such a property right be defined? Who owns it? Who has a reasonable interest in governing its use, transfer, or alteration? Property rights mostly arose from, and for a long time mostly attached to, physical objects or to the use of physical objects. But property values may exist where there is little or no corresponding physical object, and legal rights may be established to such property. Before society can do much to maximize the as yet poorly defined external values from land uses in urban settings, it must find a way to define the property rights and to control their creation, transfer, increase or decrease, or modification in any way. Here is an intellectual task for the lawyers, working closely with the economists.

3. To devise and develop institutional forms for the creation, maximization, and management of the externalities in land use values. Since external values are, by definition, outside the control of the individual, then it would seem to follow that the institutions concerning them must involve groups also. Perhaps the approach must be the formation of urban improvement districts to promote external values. But how shall the area of such a district be determined? One answer might be: by the area within which significant external values exist for a possible land use or property change; but this implies that one can measure the extent of such value flows. Moreover, what about overlapping areas? What legal and financial powers should a district have? How shall it be governed? How can values created by an action be captured and used to recompense the agent of that action? These are but some of the questions that arise about urban improvement districts; if some other approach were chosen, somewhat similar questions would surely be raised about it. A major job of institutional invention is called for. Some clues may come from experience with other institutions in other settings—especially in agricultural ones, where the long experience is mostly unknown by urban planners.

If intellectuals of various disciplines did their conceptualizing and testing jobs thoroughly, until there was a reasonable consensus of how to measure, define, and maximize these positive external values and to minimize the negative ones, there would still remain two other tasks, of equal or greater magnitude. There would be a major job of public education. The average householder might agree that the attractiveness and value of his house depends in some degree on good schools, good opportunities for employment, good shopping districts, good recreation areas; but getting him to agree to pay more taxes to support such other land uses has been difficult enough for the public land uses and might well be impossible for private uses. He might agree that all the houses in the neighborhood should be properly painted or otherwise kept up; but getting him to agree to carry out specific actions on his house might be another story. It is most unlikely that there can be effective group action without substantial understanding among members of the group. At best, an educational job of considerable magnitude is involved, even assuming that the intellectual job of defining and measuring externalities in land values has been done satisfactorily. Citizens or homeowners associations might be helpful here.

A final job of actually carrying out some measures for improvement of urban and suburban areas, in order to increase if not to maximize the external land values, would be a major undertaking. To some degree, the Model Cities program of the federal government is a step in this direction, though not described or defended in these terms. Programs could be devised which would create such significant new land and property values that it would be in the interest of private parties to carry them out—if these values could be defined and measured, their incidence accurately estimated, and the appropriate legal and institutional mechanisms created. But at this stage, this is merely a hope.

Potentials of a Package of Measures

Discussion thus far in this chapter has been in terms of single measures that might improve the processes of suburban land conversion and all the activities associated therewith, with only passing reference to the interaction of various measures. This section will explore the possibilities of combining several measures, to try to show how far one possible line of improvement would strengthen another or possibly conflict with it. Since half a dozen major lines of improvement, some with specific subdivisions have been discussed, the possible combinations of programs into packages are very numerous, and only the more important variants will be mentioned here.

In economic literature it is common to speak of measures or actions which are *sufficient* in and of themselves to bring about some specific result, and of other measures which alone are not sufficient but which are *necessary* if the desired result is to be attained. Perhaps we need to add a third major category: measures which are neither sufficient nor necessary but are *helpful* or *useful*. An example may help. You propose to open a new restaurant in a small town which now has a single restaurant. Having a good cook would be helpful because it would be easier to attract customers in that way; but it may not be necessary, because your competitor may have a bad cook, and you might succeed in spite of poor cooking; and it surely would not be sufficient, for you might serve delectable meals and still go broke. It is probable that, in economic and social affairs, the number of measures that are helpful vastly exceeds the number that are either necessary or sufficient.

Perhaps no one of the measures for the improvement of the suburban land conversion process discussed in this chapter is sufficient in and of itself to accomplish very much in the way of improving that process. This is simply another way of saying that there is no single road to improvement which is guaranteed to produce results. It is not altogether clear how many of these possible measures are strictly necessary. It is enough to say that an urban area might succeed in making a lot of improvements in spite of some serious deficiencies in one or more of the factors discussed herein. But we can say that all of the measures enumerated would be helpful.

Improvement in the process of urban and suburban planning would surely be helpful to zoning. Indeed, it was suggested that zoning be confined to those situations in which comprehensive or overall plans had been prepared and adopted by the relevant general governing body. However, some zoning has proceeded in the past with almost no planning to guide it, and presumably some may do so in the future. Good plans would be extremely helpful if a serious effort were made to schedule public improvements as a conscious tool in suburban development. If measures were undertaken to improve the functioning of the suburban land market, then competent overall plans would be very useful. If better planning is to be done, then some reorganization and improvement of local government may be necessary; one major reason for the weakness of much land planning to date has been the weakness of local government or its commitment to general planning. If local government could be strengthened, one place where this would show up is in the competence of the planning effort. If large-scale public purchase of undeveloped suburban land for later sale or long-term lease to private developers were to be undertaken, it would almost certainly have to proceed in the framework of some kind of a general long-term plan for the whole area. If the official planning agency did not come forth with one, the public land acquisition agency would have to do so—even if its plan were unofficial, informal, and not necessarily reduced to writing. But a good general plan would be extremely helpful to such a land acquisition and development program. Any efforts at stimulating renewal of older urban areas would almost require an overall plan; it will be recalled that one of the conditions proposed for attachment to the private use of the power of eminent domain was that the resultant land use conform to the public plan for the area. Likewise, if any effort were made to stimulate social integration on a neighborhood or any other scale, then a general plan of some kind would be a necessary guide. Lastly, any effort to maximize the positive externalities in land use must be based on some kind of a plan for the specific area and usually for the whole urban complex. Thus, in many ways better land use and general planning is highly useful, and perhaps even necessary, for the success of the other measures described.

Similarly, better land zoning, programs for more careful timing of public improvements and for allocating their costs to beneficiaries, improvement of the suburban land market, and strengthening of local government would have important interactions among themselves and with the other measures discussed. Marked improvement in any one of them would make possible more effective operation of all the others, and this in turn could reinforce the first.

Public purchase of large areas of undeveloped suburban land for later private development under sale or lease would have many interrelations with the other measures suggested. It could be a means of implementing a large part of the planning and zoning and of scheduling the timing of public improvements. In itself, it would go far to deprofitizing the suburban land market, if it could be made more efficient than the private land market; and at the same time its tasks would be easier to the degree that this market was deprofitized by other means. The particular interaction between public land purchase and taxation of idle suburban land was discussed earlier; if the public land agency made firm offers to buy, then this price establishes the basis for real estate taxes; and the latter, on the same percentage of true market price as improved property is to its market price, would provide one of the strongest incentives to sell or develop idle land. Indeed, this incentive would make it possible for the land agency to operate without the power of eminent domain to acquire land. An extensive program of public purchase of suburban land could greatly facilitate zoning in an analogous way. That is, an owner who objected to a proposed zoning of his land might be given the alternative of selling it to the public purchase organization. While this might not remove all his objections, it surely would reduce their appeal to the public. The owner of land which was planned for much later development could sell it to the public body, as one alternative. Large-scale public purchase of undeveloped suburban land may be the only way families of somewhat less than average income (not the really poor) are ever going to be able to buy new housing, for only in this way could land prices be set low and less expensive houses be built, which such people could afford to buy. Public purchase may be necessary or helpful in some other situations of urban development and redevelopment.

The abolition of poverty, at least in its more extreme or absolute form would have great impact on a number of the other measures discussed. Poverty programs would be less influenced, by and large, by specific land programs than the latter would be influenced by the poverty programs. If every family had an income equal to or above some defined poverty level, the impact upon renewal of decaying areas and upon development of new suburbs might be considerable, though often indirect.

These are some possible pairings of measures to improve suburban land conversion and all the processes associated with it. But combinations of measures need not stop with pairings; they might include a much larger number of measures than merely two. Indeed, all the measures described earlier in this chapter could be combined into one program of wide coverage; each would in some measure benefit from all the others and would in some degree contribute to all the others.

Who Initiates Change?

This chapter has been concerned with ways in which the general process of suburban land conversion might be improved. All of the suggestions involve changes in economic, political, management, and institutional arrangements and practices.

And such arrangements and practices are not easily changed; they have a tenacity and a stability which is at the same time one of their chief strengths and one of their serious disadvantages. Change requires an initiating agent or agents and, where public or semipublic actions are involved, popular acceptance as well. Who might be, or is likely to be, the initiating agent for the changes in the suburban land conversion process which have been described in this chapter? Any one of several groups, organizations, or persons might well be the initiator. The danger is that what may be anyone's business ends up by being no one's business. Some changes could come from only one source—e.g., only the federal government can make certain types of laws. But the impetus to federal legislation in turn may come from various sources. Other changes might come from any of several sources —the drafting of a new model zoning law perhaps falls in this category.

Only the federal government can change the federal income tax laws, to provide that increases in value of relatively unimproved land are ordinary income, not capital gains; this would have a powerful effect upon land speculation and other dealings in unimproved suburban land. Only the federal government can modify the federal income tax law to provide that rental residential property can be depreciated once only in its lifetime, regardless of how many owners it may have. These basic changes in law have significance far beyond suburban land conversion and would be judged on the basis of their total repercussions. Although only the federal government could make such changes in law, stimulus to the actions of individual lawmakers and to the President could come from many sources.

The federal government in the future, as in the past, could use subsidies as stimulants to other governmental and private action. It has been suggested above that federal subsidies could be used to stimulate local governmental reform of real estate taxes, in at least two directions: (1) assessment of idle suburban land on the same basis with respect to its market value as improved property was assessed with regard to its market value; and (2) lower assessment of improvements and higher assessment of land. The federal government could stimulate the formation of urban reconstruction districts, perhaps by outright grant, perhaps by funnelling various federal programs through such districts when they had been established in any area. The federal government could readily find ways of stimulating the reorganization and strengthening of local government, if a little thought and inventiveness were directed to this end. The mere placing of federal offices in various locations can either accelerate or retard change in local government; but more direct forms of stimulation to reform of local government are easily possible.

If there is to be large-scale public purchase of unimproved suburban land in many (perhaps in any) metropolitan areas, then a source of federal loan funds for this purpose would be extremely helpful, if not necessary. The federal government has long subsidized investment in rural natural resources; an extensive farm credit system owed its beginning wholly to federal action. There is the further precedent of large-scale federal holdings of land, not only in the past, but today; and many cities in the United States were begun on federally established town sites. Large-scale public purchase of unimproved suburban land is an investment; if wisely conducted, the value of the assets at all time would equal or exceed the purchase cost, and the land when sold or leased for long terms would return income that would fully liquidate the investment, and more. But it would require substantial capital investment, which would often be beyond the ability of many local governments to originate. A substantial federal investment bank, making loans that could be repaid fully and at reasonable interest, would be a dominant factor in any program of large-scale public purchase of suburban land.

There are several measures where state government initiative is required and others where it might be helpful. In the past, state government was often dominated by rural legislators who were often antagonistic to the cities or at best indifferent to their problems. The one-man-one-vote revolution has shifted a great deal of legislative power from rural areas to suburbs. The latter may be no more liberal than the former in a political sense; but at least they are aware of urban problems and are more likely to do something about them. The planning, zoning, subdivision controls, and timing of public improvements as carried out by local government are under state laws, which could be modified to greatly strengthen any or all of these processes. The states might be nudged by federal legislation and/or subsidies, but in the end the responsibility must lie with them. In particular, state law will govern any efforts at reorganization and strengthening of local government. One weakness of states has generally been that they lacked funds to carry out large-scale activities; but reform of laws does not require much money— only brains and a will to do something constructive.

Not only might the states provide very much better laws under which suburban land conversion (and other aspects of local government) could go forward, but they might also provide a degree of supervision over local government. This is politically touchy ground, and one can feel local officials bristling at this statement. But the authority which virtually every state constitution conveys to the state to enact laws relating to local government carries an obligation to accept responsibility for what the legislative child does; in both government and private activities, responsibility must accompany authority. One specific way in which states might exercise some control over local planning and zoning would be to permit appeals from local decisions to some form of higher government, either a special court or special state agency. Or states might require neighboring local governments to resolve the matter of discrepancies in planning and zoning along their boundaries, on pain of having the state make the determinations if the local governments concerned could not agree or failed to act. In recent decades, a good deal of federal legislation has offered the states the oportunity to enact laws up to some minimum standard but has provided that the federal laws should be operative if the states failed to act satisfactorily. The same procedure might be applied by states to local government. In the Springfield case, for example, the towns might be given the option of cleaning up their own sewage disposal, or of having the state do it for them—at their expense. States cannot logically decry the tendency of the cities to bypass them on the way to the federal government, and of the federal government to bypass state governments, unless states are willing to assume a greater responsibility for what their local governments do.

If there were to be suburban development districts or special urban redevelopment districts, or any other new form of institution at the local governmental level, then the states would have to pass the necessary enabling legislation. This would call for innovation and pioneering. In spite of the theory that in the federal system of government the states may act as governmental innovators or laboratories, in fact the states have shown themselves reluctant to undertake innovation. In the past generation, far more innovative legislation has come out of Washington than out of most state capitals.

One should not rule out direct state participation in the suburban development process, or in rebuilding and revitalizing of older cities. New York State has passed some quite broadly conceived legislation of this kind in recent years; it is too early yet to see how effective it will be in operation. Other states may have taken similar moves. There are serious problems of direct involvement of states in urban redevelopment and in suburban development. Most could not put enough capital into such operations to be very effective, but states, like local governments, might borrow from special federal funds for this purpose. Many states have governmental structures with limited power in the hands of the governor and a wide dispersal of power among many elected officials, each of whom seeks to be different from his colleagues, in order to establish some sort of a separate image with the electorate. Many state legislatures are too weakly manned, sessions are to infrequent or brief, and they lack general capability for constructive action. And yet some states might be highly effective, in providing a test for ideas if nothing else.

There is much that local government could do, with or without state and federal help, to improve suburban land conversion and city rebuilding within its borders. Even within existing legislation, there are many opportunities for local governments to strengthen themselves, through reorganization or through improved operation. The legislation within which local government operates is enabling and to some extent restrictive; but actual operations depend not only on the legislation but also on how well the area manages its own affairs. The intellectual level of the public debate, the character and ability of elected local officials, and the action on bond issues or other matters put to popular vote are determined by the local citizenry, not by legislators. The board of supervisors in Fairfax County allowed itself to be continuously swamped by masses of zoning detail and other specific actions; it never saw the forest for the trees; and one suspects it wanted to operate this way, in the belief that favors for or actions involving individuals were the source of political strength for its members. Cities and counties in metropolitan areas struggle with many difficult economic and social problems and often lack the legal and governmental tools best adapted to their needs, yet they do have some room for decision and action and must accept the responsibility for the results.

Local governments might join in cooperative regional efforts to solve some of the problems of metropolitan-wide or greater scope—pollution control, for instance. Some efforts in this direction have been made in many metropolitan areas; most procede slowly and only within a very limited range. More progress on truly regional or metropolitan problems might be possible if there were a clearer definition of activities that could just as well, or better, be the province of a single local government and those which necessarily must require a broader approach. The threat of direct state or federal action would be a powerful stimulus to cooperation among local governments.

While legislation to permit improvements in planning, zoning, subdivision control, and scheduling of public improvements is greatly needed in most states, it would appear that most cities and counties have legal power to do a lot better job than they have shown the will or the management capacity to do. It has been suggested above that planning might be done more in cooperation with private interests than it usually has been in the past; some improvement in realizing positive externalities might be achieved in this way, as well as better enlistment of private enterprise to carry out the plans made. This is something that could be done at the local governmental level. At present, many units of local government seem to act only in response to an immediately critical problem. If they cannot learn to look forward and to set the stage for their own development, then they are likely to see some other level of government or private interests assume the power that they do not use.

If there is to be large-scale purchase of undeveloped suburban land, presumably this will be done by some unit of local government, although it might be a new, special unit, such as a land development authority or suburban development district. An activity of this kind would impose new responsibilities on such units of local government which many of them today are ill-equipped to assume. Likewise, if local government were to assume responsibility for stimulating urban renewal in some of the ways described, this would put new burdens on them. However, there is great variation among local governments in their capacity to carry out such activities, and in general one may assume that only the larger and more capable units would be likely to undertake such programs.

Private groups of many kinds could help initiate change in the process of suburban land conversion. Above all, they could support proposals for public action along any or all of the lines discussed. Federal or state action inevitably means the involvement of substantial numbers of individuals. Government at every level is no better than its electorate demands of it—and may, sadly, be worse. Private actions in buying houses, investing in buildings, and in other direct ways will continue to be important in suburban land conversion and all that goes with it. The individual will continue to act in his own personal interest, within the broad legal and institutional framework confronting him, of course; but he may be informed as to where his actions and those of many others like him are leading.

If all or a large portion of the measures outlined in this chapter were adopted and carried out efficiently, the kinds of suburbs that would be built and the kinds of older city rebuilding that would be carried out would be significantly better than has been the case in the past or at present. Economies in public services and private costs could be achieved, aesthetically more pleasing areas would develop, and—above all—greater opportunities for good housing and good neighborhoods would develop for the lower-income half of the population. Under the greatest possible improvement in suburban land conversion, many difficult problems of the whole city will remain. If the various alternatives outlined in this chapter are not pursued vigorously, then the suburban land conversion process will remain less helpful in the solution of pressing social and economic problems than it might be. Suburban expansion can go on following the pattern of the past two or three decades and produce a lot of comfortable housing; but the deficiencies would persist and probably grow in seriousness.

APPENDIX TABLES

APPENDIX TABLE 1

Number of Urban Places and Population According to Size of City and Type of Rural Location 1790–1960, and Projections for 1980 and 2000

1. Number of places

Year	Urban population											Rural population					
	1,000,000 or more	500,000 to 1,000,000	250,000 to 500,000	100,000 to 250,000	50,000 to 100,000	25,000 to 50,000	10,000 to 25,000	5,000 to 10,000	2,500 to 5,000	Under 2,500	Total	1,000 to 2,500	Under 1,000	Total	Other rural population[1]	Farm population[1]	Total
1790	—	—	—	—	—	2	3	7	12	—	24	—	—	—	—	—	—
1800	—	—	—	—	1	2	3	15	12	—	33	—	—	—	—	—	—
1810	—	—	—	—	2	2	7	17	18	—	46	—	—	—	—	—	—
1820	—	—	—	1	2	2	8	22	26	—	61	—	—	—	—	—	—
1830	—	—	—	1	3	3	16	33	34	—	90	—	—	—	—	—	—
1840	—	—	1	2	2	7	25	48	46	—	131	—	—	—	—	—	—
1850	—	—	—	6[2]	4	16	36	85	89	—	236	—	—	—	—	—	—
1860	—	2	1	6	7	19	58	136	163	—	392	—	—	—	—	—	—
1870	—	—	—	14[2]	11	27	116	186	309	—	663	—	—	—	—	—	—
1880	1	3	4	12	15	42	146	249	467	—	939	—	—	—	—	—	—
1890	—	—	—	28[2]	30	66	230	340	654	—	1,348	1,603	4,887	6,490	—	—	—
1900	3	3	9	23	40	82	280	465	832	—	1,737	2,128	6,803	8,931	—	—	—
1910	3	5	11	31	59	119	369	605	1,060	—	2,262	2,717	9,113	11,830	—	—	—
1920	3	9	13	43	76	143	465	715	1,255	—	2,722	3,030	9,825	12,855	—	—	—
1930	5	8	24	56	98	185	606	851	1,332	—	3,165	3,087	10,346	13,433	—	—	—
1940	5	9	23	55	107	213	665	965	1,422	—	3,464	3,205	10,083	13,288	—	—	—
1950—old	5	13	23	67	129	283	831	1,129	1,574	—	4,054	3,404	9,831	13,235	—	—	—
1950—new	5	13	23	65	126	252	778	1,176	1,846	457	4,741	4,158	9,649	13,807	—	—	—
1960—old	5	16	30	80	203	427	1,146	1,326	1,789	—	5,022	3,545	9,873	13,418	—	—	—
1960—new	5	16	30	81	201	432	1,134	1,394	2,152	596	6,041	4,151	9,598	13,749	—	—	—
1980[3]	12	15	29	100	191	405	1,252	1,930	4,166	—	8,100	—	—	—	—	—	—
2000[3]	19	22	39	150	234	538	1,595	2,975	4,828	—	10,400	—	—	—	—	—	—

2. Population (1,000)

Year	(1)	(2)	(3)	(4)	(5)	(6)	(7)	(8)	(9)	(10)	(11)	(12)	(13)	(14)	(15)
1790	—	—	—	62	48	48	44	—	202	—	—	—	—	—	3,929
1800	—	—	61	68	54	94	45	—	322	—	—	—	—	—	5,308
1810	—	—	150	80	109	116	70	—	525	—	—	—	—	—	7,240
1820	—	124	127	70	122	155	96	—	693	—	—	—	—	—	9,638
1830	—	203	222	105	240	231	126	—	1,127	—	—	—	—	—	12,866
1840	313	205	187	235	405	329	172	—	1,845	—	—	—	—	7,200[4]	17,069
1850	267	1,175[2]	284	611	561	596	316	—	3,544	—	—	—	—	10,200[4]	23,192
1860	1,379	993	452	670	884	976	595	—	6,217	—	—	—	—	13,300[4]	31,443
1870	1,301	4,130[2]	768	930	1,710	1,278	1,086	—	9,902	—	—	—	—	—	39,818
1880	1,206	1,787	948	1,446	2,189	1,717	1,618	—	14,130	—	—	—	—	20,000[4]	50,156
1890	1,917	9,698[2]	2,028	2,269	3,451	2,384	2,277	—	22,106	2,509	2,249	4,758	13,284	22,800[4]	62,948
1900	1,465	3,272	2,709	2,801	4,338	3,204	2,899	—	30,160	3,298	3,004	6,302	10,833	28,700[4]	75,995
1910	3,011	4,840	4,179	4,023	5,549	4,217	3,728	—	41,400	4,234	3,931	8,165	10,330	32,077	91,972
1920	6,224	6,519	5,265	5,075	7,035	4,968	4,386	—	54,158	4,712	4,255	8,967	10,612	31,974	105,711
1930	5,764	7,541	6,491	6,426	9,097	5,897	4,718	—	68,955	4,821	4,363	9,184	14,107	30,529	122,775
1940	6,457	7,793	7,344	7,417	9,967	6,682	5,026	—	74,424	5,027	4,316	9,343	17,355	30,547	131,669
1950—old	9,187	9,724	9,138	9,876	12,768	7,832	5,579	—	89,749	5,383	4,129	9,512	28,389	23,048	150,697
1950—new	9,187	9,479	8,931	8,808	11,867	8,139	6,490	578	96,468[5]	6,473	4,031	10,504	20,677	23,048	150,697
1960—old	11,111	11,548	13,959	14,776	17,731	9,350	6,332	—	113,056	5,616	4,032	9,648	43,145	13,474	179,323
1960—new	11,111	11,652	13,836	14,951	17,568	9,780	7,580	690	125,269[6]	6,497	3,894	10,391	30,190	13,474	179,323
1980[3]	12,000	19,000	16,000	16,000	23,000	16,000	16,000	—	185,000	—	—	—	40,000	15,000	240,000
2000[3]	15,000	26,000	18,000	20,000	29,000	22,000	18,000	—	255,000	—	—	—	43,000	12,000	310,000

Sources: U.S. Bureau of the Census, *Statistical Abstract, 1955 and 1966* and *Historical Statistics of the United States, 1789–1945*.

1 Calculated as difference between other enumerated items and total; ignores fact that some farm population lives in towns and cities.

2 Including numbers of cities and population of all cities 100,000 and over.

3 Projections of the author. Total number of cities estimated on basis of past trends in average population per city. Number of cities and population for cities of each size class estimated from rank-size distribution.

4 Estimated on basis of 5.0 persons per farm reported by Census.

5 Including 7,344,026 persons in unincorporated urbanized areas, in addition to those in places of under 2,500.

6 Including 9,851,000 persons in unincorporated parts of urbanized areas.

APPENDIX TABLE 2

STANDARD METROPOLITAN STATISTICAL AREAS, AND THEIR CITY AND COUNTY COMPONENTS, NORTHEASTERN URBAN COMPLEX, 1960

Standard Metropolitan Statistical Area	Cities of 25,000 or more included		Counties included	
	State	City	State	County
1. Lawrence-Haverhill	Mass.	Lawrence, Haverhill	Mass.	Essex (part)
			N.H.	Rockingham (part)
2. Lowell	Mass.	Lowell	Mass.	Middlesex (part)
3. Boston	Mass.	Beverly, Lynn, Peabody, Salem, Cambridge, Everett, Malden, Medford, Melrose, Newton, Somerville, Waltham, Woburn, Quincy, Boston, Chelsea, Revere	Mass.	Essex (part), Middlesex (part), Norfolk (part), Plymouth (part), Suffolk (part)
4. Brockton	Mass.	Brockton	Mass.	Bristol (part), Norfolk (part), Plymouth (part)
5. Fitchberg-Leominster	Mass.	Fitchberg, Leominster	Mass.	Middlesex (part), Worcester (part)
6. Worcester	Mass.	Worcester	Mass.	Worcester (part)
7. Springfield-Chicopee-Holyoke	Mass.	Chicopee, Holyoke, Springfield, Westfield, Northampton	Mass.	Hampden (part), Hampshire (part), Worcester (part)
8. Providence-Pawtucket	R.I.	Warwick, Cranston, East Providence, Pawtucket, Providence, Woonsocket	R.I.	Bristol, Kent (part), Newport (part), Providence (part), Washington (part)
9. Fall River	Mass.	Attleboro	Mass.	Bristol (part), Norfolk (part), Worcester (part)
	Mass.	Fall River	R.I.	Bristol (part) Newport (part)
10. New Bedford	Mass.	New Bedford	Mass.	Bristol (part), Plymouth (part)
11. Hartford	Conn.	Hartford	Conn.	Hartford (part), Middlesex (part), Tolland (part)
12. New Britain	Conn.	New Britain	Conn.	Hartford (part)
13. New London-Groton-Norwich	Conn.	New London, Norwich	Conn.	New London (part)
14. Meriden	Conn.	Meriden	Conn.	New Haven (part)
15. Waterbury	Conn.	Waterbury	Conn.	Litchfield (part), New Haven (part)
16. New Haven	Conn.	New Haven	Conn.	New Haven (part)
17. Bridgeport	Conn.	Bridgeport	Conn.	Fairfield (part), New Haven (part)
18. Norwalk	Conn.	Norwalk	Conn.	Fairfield (part)
19. Stamford	Conn.	Stamford	Conn.	Fairfield (part)
20. New York	N.Y.	New York City, Freeport, Hempstead, Long Beach, Mt. Vernon, New Rochelle, Rockville Centre, Valley Stream, White Plains, Yonkers	N.Y.	Bronx, Kings, New York, Queens, Richmond, Nassau, Rockland, Suffolk, Westchester

No.	SMSA	State	Cities	State	Counties
21.	Paterson-Clifton-Passaic	N.J.	Bergenfield, Clifton, Englewood, Fair Lawn, Garfield, Hackensack, Passaic, Paterson	N.J.	Bergen, Passaic
22.	Jersey City	N.J.	Bayonne, Hoboken, Jersey City, W. New York	N.J.	Hudson
23.	Newark	N.J.	Kearny, Union City, Belleville, Bloomfield, East Orange, Elizabeth, Irvington, Linden, Montclair, Newark, Nutley, Orange, Plainfield, Rahway, Westfield, West Orange	N.J.	Essex, Morris, Union
24.	Trenton	N.J.	Trenton	N.J.	Mercer
25.	Atlantic City	N.J.	Atlantic City	N.J.	Atlantic
26.	Allentown-Bethlehem-Easton	Pa.	Allentown, Bethlehem, Easton	Pa.	Lehigh, Northhampton
				N.J.	Warren
27.	Reading	Pa.	Reading	Pa.	Berks
28.	Philadelphia	Pa.	Chester, Norristown, Philadelphia, Pottstown	Pa.	Bucks, Chester, Delaware, Montgomery, Philadelphia
		N.J.	Camden	N.J.	Burlington, Camden, Gloucester
29.	Lancaster	Pa.	Lancaster	Pa.	Lancaster
30.	Harrisburg	Pa.	Harrisburg	Pa.	Cumberland, Dauphin
31.	York	Pa.	York	Pa.	York
32.	Wilmington	Del.	Wilmington	Del.	New Castle
				N.J.	Salem
				Md.	Cecil
33.	Baltimore	Md.	Baltimore	Md.	Baltimore, Baltimore City, Anne Arundel, Carroll, Howard
34.	Washington	D.C.	Washington	D.C.	D.C.
		Md.	Rockville	Md.	Montgomery, Prince Georges
		Va.	Alexandria	Va.	Alexandria City, Falls Church City, Arlington, Fairfax

In addition, following counties not included in any SMSA have been included in the Northeastern Urban Complex:

	State	Counties
	Conn.	Windham
	N.J.	Hunterdon, Somerset, Middlesex, Monmouth, Ocean
	Md.	Harford

as well as all remaining parts of any counties partly included in any SMSA

Source: Bureau of the Census.

APPENDIX TABLE 3

AREA, POPULATION, AGGREGATE INCOME, LABOR FORCE, AND HOUSING, BY PARTS OF THE NORTHEASTERN URBAN COMPLEX, 1940, 1950, AND 1960

Name[1]	Kind of area[2]	Land area (sq. mi.)[3]		Total population (1,000)[4]			Population per square mile[5]		Families (1,000)		Aggregate personal income, 1960 (million $)	Labor force 1960 (1,000)		Housing units 1960 (1,000)
		1960	1950	1960	1950	1940	1960	1950	1960	1950		Total	Manu-facturing	
Lawrence-Haverhill	SMSA	163	87	189	126	125	1,151	1,448	50	33	361	82	38	63
Lawrence-Haverhill	urban area	70	16	116	112	—	2,356	6,976	44	30	314	73	35	56
Lawrence	city	7	7	71	81	84	9,852	12,020	19	22	120	31	15	24
Haverhill	city	32	32	46	47	47	1,448	1,478	12	12	92	21	11	16
Lowell	SMSA	123	105	158	134	131	1,284	1,276	39	32	275	63	25	49
Lowell	urban area	30	17	119	107	—	3,952	6,425	30	27	208	49	20	38
Lowell	city	13	13	92	97	101	7,031	7,539	23	24	159	39	16	30
Boston	SMSA	969	770	2,589	2,370	2,178	2,672	3,078	641	586	5,809	1,064	294	814
Boston	urban area	516	345	2,413	2,233	—	4,679	6,478	599	555	5,365	1,003	278	760
Boston	city	48	48	697	801	771	14,586	16,767	164	193	1,338	303	70	239
Beverly	city	15	15	36	29	26	2,391	1,913	9	7	75	14	5	11
Cambridge	city	6	6	108	127	111	17,098	19,474	24	29	246	48	12	35
Chelsea	city	2	2	34	39	41	14,062	19,456	9	10	56	13	4	11
Everett	city	3	3	44	46	47	13,195	14,369	12	12	81	19	6	14
Lynn	city	10	10	94	100	98	9,084	9,590	25	26	182	39	16	33
Malden	city	5	5	58	60	58	12,016	12,459	15	15	113	24	8	18
Medford	city	8	8	65	66	63	8,021	8,162	17	17	134	27	7	19
Melrose	city	5	5	30	27	25	6,171	5,623	8	7	73	12	3	9
Newton	city	17	17	92	82	70	5,340	4,740	23	20	335	38	9	26
Peabody	city	17	—	32	23	22	1,894	—	8	6	64	13	6	10
Quincy	city	17	17	87	84	76	5,203	4,990	23	22	187	36	10	27
Revere	city	6	6	40	37	34	7,157	6,565	11	10	73	16	4	13
Salem	city	8	8	39	42	41	4,901	5,235	10	10	76	17	6	13
Somerville	city	4	4	95	102	102	23,097	24,964	24	26	173	41	12	29
Waltham	city	14	12	55	47	40	4,074	3,805	13	11	109	23	9	15
Woburn	city	13	—	31	20	20	2,477	—	8	5	58	12	4	9
Brockton	SMSA	164	166	149	129	119	911	780	37	34	274	59	21	46
Brockton	urban area	41	30	111	92	—	2,728	3,020	28	24	207	45	16	35
Brockton	city	22	21	73	63	62	3,387	2,937	19	17	136	30	11	24
Fitchburg	SMSA[6]	99	—	82	—	—	833	—	22	—	153	33	17	26
Fitchburg	urban area	58	—	72	—	—	1,254	—	19	—	136	30	15	23
Fitchburg	city	27	27	43	43	42	1,570	1,552	11	11	78	18	9	14
Leominster	city	30	—	28	24	22	947	—	7	6	55	12	6	9
Worcester	SMSA	428	286	323	276	253	755	966	81	69	619	129	51	100
Worcester	urban area	61	44	225	219	—	3,678	5,031	57	56	438	92	34	71
Worcester	city	37	37	187	203	194	5,043	5,500	47	52	360	76	28	59

Place	Type													
Springfield	SMSA	429	333	479	407	365	1,116	1,223	121	105	939	189	71	152
Springfield	urban area	239	167	450	357	–	1,883	2,133	114	92	869	177	67	143
Springfield	city	33	32	174	162	150	5,271	5,123	45	43	331	71	23	59
Chicopee	city	18	19	62	49	42	3,345	2,646	15	11	111	21	11	18
Holyoke	city	23	21	53	55	54	2,311	2,603	14	15	102	22	9	19
Northampton	city	35	34	30	29	25	859	860	6	6	52	11	3	9
Westfield	city	46	–	26	21	19	568	–	7	5	53	11	4	8
Fall River	SMSA	144	144	138	137	135	959	953	37	35	234	60	28	47
Fall River	urban area	48	35	124	118	–	2,604	3,346	34	30	210	54	26	42
Fall River	city	34	34	100	112	115	2,948	3,303	27	29	165	44	22	34
New Bedford	SMSA	142	111	143	137	134	1,008	1,238	38	36	245	62	28	52
New Bedford	urban area	30	24	127	125	–	4,265	5,340	34	33	216	55	26	45
New Bedford	city	19	19	102	109	110	5,365	5,717	28	28	171	45	22	37
Providence	SMSA	634	494	816	737	677	1,287	1,492	212	187	1,496	331	132	270
Providence	urban area	188	143	660	583	–	3,508	4,091	172	150	1,229	271	105	217
Providence	city	18	18	207	249	254	11,592	13,892	54	63	377	85	28	73
Attleboro	city	27	–	27	24	22	993	–	7	6	53	12	7	9
Cranston	city	29	29	67	55	47	2,326	1,918	17	13	133	26	9	19
East Providence	city	14	–	42	–	–	3,040	–	11	–	81	17	6	13
Pawtucket	city	9	9	81	81	76	9,419	9,469	22	22	146	36	17	28
Warwick	city	36	34	69	43	29	1,887	1,284	18	11	135	26	9	22
Woonsocket	city	9	9	47	50	49	5,474	5,838	13	14	77	20	11	16
Hartford	SMSA	514	346	525	358	296	1,022	1,035	134	92	1,260	228	76	164
Hartford	urban area	131	53	382	301	–	2,909	5,686	98	78	947	171	53	123
Hartford	city	17	17	162	177	166	9,321	10,195	41	46	341	78	22	58
New Britain	SMSA	84	133	129	147	127	1,535	1,105	34	39	275	56	28	40
New Britain	urban area	23	46	100	123	–	4,420	2,681	27	33	213	44	22	31
New Britain	city	14	14	82	74	69	6,000	5,381	22	20	174	36	18	26
Waterbury	SMSA	182	182	182	155	139	998	850	47	40	395	77	38	57
Waterbury	urban area	50	47	142	132	–	2,810	2,802	37	34	303	62	31	45
Waterbury	city	28	28	107	104	99	3,882	3,785	28	27	225	47	22	34
Meriden	SMSA[6]	24	–	52	–	–	2,206	–	14	–	110	22	10	17
Meriden	urban area	24	–	52	–	–	2,206	–	14	–	110	22	10	17
Meriden	city	24	23	52	44	39	2,206	1,917	14	11	110	22	10	17
New London	SMSA[6]	286	–	157	–	–	549	–	39	–	320	54	20	50
New London	urban area[7]	(40)	–	(85)	–	–	–	–	8	–	–	–	–	–
New London	city	6	6	34	31	30	5,604	5,008	8	7	75	12	3	11
Norwich	city	29	–	39	23	24	1,314	–	10	–	76	16	6	13
New Haven	SMSA	200	154	312	265	241	1,558	1,718	81	68	711	132	41	101
New Haven	urban area	84	47	279	245	161	3,327	5,232	72	63	614	120	37	91
New Haven	city	18	18	152	164	–	8,494	9,187	39	42	319	67	20	51
Bridgeport[8]	SMSA	161	108	335	258	213	2,040	2,390	87	69	734	140	61	106
Bridgeport[8]	urban area	148	43	367	237	–	2,471	5,574	96	63	795	153	68	116
Bridgeport[8]	city	15	15	157	159	147	10,381	10,870	41	42	307	68	29	52

APPENDIX TABLE 3—Continued

Name[1]	Kind of area[2]	Land area (sq. mi.)[3] 1960	Land area 1950	Total population (1,000)[4] 1960	Total pop 1950	Total pop 1940	Population per square mile[5] 1960	Pop/sq mi 1950	Families (1,000) 1960	Families 1950	Aggregate personal income, 1960 (million $)	Labor force 1960 (1,000) Total	Manu-facturing	Housing units 1960 (1,000)
Norwalk[9]	SMSA	72	–	97	–	–	1,351	–	25	–	292	41	14	31
Norwalk[9]	urban area	39	–	82	–	–	2,120	–	22	–	228	35	12	26
Norwalk[9]	city	25	25	68	49	40	2,744	2,002	18	13	175	30	11	21
Stamford[9]	SMSA	120	–	178	–	–	1,487	–	46	–	675	76	23	55
Stamford[9]	urban area	98	–	167	–	–	1,702	–	43	–	598	72	22	52
Stamford[9]	city	38	38	93	74	48	2,414	1,976	24	19	266	41	14	29
Stamford-Norwalk[9]	SMSA	–	133	–	196	160	–	1,474	–	50	–	–	–	–
Stamford-Norwalk[9]	urban area	–	82	–	174	–	–	2,119	–	45	–	–	–	–
New York	SMSA	2,149	2,149	10,695	9,556	8,707	4,977	4,447	2,808	2,536	25,908	4,586	1,127	3,643
Paterson-Clifton-Passaic	SMSA	427	427	1,187	876	719	2,780	2,055	320	239	2,973	493	181	371
Jersey City	SMSA	45	45	611	647	652	13,572	14,388	165	173	1,246	268	96	205
Newark	SMSA	698	679	1,689	1,468	1,291	2,420	2,160	444	387	4,254	713	243	536
New York-Paterson-Clifton-Passaic-Jersey City-Newark	urban area	1,892	1,253	14,115	12,296	–	7,462	9,810	3,725	3,266	34,139	6,059	1,685	4,687
New York City	city	315	315	7,782	7,892	7,455	24,697	25,046	2,080	2,114	17,946	3,488	870	2,759
Bronx[10]	city	43	43	1,425	1,451	1,395	33,135	33,440	391	397	2,837	618	153	473
Brooklyn[10]	city	76	76	2,627	2,738	2,698	34,570	35,981	712	741	5,179	1,107	314	876
Manhattan[10]	city	22	22	1,698	1,960	1,890	77,195	87,897	415	496	4,944	863	177	727
Queens[10]	city	113	113	1,810	1,551	1,298	16,014	13,724	508	432	4,528	816	210	617
Richmond[10]	city	60	60	222	192	174	3,700	3,177	55	47	456	84	16	66
Freeport	city	5	–	34	25	20	7,482	–	9	7	93	14	3	11
Hempstead	city	4	4	35	29	21	9,116	7,874	9	8	87	16	3	11
Long Beach	city	2	–	26	16	9	12,606	–	7	4	74	10	2	14
Mt. Vernon	city	4	4	76	72	67	18,539	17,536	21	20	196	35	8	25
New Rochelle	city	11	10	77	60	58	7,179	6,033	20	15	257	33	6	23
Rockville Centre	city	3	–	26	22	19	7,986	–	7	6	104	11	2	8
Valley Stream	city	4	4	39	27	17	10,730	7,459	10	7	95	15	3	11
White Plains	city	9	9	50	43	40	5,371	4,624	13	11	165	24	4	17
Yonkers	city	18	17	191	153	143	10,417	8,884	52	40	513	82	20	62
Bergenfield	city	4	–	27	18	10	7,159	–	7	5	65	11	3	8
Clifton	city	12	12	82	65	49	7,016	5,514	23	18	195	36	18	26
Englewood	city	5	–	26	23	19	5,318	–	7	6	90	12	3	8
Fair Lawn	city	5	–	36	24	9	6,872	–	10	7	97	14	5	10
Garfield	city	2	2	29	28	28	13,297	12,523	8	8	59	13	7	10
Hackensack	city	5	5	31	29	26	6,635	6,352	8	8	77	14	4	10
Passaic	city	3	3	54	58	61	17,407	18,614	15	16	113	25	11	19

Place	Type	(1)	(2)	(3)	(4)	(5)	(6)	(7)	(8)	(9)	(10)	(11)	(12)	(13)
Paterson	city	8	8	144	139	140	17,103	17,202	39	39	265	61	25	48
Bayonne	city	8	5	74	77	79	9,895	14,847	20	20	154	31	12	23
Hoboken	city	1	1	48	51	50	37,262	50,676	13	13	87	21	8	16
Jersey City	city	13	13	276	299	301	21,239	23,001	73	79	542	119	37	92
Kearny	city	9	9	37	40	39	4,210	4,489	10	10	86	17	7	12
Union City	city	1	1	52	56	56	40,138	42,721	15	16	103	24	10	19
West New York	city	1	1	36	38	39	32,315	34,257	10	11	75	17	7	13
Belleville	city	3	3	35	32	28	10,939	10,006	10	8	78	15	6	11
Bloomfield	city	5	5	52	49	42	9,605	9,131	15	14	130	23	9	17
East Orange	city	4	4	77	79	69	19,315	20,344	20	22	204	37	10	28
Elizabeth	city	12	12	108	113	110	9,205	9,642	29	30	234	48	20	35
Irvington	city	3	3	59	59	55	19,155	19,097	18	17	138	28	10	21
Linden	city	11	11	40	31	24	3,597	2,761	11	8	90	17	8	12
Montclair	city	6	6	43	44	40	6,956	7,085	11	11	167	18	4	14
Newark	city	24	24	405	439	430	17,170	18,592	104	115	726	177	59	135
Nutley	city	4	3	30	27	22	8,432	7,939	8	7	75	13	5	9
Orange	city	2	2	36	38	36	16,268	17,290	10	10	80	16	5	12
Plainfield	city	6	6	45	42	37	7,555	7,061	12	11	120	20	6	14
Rahway	city	4	-	28	21	17	6,756	-	7	6	62	12	5	9
Westfield	city	6	-	31	21	18	4,992	-	8	8	115	11	4	9
West Orange	city	11	12	40	29	26	3,594	2,288	11	8	127	16	5	12
Trenton	SMSA	228	228	266	230	197	1,168	1,008	66	56	590	113	35	79
Trenton	urban area	75	26	242	189	-	3,219	7,282	61	47	504	102	35	73
Trenton	city	7	7	114	128	125	15,428	17,779	27	31	216	49	16	35
Atlantic City	SMSA	575	575	161	132	124	280	230	42	34	289	65	9	65
Atlantic City	urban area	60	55	125	105	-	2,082	1,911	32	28	237	50	4	61
Atlantic City	city	12	12	60	62	64	5,178	5,361	15	16	95	26	2	25
Allentown-Bethlehem-Easton	SMSA	1,082	1,082	492	438	397	455	405	131	112	950	206	96	158
Allentown-Bethlehem-Easton	urban area	60	49	256	226	-	4,260	4,583	68	-	516	109	50	81
Allentown	city	18	16	108	107	97	6,156	6,714	29	28	224	48	19	36
Bethlehem	city	19	19	75	66	58	3,969	3,567	20	17	150	30	15	23
Easton	city	4	4	32	36	34	8,636	9,898	8	9	57	13	6	11
Reading	SMSA	864	864	275	256	242	319	296	74	66	532	122	54	92
Reading	urban area	33	26	160	155	-	4,843	5,869	44	42	334	73	31	56
Reading	city	10	9	98	109	111	10,277	12,423	26	29	187	45	19	35
Philadelphia	SMSA	3,549	3,550	4,343	3,671	3,200	1,224	1,034	1,087	921	9,073	1,730	588	1,334
Philadelphia	urban area	597	312	3,635	2,922	-	6,092	9,379	916	744	7,632	1,470	487	1,129
Philadelphia	city	127	127	2,003	2,072	1,931	15,743	16,286	501	523	3,755	843	262	649
Chester	city	4	5	64	66	59	14,468	14,051	16	17	103	25	10	20
Norristown	city	4	4	39	38	38	11,121	10,893	9	8	67	16	6	11
Pottstown	city	5	-	26	23	20	5,229	-	7	6	53	11	6	9
Camden	city	9	9	117	125	118	13,467	14,483	29	32	197	46	19	37

APPENDIX TABLE 3—Continued

Name[1]	Kind of area[2]	Land area (sq. mi.)[3]		Total population (1,000)[4]			Population per square mile[5]		Families (1,000)		Aggregate personal income, 1960 (million $)	Labor force 1960 (1,000)		Housing units 1960 (1,000)
		1960	1950	1960	1950	1940	1960	1950	1960	1950		Total	Manufacturing	
Lancaster	SMSA	944	945	278	235	213	295	248	70	59	515	117	46	84
Lancaster	urban area	29	8	94	76	–	3,214	9,302	24	20	204	41	16	30
Lancaster	city	7	4	61	64	61	8,364	14,831	16	17	113	27	10	20
Harrisburg	SMSA	1,075	1,075	345	292	252	321	272	89	73	661	140	32	111
Harrisburg	urban area	48	29	210	170	–	4,346	5,790	55	44	434	88	16	70
Harrisburg	city	8	6	80	90	84	10,486	14,213	20	23	154	35	5	29
York	SMSA	911	914	238	203	178	262	222	64	53	437	100	42	78
York	urban area	28	9	101	79	–	3,590	8,659	27	21	204	44	18	34
York	city	5	4	55	60	57	11,597	14,275	14	16	97	24	10	19
Wilmington	SMSA	787	787	366	268	222	465	341	92	67	825	144	51	114
Wilmington	urban area	81	47	284	187	–	3,506	4,012	72	48	650	112	40	88
Wilmington	city	10	10	96	110	113	9,778	11,261	24	28	200	42	10	33
Baltimore	SMSA	1,807	1,106	1,727	1,337	1,083	956	1,209	423	335	3,397	679	194	520
Baltimore	urban area	220	152	1,419	1,162	–	6,441	7,654	352	298	2,805	574	171	429
Baltimore	city	79	79	939	950	859	11,886	12,067	229	242	1,753	387	102	290
Washington	SMSA	1,485	1,488	2,002	1,464	968	1,348	984	479	370	4,991	815	60	618
Washington	urban area	341	178	1,808	1,287	–	5,308	7,216	438	330	4,615	753	55	570
Washington	city	61	61	764	802	663	12,442	13,065	174	198	1,836	356	21	263
Rockville	city	7	7	26	7	2	3,727	–	6	–	50	9	1	7
Alexandria	city	15	8	91	62	34	6,068	8,238	24	17	228	38	3	30
Total of all above enumerated items (including averages calculated from totals):														
SMSAs		21,564	19,466	31,708	26,905	23,738	1,475	1,384	8,139	6,956	71,818	13,189	3,872	10,248
Urbanized areas		5,382	3,283	28,522	24,012	–	5,300	7,325	7,354	–	65,274	12,003	3,485	9,239
Cities		1,894	–	19,375	19,507	18,249	10,230	–	5,024	–	41,847	8,450	2,399	6,558

ADDITIONAL TERRITORY in counties partly but not wholly included in SMSAs, or in counties enclaved by SMSAs, or closely adjacent to SMSAs (see Figure 12):

1. Rockingham County, New Hampshire; Essex, Middlesex, Suffolk, Norfolk, and Plymouth counties, Massachusetts, all minus Lawrence-Haverhill, Lowell, Boston, and Brockton SMSAs:

		1,718	–	372	–	–	–	–	–	–	–	–	–	–

2. Worcester County, Massachusetts, minus Fitchburg and Worcester SMSAs:

		989	–	178	–	–	–	–	–	–	–	–	–	–

3. Hampshire and Hamden counties, Massachusetts, minus Springfield SMSA:

		720	–	53	–	–	–	–	–	–	–	–	–	–

4. Bristol County, Massachusetts; and entire state of Rhode Island, minus Providence, Fall River, and New Bedford SMSAs:

		694	–	160	–	–	–	–	–	–	–	–	–	–

5. State of Connecticut, minus Hartford, New Britain, Meriden, Waterbury, New Haven, New London, Bridgeport, Norwalk, and Stamford SMSAs:	3,256	—	568	—	—	—	—	—	—
6. Hunterdon, Somerset, and Middlesex counties, New Jersey (not included in any SMSA in 1960):	1,054	—	632	—	—	—	—	—	—
7. Monmouth and Ocean counties, New Jersey (not included in any SMSA in 1960):	1,116	—	442	—	—	—	—	—	—
8. Harford County, Maryland (not included in any SMSA in 1960):	448	—	77	—	—	—	—	—	—
Sum of foregoing eight numbered items:	9,995	—	2,482	—	—	—	—	—	—
GRAND TOTAL, ALL SMSAs PLUS ADDITIONAL TERRITORY DESCRIBED ABOVE:	31,559	—	34,190	—	—	—	—	—	—

Sources: These data have been taken from various publications of the Bureau of the Census; most came from *County and City Data Book 1952* and the same publication for 1962.

1 To save space in this table, names have been abbreviated in some cases; i.e., the New London SMSA is given in Census publications as New London-Groton-Norwich. In every case, the first listed name is used here.

2 For definitions of the various kinds of areas, see Chapter 2. In general, definitions for 1950 and 1960 are closely comparable, although the 1960 urbanized areas (in col. 2, "urbanized area" is abbreviated to "urban area") seem to be more inclusive (even allowing for growth) than those for 1950. Where boundaries or any area were extended between censuses, this is evident from area at each census.

3 Data for urbanized areas and cities have been rounded to nearest whole square mile; original published data given to nearest tenth square mile.

4 Data unavailable for total population of urbanized areas in 1940, since such areas were first delineated in connection with the 1950 Census.

5 Data on population per square mile as published; calculated from unrounded data.

6 Not an SMSA in 1950; lacked 50,000 population in that year.

7 New London-Groton-Norwich SMSA is included under the "twin city" rule of Census; each city lacks 50,000 population, but together they exceed it and they are considered as "constituting, for general economic and social purposes, a single community." An urbanized area was not established under these conditions; personal letter from A. Ross Eckler, Director of the Bureau of the Census, to Marion Clawson, March 8, 1967. In order to make the data on total land area and total population for SMSA's and urbanized areas more nearly comparable, the authors have estimated the data shown in parentheses.

8 Although urbanized areas generally fall within SMSA's of the same respective name, some may include urban fringes outside the SMSA boundaries. This is the case for Bridgeport; its urbanized area includes some towns in New Haven County which are not included in the Bridgeport SMSA. Letter from Eckler to Clawson, March 8, 1967.

9 Norwalk and Stamford were considered one SMSA in 1950, but by 1960 each was an independent SMSA.

10 Included in New York City total.

ESTIMATES OF COMPONENTS OF CHANGE IN RESIDENT POPULATION, NORTHEASTERN URBAN COMPLEX, BY COUNTIES, 1950–60

County	Population		Net change, 1950–60	Components of change, 1950–60		
	1960	1950		Births	Deaths	Net total migration
New Hampshire						
Rockingham	99,029	70,059	28,970	18,362	8,739	19,347
Massachusetts						
Essex	568,831	522,384	46,447	114,950	63,692	−4,811
Middlesex	1,238,742	1,064,569	174,173	267,785	116,306	22,694
Suffolk	791,329	896,615	−105,286	182,044	104,845	−182,485
Norfolk	510,256	392,308	117,948	100,182	43,754	61,520
Plymouth	248,449	189,468	58,981	49,103	24,586	34,464
Subtotal of foregoing, which includes Lawrence-Haverhill-Boston-Brockton SMSA group:	3,456,636	3,135,403	321,233	732,426	361,922	−49,271
Worcester	583,228	546,401	36,827	122,745	60,175	−25,743
Hamden	429,353	367,971	61,382	94,773	41,409	8,018
Hampshire	103,229	87,594	15,635	19,354	8,807	5,088
Subtotal of two foregoing, which includes Springfield SMSA:	532,582	455,565	77,017	114,127	50,216	13,106
Bristol	398,488	381,569	16,919	79,244	44,296	−18,029
Rhode Island (all)	859,488	791,896	67,592	178,683	84,774	−26,317
Subtotal of two foregoing, which includes Providence-Fall River-New Bedford SMSA group:	1,257,976	1,173,465	84,511	257,927	129,070	−44,346
Connecticut						
Fairfield	653,589	504,342	149,247	124,220	53,824	78,851
Hartford	689,555	539,661	149,894	144,053	54,718	60,559
Litchfield	119,856	98,872	20,984	23,433	11,355	8,906
Middlesex	88,865	67,332	21,533	16,558	7,374	12,349
New Haven	660,315	545,784	114,531	132,792	60,554	42,293
New London	185,745	144,821	40,924	40,017	15,513	16,420
Tolland	68,737	44,709	24,028	13,396	4,374	15,006
Windham	68,572	61,759	6,813	14,082	7,063	−206
Connecticut: All—includes New London-Groton-Norwich, Hartford, New Britain, Meriden, Waterbury, New Haven, Bridgeport, Norwalk, and Stamford SMSAs:	2,535,234	2,007,280	527,954	508,551	214,775	234,178
New York						
Richmond	221,991	191,555	30,436	44,345	21,304	7,395
Kings	2,627,319	2,738,175	−110,856	552,245	280,098	−383,003
Queens	1,809,578	1,550,849	258,729	347,574	156,724	67,879
Nassau	1,300,171	672,765	627,406	236,310	71,799	462,895
Suffolk	666,784	276,129	390,655	105,161	36,459	321,953
Bronx	1,424,815	1,451,277	−26,462	275,810	146,109	−156,163
New York	1,698,281	1,960,101	−261,820	352,355	249,774	−364,401
Rockland	136,803	89,276	47,527	22,136	9,061	34,452
Westchester	808,891	625,816	183,075	141,495	66,659	108,239
New York SMSA:	10,694,633	9,555,943	1,138,690	2,077,431	1,037,987	99,246
New Jersey						
Passaic	406,618	337,093	69,525	79,479	37,322	27,368
Bergen	780,255	539,139	241,116	143,380	55,111	152,847
Hudson	610,734	647,437	−36,703	133,020	71,480	−98,243
Essex	923,545	905,949	17,596	193,630	101,106	−74,928
Morris	261,620	164,371	97,249	47,018	18,325	68,556
Union	504,255	398,138	106,117	96,418	39,713	49,412
Total for Paterson-Jersey City-Newark SMSAs:	3,487,027	2,992,127	494,900	692,945	323,057	125,012
Hunterdon	54,107	42,736	11,371	9,676	5,487	7,182
Somerset	143,913	99,052	44,861	27,077	9,586	27,370
Middlesex	433,856	264,872	168,984	84,412	27,469	112,041
Subtotal	631,876	406,660	225,216	121,165	42,542	146,593
Monmouth	334,401	225,327	109,074	64,909	29,002	73,167
Ocean	108,241	56,622	51,619	18,411	8,941	42,149
Subtotal	442,642	281,949	160,693	83,320	37,943	115,316
Mercer	266,392	229,781	36,611	54,127	25,106	7,590
Atlantic	160,880	132,399	28,481	29,245	19,507	18,743
Warren	63,220	54,374	8,846	12,422	6,946	3,370

APPENDIX TABLE 4—*Continued*

| County | Population | | Net change, 1950–60 | Components of change, 1950–60 | | |
	1960	1950		Births	Deaths	Net total migration
Pennsylvania						
Lehigh	227,536	198,207	29,329	43,165	21,534	7,698
Northampton	201,412	185,243	16,169	39,950	19,884	−3,897
Total for Allentown-Bethlehem-Easton SMSA:						
	492,168	437,824	54,344	95,537	48,364	7,171
Berks	275,414	255,740	19,674	50,381	28,514	−2,193
Lancaster	278,359	234,717	43,642	61,497	25,061	7,206
Adams	51,906	44,197	7,709	11,431	4,488	766
York	238,336	202,737	35,599	49,928	21,307	6,978
Total, York SMSA:	290,242	246,934	43,308	61,359	25,795	7,744
Bucks	308,567	144,620	163,947	60,593	16,857	120,211
Chester	210,608	159,141	51,467	42,428	17,103	26,142
Delaware	553,154	414,234	138,920	116,968	42,445	64,397
Montgomery	516,682	353,068	163,614	93,333	39,325	109,606
Philadelphia	2,002,512	2,071,605	−69,093	458,342	242,882	−284,553
New Jersey						
Burlington	224,499	135,910	88,589	40,842	13,648	61,395
Camden	392,035	300,743	91,292	80,474	34,069	44,887
Gloucester	134,840	91,727	43,113	26,896	10,621	26,838
Total Philadelphia SMSA:	4,342,897	3,671,048	671,849	919,876	416,950	168,923
Pennsylvania						
Cumberland	124,816	94,457	30,359	25,328	9,758	14,789
Dauphin	220,255	197,784	22,471	47,210	22,378	−2,361
Perry	26,582	24,782	1,800	5,956	2,715	−1,441
Total Harrisburg SMSA:	371,653	317,023	54,630	78,494	34,851	10,987
Delaware						
New Castle	307,446	218,879	88,567	69,534	24,490	43,523
New Jersey						
Salem	58,711	49,508	9,203	12,874	5,318	1,647
Total Wilmington SMSA:	366,157	268,387	97,770	82,408	29,808	45,170
Maryland						
Anne Arundel	206,634	117,392	89,242	38,601	10,497	61,138
Baltimore	492,428	270,273	222,155	95,267	25,625	152,513
Baltimore City	939,024	949,708	−10,684	235,970	109,094	−137,560
Carroll	52,785	44,907	7,878	9,867	4,797	2,808
Howard	36,152	23,119	13,033	7,032	2,252	8,253
Total Baltimore SMSA:	1,727,023	1,405,399	321,624	386,737	152,265	87,152
Harford	76,722	51,782	24,940	18,065	4,730	11,605
Montgomery	340,928	164,401	176,527	67,440	15,164	124,251
Prince Georges	357,395	194,182	163,213	78,412	14,873	99,674
Washington, D.C.	763,956	802,178	−38,222	206,273	86,210	−158,285
Virginia						
Arlington	163,401	135,449	27,952	40,851	8,480	−4,419
Fairfax	275,002	94,856	180,146	48,456	6,935	138,625
Alexandria*	91,023	65,488	25,535	26,349	6,182	5,368
Falls Church*	10,192	7,535	2,657	2,643	667	681
Total Washington SMSA:	2,001,897	1,464,089	537,808	470,424	138,511	205,895
Total	34,271,638	29,269,916	5,001,722	7,018,787	3,207,149	1,190,084

Source: U.S. Bureau of the Census, *Current Population Reports: Components of Population Change, 1950–60, for Counties, Standard Metropolitan Statistical Areas, State Economic Areas, and Economic Subregions.* Series P-23, No. 7, November 1962. Population includes persons in the Armed Forces stationed in each area, but excludes members of the Armed Forces abroad.
* Indicates independent cities.

APPENDIX TABLE 5
LAND USE (ON A COUNTY BASIS), BY MAJOR PARTS OF NORTHEASTERN URBAN COMPLEX

(1,000 acres)

State	County	Land use data, NE Corridor Study[1]						Land in farms, Census of Agriculture, 1959[2]					Unaccounted for[4]
		Total area	Residential area	Commercial area	Industrial area	Public area[3]	Other area	Total	Cropland harvested	Woodland Pastured	Woodland Not pastured	Other pasture	
N.H.	Rockingham	442.2	9.9	1.0	0.1	0.8	430.4	116	26	8	59	4	314
Mass.	Essex	320.0	40.7	4.1	3.1	23.9	248.1	58	20	3	13	5	190
	Middlesex	530.6	80.5	7.2	6.4	33.7	402.8	96	28	4	34	4	307
	Suffolk	35.2	11.6	3.9	1.0	7.3	11.4	—	—	—	—	—	11
	Norfolk	254.7	44.5	3.6	4.0	10.9	191.7	30	8	1	11	2	162
	Plymouth	425.0	10.8	2.0	2.8	38.0	371.4	96	21	1	38	2	275
Subtotal of foregoing, which includes Lawrence-Haverhill-Boston-Brockton SMSA group:		2,007.7	198.0	21.8	17.4	114.6	1,655.8	396	103	17	155	17	1,259
Mass.	Worcester	970.2	35.1	3.0	4.2	87.3	840.6	259	65	29	94	26	582
Mass.	Hamden	397.4	29.8	2.4	3.4	28.8	333.2	91	21	8	37	4	242
	Hampshire	337.9	11.8	1.5	0.7	24.6	299.4	123	33	11	48	11	176
Subtotal of two foregoing, which includes Springfield SMSA:		735.3	41.6	3.9	4.1	53.4	632.6	214	54	19	85	15	418
Mass.	Bristol	355.8	39.0	0.4	8.5	22.0	285.9	68	20	4	22	5	218
R.I.	All	677.1	54.6	5.8	18.7	52.6	545.4	138	34	8	54	10	407
Subtotal of two foregoing, which includes Providence-Fall River-New Bedford SMSA group:		1,032.9	93.6	6.2	27.2	74.6	831.3	206	54	12	76	15	625
Conn.	Fairfield	405.1	72.3	3.5	3.4	12.4	313.5	32	10	2	5	4	282
	Hartford	473.6	66.5	5.6	8.1	14.7	378.7	134	50	8	27	13	245
	Litchfield	600.3	20.3	1.0	1.1	10.6	567.3	214	52	22	71	35	353
	Middlesex	239.4	13.3	0.7	1.0	5.8	218.5	57	16	4	21	6	161
	New Haven	390.4	50.3	3.0	4.5	20.2	312.4	73	25	6	15	8	239

Area												
New London	430.1	22.3	1.3	1.8	12.6	392.0	160	34	24	47	25	23
Tolland	266.2	12.0	0.7	0.7	10.4	242.5	91	22	10	31	10	151
Windham	330.2	8.6	0.7	1.1	1.0	318.8	123	28	12	43	9	196
Conn. All—includes New London-Groton-Norwich, Hartford, New Britain, Meriden, Waterbury, New Haven, Bridgeport, Norwalk, and Stamford SMSAs:												
SMSAs:	3,135.3	265.6	16.5	21.7	87.7	2,743.7	884	237	88	260	110	1,860
New York Richmond	38.4	12.3	0.8	4.8	8.0	12.5	1	—	—	—	—	11
Kings	48.6	24.6	2.7	7.1	12.4	1.8	—	—	—	—	—	2
Queens	72.3	35.1	2.8	13.8	15.6	5.0	—	—	—	—	—	5
Nassau	192.0	96.9	4.9	7.4	25.9	56.9	7	4	1	1	—	50
Suffolk	590.1	99.0	7.1	12.7	62.6	408.6	90	62	—	11	2	319
Bronx	27.5	11.4	1.9	3.0	8.3	3.0	—	—	—	—	—	3
New York	14.1	6.2	1.9	2.2	3.7	0.1	—	—	—	—	—	—
Rockland	113.9	18.5	2.6	11.6	32.6	48.7	7	2	—	1	1	42
Westchester	278.4	114.1	6.6	5.1	58.2	94.5	25	7	3	4	2	70
New York SMSA	1,375.3	418.1	31.3	67.7	227.3	631.1	130	75	4	17	5	501
N.J. Passaic	124.2	45.2	1.2	2.4	7.7	67.7	4	1	—	1	—	64
Bergen	149.1	83.8	2.2	3.6	7.6	51.9	7	4	—	1	—	45
Hudson	28.8	8.5	0.4	8.6	2.2	9.1	—	—	—	—	—	9
Essex	81.9	43.2	1.2	5.3	6.4	25.8	4	1	—	1	2	22
Morris	298.9	72.3	1.9	3.6	15.2	205.8	48	17	1	12	—	158
Union	62.2	39.2	1.2	6.6	6.5	8.7	2	1	—	—	—	7
Total for Paterson-Jersey City-Newark SMSAs:	745.1	292.2	8.1	30.1	45.6	369.0	65	24	1	15	2	304
N.J. Hunterdon	278.4	40.9	1.1	0.4	10.2	225.8	153	73	3	17	12	73
Somerset	196.5	40.8	1.1	3.5	5.1	145.9	65	32	1	6	6	81
Middlesex	199.7	62.5	2.0	13.6	11.7	110.0	43	26	—	6	1	67
Subtotal, 3 foregoing:	674.6	144.2	4.2	17.5	27.0	481.7	261	131	4	29	19	221
N.J. Monmouth	305.3	77.0	2.0	1.2	19.6	205.5	106	57	1	13	3	100
Ocean	409.0	26.1	0.7	0.1	60.4	321.7	28	6	—	10	1	292
Subtotal, 2 foregoing:	714.3	103.1	2.7	1.3	80.0	527.2	134	63	1	23	4	393
N.J. Mercer	145.9	43.9	1.2	3.2	4.9	92.7	63	40	1	7	3	30
N.J. Atlantic	368.0	27.9	0.7	0.4	38.3	300.7	46	18	—	15	1	255
N.J. Warren	231.0	36.3	1.0	0.7	8.3	184.8	113	56	4	15	8	72

391

APPENDIX TABLE 5—*Continued*

State	County	Land use data, NE Corridor Study[1]						Land in farms, Census of Agriculture, 1959[2]		Woodland			
		Total area	Residential area	Commercial area	Industrial area	Public area[3]	Other area	Total	Cropland harvested	Pastured	Not pastured	Other pasture	Unaccounted for[4]
Pa.	Lehigh	222.1	85.6	5.0	3.6	6.1	121.8	133	86	1	12	5	−11
	Northampton	239.4	64.0	3.8	8.0	2.9	160.7	145	97	2	11	6	16
	Total for Allentown-Bethlehem-Easton:	692.5	185.9	9.8	12.3	17.3	467.3	391	239	7	38	19	76
Pa.	Berks	553.0	11.7	2.1	3.2	45.1	490.8	322	192	4	33	27	169
Pa.	Lancaster	604.2	11.8	2.2	4.4	45.5	540.3	483	320	6	37	57	57
Pa.	Adams	336.6	12.3	0.3	1.0	24.0	299.0	237	125	6	34	23	62
Pa.	York	583.0	8.2	1.3	4.2	6.0	563.3	408	228	5	60	41	155
	Total, York SMSA:	919.6	20.5	1.6	5.2	30.0	862.3	645	353	11	94	64	217
Pa.	Bucks	394.9	32.2	2.3	7.2	18.1	335.1	190	119	2	17	12	145
	Chester	486.4	44.8	12.1	2.5	24.3	402.8	293	136	4	33	49	110
	Delaware	118.4	35.1	1.4	5.0	8.4	68.6	20	8	–	3	4	49
	Montgomery	314.2	30.0	2.0	8.9	12.8	260.6	111	66	1	6	9	150
	Philadelphia	81.3	23.6	4.8	3.8	12.4	36.6	3	2	–	–	–	34
N.J.	Burlington	524.2	13.1	0.4	1.4	123.0	386.2	185	76	2	44	11	201
	Camden	141.4	78.1	2.1	2.7	19.5	39.1	19	10	–	3	1	20
	Gloucester	210.6	43.8	1.2	4.3	3.3	158.0	92	51	–	13	2	66
	Total, Philadelphia SMSA:	2,271.4	300.7	26.3	35.8	221.8	1,687.0	913	468	9	119	88	774
Pa.	Cumberland	355.2	15.5	4.0	0.5	30.0	305.2	204	124	4	16	14	101
	Dauphin	332.8	55.0	2.0	1.5	28.0	246.3	145	79	2	20	11	101
	Perry	352.0	8.5	0.2	0.7	3.0	339.6	173	69	2	60	9	167
	Total, Harrisburg SMSA:	1,040.0	79.0	6.2	2.7	61.0	891.1	522	272	8	96	34	369
Del.	New Castle	279.7	22.5	2.9	4.3	9.2	240.8	130	61	2	18	12	111
N.J.	Salem	224.0	15.1	0.4	1.8	10.1	196.5	121	63	1	15	4	76
Md.	Cecil	225.3	2.6	0.5	1.5	0.7	219.9	139	60	4	25	22	81
	Total, Wilmington SMSA:	729.0	40.2	3.8	7.6	20.0	657.2	390	184	7	58	38	268

Md.	Anne Arundel	266.9	22.8	2.0	7.3	25.1	209.7	82	25	4	20	3	128
	Baltimore	389.1	42.3	1.4	14.8	36.1	294.5	150	56	4	27	28	145
	Baltimore City	51.1	16.4	2.4	7.3	9.3	15.6	–	–	–	–	–	16
	Carroll	289.9	4.4	0.3	0.8	8.5	275.9	225	117	3	28	40	51
	Howard	160.0	3.9	0.6	1.9	7.2	146.4	96	37	4	15	17	50
	Total, Baltimore SMSA:	1,157.0	89.8	6.7	32.1	86.2	942.1	553	235	15	90	88	389
Md.	Harford	286.7	9.3	1.2	1.5	6.7	268.1	166	67	5	28	44	102
Md.	Montgomery	323.8	24.4	1.0	2.2	15.8	280.5	170	61	7	23	36	110
	Prince Georges	317.4	20.7	1.9	2.9	31.1	260.9	124	32	5	41	4	137
D.C.	Washington	39.0	9.1	0.4	1.3	14.7	13.5	–	–	–	–	–	14
Va.	Arlington	15.4	6.9	0.5	0.4	3.6	3.9	–	–	–	–	–	4
	Fairfax	259.2	39.2	1.7	0.8	21.7	195.8	62	15	3	19	9	134
	Alexandria[5]	9.6	3.5	0.2	0.7	1.4	3.7	–	–	–	–	–	4
	Falls Church[5]	1.3	0.8	0.1	–	0.3	0.2	–	–	–	–	–	–
	Total, Washington SMSA:	965.7	104.6	5.8	8.3	88.6	758.5	356	108	15	83	49	402
	Total for all areas listed in this table:	21,123.7	2,516.8	165.3	307.9	1,462.9	16,671.1	7,399	3,302	263	1,452	725	9,272

[1] Unpublished data from Northeastern Corridor Transportation Project. (See Chapter 10 above.)

[2] The enumerated subclasses do not include all land in farms, hence do not add to total.

[3] Includes semi-public areas also.

[4] Difference between "other," NE Corridor study and total in farms.

[5] Independent cities, not included in counties.

APPENDIX TABLE 6

RESIDENTIAL, COMMERCIAL, AND INDUSTRIAL INTENSITY OF LAND USE, BY COUNTIES IN NORTHEASTERN URBAN COMPLEX

State	County	Population 1960[1] (1,000)	Residential area[2] (1,000 acres)	Persons per residential acre	All retail sales 1960[3] (mil. $)	Commercial area[2] (acres)	Retail sales per acre (1,000 $)	Total employees in manufacturing 1958[4]	Industrial area[2] (acres)	Manufacturing employees per industrial acre
New Hampshire	Rockingham	99.0	9.9	10.0	115	990	116	6,320	119	53.2
Massachusetts	Essex	568.8	40.7	14.0	664	4,057	164	87,892	3,147	27.9
Massachusetts	Middlesex	1,238.7	80.5	15.4	1,328	7,196	184	140,780	6,382	22.1
	Suffolk	791.3	11.6	68.2	1,432	3,943	363	92,208	1,007	91.6
	Norfolk	510.3	44.5	11.5	540	3,600	150	44,361	4,024	11.0
	Plymouth	248.4	10.8	23.0	272	2,000	136	18,924	2,800	6.8
Subtotal of the foregoing, which includes Lawrence-Haverhill-Boston-Brockton SMSA group:		3,456.5	198.0	17.5	4,351	21,786	200	390,485	17,479	22.4
Massachusetts	Worcester	583.2	35.1	16.6	630	2,983	211	99,469	4,154	23.9
Massachusetts	Hamden	429.4	29.8	14.4	514	2,360	218	63,512	3,375	18.8
Massachusetts	Hampshire	103.2	11.8	8.7	88	1,480	59	8,453	690	12.2
Subtotal of two foregoing, which includes Springfield SMSA:		532.6	41.6	12.8	602	3,840	157	71,965	4,065	17.7
Massachusetts	Bristol	398.5	39.0	10.2	418	420	1,000	74,250	8,500	8.7
Rhode Island	Bristol	37.1	3.4	10.9	27	275	98	4,718	256	18.4
	Kent	112.6	9.9	11.4	100	859	116	8,755	2,063	4.2
	Newport	81.9	7.1	11.5	62	749	82	742	849	0.9
	Providence	568.8	24.7	23.0	681	3,079	221	94,718	14,123	6.7
	Washington	59.1	9.5	6.2	60	870	69	3,947	1,417	2.8
Subtotal of the six foregoing, which includes Providence-Fall River-New Bedford SMSA group:		1,258.0	93.6	13.5	1,348	6,182	202	187,130	27,208	6.9
Connecticut	Fairfield	653.6	72.3	9.0	848	3,516	241	99,698	3,405	29.3
	Hartford	689.6	66.5	10.4	904	5,550	163	119,559	8,104	14.8
	Litchfield	119.9	20.3	5.9	128	970	132	16,062	1,148	14.0
	Middlesex	88.9	13.3	6.7	99	685	145	10,093	1,007	10.0
	New Haven	660.3	50.3	13.1	781	3,021	259	98,122	4,473	21.9

New London	185.7	22.3	8.3	213	1,343	159	23,667	1,751	13.5
Tolland	68.7	12.0	5.7	41	655	63	2,823	661	4.3
Windham	68.6	8.6	8.0	89	690	128	10,307	1,060	9.7
Connecticut All—includes New London-Groton-Norwich-Hartford-New Britain-Meriden-Waterbury-New Haven-Bridgeport-Norwalk-Stamford SMSAs:	2,535.3	265.6	9.5	3,103	16,430	189	380,331	21,609	17.6
New York Richmond	222.0	12.3	18.0	195	771	254	9,879	4,849	2.0
Kings	2,627.3	24.6	106.8	2,488	2,718	915	227,958	7,128	32.0
Queens	1,809.6	35.1	51.6	1,704	2,832	602	134,322	13,770	9.8
Nassau	1,300.2	96.9	13.4	1,727	4,927	350	79,274	7,389	10.7
Suffolk	666.8	99.0	6.7	704	7,137	99	32,139	12,722	2.5
Bronx	1,424.8	11.4	125.0	1,173	1,852	634	52,471	2,959	17.7
New York	1,698.3	6.2	273.9	4,338	1,869	2,321	471,208	2,234	210.9
Rockland	136.8	18.5	7.4	128	2,566	50	11,477	11,626	1.0
Westchester	808.9	114.1	7.1	1,125	6,560	171	55,833	5,100	10.9
New York SMSA	10,694.7	418.1	25.6	13,582	31,232	435	1,074,561	67,777	15.9
New Jersey Passaic	406.6	45.2	9.0	547	1,221	448	74,632	2,380	31.4
Bergen	780.3	83.8	9.3	905	2,241	404	81,698	3,589	22.8
Hudson	610.7	8.5	71.8	640	438	1,460	120,678	8,555	14.1
Essex	923.5	43.2	21.4	1,278	1,245	1,026	125,708	5,348	23.5
Morris	261.6	72.3	3.6	276	1,947	142	22,153	3,641	6.1
Union	504.3	39.2	12.9	689	1,177	585	78,790	6,643	11.9
Total for Paterson-Jersey City-Newark SMSAs:	3,487.0	292.2	11.9	4,335	8,269	524	503,659	30,156	16.7
New Jersey Hunterdon	54.1	40.9	1.3	61	1,059	58	4,473	389	11.5
Somerset	143.9	40.8	3.5	135	1,136	119	18,139	3,531	5.1
Middlesex	433.9	62.5	6.9	446	1,950	229	64,045	13,553	4.7
Total, three foregoing:	631.9	144.2	4.4	642	4,145	155	86,657	17,473	5.0
New Jersey Monmouth	334.4	77.0	4.3	404	2,007	201	14,484	1,190	12.0
Ocean	108.2	26.1	4.1	164	672	244	2,008	103	19.5
Total, two foregoing:	442.6	103.1	4.3	568	2,679	215	16,492	1,293	12.0
New Jersey Mercer	266.4	43.9	6.1	361	1,209	299	35,077	3,216	10.9
Atlantic	160.9	27.9	5.8	240	726	331	7,132	363	19.6
Warren	63.2	36.3	1.7	66	950	69	10,412	736	14.1

APPENDIX TABLE 6—Continued

State	County	Population 1960[1] (1,000)	Residential area[2] (1,000 acres)	Persons per residential acre	All retail sales 1960[3] (mil. $)	Commercial area[2] (acres)	Retail sales per acre (1,000 $)	Total employees in manufacturing 1958[4]	Industrial area[2] (acres)	Manufacturing employees per industrial acre
Pennsylvania	Lehigh	227.5	85.6	2.7	275	5,003	55	32,872	3,570	9.2
	Northhampton	201.4	64.0	3.1	210	3,785	55	45,051	7,970	5.7
Total for Allentown-Bethlehem-Easton:		492.1	185.9	2.6	551	9,738	56	88,335	12,276	7.2
Pennsylvania	Berks	275.4	11.7	23.5	300	2,138	140	48,170	3,226	14.9
Pennsylvania	Lancaster	278.4	11.8	23.6	309	2,200	141	42,295	4,400	9.6
Pennsylvania	Adams	51.9	12.3	4.2	44	293	150	6,763	1,000	6.8
	York	238.3	8.2	29.1	271	1,300	209	41,178	4,200	9.8
Total, York SMSA:		290.2	20.5	14.2	315	1,593	198	47,941	5,200	9.2
Pennsylvania	Bucks	308.6	32.2	9.6	299	2,315	129	27,633	7,180	3.8
	Chester	210.6	44.8	4.7	215	12,066	18	24,019	2,476	9.7
	Delaware	553.2	35.1	15.8	552	1,400	394	45,179	5,000	9.0
	Montgomery	516.7	30.0	17.2	619	2,000	309	63,017	8,900	7.1
	Philadelphia	2,002.5	23.6	84.9	2,528	4,844	522	287,029	3,794	75.7
New Jersey	Burlington	224.5	13.1	17.1	169	373	454	15,080	1,429	10.6
	Camden	392.0	78.1	5.0	440	2,073	212	43,721	2,710	16.1
	Gloucester	134.8	43.8	3.1	120	1,231	98	9,494	4,258	2.2
Total, Philadelphia SMSA:		4,343.0	300.7	14.4	4,942	26,302	188	515,172	35,747	14.4
Pennsylvania	Cumberland	124.8	15.5	8.0	133	4,000	33	8,429	500	16.8
	Dauphin	220.3	55.0	4.0	284	2,000	142	23,289	1,500	15.5
	Perry	26.6	8.5	3.1	18	180	100	821	700	1.2
Total, Harrisburg SMSA:		371.7	79.0	4.7	435	6,180	70	32,539	2,700	12.1
Delaware	New Castle	307.4	22.5	13.7	393	2,860	137	28,697	4,324	6.6
New Jersey	Salem	58.7	15.1	3.9	63	434	145	10,481	1,797	5.8
Maryland	Cecil	48.4	2.6	18.6	42	525	80	4,530	1,496	3.0
Total, Wilmington SMSA:		414.5	40.2	10.3	498	3,819	131	43,608	7,617	5.7

Maryland	Anne Arundel	206.6	22.8	9.1	159	1,955	81	8,321	7,303	1.1
	Baltimore	492.4	42.3	11.6	326	1,438	227	70,085	14,817	4.7
	Baltimore City	939.0	16.4	57.3	1,396	2,448	570	111,757	7,349	15.2
	Carroll	52.8	4.4	12.0	50	333	150	4,716	847	5.6
	Howard	36.2	3.9	9.3	24	551	44	1,047	1,933	0.5
Total, Baltimore SMSA:		1,727.0	89.8	19.2	1,955	6,725	291	195,926	32,249	6.1
Maryland	Harford	76.7	9.3	8.2	68	1,181	58	3,187	1,488	2.1
	Montgomery	340.9	24.4	14.0	353	979	361	3,925	2,201	1.8
	Prince Georges	357.4	20.7	17.3	298	1,896	157	5,221	2,873	1.8
District of Columbia	Washington	764.0	9.1	84.0	1,304	400	3,260	20,818	1,330	15.7
Virginia	Arlington	163.4	6.9	23.7	242	499	486	1,199	439	2.7
	Fairfax	275.0	39.2	7.0	132	1,722	76	637	820	0.8
	Alexandria[5]	91.0	3.5	26.0	136	226	602	2,125	721	2.9
	Falls Church[5]	10.2	0.8	12.8	36	87	418	121	10	12.1
Total, Washington SMSA:		2,001.9	104.6	19.1	2,501	5,809	431	34,046	8,394	4.1
Total, all counties		34,320.0	2,516.8	13.6	41,636	165,236	252	3,904,277	308,090	12.7

[1] Bureau of Census, County and City Data Book, 1962, item 3.
[2] Area data from Northeast Corridor Transportation Study, see Appendix Table 5.
[3] Bureau of the Census, County and City Data Book, 1962, item 100.
[4] Ibid., item 89.
[5] Independent cities not included in counties.

INDEX